INTRODUCTION
TO
RECREATIONAL SERVICE

ABOUT THE AUTHOR

At present Dr. Jay S. Shivers is Professor and Coordinator of the Recreational Service Education curriculum in the School of Education at the University of Connecticut. He received his Bachelor's degree from Indiana University, his Master's degree and Directorate in Recreational Service Education from New York University, and was the first person to graduate with a Ph.D. in Recreational Service Education at the University of Wisconsin, Madison.

Years of practical experience serving as a programmer, supervisor, and administrator in various parts of the United States have provided him with the insights and knowledge that have resulted in numerous articles in refereed journals, and other publications.

He is currently cited in *Who's Who in Education,* a recipient of the National Literary Award from the National Recreation and Park Association, 1979; the Distinguished Service Award of the National Therapeutic Recreation Society, October, 1983; a founding fellow of the Academy of Leisure Sciences, 1980; and the Hollis Fait Scholarly Contribution Award from the National Consortium on Physical Education and Recreation for the Disabled, 1990. He is the author of twenty-three texts in recreational service, and has presented papers at International congresses and forums each year since 1970.

INTRODUCTION
TO
RECREATIONAL SERVICE

By

JAY S. SHIVERS

Department of Sport, Leisure and Exercise Science
The University of Connecticut
Storrs, Connecticut

CHARLES C THOMAS • PUBLISHER
Springfield • Illinois • U.S.A.

Published and Distributed Throughout the World by

CHARLES C THOMAS • PUBLISHER
2600 South First Street
Springfield, Illinois 62794-9265

© *1993 by* CHARLES C THOMAS • PUBLISHER

ISBN 0-398-05858-X

Library of Congress Catalog Card Number: 93-22309

Printed in the United States of America
SC-R-3

Library of Congress Cataloging-in-Publication Data

Shivers, Jay Sanford, 1930–
   Introduction to recreational service / by Jay S. Shivers.
      p.   cm.
   Includes bibliographical references (p. 599) and index.
   ISBN 0-398-05858-X
   1. Recreation — Management.   2. Recreation leadership.   I. Title.
GV181.5.S54   1993
790'.06'9 — dc20   93-22309
                                                                  CIP

In Memoriam

RHODA SHIVERS
June 5, 1930–January 9, 1989

Omnia Vincere Debet Amor

PREFACE

Recreational service education in professional preparatory curricula, as well as the practicing field, requires a textbook that will offer information for learning and performance. This text offers basic conceptual information dealing with the origin, forces, and political realities which coincided over time and resulted in the modern recreational service movement. Students will be able to understand why some practices and behaviors are given credence and precedence over others.

This book is primarily concerned with the public or governmental sector of recreational service, but is also involved with the private and quasi-public sectors. Although specific legal impingements and financial accountability have bearing only upon the public sector because of legal requirements, almost every chapter has direct meaning and value for the provisions of recreational service in this society regardless of where they originate.

The text treats the organization of recreational service departments, administrative functions, and responsibilities which are based upon legislative enactments and requirements, as well as on political realities insofar as daily operation of the agency is concerned. Emphasis is placed upon fundamental principles and practices of recreational service and the role of the recreationist in the community setting. Additionally, information is given to the expanding specialization of therapeutic recreational service and the need to deal with disabled populations.

The book is pragmatic and indicates why the field developed the way it did and what is currently being done by practitioners in the field as they carry out their mandate. It provides well-supported methods for handling theoretical questions as well as those concerned with practical considerations in the organization and operation of public departments.

The book is arranged in four major divisions: Foundations for Recreational Service, Standard Practices for Recreational Service, External Influences on Recreational Service, and The Making of the Recreational Service Profession. The advantage of organizing it in this manner is so the reader gains the clearest explanation possible in order to comprehend the origin, nature, and sociological manifestations of recreational service. Precise information for intelligible description is provided. The reader is introduced to the topic by definition and narrative discussion. Each chapter, although it may stand alone and be perused independently or in conjunction with others, is complete in itself and has been placed to supplement and complement successive chapters. Thus, the reader can follow the complete development and current practices of recreational service from origin to contemporary experience.

The book approaches the subject by dealing with the essential background information, principles, problems, and practices as they relate to the institution and administration of public recreational services. Historical facts are liberally provided, and assertions are substantiated.

The book was written to enable students to gain greater knowledge of the field. Of considerable significance, as well, is its utility as a handbook of preferred practices for professionals in the field. It is useful in that it illustrates and exemplifies techniques for successful accomplishment of operational phases of recreational service in all of its ramifications. It details the most worthwhile idea dealing with administrative aspects of the agency, and all the management and supervisory methods designed to achieve success when working with laymen and professionals alike. Political actuality is stressed, as are guidelines for policy statements, coordination, public relations, and techniques for effecting the most competent and comprehensive service possible.

The text deals with facts that students must have if they are to become recreationists. There is both historical and eminently pertinent information that fulfills the needs of those who seek careers in recreational service.

JAY S. SHIVERS

CONTENTS

INTRODUCTION
TO
RECREATIONAL SERVICE

PART I
FOUNDATIONS FOR
RECREATIONAL SERVICE

Chapter 1

INTRODUCTION TO PUBLIC PARK
AND RECREATIONAL SERVICE

P ublic recreational service encompasses all resources of the locality in an effort to provide various constituencies with opportunities for obtaining recreational experience. This means that community-situated agencies, whether in the public, quasi-public, or private sector, render primary services designed to satisfy one or more parts of the population by offering activities, facilities, instruction, counseling, and leadership under conditions considered to be enjoyable by recipients. The performance of community recreational services is typically guided by certain precepts to which most organizations adhere. Some commercial enterprises which purvey aspects of recreational activity, for example, places of entertainment, spas, sport centers, or specialty athletic clubs, may not be inclined to follow principles which have come to be accepted as fundamental to recreational service. These businesses cater to individuals who are buying space, equipment, or passive amusement on a personal basis and who therefore seek values known only to themselves. However, those agencies attempting to serve the common good through the provision of recreational activity are guided by generally acknowledged concepts. These concepts have developed as the field has matured. They are at once the distilled facts and essential truths by which practitioners in the field have learned to conduct their operations. They apply wherever people are to benefit from engagement in recreational activity sponsored by community-based organizations. How have these principles been formulated?

Development of Principles

Historically, a variety of factors has focused attention on man's recreational experiences and the opportunity for organized recreational experience provided by public or private agencies. The application of comprehensive activities operating for the social, physical, and cultural benefit of people has been supported by a varied group of agencies and individuals in many societies. Recreational activities are so manifold and extensive in expression that they represent nearly every form of approved human behavior. The scope and medium of experiences emphasize their necessity and value in whatever culture they have appeared. The diverse manifestations of leisure acts and the services incidental to them clearly indicate that salient or covert principles are in effect. Primary hypotheses and assumptions do exist, and they account for the widely separate means developed by different agencies and for the stressing of certain program instruction and experiences in these varied groups and places.

Principles are truths whose bases stem from scientifically corroborated facts and logical concepts. The sources of principles are primarily from logic, biology, philosophy, anthropology, sociology, and education. Facts derived from these studies become the fundamental premises upon which are built systematic concepts for behavioral guidance. However, it should be noted that some individuals may base their beliefs on nonsense, prejudice, emotional bias, or reasons that cannot be corroborated. Under these conditions, discriminating and valid action is unlikely, but nonetheless undertaken. Generalizations, for example, are quite often based upon knowledge which is predicated upon thinking that cannot be verified. The person who justifies his actions on the stated belief that "nice guys finish last" bases his view on a falsely interpreted fact. Attitudes held and supported by misrepresentations have just as much power to influence subsequent actions as do valid principles. The significant fact is that principles denote statements that can be validated, whereas attitudes, even those resting upon long use without adequate factual confirmation cannot be termed principles even though they influence behavior.

As a consequence of research, specific facts are established and give rise to a need. This need develops in terms of the explication and application of the findings of verified research. Many persons know what to do but are uncertain about putting their knowledge to practical use. They are acquainted with theory but are strangers to methods of practice. Scientific data need interpretation for action. Agencies of recreational service functioning within the private as well as the public sphere will progress more rapidly when they rely upon the twofold system comprising principles, for example, scientific foundations of research plus logical implementation through careful and accurate interpretation and application.

Principles are the best compilation of ideas which standardize behavior so that the most effective performance can be accomplished. It is unusual to find step-by-step sequential organization of principles in the writings of recreational service. Instead, students must analyze the content of volumes and determine the principles experts have deposited there. Thus, the development of a sound body of principles for the field has been somewhat hindered by lack of clarification. The principles herein presented are organized in such a way that there is a logical progression from a broad base of social-historical data to a narrowly specific rationale of application of principles which practitioners can utilize.

Standards

Standards are immediate and direct outgrowths of principles, a standard is a commonly held practical procedure for the implementation of the principle. Standards are developed as precise means for executing generalized rules of action. Because they are more numerous than principles, they are influenced by distinct situations and conditions. They are relatively flexible and subject to modification and do not have the same total commitment to invariability as do principles. The principle serves as the ideal goal toward which all activity is aimed. The standard is the action taken in attempting to reach the ideal. The need for standards is discovered in the requirement for organization, consistency, reliability, identification, and the sense of security and endurance in the conduct of social institutions.

Standards may be correctly or incorrectly oriented, purposeful or ambivalent, stable or short term; but whatever they are and however they are placed in effect, they include the operational techniques and are supposedly guided by principles. It seems inconceivable that standards disoriented to the clear purpose identified by principles can be set. Nevertheless, value judgments are made by human beings and are subject to the same biases and miscalculations that influence their creators. There are other reasons for a less-than-perfect standard implementing any given principle. More numerous than principles, standards attempt to meet the ideal from polar positions. The end result may be the same, but the actions taken to gain the end in view may be quite devisive. Standards are only as strong, reliable, and permanent as the human mind that formulates them can make them. Again, the human ego, personality, behavioral dynamics, and the pressures of environment upon the standard maker at any given time may result in measures which fail to fulfill the functions for which they were designed. Allowance for the role of human nature and personal motives cannot be omitted from the concept of standard making.

Standards are particularly significant to the purposes, range, and stability of recreational service. Principles of recreational service cannot operate without effective standards for their implementation. However valuable a principle may be, it will be of small benefit if the standards that are supposed to effect its idealization are static and without the necessary means to innovate, initiate, or boldly question current practices. If, on the other hand, standards are developed which forthrightly provide the *modus operandi* for producing services that comply in every respect with the principle, then recreational service and the persons who constitute its clientele will be well served.

Techniques

Even more numerous than standards, techniques are the practical day-to-day means for performing the work of the agency of recreational service. Just as standards serve as the implementation of principles, so too do techniques become the specific devices for the implementation of standards. Techniques are even more subject to variation and impermanence than the aforementioned factors. Techniques are often expedients and are used pragmatically. If a practice is successful it will be utilized regardless of whether it meets the requirement set forth by the principle and standards of which it is a consequence. Thus, for example, a basic principle is the provision of recreational service for all persons. This principle demands a wide range of activities which will appeal to the greatest number of people within the community to be served. However, the technique used may be to offer opportunity to a limited number of people through the inclusion of sports and games without adequate arrangement for other experiences. The basis for such thinking is that the routine provision of sports and games invariably succeeds in attracting a definite number of participants. The stability of numbers of participants in such activity will help to justify the department's request for funds or facilities. The inclusion of other activities within the program may be considered too unsure in terms of the number of individuals who might participate and therefore leaves the department open to harassment or censure for using public funds without justifiable results. Farfetched as this example may appear, it is nonetheless used time and again by some administrators to vindicate their extremely limited program and policies. In fact, there is no defense for the omission of a well-rounded and extensive program of various activities. The pragmatic view prevails among those who have not been professionally prepared to assume recreationist positions or among those who do not recognize or understand the nature and function of recreational service agencies.

These criticisms are not to be taken as an attack upon techniques. A good technique is practical and sure. It guides the necessary work according to the policies, standards, and principles to which it is oriented. It is a way of performance or rapid execution of some appointed task. It may be simple or complex, but in any case, the technique must conform to and be absolutely guided by principles. Briggs and Justman assert:

> The surest way of finding a solution for a new problem is not to draw solely on a composite of old experiences, but to possess sound fundamental principles and to know how to apply them.[1]

There is little question that a series of techniques is requisite for competency in carrying out the principles of recreational service, but as will be obvious, complete reliance upon the technique of expediency without guidance or understanding of principles can result in experiences and values which are less than standard at best, and unfortunate or negative at worst. The main difficulty in attempting to resolve problems that occur in recreational service by the use of common techniques is that two program situations are rarely if ever identical. Intrinsic and conditional factors vary from individual to individual, time to time, activity to activity, group to group, and environment to environment.

A technique that proves successful in one situation may not be successful in the next. More is needed than an array of techniques on which to rely when a situation demands improvisation and creativity by the recreationist. Principles are necessary to guide the selection and steps of action for appropriate techniques, as well as to indicate new methods when conditions require them. Recreational service must be controlled and guided by a definite set of principles by which optimal values can be gained for and by people. Otherwise, recreational service continues in a

---

[1]T.H. Briggs and J.L. Justman, *Improving Instruction Through Supervision* (New York: The MacMillan Company, 1952), p. 406.

haphazard, trial-and-error, and inept manner. Such operation is not only wasteful of time, money, and effort, but it tends to deteriorate the image of the field, which needs all of the public support it can gain.

The previous statements should not be understood as a condemnation of techniques nor as a suggestion that techniques are not absolutely essential for carrying out the practices of recreational service. Techniques are basic to the provision of recreational service. Skillfulness and technical information are necessities. When the objectives are defined and standards have been set, then the achievement of the entire operation hinges upon the technical competence and adroitness of the recreationist. Recreational service is a technical field which calls for specialized and prolonged education and sound experiences before one is adequately prepared in its various techniques. Principles are essential if techniques are to be correctly channeled, but principles can never abrogate the basic role which techniques play in the execution of the procedures and practices of daily recreational service.

Services

All efforts by community-based agencies designed to help people lead more satisfying lives through the enhancement of their physical, mental, social, and cultural capacities by active or passive participation within recreational experiences may be deemed services. Services may be performed for monetary return, for altruistic purposes without extrinsic motives, for a combination of these reasons, or out of necessity created by cultural forces requiring such endeavors if the organization of a specific society is to survive.

Commercial enterprises perform services for profit. Humanitarians provide services because of their belief in, and need to promote, human dignity. Certain individuals and organizations are motivated by a blending of humanitarian dedication and economic gain. Only public services, growing out of governmental establishment, perform functions thought to be essential for the preservation, stabilization, and advancement of the ideological order through the promotion of the public well-being. Services are usually intangible products, the effects of which enable recipients to perform their individual functions better. The improved performance, in turn, either modifies the environment (social or natural), so that particular activities may be engaged in, or mitigates conditions to the extent that the individual is able to achieve some satisfaction or enjoyment as a result of a given experience.

Functions and Responsibilities of Recreational Service

All functions and responsibilities undertaken by the recreational service agency are necessary but incidental to the chief reason for the establishment of such agencies. Everything the agency does is performed with one objective—the direct or indirect sponsorship, operation, management, and administration of activities of a recreational nature within a comprehensive program. All other acts are important only to the extent that they contribute to a more effective end product, that is, the creation of an environment in which participants may engage in a variety of recreational endeavors.

The recreational service triad consists of leadership, finance, and facilities. Each of these aspects is necessary if a well-planned, comprehensive program containing a variety of activities is to be offered. No one questions the fact that people are capable of assuming individual responsibility for achieving recreational experiences by themselves. However, in an ever-expanding society of specialists, many persons simply do not have the monetary means to construct suitable areas or facilities for participation in motor skills, dramatics, art, craft, and other experiences requiring special spaces, places, direction, or financial outlay. The community recreational service agency makes all these things available to the greatest number of people at the least possible cost to them, and further provides the competent personnel to guide, instruct, or lead activities of this type.

Analogous to the services rendered by a public recreational agency is the example of those an obstetrical team offers a mother during childbirth. For thousands of years women gave birth with little, if any, assistance from anybody. More recently, the science of medicine has developed techniques for the more efficient and safe handling of mother and child during parturition. Aseptic methods in modern delivery rooms have decreased death rates from puerperal infections, toxemia, and a host of other diseases. Obstetrical methods have progressed to the point where a great deal of pain, complicated delivery, injuries, and other traumata to the mother and child are either minimized or eliminated. Women can still give birth to children without medical assistance, but if assistance is available, the experience is safer, healthier, and with less likelihood of undue complication. The same holds true for recreational service and the integral experiences produced for the participating recipient. These services are available, and practitioners are more highly competent and technically qualified than ever before to perform functions which will enable participants to achieve a greater degree of satisfaction in a wider variety of activities. Why, then should not the general public make use of these services?

Among the coincidental services the community agency performs in carrying out its prime responsibility are organization, administration, education, coordination, conservation, planning, supervision, programming, and evaluation. The net outcome of the sum of these functions is the offering of the broadest schedule of recreational activities from which the individual may choose for his satisfaction.

Organization

In order to carry out the objectives of bringing participants into contact with recreational activities, a certain amount of organizational arrangement must be made. Basically, organization concerns the establishment of the agency, the specifications of its functions and responsibilities, the structure of its internal system—that is, employment of line and staff personnel to operate the agency and produce those services which result in recreational activities—and the performance of those necessary adjustments within the community so that the most effective, efficient, and economical utilization of available professional leadership, volunteers, spaces, areas, facilities, equipment, and financial support can be made. The objective of organization is attained when the most complete provision of recreational experiences is formulated so that individuals have the opportunity to satisfy their individual needs.

Administration

To carry out the policies assumed as a result of the institution of the community recreational service agency and guided by the principles adopted during organizational establishment, the process of direction, management, and control that is termed *administration* is initiated to operate the agency. Administration is the medium by which all segments of the agency are coordinated in the production of activities for the recreational benefit of agency constituents. Operationally, administration is divided into at least eight subdivisions for the most efficacious outcomes relating to activity offerings: personnel management, fiscal management, recording, planning, maintenance, public relations, research, and programming. Administration within community recreational agencies should be wholly concerned with techniques for the conduct of effective services that can be supplied to the citizens of any community at minimal cost, maximal efficiency, and without repetition of other agency functions.

Education

Every recreational service agency has an obligation to keep its patrons informed about the agency, but beyond that, it has an instructional obligation to perform. It should attempt to educate people to the variety of activities in which they can engage, not only for public relations purposes, but also in terms of equipping the individual for enjoyable and valuable pursuits during leisure. The enrichment of life, enhancement of personality, enlargement of personal viewpoints, teaching of skills, and the guidance of people in selecting leisure activities that will be reflected in creative achievement are all part of this procedure. The significant development of appreciation for and participation in worthwhile leisure activities in an instructional goal. An ofttimes neglected, but nevertheless important, contribution that recreational service agencies may make to the steady utilization of common means of enjoyment is the effort to make available opportunities in an environment wherein people find it conducive to learn. This instruction does not have to be formal education. The entire process can be informal and concomitant with the provision of a well-balanced program. Something for everybody, rather than stereotyped and routine acts, may be the most effective method by which individuals will be educated to appreciate personal capacity and potential for achievement and the satisfaction that achievement brings.

Coordination

No single agency can provide all the services necessary to meet the needs of each individual within the community. Even when there is an established public recreational service agency, the time of operation, personnel, and experiences offered simply cannot keep pace with the diverse needs of people. The limitations upon any one agency are not insurmountable. Some coordinating effort within the community must be arranged so that all the people are reached. Public recreational agencies must cooperate and coordinate their services with all other agencies, so that the most comprehensive program of recreational experiences can be offered.

Each agency in the community, whether public, private, or quasi-public, has something in its program, structure, or orientation to offer to people. These agencies exist to serve people. They have the specialized personnel, financial resources, and physical plants, material, or equipment necessary to supplement and complement the natural and physical resources of other agencies. By judicious counsel, joint planning, and cooperative attitudes, all agencies within any community may more effectively meet the social recreational needs of people. These efforts may very well provide recreational services to almost all the people all the time without jurisdictional dispute, duplication of functions, or expensive and needless monetary expenditures. Coordination may be the purposive process by which strangulating competition for the same group of participants at the same time is eliminated, and by which each person may be the recipient of a more highly competent and extensive series of services.

Conservation

Public recreational agencies in particular must acquire, develop, and otherwise maintain areas for the recreational values derived from the utilization of such spaces by the public. Insofar as is possible these agencies must protect any natural resources within their jurisdiction. Such preservation is extended to fish and wildlife as well as flora and whatever wilderness exists within the area under control. The entire concept of conservation deals not only with the continuing use of natural resources in such a manner as to avoid depletion, pollution, or destruction, but also with the controlled maintenance through scientific management and the sustained development of resources that can be replenished.

Because the public is poorly informed on the current status of the nation's natural resources, it behooves agencies involved in conservation to establish lines of communication with every means applicable and at their disposal. Unfortunately, the day of unlimited natural recreational resources is largely over because of the exploitation and spoilage by private interests and shortsighted governmental officials. To this must be added an increasing population with higher demand for outdoor recreational resources to use and the consequent impaction of some of these resources. Unquestionably, the time has arrived when properties must be operated with a minimum of waste and destruction. It has become necessary for governmental agencies to regulate natural resources and areas for the benefit of the country as a whole. Local agencies have the responsibility to provide the same control in their jurisdictions.

Land and water areas are necessary for comprehensive recreational activities. Unless space is preserved against encroachment for any reason, it is used up and cannot be replaced.

In order that the public may enjoy whatever primitive or wilderness areas remain, recreational service agencies must acquire and set aside these spaces, in perpetuity, so that present and future generations have the opportunity to see and appreciate the wonderful scenery and wildlife, and so that those who wish to enjoy wilderness experiences may be accommodated. It is unlikely that any municipality will have an area that can be remotely termed primitive or wilderness, but to the extent that open and natural places are still available, they should be preserved. This need is particularly crucial in large urban centers where the density of population far outstrips any of the reserved natural areas.

Planning

The systematic acquisition and logical development of property and physical plants based upon a long-term priority schedule is one aspect of planning. Community recreational agencies must provide adequate facilities in order to safeguard the health and welfare of the participants, to provide for the conservation of accessible natural areas and resources for the perpetual use and value of the people, and to control expenditures on a need basis in coordination with local, district, and regional plans.

Planning is the process by which current status of the locality under investigation is determined. It is concerned with the collection, analysis, and evaluation of the physical and natural areas and resources of the community in order to assess whether there are adequate recreational spaces and structures; it compares population movement, trends, and density with property and facility needs; it provides a method by which the agency may incorporate community preparedness for future growth and cooperative endeavor in realizing the significance of recreational service to the community; and it is a device whereby undesirable conditions may be alleviated.

Planning is an exploratory technique in which an attempt is made to develop sound procedures for the orderly selection, acquisition, construction, and maintenance of land and water spaces which can serve the immediate and future needs of residents and transients of the local community. It is the principal means of gathering information upon which a master plan can be based so that a more highly skilled and effective service can be rendered. The main purpose of planning is the collation of evidence, both existing and predictable, that affects the jurisdiction's competency to initiate and administer an ever more valuable and effective recreational service to its people. Planning for recreational service is an integral part of total community planning. The interrelationship of all community factors, of which recreational service is but one, is a necessary objective in the analysis of local and agency needs.

Supervision

Supervision, the leadership process, has two distinct functions: guidance and direction of participants within the program of recreational activities sponsored by the agency; and the maintenance of personnel standards of competency and effectiveness of all employees. Supervision may be effected by authority and headship, or by communication and understanding among persons. If the latter technique of human relationship is used, as it should be, then more satisfactory behaviors can be expected, feelings of reliability and loyalty may be engendered, and the personality needs of personnel will be met better. Being able to understand individual behavior patterns is one of the important areas of specialized knowledge acquired by the professional, and is a skill especially necessary for the supervisor.

The highly successful supervisor is an individual whose participating followers are not aware of being led, whose supervision is indirect, and who works with and through others. Naturally, this type of leadership depends upon the previous experiences, level of competence, motivation, intelligence, and status of those participating in the activity. Supervisory factors depend, to a great extent, upon the mental contact, desire, enthusiasm, age, and skill of participants and the environment in which the recreationist works.

Supervision is important in terms of encouraging worker resourcefulness on the job. The supervisor is also responsible for the guidance and in-service education of line employees, direction of certain phases of the overall program of activities, interpretation of administrative policies to lower echelons, and the elimination of grievances, which tend to undermine staff effectiveness. The success of supervision can be measured in relation to increased worker competence and participant attendance and enjoyment of program offerings. In general, the supervisor will perform a variety of functions, such as:

1. Understand the recreational needs and interests of those the program will serve.
2. Provide direct leadership, when required, of individuals within the program.
3. Guide volunteers toward providing better service in their performance.
4. Direct, control, and maintain facilities in order to produce a maximal amount of service at the lowest possible cost.
5. Coordinate, through scheduling and conference, the use of recreational structures, facilities, and spaces.
6. Keep abreast of current techniques and practices in recreational service in order to assist and guide program workers as well as to make supervisory personnel more competent.
7. Offer direct counseling and inservice education, and participate in field observation to enhance worker competence and morale, and be in a position to offer valid advice and reliable appraisal of worker performance.

Programming

The *sine qua non* for any recreational service agency is the provision of opportunities for the public to engage in recreational experiences. Programming is the chief means of carrying out the prime responsibility for which the agency was created. Adequate programming is derived when the agency can offer a varied, stimulating, and well-balanced selection of activities that meet both individual and group needs. The program itself must appeal to different age groups of both sexes and take into consideration such aspects of social life as economic means, educational background, vocational experiences, religious beliefs, ethnic, racial, and environmental status, and physical and mental capacity to perform. Some activities will be routine because they appeal to all. However, some activities will be programmed on the basis of individual differences and special needs or interests.

Programming is the process by which the agency brings together the participant, the activity, any specialized facility or space, and whatever instructional direction or leadership is necessary for the participant's enjoyment of the experience. It involves the establishment of a master calendar of events on a community-wide basis, which is subdivided into hourly, daily, weekly, and monthly activities. These activities may be programmed to direct attention to some common theme, so that there is, or appears to be, a progression of experiences culminating in a central event. There are routine activities whose universal appeal makes their inclusion on a daily basis mandatory. There are intermittent or irregular activities with application, but whose more frequent use might lead to undue fatigue, harassment, or boredom. There are singular events or unique spectaculars performed once or less than three times throughout the year, and there are special interest experiences, which may coincide with holidays, memorials, anniversaries, ceremonial occasions, or ethnic and religious patterns.

The main purpose of programming is to create opportunities whereby people are assisted in achieving the maximal benefit from active or passive participation in any given activity. Programming has extreme ramifications, the details of which cannot be fully explained here. However, the program of any recreational agency should contain as many activities as there are professional staff and volunteer workers to give guidance and instruction on a continual, regular, and adequate basis. The program may include some of the following activities, offered on a fee or free basis, and with any necessary instructions in order for participants to achieve satisfaction: athletics, games, art, crafts, dancing, dramatics, outdoor and nature experience, music, hobbies, and social, educational, service, and special projects. Such activities should be scheduled either where there is a high degree of interest and potential participation, or for exposure of people to activities which may stimulate participation by their very unfamiliarity. Programming is clearly one of the most vital segments of the agency's work. Through this function, the justification for the establishment of the agency is readily explained.

Evaluation

Evaluation, the comparison of present recreational services to proposed services, and the contrast between one agency's or one community's recreational service operation with another of the same type, is the process utilized to determine the adequacy, ability, and comprehensiveness of organizational offerings. Evaluation is concerned with every aspect and function of the operation. It is a technique designed to measure current output against specified goals.

Every recreational service agency must undergo evaluation continually in order to establish and maintain an optimal recreational service for the people it serves. Significantly, objectives of evaluation are not the same as the process of evaluation. The objective, or end product, is improvement, whereas the procedure is simply one of contrast and qualitative measurement. Thus, evaluation seeks to determine:

1. The actual level of performance or adequacy of the subject under consideration.
2. Any shortcomings that currently exist.
3. Unsatisfactory fulfillment of service needs.
4. Personal and physical or natural resources that may be utilized.
5. Suggestions for favorable reform.
6. Policy relating to priority for action.

There is no function of the agency that may not profit from evaluative action. Just as the operational procedures and standard duties of the department may be studied for improvement, so too, can all personnel and their respective responsibilities be subjected to the same evaluative procedure. The objectives will remain, but they will tend to fall in the qualitative rather than in the quantitative category. Objective and subjective examination of personnel efficiency is within the purview of evaluation. Unless all factors relating to the provision of recreational service within the community are adequately considered, the inquiry will be deficient and indecisive and will not offer any substantial, accurate, or valid means for effecting improvements and abolishing the insufficiencies in the subject under investigation.

Chapter 2

VALUES OF RECREATIONAL EXPERIENCE

Many values have been ascribed to recreational activity and these are essentially why recreational service has been promoted for the well-being of participants. The movement has promulgated a wide variety of experiences which include these basic values thought to be of extreme importance in enhancing life itself.

Physical Fitness

Although physical fitness is a specific state of physiological conditioning which is subject to change in terms of muscle tone and endurance, certain gross motor activities suited to the needs of the individual will, with the person's regular participation, contribute to the development of his functional power and stamina, and have a significant effect on the physiological structure of his musculature, skeletal system, and vital organs. Vigorous muscular activities develop the individual's ability to work to capacity with less fatigue and more effectiveness.

The improvement of physical vigor and the release of hostility, caused by the sublimation of certain feelings, through competitive experiences or individual acts in a social setting provide satisfaction for the participant in motor activities. Because a great number of persons take part in physical activities for the sense of achievement they attain, the experience is one in which significant behavior toward others is highly developed.

Health

Among the many factors which contribute positively to the development of health is joyous activity. Certain activities have an important hygienic effect. Of equal significance from the standpoint of health is the emotional release which nearly all recreational activity affords, and the joyous effect of activity upon the person through the functioning of the endocrine glands.

Recreational service seeks to provide activities largely out-of-doors because of the appreciation of its health-building and health-conserving values. The programs of community recreational service are designed in part to counteract the effects of sedentary occupation and the strains of daily life, which promote degenerative conditions because of insufficient motor activity. During leisure, community recreational programs afford opportunities for continuation of good health habits, moral conduct, and increased individual development. Activities for all ages are thus employed to supply that form of exercise and mental or emotional involvement which may be missing from other aspects of living. Therefore, these activities contribute to the maintenance of the whole person.

Satisfaction

The limited satisfaction many individuals receive from their employment enhances the importance of recreational activity and provides an objective toward which recreational service may move. More and more, people must depend upon their recreational outlets for the continuation of the developmental processes begun during childhood. When a person enters a vocation, usually he employs only a limited range of his skills; his other skills should be expressed and developed further by recreational offerings. Community recreational service, through such activities as may be provided, creates an opportunity for balanced development and for a continuation of education in lines pursued, for utilitarian and nonutilitarian purposes, both of which may bring pure satisfaction.

The impulses that are the bases for creative art, music, literature, and drama are to be found in almost everyone to a variable degree. Potentially, everyone is an artist, a musician, an interpreter, and a dramatist. There is no more thrilling experience for the individual than to discover some modicum of creative capacity in one of these media. People may be literally born anew by such discoveries in their recreational experiences. Through well-planned leisure programs, opportunities for discovery of latent talent may be created and a new type of art patron developed, namely, one who has had personal experience in the arts and whose appreciation for the creative efforts of others is, therefore, more real. For too long the development of art has been left to the professionals. Through planned leisure, art may be restored to the amateurs and a real folk art may emerge, making for a happier people.

It is not necessary to justify recreational service as a means of accomplishing preconceived objectives. It is true, however, that benefits will accrue to participants in recreational activity. But the participant is not always conscious of them. Accomplishment of objectives is somewhat impeded by too serious contemplation of them by the subject. The individual is primarily interested in the *affect* and only incidentally in the *effect* of the experience. The affective state of satisfaction is, therefore, the primary objective of recreational participation.

Individual satisfaction must be recognized in planning all recreational services. At the same time, it is necessary to discriminate between levels of satisfaction. There must be an effort to improve the quality of appreciation and response. This raises the inevitable question as to whether a community recreational agency should provide a program in accord with what people want or what people should have. This question is usually answered in the codes, philosophy, or charter that gave original authorization for creation of the agency or inauguration of the program. For example, state enabling laws authorizing the establishment of systems of public recreational service frequently set forth the purposes of the legislature in enacting the legislation, and are almost always stated in terms of public welfare. The view may be justified, therefore, that it is a mandatory obligation of a public recreational agency to offer facilities and a program of activities which attempt to accomplish the desired social objectives. At the same time, the facilities and program must meet with public approval, or participation in the activities will not eventuate. The problem is one of providing facilities and programs which induce participation in activities that contribute to desired objectives, in a manner immediately and primarily satisfying to the individual. This, of course, calls for the greatest skill in planning and the highest degree of leadership.

Safety

Another aim of community recreational service is safety education and prevention of accidents. The earliest playgrounds were advocated as necessary in order to get small children off the streets, which were becoming unsafe as play places. This continues to be an important objective because, in most congested urban areas, the only alternative to playing on a playground is playing on a public street. The recreational center goes further than this, however, for it eliminates the most dangerous practices in play, provides safe equipment, and through competent leadership instructs safe practices. By developing skill in recreational activities, much of the hazard inherent in body contact games or in activities which require individual strength, coordination, and flexibility is avoided. Awkwardness and dangerous acts are replaced with skilled practice when professionals supervise the program. Personnel of modern recreational agencies also make continual studies of causes of accidents and unsafe conditions on the operated areas and devise means for their removal. Additionally, outdoor recreational areas may be designed, where appropriate, to eliminate obvious hazards without destroying aesthetic appearances.

Social Intercourse

Social needs have to be satisfied throughout life. There are always situations wherein people have to meet, mix, get along, or adjust. Social activities of a wide scope have a place in any program in which socially approved actions are desired and good mental health is an objective. The relationships developed as a result of such social intercourse contribute to the development of empathy, understanding, catharsis, personal value, and self-expression.

Through recreational activity a person may find a satisfying place among peers. Cultivating the basic human virtues of courage, justice, patience, and fairness may be enhanced. Learning to live happily among peers, making a contribution to the good of all, and feeling wanted, needed, and appreciated are the basic needs of the social person. In playing together people learn to live together and to adjust to the ramified and complex relationships which society imposes upon them.

Cultural Achievement

At the present time, the tremendous drop in the number of working hours which today's machines make possible allows for vast opportunities for everyone, in a recreational context, to select and move toward the ends that seem good to him. His selection of leisure activities may be wise or foolish, worthwhile or stupid, but it will be only by educating him that he will choose the wise and worthwhile ones. Individual satisfaction and self-realization will be a consequence of how well the educational process has taught the individual to enjoy and employ free time in recreational experiences.

All decisions concerning human behavior patterns are important. Every alternative relating to the activities in which people engage is an educational selection because it gives guidance and direction to the path of human development. For this reason, recreational opportunities have a marked influence on the maturation and development of personality and character. Because it is an individual choice, recreational activity is an accurate indicator of personal interests and goals. If this is true, then recreational activity is a concern of education and the agencies by which education is transmitted. Individual growth through recreational experiences must not, cannot, be left to chance situations or accident. Recreational living must receive the careful and deliberate planning of those whose professional duty it is to provide service to the public in an educational capacity. Provision for recreational experience must be as skillfully guided as is preparation for a job. In many instances, educational opportunity for cultural development through recreational experiences is even more pronounced than are opportunities on the job.

Heretofore, the total amount of leisure not only has been small in quantity but also has been in the possession of few. Now it is an almost universal possession. Some persons question whether the American people will prove themselves equal to the opportunities which this heritage bestows upon them by using their leisure for the improvement of the national culture, or whether through its misuse the culture will be profaned. Civilization, according to H.G. Wells, is a race between the forces of education and disaster. Community recreational service, having a broad educational impact upon people, can have a significant part in this race.

Ethical Practices

A distinctive ethical code is the characteristic of a professional field. It is a primary objective of the recreationist to provide service to all individuals under the auspices of the agency and to perform in a way that can cast no shadow of doubt upon his ethical practice. The professional's unique knowledge and skill carry with them certain moral responsibilities. The ethical code of professional practice is a special instrumentation of ideal precepts, formed from an awareness of the particular functions attributed to the unique field for which it was established.

The ethics of practice require the recreationist to provide the best possible service which professional preparation and experience make available. It is the recreationist's duty to afford varied opportunities of a recreational nature where people may satisfactorily achieve such experience. The practice of the recreationist must adhere to the principle of equalitarian service, regardless of the social, economic, racial, religious, educational, health status, physical or emotional limitation, or political affiliation of prospective clients. It is an item of the professional ethic that equal opportunity for recreational satisfaction be offered in the most attractive manner possible.

By definition, the recreational experience is inherently moral. Nothing about the term reveals any intent for physical, social, or psychological disintegration. On the contrary, recreational activity is conceived to be of benefit to the participant. Leisure may be utilized immorally or morally, and it is the function of the professional practitioner to guide people into activities that have been proved beneficial. The recreationist is concerned ethically with human behavior. He must provide services that will induce people to participate in recreational activities rather than in wanton activities.

Democratic Ideals

Recreational service recognizes the essential dignity and worth of the individual and accords a place commensurate with the individual's capacity and willingness to serve. A person's success is determined by his ability to produce and to cooperate with others. Democratic ideals are concerned in the individual's acceptance of the rights of others and in the use of processes which preclude infringement upon the equitable actions of others. Recognition of the rules of the game is necessary in the same way as the regulations of society are recognized. The individual may select specific recreational experiences, the time devoted to them, and those who will also participate in such a venture. Yet, full enjoyment of recreational activity requires submission to collective choices and self-imposed laws. This is the essence of democracy. If it becomes the rule of life in recreational pursuit, it will be difficult to follow another principle in other areas of living. Recreational opportunity in America conforms with the democratic ideal and fosters its general acceptance and application.

As the economic, civic, and social organization has become more complex, requiring increasing regimentation of individuals even in a democracy, the freedom which people may still enjoy in leisure stands out in bold relief. The democratic principle of freedom strongly persists in leisure. The necessity for regimentation that exists in productive industry does not exist in leisure, although there is an ever-present danger that people might unwittingly yield this freedom to self-appointed or elected dictators. Dictators in totalitarian nations have demonstrated how leisure may be organized to serve the will of the dictator and the purpose of the state. The Declaration of Independence declares that "life, liberty and the pursuit of happiness" are among "certain unalienable rights" with which "all men are endowed by their Creator." The right to pursue happiness in leisure must be considered a basic precept in American democracy. In protecting this principle in leisure, the democratic ideal is sustained.

It is the concept of freedom in leisure that imposes upon society the necessity of educating people for leisure. Democracy has been said to contain the seed of its own destruction. This is certainly true in relation to leisure. Individuals may interpret liberty as license, rather than as freedom with concomitant responsibility. The individual, therefore, may freely neglect to take advantage of leisure for purposes of growth and development; the individual may even waste it in vulgarity, mediocrity, and debauchery. Any person may destroy body, mind, or the finer sensibilities by excesses in leisure, or may develop powers and enhance knowledge, talent, and satisfactions by creative utilization of leisure through recreational endeavors.

The Principle of Equality

Every person has the innate right to pursue his dreams and must be given the opportunity to fulfill personal needs within societally accepted bounds without artificial hindrance or restriction as he has the capacity to achieve. The only limitations upon individual achievement should be biological potential and social acceptability. Age, sex, race, ethnic origin, religion, economic worth, political affiliation, social status, and physical or mental handicap are all considered artificially contrived restrictions if, because of them, any person is prevented from participating in an activity which would otherwise be socially acceptable. Social acceptability in this instance has nothing to do with regional traditions or biases. Social acceptability simply means that the activity is not immoral, injurious to life, detrimental to the health, welfare, or safety of the individual so engaged or to anyone directly or indirectly associated with the experience.

The only criterion of equality utilized for recreational service is whether each individual has had an opportunity to take advantage of activities offered, not whether he has actually participated. There is no stipulation as to the amount of service received. In fact, equality of service is neither possible nor feasible because of the great disparity in individual differences.

To the extent that some persons need a good deal more attention than others in instructional assistance, personal guidance, activity direction, or other supervision, there will always be a disproportionate amount of services administered because of the very nature of recreational services. There are too many people in comparison to the number of professional personnel employed within the field. In no way can every person be reached; it is a physical and economic impossibility. The usual way of fulfilling the recreational needs of people is by attracting a small group so that specific individual service can be performed or by programming for mass activities. Only in special situations will the recreationist be able to work on a one-to-one basis, and these will be instances in which the physical or mental capacity of the participant is so limited as to make any other possible method untenable.

Thus, recreational service is concerned with equality of opportunity. Every person must be given a share, an opportunity to perform, whether the opportunity is taken or not is incidental. That the chance to take part is available is the only fact. Insofar as this opportunity is one of recreational experience, it is limited to those satisfactions which may be gained through activities in a recreational context. But beyond the opportunity to participate or not to participate, recreationists have the professional obligation of providing stimulating activities covering all phases of human living. There must be something for everybody. Activities should range as wide as the human mind is capable of expanding, with emphasis upon those events which tend to inculcate achievements in social, cultural, and educational experiences.

It is meet that recreationists have an educational function as well as a program function because only when attractive and positively suggestive activities are offered will individuals want to take part. Although it is important to make the experience available, it is of equal importance that the activity be of such a nature as to excite persons and entice their participation; particularly is this true when they have had no previous experience. Professionalism demands that each person's personal horizon be widened so that he has a better chance to enrich his life. If the recreationist can open a new door to satisfaction and achievement through presentation of ingenuity and attractive activities, then competent performance is forthcoming. After all, this is the purpose for which the recreationist is employed.

Social Limitations on Equality

All men are not created equal, nor does the Constitution of the United States attempt to make such a statement. The true meaning of the constitutional statement is an idealistic concept of all men being equal under a justly administered legal system, under God (if such a belief is part of the individual's rationale), and because all men are endowed with the unalienable right to life, liberty, and the pursuit of happiness, equality of opportunity. All men are different by virtue of genetic identification, environment, and other factors. Even identical twins have some basic personality, physical, and social distinctions, because according to Newton's law, two bodies cannot occupy the same space at the same time. Each individual, therefore, sees objects just a little differently from anyone else. This is not only a physical phenomenon, but an emotional or a psychological one as well. Environmental stimuli and pressures cause different reactions to the same set of facts or conditions in different individuals and give rise to differing opinions, attitudes, biases, and extremes of behavior.

Because we cannot all have the same points of view, and because we are characterized by specific physical, mental, and other differences, the idea of equality, except as an abstract form, is meaningless. Yet, there is, or should be, equality. Even in a great working democracy, where the law is supposed to be administered impartially and where justice is tempered with mercy, equality is a sometimes thing.

Economic means has often played an important role in securing one verdict from judge or jury when, in fact, another judgment should have been handed down. However, discrepancies are rapidly dying as great new legal gains are made in jurisprudence. The American Civil Liberties Union, state laws which provide indigents with court-appointed defenders, and the Supreme Court of the United States have done much to eradicate inequalities due to economic status while giving greater protection to defendants in criminal cases. But this is an imperfection of human nature rather than a revocation of the principle of equity. Until the last few years it could also be said that a wealthy individual by reason of wealth might secure more highly competent and effective counsel before the law. The poor person was either denied access to highly polished advocates or limited means incapacitated his understanding or denied him an adequate defense. Affluence is itself an unequalizing force in society and nowhere has this been more apparent than in the law courts. Fortunately, these circumstances have been reduced through more enlightened legislation and private interest groups. Even where there is a blatant misuse of office, or where felonies occur, the wealthy rarely suffer the degree of punishment, in terms of penal servitude, high fines, or both, as do the poor. Nevertheless, all people should be equal before the law.

As far as equality of opportunity is concerned, social custom, ignorance, bigotry, and other impingements tend to lessen or make unequal the opportunities that are available to different persons. Education, aside from wealth, is still the great leveler in a democracy. But opportunity to obtain the kind of education that could equalize a disproportionate allocation of wealth, social control, status, and other societal advantages is often denied even the person with the most highly endowed intelligence because of lack of funds, and other cultural strata may prevent an individual from gaining access to institutions of first rank. In other words, many barriers are raised against those who do not have the financial means even if they have the natural talent and intellectual ability. The vicious cycle of inequality seems to be that if one does not have it, one cannot get it because no matter how hard one tries, one does not have it. Certainly there are exceptions, but they serve only to prove the rule.

Cynicism aside, and with knowledge of the inability of humans to achieve perfection in many or all aspects of social intercourse, all who seek to serve other people must work toward the ideal of equality. Wherever professionals view human dignity and the pursuit of excellence above materialism, there equality for all has a chance for development as a common part of life instead of as the rarity it is.

Prejudice

Prejudice is widespread in this society, and it is this bias that accounts for the development and constancy of unequal social opportunities. Inequality of opportunities to participate in many cultural experiences causes, in turn, behavior and personality characteristics which are analyzed as proof of inferiority by the majority group and produce additional so-called evidence giving rise to further bias. All prejudice is nurtured, it is not inborn. The attitudes of any bias against a minority group are taught either directly or vicariously by contact with bigotry in the home, neighborhood, school, church, and other social environments. It is indirectly manufactured through literary, popular magazine, radio, theater, motion pictures, and other media by which common stereotypes are mass produced.

The most valid reasons for bigotry can be ascribed only to economic and psychological disturbance. In the former example, the exploitation of minority groups has had distinct advantages for the majority group. Minority groups have always undergone economic exploitation in this country. Every new wave of immigration brings with it a racial, a religious, an ethnic, or a political group against whom prejudice is leveled, so that the dominant group can arrogate for itself the best occupational positions, the amassment of the most wealth, and the highest status in society. Another reason for the development of bigotry is the emotional or psychological factors which the least secure, least educated, and least recognized within the social hierarchy manifest against minority groups. Those who are thwarted in any way, and are unable to cope with such frustration, seek the rationalization of scapegoating. Frustrations are not resolved by casting aspersions against minority groups, but they tend to ease the feelings of individual guilt and reduce the need for acceptance of self blame.

Age

During no other period of American life has there been such a concern for the problems of old age as during the last 15 years. More than 33 million persons are classified as aged because they have reached 65 years or more. Public concern continues to grow as an increasing number of persons reach the age when they are considered to be economically useless, victims of advancing health hazards, and dependent or partially dependent upon others for basic necessities. The elderly have long since learned the efficacy of a united front and the power of the ballot.[1] Old people are the most consistent voters of all our groups able to vote. One outcome of this fact is that all legislators are wary of dismissing the desires or demands of the elderly in terms of health insurance, job retention, discrimination against them, and other empowerment rights. All too frequently, society arbitrarily assumes that old age makes a sudden appearance at 65, as may be seen from the commercial propensity of forcing retirement at 65. It is fallacious to presume that there is any specific age at which a person becomes old. This psychophysiological process may occur at any time. Just as individual differences are

---

[1]*U.S. News and World Report,* "The Elderly Fight Back," (Vo. 109, No. 4, July 23, 1990), p. 46.

noted in personality, so are there individual differences in the degree of aging. Physiologically, the internal organs age at varying rates and with different intensities. Externally, eyes and ears are not necessarily impaired in their functions at the same rate nor to the same degree. In fact, some individuals never lose these sensory functions.

Not only are there great individual differences in onset of specific physical decline, there is also the psychological aspect of aging which is probably more apparent and important. Psychological deterioration is the more likely manifestation, although its measurement is more difficult. Intense forms of senescence are readily observed in loss of memory, inability to concentrate, inability to learn new skills, insecurity, suspiciousness, living in the past, and other features. It must be understood, however, that these indications of aging do not occur in all individuals, and even if some do, they do not occur at the same time nor at the same rate. At least 4 million persons have Alzheimer's Disease, which produces these symptoms.

Adjustment to the changes of aging is essentially a subjective matter. It can be achieved when there is opportunity rather than rejection. Because society as a whole creates roles, biases, social values, status, agencies, organizations, and services, the personal problems of old age have their mirror image in the social environment. Society and the individual communities have provided a favorable environment for the development and self-fulfillment of other age groups and they have now created the same climate for the elderly adult. American society recognizes and rewards self-sufficient and contributing citizens. It ignores or allows disproportionate existence to those who have outlived their usefulness—at least as far as some persons are concerned. Medical science has discovered ways by which life can be prolonged for 10 to 25 years after an individual reaches 65. With prolongation of life, there has been concurrent societal efforts, either to utilize productively the knowledge and experiences assimilated by willing individuals, or to make sure that the elderly adult is not screened out of the events which constitute the mainstream of life.

The denial of a worthwhile role for the aged in any of the areas comprising social existence that excludes them from equal opportunities to achieve in economic enterprises (unless they are financially independent), in civic responsibility, and even within the family, is increasingly unlikely. The elderly are better served today than ever before and recreational agencies of all types are in the forefront in the delivery of such services.

Youth

The limitation on youths in a society which dotes upon them seems to have built-in contradictions. Nevertheless, this society attempts to give with one hand while taking with the other. The adolescent is expected to act in a manner that conforms with adult societal standards, although he is, in fact, treated as a child. Confusion as to moral attitudes and standards confronts the adolescent on all sides. He is at once admonished to go to school, stay in school, and then select a vocation in which he will be able to earn his livelihood. This has been the time-tested formula since societies were first organized. Unfortunately, in this era of modern technology and varied occupations, there is an attempt to force the individual, from early childhood through young adulthood, into preconceived molds that actually may not meet the individual's particular needs and differences. All too often, great emphasis is placed upon peer competition. "Why can't you be like Johnny? He always gets high marks!" is an anguished cry from some parents who refuse to believe that their child cannot perform as well as someone else's child.

"You're going to college whether you want to or not!" is another common parental statement. For whom is this college education? In many instances, it is not for the recipient, but for the parent or for the parent's unconscious desire to have his child accepted into a society where a college education has become a partial open sesame to economic and social status. The plethora of blatant sexual stimulation at the most provocative age is completely inconsistent with moral preachments concerning the conduct of sexual relationships. Adolescent behavior, imitative of adult behavior, is consistently rejected by the adult community even though adult morality and conduct under certain conditions are either absolutely reprehensible or questionable at best.

Adolescents, like adults, have leisure. What they do with that free time concerns the entire community, and by ramification, society as a whole. They may have no inclination to use whatever leisure they have in antisocial ways, but in not a few instances, this is the only way possible to them, because no other avenues are open. Recreational activity based upon what the traffic will bear proves too costly and usually does not meet adolescent needs. The growing youth wants an interesting, exciting, absorbing, and long-term experience. He wants to be with his own kind and not be dominated by adults, although he is generally willing to concede that social standards must be maintained for the benefit of all.

Public recreational service may be able to meet the needs of youths through the variety of activities available within the departmental program, or the department may serve as a cosponsor with another agency to provide youth-oriented activities not usually offered by the department. Recreational service that provides equal opportunities for all youths to participate in valuable and creative experiences is a most constructive proposal. Communities should provide extensive year-round public recreational services for adolescents. Even when the total cost of such a program appears out of proportion, the per capita cost of such a system to the taxpayer is extremely low.

However, the provision of such activities by the public recreational service department is not the entire answer to the problem of adolescence. Most, if not all, problems of youths are reflected in society at large. Economic deprivation, poor mental health, sexual frustration, delinquency, and other failures are not to be found only in adolescence. They are integral parts of the social order. The cause may be adult ineptitude and an ineffective or unresponsive society. The recreational inequality engendered by this inefficiency may be observed through the following:

1. Lack of cooperative effort on the part of the entire community. Disunity and bickering among those community agencies that should be interested in and manifest concern about youths. Misunderstanding about youth's needs and leadership.
2. Inability of community agencies to reach all youths. Ineffectiveness of program and understaffing of agencies make this effort a failure.
3. Adult domination of youth activities. The adult planners leave youths out of program planning and operations. As a result, adolescents react by nonparticipation or hostility. Too often, activities derived from adult opinion are based upon recall rather than inventiveness and have no connection with the needs of today's youths. What was "good enough for my grandfather" is no longer good or even necessary.

Sex

Except in the Ancient Near-East, all cultures have traditionally held the female as an inferior creature. The manifestation of this fact can be validated by scanning recent history and recalling the suffragette movement. That this has been a worldwide disservice to the distaff side does not make it any more logical or right. Although this country has grown beyond its rural "American way of life" and has now entered upon a growth rate with urbanized foundations, it is still bound to old mores. Only in recent years has there been any noticeable modification in programming for women and girls. Most public and private recreational service agencies are content to program for men and boys. Enter any agency on any given day and the physical activities in progress will provide the accuracy of that statement. Whether this is true because of incompetence or ignorance of the programmers, or both, is a moot point.

Recreational agencies have historically been devoted to youth rather than any other age group, to males, and to those who utilize the center or facility. There has never been a concerted effort to recruit female participants into the program. Even when concerned individuals protest against this inequitable arrangement, little is done to change the pattern. Frequently, the program is developed around gross motor skill activities which appeal to young males. Thus, football, basketball, baseball, soccer, and other team sports are initiated. These grow into major or minor leagues and tournaments, as the case may be, and have as their devotees boys and young men.

Once there might have been an intrinsic feminine disdain for gross motor activities because of the so-called "perspiration concomitant" which happens to be part of the activity. It once may have been considered unfeminine to participate in strenuous sports, and females simply did not wish to appear unfeminine. Nevertheless, females' bias against game participation is being countered successfully as a result of the popularization of gymnastics, yoga, and belly dancing, swimming, and bowling. There has been a noticeable upsurge in women's track-and-field events as a consequence of the past few Olympic Games, and more and more women are participating in golf, snow skiing, horseback riding, as well as aquatic activities such as waterskiing, scuba diving, and surfing. Perhaps even more important are the recent court cases which tend to abolish the last, though reluctant, vestiges of sex discrimination against females. Moreover, many females are now able to compete with males when the nature of the activity permits.

Still, recreational agencies continue to neglect the program experiences which are more likely to draw a feminine crowd. Perhaps this is in part the result of the inability of those in charge to lead or direct such activities. Many times the department has a former athlete as its executive. Such an individual cannot or does not appreciate nonathletic and noncompetitive experiences. It may well be easier to organize and operate many leagues and tournaments than to direct and produce community theater presentations, to lead a chorus, to supervise an orchestra, to conduct a dance festival, to organize an art or a sculpture class, book group, and literary program, or to find the skilled people who are employable or who will voluntarily undertake these functions. For these reasons, women and girls have been neglected and are being omitted from obtaining an equal share of recreational service by the public agency charged with this responsibility. Some private agencies with direct interest in females, for example, YWCA, Girl Scouts, Future Homemakers of America, Girls' Clubs, Junior League, and so on, do have activities specifically geared to appeal to females. But this does not make for equal opportunity within public agencies.

A noticeable gap exists on the playgrounds where even the youngest children, both boys and girls, should find equal opportunity. If there are organized activities available, they have typically been of the Little League, Little Guys, midget or some other appellation signifying that the game is for little boys, not for little girls. Attempts to include coeducational activities have been skimpy affairs at best and farces at worst. The tendency to relegate females to the role of spectators, passive participants, and "off-to-the-siders" remains a real part of current recreational practice. Within the past few years, however, these practices have been seriously challenged, and many barriers to female participation of every kind are being overturned.

Economic and Social Status

Part of the initial social movement which later came to be known as the recreational service movement was instigated as a welfare or relief program. It was born as a result of waves of immigrants being tossed into the melting pot of this country, and as the result of the new urbanization with its slums, ghettos, and demoralizing human values. The concept of service to the poor, slum-ridden, foreign-born, illiterate, and low status person has never been completely erased from the practice of recreational service. As Hutchinson wrote:

> Such entity as a special recreation neighborhood should exist in a city officially supporting recreation activities by taxes. Residential neighborhoods, slum districts and those in between deserve consideration only because of need. Neither superficial standards nor pressure group activities should influ-

ence recreation efforts so that one section of the community gains at the expense of the other.[2]

That such neighborhoods do exist in our largest cities cannot be disputed. Why they exist at all is the prime question. The special neighborhood is a throwback to the social welfare aspect of the movement. It has been thought that certain classes of people, particularly low-end socioeconomic groups, should receive the greatest share of public facilities, leadership, and organized program activities. On the other hand, there are those who think that recreational facilities, leadership, and activities should be parceled out to the better neighborhoods because the people who count live there. Little thought is given to any concept of equality when either of these conditions prevails.

On occasion, political, social, or economic pressure groups will demand the construction or development of certain recreational facilities within the immediate environs of the neighborhood they represent. The ward heeler does this as a part of his campaign pledge made to voters in his district or as a sop to his supporters. Well-to-do persons ask for parks and other beautifying facilities because such areas tend to raise property values when they are adjacent to or within a reasonable distance of a given place. All these factors make demands upon the type and quality of service which the public department can render to all residents of the community. The function of the public department is to provide equal opportunities for all persons without distinction as to economic or social status. Recreational service, as a public tax-supported function, exists for all people regardless of their economic or social characteristics. The public agency can no more provide one type of facility, program, and leadership to a specific class or group, and do a creditable job for the entire community, then it can afford to plan for only one neighborhood and leave the rest of the community to fend for itself. Such inequity would surely meet with honest cries of outrage from the citizens who were being discriminated against—at least one is led to believe this would happen. But it does not, for many departments do function in precisely this discriminatory way, either for one segment of the total population with token activities for the rest or with inequitable expenditures of budget for one group and nothing for anybody else. As Butler has written:

---

[2]J.L. Hutchinson, *Principles of Recreation* (New York: A.S. Barnes and Company, 1951), p. 178.

Every community recreation program should:
1. Provide equality of opportunity for all. This democratic principle applies particularly in the field of recreation. For example, as far as possible, *all* neighborhoods should have adequate playgrounds, not just a favored few. Facilities and programs should be sufficiently broad and well distributed to enable all the people to be served.[3]

Some progress is being made to offset the pressures that tend to favor the few at the expense of the many, but the condition is a current problem. Practices attempting to operate facilities and administer activities for one group militate against the common principle of equal opportunity for all. To overlook the whole so that one part may benefit is not merely shocking, but may eventually prove disastrous to the public agency. As improved communications are developed, better understanding and recognition of the function of recreational service will also grow. The public will disavow its support of any agency that cannot or will not provide the service for which it was created. The function of community recreational service is to mobilize *all* forces so that inequality can be reduced or abolished.

Education

To the extent that individuals have not had prior experience with or instruction in leisure skills other than a few motor activities, they are particularly hindered from participating in the remarkable variety of recreational activities available within public programs. This lack of exposure to enjoyable experiences does much to mitigate potential performance. If the individual has not previously attempted specific activities, it is unlikely that he or she will be inclined to do so because people do not like to be placed in uncomfortable or unfamiliar situations or positions. When the individual must function on a low level of competence, under conditions that make that person either defensive or frustrated, or without any appreciation for activities that have not been a part of that person's educational preparation, he is hindered from considering these activities and is thereafter offered an unequal share of recreational items from which to choose. Such a condition may be largely brought about by the individual, but in many communities throughout the country, inequitable educational programs prevent individuals from

---

[3]G.D. Butler, *Introduction to Community Recreation*, 4th ed. (New York: McGraw-Hill Book Company 1967), p. 260.

achieving through leisure arts because the activities are not included in the curriculum.

Channeling the development of people is not sufficient if the outcome of such direction does not consider off-the-job living as well as vocational experiences. Occupational provision through formal schooling facilitates the essential functions by which society carries on. However, life is more than existence, and the process of education influences living (in the fullest meaning of the word) and is, in turn, affected by it. Living is not only occupational; it has recreational connotations as well.

Education must prepare the individual to appreciate worthwhile leisure activities. Individual proclivity for one kind of activity instead of another is generally learned. Activity fulfilling to one person may be dissatisfying to someone else without the same experience and education. Biological factors may have some bearing upon a given predisposition toward a specific form of activity, but the individual's attitude toward and taste for one form of leisure activity as opposed to another is largely acquired. Therefore, learning is of primary significance in defining what activities a person will engage in with a maximum of satisfaction. No individual is born with a taste for reading good books, skillfully participating in a variety of motor activities, or performing great music. These proficiencies are acquired slowly and usually only with painstaking care. During the learning phase much support must be rendered to the potential performer, by way of praise, stimulation, and prediction of potential ability, in order to compensate for the often painful predicaments he experiences when he attempts something new or unfamiliar. With diligence, the practice of new functions becomes pleasurable, as increasing skill makes the performance smooth and easy, and thus provides satisfaction. Nevertheless, in the procedure of educating toward desirable kinds of activity, supplemental rewards having some extrinsic value will do much to reinforce individual perseverance and productivity. In this connection, Phenix has written the appropriate statement:

A considerable segment of most people's time is spent in recreation. Furthermore, unlike work, there is an almost universal presumption in its favor. It is neither punishment nor an evil or unpleasant necessity. It is usually regarded as a reward and an undeniable good. Being freely chosen, it is also a reliable reflection of personal interests and goals. For these reasons recreation is certain to exert a marked influence on the development of character. It is therefore not appropriate that recreation should be considered a subsidiary educational concern. Personal growth through recreation cannot safely be left to haphazard

arrangement, accidental circumstance, and the vagaries of momentary inclination. Provision for recreation needs as careful deliberate consideration as
preparation for the job. In some respects the educational opportunities in the
former are even greater than in the latter.[4]

The education of people to choose valuable and worthwhile leisure
activities is a function of the learning process. Whenever the educational
process is tainted by poorly prepared and equipped instructors, by bias,
or by authorities with no conception of the need for such education, the
individual will be slighted and the criteria by which people judge
the relative value of activities will be impaired. To the extent that this
impairment of judgment exists, the individual cannot fairly distinguish
between the more and the less desirable and worthy forms of leisure
experience. If the individual does not have a basis from which to select
recreational experiences which may prove to be of greater satisfaction,
enjoyment, and value to him, then he has been the victim of inequity
within the educational system and is ill-prepared to find living outside
of existence.

Disabled Populations

Perhaps the greatest inequity relating to recreational service is in the
basic principle of equal opportunity for all the people all the time.
Certainly, this principle has had little application toward disabled persons,
whether they be in treatment centers or in the community itself. This
principle has been warped to the point where it must be translated to
mean equal opportunity to all, except the disabled. What has been
behind this apparent indifference of community recreationists? Even
more startling has been the disinclination of competent medical authorities to utilize recreational services within the treatment environment.
Recreational service has largely been confined to long-term, custodial,
or chronic treatment centers, the Veterans Administration Hospitals,
and mental health institutions or adjunctive therapeutic aid.

Recreational service is a relatively recent addition to commonly accepted
medically oriented treatments. It is not surprising, therefore, to discover
that little is known of the therapeutic outcomes of such programs. Although
recreational services may not yet be considered therapy in the true sense
of the term, because no experimental cause-and-effect research has been
performed to show the worth of recreational experiences to patients

---

[4]P.H. Phenix, *Philosophy of Education* (New York: Holt, Rinehart, and Winston, 1958), pp. 243–244.

under different circumstances and with various physical and mental disabilities, some investigatory procedures appear promising. No conclusive evidence that would unhesitatingly assure physicians that the involvement of patients in recreational activities would materially benefit the patients has yet been brought to medical attention. A great deal of personal observation supports the inclusion of recreational services within treatment centers to assist, in some way, the rehabilitation of patients afflicted by some mental disorder, but beyond these subjective *medical* opinions there is little empirical proof. Nevertheless, recreational programs are carried on in hospitals, nursing homes, and some general hospitals. The only reasonable explanation for including such a function as a part of the medical program is that it seems to help.

There is almost universal agreement on the futility of providing a recreational service program in a general hospital which deals only with acute medical incidents. However, even the smallest general hospital will have not less than half of its beds occupied by patients who either have progressed beyond the acute stage in their recovery or were never on the acute list at all, for example, those in the hospital for tests, examinations, observation, or prolonged treatment (anything lasting more than three days). The acutely ill patient's stay in the hospital generally lasts between three and eight days, depending upon the specific reason for his initial admission. After minor operation, the patient will be in pain, traumatized, and in no condition to know or care what is happening around him during the first 24 hours. Within three days he may be sufficiently recovered to be released from the hospital. The duration of pain and other postoperative shock and weakness depends upon the severity of the incident, whether major or minor repair was made, the patient's physical condition prior to the operation, and his ability to recuperate. The more drastic the operation or treatment, the longer will be the required recovery period and the hospital stay. What do these patients do after they have recovered sufficiently to begin to take notice of their surroundings? Aside from the normal routine of injections, tests, periodic visitation by medical personnel, feeding, and eliminatory acts, what do these recuperating patients do for the next one to eight days and nights? In many instances, nothing, with concomitant boredom, impatience, and other frustrating manifestations. "Well, we are not running a resort hotel," "My patients cannot do anything," are comments made frequently by hospital administrators. "Funds are limited, costs are high and getting higher, only those vital medical services which are

proved essential to the competent treatment of patients can be provided."
These answers are obviously designed to relieve the needs of patients.

As if to complement the lack of recreational service within the treatment center, the external community has offered little in the way of
recreational services to the disabled. Shut-ins, permanently disabled,
mentally retarded, blind, deaf, mute, outpatients of mental hospitals, all
but those with communicable diseases require the same recreational
services as do normal people, because as human beings they have the
same physical, social, and psychological needs. Like some hospitals,
some community agencies are either unwilling, unable, incompetent, or
ignorant of the need to provide such services. There is the question of
the value of recreational service, as an unknown quantity, in terms of its
effect on disabled citizens. Surely there are other more essential functions that need to be performed, namely, fire, police, sanitation, public
health, and so on. That recreational activity falls within private purview
anyway seems to be the general opinion.

Some reactionary community and economy-minded hospital authorities will continue to deprive the disabled of their fair share of services
which they should receive.

Advocates of recreational services to disabled populations in whatever
environment they inhabit are, if not reviled, ignored, or openly opposed,
consigned to intolerable situations, in hopes that they will just go away.
Disabled populations will always be among us and as citizens should
receive opportunities for recreational experiences.

Explicit evidence as to the therapeutic value of recreational activity
for the ill, handicapped, and disabled person has not yet been confirmed.
But to the extent that recreational experience has proved to be of value
to people in general, there is no reason to believe that disabled persons
would not also benefit from such participation. Confronted with the
same problems, in many cases much more complex as a consequence of
the disability, the disabled person requires at least the same chance as
other more fortunate persons to associate with various groups which
offer the possibility of enjoyment through recreational activities.[5]

With the passage of the Americans with Disabilities Act of 1990, which
bans discrimination against the nation's 43,000,000 disabled people, a
strong measure of protection now exists. Those who flout the law and do

---

[5]J.S. Shivers and H.F. Fait, *Therapeutic and Adapted Recreational Services* (Philadelphia: Lea and Febiger,
1975), pp. 51–52, 57–59.

not provide equal opportunity and access to public recreational facilities and programs will risk a variety of sanctions, including litigation.

Regional Deficiencies

The vagaries of nature being what they are, certain regions within the territorial limits of the United States have been fortunate to have an abundance of scenic vistas, mountains, caverns, deserts, glaciers, gorges, inland waters, coastal areas lapped by ocean, sea, sound, or gulf, temperate climates, and other natural phenomena which make the region more susceptible to leisure experiences. Conversely, the absence of natural wonders has created areas of flat uninteresting land, cold in winter, hot and humid in summer, wet in spring, but perhaps magnificent in autumn. These areas, too, have capitalized on whatever nature has presented. However, there are areas that have nothing whatever to recommend them as recreational settings. These may be the island communities dotting the great plains or the numerous industrial towns which are now drying up in an economy that no longer needs the labor or raw material.

Little can be done about the imbalance of nature. Man may create artificial waterways and lakes by damming and constructing canals, but he can do less when it comes to repairing desolate, stark, featureless terrain. These factors may come under human domination and control eventually, but such deficiencies of geographical location, topography, and weather are not validly included in regional dislocation. They may be partially contained by the development of manmade facilities and structures which can compensate in some way.

The real regional disparity comes in terms of political understanding or the lack of it, economic means or the lack of it, local mores, urban congestion, rural sparsity of population, apathy on the public's part, the desire to reduce social services whenever costs rise during periods of recession or inflation, population movements, and the establishment of recreational service agencies to provide the leadership and direction for equalizing opportunity.

Political shortsightedness accrues from elected officials who view the recreational service department as a waste of taxpayer's money and an agency that can be lopped off the municipal budget during times of retrenchment. Coupled with this lack of appreciation of the functions of the recreational authority is the politician's constant compromise toward a variety of pressure groups which force him into expedient rather than logical actions, the consequence of which are blighted recreational areas within the community. Particularly is this true of the great urban centers of the United States, where the costs of acquisition of built-up property, demolition of condemned buildings, and construction of modern public structures and facilities are extreme. The covetous politician casts his eye upon parklands as a means of reducing some of the cost of appropriation. The sad fact is that such encroachment is not only for parking lots, streets, and other mundane reasons, but for vitally required schools, hospitals, police stations, and so on. In spite of the apparent justification for taking park and other recreational spaces for public building, the end result is to create a city without breathing space. Once the land is taken over by asphalt or concrete, it can never be utilized as a park. The expedient of saving the taxpayers' money generally ends with a future appropriation of many times the original "saving" when, if ever, the community has to buy new property for its recreational areas, presuming that such property is acquirable. The fallacious idea is that it costs the city less if parkland is taken. In reality, the city is denuded of its necessary green places, which are never replaced. The danger then is that the politician and appointed officials have not planned for construction needs and often transfer open space to another department because it is easier to do this than to buy on the open market. Without adequate facilities, for example, parks and reservations, there is a reduction in the kinds of recreational experience which can be programmed. Lacking open spaces, people are denied equal opportunity to participate in activities requiring places of this type.

Limited economic resources prevent the community from establishing a department geared to the provision of recreational service. Communities without the financial means cannot afford to develop facilities, much less employ qualified leaders for the direction and operation of a department. Whenever funds are in short supply, the program deteriorates or those who would ordinarily benefit from participation in the program suffer because they have to do without.

Urban congestion, which presses more people into less space and limits the amount of service, and the number of opportunities available to each individual because of the absolute disproportion between professional workers and recipients of the service lead to inequality. Inadequate facilities and recreational spaces to serve the needs of the inhabitants tend to appear in highly congested neighborhoods of cities. In too many instances, slum areas and the center section, or core, of the city have been allowed to degenerate, as the rim has expanded and become increasingly more residential. Allowing recreationally blighted areas to exist leads to a movement away from the heart of the city, lack of open space, and by default, commercial, light manufacturing, loft, and warehouse establishments take over.

The scarcity of rural population often negates governmental provision for recreational services. When the population of any given area is small, as it is in many rural regions, there are economic limitations upon the agencies that can provide services. Usually, rural areas can count only upon the school district because county government is not adequate to the task of supplying leadership. Often, rural dwellers have been unwilling, or uncaring enough, to tax themselves so that some central authority is enabled to undertake the responsibility for performing those functions designed to establish recreational services. Rural populations, generally made up of agricultural workers and exurbanites, have been disposed to view governmental organization of any form in a dismal light. With millions of rural residents leaving their districts to migrate to cities, the disparity between land area and people living in the rural region has become extreme. To those families who remain, the lack of an established agency to which the individual may turn when seeking services of a recreational nature, the poor or limited financial resources, and the inadequate facilities, program, or direction all indicate a basic inequality due to sparse population. The state seems to be the final source of redress, and many state governments, finding themselves heavily taxed to offer aid to great urban centers with their millions of people, consider rural districts with few people to be somewhat less important. However, movements of population show that major metropolitan regions are losing people to exurban locations. The flight away from the big cities and suburbia to rural and more remote sections of the country has increased dramatically during the decade of the seventies. New York, for example, lost 7 per cent of its population while Arizona was expanding by 25.3 per cent. Rural counties that were losing population in the 1960s show the greatest gains in the 1970s. In light of these facts there may well be a reversal of legislator's inattention to the needs of rural areas. State legislators may be persuaded to pass money bills favorable to rural sections and thereby provide services which have not been forthcoming previously. Then, too, private agencies such as the Grange, churches, civic organizations, and others have offered recreational resources to rural residents. For the most part, however, rural dwellers must provide for themselves.

Inadequacies in Leadership

Incompetence, like illiteracy, steals opportunity from people. Those who cannot read find that many of life's enjoyments, as well as necessities, are beyond them. Incompetency, or the inability to perform adequately, is perhaps the most damaging factor to the provision of equal recreational opportunity and service to people. Almost every other inequity can be overcome if the recreationist has the intelligence, drive, ingenuity, and dedication it takes to function under adverse circumstances. When the worker is incompetent, every advantage working to benefit the program is negated, because the success of organized recreational service depends chiefly upon the quality and effectiveness of the leaders available to it. Inept individuals either are poorly prepared to negotiate the sometimes delicate public relations so necessary to the maintenance of a sound public image or are incapable of offering attractive activities which make up a well-balanced program appealing to all potential participants.

Incompetency in the worker cannot be hidden because it is always and immediately reflected in the program. A worker who does not have the skill or knowledge required of the recreationist cannot offer the variety of recreational experiences which must be afforded if people are to be well served. Usually, there is a tendency to present activities that limit participation to those who are highly skilled or that call for overloading the program with athletics, thus eliminating a majority of the public without offering compensating efforts. Activities may be proposed without prior plan or consideration of people's needs. This action often develops because chance rather than purposeful choice is depended upon for success. In many cases, the incompetent person relies upon a specific group of activities, whether they fit the situation or not, and these are offered continuously. Under such conditions the program becomes stagnant and denies ample opportunities to citizens to perform in patterns which may be more meaningful to them.

Incompetency results from any of the following factors: 1) a lack of intelligence which precludes any satisfactory performance; 2) a lack of knowledge necessary for the provision of comprehensive recreational services in a given environment; 3) a lack of skill and/or experience for functioning in a particular assignment; or 4) a lack of initiative, desire, or enthusiasm for the accepted responsibility. Any of these, by itself or in a combination, when applicable to a worker results in inefficient operation, ineffective rapport with the public, disorganization or deterioration of the program, and an intense form of inequality.

It is the responsibility of all community recreational service agencies to coordinate their functions, thereby providing opportunities of a comprehensive and varied recreational nature for all persons within the community. To this objective, all duties, obligations, and standard operating procedures performed by the agency are supportive but incidental to the chief goal. Everything the agency does, it does in order to carry out the purpose for which it was established, namely, furnishing competent leadership, providing adequate and safe places, and financially supporting the most balanced and varied recreational program possible. Anything less than this standard is unfortunate and inadequate. When the public places its trust in some agency and the agency fails to deliver satisfactory service, the consequences are often disenchantment with the program and ultimate replacement or abolishment of the agency. Sometimes, nonfeasance by a public recreational service agency may be caused by political intrigue, a nonsupportive city administration, or incompetence within the department. Whenever any of these factors is operational, the taxpaying citizens will bear a heavier burden than usual. Other community agencies also have a responsibility for responding to the recreational needs of their members. Should they fail in this task, then lack of support swiftly follows.

In order to perform its vital function, the public recreational service agency must also maintain adjunctive services for greatest efficiency, economy, and effectiveness. These staff, or technical, services include organization, administration, education, coordination, conservation, planning, supervision, and evaluation. The outcome of such supportive functions is the offering of the most comprehensive schedule of recreational opportunities from which each person in the community may choose for his individual satisfaction and enjoyment. Coordination is the mobilization of total community resources in a smoothly functioning and complementary effort in order to supply effective recreational services.

Essentially, recreational experiences provide specific values to individuals who participate, thus promoting intellectual, physical, and emotional development. Recreational activities engender a sense of well-being and may best bring about self-expression, involvement, enjoyment, satisfaction, self-control, and an enhancement of life not offered by other experiences. Among these values are thought to be physical fitness, health, aesthetic appreciation, socialization, equality, sound value judg-ments, and freedom of choice.

The provision of recreational service demands a high degree of skill, knowledge, sound judgment, reliability, and intelligence. The burden of programming falls upon the recreationist, who must bring all of his natural and learned forces to bear on the problem of comprehensive and varied experiences which can satisfy diverse public demands. There must be constant evaluation of the program. The recreationist cannot allow the program of activities to become static. Basic activities, such as motor skills, arts, crafts, music, drama, camping, interest groups, and so on, should always be available. However, the recreationist must be cer-tain to build continually on these experiences as demand is created for them and as competent leadership becomes available to promote them. Departments of recreational service must consistently offer opportuni-ties for persons to grow recreationally. They must provide the means and the leadership to allow participants and potential participants ample opportunity to select experiences which can widen their horizons and achieve satisfaction for them. Recreationists must indeed be leaders of leisure and serve as resources for the public. Community involvement in supplying recreational service must be strengthened continually, as experi-ments with new ideas to create additional opportunities for the people which they serve are attempted in response to request, expressed interest, and changing tastes.

Chapter 3

THE ORIGINS OF RECREATIONAL SERVICE

R ecreational service as a comprehensive movement did not spring into being overnight. From various modest beginnings it developed gradually over the years and was shaped and channeled by many events and influences. This chapter will define what a movement is and trace it back to its roots.

Historical Background

The first settlers who came to America brought with them a recreational tradition from the Old World that was based on the leisure which, by the seventeenth century, all free persons possessed to a limited extent. So it is not surprising that the early colonists, in the face of all their hardships, managed to set aside some time for enjoyment and relaxation. Although there were strictures against recreational pursuits among all thirteen of the original colonies, as soon as survival needs were met the settlers once again took up those leisure pursuits which we call recreational. There is evidence in the records of the Massachusetts Bay Colony and the Connecticut Colony that recreational pursuits had a place in the lives of the people.

One important early influence was the tradition of fencing off common pasture lands. In this custom can be seen the genesis of future municipal parks and gardens that would reach a zenith in the twentieth century. Parks had their inception as plazas or central open space after the Spanish explored and settled Florida. Boston Common, originally a pasture, was designated in 1634 as a public meeting ground where people could congregate for open discussion of daily issues. Today this area is part of the most important and centrally situated park in Boston. The first ground, designated originally as a park, was five squares set aside by William Penn, who designed the city of Philadelphia. The recognized need for parks in cities, indeed the park movement itself, took its impetus from these earliest beginnings.

The westward migration of the eighteenth century required new roads and routes to be opened. As early as 1770, Daniel Boone of North Carolina explored and marked a trail to Kentucky. By 1800 water routes to the West had been explored and were in constant use. The Monongahela and Allegheny Rivers carried small craft to the Ohio at Pittsburgh. After 1800 the settlers used the Great Lakes as their main water route. By 1834 a trading post had been established at Fort Dearborn on Lake Michigan; the city of Chicago developed around this fort. The pace of migration west quickened. The new pioneers brought their customs with them. A number of recreational activities were of a utilitarian nature—bringing people together in some cooperative effort which was enjoyable. The activities might be based upon agricultural work such as sheep shearing, corn husking, wheat threshing, or the like. It could have been church socials, horse racing, animal fighting, or some other event. Whatever leisure these people had afforded them recreational opportunities on a personal or private basis. There was no concept of public recreational service as such during the formative years of the American Republic.

The Recreational Movement

The recreational movement grew out of social situations which were products of population migrations, urbanization, industrialization, mass education, mobility, mechanization, and leisure. According to Clarence Rainwater, the cavaliers of the Tidewater region in the Virginias and Carolinas lived a rich recreational existence. Even Puritan New England, which at first suppressed recreational opportunities, was forced to concede recreational activity in the life of the people. Colonial America had a rich heritage of recreational life. Nevertheless, the recreational tradition in the American culture suffered a decline during the formative years of national growth and development because of an expanding urban structure with its congestion, an overwhelming devotion to materialism and commercialism, and the basic isolation of rural districts. However, with the passage of time a movement of great impetus and inherent value spread throughout the country. Its inception may have been from a parallel development in education in the middle 1800's or with the establishment of sand gardens for children in Boston in 1885. Regardless of the initial stage, this social movement has revitalized American life. The Neumeyers have this to say:

Pioneer leaders sensed the situation and called attention to the necessity of providing recreation for the masses, especially for the underpriviliged groups. Various organizations and agencies began to do something about it and pioneered in establishing new ways of meeting a felt need. One event followed another, resulting in a more concerted effort and a spread of attempts to provide new forms of recreation for people who otherwise lacked opportunities for them. As the movement progressed, objectives and standards emerged, leaders were trained for the supervision of recreation, transitions took place in the program of activities, and the movement progressed through various stages of development.[1]

The growth of a public movement usually proceeds without much reference to plan. It arises out of a recognized need. In its early stages there is considerable groping and searching for detailed solutions to the problems which the need creates, but which are amorphous. Experimental efforts appear intermittently to solve these problems, and gradually through the sharing of experience and the influence of imitation, common practice and procedures develop.

Recreational Service as a Social Movement

Imbalances in society inevitably generate a counterforce or an action designed to alleviate such conditions. Generally, dissatisfaction with mores, disintegration of traditions, disparity of economic power, bigotry, political negligence, or lack of essential needs has caused social upheavals, both of a positive and negative type. Such activity may result in movements.

When there is social unrest or dissatisfaction, a case of social dislocation, the situation may be just the trigger for the ascendancy of some individual who will lead the disenchanted in a reform effort. This person may or may not be the ultimate leader of the organized, social movement who will be heard. A prime concern is to function as a catalytic agent, to foment anger at passivity, to make concrete the vague discontent that people feel in order to gain action on a significant issue. In some instances, the first person to arise will be a fanatic, an idealist, or one who is simply surfeited with the conditions that prevail and has the intestinal fortitude to voice what other people are thinking. In this way, the leader's mantle is assumed. In stirring the masses, the first leader may offer goals that are unrealistic, but appeal to those who follow.

---

[1]M.H. Neumeyer and E.S. Neumeyer, *Leisure and Recreation: A Study of Leisure and Recreation in Their Sociological Aspects,* 3rd ed. (New York: The Ronald Press Company, 1958), p. 64.

When there is a conscious understanding of dissatisfaction, when people are aroused and emotional about a given issue, almost any vociferous and hostile person with a gift of speech and the will to perform can spark some action. It is only when the imbalances are not clearly perceived or are moderate, or, if salient and harsh, are accepted as a fact of life which cannot be changed that someone with real leadership abilities is required to influence change.

The Provocateurs of social movements are not always among those who have endured the condition which is the focal point of modification. Often the have-nots are stimulated to act to serve the intent of demagogues and would-be dictators who wish to seize power as a consequence of the discontentment that has been instigated by their henchmen. There are special interest groups who hope to profit by any reform which may occur. But there also are those who because of race, religion, economic, political, or other social status have a valid grievance against the existing social order, and who seek change and the satisfaction of their wants. These latter groups may be used for cynical purposes, but sooner or later they become aware of what has been done to them and they seek redress of wrongs and frustrations that have beset them.

Opposition to Change

The *status quo* always appeals to those who have found it to their benefit to resist any modification in the social structure. Whenever there is a suggestion to reform things, conservatives and others who deem it expedient to save whatever privileges they see jeopardized by change immediately close ranks. Thus, the success that any social movement has will depend in full upon its enthusiastic support by those who visualize a chance for an improved status or other gain through the reorganization of the social order.

The most serious obstacle to the movement will be the conditioning factors of habit which inhibits any attempt at change. Even though habitual methods have not produced satisfactory conditions, they are at least familiar and people are used to them. Ignorance of the unknown is the most militant factor against innovation. Individuals are secure and confident in what is familiar and afraid of those things that are new. This natural conservatism causes inertia. Although there may be dissatisfaction with present conditions, little is done to remove the cause of such situations because of implied risk to any security that the individual has attained. It is easier to be dissatisfied, but apparently safe, than it is to take a decisive stand which would topple the old regime and, perhaps, the safety which the individual is conditioned to accept.

The would-be social engineers invariably split their own unity of purpose by disagreement. Nowhere has this been seen more clearly than in the AIDS movement of the 1990s in the United States. Not content with the slow progress being made, several splinter groups, such as UPSET, have entered the equal rights movement with the hope of speeding progress in better education, housing, occupational status, and other social benefits. The result has not been greater speed, but possible increased resentment and more concentrated prejudice in some circles against this movement. Conservatives against this movement have united to form common cause in opposition to it, whereas the more liberal elements for reform and moderation are in schism among themselves. This devisiveness is characteristic of most social movements, for as Hertzler states:

> The conservative minority opposing the progressive move are in agreement. On the other hand the 60 percent (and it may just as well be more), while they are in favor of progress along the particular line, are not agreed on just what they want or how they want to bring it about, and pull in different directions, thus neutralizing each other's progressive efforts, and are stopped or even dominated by the unified "won't" power of the conservatives.[2]

Social Action

In order for a social movement to grow and actually produce those things originally inciting its creation, it must have an efficient organization and an effective program. The structure of the organization will depend upon certain essentials, chiefly the persons the movement wants as followers, the economic and power resources of the leader or leaders of the movement, and the consequences of the movement. Whether the original proponent or agitator of the discontent will remain in charge of the movement is of little note.

As the organization develops in the three major aspects which give it form, additional workers will be necessary, new and stronger voices may have to be heard, more highly competent or unethical individuals may have to be called upon to produce action toward the goal of reform. The

---

[2]J.O. Hertzler, *Social Progress* (New York: D. Appleton-Century Company, 1928), p. 118.

organization operating the movement may achieve success. If this happens, there will be no further need for the organization and it should dissolve. But this is easier said than done, for there will be pressure from within by working staffs and personnel who now have a vested interest in maintaining the organization. Perhaps they will seek new social aims in order to continue in power. Usually, the organization simply becomes an institution which in fact supports a particular point of view—tending to become conservative and opposed to change with the passage of time. Eventually, new groups arise to tear down its mechanism, thus continuing the cycle of social engineering.

Social movements created out of protest against the *status quo* or in terms of social need may be of such value as to continue for many generations, as the feminist movement has. If the movement can furnish a program by which action will be generated for the betterment of the public, it may very well be kept and supported. Usually, the movement is characterized by a specific program, and it is on the basis of its proposals that the movement gains its support.

Programs may be general or specific, corrective or innovational. Whatever they are, they must be practical and possible of success if any hope of survival is contemplated. Yet, human nature being what it is, modification of society by social movement cannot be so radical as to be outside the comprehension of its supporters. Social change is generally slow and movements develop with the times. Science and technological advances tend to speed the movement because of great mobility, communication, and education of those seeking the change. It is now possible to enlist the aid of persons far removed from the arena of conflict by utilization of propaganda through the mass media. It is possible to transport great populations cheaply and easily because of new and faster means of mobility. It is feasible to put forth more highly complex and intricate schemes and expect greater understanding and sympathy for their progress because of a more highly literate and intelligent society. Nevertheless, even in a society as modern as that of the United States, with all of the great scientific, educational, and cultural advances which have been made, programs of social change must be activated in terms of those whom the changes will benefit most. Intellectuals may understand and accept the need for reform, but most individuals will still be guided by what they know rather than by what they hope for.

The efforts of society to rearrange itself in order to provide a better life for its people is a social movement. When the reform group spearheading this movement wins converts to its cause, continuously expands from community to community until there is a widespread acceptance of the movement's goals, and realizes the need to maintain distinct unity, then some institutionalization will occur. In this way, the movement which began as a highly desirable idea, with the dedicated and enthusiastic support of a few, begins after some rapid growth to settle down to a development that is less spectacular than the one first advanced by the visionaries who initiated the movement. The social order has been revised to a certain extent and the movement comes of age. Its future will probably be one of development until the saturation point is reached and then consolidation will occur.

Recreational Service and Divisions of Culture

The recreational service movement is in part a response to the changing functions of the family. Urbanization, mass mobility, and communication have removed the family from its former position of centrality and placed the recreational pattern surrounding the home into the school, the church, the neighborhood, the recreational center, and the community at large. Because now more than ever before there is more leisure, more money with which to do things, and wider horizons as a result of mass communications and education to identify a variety of leisure pursuits, the home is the scene of less recreational activity. But with this apparent family-recreational disintegration, there has been an upsurge in individual interest in community patterns of recreational service and public affairs.

Among the trends to be observed in the current pattern of recreational services are the provision of spaces and facilities in which mass as well as individual recreational opportunities may be fulfilled and the increasing diversity of comprehensive programs which include aesthetic, educational, cultural, social and physical experiences. More and more communities throughout the nation are organizing and operating full-time or part-time recreational service departments financed from public funds. Educational devices to inform the public of the massive opportunities available are in keeping with identification of governmental functions for the promotion of public welfare.

The broadening of recreational horizons by stimulating interest and effort of would-be participants to the possibilities that await them may have to begin artificially. However, once the experiment has started, the activity generates enough interest to perpetuate itself and ignite the individual's ideas of further experiences. This objective is often accomplished through the organizational efforts of the recreational service movement. The agencies that make up the movement and the personnel involved form the resources for stimulation. In the final analysis, it is to the schools that the entire movement must turn for the educational emphasis of skills for leisure. A main responsibility of the educational system must be for the beneficial uses of leisure and the enrichment of recreational living.

One of the great social movements to appear in the era of technological change is that of recreational service and its objective of providing a great opportunity for the enhancement of life. Although there is no one national recreational program, there are many community patterns which would appear to make the movement one of national significance. Increasingly, state and federal governments are providing agencies, finances, and leadership in securing perpetually dedicated areas and facilities for the development of recreational pursuits.

In the past, the focus of municipal politicians was on an expanding economy. Together with a lack of citizen enlightenment and an aroused public opinion, there resulted recreationally blighted communities. The consequences of this political ineptitude allowed forests to be cut down indiscriminately and replaced by brick, steel, and cement structures; streams to be dammed and rerouted to accommodate thoroughfares; rivers to become polluted by industrial and domestic waste; warehouses and wharfs to obliterate the waterfronts. We reap the harvest of this imprudent action. Traffic, both pedestrian and vehicular, filled the streets as homes with open spaces disappeared from the American scene. Railroad apartments and multistoried dwellings replaced private homes in the urban center. In rare instances, some municipalities actually planned for park and other recreational spaces, but in nearly all cases, urban development meant urban blight.

Supportive and Contributory Movements

The industrial revolution gave a major thrust to the recreational service movement in America. With the rise of factories, industrial expansion, mass production, and other new developments, came an increasing need for recreational activity to make use of the increased leisure that was now available. Although industrialization brought prosperity and built a wealthy nation, it also raised some social problem in regard to how citizens should spend their free time.

Increasing industrialization put an end to an agrarian economy. Into the cities and manufacturing centers poured waves of new immigrants, supplying a cheap labor force for the factories and mills. Exploitation of labor was a common practice. Working fourteen hours a day, six days a week, workers had very little leisure.

The decades between 1865 and the close of the First World War signaled the transition of America from an agricultural and rural-based land to a modern industrial and urbanized one. In little more than half a century, a turbulent but secondary power became an ambitious and thrusting world leader. By 1912 continental United States numbered 48 states and whatever frontier there had been no longer remained. The population of slightly more than 30 million people in 1860 swelled to something more than 100 million by 1920. Immigrants from other countries poured into the United States in successive waves. Escape from famine, wars, and religious persecution, and a desire to seek new land, new homes, and work, brought the immigrants of the world to America — this last best hope.

The tremendous expansion of industrial production was the key factor in the United States' capacity to absorb the ready supply of cheap labor the immigrants afforded. The federal government stimulated this growth through its legislative enactments and policies. The latter part of the nineteenth century was the era of the robber barons, those captains of industry who by clever manipulation, shrewdness, merciless competition, sometimes corrupt practices and certainly criminal activity were able to put together corporate combinations that dominated transportation, manufacturing, and the fledgling basic industries that undergird all industrialized countries. American products covered both home and foreign markets.

Politically, the national government passed into the control of the Republican Party. Only Grover Cleveland's two terms in office interrupted Republican entrenchment between 1865 and 1913. The federal government advocated high tariffs, free land, civil-service reform, and "sound money." All these policies were particularly favorable to business and industry. A growing discontent among the rural and nonbusiness populations found expression in the growth of new political parties. Between 1870 and 1896 a variety of third parties existed, but their efforts could not prevail against the vested interests of the commercial classes of the nation.

The growth of industry was based upon America's raw materials; forests, coal, iron ore, copper, sulfur, lead, zinc, phosphates, silver, and oil. Additionally, natural gas and waterpower were available to furnish energy to turn the wheels of industry. Considerable Congressional aid buffered American industry against the competition of cheaper European imports. Immigration provided a steady source of unskilled labor to work the machines. The increased population and its concentration in urban centers offered a ready market for manufactured goods. But the new machines did not provide benefits for all who served them. Exploitation of workers was unprecedented. Not even England, which had trampled on workingmen's rights for so long, equaled the ferocity with which company bosses treated their employees. Children, women, and men were typically forced to labor up to 16 hours, 6 days each week in intolerable sweatshops. The pay was meager and working conditions bordered on the inhumane. Safety and health hazards abounded. Under certain circumstances industrial employment could be likened to involuntary servitude.

The Labor Movement

Beginning in 1830, labor leaders had agitated for organization. By 1860, the miniscule labor movement had enrolled an insignificant percentage of American workers with commensurate power. By 1918, American workers realized that they could not endure against the exploitation and abuse which characterized industrial policy and began to join in labor organization. The first labor union organized nationally was started in 1866 and was disbanded in 1872. The 1870's marked a period of violent confrontation between members of labor organizations and both company hoodlums and police. The infamous Molly Maguires of the Pennsylvania coal mines were typical of the terrorist groups who operated at the time.

The stresses of the 1870s gave way to a more systematic labor appeal in the 1880s. The Knights of Labor, organized in 1869, worked "to secure to the toilers a proper share of the wealth that they create; more of the leisure that rightfully belongs to them; more societary advantages." In 1884 the Knights conducted a successful strike against Jay Gould's railroad, which greatly strengthened them, but in 1886 the Haymarket Square riots in Chicago so damaged their image that their support decreased and finally disappeared. As the Knights declined, the American Federation of Labor (AFL), organized on a craft basis, started to recruit skilled workers. From 1870 on, there was a variety of railroad employee organizations. The AFL had enrolled less than 500,000 workers by 1900 and faced great odds as industrial concerns attempted first to stop and then to hinder the development of unionism. Despite all of the forces arrayed against it, the AFL continued to gain membership and by 1917 had 2 million members. It was not long before workers realized that only through a concentration of power could they hope to deal with the "bigness" of business. Once this movement for organization had begun, it developed the capacity to wield power in legislatures and with other organizations. More and more workers turned to the national government for assistance and received it, grudgingly at first, and then with alacrity as labor's growing power became more apparent to politicians.

With unionization and the betterment of employee working conditions, there also was a concomitant desire for a share in the salutary benefits of life. Labor demanded some equalization for the leisure of its members. Unions were concerned about the free time of their membership and wanted to accommodate employees in settings that were conducive to the good life. Of course, all these requests were fulfilled to a certain extent after the unions achieved their power base. In the early days of unionization, the unrealized yearning of the workingmen to have some free time, to see their children in more pleasant surroundings, to take them out of the congestion of cities, became part of the package which would be used in collective bargaining sessions of the future. A better life meant more time for recreational activity, schooling, and the means to achieve these ends through economic reward.

Unions have contributed to the recreational service movement through the organization and operation of employee recreational programs, participation in local, state, and national efforts at supplying public recreational services, and in introducing a broad gauge of recreational activities to unionists who then become effective lobbyists for more governmental recreational opportunities. Union recreational activities have also fostered a greater willingness on the part of employers to provide recreational services to their employees. Company sponsored recreational programs are an outgrowth of unionization. Whatever the motives of management, such programs have benefited employees and their families and made them aware of the need for recreational experiences. This exposure exerts an important influence at the ballot box when votes are cast affecting the public provision of recreational service. Those who have enjoyed well-operated programs will be inclined to support more public funding for them.

The Settlement House Movement

While the philanthropic or welfare trend began in England as early as 1640, its dominant establishment did not come to American shores until organization of the Neighborhood Guild in New York City in 1886. The American reformers focused attention on the prevailing inequities which were obviously an outcome of industrialism and urbanization after 1865. Poverty, sickness, crime, and vice were rampant in the fetid slums of the cities. Influenced by similar manifestations which had occurred in England, a number of social workers organized settlements in American cities during and following the 1880s. The most illustrious was Hull house, founded by Jane Addams and Ellen G. Starr in Chicago in 1889, on land which was later incorporated into the first model playground. Recreational programs in such play areas included apparatus, sport activities for older children, and supervised games of low organization. In this and other such settlements, social workers lived among those for whom they were responsible and organized a variety of activities designed to enrich the lives of slum dwellers. Other philanthropic groups and individuals worked in a multitude of ways to solve some of these social ills. All these efforts contributed to the slowly awakening awareness of the need for some kind of organized recreational service.

The initiation of social welfare facilities for the foreign born, the poor, and the uneducated or illiterate appeared to be catering to those who could not afford leisure expenditures. This gave rise to the notion that any agency which provided some free services was a welfare agency. Consequently all public recreational departments were stigmatized as having to do with pauperism. The traditional dislike for having to depend upon someone else caused many to shun public recreational systems after the turn of the century. Although recreational service has come into its own as a tax-supported government function, controlled by public authority on the local, state, and national levels, some people still regard it as a form of welfare associated with poverty status.[3]

Neighborhood houses, carrying on the tradition established by Jane Addams and Elaine Starr, are operating in cities throughout the United States. Particularly are they found in the Mid-west and in East coast cities. They have become more group work oriented, although they still provide recreational opportunities for their clients.

The Physical Development Movement

Harvard and Yale colleges were the first institutions of higher education to organize athletic activities for their students. Both colleges were advocates of interscholastic competition on the athletic field. The first football game was played in 1869 between Princeton and Rutgers. Sports activities such as football, baseball, rowing, and swimming were quite popular. Before long amateur athletic clubs, sectarian organizations, and ethnic groups were running sport and game activities on both a competitive and noncompetitive basis.

German, Czechoslovakian, and Swedish immigrants promoted gymnastics. The teachings of Johan Guts Muths, Friedrich Jahn, and others were bearing fruit in the United States after the Civil War. *Turnvereins* and *Sokols* did much to popularize gymnastic participation, exhibitions, and instructions.

Churches and other sectarian organizations soon recognized the need for physical activity. The Young Men's Christian Association, established in 1844, constructed over two hundred gymnasiums in a number of cities. By 1880 the provision of organized physical activities at Y centers rapidly built their membership. The use of athletic activities to attract members to sectarian associations is a technique that continues to this day.

Men were not the only beneficiaries of the changing attitude toward participation in athletics. Women, too, could now take part in a number of sports that were regarded as respectable and appropriate for females. Between 1858 and 1875, the forerunners of modern professional baseball

---

[3]Clarence E. Rainwater, *The Play Movement in the United States,* 1922, The University of Chicago Press, pp. 230–33.

came into being and several professional teams were organized to play before spectators. Track and field meets offered widespread opportunity for amateur participation. Additionally, croquet, archery, bicycle riding, lawn tennis, and other outdoor pursuits gradually grew in popularity.

Sectarian agencies and church leaders came to realize that their co-religionists would no longer be bound by arbitrary restrictions against recreational activities. To deter them from inappropriate leisure activities, churches began to sponsor programs deemed more desirable. Thus, physical facilities were constructed for use by the congregations and social meeting rooms were provided as were reading rooms. In the closing decades of the nineteenth century, recreational activities were broadened to include concerts, dances, and other programs.

Physical education in the schools found support in Luther Halsey Gulick. A graduate of the New York University Medical College in 1889, he upheld vigorous activity and the psychology of play. In 1899 he organized and taught a course in play at the Springfield School for Christian Workers, now Springfield College, in Massachusetts. As physical education director for the YMCA, he promoted physical fitness through a variety of gymnastic exercises. In 1903, as Director of Physical Education for the City of New York, he organized the first Public School Athletic League in the United States. This municipal program which provides competitive opportunities for all school-age children, remains a significant part of the extracurricular program in New York City. Dr. Gulick was also instrumental in organizing the folk dance movement in this country, which still carries on through public and private interest clubs, as a way of promoting healthful exercise, cultural preservation, and recreational activity.

The Camping Movement

In 1861 Frederick William Gunn, headmaster and founder of the Gunnery School of Boys in Washington, Connecticut, inaugurated the first school camp in America. Gunnery Camp sought to provide outdoor experience as an integral part of the school curriculum. This early effort was the forerunner of the many kinds of camps that we have today.

The first private camp dates from 1876, when Dr. Joseph T. Rothrock set up a tent camp in the hill country of Pennsylvania offering a healthy outdoor experience to boys in poor health. Although the camp was soon a financial failure, it set the stage for future ventures. From 1881 to 1889

Ernest B. Balch operated Camp Chocorua, the first commercially success-ful private camp, located on an island in Asquam Lake, New Hampshire. Campers were recruited from affluent families, a technique that has been followed with few variations to this day. The Balch camp was staffed with qualified counselors and the program consisted largely of competitive activities. A camp uniform was required, and this established a trend for private commercial camps for many years.

The first sectarian camp was founded by the Reverend George S. Hinckley in 1880. This camp was so successful that Hinckley established a permanent camp in Maine where organized outdoor activities and religious services were a mainstay of the camp program.

The camping movement really gained impetus when, in 1885, Sumner F. Dudley instituted the first agency camp. Dudley and the YMCA orga-nized a fishing trip to Orange Lake near Newburgh, New York, and this first expedition became a permanent camp. It is the oldest continually existing camp in the United States and is still operated under the sponsorship of the State Executive Committee of the YMCA of New York.

The first camp for girls was started by Laura Matoon in 1902, on Lake Winnepesaukee, New Hampshire. Similar camps were soon organized. In short order coed camps appeared and the camping movement really caught on.

The camping field began to professionalize with camp director meetings, the first held in Boston in 1903. By 1910 it was apparent that some organization was needed to set and maintain camping standards so that the health, welfare, and safety of campers could be protected and enhanced. This resulted in the organization of the Camp Directors Association, and in 1916, its affiliate, the National Association of Directors of Girls' Camps. This was followed in 1921 by the Midwest Camp Directors Association and in 1923 by the Pacific Camping Association. These three groups joined together in the Camp Directors Association in 1924. In 1935, at a Cleveland convention, the organization was re-named the American Camping Association. Today this organization is the chief advocate of organized camping in the United States and represents nearly all camping elements in its membership.

In 1989 the number of established camps of all types was 8,000 serving almost 6 million children during the summer.[4] Despite fluctuations in the economic ability of American parents to send their children to camp,

[4]American Camping Association

camping has become firmly embedded as a recreational experience. The number of school children currently available to go to organized camps is estimated to be in excess of 40 million. At least 8 million of all school age children participate in organized camp experiences. It seems certain that camping will continue to provide recreational opportunities and make contributions to leisure activity as a component of the recreational service movement.

The Public Education Movement

The American dream of a free public education had already been pronounced by the time of the Civil War. Although it had not been realized, the extent of the ideal had been clearly perceived and was in practice by 1865. Despite major shortcomings and inequities, the movement for a common education for all America's children was being legislated and would, after overcoming both sectarian and political difficulties, evolve into an edifice which would permit quality instruction for all, from kindergarten to university. But this latter aspect was as yet in the future. In 1865, the South lay in ruins, and most public education was being carried on in cities. The objections to compulsory attendance were finally overcome when the argument reached the crucial question of the states' right to promote the general welfare. Universal free public education was a decision reached only after serious, prolonged, and hotly contested debates that touched every individual in the country. Equal educational opportunity became the touchstone on which unbounding determination to succeed was based. Here was a condition favorable to the masses of people who had come into the United States seeking freedom and opportunities to flourish along with the rest of the country. Now the means for realising individual potential was at hand. During the 1885 convention of the National Education Association, the discourse rose to new heights as John Seaman invoked the meaning that education had for a free and democratically oriented people. He stated:

> We contend that the circumscribed course of rudiments taught in the lower schools is not education. They are the tools only . . . If the ultimate object of a public school education is to lift up man to the dignity of a reflecting, self-guiding, virtuous member of society, then the instruction, scrupulously limited to the three Rs, is a lamentable failure.[5]

---

[5]J.E. Seaman. *"High Schools and the State,"* National Education Association *Proceedings* (1885), pp. 173–180.

Only through the full range of education beyond the primary grade schools can an enlightened citizenry deal with the numerous problems which confront it. This was the call that resounded through the halls of numerous conferences and served as the inspirational message which eventuated in the establishment of free public education throughout the United States. Education, it was thought, could be the means by which each person would be enabled to develop both latent intellectual ability, or talent, and aptitude for the choices which they would make in vocational and trade careers. In addition, education would benefit the person as a citizen in helping to make wise choices, whether in the election of public officials, in participation in civic affairs, or in the recreational use of his leisure. School would be effective in promoting the discrimination that would battle the bleak lives led by the children of the poor and those who lived in urban slums. As Jacob Riis indicated, only by a concerted effort of the entire community could the influence of the street be negated. The school stood as one bastion against the corrupting influence which *the streets* inculcated.

Henry Barnard and the Recreational Service Movement

By the middle of the nineteenth century, a strong movement toward free public education had already appeared in the United States. In fact, the bottom rungs of the educational ladder included a well-developed public elementary school system. Among the most illustrious names associated with this trend is Henry Barnard—educator, editor, and protagonist of universal free public education. He stands as the connecting link between the philosophic play concepts of the European continent and the first stirrings of what was later to take shape as the recreational service movement in the United States. Yet Henry Barnard was not a philosophic contributor to recreational service nor did he conceptualize about leisure. His contribution is as a reproducer, rather than as a producer, of play theory. His outstanding role came as an interpreter of the educational theories of Pestalozzi and Froebel, whose works he translated and transmitted to the American educational scene.

Barnard's profound knowledge and scholarship placed him in a position of preeminence, along with Horace Mann, James G. Carter, and others who influenced and shaped educational content and philosophy during its transitional phase from mere toleration to widespread public acceptance. In his European travels and studies Barnard was strongly influenced by the educational concept of Pestalozzi and Froebel. He was especially attracted to their ideas of every individual's being potentially educable for well-rounded characteristics that would enhance, rather than hinder, the individual's role in the welfare and development of the community regardless of environmental background.

Barnard recognized the importance that Froebel's concept of play had for education and did much to encourage the opening of kindergartens in the United States. Although being aware of the significance of this movement and its impact upon the educational discipline at that time, he nevertheless was analytical enough to realize the inadequacy of the psychology and physiology of his day for explaining the child and its play.

Materials that he edited indicated that the Froebelian system contained an indirect contribution to growth through symbolism produced in the use of gifts, occupations, and games.[6] He undoubtedly recognized the error which the pantheistic philosophy of Froebel made by introducing the element of sentimentality into the system. However, it is to Barnard's credit that he made every effort to translate the indirectness, in which play activities were utilized for maximal benefit to the individual, rather than for the value such activities were supposed to have as symbols.

Barnard's main contribution to recreational service was as an outstanding champion of play and other creative activities within the educative system. He recognized the value of play activities and strongly advocated their inclusion in the curriculum. He believed that a broad range of experience should be brought to students through the use of industrial, mechanical, creative, expressive, manual arts, physical, and other play activities.[7]

He thought that the educative value to be found in recreational activities would provide benefits beyond mere enjoyment. Sound social attitudes, personal habits, character development, and physical skills were to be gained from recreational activities and were urgently needed by individuals if they were to become ideally educated. Barnard was aware that interesting subjects were assimilated readily, and if students were interested in what they were doing, learning could be promoted through real rather than vicarious experience. As a reformer in education, he placed major emphasis on activity concepts of learning and in this

---

[6]H. Barnard, Ed., *Kindergarten, and Child Culture Papers, Papers on Froebel's Kindergarten, With Suggestions on Principles and Methods of Child Culture in Different Countries,* American Journal of Education (Hartford: F.C. Brownell, 1890), p. 330.

[7]H. Barnard, "Public High School." *American Journal of Education, VIII.* (March, 1857), pp. 185–188.

area became the medium by which play, as an educative device, was injected into the curriculum.

Barnard felt repugnance for ignorance and sought to provide a way for the great mass of people in the United States to gain some education and thus attain a measure of social mobility. His writings and speeches reflected his abhorrence for the blighted living conditions existing in industrial slums. He called for the removal of slums and conditions causing slums. He was cognizant of the relationship between the dullness of uninspired toil and the human need for satisfying emotional outlets. His plan for adult education and public school systems had as a central theme the universalization of culture and intellectual development. He did much to further utilitarian education in the schools, the aims of which he believed were to serve the practical needs of society.[8]

As the founder and editor of the *American Journal of Education,* Barnard actively publicized and promoted play in education. When he became the first Commissioner of Education in the United States in 1867, he held to this same course of action. Some statements that have appeared on play and recreational activity in the *Journal* illustrate his approval of this area of human behavior. He thought, as did Susan E. Blow, that play develops a healthy objectivity and emphasizes mental activity in children.[9] Among other things, he felt that play in kindergarten developed a capacity for individual self-expression instead of dependence upon others for mere amusement.

In 1879, he wrote to Elizabeth P. Peabody, then President of the American Froebel Union to describe his plans for and interest in the work of Froebel.

> I propose to do more in 1880 than I have done as publisher since 1838, in any one year for the elucidation of Child-Culture, and particularly of the Kindergarten as devised by Froebel, and developed by himself and others who have acted in his spirit and after his method . . . But the suggestion in my Special Report as Commissioner of Education to the Senate in 1868, and again to the House of Representatives in 1870, on the System of Public Instruction for the District of Columbia, "that the first or lowest school in a graded system for cities should cover the play period of a child's life," and that "the great formative period of the human being's life in all that concerns habits of observation and early development, should be subjected to the training of the

---

[8]*Report of the Commissioner of Education,* 1867–68, pp. XVII, 831.

[9]S.E. Blow, "Some Aspects of the Kindergarten," *Child Culture Papers,* H. Barnard, Ed. (Hartford: *American Journal of Education,* 1890). p. 614.

Kindergarten"... must be received now under at least the conditions of the original recommendation.[10]

In introducing an article on play in his *Journal* he wrote: "We are firm believers in the efficacy of play—in the ring of happy voices of boys and girls engaged in their innocent sports—"[11] He realized the importance of play for education and sought to nourish its growth by designing playgrounds and recreational spaces where healthful activity could flourish under competent supervision. His school architectural designs abound in descriptive detail of playground and play space construction.[12]

Henry Barnard is important to recreational service because of his unique station in the history and development of education and subsequently of a professional recreational service movement. He, more than anybody else, bears the distinction of having recognized play as an educative function in the early days of the United States' school system. His active interest assured the place of play in education and prompted the inception of the recreational service movement prior to 1865.

It is commonly believed that the earliest phases of the modern recreational service movement occurred in 1885 with the initiation of the Boston Sand Gardens. Yet, one is compelled to accept the fact that Barnard was already promoting the play concept in Kindergarteners, those teachers who, in the best Froebelian manner and tradition, were certainly the ancestors of today's recreationists. The Kindergartners were professional in every sense of the word and were devoted to the theory of play as the highest expression of child life. Surely, dedicated recreationists of this age will recognize their immediate predecessors and accord them a rightful place in the history of the American recreational service movement.

Barnard's life spanned almost 90 years. In that time, he witnessed what has just been described as the first stirrings of professional leadership. His interest and effort on behalf of play provided a place for it in the American school. Towards the end of his life he also saw the emergence of new play theories, each more detailed and definitive than the ones before.

In Barnard, the best of the European play theories were combined,

---

[10]H. Barnard, Ed., *American Journal of Education, XXX* (1880), p. 1.

[11]H. Bushnell, "Plays, Pastimes, and Holidays of Children," *American Journal of Education, XIII.* (1863), p. 93.

[12]H. Barnard, Ed., "General Principles of School Architecture," *American Journal of Education, IX* (1860), pp. 527–545.

actively promoted, and transmitted to America. As a translator of play and the father figure whose career coincided with the transitional phase of European to American play theory, Barnard has a lasting place as one of the guiding lights of the professional recreational service movement.

Luther H. Gulick—Pioneer Recreationist

Gulick's educational background was varied and interesting. In 1889 he graduated from New York University Medical College with the degree of Doctor of Medicine. In 1899 he instituted and taught a course in the psychology of play at the Springfield School for Christian Workers, now Springfield College, in Massachusetts. He was interested in physical education and through this field he developed play as physical education. As physical education director for the Young Men's Christian Association, he taught and thought of physical exercise in terms of play and of gymnastics as recreational, hygienic, and educational.[13] According to Gulick, recreative exercise did not require thought, but involvement took the mind of the participant from other worries or problems.

In 1903 he was nominated for and accepted the position of Director of Physical Education for the city of New York. In this position he organized and directed the Public School Athletic League. This organization was designed to make room for all children to participate in competitive sports and games whether they were outstanding athletes or not. He promoted the folk dance movement and saw the value that could be garnered through participation in this type of play. He stated of this activity:

> If we can enrich childhood by giving out to children dance games; if we can add to the social resources for the leisure time of adults—then this movement for the resurrection of the folk dance will be worthwhile, for it will help to make life more vivid, happy, and wholesome.[14]

In this way, social recreational activity as a distinctive phase in the structure of the recreational service movement was stimulated and actively promoted.

Gulick had been identified with the playground movement in the United States and his concept of play has, to a great extent, been taken as

---

[13]Editorial in *Physical Education II* (October 1893), pp. 118–121.

[14]L.H. Gulick, *The Healthful Act of Dancing* (Garden City, N.Y.: Doubleday, Page and Company, 1910), p. 9.

a foundation for the work of many others. In 1906, as a result of his interest and activity in the area of play, Gulick and some of his contemporaries officially formed the Playground Association of America, now the National Recreation and Park Association. Concerned with promoting interest in play throughout the country, he believed that the playground was the logical place for this educational experience to occur. His efforts to aid the development of positive attitudes regarding play spurred him to write a series of articles, one of which, "The Social Function of Play," appeared in the *Journal of Education* in 1915. In this article he defined recreation as recuperation from the strain of living, and play as a voluntary activity whose drive was sustained through its own action, that is, self-activity. He conceived of play as those pleasurable activities engaged in during leisure, being of the creative, artistic, and social nature.[15]

The recreational service movement has closely paralleled that of education, although it still has not achieved the status that education enjoys. Recreational service began, as did education, with very little support, hardly tolerated by the people and suppressed in many instances. It was considered to be within the operational confines of private enterprise or individual discretion during the first 250 years after the establishment of the American colonies. Today, much of the recreational activity carried on in the United States is still subjective and highly individualistic. However, recreational service has also been seen as a vital governmental function. Supported in many instances by public tax funds, recreational service provides needed physical facilities, organized experiences, and professional personnel beyond individual means that only a pooling of tax resources can provide.

The Chautauqua Movement

The original chautauqua was inspired by religious considerations. Established in 1874 by Lewis Miller and John H. Vincent, it started as a summer training program for religious workers at Lake Chautauqua in New York State. The meetings rapidly developed into a large-scale public forum where public issues of the day were debated, where lectures covered a multitude of subjects, and where the old-fashioned revival

---

[15]L.H. Gulick, "Popular Recreation and Public Morality," *Annals of the American Academy of Political and Social Science*, XXXIV, (July, 1909), p. 34.

and mass meeting served as a medium of entertainment and delight. Eventually, hundreds of local chautauquas appeared throughout diverse communities in the United States and served as the organization which brought popular culture and arts to rural towns. Any local chautauqua series might include entertainers, humorists, and inspirational speakers. William Jennings Bryant was typical of the speakers who traveled the chautauqua circuit.

The Public Library Movement

The public library movement, which had received its initial impetus prior to the Civil War, continued to flourish throughout the United States after the war. By 1900, 37 different states had appropriated public funds for the support of libraries, and in 1895 New Hampshire enacted laws which made public libraries compulsory. The founding of the American Library Association in 1876 influenced the direction and speed which this movement would generate. Andrew Carnegie and other philanthropists materially assisted in the growth of the library movement by making huge bequests for the construction and support of libraries. Carnegie donated over 31 million dollars. Other gifts to American libraries during the last decade of the nineteenth century totaled more than 46 million dollars. More than 9000 free circulating libraries were reported in 1900. Libraries opened their doors to everyone, promoting not only informal education but also reading, one of the great recreational activities which people engage in during their leisure. Libraries appeal to those who seek an enriched life through the joys of reading.

The Park Movement

Parks in the American culture had their beginnings as far back as 1565, when the first known municipal plaza, or central open space, was built in St. Augustine, Florida. Many regions were first settled by the Spanish, who had a decisive influence on the architectural style of the facilities constructed. Spanish architecture always employed open porticos and plazas to enhance a structure, and this custom was repeated in the New World. Moreover, it is quite logical that cities in the southern and southwestern sections of the country would construct open spaces within their cities, for in this way the inhabitants could take advantage of the relatively mild climates which prevail in those regions.

The older and larger American cities of the North and Midwest early set aside or accepted gifts of land squares for local parks. As new town sites were laid out, the rule of providing an open place at the crossroads which marked the center of the town was generally followed. The local parks were largely places of assembly but they were improved with landscaping, walks, statuary, and benches. They were not considered as places for vigorous recreational activity; on the contrary, they usually were posted with signs prohibiting play in them.

Boston Common was set aside as a meeting place, outside of a church, where things more important than leisure activity were discussed. This ground was developed in 1634, probably out of former common pasturage acres. It was William Penn, however, a forerunner of the modern city planner, who assigned five open squares as parks in the Philadelphia city plan which he designed in 1682. The first large city parks were established in 1853 when New York purchased the land for what is now Central Park. Other cities followed the lead of New York, and in 1854, Fairmount Park of Philadelphia was created by legislative act, as was Bushnell Park of Hartford, Connecticut.

In 1885, Boston became the first city to recognize the benefit that a public recreational activity might provide and appropriated funds to support the Mission Sand Gardens. In 1892, Boston established its Metropolitan Park Commission. New Jersey authorized the initiation of its county park systems thereafter. Other cities, such as Chicago, Buffalo, Denver, Baltimore, Cleveland, and Louisville, also developed municipal parks and park systems. By 1902, 792 cities had some land set aside for park spaces.

The authority for parks in cities was originally derived from the doctrine of eminent domain under police power. However, rapid urbanization, faster methods of transportation, a rapidly expanding technological industrial growth, and economic factors combined to force legislation through the various state and local legislatures in order to create parks, parkways, and reservations.

Nor was the federal government slow to accept the responsibility for the conservation and maintenance of scientific and natural wonders. In 1832 Congress passed legislation authorizing federal control of the Arkansas hot springs. Hot Springs National Park opened in 1921. By the Antiquities Act of 1861 the President was empowered to designate as historic landmarks sites and structures of scientific or historic interest. In 1864 Congress set aside Mariposa Big Tree Park for the State of California.

This grove is now part of Yosemite National Park. Yellowstone National Park was established in 1872, and the use of national forests for recreational purposes was authorized in 1897. In 1916 the administration of all national parks was placed under the Department of the Interior.

Just as the federal government saw opportunity and advantage in establishing national preserves and parks during the nineteenth century, the several states also acted to claim open spaces for the benefit of their people. The first state parks were established in California, New York, Michigan, Minnesota, and New Jersey between 1870 and 1890. The first state forest was established in the Adirondack mountains in New York State on 800,000 acres in 1885. The advent of the automobile stimulated a growth in other than urban recreational facilities, and in order to meet the travel and camping needs of people, more parks were opened.

At first the park movement in the United States was chiefly a method for improving the appearance of specified areas. The early years saw a rapid rise in the number of parks created, but the most significant change has been the shift in use. In the initial stages of the park movement, parks were looked upon as aesthetic areas to be preserved for study, contemplation, and passive appreciation. In the twentieth century, parks have come to be regarded as primary recreational areas, which also happen to be scenic.

As the public became more mobile through the use of private automobiles, there developed a movement toward large regional parks removed from urban centers. Regional parks are usually authorized by county government. The first was in Essex County, New Jersey, in 1895. Since then there have been several outstanding county park systems, notably Cook County in Chicago, Los Angeles County, and Dade County, Florida. Today, most counties that overlap urban centers have large park and recreational systems.

Many county systems have shown a dramatic growth in recent years. Some counties are recognizing the need for public recreational areas and are providing the necessary spaces. Thus, Westchester County in New York, Orange County, California, Maricopa County, Arizona, and others have been acquiring land for incorporation into a regional park development system. All of this activity has contributed immeasurably to public recreational service in America.

The Playground Movement

Some say that the Kindergarten movement, introduced by Henry Barnard in 1835, was the predecessor of the recreational service movement in the United States, but most professionals feel that the recreational service movement got its start in 1885, with the establishment of the Boston Sandgardens. The first public recreational facility was created in Boston when a sand pile was placed in a mission yard to provide a safe area where children could play. The idea, brought back from Germany by Dr. Maria Zakrewska, was so popular that school grounds soon had sand piles on them. The concept was borrowed from the public parks of Berlin, Germany, where piles of sand were available for youngsters to play in. The Massachusetts Emergency and Hygiene Association started its experiment as a private project, using volunteers to supervise the activities. Later, paid matrons were used, and after that, teachers and other trained personnel were employed. In 1889, Boston budgeted tax money to meet part of the expense which the provision of a directed program made necessary. Boston also established the Charlesbank Outdoor Gymnasium in 1889, and created the 40-acre Franklin Field in 1894. The Boston School Committee appropriated $3,000 for public recreational purposes in 1898. From Boston the playground idea spread to such cities as Philadelphia, Milwaukee, Pittsburgh, Denver, Minneapolis, New York, Chicago, Providence, and Baltimore. Although the sandgardens initially included only sand piles for the children, in time they also incorporated play areas with various apparatus as well so that older children might be attracted.

In New York City, two model playgrounds were constructed in underprivileged neighborhoods by the New York Society for Parks and Playgrounds in 1889 and 1891. These operated with private support. The playground movement was firmly entrenched during the last decade of the nineteenth century. New York City converted a tenement area into what is now known as Seward Park, under the promptings of Jacob Riis and his antislum newspaper campaigns. This park was developed at a cost of $1,800,000, a phenomenal price for the year 1897. Jointly financed by the Outdoor Recreation League and New York City, substantial funds were raised to finance the operation and take care of any litigation that might occur as a result of any unsafe incidents. In 1899 the New York City School Board permitted its property to be used for recreational purposes specifically for playground activities.

The early playground movement contributed enthusiasm and vigor to an awakened public which, under the urgings of farsighted leaders such as Jacob Riis, Luther Halsey Gulick, Jane Addams, Henry Curtis, Joseph Lee, and others, insisted that adequate provision be made for city children. What had started as a desire on the part of social reformers and concerned persons to set aside safe areas where children could play blossomed in the twentieth century into a comprehensive range of recreational activities and facilities.

The Entertainment Industry

The early colonists disapproved of theatrical productions as they did of other recreational activity. Nevertheless, players (both male and female) performed Shakespeare and Marlowe on makeshift stages wherever audiences could be found. The classics soon gave way to more popular forms of entertainment. With the lecture fad hitting full stride after 1840, the audience for legitimate theatre dwindled, and there was a concomitant rise in variety shows and stage farce. It was not long before burlesque, vaudeville, and melodrama enthralled a public that wanted to be entertained.

The circus, which was to bring to rural populations what the variety shows already offered to city dwellers, was the response to relatively isolated communities in the early nineteenth century. These shows had animal exhibits, acrobats, jugglers, and tight-rope artists. The traveling tent shows with their bands, animals, and parades, gradually consolidated and began to give more elaborate performances in rings, either in a large auditorium or under a canvas top. By 1850, the genesis of the circus as a great entertainment spectacle was complete. It only needed a P.T. Barnum, one of the great popularizers of entertainment that America has ever seen, to capitalize on the trend toward the big business of amusement.

During the decade from around 1840 on, the minstrel shows introduced a comic variety entertainment by performers in blackface, featuring songs, dances, and jokes. This form of entertainment declined after the Civil War because it failed to keep pace with what audiences wanted.

Throughout this period, particularly in urban centers, commercial enterprises were competing for the public's dollar and leisure. Dance halls, shooting galleries, pool halls, beer gardens, amusement parks, and the ever-popular spectator sports all beaconed to the public to spend their money and leisure in these recreational pursuits.

The demand for mass spectator activities has continued unabated up to the present. Despite war, depression, mass unemployment, drought, and other disasters, the entertainment industry has been able to introduce new ideas, performers, and attractions that capture the attention of the buying public.

Professional sports, motion pictures, radio, records, and television have contributed to the monumental growth of the entertainment industry. In 1929, more than 110,000,000 or 80 percent of the population was attending the movies once a week. During the worst years of the Depression no less than 70 million people patronized the movies. In 1980, however, attendance at movie theaters was down to 50,000,000 per week, largely due to the inroads of television, especially cable TV.

The entertainment industry satisfied a general need to escape from the tedium and frustration of society. It provides relaxation and enjoyment to millions of viewers who cannot get to see in-person performances. Furthermore, spectator involvement can stimulate individual desire to emulate the athletic prowess, singing, acting, or other skill depicted on the screen. Television has probably motivated millions of youngsters to participate in hockey, soccer, skiing, gymnastics, swimming, tennis, and many other sports and games. Televised marathons have boosted interest in running a hundredfold. On the negative side, however, television has also produced a nation of watchers who do not participate, and are thus depriving themselves of the benefits of active participation in wholesome activity.

At the beginning of the twentieth century, some municipalities had undertaken financial support—by bond issues, special assessments, and taxes—of agencies which could administer programs and facilities for leisure activities. The employment of professionally prepared leaders to carry on the functional operation of the agency was also considered, however, not until after 1910 was any strong trend noticeable toward the provision by municipalities of public recreational departments as governmental services, along with police and fire protection. Another three decades passed before twenty states recognized the need for setting up some sort of recreational committee, agency, commission, or office to handle their growing problems of leisure facility deficits. Even today, relatively few states actually employ full-time professional recreational service personnel to coordinate, direct, or advise on state services in this field. This view places recreational service in the unenviable position of being a governmental function but having no centralized authority of a legal nature to help disseminate program material or stimulate local governments in the provision of at least a minimal level of public recreational service. On the positive side, several states notably California, now have a recreational service license issued by the State. In most instances, however, licenses are only mandatory where personnel are employed by boards of education.

Recreational service is a function of government on every level; federal state and local. The field of recreational service attempts to satisfy felt needs for achieving happiness, refreshment from stress, and the optimistic creation of a new outlook on life—at least this is the idealized statement which guides personnel in the field. To date there is still little in the way of equalization of service or the promotion of interracial and ethnic harmony among the multi-cultural populations of the United States.

The current decade may force professionals in the field to do more than carry out routine and mechanical functions which culminate in programs that may or may not be responsive to citizens' needs. In many cases it is only by chance that the typically parallel lines of field practice and citizen expectations interact. Few administrators appear to be influenced by the field's potential for affecting people's lives. That recreational programs might be instrumental in bringing people together, despite racial, religious, or ethnic biases, has received scant attention. Important too, are the conservation of natural resources and a determined effort to assist people to use modern technology to their own best advantage during their respective leisure.

Chapter 4

TRANSFORMATIONS OF RECREATIONAL SERVICE

The following section will review the social developments that gave impetus to the recreational movement in America and continue to mature while serving the needs of people.

1900 to 1910

In the early 1900's, the public recreational service movement gained momentum. As earlier suspicions of leisure activity gave way to a new understanding of the needs of people, the church and school made substantial efforts to begin educating for the new leisure. During this period the cumulative effects of social, economic, and cultural factors decidedly offered a place to the burgeoning field of recreational service. There appeared at this time an almost catholic appeal and recognition of the fact that recreational experience was a real need, and that one of the best means of providing satisfaction of this need was through public recreational service. Public awareness was not generated easily. After all, almost 50 years previously the first play programs had been organized for children.

Prior to 1850, private influence was the dominant force in the progress of the recreational service movement. It was not until 1899 that tax funds were utilized to support recreational functions in the Boston school system. Citizen petitions to the School Committee of Boston forced approval of the use of school property for recreational purposes in 1901. Following suit, New York City's school board established recreational centers in several schools. This plan was the forerunner of the school-community center plan not extant in New York City. Rochester, New York, was the first city in the nation to allow use of school buildings for a community center (1907), and a year later Gary, Indiana, provided the same service. In 1903, New York City organized the Public School Athletic League, which has enabled millions of students to participate in sport and game events ever since.

Only after the turn of the century could any real public recreational service movement be discerned. In 1902, Chicago erected two large field houses in the South Park system which were financed by a $3,000,000 bond issue. Los Angeles created its Board of Playground Commissioners in 1904 and was the first city to operate recreational services on a communitywide basis.

In 1906, a group of farsighted men and women met to form a new organization which would become the spearhead of the American recreational service movement. The interest aroused in developing playgrounds and other recreational facilities stimulated the need for sharing and disseminating information about the best methods for operation. Answering this need, Henry Curtis, Luther H. Gulick, and others organized the first national body concerned with the recreational needs of children—the Playground Association of America (PAA). The PAA focused its attention on satisfying the recreational deficits caused by urban congestion. In so doing, the organization became the guide and voice for a movement which required leadership. Employees of the organization traveled from city to city meeting with and giving point to the provision of recreational services. Consultations were held, information was exchanged, and assistance was offered in the establishment and operation of recreational facilities and programs. Responding to a broadening concern which included the recreational needs of all persons, not only those of children, the PAA changed its name in 1911 to Playground and Recreation Association of America. Sometime later it became the National Recreation Association.

By 1907, St. Louis, Oakland, and Minneapolis had organized recreational service authorities. The important Playground Law was passed in Massachusetts in 1908, a milestone in the recreational service movement. In short order, the cities of Newark, Milwaukee, and Boston opened their school buildings as recreational centers, and this established a pattern for other communities to model themselves on. School administrators seemed to be the first professionals to apply the concept that recreational service was a fit subject and responsibility for municipal concern. It was the school systems of several cities that pioneered the provision of recreational service years before municipal government finally accepted recreational service as a public function.

Developments in the Playground Movement From 1900 to 1910

The years between 1900 and 1910 enhanced the growth of community recreational service.

The following chronology indicates the events that had a decided effect upon the young recreational service movement.

- 1902 Chicago erects two large field houses in the South Park System financed by a $3,000,000 bond issue.
- 1903 New York City establishes the first Public School Athletic League.
- 1904 Los Angeles creates the first Board of Playground Commissioners.
- 1906 The Playground Association of America is established.
- 1907 St. Louis, Oakland, and Minneapolis organize public recreational service authorities.
- 1907 Rochester, New York is the first city to open its school buildings as community centers.
- 1907 The first playground convention, organized by the Playground Association of America, is held in Chicago.
- 1908 Massachusetts passes the Playground Law.
- 1908 Gary, Indiana opens its school buildings as community centers.
- 1910 The Boy Scouts of America is organized.

School administrators were quick to discern the need for recreational service as a municipal function. The school systems of a number of cities, among them Newark, Milwaukee, New York, Boston, and Rochester, opened their school buildings as recreational centers thereby setting patterns for other communities to emulate. School systems were in the forefront of providing recreational services to communities long before local governments reluctantly assumed this function.

Growth and Change From 1910 to 1920

1910 to 1920. The second decade of the twentieth century actually brought recreational service, as a public function, to the attention of municipal authorities. The progress made during that time was tremendous by virtue of the then innovational idea of promoting these services. It should be understood that the concept of operating public agencies for the purpose of making recreational opportunities available through tax support was considered radical. Indeed, there are communities today which still have that notion. Nevertheless, there was a determined movement by progressive jurisdictions to enact statutes, codes, and other legislative implementation whereby recreational services could be offered as widely as possible by public agencies.

The years between 1911 and 1914 were characterized by an increase in the number of private and public camps that were established. The Boy Scouts had been organized in 1910, and two years later the Campfire Girls and Girl Scouts were established. Significantly, the National Education Association approved the use of school buildings and grounds for recreational functions in 1911, and in 1918, authorized formation of the Commission on the Reorganization of Secondary Education which issued the now famous *Seven Cardinal Principles of Secondary Education.* Among these principles, which were directly concerned with the personal and social competencies of life in general, was the worthy use of leisure. This one point has vastly greater implication for the expanding field of recreational service than did the others.

College and high school athletics made considerable headway during the two years prior to America's entry into World War I. With better facilities available, larger numbers of participants were recorded. Intramural programs gained a foothold and made continuous progress. The National Park Service of the Department of the Interior was established in 1916, and a year later, the War Camp Community Services (WCCS) program under the leadership of the Playground and Recreational Association of America was created. Although American participation in the war lasted for only one and a half years, the WCCS was able to organize a large number of communities and industrial districts across the nation. The major effort of this service was to initiate recreational services by mobilizing community resources for the purpose. The impact the program had upon the communities in which it was situated, as well as upon members of the military who profited by association with organized recreational activities, could be observed after the service was terminated at the end of the war. Both military servicemen and citizens in these communities who had been exposed to well-organized and competently led recreational programs found the means for continuing them as integral parts of the life of the community.

Various social, civic, business, religious, and educational agencies whose members had obtained satisfaction from the inception of community recreational services now desired to maintain such programs for the benefit which could accrue to the community's residents. Having seen the contribution that organized recreational service could make to the life of the community, these civic-minded persons influenced their communities to provide support for public recreational service.

The number of communities operating playgrounds, employing personnel, and spending money for the maintenance of facilities and the supply of programs increased dramatically. In 1900, less than 15 cities reported that they were providing recreational service with public funds. Twenty years later more than 450 cities reported their organization and administration of public recreational service departments.

Between 1910 and 1914, the number of public and private camps increased many times over. The following list of events is indicative of the burgeoning recreational movement.

- 1911 The Playground Association of America changes its name to the Playground and Recreation Association of America (PRAA).
- 1911 The National Education Association approves the use of school buildings and grounds for recreational function.
- 1912 The Girl Scouts and Campfire Girls are established.
- 1916 The National Park Service of the Department of the Interior is established.
- 1917 The War Camp Community Service program is set up under the leadership of the PRAA.
- 1918 The N.E.A. Commission on the Reorganization of Secondary Education issues *Seven Cardinal Principles of Secondary Education.*
- 1918 American involvement in World War I.

Clarence E. Rainwater was able to discern nine transitions that the play movement had undergone from the turn of the century until 1920:

(1) From provision for little children to that for all ages of people; (2) from facilities operated during the summer only, to those maintained throughout the year; (3) from outdoor equipment and activities only, to both outdoor and indoor facilities and events; (4) from congested urban districts to both urban and rural communities; (5) from philanthropic to community support and control; (6) from "free" play and miscellaneous events to "directed" play with organized activities and correlated schedules; (7) from a simple to a complex field of activities including manual, physical, aesthetic, social, and civic projects; (8) from the provision of facilities to the definition of standards for the use of leisure time; (9) from "individual" interests to group and community activities.[1]

---

[1]Clarence E. Rainwater, *The Play Movement in the United States,* (1922) The University of Chicago Press. p. 192.

Expansion and Prosperity From 1920 to 1930

Following World War I, recreational service increased in importance. In the next ten years after the war, many new parks, community houses, swimming pools, beaches, golf courses, picnic areas, skating rinks, and bowling alleys were constructed. The public began to realize that a well-organized recreational program could accomplish much in the way of a better life style for Americans.

The accelerated growth of the municipal recreational service movement in this decade was due largely to the influence of wartime experiences. Tremendous impetus was given to enactment of municipal legislation for recreational services by the consequent rise of free time and the effect which an economic boom had on services provided by cities. During the decade of expansion that followed the end of World War I, the first venture into professional preparation occurred. Concurrently, an emphasis on legislation for recreational service was evidenced, and public appropriations for recreational facilities rose to almost $30 million by 1922. Furthermore, educational institutions joined the recreational movement by mandating compulsory physical education programs. Schools broadened their curricula to include intramurals along with hiking, winter sports, social affairs, and other recreational activities. President Coolidge added to the prestige of the recreational movement when, in 1924, he called into being the National Conference on Outdoor Recreation. The meeting of this group centralized a great deal of attention on the need for added recreational facilities to handle the growing leisure problem.

The following events are indicative of increased leisure, greater wealth, and public involvement in recreational activities of all kinds.

- 1922 The National Conference on State Parks is established.
- 1922 The Izaak Walton League is established.
- 1924 The American Association of Zoological Parks and Aquariums is established.
- 1924 President Calvin Coolidge calls for a National Conference on Outdoor Recreation in Washington, D.C.
- 1926 The National Recreation School is established by the National Recreation Association (formerly the Playground and Recreation Association of America).
- 1929 President Herbert Hoover's Research Committee on Social

Trends gives special consideration to recreational activity as a use for leisure.

In summary, the decade of the twenties had developed a firm foundation for organized recreational services. Public and private agencies were widely recognized and operated for community benefit. As the nation prospered, the recreational movement gained added momentum. The mass production of the automobile allowed the tourist industry to provide the individual with a form of transportation that was also recreational. Thousands of persons flocked to the movies and other places of entertainment to spend their leisure. Stuart Chase estimated that in 1927 out of a national income of $92 billion the American people expended over $21 billion on recreational activities and for commodities consumed during leisure.[2]

Recreational Advance During the Great Depression (1930–1940)

In the 1930's the Great Depression brought home the dramatic dependence of people on simple recreational activity. With direct impact, the nation's attention was focused on the need for public recreational service.

The Depression of the 1930s resulted in an increased emphasis on recreational service. The modified work week, shortened to give more jobs to more people, resulted in more leisure for all. The Depression resulted in a downturn in business and industry, and some commercial recreational enterprises had to be closed. In light of the shortage of recreational programs, voluntary and community agencies attempted to supply needed recreational services, but fell far short of the demand. As a result, the federal government, through its various agencies, gave the recreational service movement an invaluable forward push by providing jobs for those who were unemployed, by constructing new or refurbishing old recreational areas and facilities, and by providing the funds for employing recreationists to provide leadership for programs throughout the country.

Federal intervention created several agencies to carry on the function of supplying needed recreational services for Americans. Although there were less public and private funds to support the movement, there was, nevertheless, a great demand for federal assistance in the provision of

---

[2]Stuart Chase, "Play," in C.A. Beard, *Whither Mankind* (New York: Longmans, Green and Company, 1928) Chapter XIV.

qualified leadership and recreational facilities. The Recreation Project of the Federal Emergency Relief Administration (FERA) was created in 1935, with the two-fold job of constructing facilities and developing adequate recreational programs supervised by effective leaders. By 1936, the Works Progress Administration (WPA) had been established to replace the old FERA. With its Division of Recreation Projects, the WPA was able to supply close to 45,000 full-time recreational workers to communities throughout the country. By 1937, about 10 per cent of the entire WPA budget had been expended on the construction of more than 10,000 recreational structures, facilities, or places. The federal government also organized the Civilian Conservation Corps which gave employment to jobless young men, and enlisted more than 3,000,000 into its administration during its tenure of operation between 1933 and 1942.

The reaction to the Great Depression again demonstrated the fact that Americans insisted upon having recreational activities provided by local authorities. Federal, state, and local relief funds were utilized to establish and administer recreational programs throughout the nation. Attendance at municipally operated recreational facilities and activities increased dramatically during this period; taxes for the support of such programs declined even faster and budgets had to be slashed. By propitious use of volunteers to run activities and curtailment of construction of some facilities, municipal administrators were able to accommodate some of the 15 million people who were unemployed.

The 10 years of depression following the boom years of the 1920s served as a great stimulus to the recreational service movement. Municipalities, acting with federal funds, put people to work in construction of facilities and development of property which, upon completion, were utilized for recreational activities. Local communities reacted to the deepening calamity by making new efforts to provide for citizen betterment. Laws were passed whereby public and private agencies might work out cooperative actions. Federal recreational projects greatly multiplied local jurisdictional activities. The municipalities responded with emergency measures to gear federal aid and developmental programs to supplement and complement existing programs. The means for setting up a municipal establishment to assume complete authority for the operation of recreational services after the withdrawal of federal assistance was nothing short of phenomenal. Cities, which never before had considered such responsibility, reacted to the emergency with plans, personnel, and action supported by new legal enactments. On the whole, then, the principle of recreational service as the direct responsibility of city government was really espoused and accepted during this time. Significantly, state enabling legislation for recreational services also received much stimulation, resulting in the provision of a stable base for local improvement and consideration of recreational service as an important segment of municipal function.

Wrenn and Harley summarized the view of the depression's influence on recreational service when they wrote:

> The effect of the Depression—while it was devastating in other ways—was positive in terms of recreation. Instead of simply channeling off billions of dollars in direct relief, according to the European dole system, people were put to work meaningfully. The lives of millions of people in thousands of communities were enriched. Recreation training was given to hundreds of thousands of leaders. Great numbers of indoor facilities were built and outdoor recreation areas constructed and improved. Recreation and park development, in the view of one analyst, was set ahead at least a decade by the services provided by the Civilian Conservation Corps along.[3]

The following events indicate the ways in which the federal government participated in the recreational service movement during the Depression.

- 1932—15 million people were unemployed.
- 1933—The Civilian Conservation Corps (CCC) is established.
- 1933—Tax revenues of municipalities decline by more than 50 percent.
- 1935—The Federal Emergency Relief Administration (FERA) is created and establishes the Recreation Project to construct recreational facilities and develop supervised recreational programs.
- 1936—The Works Progress Administration (WPA) is established with a Recreational Division responsible for a variety of projects serving millions of people through art, music, and theater activities.
- 1937—Ten percent of the WPA budget is consumed in the construction of 10,000 recreational structures.
- 1939—300 CCC camps are operated. The Corp also constructs parks and other recreational facilities and areas throughout the United States.

---

[3]C.G. Wrenn and D.L. Harley, *Time on Their Hands: A Report on Leisure, Recreation and Young People,* (Washington, D.C.: American Council on Education, 1941), p. 221.

- 1940—More than 9,000 structures constructed by the National Youth Administration were for recreational purposes.

The many federal agencies and projects set up to alleviate the Depression greatly enhanced the recreational service movement by providing jobs for unemployed persons, by building and improving such facilities as parks, picnic areas, roads, and trails, and by training volunteers and recreational workers. The primary example of federal intervention was the Works Progress Administration, a "grass-roots" program aimed at increasing community involvement. Various works projects were developed in the field of community public recreational service. Their objective was to stimulate mass recognition of, and action in, community recreational service. The WPA had previously concentrated on organized games and sports for children and youth. This was broadened to include an increased emphasis on, and participation in, a cultural program of aesthetic and intellectual activities. Professional artists, whose areas of expertise included art, music, drama, and writing, were added to the recreational movement. An important feature of the WPA experiment was its attempt to develop a community leisure program by integrating physical activities, education, and art programs.

Recreational expansion as a result of federal assistance provided many new jobs and also resulted in many new and better facilities. The WPA and the Public Works Administration funds financed and constructed school sports facilities, swimming pools, tennis courts, and athletic fields. New employment opportunities were created, such as camp and community center personnel, crafts specialists, swimming instructors, consultants, and plant, program, and facility managers.

Federal programs also made it possible for small as well as large communities to benefit from recreational programs. Facilities were built, personnel hired, and services provided in many of the nation's small counties, cities, towns, and villages.

Outdoor recreational activities also gained popularity during the 1930's. Federal funds that financed state park and forest systems contributed to a sharp rise in state outdoor recreational developments. Forty-six recreational demonstration areas, initiated under the National Park Service in 1936, were later turned over to federal and state agencies. The states' work in protecting and improving game resources was accompanied by an increase in the already popular outdoor sports of hunting and fishing. Private agencies added skiing to the choices of activities available in the outdoors.

Modifications of the movement were continuous during these twenty years. Experts could see the differences which were produced as the movement matured. Writing in 1940, George Hjelte was able to note five additional transitions that had occurred: (1) From a "play" movement to a "recreational" movement; (2) from a local municipal movement only, to a state and national movement; (3) from programs detached from public education, to programs integrated with the educational curriculum and system; (4) from organization limited to urban communities to the inclusion of suburban and rural areas as well; (5) from an organization largely under quasi-public control with subsidies from public funds to full acceptance of recreational service as a public function.[4]

Colleges and universities recognized that recreationists required special preparation. In 1937 a conference concerning the education of recreationists was sponsored by the University of Minnesota and the recreational division of the WPA. The impetus for this training had been given by the WPA and its leadership preparation program for supervisors, leaders, and lay personnel participating in its program. This program, and the techniques developed, influenced recreational methods and materials in thousands of communities.

World War II and Economic Boom (1940–1950)

The emergence of the economy from the Great Depression coincided with the advent of World War II. Again the federal government was called upon to aid both its civilian population and military components. The Federal Security Agency's Office of Community War Services established a Recreation Division whose primary job was to help organize and develop community recreational services. Through its local field offices, the Recreation Division was able to assist many communities located near military posts with the operation of recreational services, and helped to certify the need for Lanham Act funds which subsidized the maintenance operation of recreational projects.

World War II emphasized the need for increased funds and leadership within municipal programs. With 10 million men and women in the

---

[4]George Hjelte, *The Administration of Public Recreation,* (New York: The MacMillan Company, 1940), p. 16. Used by permission of George Hjelte.

armed services and millions more employed in defense-related industries, towns were forced to plan for a mobile and newly rich population. Small communities that never before had experienced transient populations were inundated by members of armed forces from nearby centers. Cities had to organize to compensate for the needs developed by war conditions. Many citizens took the opportunity to become active in community affairs on a scale hitherto unknown, and recreational councils, committees, and boards were established. Public and private agencies were forced to coordinate their activities, and this association led to increased confidence and cooperation in the planning and direction of recreational services to meet community needs.

With World War II came the realization that recreational service was indispensable. The physical examination undergone by draftees showed the poor physical condition of our population. Programs geared toward improving both the physical and mental health of servicemen were undertaken by the American Red Cross, Army Special Services Division, the Welfare and Recreation Section of the Bureau of Naval Personnel, and the Recreation Service of the Marine Corps. The objectives of these organizations included relieving war-induced tension, bolstering morale, and decreasing the psychological impact of the servicemen being separated from home. The worth of this work was demonstrated by the increased efficiency of the fighting force, a program for the relaxation and diversion from work responsibilities for servicemen, and improvement of conditions for millions of Americans living in congested areas.

Three groups were outstanding in providing leisure activities during this war period. The first of these were organizations that functioned under the auspices of the Armed Forces—the Army, Navy, Merchant Marine, and Red Cross. The Special Services Division of the United States Army was empowered to provide facilities, programs, financial support, and leadership for the recreational activities of the soldiers. The Navy Welfare and Recreation Section offered personnel, facilities, equipment, and funds for recreational programs at sea and at naval bases. The United States Seaman's Service was responsible for the Merchant Marine and served the men of the country's civilian fleet, which transported war materials to the Armed Forces. The American Red Cross was officially requested by the War Department to provide recreational centers, posts, facilities, programs, and other recreational opportunities for soldiers overseas.

The second group that contributed so importantly to the wartime recreational service movement was the United Services Organization (USO). This agency was comprised of six divisions: the Jewish Welfare Board, the Salvation Army, Catholic Community Services, Young Men's Christian Association, Young Women's Christian Association, and the National Traveller's Aid. Its purposes were to serve the leisure needs of the armed forces in community settings and to provide recreational opportunities for industrial workers engaged in the war production effort. The USO is still a primary agency providing recreational services to military personnel world-wide.

Youth-serving agencies also were caught up in the spirit of the times and did much to develop enthusiasm for the various drives for materials such as paper, fat, scrap metal, and the like, which were used for war material. The abnormality of war, the feverish activity, the war industries working around the clock, all contributed to the rapid expansion of public recreational services. Many public departments inaugurated 24-hour programs to accommodate war plant workers and others whose leisure fell at odd hours.

The Federal Security Agency also played a key role in the recreational programs that were developed during the second World War. This agency helped communities to initiate, organize, develop, and maintain recreational services to meet the increasing demands of the war effort through such means as surveys, publicity, publications, and by providing the motivation and support for communities to initiate their own recreational service.

It is probably true that the intervention of the federal government in the provision of recreational programs to communities and to members of the armed forces, along with the supplementary help of quasi-public and private agencies, did much to stimulate the entire recreational service movement. There is little doubt that the attention and concentration of effort to initiate, maintain, and operate recreational service programs duly affected the public recreational service field and subsequently led to its enlargement and recognition as a basic function of government on all levels.

As Butler states:

> The effects of World War II upon local recreation were even more striking than those following World War I. Large numbers of servicemen and service-women for the first time has an opportunity to enjoy extensive recreational facilities and diversified recreational programs. Furthermore, every community felt the effects of home-front recreation activities during the war. The

Recreation Yearbook for 1946 revealed great forward strides since 1941, the last prewar year, and a greater volume of service than ever before recorded. A renaissance of the movement for living war memorials, initiated after World War I, took place and prompted the construction of memorials in the form of recreational buildings, playgrounds, parks, and athletic fields, swimming pools, band shells, and forests.[5]

Service in the armed forces by 10 million Americans brought many of them into contact with programs of an organized recreational nature. These servicemen and servicewomen experienced the entertainment, social, and physical values of recreational pursuits through such media as the USO shows, intramural and intermural sports, arts, crafts, and library activities. It is not surprising, therefore, that they would desire the same types of experiences when they returned to civilian life. Under such pressures, communities were forced to organize and, in many cases, expand departments of recreational service to meet the demand.

In 1945, a bill was introduced in the Congress which, for the first time, indicated a need for one federal agency to be solely responsible for the implementation and coordination of recreational services on a national level. The Federal Inter-Agency Committee on Recreation was brought into being in 1946 to coordinate plans and disseminate information concerning a variety of governmental agencies which performed some function in, or were responsible for some aspect of, recreational service. Such diverse agencies as the United States Army Corps of Engineers, the Children's Bureau of the Department of Health, Education and Welfare, the Bureau of Roads, and the National Park Service of the Department of Interior became part of this relationship, as did others. However, the agency has never lived up to its promise and does little in the way of national leadership.

Among the events that had implications for the movement we may cite the following:

- 1945—First introduction of a Congressional bill requiring a federal agency responsible for national recreational services. The bill fails of passage.

---

[5]G.D. Butler, *Introduction to Community Recreation* 5th ed., (New York: McGraw-Hill Book Company, 1975) p. 83.

- 1946—The Federal Inter-Agency Committee on Recreation is established.
- 1947—Vermont establishes a state recreational service board commission.

World War II emphasized the need for increased funds and leadership within municipal programs. With men and women in the armed services and millions more employed in defense-related industries, towns were forced to plan for a mobile and newly rich population. Small communities that never before had experienced transient populations were swelled by nearby armed forces centers. Cities had to organize to compensate for the needs developed by war conditions. Many citizens took the opportunity to become active in community affairs on a scale hitherto unknown, and recreational councils, committees, and boards were established. Public and private agencies and organizations were forced to coordinate their activities, and this association led to increased confidence and cooperation in the planning and direction of recreational services to meet community needs. After the war there was some reduction in the feverish activity that had characterized a mobilized society. Everyone expected some recession to come after the war years. A series of cutbacks were initiated as departments were consolidated for economic reasons. But the economy maintained an upward thrust and governments at all levels were made to recognize the importance of supporting public recreational service.

Internationalism and Expansion (1950–1960)

The momentum gained by the recreational service movement during wartime was continued in peacetime. Those persons who had assumed leadership roles in the recreational service movement during World War II became advocates of new recreational programs. Many cities had discovered, as a result of the war, the value and need for recreational programs. Also, millions of dollars worth of facilities built to meet wartime recreational needs were available for peacetime use. Furthermore, the extended evidence of recreational activity on the community level bore witness to the notion that recreational service and leisure had become a national concern and necessity.

By 1950, a well-established need for recreational service on every level of government had developed in the United States. In this year, the National Recreation Association received reports from more than 2000 communities operating public recreational service agencies.[6] These reports showed that the number of playgrounds had increased 12 times since 1910, and indoor recreational centers had increased 33 times during the same period. The first national conference on aging was held in 1950, during the Truman Administration, and another was held in 1961 and another in 1970. One of the 10 topics devoted to gerontological problems was that of free-time activities.

The Korean police action, followed by a resumption of the cold war, caused considerable apprehension and once again placed the United States on a limited war footing. The young men who went to war and returned had been exposed to a better recreational provision than had their relatives of the two preceding wars. Inasmuch as the Selective Service Act, originally passed in 1939, had never been repealed, many young men were exposed to a variety of well-organized and -operated recreational services administered by Special Services in the various military branches. When the soldiers returned to civilian life it seemed natural to expect such services to be provided by local government. A new round of committee and council hearings took place in the municipalities across the United States, and communities of all sizes were witness as this younger generation sought to convince local authorities of the need for expanding existing departments or establishing new services of a recreational nature.

Perhaps the most visible program to take place was Mission 66, a 10-year master plan for the development of modern recreational facilities and sites in the national parks. The program was started in 1956, and has been responsible for the construction of a new lodge at the Mt. Rushmore Memorial, campgrounds of excellent quality at Theodore Roosevelt National Memorial park in North Dakota, recreational facilities at Lake Meade National Recreational Area in Nevada, and many other observable and highly necessary constructions. Operation Outdoors was the Department of Agriculture's Forest Service corresponding program and effort to keep up with the expanding use of the national forests. Of course, not all governmental programs succeed regardless of their intent. That Mission 66 and Operation Outdoors did not live up

---

[6]*Recreation and Park Yearbook: Midcentury Edition* (New York: National Recreation Association, 1950), 1950.

to their stated aims occurred because of weak prognostication by departmental planners. Thus Jubenville was able to assess both programs as having been failures because:

" . . . these programs were set up to update facilities and area developments and also to expand the construction and development phases of the programs to meet the recreation needs of *tomorrow*. The lack of total success of these two programs was directly attributable to the poor predictions of future needs. The predictions were so inadequate that by the middle 1960's the developments were further from the intended goals than when the programs were started.[7]

In 1958, the Outdoor Recreation Resources Review Commission was activated, and the survey performed by this group led to the creation, in 1962, of the Bureau of Outdoor Recreation administered in the Department of the Interior. This Bureau, as an action agency, served as consultant to state and local subdivisions concerning the planning and development of parks, historical areas, wildlife and waterfowl areas, and other outdoor recreational spaces. The Soil Conservation Service of the U.S. Department of Agriculture under Public Law 566, as amended by the Food and Agriculture Act of 1962, may provide up to 50 percent of the cost of the land, easements, and rights-of-way for reservoir and other facilities required for recreational activity. These are only a few examples of the continual assistance given by federal agencies to the recreational service movement.

The states, too, had been partially effective in promoting services of a recreational nature to their constituents during the sixties. Many states had begun to implement a shared cost system for the acquisition of open spaces for recreational purposes and not a few have long-term plans for regionalizing within their borders to develop more efficient recreational service. Most states have planning boards or departments that have primary responsibility for the planning and construction of regional recreational facilities, which tend to equalize recreational opportunities for persons. Some states even provide consulting services to local communities.

The growth of recreational service as a function of government, which parallels in time the acquirement of almost universal leisure, represents one of the interesting public developments of the present century. Previously regarded as purely the prerogative of individual citizens in their private capacity, recreational service is now considered a human activity in which government must manifest some concern and render

---

[7]A. Jubenville, *Outdoor Recreation Planning* (Philadelphia: W.B. Saunders Company, 1976) p. 108.

some aid. Under the police power authorized by the supremacy of organized government, leisure activities, which were early stigmatized as being harmful and destructive, were regulated or prohibited. The laws restricting certain activities on the Sabbath, laws regulating hunting, fishing, prizefighting, gambling, traveling circuses, and dispensing of alcoholic beverages are examples in point. Only in the present century, and then only in the last 60 years, has government in the United States generally gone beyond the province of regulation and control to assume a more positive function of "promoting the general welfare" through recreational service.

Among the events that occurred in this decade the following are significant:

- 1950—The first national conference on aging is held.
- 1950—The Korean War begins and provides additional impetus for recreational service both in communities and the armed forces.
- 1952—The first National Workshop in Recreation for Leaders in Religious Organizations is sponsored by the Department of Recreation at Indiana University.
- 1956—Mission 66 is begun, a ten-year master plan for developing modern recreational facilities in the national forests.
- 1956—The International Recreation Association is founded.
- 1957—Washington Conference on Recreational Service for the Mentally Ill, sponsored by the American Association for Health, Physical Education, and Recreation is convened.
- 1958—The National Cultural Center for Performing Arts is founded.
- 1958—Congress creates the Outdoor Recreational Resources Review Commission.

During the decade between 1950 and 1960, leisure pursuits of Americans underwent changes. In this time one-twelfth of the total income was spent on recreational activities. There was renewed interest in active participation in tennis, bowling, and golf. In fact, money spent for active sports participation far exceeded expenditures for spectator sports.

Increased national attention in the performing arts had direct impact on recreational services. Programs were demanded in music, art, concerts, exhibitions, dance, and theater, necessitating additional appropriations for this purpose. Moreover, a greater portion of the program was concerned with the performing arts as well as the employment of specialists who could offer leadership and guidance to these activities.

International relationships acquired singular importance when Tom Rivers was appointed Director General to administer the international phase of the world recreational service movement. Each year an international conference was organized to facilitate the exchange of techniques and learn about innovative facilities, programs, and other pertinent information vital to the provision of recreational services. The first International Cooperative Community Recreational Exchange, begun in the late fifties, enabled America to exchange recreationists with foreign countries.

The Cultural Revolution (1960–1970)

The "rebellious" years started peacefully enough, but in 1961 the United States indirectly became involved in an undeclared war in Vietnam. This was America's most unpopular war and, although at its peak more than 500,000 of the armed forces were involved, it never generated the conformity or enthusiasm which previous wars had inspired. Young people everywhere, but particularly those who were registered in America's most prestigious institutions of higher education, challenged established systems. They espoused an existential life style which made a virtue of not complying with customary mores. Traditional recreational activities were discarded as many of these young people adopted a more permissive attitude toward sex, drug taking, rock music, sound and light shows, and other experiences to induce a "hyper" state. Some of the key expressions used at this time are indicative of the type of attitude held. Thus, the "me" generation was born. "Doing your own thing" became the in phrase. Being "turned on" or "turning off" were ways in which young people looked at themselves, their relationships, and society.

A new generation of Americans viewed the system and society, on the whole, as a conglomeration of static, manipulative, materialistic, and cynical power wielders. The first salvo of six years of youth rebellion was fired at the University of California's Berkeley branch, where a free speech movement rapidly deteriorated into a filthy speech movement. Members of the radical left had been moving into higher education and now looked upon the United States' involvement in Viet Nam as their make-or-break opportunity. A wave of student protests, strikes, and some violent confrontations between militant students and campus security forces, city police, or state police occurred. The pictures of students rioting at San Francisco State College in California, Columbia University, and Cornell University will not soon fade away.

The terms generation gap, alienation, co-option, drop-out, acid head, flower child, black power, women's lib, and SDS seem to have been pronounced by almost anybody who took part in any discussion during the late sixties. The United States experienced the assassination of President John F. Kennedy, Senator Robert Kennedy, and Nobel prize winner Martin Luther King. It went through a continuous series of agonizing reappraisals, as vociferous individuals and groups purported to report on the alleged failings of American democracy. In some instances, radical groups likened the United States to a warmongering imperialist aggressor only interested in enlarging its hegemony throughout the world. The chief writings, which seemed to give point to all these fanatical self-hating and guilt-inspired persons, were by Herbert Marcuse who wrote about one-dimensional man. Charles Reich who stressed consciousness rising in *The Greening of America,* and Alvin Toffler whose *Future Shock* showed the confrontation of human values, time, and accelerated life styles trying to keep pace with technological change. As late as 1975 the doomsayers and irresponsible literati were still promoting a concept of ill-favored solutions for their warped view.[8]

Despite an apparently endless revolutionary rhetoric and some antisocial activities, there was also a concomitant upsurge in traditional recreational forms. The federal government embarked upon a model cities program whose objective was to rehabilitate urban ghettos and supply needed services to inner-city residents. Many cities took advantage of federal largess and did upgrade, among other things, recreational services and facilities. But the financial resources were unsteady and never really began to meet the needs of inner-city dwellers.

This was the era of urban riots. Under the driving force of black militancy some of the largest cities were subjected to rampaging mobs and arson.[9] Perhaps of greatest interest to recreationists everywhere was the demand by ghetto residents that recreational services and facilities be improved. Local government response to these demands was less than inspiring, although some city recreational departments actually moved to eradicate some of the recreational deficiencies which had been allowed to exist. There was a use of mobile recreational facilities and

---

[8]A.A. Rogow, *The Dying Light* (New York: G.P. Putnam, 1975), 384 pp.

[9]Theodore H. White, *America in Search of Itself* (New York: Harper and Row, Publishers, 1982), p. 20.

attempts were made to recruit and employ minority group members for departmental positions. More women were given an opportunity to achieve supervisory and management levels than ever before.[10]

America could still try to spend its way out of stressful situations in this decade. There was more affluence, mobility, and leisure. The performing arts received great support and innumerable orchestras, museums, art galleries, dance groups, and repertory theaters flourished under the bounty of federal aid. The Great Society was in full swing but it could not stamp out poverty, provide jobs, underwrite the indigent, and supply an unending reservoir of financial expenditures indefinitely.

But the decade of the 1960s was not all rebellion, confrontation, and know-nothing irrationalism. It was a time of unprecedented economic growth and cultural expansion. The federal government underwrote this cultural blossoming by enacting the Arts and Humanities Act of 1965. The performing arts received tremendous impetus, and orchestras, museums, art galleries, and dance centers proliferated during this period. There was a marked concern with physical fitness and notable increases in sport and game participation of all groups and both sexes.

The federal government began to implement the Great Society programs under the administration of President Lyndon B. Johnson. The civil rights movement gained rapidly, and there was a new and sustained effort to reconcile the provision of governmental and other services with the ideal of the Constitution's concept of equality. To that end, a variety of civil rights laws attempting to ensure equalization for the poor, the aged, women, and racial minorities was passed. Congressional action on the passage of the Open Space and Urban Development Act and the Land and Water Conservation Fund appeared to open the way for a new era of federal recognition of the need for land acquisition and reservation for recreational purposes, as well as the need for assisting in the funding of programs for populations residing in urban centers.

A number of urban riots occurred during this decade. Among them were the violent upheavals in the Watts section of Los Angeles, Newark in New Jersey, Detroit, Washington, D.C., and elsewhere. Of interest to recreationists was the demand by inner-city residents for more and better recreational facilities and programs. In responding to these demands, cities actually began to provide mobile recreational equipment, activi-

---

[10]Pamela Leish, "The Managerial Women in Parks and Recreation," *Parks and Recreation,* Vol. 17 No. 10 (October 1983), pp. 40–46, 71.

ties that satisfied some of the recreational deficiencies about which inner-city dwellers complained, and highly visible recreational activities in which individuals could express themselves. Other communities, notably Cleveland, abolished its public recreational service department and employed more police and fire protection.

One distinctive type of program which came to the fore during the decade of the sixties was an increased concentration upon the needs of the ill, disabled, and homebound persons who previously had not been delivered the kinds of recreational services they needed. During this period many public recreational service departments initiated programs for the mentally retarded, the physically disabled, and in a few instances, attempted to work with institutions which promoted halfway houses for the rehabilitation of those with mental health problems.

In 1965, the National Recreation and Park Association (NRPA) was organized by the merger of the American Recreation Society, the American Institute of Park Executives, the National Recreation Association, and the National Conference on State Parks. This combination of diverse organizations with some overlapping concerns was brought about because it was thought that a single representative organization might have greater political and more broadly based support than separate agencies. Even though there is an overriding concern for the provision of recreational service, each specialized branch views its own perception of that service with the biased eye of vested interest. The organization was instigated to raise the standards of the professional field and to promote national interest in the movement, as well as to gain Congressional support for recreational-oriented legislation; it has sometimes succeeded. The bright promise of professionalism, consciousness rising, focused attention on the problems confronting recreationists, higher standards of leadership, and other formidable tasks taken on by the NRPA, has done much to inspire a new wave of enthusiasm that the organization can live up to its potential as the cutting edge of the American recreational service movement.

The following chronology indicates some of the salient developments of the decade.

- 1960—A Special Assistant for Aging is authorized in the HEW Department.
- 1960—White House Conference on Children and Youth is convened.
- 1960—Forest Service Multiple Use Act is passed.

- 1961—Urban Open Space Land Program is enacted.
- 1962—The President's Panel on Mental Retardation expands services for retarded children and youth, giving rise to many new recreational programs.
- 1962—Lincoln Center for the Performing Arts opens in New York City.
- 1962—The Food and Agriculture Act provides up to 50 percent of the cost of land acquisition for recreational purposes.
- 1962—Recreational Use of Fish and Wildlife is legislated.
- 1964—Land and Water Conservation Fund Act is enacted.
- 1965—The Arts and Humanities Act enables organizations to receive financial support for the performing arts.
- 1965—The National Recreation and Park Association (NRPA) is organized by the merger of the American Recreation Society, the American Institute of Park Executives, the National Recreation Association, and the National Conference on State Parks.
- 1965—Federal Water Project Recreation Act is passed.
- 1966—The International Rehabilitation Association meeting in Weisbaden, Germany initiates a leisure concerns section.
- 1966—National Historic Preservation Act is passed.
- 1968—Wild and Scenic Rivers Act is passed.
- 1968—National Trails System Act is passed.
- 1969—National Environmental Policy Act is passed.

These years manifested a new orientation by the federal government and the private sector. In 1960, state park attendance figures had reached nearly 260 million. Recreational activities were mainly of the overnight tenting, hiking, and birdwatching type. In 1970 double that number of visits were recorded and the activities also included bicycling along wooded trails, arts, and crafts, scuba diving, climbing, spelunking and camping.

The interrelationships between mental and physical health were more widely recognized and greater concern for mental health within the context of recreational programs was an important consideration among professional practitioners.

The needs of youth and children has always been a major concern of the recreational service movement, but the golden anniversary conference of 1960, with its theme "For each child an opportunity for a creative life in freedom and dignity," gave the recommendations greater impact.

Some of these recommendations included community program development, encouragement of leisure reading, greater emphasis on the arts, and an increased effort to research the value of recreational activity for this age group.

Recreational programs for the aged began to receive greater attention. The year 1960 saw the Fourth Annual Convention of the Golden Age and Senior Citizens in New Orleans. Subsequently, this became a formal national organization. Recognition that the needs of the older population must be met was evidenced by the kinds of activities that the Federal government provided. The first White House Conference on Aging was held in Washington, D.C. in 1961. Prior to this conference, federal grants had enabled states to conduct their own studies on aging. At the conference some 3,000 delegates recommended more programs of activities for the aging, better facilities, cooperative planning, better leadership, more research, and more adequate preparation for retirement. This concern for the nation's older population continues to have a high priority in the country's recreational programs.

By 1969, several states had begun to recognize the need for interstate cooperation in order to meet the recreational needs of their citizens and visitors. One such compact was initiated when, on April 1, 1969, the states of Vermont and New Hampshire signed a Plan of Cooperation whereby the recreational services of each state are to work cooperatively. This was the first such formal agreement between the recreational services in two states, and it is expected to develop into a trend throughout the country as the demand for recreational service increases. The Vermont—New Hampshire plan of cooperation calls for an interchange of publications, discussions between state directors of recreational service, and leadership development programs.

A new approach to the provision of local recreational service made its appearance. Community—school cooperation has become greatly assistive in the administration of recreational programs. Two examples of such cooperation exist in Flint, Michigan and Los Angeles, California. In Flint, as a consequence of the philanthropy of Charles Steward Mott and The Mott Foundation, recreational programs exist in schools, which bring together people of all backgrounds. The program includes recreational activities from roller skating to an international program that involves approximately 1,000 athletes and their families in both Flint, Michigan and Hamilton, Canada. In Los Angeles, the city school district, through its Youth Services Section, sponsors a program in which millions of people participate each year. More than 550 recreational sites are used and more than 4,000 full-time and part-time personnel are involved in the leadership phase of the program.

The National Recreation and Park Association has attempted to provide overall professional leadership as well as involving laymen who serve their communities on various commissions, committees, and boards. The association combines the efforts of the leading professional people in the field of recreational service for the furtherance of recreational service and all of its concomitant functions in America. Concerned with both natural and man-made beauty in America and the human environment, it is attempting to help Americans have a better and healthier place in which to live, work, and enjoy their leisure. Its goals are to provide good recreational facilities of all kinds and to instill the need for the proper use of the natural resources.

The field remained dynamic and transitions could be traced easily. Writing in 1967, the author was able to add three additional modifications to the ones previously mentioned:

1) From programs operated by laymen to those operated by professionally prepared and, in most instances highly qualified, practitioners; 2) from an amenity service to one which is considered essential to the health, welfare, and cultural development of all people; and 3) from a voluntary field of service to a professionalized occupational field of applied social science.[11]

Recession and Ecology (1970-1980)

The alienation which had begun as a demonstration of political and social rights in the sixties took on the added concern of ecology during the early years of the decade. Anxiety about population explosions, pollution of air, water, and land, and a dimly perceived end to fossil power sources began to grow. The decade of the seventies offered the field of recreational service certain challenges and priorities. One problem which confronts all citizens, and particularly recreationists, is in the area of ecology—that balance between nature's resources and our technological production. Our beaches, for example, are being eroded and polluted. The dumping of industrial wastes, oil-tank spills, and improper care may mean that these beaches will cease to exist for recreational purposes unless certain controls are established.

---

[11]Jay S. Shivers, *Principles and Practices of Recreational Service*, (New York: The Macmillan Company, 1967), p. 117.

From the first warnings in Rachel Carson's *Silent Spring* and the dire predictions in Paul Erlich's *Population Bomb,* there developed in the public's consciousness a vital interest in preserving "spaceship" earth. Not everybody was convinced that a burgeoning population was disastrous to what had always been looked upon as earth's unlimited natural resources and limitless space. Surely, people dimly realized that the earth is finite, but they never understood that natural resources could be used up or that even the vast oceans could become polluted. Throughout the late sixties and to the present, there were unmistakable signs that the population explosion and the wastral ways of user societies were finally catching up to the formerly easily exploited energy and mineral resources.

The last year before the economic recession struck the major industrialized Western nations was 1972. The immediate cause of this was the alliance of all major oil-exporting nations into a cartel that drove up the price of oil. All nations experienced a surge in inflation, one third of which was directly attributable to the jump in oil prices. As the prices went up, consumers began to feel the pinch. Everything dependent upon oil increased in price. The most notable effect was the slump in foreign travel. Tourist rates shot up so fast that travel fares, hotel rates, and restaurant food prices literally doubled and tripled overnight. Many middle-class Americans, who formerly made up the bulk of the overseas travel group, canceled their travel plans.

As inflation worsened and domestic prices soared, labor attempted to negotiate wage increments to meet higher costs. Naturally, this set off another wage-price spiral. Despite short-lived attempts by the federal government to freeze wages, inflation continued to eat away at American buying power. The war in Viet Nam was still raging, and militant groups as well as usually passive protestors demanded that the war be brought to a close, in any way possible. The Nixon Administration squirmed at the possibility of not winning the war, then in the end acceded to a citizenry which was more and more polarized and discontented about the 10-year war.

An imbalance of foreign payments produced yet another shock to the American monetary system, and for the first time in modern history, the dollar lost ground to other money. In fact, the dollar was devalued, and an economic recession settled onto the business world. Automakers could not sell their products and laid off tens of thousands of workers. This had a rippling effect throughout all American industry and business. More and more people were furloughed or simply laid off, and eventually the unemployment figure reached 8 million persons. Some were out of work for two years before the necessary belt tightening took hold. America's balance of payments problem was corrected when food production increased and farm commodities were sold on the international market. Inflation fell to single digits from the 12 percent at which it had been. Slowly the basic industries rehired their workers. By the end of 1975, the economy had started a slow but steady rise. The worst economic recession since the Great Depression of the thirties was over. Unemployment figures showed that more than 7 million were out of jobs, but this was overcome as the federal government organized programs in which people could find work.

The environmental problems, which all countries face, did not disappear. Writing in 1975, Thor Heyerdahl could still report:

> The misconception of a boundless ocean makes the man in the street more concerned about city smog than about the risk of killing the ocean. Yet the tallest chimney in the world does not suffice to send the noxious smoke away into space; it gradually sinks down, and nearly all descends, mixed with rain, snow, and silt, into the ocean. Industrial and urban areas are expanding with the population explosion all over the world, and in the United States alone, waste products in the form of smoke and noxious fumes amount to a total of 390,000 tons of pollutants every day, or 142 million tons every year.[12]

Myopic individuals, who need scapegoats to rationalize their desire to make money, quickly turned on environmentalists as the prime cause of inflation. They pointed to the delay in the Alaskan oil pipeline and the hindrance of construction of atomic energy plants to produce electrical power as evidence of environmentalists' meddling, which unnecessarily drove up prices. One really has to understand the situation produced by uncaring entrepreneurs on the one hand and concerned individuals and groups on the other to appreciate the conflict of interest which ecological and consumer issues turned up.

The effect upon the recreational movement was sharp and relatively immediate. Vast cutbacks in personnel necessary to man agencies were undertaken. Losses in personnel by retirement or resignation were not made up, as hiring freezes were placed in effect. Physical plants were allowed to deteriorate without maintenance, as work crews were limited and supplies, materials, and equipment were not obtained in the quantity required. Programs suffered because competent personnel were not employed to provide needed instruction, organization, or planning. The

---

[12]TM Heyerdahl, "How to Kill an Ocean," *Saturday Review,* (November 29, 1975), p. 16.

total impact of the recession of the mid-seventies terminated the once unbounded optimism which always characterized recreational service.

Nevertheless, people still demanded recreational services, and the great contradiction was that citizens, especially in urban centers, wanted recreational facilities and programs but did not want to pay for them. Cities suffering from an inability to obtain money in the bond market for the construction of facilities or to pay for many municipal services terminated thousands of city employees in order to remain solvent. During the latter part of 1975, New York City was saved from bankruptcy by the intervention of the federal government, which granted it a loan of 2.3 billion dollars. However, the short-term loan required the city to balance its budget and to reduce many more services than it already had. These disastrous affairs reverberated across the United States, as many cities found that their bond issues were no longer being taken at low rates of interest payment. This situation prompted a new wave of budget cutting, and municipal recreational service departments felt the sharp edge of reduced financial support. Recreational service department employees were furloughed or discharged in a retrenching move.

The economic recession, which developed as one consequence of the major oil exporting countries banding together into a cartel, struck the industrialized Western nations in 1973. All materials made from oil-based products and things that depend upon oil to operate, increased in price dramatically. A wave of inflation cut the purchasing power of most Americans. Tourism to foreign countries was noticeably affected. Travel, food, and accommodations doubled or tripled.

Citizens were urged not to travel abroad, and many persons did attempt to utilize the parks, forests, and other recreational facilities administered by federal, state, and local governments. Unfortunately, the impact of millions of individuals had an adverse effect upon outdoor recreational facilities. The national agencies also had to trim their services and reduce spending. This cutback meant loss of interpretative services in the parks and less maintenance of trails, cabins, and waterways. As people turned to their local recreational service departments for a greater number of activities, there was a concurrent attempt to lower budgets and make do with far less personnel than was required if adequate services were to be offered. Only after an upturn in the economy during 1976 was there a noticeable attempt to employ qualified recreationists as hundreds of agencies competed for workers.

Coupled with rising inflation, the war in Viet Nam still continued.

Society became more polarized. More and more demonstrations against the war finally compelled the Nixon Administration to end this ten-year struggle ignominiously.

Outflow of money spent overseas was so unbalanced that the dollar's value was weakened against foreign currencies. Its devaluation caused further economic displacement in the United States. The automobile industry could not sell its output at the rate that it formerly enjoyed and thousands of workers were laid off. This inability to earn money was felt in all of the industries related to automobile production as well as to industries and businesses more remotely concerned. At the height of the recession, more than 8 million persons were unemployed and the inflation rate reached 12 percent. It was not until 1975 that food exports and belt tightening finally managed to bring the recession under control inflation fell to 4½ percent.

The euphoria lasted two short years. By 1978, OPEC ministers relentlessly raised oil prices and world-wide inflation became endemic. All of the social pressures which could not be relieved when the United States did not suffer from inflation and monetary weakness surfaced and harried all sectors of society. Ethnic and racial minorities, women's groups, older adult groups, people on welfare, and other concerned citizens became more militant in their demands. Prejudices which had been held in check were now boiling furiously and numerous confrontations and dangerous incidents occurred. Some people took to cult-like organizations in an attempt to find a way of coping with a social system that, at times appeared in disarray.

The residual outcome upon the recreational service movement was swift and cutting. Public agency budgets were severely curtailed necessitating the discharge of personnel. This left many large city departments with depleted manpower to operate. Hiring freezes were the order of the day. Physical plants deteriorated because maintenance workers would not be employed and those who were working couldn't keep up with the job. The impact of the recession had both short and long term effects and did much to lend a pall of pessimism to a field which had always been identified by its limitless optimism.

Because of negative payment balances, citizens were urged to stay at home. The tourist business dropped off accordingly. However, as more people made use of local, state, regional, and national recreational resources these facilities deteriorated as well. Under assault by millions of recreators, governmental departments were still curtailing services in order to meet reduced budgetary allocations. The public sector delivering recreational services has never recovered from the personnel attrition, supply deficiencies, and lack of facility maintenance and refurbishment. Smaller budgets wiped out many recreational programs.

The capstone to a disheartening decade was the passage, in California, of the Jarvis-McGann Act, or the notorious Proposition 13. The people voted to limit the amount of money which the state could assess as a percentage of property value to one percent. This effectively mandated governmental budget slashes at every level. Only during the first year after passage of "Prop 13" was there a cushioning effect because of a $5 billion state surplus which was shared out to all subordinate governments. However, once the surplus was used up, cities, counties, and other public levels were hard pressed to maintain services. Most violently hit by cruel restrictions were public recreational service departments, public libraries, and other social service organizations. Some county governments lost up to 60 percent of their budget with concomitant layoffs of personnel, elimination of recreational programs, and the closure of many recreational facilities which could no longer be manned or maintained. This was the first in a series of tax-reducing referenda in a number of states as citizens began to rebel against outrageously heavy property taxes which fuel the state's ability to provide services. Proposition 2½ in Massachusetts, passed in November 1980, effectively sliced governmental budgets in that state to a point where many public services, including recreational services, had to be curtailed or eliminated entirely.

The spectacle of taxpayer revolts spreading throughout the United States was one consequence of bureaucratic indifference to people and the non-response of government to the heavy burdens placed upon most property owners. As the rate of inflation grew to 12½ percent in 1980, many people simply could not afford the costs which governmental services were draining out of them. An entirely new political and economic philosophy began to pervade the American scene. A much more conservative orientation was noted. Many cutbacks in social programs were immediately put into effect. From some quarters it was continually stated that the day of public recreational service had run its course and that in order to save taxpayers' money, government would simply become the conduit for contractual operations wherein private companies, who successfully bid for the provision of recreational services, would be paid for specific activities, facilities, or maintenance operations so that tremendous costs of fringe benefits to workers in the public sector could be eliminated. Moreover, it is also repeated that private enterprise would be much more productive than are public employee counterparts in the delivery of recreational services. For the time being this remains sheer speculation. Very few contracts have been let to private entrepreneurs at this time. Those that have been are being monitored closely. Whether privately employed personnel are, indeed, more productive in their performance than are their public peers is still open to question. However, this was one of a number of solutions then being advocated in response to the economic climate which was experienced in the United States at that time.

Among the events of the seventies, the following illustrate some of concerns and influences at work here and abroad.

- 1970—First Biennial Leisure Conference is held in Geneva, Switzerland.
- 1970—White House Conference on Children and Youth.
- 1971—White House Conference on Aging.
- 1971—American Association of Zoological Parks and Aquariums resumes its independent status away from the NRPA consortium.
- 1972—Gateway National Recreational Areas on the East and West coasts are introduced by the federal government.
- 1973—The International Recreation Association becomes the World Leisure and Recreation Association as nations form their own associations of recreational and leisure organizations.
- 1973—Older Americans Act is amended.
- 1973—First World Congress on Leisure is held in Brussels, Belgium, by the Van Clé Foundation.
- 1974—Community Schools Act is passed.
- 1974—National Conference on State Parks becomes the National Society for Park Resources.
- 1975—First national conference on leisure education is held.
- 1976—Federal Land Policy and Management Act is passed.
- 1977—White House Conference on Handicapped is convened.
- 1978—Heritage Conservation and Recreational Service (HCRS) replaces the Bureau of Outdoor Recreation (BOR) in the Department of the Interior.
- 1978—National Parks and Recreation Act grants $1.2 billion for urban and national parks improvements.

- 1980—International Organization of Park and Recreational Administrators holds its world conference in West Berlin, Germany.

There is little doubt that the field of public recreational service still commands a remarkable following despite political and economic misfortunes. The very people who require delivery of public recreational services are the ones who are forced to do without when economic retrenchment pares budgetary allotments and services have to be reduced or eliminated. But politicians also realize that they must tread a very narrow line insofar as providing services to millions of people and placing an unendurable tax burden on a relatively few property owners. It appears likely that public recreational service will continue to be financed, although fees and changes are being added or increased to assure that recreational opportunities are maintained.

The 1970s also saw a resurgence of vigorous physical recreational activity due, primarily, to a confluence of forces, namely, the energy crisis, inflation, the high cost of everything, and a conscious recognition on the part of many that active participation in energetic physical programs might be conducive to good health and fitness. Phenomenal growth was observed in jogging, long distance running, swimming, tennis, racquetball, bicycle riding, roller skating, figure skating, and gymnastics. The latter event was particularly popularized by television coverage of the Olympic Games in 1968, 1972, 1976, and 1980. The names of Olga Korbet, Nadia Comaneci, and other heralded an appreciation and participation by hundreds of thousands who previously could not have differentiated a handspring from a handstand.

The Housing and Community Development Act of 1974, which provided for full funding of a variety of urban services, including those of a recreational type, was a compelling feature in the public sector just before the bubble burst. However, as late as 1978, the Urban Park and Recreational Recovery Program was funded in the amount of $650 million and this was seen as a key event in improving local public recreational areas and facilities. In appraising the previous ten years, it can be asserted that the entire recreational service movement, but particularly the public sector, has made tremendous strides. Now, unfortunately, the forces of reaction and conservatism have taken the helm and recreational experiences are no longer held in the same high regard as they once were. The HCRS, considered to be a positive indicator of federal government's concern for recreational service, was abolished in

1981. Of course, everybody believes that recreational activities are worthwhile, but they are no longer willing to support such activities through public funds. Instead of being seen as a vital aspect of each person's life, recreational activities were downgraded in status in the eyes of taxpayers and politicians.

Recreational Service Demand and Austerity (1981-1990).

In the 1980s the demand for recreational services continued unabated in the private sector while public agency operations were scaled back. The field of recreational service faced a dilemma. People were perfectly willing to spend money on their own leisure enjoyment, but not permit themselves to be taxed for such purposes. Perhaps the taint of welfarism and the stigma of pauperism lingered in the minds of some.

It is commonly perceived that recreational service applies great value to people and must be publicly administered for everyone's benefit. Despite this apparent recognition a contradiction also exists. Commercial recreational services are expanding while public service faltered and was subject to every quiver in the economy. Recreational businesses are guided by market considerations, but public departments must consistently be concerned about bureaucratic encroachment on their prerogatives. Companies may buy political favors while public agencies have become increasingly politicized as departmental administrators maneuver for positions from which they expect to gain advantageous decisions from those elected or appointed officials who hold power.

Special interest and other pressure groups had not been quiescent either. Those groups generating the greatest degree of public sympathy for their disability were also able to use the publicity to demand programs which hard-pressed departments find difficult to carry out. Because of the political impact and favorable media coverage that these groups tended to receive, departments responded even when it meant lessened services to others in the community.

The inauguration of the administration of Ronald Reagan as President of the United States began a decade of massive military spending, tremendous cut-backs in federal funding of social services, and an immense public debt. After holding office for two terms and heading an administration that was one of the more corrupt in U.S. history, more than 300 bureaucrats, including the National Security Director, went to prison or were found guilty by the courts. Ronald Reagan completed his tour of office in 1988. During his Presidency more foreign policy political mistakes and judgmental errors were made than ever before. Even the hapless Carter did not commit as many blunders. However, Reagan's popularity was so great that no scandal, regardless of noteriety, could touch him and he was dubbed "The Teflon President."

Public recreational service was badly mauled between 1980–1988. During this period the termination of the CETA (Comprehensive Employment Training Program) was ordered. Cities dependent upon federally supported job programs, particularly for inner-city minority youngsters, were no longer able to stabilize labor forces at a time of decreasing financial resources. The withdrawal of funds almost caused the collapse of many park systems as personnel cuts had to be made. One basic result was an increase in mechanization to compensate for lost labor. While this has proved to be somewhat beneficial to departments in terms of efficiency and costs, it has had a negative outcome on maintenance effectiveness, as well as an employment mechanism or pathway for individuals who seek careers in the maintenance side of recreational service.

The introduction of computer technology over the past fifteen years has changed the style of management in the field from a hierarchical orientation, where centralized decision making set policy and practice for an entire community, to a horizontal or decentralized system, where specialists rather than generalists can be employed. The computer has eliminated an entire cadre of middle managers. Although the competent and comprehensive use of computers readily lends itself to better planning, analysis, costing, and patron carrying capacity, it also reduces the pool of managers who can assume the mantel of top leadership after having served in the middle management ranks for a seasoning period. How this will affect career choices remains to be seen.

During the 80's, city managers turned more and more toward municipal department consolidation. Smaller communities have not yet chosen this avenue to serve the public. There was a noticable swing to combined departments which included such traditionally separate line agencies as parks, recreational service, health, older adults and youth serving municipal organizations under the rubric of Human Services. Managed by a super commissioner, or other designator, the formerly separate departments were joined to provide a comprehensive plan of services to community citizens while diminishing overhead and administrative costs. This seems to be an ongoing transition.

Interestingly, citizen involvement in governmental decision making has almost paralyzed local political authorities. Hailed as a grass roots democratic demonstration of full citizen participation, special interest, lobbyist, and pleader groups have virtually halted many planning designs and proposals. Of course, citizens should be involved in any planning process that will have a significant impact on their environment and quality of life. However, when special interest groups decide that they, and they alone, know what is best for society at large, then the result can be outright bias against beneficial plans and vociferous prevention of such plans from becoming viable and translatable into programs or facilities.

This past decade has witnessed a move to the privatization of formerly public functions. Privatization has become institutionalized because the infrastructure costs are too expensive to maintain. In an era of tax-payer revolts and continual referenda to force politicians to reduce real estate taxes throughout the country, government has simply become hard pressed to perform its traditional roles in supplying needed services. Instead many local authorities find it expedient to let contracts to the private sector. New York City, for example, gave a contract to Donald Trump to complete the Wollman Ice Rink in Central Park when the city's own construction efforts failed. In other communities contracts were given for operation of pools, beaches, tennis courts, golf courses, and other facilities.[13]

All was not moribund despite an often hostile federal attitude and niggardly funding. Community Arts enjoyed a renaissance with help from the National Endowment. Foreign travel and tourism, which had been hurt by the "oil weapon" once again began a notable resurgence in the mid and late 1980s. At home, travel increased annually until more than 3 million persons were taking trips of one kind or another.

In the late 1980's, cities were again in a relatively healthy financial posture. Economic resurgence permitted once financially embarrassed municipalities to revive and begin new programs along with the personnel to operate them.

Along the notable occurrences during the decade of the 80's, the following appear to epitomize the times:

- 1980—National Heritage Section omitted from Heritage Act.

A National Council for Therapeutic Recreation Certification is

---

[13]Review and Outlook, "Democrats Go Private," *The Wall Street Journal* (June 8, 1991) p. A18.

begun and is a completely independent organization designed to credential practitioners.

- 1981—A marketing orientation is introduced to finance local recreation programs.
- 1982—National Park Service reports on deteriorating conditions of park facilities and external threats to park system because of development focus of the Reagan administration. Residential Facility Standards for practice are made available by NTRS.
- 1983—Federally supported Land and Water Conservation Fund is drastically reduced.
- 1984—Certification Standards for TRS personnel were made more stringent. Minimum degree requirements at the undergraduate level must be met regardless of advanced graduate education. The ATRA is founded to stimulate more growth of clinical practice and specialization within the field of Therapeutic Recreational Service.
- 1985—Resignation of Interior Secretary William Clark—a supporter of the NRRRC.
- 1986—NRPA appeals to Education Secretary Terral Bell to fund the Special Olympics Winter Games from funds other than that requested for Section 36 of the Rehabilitation Act of 1973. Urban Park and Recreation Program Funds cut.
- 1987—House of Representatives approves legislation to extend LWCF for 25 years. The National Council on Post-Secondary Accreditation formally recognizes the NRPA as an accreditation agent.
- 1988—Public Laws 100–203 requires that a qualified professional be employed to direct nursing home recreational programs.
- 1989—An American Heritage Trust Bill was re-introduced into the House and a companion measure was filed in the senate to create trust funds. Feminist literature depicting women's leisure needs is sharply defined.
- 1990—Americans with Disabilities Act is passed; requires reasonable accommodation of disabled individuals' in public park and recreational systems. First National Examination for Certification of Therapeutic Recreationists is given under the auspices of NTRS. Title XII of the Food, Agriculture, Conservation and Trade Act

creates authority for federal assistance to state and local governments for urban forestry and related concerns.

The sudden collapse of the Soviet Union's economy in 1989 and the demand for sovereignty from former republics incorporated into the Soviet empire did much to relax tensions at the beginning of 1990. The advent of *peristroika* and *glassnost,* first introduced by the Soviet Chief of State and Communist Party, Mikail Gorbachov, was the linchpin that finally brought about the end of Communism in Eastern (Middle) Europe and opened the way for a reduction of armaments between the East and West.

Iraq, under the dictatorship of Saddam Hussein, had engaged in a series of wars between 1980–1988. A war of expansion against Iran ended in stalemate and concession despite a reputed $80 billion expenditure and the loss of one million lives during the conflict. Savage attacks against the Shi'a majority of Iraq as well as the Kurds produced thousands of casualties as Hussein loosed poison gas to smash opposition. In 1990, Iraq invaded the neighboring Arab state of Kuwait. This brought an abrupt dislocation of relationships between the United States and Iraq as President Bush organized a world coalition to combat the growing menace represented by Hussein's ambition for self-aggrandizement and hegemony in the Persian Gulf region.[14]

On October 3, 1990, East Germany ceased to exist and the Federal Republic of Germany came into being. This would, at once, make the newly reunified country the richest, most populous, and economically powerful countries in Europe. How this would affect the European Economic Communities and the eastern European states, no longer dominated by the Soviet Union, created some anxiety among sectors of the East and West who were victims of Naziism.

It is always intriguing to speculate about coming events. No one can predict the future—at least with any certainty, but there are signposts which indicate what might be expected. One simply cannot make straight line projections into the future based upon what has happened in the past and present. However, careful analysis of past events and contemporary attitudes and experiences often provides us with some reasonable foundations on which to suggest the future.

Voices of reaction will always attempt to diminish or abolish recreational service. There will always be individuals in this country who view public

---

[14]The Economist, January 19, 1991.

recreational service as a waste of their tax dollars. Those who represent a conservative philosophy believe that recreational service is a frill of government and perceive recreational activity as the individual's responsibility. Such objectors have been a part of the history of the movement and, no doubt, will continue to attempt to reduce the services which the movement upholds routinely. Whether the views of those who decry public recreational service prevail or the opposite occurs depends largely upon the educational impact which professionals can make upon the varied constituencies which their respective departments serve. Additionally, economic capacities will play a large role in determining public service priorities in the foreseeable future.

The recreational services that will be upgraded in the months and years ahead will be those dealing with the needs of elderly persons, those for individuals who are homebound, ill, or disabled in some way. More emphasis will be placed on appreciation for and use of therapeutic recreational service in treatment centers of all kinds. Moreover, there will be a continuation of emphasis upon programs stressing outdoor recreational resources which comprise conservation of depletable resources, preservation of wilderness areas, implication for primitive camping, hostels, orienteering, and those activities which utilize waterways as the basis for experience.

In the inner-city districts, major recreational activities will center around mobile units which can be shifted to high-density residential areas as the season and need arise. Such units will include swimming pools, roller-skating equipment, zoological and astronomical exhibits, bookmobiles, puppetry theaters, dramatic presentations, music ensembles, craft shops, and any other activities which can be transported by truck or bus to neighborhoods that lack a facility.

Personnel employment will probably undergo some drastic changes, as new tactics are planned to offset the time-consuming and often ineffective procedures undertaken by civil service programs.

It is probable that the public sector will see a rise in contract work specialty or task force operations.[15] The employment of provisional recreational workers, and then only specialists and seasonal employees, will be a major factor in urban departments in the next few years.

The decade of the 90s should, with a few exceptions, i.e., the Middle

---

[15]G. Goldsmith, "Indianapolis Competition," The Wall Street Journal (Dec. 3, 1992), pg. A14 and S. Games, "Cleaner Streets in Newark," The Wall Street Journal, Dec. 3, 1992), pg. H14.

East, the Philippines, and some African countries, be given over to peaceful development. In fact the money formerly expended for arms should be redeployed into social programs that can do much to strengthen the educational, vocational, residential, and recreational aspects of the lives of America's citizens.

Whether this will occur depends on a number of variables currently operating throughout the world. Although a peace conference, to mediate Arab-Israeli differences, has been set up, the self interests of the participants may be irreconcilable in the short term.

Break-away republics in what was the Soviet Union and Yugoslavia are proving to be daunting problems, while coups and violent passions mount against a flow of migrants in Germany, Italy, France, England, and other western states.

The United States continues to confront an economic recession with the several states and many municipalities facing huge debts brought about by profligate spending without rational restraint. All of these concurrent situations tend to complicate and frustrate attempted resolutions. For some political nail-biters this is a time for withdrawal, nationalism, and pessimism. However, all human problems produced in the superheated climate of bias and ignorance are amenable to resolution—if there is enough time. We will just have to wait and see.

With the election defeat of the Bush Administration on November 3, 1992, Democrats finally elected a President. Bill Clinton of Arkansas, a post World War II politician, will attempt to bring the country's economy out of recession and reduce the gigantic national deficit which has sapped economic vitality. It also appears likely that social programs will be supported. This bodes well for the field of recreational service.

It is feasible to suggest that the function of public recreational service departments in the future will be that of advising and counseling individuals about their leisure, insofar as recreational possibilities are concerned. The coordination of individuals (constituents) with specific activities, facilities, and resources in conjunction with the time and money they have at their disposal is certainly one form of service which cannot be overlooked. Computerized scheduling of consumer profiles will be routine, as public departments become the centralized repository of potential leisure informational systems.

Chapter 5

LAW AND ESTABLISHMENT
OF RECREATIONAL SERVICE

T he establishment of agencies providing benefits to the public which are considered essential to their general health, education, and welfare is sanctioned by the state through constitutional measures. The administration of certain functions for effecting promotional services cannot be left to happenstance or private exploitation and, therefore, becomes the foundation for legislation to advance both governmental responsibilities and other enterprises of the nonpublic sectors of society.

The Public Sector

Constitutional provision for governmental undertakings to enhance, protect, or secure a better life for the constituency has been a part of the American system since the inception of the republic. While constitutional enactment has been the living frame of reference for the restriction of governmental power over the life and liberty of individuals, it has also been the document on which justifiable governmental arrogation of power to enable it to carry out its functions is based. This interesting and apparent dichotomy developed because of the time in which the framers of the Constitution lived as well as their own ideology. It must be remembered that those who formulated the Constitution were products of enlightened humanism. They were steeped in the German romantic tradition and were passionately devoted to the doctrine of individual liberty and the natural rights of free men. Therefore, it is not surprising that the Constitution is a document of limitation on government, with more emphasis on the restriction of governmental power than on its utilization. However, the men who designed it never foresaw the growth and development of the United States to the degree that it has attained; yet they provided for an elasticity which enabled the

Constitution to develop with the changing times. The Constitution is not a document of specificity but of generality. Thus, the original source of power by government has been able to keep pace with the exigencies that time brings. Still, if the framers wanted less government control, how is it that such a powerful force as *police power* came into being?

Supremacy, Sovereignty, and Police Power

In the aftermath of the American Revolution, a constitution enumerating a tripartite central government which also established two levels of government existing side by side was drawn up. However, the constitutionalists did not want to repeat the same mistakes and weaknesses found in the original Articles of Confederation. To offset the possibility of a central government without the necessary power to perform its functions and to prohibit the assumption of sovereignty by the states, with all of the prerogatives which the term *sovereignty* implies, the framers created a document that draws its strength, centrality, and power from "We the people" rather than from the states. The Constitution is itself irrevocably opposed to the concept of state sovereignty. Although the United States is composed of 50 autonomous political entities, by design and fact the law of the land was not created from them as sovereign states. The Preamble essentially explicates that the Constitution was the act of the nation not of the states. All the states form, but they did not create, the United States.

Supremacy. The supreme law in this country is the Constitution. The supremacy clause has been challenged several times, but there has never been any question as to what level of government is sovereign or what foundation provides it with that supremacy. If there had been any question, it was effectively settled by the Civil War and reaffirmed in Supreme Court decisions after that time. The acts of the national government are defined as the operational supreme law in the United States. This status is conferred upon them as a result of their independence from other sources for enforcement. Thus, federal mandate is enforceable in every court because there is no dependency on state origin. The states do not have the authority to hinder in any way or to supervene the performance of federal law. The Constitution is "the written instrument agreed upon by the people . . . as the absolute rule of action and decision for all departments and officers of the government . . . and in opposition to which any act or rule of any department or officer of the government, or even of the people themselves, will be altogether void.[1]"

Sovereignty. The absolute, incontestable, and arbitrary right to govern is unknown in the United States. Sovereignty, then, is antithetical to the concept of government under which the United States was founded. The federal government itself is one of limited powers, expressly enumerated, delegated, or implied by the Constitution. In such an instance, the Constitution is itself sovereign, with the supreme power to govern not residing in any legal or executive body. Only in the sense that the United States of America does not owe allegiance to a superior form of government and that it may, if it so desires, carry out its functions on a unilateral basis (which acts it may have to enforce with arms) can it be called sovereign. In reality, however, there is only the sovereignty of law. The reasons for this are plain. In a free society disputes must be weighed in the courts and, regardless of the judgment handed down, the verdicts must be accepted.

In the United States, the establishment of fundamental precepts in an organic law enforced by a judiciary branch as the supreme law is necessary because of the extreme diversity of population. There can be no arbitrary enactment by government because of the separation of powers within the federal government, as well as between the nation and the states. Finally, each state is submissive and answerable to the supreme law. As Schwartz has maintained:

> One can go further and assert that the rule of law is utterly dependent upon the existence of a free society whose political institutions are endowed with authority to promote such freedom ... The rule of law is thus both the effect and the cause of the American system of government. Representative democracy without the rule of law is a contradiction in terms. At the same time, the supremacy of the law, enforced by the courts, can only be effective in a democratic society; it is that kind of society alone that is really willing to submit conflicts to adjudication and to subordinate power to reason.[2]

The several states have never had total autonomy nor have they ever been sovereign. Never in American history was any state ever recognized as sovereign. Regardless of common misconception of states' rights or the statement that each state is supreme within its own border, no state has any unbridled right to act without subordination to the Constitution.

---

[1]T. Mel. Cooley, *A Treatise on the Constitutional Limitations Which Rest Upon the Legislative Power of the States of the American Union* (Boston: Little, Brown and Company, 1868).

[2]B. Schwartz, *The Powers of Government*, Vol. I (New York: The MacMillan Company, 1963), p. 29.

Inasmuch as all states are restrained and limited in their actions they cannot be sovereign. Furthermore, they owe allegiance to the United States and may not attempt to perform acts that are expressly set aside for the federal government to enact. But the Constitution, generalized as it is, leaves to administrative discretion the formulation and substantive activities by which daily government becomes operational. It is this fact of law to which attention is turned.

Police Power. Because the Constitution does not specify the precise functions of government nor makes any mention of state regulations for internal security, other than to indicate the limitations of the federal government, no ready device for protection and service remains to each state except police power. Until recent years, police power has meant simply regulation of conduct, prohibition of certain actions, and the maintenance of public order and safety. Government, particularly in the states, was of a restrictive nature. It seemed to exist to inhibit life rather than to promote it. This concept of governmental function was largely negated as a result of the depression years, 1930 to 1940, although there had been inroads into the purely regulatory aspect of government prior to 1835. Those functions of government we take for granted, such as police and fire protection, were originally in the hands of private citizens, as was the postal service and education. When it was determined that these responsibilities of public safety and welfare could be performed most effectively by publicly controlled agencies, the government undertook to carry them out.

The power to provide protective and preventive services by governmental bodies within the state is police power. This power literally controls all citizens' behavior within the state's boundaries. Essentially, it was originated to establish laws and ordinances of reasonable and wholesome content, with or without penalties, and not in conflict with the constitution, for the security and the enhancement of the general health, safety, morals, education, welfare, and prosperity. It is this power that provides the state with the right and responsibility for the provision of services of a recreational nature. Initially, this may have been used as a restrictive device, namely, for the control of prostitution, gambling, and licensing of certain activities to prevent the depletion of natural resources, but with the passage of time its effects have taken much more of a promotional form than formerly. Today, the state is largely concerned with provision of social, educational, cultural, and developmental opportunities which are actively encouraged in recreational experiences. Other legislative forms, rather than the police power, have been passed at every level of government to provide recreational service to all persons.

Establishment of Recreational Service and Legislation

Recognition by government that recreational service, and the concomitant experiences thereby produced, is a vital and necessary part of society and a proper function of public agencies has done much to establish the movement as an important social force. Indication of governmental effect upon the impetus of the movement may be seen in its most salient form at the community or municipal level. Nevertheless, federal and state governments have had profound influence upon the provision of recreational services by acquiring regional and extensive areas whose recreational capacity and potential have been invaluable in supplementing local services. State legislation has paved the way for local implementation of recreational services. The federal government has done much to promote state action by undertaking surveys, offering consultation, and in many ways provoking state legislatures into expanding their respective views for the provision of recreational service.

Federal Interest

An example of governmental influence on the recreational service movement may be illustrated by the Congressional enactment of 1832, whereby the Arkansas Hot Springs area was set aside for public ownership and utilization, instead of private exploitation, because of the supposed therapeutic value of the springs. This act was the forerunner of acquisition of additional areas which subsequently culminated in the establishment of the National Park Service. The national parks are essentially recreational areas administered by the National Park Service, a bureau of the U.S. Department of Interior. These parks are maintained, to a great extent, in their natural condition for the benefit of all the people. Preserved in national parks are spectacular canyons, caves, mountains, wilderness regions, volcanoes, glaciers, lakes, hot springs, giant trees, and paleontological remains. The National Park Service has constructed roads and trails to enable visitors to reach various points of interest. Hotels, lodges, cabins, and campgrounds also have been made available. Park naturalists and rangers are on hand in several of the parks to conduct those interested on hikes and nature study walks, and to explain the phenomena encountered along the trails. In the evening, they conduct campfire programs, illustrated lectures, and other recreational activities. Some parks have museum and library collections. New parks are being acquired as the growing population demands additional space. Delaware Water Gap National Recreation Area, Indiana Dunes National Lakeshore, Assateague Island National Seashore off the Virginia coast, and the world's only underwater park at Key Largo Coral Reef off the Florida Keys are some of the acquisitions over the past fifteen years.

Although Yellowstone National Park was created in 1872, followed by Yosemite and Sequoia in 1890, the National Park Service was not established until 1916. This service has as its major function the administration of all the national parks, 84 national monuments, 54 military and historic parks and sites, 3 national parkways, and the system of National Capital Parks in the District of Columbia and its environs. This includes administration of the National Recreational Demonstration Areas and Reservations, the best known of which are located at Lake Mead, Nevada, Shadow Mountain, Colorado, and Grand Coulee Dam in Washington.

Many federal agencies have recognized the essential aspect of recreational experience in the lives of individuals and have acted to provide opportunities that might otherwise be lost. More than 40 federal agencies in seven departments have responsibilities for offering direct or indirect recreational services. Among these are the Department of the Interior with the National Park Service, mentioned previously, the Fish and Wildlife Service, the Bureau of Roads, Bureau of Indian Affairs, Bureau of Reclamation, and the now defunct Heritage, Conservation and Recreational Service; the Department of Health and Human Services with the Children's Bureau; Department of Education, with the Office of Vocational Rehabilitation Administration; the Department of Agriculture with the National Forest Service, the Soil Conservation Service, and the Extension Service which offers advisory recreational service to state departments of agriculture as well as the 4-H Club activities; the Department of Commerce with the Area Redevelopment Administration; and the Department of Defense with the Corp of Engineers, who have done much to augment recreational spaces and specialized sites through dam building, flood control, and construction of rivers and harbors. The Tennessee Valley Authority, the Veterans Administration, the Urban Renewal Administration (formerly the Federal Security Agency), the depression-inspired Works Progress Administration, the Civilian Conservation Corps, all made notable achievements in direct and incidental provision of recreational service and did much to inspire a great deal of state and local legislation for the organization and operation of recreational service departments during the depression years.

It is not my intent in this chapter to supply the names, duties, and offerings of a recreational nature of all the federal agencies involved, but merely to suggest that such legislation as was enacted by the national government to initiate these services did more to develop the legal establishment of recreational service as a governmental function than almost anything else. Surely, private groups and individuals such as Jane Addams, Jacob Riis, Joseph Lee, Luther Gulick, Howard Braucher, and others did an enormous amount of work in pioneering the American recreational service movement. Nevertheless, it was still necessary for government to pass suitable legislation for the movement to gain legal status and initial impact.

State Intent

Early state interest and recognition of recreational service as an important facet of social living were manifest in the beginning of state park development and systems. Such acquisitions for this type of area probably resulted from a desire on the part of the state to emulate the federal government's reservation of natural sites as potential recreational spaces. However, it is in the enactment of legislation that the state has recognized the general need of the total population for recreational services. Perhaps the first instances of state awareness came through the passage of legislation allowing the utilization of school properties for recreational and other civic purposes. In addition, the subsequent development of recreational services by some state agencies, including consultative and direct leadership from universities and colleges, extended such activities. Today, many state recreational services are rendered by the following agencies: conservation, agriculture, natural resources, parks, planning, youth, library, education, higher education, highway, fish and game, forests, when created, recreational service commissions, departments, boards, or other state-designated authority.

The first state to enact legislation allowing schools to be used for community recreational purposes was Indiana in 1859, although no school funds were permitted to support this project. However, when New York State authorized the city of Rochester to provide community schools for recreational purposes in 1907, it also allowed school funds to be made available. This was the first time that such a step had ever been taken by a state legislature, and the experiment attracted much favorable attention and emulation. A logical question which arises is why such a long period of time was necessary between the Indiana enactment, the Rochester experiment, and the major state developments for recreational service in 1945. The following factors may be cited for this retarded pace and may lead to some answers.

1. Inadequate knowledge of the need for and significance of recreational experiences in human life.
2. Failure to understand the need for planned provision of recreational opportunities.
3. Recreationists' inadequate education of state legislators about the need for state action and their concern for recreational services.
4. A disinclination to organize and coordinate the recreational functions charged to various state agencies, such as they were.
5. Lack of understanding concerning the need for a state authority to undertake primary responsibility for the provision of leisure opportunities and recreational services at the state level.
6. A disinclination to expend or appropriate funds for promotional projects.
7. The prevailing political philosophy that the state was a restrictive rather than a promotional body.

With all the detrimental aspects, it is remarkable that such permissive legislation was ever enacted in the latter half of the nineteenth century. It took two world wars, a panic, a depression, and a vast communications network before state governments awoke to common needs. Even after 1920, only 20 states had passed enabling legislation for public recreational service. The first true state authority was established as recently as 1945, when North Carolina passed a law creating its Recreational Commission. In 1947, California passed a bill creating a state recreational service commission, which in 1959 was consolidated into the Department of Natural Resources. Vermont established a state board in 1947, after the governor had appointed a state director of recreational service in 1944. Other states have legislated the creation of recreational bureaus, divisions, or other appropriate office designations in a variety of state departments whose primary function may or may not be recreational. Often, recreational service is incidental to the major concern of the agency; in some instances, it is the primary function of the agency. New Hampshire, Florida, and Missouri have a recreational service division in their respective Development Commission; Kentucky has a similar division in its conservation department; Louisiana has a little-used recreational division in its Department of Parks. The states of Wisconsin, New York, Pennsylvania, Indiana, Connecticut, Illinois, and Washington employ recreationists in a variety of departments including their respective Youth Boards or Commissions, Mental Health Departments, or Health Departments to provide consultative and demonstration projects throughout the state; Indiana, by comparison, recently appointed a state director of recreational service, as did Washington.

State Enabling Legislation. The chief legislative enactment by which the state recognized its responsibilities for the provision of recreational services to its constituents has been broad enabling acts. For the most comprehensive, intensive opportunities and tangible means of offering state support for these functions, permissive legislation signifying local prerogative for the operation and administration of departments supplying recreational programs has been most effective. During the initial phase of the recreational service movement, when children's playgrounds were being established in cities, state enabling laws for local recreational service were not significant, because after the historic Missouri act of 1875, which gave rise to the "Home Rule" law, large municipalities depended upon their charters for the required power.

No state is without some legislation on its books applicable to or affecting some aspect of state and local provision for recreational services. In many cases, state law stipulates the local bodies in which the operation of public recreational service will reside. Generally, but not always, such authorization includes the power to appropriate funds, acquire land, develop areas, construct facilities, and employ suitable personnel. In a few states, laws directing the operation of recreational services designate specific cities by class, counties, townships, special districts, regional government, and school districts as the recreational authority. Several states have passed a single organic law of such an inclusive nature that the local legal subdivision has complete autonomy in selecting the agency to provide recreational services.

The characteristic feature employed by broad general recreational service enabling legislation is the empowering of any division of local government to organize, operate, and administer a public tax-supported recreational program for all persons. The general law also permits legal cooperation between two or more corporate entities, for example, city-county relations, municipality-school district relations, or special district-city relations. It must be remembered that enabling acts are permissive and not mandatory in binding local governments to perform recreational functions. Special purpose and regulatory acts, aimed at the conduct or operation of a specific phase of recreational service, are authorizations and requirements to act. Typical of the language usually written into broad enabling legislation is the following statement:

> Any local legal subdivision of the state may select an existing agency of government or create and establish a new agency to have direct responsibility for the organization and operation of recreational services for the citizens of the community. The agency shall be directed to do all of those things necessary and incidental to the provision of such services and shall be supported by tax funds. Said agency shall join or cooperate with one or more extracorporate or other legal subdivisions of the state in executing the functions for which it was established.

In some instances, however, state enabling legislation is quite narrow and restrictive. Such legislation not only designates the agency to be authorized to administer recreational services, but usually is explicit in dealing with how the agency will be financed, how much of the tax dollar can be expended on facilities, the type of facilities and their number, the titles of personnel to be employed, the classification of local government to which this act may be applied, and other regulations which are tacked onto the bill. Enabling legislation, other than to focus the attention of local government on the need for recreational service, in recent years has not been as important as formerly because of the wider use of home rule legislation. Even in states where home rule has not been universally adopted, recreational enabling legislation is getting away from the narrow form and moving toward broad acts which can encompass most local customs and probabilities.

State enabling acts for recreational service should be of the broadest type to provide the widest latitude to local governments in determining the procedures best suited for them in their organization, and operation of public recreational service. Any restrictive provisions that tend to hinder or prohibit the logical development of recreational services should be shunned.

Progress is being made, but it is neither constant nor uniform. Variability is justified and desirable, depending upon the traditions and financial resources available for funding specialized agencies. However, the states are and have been notoriously slow to approve recreational service as a primary responsibility and direct function of the state. This unfortunate situation is being improved, as the request for recreational services continues to grow unabated and focuses pressure upon legislatures. With a highly literate and vastly informed public, the states are finding it difficult to turn a deaf ear to the incessant demand for more competent services of a recreational nature in order to take advantage of leisure opportunities available to nearly all citizens. Particularly is this true when older adults and minorities descend en masse upon state legislatures and begin to clamor for services, among which are those of a recreational nature.

American cities are no longer dominated by absolute state control. State constitutions have been amended or completely rewritten, in some instances, to grant municipalities a large measure of autonomy, whereas in other states measures have been taken to limit the worst abuses of the legislature's power. The state is no longer free to handle purely local matters or to regulate local jurisdiction. States must adhere to constitutional law. One of the greatest acts of emancipation of cities from state legislative abuse and regulation was municipal home rule. The exact meaning of home rule does not suggest complete freedom from state influence. Rather, it means that state control will be exercised where such matters of statewide concern are involved, and that in problems arising from local situations, authority will reside with the community so involved. Essentially, municipal home rule may be defined as the power of the city to control, regulate, and dominate its own affairs. Chiefly, the whole home rule concept has to do with local autonomy and the way in which public services are carried out. Until the great recessions of 1974–1976 and 1990–1992, municipalities, particularly the urban giants, were attempting to provide comprehensive recreational services. However, public recreational service in major urban communities fell on hard times. Some metropolitan cities have permitted a reduction in personnel through attrition and job freezes over a period of 15 years. This has had an immediate impact upon what the remaining personnel could perform in the way of program services, maintenance programs, and other necessary but costly operations. With rising costs, lessening revenue, and manning priorities far below those required to provide comprehensive recreational services, city departments have not fulfilled the mandate exemplified by law. On the contrary, and through no fault of recreationists, public recreational service in the largest cities has been steadily declining. The slow erosion of services has produced deteriorated morale among personnel which can be offset only by ingenious administrative manipulation of staff and the infusion of supporting funds from both public and private means.

The Private Sector

The law pervades every aspect of life. From birth to death, through the most intimate acts of persons, the law infringes on the behavior of individuals and the conduct of organizations. Perhaps this is one of the requirements of living in a social system governed by law and not by people. It is true that the law may be changed to reflect new ideas and life styles, but it changes deliberately. Social organization is not yet dictated by individual whim and the vagaries of human nature.

In the private sector of society a number of agencies have developed either the expertise or the reputation for being able to satisfy certain recreational needs which segments of the population desire. Thus, youth-serving agencies, such as Boy and Girl Scouts, Boys' Clubs, Catholic Youth Organization, Police Athletic Leagues, camps, Campfire Girls, Little League, and adult-serving agencies, such as social, civic, benevolent, protective, union, commercial enterprise, service, professional, and religious organizations, exist to assist in meeting, in part or whole, the recreational needs of adults. Elderly adults may have their recreational needs satisfied by these same agencies, but to these can also be added nursing homes, convalescent homes, hospitals, older adult communities, and age-oriented centers.

Naturally, there are individuals who do not rely upon organizational formats to satisfy their recreational interests, and this probably represents the majority of the population. However, the number of persons who look to private entrepreneurs or organizations to plan, guide, instruct, structure, or otherwise formulate recreational situations and experiences for them is still formidable. All these private sector functions are influenced by the law in some way.

Automobile driving, or any use of motorized vehicles for pleasure, is strictly controlled by law. How fast or slow, on what side of the road or waterway, or in what area, the need for a license or permit, even kinds of equipment used, is dictated by law. Individuals who hunt, trap, or fish are governed by legislation which details the time of activity, the size, sex, and quantity of catch as well as the method employed.

When it comes to commercial development of care services to any part of the population, then an entire series of legislative enactments becomes a decisive factor in the administration of such practices. There are innumerable laws concerned with health care, sanitation, building codes, fire protection, and personnel management directly aimed at private enterprises which engage in the provision of primary or secondary recreational services. Establishment of corporations or companies which promote recreational activity is usually by charter and fulfills certain legal requirements. Newly enforced civil rights legislation clearly prohibits employment discrimination for reason of sex, age, religion, disability, or ethnic origin. In some states, laws require that particular agencies, such as nursing homes, hire recreational specialists in order to gain or remain in compliance with regulatory legislation designed to control such establishments.

Laws have been passed to control or guide the behavior of individuals and groups since the Colonies were first settled. In fact, many original laws were promulgated especially to restrict the recreational activity of private persons. The Blue Laws of the New England Colonies are still somewhat in effect today. Although the laws are not as rigidly enforced insofar as most recreational activities are concerned, some communities do prohibit organized sports and games from being played on Sunday.

Legislation aimed at the control of businesses that provide entertainment, amusement, or other recreational experiences was originally passed to suppress nuisances which developed from the activity in which private companies were engaged. Thus, carnivals were required to obtain permits after many persons were cheated out of money in side show games, and saloons and other drinking places were licensed to make sure that undesirable activity was curtailed. Gambling establishments were licensed to ensure that known criminals could not own or control the business to the detriment of the patrons who frequent such places.

Legislation setting minimal health, safety, and fire protection standards was passed to make sure that children would not be ill-treated or placed in danger at camps, in agency-operated buildings, or other situations where communicable diseases might be spread indiscriminately, where sanitary facilities were primitive, or where food handling was a part of the service. Recently, new legislation that restricts private enterprise even further than before has been proposed. It has been focused upon the camping field for which guidelines have been set on the ratio of counselors to campers on permissable activities in which there is some danger to the participant, and on even stricter control of health measures.

As society grows more complex, and as individuals seek newer and more adventurous activities in which to satisfy their craving for recreational experiences, there will be private sector firms which purvey equipment, facilities, or services designed to take advantage of such demand. When sufficient pressure is built up to regulate activities because of injury to persons, damage to property, or annoyance to the tranquility of the community, legislative enactments concerned with controlling or prohibiting experiences will be made. It is only when life and property become jeopardized that restrictive laws are passed. Also being passed are laws attempting to promote recreational activity by making recreational resources available to individuals who otherwise would not be able to enjoy them. The influence of the law, whether to restrict or promote recreational activity, is ubiquitous. Typically, the law has developed in response to inequities, to demands for protection, or from the need to enhance the opportunities of citizens to enjoy experiences of a recreational nature. There is a new leisure, greater economic means, a higher incidence of mobility, faster methods of transportation, a mass means of communications today that offers tremendous news coverage and instantaneous appreciation of the facts while they are becoming history. Most Americans have the wherewithal to do what they want to do when they want to do it. This places increased responsibility for the planning, development, and conservation of recreational facilities and spaces on all levels of government and on the legislative intent which controls activities and resources.

How are the various levels of government meeting this challenge? There is a vast appreciation of the need for recreational services by all people. This is manifested in the coordination and joint planning by all levels of government and in the pumping of tax dollars by the federal government directly into local and state coffers to be spent for acquiring recreational areas and open space, albeit at a lessened rate than in previous decades. The assumption of state responsibility for recreational services, the passage of new legislation for the establishment of state authority in which this primary function will reside, and the increased incidence of state stimulation to local government, as well as tax support for planning and developing recreational service systems, have had a considerable influence in several sections of the United States. Since the beginning of the organized recreational service movement in America, considerable pressure has been exerted upon local jurisdictional phases of organized recreational opportunities. The communities' actual provision of recreational services to all within the last 50 years represents a considerable accomplishment and a great step forward in social adjustment.

To this significant advance must be added the beating down of bigotry and ignorance by law and public opinion.

Changing Times and Legislation

Additional progress is being observed daily as recreational service gains the interest and effort of state and national legislators. However, recreational service is a long way from reaching its goal, although municipal and other local governments are attempting to satisfy public requirements. The widespread importance of recreational opportunity and experience in the American way of life makes mandatory additional legislative enactment to fulfill the early promise of comprehensive service and equal opportunity for all people.

State Legislation

Coordinated planning and action on a statewide level seem to be the means of ensuring adequate provision of recreational opportunity to all persons. Current action of states in the development of recreational services is one consequence of the deficits which the states have allowed to build up over the years. Although there is realization of the importance, to many groups, of a service of a recreational nature, and states are attempting, even if belatedly, to secure legislation that can facilitate ways to satisfy needs; the economic recession of 1990–1992 has prevented states from following through. The structure of state government, together with the collection of agencies having some responsibility for recreational service, requires a plan that can meet the diverse needs of individuals and the special needs of the particular state. The whole concept of statewide planning must be developed with the same scrupulous care for the degree of difference to be encountered in individual states as is made for variability at the local level. As the economic health of society improves, so does the expenditure for state services. The characteristic aspect of recreational experience is its wide latitude and impact upon human life, and this factor does not change regardless of the governmental level which endeavors to promote it. For this reason, the several states, in the past, have undertaken particular recreational responsibility and interest, motivated, no doubt, by the same stimuli which have prompted local actions along the same lines. This will undoubtedly reoccur in the future.

Any legislation that is proposed will have to consider:

1. The collection, arrangement, and analysis of all legislation pertaining to the recreational service within the given state, as well as the nature of legislation enacted in other states relating to the same issue.
2. The thorough investigation of recreational service responsibilities and functions currently assumed by state agencies, and the means whereby improved cooperation between such departments may be facilitated.
3. The determination of various means by which public awareness and recognition for recreational services in community life can be fostered, organized, and maintained.
4. The assembly, collation, and classification of current investigations on recreational service within the state, conducted by both state and local agencies.
5. The implementation, insofar as is feasible, of legislation authorizing one central state body to be responsible for the major functions of providing recreational services to the state at large.
6. From these studies, the development of a statewide plan for the design, construction, and maintenance of recreational facilities; systematic acquisition of land and water areas, to be held in perpetuity for recreational purpose; the development of space and facility standards to which all local governments may apply for matching grant-in-aid; and personnel standards, set in cooperation with institutions of higher education offering preparatory curricula in recreational service education, and professional organizational personnel policy statements, to ensure competent practices.

State governments must be encouraged to pass legislation for the establishment of a recreational service authority independent of other state departments and directly responsible to the governor. Only with the proper legislation establishing a central state authority can it be hoped that the essential services will be effected. Total recognition of individual, as well as group and corporate, needs will serve as the motivational factors for providing those functions which are an integral part of any state level agency. Legal enactment of bills for the authorization of recreational service as the sole responsibility of *one* state agency will be reflected throughout the state by increased assistance to local communities in the organization and administration of recreational provisions. Devices such as a consulting program available to all communities upon request can be attainable only when it becomes a prime duty of the state authority. Although other state agencies may rightly have primary, secondary, or incidental recreational responsibility, their respective functions should be facilitated through a high degree of coordination so they can be aided in offering such services. The state authority, in its coordinative capacity, can also act as the medium by which the collection, analysis, and dissemination of recreational service information of all kinds may be exchanged among agencies. Furthermore, the state is the only level at which responsibility is at once the basic focus of attention in urban and rural regions. Thus, both corporate and unincorporated areas and their populations are assured of continuing recreational services. Finally, the state agency is in the best position to promote, as well as determine, professional personnel standards for potential licensing procedures and to assist in the recruitment and placement of recreationists.

Local Legislation

The entire concept of recreational service being a proper function of local government has received widespread recognition. As government is a social institution created by people for the provision of necessary and elemental services, which by individual means could not be so economically or effectively performed, the processes by which recreational opportunities are made available to citizens are especially adapted to the province of local administration. Every person in the community supports local governmental functions by a system of taxes and other money-raising measures and obtains in return a level of service consistent with the ability of the community to provide these services. The history of the recreational movement indicates the past recognition of the local jurisdiction to concern all people all the time presents communities with the precept that total opportunity means financial responsibility and operation of a public department whose prime purpose it is to place at everyone's disposal the program, leadership, and facilities for wholesome enjoyment of leisure.

There is no intent here to discuss the administration of public recreational service, but to treat the procedure by which local authority can be empowered to perform. Essentially, the local civil subdivision must take advantage of either a charter or home rule grant, or if these enactments are not established, of any existing state enabling legislation for the declaration of legal assumption of recreational service functions. As it is well known, there are many legislative forms for the establishment of local community recreational service. Whatever type of ordinance or statute it takes to create a department according to local tradition, and influenced by state grants of powers to perform, should be taken.

The organizational patterns and legal recourses for the establishment of operating authorities for local recreational service administration are as varied as individual communities make them. One outstanding factor which remains, however, is the need to accept, as an integral part of government, the function of recreational service. Once this is recognized, the creation of a separate authority becomes almost mandatory. There is increasing evidence, based upon historic precedence, current social mores, and potential technological progress, that leisure and opportunity for recreational experience are primary factors of the American way of life. Where required, in the absence of established governmental forms to perform, special recreational service districts of a regional character should be organized. Such agencies would have legal authority to function within or without corporate areas, and not be limited by geopolitical boundaries if the agencies' functions could be carried on successfully. This kind of recreational authority is provided with grants of power formerly enjoyed by both city and the county, and assigning it explicit functions for designated recreational services, would make it an effective instrument.

When some aspect of social existence has been found to be of importance to the general welfare, then legislation is applied to bring that experience into public domain by empowering some agency with the necessary authority, financial support, and personnel commensurate with its significance in individual, local, state, and national life. Such has been the case of recreational service and the myriad opportunities which it offers to all persons. Acting for the common good and without dependence upon other governmental agencies, the recreational service authority must possess the same status and receive the same treatment as other local or state departments enjoy. Sound and broad legislative enactments are the most reliable measures to ensure adequate, effective, and official recognition of this logical public service. The people are best served when enlightened legislators enact laws which provide for wide latitude and great discretionary powers in the provision of recreational services.

Chapter 6

COMMUNITY ORGANIZATION
FOR RECREATIONAL SERVICE

Historically, municipal government has been exercised through a legislative body usually referred to as a common council, whose members are elected for stated terms by the qualified voters of the city. In very small cities the common council legislates and regulates all the affairs of the city; managerial or administrative duties are assigned to a competent city manager and to department heads.

As municipal responsibilities increased in number and complexity, there arose a need for larger representation of the citizenry in public affairs. The plan evolved of appointing commissions of laymen to preside over the affairs of the separate departments. In essence these commissions were appendages of the common council. Their members, citizens presumably well-informed in their respective special fields, were deemed to be competent advisors of the common council and the city manager—if such there was—and of the executives of their respective departments and to provide an effective communication between citizenry and government.

In discussing the organization of recreational service within the structure of municipal government, and the role of lay commissions it is necessary to distinguish between government as an instrument for the preservation of society, and government as an agency for the rendition of services desired by the citizenry. The view of government as an instrument of services is a comparatively recent one, dictated largely by necessity stemming from the complexity of urban living. Many services presumably required by all citizens have now, by common consent, been taken over administratively by local government.

Some of the functions of municipal government can be performed best by ministerial agents (city treasurer, city clerk, city auditor, etc.) without the aid of commissions. Law enforcement functions (police, fire, zoning, building regulation, sanitary inspection etc.) may well be provided with

137

commissions, not only to advise but also to establish regulations according to legal authority and to hear appeals from decisions made by law enforcement agents. Their procedure must be formal and their findings recorded because they often are put to the test of litigation. Commissions provided for service departments (recreation and/or parks, libraries, art, etc.), also valuable in an advisory capacity, have little or no law enforcement duties in the customary sense, hence are rarely required to hear appeals. Their proceedings may be largely informal. Their functions may be regarded as promotional rather than restrictive. Whether there shall be commissions, how they shall be appointed and organized, and what their responsibilities shall be will be set forth in the city charter. Their legislative duties are delegated by the common council; hence the council must confirm their actions as, for example, in the setting of fees for special services, or the fixing of salaries. Their administrative prerogatives may be prescribed by the charter or delegated by the common council or the mayor (in cities of the so-called strong mayor type).

For convenience, commissions are often differentiated according to whether they are *advisory* or *administrative.* In fact, it is not an either/or situation: there may be commissions with limited or full administrative powers; in all cases their functions are advisory.

There is a difference of opinion among students of government as to whether or not a recreational service department should or should not be provided with a lay commission. Administrators of recreational service departments heretofore have preferred commissions. This preference appears to be waning. Commissions are often thought to be the most effective means whereby local government may learn of the needs of the people it serves, but in many instances this is no longer true. Commissions may either hinder efficient operations or help in securing effective service.

Up to 1940, more than three-fourths of American urban departments of recreational service were governed by commissions consisting of lay citizens. Over the past forty years, the trend has been reversed. Although commissions still survive they are gradually being discontinued. Executive directors or managers are being made responsible to city managers or to city councils rather than to recreational and/or park commissions.

Departmental Organization

There is still much discussion among recreationists as to whether recreational services are best administered under a special agency, under a park department, under a board of education, or under some plan joining two or more agencies in a coordinated manner. It has been concluded by many that all plans have their advantages and disadvantages and that what is best for any municipality depends in large measure upon local conditions. Although each specific plan has something to commend its instigation, there are forms of organization which are decidedly more advantageous regardless of size, condition, or economic ability of the community. There is at least one type of agency which will serve the community best.

During the last few years there has been an unmistakable movement toward more effective organization and integration of the several functions of municipal government. This has been due to a number of factors. The universal expansion of municipal functions since the beginning of the twentieth century resulted in the establishment of so many new departments and bureaus that consolidation of some for efficient administration became inevitable. The economic depression of the 1930's and the insistent demand for reduction of taxes on property dictated a necessity for more economical operation and elimination of duplicated services. The growth of certain agencies—notably those concerned with education, library, park, and recreational services—has been such that a certain amount of overlapping of functions has developed. This pointed up the need for greater coordination of these services and more effective organization. As a result of this need, standardized organizational structures began to be defined.

The Nature of the Recreational Service Function

Before endeavoring to describe the several types of municipal organization of recreational services, it will be desirable to consider in more detail the nature and function of community recreational services.

The basic function of the recreational service agency is the provision of recreational service the year round to all of the citizens of the community, utilizing both indoor and outdoor facilities and activities. The proper performance of this function involves the organization of the community and its resources. Thus both personal and physical (natural) resources have to be discovered, listed, classified, and integrated into the total organizational pattern. Physical resources include natural, inanimate, and artificial resources such as land, water, buildings, structures, and other material assets. Personal resources include individual skills, talents, aptitudes, leadership ability, interests, and the history, traditions, cultural patterns, and groupings of people to be found within the community. The problem of organizing the community for recreational services may be viewed as having to do on the one hand with the organization of people—including professional and volunteer leaders—and on the other with the establishment of recreational places, and the operation, maintenance, and the administration of materials, funds, and activities. It must be remembered that material resources are of value only insofar as they contribute to the satisfaction of human needs and realization of human aspirations.

The real nature of the recreational service function can be made clearer by drawing an analogy between the work of recreational agencies and that of educational departments. The primary function of an educational agency is not to build schools and to maintain grounds and buildings, but to provide children with activities which will contribute to their growth and development in accordance with ideals of good citizenship. Similarly the effectiveness of a recreational service agency is to be judged not so much from the standpoint of the material facilities it provides (playgrounds, swimming pools, tennis courts, baseball diamonds, auditoriums, stadiums) and the manner in which they are maintained, but from the standpoint of the activities which it carries on and their contribution to individual satisfaction, personal growth, and social objectives.

The establishment of separate departments of recreational service in many cities has probably speeded the development of the function of municipal recreational service. Departments charged with a special and clearly differentiated function usually give its development more consideration than those which have other functions to perform and which are likely to view the new function as secondary. Moreover, the special departments are freer to undertake experiments, are less bound to traditional practice, and more militant and aggressive in the defense of their function during times of stress and retrenchment.

The Nature of Organization

Organization may be defined simply as a systematic combination of people involved in the achievement of definite goals. Organization is concerned with internal structure, and is created for the purpose of assigning and understanding duties, establishing lines of responsibility and communication, and effecting economy in the use of employee time and funds. It should give order to the work of all employees. It should be capable of being charted and should be fixed by official approval. To accomplish these purposes, it must be simple in its conception.

In the field of recreational service, the various elements which must be brought into correlation and cooperation by effective organization are:

PHYSICAL RESOURCES

Land and Water Areas

1. Intended primarily for recreational activity:
    a. Play spaces, fields, reservations, grounds
    b. Lakes
    c. Beaches
    d. Rivers and streams
    e. Park lands
2. Intended secondarily for recreational activity:
    a. School lands
    b. Forest lands
    c. Harbor areas
    d. Reservoir and watershed areas and adjacent lands
    e. River basins, deltas, and adjacent lands

Buildings and Structures

1. Intended primarily for recreational activities:
    a. Recreational centers, field houses, courts
    b. Recreational apparatus and equipment
    c. Community centers or club houses
    d. Gymnasiums
    e. Bath houses, boat houses, locker facilities
    f. Swimming pools and aquatic facilities
    g. Camp structures and facilities
    h. Band shells, stadiums, and exhibition halls

   2. Intended secondarily for recreational activities:
     a. School buildings and facilities
     b. Museums, aquariums, planetariums, and observatories
     c. Zoological, botanical, and horticultural gardens
     d. Libraries and other public buildings and facilities

PERSONAL RESOURCES

People of the Community, Differentiated According to

  (a) Neighborhood
  (b) Age
  (c) Sex
  (d) Interests, skills, prior experiences
  (e) Traditions, mores, customs
  (f) National culture and/or religious traditions
  (g) Economic status, social status, educational preparation
  (h) Leisure available
  (i) Artificial groupings

PROGRAM RESOURCES

Activities, Differentiated According to Their Nature

  (a) Arts and crafts
  (b) Gross motor activities
  (c) Music
  (d) Drama
  (e) Hobbies
  (f) Environmental or nature activities
  (g) Social
  (h) Service
  (i) Educational
  (j) Dance
  (k) Special project

Activities, Differentiated According to Environment or Equipment Required

  (a) Playground activities
  (b) Park activities

(c) School activities (extra-curricula)

(d) Beach activities

(e) Swimming pool activities

(f) Camping and outdoor education activities

(g) Boating activities

(h) Stadium activities

(i) Field activities

(j) Special areas activities: i.e., golf, rifle range, etc.

(k) Workshop, studio, kitchen, laboratory activities

Activities, Differentiated According to
Degree of Expertness Required in Them

(a) Instructional and developmental

(b) Opportunity for continued practice

(c) Variety after highly skilled performance

PROFESSIONAL SKILLS

(a) Planning

(b) Leadership

(c) Supervision

(d) Management

(e) Organization

(f) Design, construction

(g) Maintenance

(h) Promotion

It is clear that the problem of organizing recreational service administration in a community is extremely complicated. If all things which serve a common purpose are to be grouped together in the municipal organization, then a single department—responsible for all services suggested in the outline—would be in order. Such an assumption is impractical since many of the resources are under control of agencies serving other than recreational purposes.

That large cities sometimes have more than one department contributing to the public recreational service function is not in itself invalid. The recreational service process in the modern community is many-sided and several departments may be involved in its administration. Insofar as the services rendered by the several departments are dissimilar, their existence violates no fundamental principle of efficient governmental organization. It is only when such departments embark upon innovations which interfere and conflict with the activities of others that efficiency requires either reassignment of activities, consolidation, or a definite plan of coordination.

As yet, no governmental organization at any level has undertaken the task of placing all of the subdivisional recreational services in the hands of one department. While consolidation of similar departments has been placed into effect i.e., park and recreational service, or department of human services, no agency has been established that would have responsibility for all of the recreational services offered in the community. Such an organization would have to be concerned with administering all functions in parks, hospitals, prisons, schools, public housing developments, and the areas, structures, and facilities usually associated with recreational service departments. Traditional practice continues to maintain separate operating departments for such services, with subordinate bureaus, offices, or sections in agencies whose primary purpose is other than recreational service.

The primary advantage in operating around purposive lines is derived from the enthusiasm and coordination which is achieved throughout the hierarchical levels as a result of each person's knowledge of what the agency's basic function is and his understanding of cooperation toward that goal. Thus administrative control is obtained not only through chain-of-command relationships and structure but also through unanimous focus on the general objective or purpose. The ideal condition within any organizational structure is maximum efficiency in the pursuit of a common goal, and personnel rapport plays a most significant part in such efficiency. As always, people are more important than flow charts.

A second advantage of purpose orientation as opposed to process or function orientation is that generalists, rather than functional specialists may be employed at managerial posts. Thus administrators with administerial skills rather than specialized program recreationists may be employed at the topmost position. Since professional preparatory and graduate programs are educating students for administrative positions, more and more such persons will become available.

ELEMENTS OF RECREATIONAL SERVICE ORGANIZATION

There are principles of organization which are sound and practicable. These serve as guiding rules to action and not as mandatory requirements.

In any case, principles serve as the rationale for structure and may vary in the particulars of application as the needs of the agency vary.

The Element of Purpose. Basic to the establishment of the recreational service department is a precise definition of the purposes to be accomplished. Such a statement clarifies agency philosophy and policy, facilitates development of plans, and focuses attention and enterprise for the achievement of the purposes. The purposes of the department as a whole are the major premises on which the agency has been founded. All other aims are minor and secondary, but whatever they are, they must further the achievement of the major goals.

The Element of Research. A thorough analysis of all aspects of the recreational service should be made so that each unit of the agency can be apprised of its specific function and the separate units may be brought into a related whole. The prime object of organizational research is to classify each factor having a bearing on the provision of service and to assign specific activities to particular units of the agency for more inclusive and effective operation.

The Element of Adaption. The activities of departments are always changing as new needs arise and as the concept of their function changes. School, for example, has undergone almost revolutionary changes in the past half-century as the objectives of education have broadened and the methodology has improved. When the first municipal playground departments were organized, the suggestion that schools open their yards and supervise the play of children after school hours and during vacations was regarded as revolutionary. The same suggestion is now generally accepted in most places, and legal, financial, and administrative difficulties have been worked out through contractual agreement or voluntary cooperation.

In many cities, a division of recreational services between municipal departments, the schools, and the recreational agency—if one exists—appears to be working in the public interest. There is a great necessity for frequent re-examination and adjustment of the services of all agencies in order to avoid duplication and promote coordinated action.

The Element of Necessity. Every activity that is necessary for the adequate and effective provision of recreational service in the community should be instituted. All activities which are merely incidental to the provision of such service should be kept in subordinate position, or eliminated.

Thus the operation of lunch counters or soda fountains by the department may be a convenience to the public but is not essential for the provision of recreational service to the community and may actually hinder effective service. If the department feels that it is necessary to institute such accessory functions, it should lease, rent, or sell the necessary space to a concessionaire and simply control the concession against excesses or abuse of the privilege.

The Element of Functionalism. The agency is only concerned with the achievement of the purpose for which it was created. Therefore the department must be organized in relation to the activities which aid in the attainment of its purpose, not around the specialized activities and personnel which serve limited, ulterior, or ancillary purposes.

When departments are based upon main functions for the accomplishment of a given purpose, there is a good likelihood that their program offerings will be comprehensive and balanced and will afford opportunities for general participation. When an agency is simply built around an individual, or group of individuals, the program merely becomes an extension of their talents, skills, or abilities. In too many instances public departments of recreational service have employed as directors those whose only competence lay within the field of sports and games. Thus the program tended to become overloaded with athletic competition to the exclusion of all other recreational activities.

The Element of Unity. The agency and its subdivisions and their respective functions should be precisely defined. The specifications for each unit of the department should be systematically coordinated so that each function contributes to the overall accumulation of effective recreational service with a minimum of cost and effort.

The Element of Centralization. Concentration of executive control in the chief officer of the department is essential if authority and responsibility are to be sharply defined and fixed. This in no way implies that the executive should perform all the duties of the agency; it means that he should delegate them to his staff and subordinates. Each person employed within the department thus comes to know his duties, to whom and for whom he is responsible, and the chain of command for the alleviation of problems which cannot be solved on his level.

At any level within the department there should be centralization of authority. The individual who is charged with the operation of any unit within the department must also be given the required authority to execute that responsibility. The failure or achievement of that unit then rests with the individual in whom authority and responsibility are vested.

Such an employee has a chance to develop ideas, whereas one who is constantly supervised lacks the opportunity to initiate action.

Centralized executive control with delegated authority and responsibility essentially calls for the establishment of a definite line organization with direct triangular communication branching out from an apex at the chief executive level down through the administrative, supervisory, and program levels. Such a structure allows for a sound foundation of control and coordinated activity.

Treatment Centers

A treatment center is an institution where health care services are delivered to resident or outpatient clients. Broadly speaking, treatment centers include any agency whose function is to provide care, assistance, or therapy to those suffering from mental or physical illness, but there are some centers that merely provide custodial rather than medical care. Hospitals, extended care facilities, specialized institutions for the retarded, and clinics are typically characterized as treatment centers. Although treatment centers have as their primary objective the health care and/or treatment of the sick or injured, among its adjunct or special programs designed to assist in the rehabilitation of clientele is therapeutic recreational service.

Treatment centers may be defined by method of support, operational mandate, specialization, or term. A governmentally operated treatment center is financed from tax funds and public donations. It may also charge patients for services rendered, depending upon the individual's capacity to pay. A privately owned treatment center is a profit-making corporation financed from fees and charges billed to patients for services rendered. Public hospitals may be sponsored by any level of government — federal, state, county, or local.

Among the types of treatment centers are those which handle all kinds of diseases and injuries. These are called general hospitals. With specialization making greater inroads into health care facilities, there are hospitals for particular pathologies, for example, joint diseases, cancer, eye, ear, nose and throat, children's diseases, orthopedic conditions, neuropsychiatric problems, and rehabilitation.

Treatment centers may also be characterized by the term a patient stays while undergoing therapy. Hospitals that handle emergencies provide intensive care, or deal with acute illnesses may be defined as short-term or acute institutions; those that handle chronic diseases, rehabilitation, or convalescent cases are called long-term or custodial institutions.

Penal institutions may also be considered as rehabilitation centers, although programs organized in these specialized places have not proved successful insofar as the recidivism rate is concerned.

All of these institutions provide a setting wherein recreational services can be supplied. In some instances therapeutic recreational services are employed to directly assist in the rehabilitation of the individual. In other instances adaptive recreational activities are offered so that a person limited by physical or mental disability may be enabled to participate in activities of a recreational nature.

There are no standard recreational spaces or programs to be found in treatment centers. Each hospital or institution operates on an individual basis—some better than others. Facilities for recreational activity and the programs delivered as a result vary from place to place. Some centers employ highly qualified recreationists; others lack the essential staff to operate a program competently. Some treatment centers have spacious grounds and indoor facilities; others have makeshift arrangements that are quite inadequate and depressing. Despite the wide fluctuation in space available, materials and equipment provided, and administrative personnel, the treatment center is recognized as a setting in which recreational opportunities may be extant.

Community Recreational Service

Recreational programs exist in a variety of settings such as the home, school, playground, park, YMWCA, and so on. For purposes of discussion these settings are grouped into four general categories: 1) voluntary organizations, 2) private organizations, 3) quasi-public agencies, and 4) public institutions and agencies.

Voluntary Recreational Settings

The characteristic features of organizations are that they are not operated for profit, they provide service to a broadly based, needy clientele, and they are organized for the primary purpose of serving the individual, community, or national interest. All voluntary organizations are private in the sense that they are not funded by tax dollars nor are they associated in any way with government. They are set up to provide one or more services to some constituency and have as their motive some altruistic or beneficial ideal.

The Home

The home is a very important and frequently overlooked recreational setting. This is where first lessons in play are learned in infancy from the mother. Many indoor and outdoor games and other recreational activities are engaged in in and around the home. The family recreational tradition and the community and national heritage of recreational participation are transmitted to each generation primarily through the family, which is the basic social unit of society. In earlier times when life was simpler, the home constituted virtually a self-sufficient agency for the direction and conduct of recreational activities. Families were large and association between members of all ages was intimate and natural. Whole families worked together, worshiped together, and played together, sometimes augmented by other families who joined them for these purposes. But this social pattern of home life and its associations has all but disappeared. The nuclear family is smaller and tends to disperse. Living quarters, both interior and exterior, are shrinking, thus crowding out activities integral to home life. Urban congestion and poverty have rendered the family less effective than formerly as an agency for the direction of the recreational activity of its members.

Efforts to reinforce the home in respect to recreational participation and to improve its effectiveness as a recreational agency are not entirely lacking. They include the better planning of cities, the improved design and construction of homes and their surrounding grounds, the education of parents in home making, the invention of devices for the improvement of home-spent leisure, and the promotion of home-centered recreational activity.

The partial failure of the home to realize its essential importance and to perform its chief function with respect to the leisure of its members has placed a burden upon other agencies which have sought to fill the need thereby generated. The responsibility, however, cannot be summarily transferred from the home to the community.

Fraternal, Benevolent, and Occupational Associations

Another voluntary type comprises benevolent and fraternal orders, labor unions, women's clubs, parent-teacher associations, business service clubs, professional societies, etc. Although these groups are organized primarily for benevolent and civic purposes, such voluntary activities constitute a significant recreational activity. Related to these primary activities within these organizations, are many secondary social activities and service functions which constitute much of their programs and which add interest and zest to membership.

The influence of these organizations may be inferred from their size. It is estimated that more than 60 million persons hold active membership in one or more organizations of this type. In addition to the recreational outlets which these agencies afford their own members, who are predominantly adults, they frequently sponsor and provide some funds for programs of a recreational nature for children.

Special Interest Clubs and Groups

A third type of voluntary organization includes the innumberable clubs and societies devoted to a specific recreational activity. In every city, large and small, there are clubs engaging in athletics, gymnastics, swimming, tennis, badminton, archery, golf, bowling, hiking, hunting, fishing, singing, drama, dancing, stamp collecting, chess, card playing, gardening, nature study, birdwatching, astronomy, and—the list goes on and on. These clubs vary from an informal grouping of a few people who get together occasionally to play to a formal organization with approved constitution and bylaws, playing rules and regulations, local, state, and national tournaments, a national headquarters for the promotion of programs or the promulgation of standards, principles, and ethical practices.

The importance of the voluntary association of people for the pursuit of common interests in recreational activity can scarcely be overemphasized. Nearly everyone belongs to one or more groups. These groups multiply the spread of recreational opportunity; they provide occasion for social contact, for comparison, for competition, for formal and informal instruction, and for the encouragement of more interest and participation. Their by-products in socialization, formation of public opinion, and dissemination of information are not the least of their values. This form of voluntary, heterogeneous organization around leisure interests probably comprises the major pattern of organization of American social life and stands in striking contrast to the regimentation of leisure and control of activity which characterizes the organization of life in totalitarian states.

Private Organizations

Private sector organizations (which include some voluntary organizations) have the following characteristics: 1) they are not affiliated with governmental agencies; 2) they restrict clientele to their own members or patrons; 3) they are operated for a profit; and 4) their primary or secondary interest is the provision of recreational services or goods. The private sector agencies may be broadly divided into two categories: commercial and amusement enterprises; and community organizations, including sectarian groups.

Commercial and Amusement Enterprises

Amusements and commercial recreational activities have become a major industry for the manufacture, sale, and distribution of commodities. Almost $250 billion was spent on some aspect of recreational participation in 1982. Commercial dance halls, amusement centers, concert halls, legitimate theaters, cabarets, night clubs, sports arenas, beach, tennis, and racquet clubs, television, cinema, tourism, memberships in various organizations, and the like, taken together constitute a vast industry catering to the demand for diversion, entertainment, amusement, and leisure engagement of the American people.

Commercial recreational activities and amusement occupy an important place in the entire array of leisure organization. They offer something for everyone regardless of individual tastes or the stage of cultural development. They are both good and bad. Some of the most elevating forms of entertainment as well as the most degrading are offered under commercial sponsorship. Degrading forms have always been under attack and under some form of regulation, not wholly effective, but there is reason to believe that the general tone has been on the upgrade. It must be remembered that the primary and, in most instances, the whole objective of commercial recreational enterprises is profit. An establishment must offer "what the people want" if it is to be successful from a financial standpoint.

The improvement of commercial forms of leisure entertainment must rest fundamentally upon the improvement of the public taste, which is a process of education. The amusement industry cannot be expected to lift itself by its own efforts—particularly in an era of permissiveness. The main educational impetus will come from other sources (the home, religious, educational, and recreational agencies) organized not for profit, but for human betterment.

One of the objections frequently raised is that amusement enterprises cater largely to the spectator and do not induce creative participation. Although this is true of many enterprises, there are some that do involve active participation, notably skating rinks, bowling centers, billiard halls, golf courses, residential private camps, skiing resorts, etc.

Community Organizations

Various kinds of community organizations are prominent in the promotion of recreational service. These differ from other voluntary agencies in that they are organized for community betterment and draw their support largely from membership fees, although some of them receive much support from philanthropic sources or fund raising activities from the general community. They are not, strictly speaking, recreational agencies but utilize recreational activity as a means of enticement and as a program through which their primary aims are accomplished. Community organizations include the settlement houses, the Ys—both Christian and Hebrew, Jewish community centers, the Catholic Youth Organization, the Boy Scouts of America, the Girl Scouts of America, the Camp Fire Girls, the Boys Clubs of America, the Girls Clubs of America, and numerous others not affiliated with a national headquarters. The total membership of these agencies exceeded 3,500,000 persons in 1981.

These agencies are primarily interested in children and youth. Some provide buildings, grounds, and equipment for varied recreational activities, but all have well-formulated programs designed to contribute to the improvement of behavior. They are often spoken of as "character building" agencies but more recently as "group work" agencies, by which is meant that they employ informal educational techniques in group activity.

Sectarian Groups

Churches and synagogues are primarily concerned with religious guidance and ethical conduct, but they have always exercised an important influence upon leisure activities. Historically, sectarian agencies have sanctioned certain forms of recreational activity and have censored and suppressed others. Since religious organizations have become more liberal in this century, they now provide settings for many recreational activities. Among the wide variety of group activities offered there are choir and congregational singing; commemorative, memorial, and festive pageants and services; forums and group discussions; socials, entertainments, suppers, and other activities. Numerous religious organizations provide gymnasium, social halls, and playgrounds, and have made their physical plants the center of recreational activities for their members, especially children and youth. Sectarian agencies must, therefore, be recognized as being among the most important organizations serving recreational needs.

Corporations and Unions

Many corporations and companies have recreational programs administered by a full-time director and staff members. Recreational programs are regarded as important because they improve employee efficiency and productivity and alleviate job boredom and absenteeism. Trade unions supply recreational services for their membership to enhance morale and build support, to show tangible union services, and to offer entertainment and recreational participation where other opportunities are not available. Recreational settings may include golf courses, swimming pools, gymnasiums, game rooms, libraries, ball fields, bowling alleys, tennis courts, and others. The number of facilities and their equipment depends upon the size of the company and the amount of space they have available for recreational purposes.

Among other diverse recreational offerings, corporations and unions sponsor athletic leagues that compete after working hours in such activities as baseball, softball, volleyball, soccer, bowling, etc. There are also hobby clubs devoted to photography, sewing, gardening, bridge, gourmet cooking, and so on. In addition, there are travel clubs which plan group vacation trips and arrange charter flights. Picnics, barbecues, outings, parties, and other events are often held to provide employees with social activities.

Community agencies make an important contribution to American leisure in several ways. Their programs are definitely for the improvement of standards of recreational behavior. Sometimes they pioneer in new fields of social endeavor which may later be accepted as public functions. (The first playgrounds, for example, were conducted by private social work agencies.) They also provide opportunities for thousands of adults who serve as volunteer leaders and workers. These experiences supplement and complement public programs and offer impetus for expanding and upgrading all recreational service.

Quasi-Public Agencies

Quasi-public agencies are those organizations which are sponsored by or affiliated with governmental agencies but do not receive any tax money for support. Additionally, these agencies usually limit themselves to a particular clientele. Although they are theoretically open to the general public, they are, in fact, restricted to serving a special segment of the public. They receive financial support from donations, fees, or charges which they impose. Among the quasi-public agencies which perform significant recreational services are the numerous police and fire department athletic leagues which operate centers, play streets, sports tournaments, and the like. Student unions at public colleges or universities may be considered in this group. Perhaps the American Red Cross is the best illustration of such an agency. Chartered by the United States Congress, the Red Cross has been charged with the provision of recreational services for hospitalized soldiers in military hospitals. The organization also provides a variety of instructional activities which qualify individuals in swimming, small crafts handling, lifesaving, first aid, and other activities which have recreational overtones.

Public Recreational Settings

Recreational programs are conducted by all levels of federal, state, county, and local governments. The settings for some of these programs include the national parks and forests on the federal level; the state parks, forests, museums, beaches, and historic sites on the state level; and the community playground programs on the local level. Public recreational agencies are those which are governmentally controlled, operated by tax monies, and open to all of the people.

Public provision of recreational service occupies an important place in the pattern of organization of leisure in American life. Public recreational service does not seek to duplicate the work being done by other agencies but, on the contrary, it tries to render those services which private, commercial, and quasi-public agencies are unable or unwilling to provide. The public functions in recreational service are supplied through such facilities as libraries, schools, auditoriums and other public places. These services, however, go far beyond the mere provision of physical facilities. They include the organization and promotion of public recreational activities and the supervision of these activities.

State Agencies

The states control and operate park, forests, and other recreational areas in excess of 39 million acres. There are approximately 1,800 state parks covering more than five million acres of land. Some of the possibilities that exist for recreational purposes offered at state facilities include trails, picnic grounds, camping areas, boating, swimming, and fishing sites, numerous hotels, lodges, and museums.

Some of the state departments chiefly concerned with providing recreational settings are the following:

1. Outdoor Recreational Services. This state agency works with the federal government in planning and administering outdoor recreational programs. In some states there may be a separate agency, while in others this responsibility is taken over by the state recreational service commission, office, or department.

2. State Park Department. The state parks provide recreational areas and protection for sites of natural beauty. Some state parks are the home of important historic sites. Some of the settings provided by the state parks include swimming pools, beaches, trails, camping grounds, boating, fishing, and swimming areas, zoos, amphitheaters, and organized field trips. Parks that are of historic interest may offer museums, outdoor displays, monuments, and burial grounds. All states differ in their administration of their parks and public facilities.

3. State Forest Departments. There are over twenty million acres of state forests excluding forest areas in the state parks. Much of the state forest land was reserved for the production of lumber and for watershed protection. The recreational settings provided by the state forests include primarily hunting and fishing areas, camping areas, and some sites for vacation homes. Other activities such as boating, swimming, fishing, and skiing (in season) may also be found.

4. State Department of Fish and Game. This agency protects fish and game in their natural habitats. It enforces game and fishing laws and regulates commercial fishing and hunting. It also provides recreational settings for fishing, hunting, and trapping.

5. State Agriculture Extension Services. This agency provides recreational settings in the form of 4-H clubs, camp programs, community programs for singing, dancing, drama, and arts and crafts.

In addition to these agencies, states provide recreational settings through state hospitals, institutions for the mentally retarded and handicapped, day-care centers, nursing homes, penal institutions, children's homes, and drug control centers. The state conducts commissions on youth, the aged, and other special groups. Recreational settings are an important factor in the development of any program for these groups.

Local Government

Local governments include the county, city, community, and neighborhood levels. Schools are also included here, as they often act independently in establishing recreational settings. For any recreational program to operate successfully, it is necessary that all levels of government, from local to federal, interact with each other in the planning, funding, and development of recreational settings. Contributions to recreational settings on the local level are:

1. **County Settings.** In recent years, counties have been playing a greater role in recreational programs. Most counties have parks that have more recreational facilities than their national and state counterparts. County parks may be relatively small, but they are developed to include picnic grounds, tennis courts, beaches, ball fields, swimming pools, golf courses, trails, camps, and playgrounds. Many counties operate on a year-round basis with full-time employees for the supervision, maintenance, and administration of recreational programs.

2. **City Settings.** The larger cities often have city planning agencies that work closely with recreationist administrators in planning for recreational settings and future growth. Cities have numerous parks for historical and recreational purposes. These parks house game, swimming, boating, and hiking facilities as well as zoos, museums, aquariums, and exhibits of special interest. The so-called vest-pocket parks are a relatively recent addition to city recreational environments. These parks, established in our larger cities, are very small areas that offer a relaxing atmosphere in the center of a bustling city. Also in many large cities, small sections, designated as "communities," often sponsor recreational settings of their own such as swimming pools, playgrounds, day-care centers, and the like. In today's society, community involvement of this sort is essential to cope with the typical urban problems of poverty, poor housing, and unemployment.

3. **Community Settings.** Communities in this sense include boroughs, townships, villages, and districts that usually have independent administrations. Neighborhoods are also included. Recently, communities have become more and more active in sponsoring recreational settings. There

are highly developed community parks that offer facilities for game playing, picnicking, arts, crafts, skating, skiing, horseback riding, tennis, and many other activities. In addition, communities sponsor drama, choral groups, orchestras, athletic meets, and community-wide celebrations offering recreational activities. Many communities have swimming pool complexes that offer swimming lessons and lifesaving courses. Community centers are separate buildings with a full-time staff that offer meeting places for all age groups as well as athletic activities, hobby centers, and dramatic and musical events. Some communities also have zoos, museums, botanical gardens, and places for exhibits of various kinds.

4. School Settings. The schools are a major source of recreational settings. Some of these facilities include park-like areas, playgrounds, swimming pools, outdoor and indoor court game areas, craft shops, art rooms, exhibit areas, gymnasiums, and track and field areas. There is a national trend to utilize school plants after school hours. Perhaps the best example of this is the community school, which is designed to provide both recreational and educational activities for clients after the school day is finished. It is essential for community groups to work closely with school boards to provide the best possible recreational programs.

Local governments also provide recreational settings in the form of libraries, museums, botanical gardens, municipal auditoriums for concerts, lectures, exhibitions, and demonstrations.

PART II
STANDARD PRACTICES
FOR RECREATIONAL SERVICE

Chapter 7

STRUCTURING THE
RECREATIONAL SERVICE DEPARTMENT

I t is well known that the complexity of relationships within an organization increases in proportion to its size. In order to understand the diverse functions and organizational structure of recreational departments in metropolitan regions and other large jurisdictions, it is necessary to examine a large-scale operation. How smaller departments operate will also be noted.

Principles of Administrative Structure

1. **Chain of Command.** All supervisory responsibility is direct and is transmitted from the top of the organization via a "chain of command" to the various employees who perform the functions for which the department is established. The worker who undertakes any aspect of employment reports to and is responsible to his or her immediate superior. No employee should be accountable to or direct the work of another employee of equivalent rank.

2. **Line Employees.** Only those employees who are directly concerned with the program function of the agency will be considered *line* employees. This means that they are occupied with carrying out the functions for which the department was created. In this instance, only those employees are on the "line" who work within the section dealing with the direct provision of recreational services.

3. **Staff Employees.** In complex organizations there will be employees who support the line personnel. *Staff* employees are specialists or technical workers whose knowledge, assistance, or guidance may be applied to make the line employees more competent or to facilitate the major objectives of the agency. The function of staff employees is to provide advice, support, and technical information and guidance. With respect to their several specialties, the advice of staff personnel is rendered

161

under the authority of the chief executive of the department. Sometimes this authorization is assigned in blanket fashion, enabling the services of the staff employees to be applied wherever they are needed. Staff personnel render assistance and provide whatever technical knowledge is necessary to make line personnel more efficient, effective, and capable of executing their functions. All employees, except ancillary workers, who are not performing a recreational program function are considered to be staff.

In small departments line and staff functions are frequently performed by the same persons. The following list contains some of the typical line and staff functions in a large recreational service department.

LINE FUNCTIONS

   a. Direct program development in any and all categories of activities.
   b. Instruction of individuals and groups in certain recreational activities.
   c. Supervision of the public in the use of areas and facilities.
   d. Organization and promotion of activities adapted to available activities.
   e. Organization, promotion, and management of special programs.
   f. Safeguarding the health and welfare of patrons who are utilizing departmental areas and facilities.
   g. Performing outreach assignments with populations who might normally not make use of department facilities or organized programming.

STAFF FUNCTIONS

   a. Maintenance of areas and equipment to facilitate all recreational activities.
   b. Maintenance of the entire physical plant of the agency or system to enhance aesthetics, promote good public relations, and ensure the health and safety of patrons.
   c. Construction of buildings, ground improvements, and equipment.
   d. Planning new areas and facilities.
   e. Publicity and public relations.
   f. Personnel management.
   g. Record keeping and filing.
   h. Accounting and auditing.
   i. Purchasing and supplying material goods and services.

j. Advising, counseling, and developing technical information concerning the methods for conducting recreational activities.

4. Job Assignments. The allocation of services or duties within a department should be established upon a sharp differentiation of the activities to be performed by the personnel involved. Duties that are similar in respect to skills, education, and experience necessary in their performance should be grouped together. Duties that are dissimilar with respect to the knowledge, skills, and experience required should not, in the ordinary course of events, be assigned to the same person.

Activity leadership should never be assigned to maintenance or janitorial staff. Housekeeping and custodial functions should not be assigned to recreationists. The consequence of assigning dissimilar duties to a single employee is usually that one function is favored over the other with the consequent neglect of the less favored one in terms of the individual's orientation, skills, or interest. Since many recreational centers have a small staff, less than four workers, this principle is often violated.

5. Administrative Responsibility. Administrative responsibility at any recreational center that is staffed by more than one person should be given to a single employee.

At any recreational center numerous tasks are performed that must be coordinated with departmental policies. Coordination must be achieved at the place where the assignments are performed. This necessitates having one person in charge at the center who is responsible for making decisions. Assignment of administrative responsibility to one person facilitates various operational contacts between the central office of the department and the several staffs at the different outlying centers. It also tends to reduce personal conflicts among the employees at a given place. This practice is, in fact, a partial decentralization of the executive function, which is certainly advisable, if not absolutely required, in a system whose work is carried out at many separate places.

At recreational centers where there are not sufficient managerial duties to require the full time of one person, the administrative duties may be assigned to someone who also performs other functions. In that event the job title should indicate managerial status, e.g., Recreationist II or III. In centers employing a large staff, the chief administrative executive is usually given the title of Director. In large centers the director is to the center what the principal is to a high school.

6. **Dual Supervision.** When an employee is responsible for the performance of two or more distinguishable functions he or she may be appropriately required to report to two (or more) superiors. This situation should be permitted only where the consolidation of functions is unavoidable because of staff limitations. Generally speaking, it is poor practice to have a single employee reporting to more than one supervisor.

7. **Organizational Flexibility.** The organization of the department must be sufficiently flexible to enable the agency to make the fullest possible use of the employed staff. Basically, of course, the functions that a department must perform define its structure and determine the kind of staff needed. Employees should be recruited and hired who can effectively perform the required duties. However, in order to meet actual needs, the organizational arrangement—especially in the lower echelons—should be adaptable to the particular skills and abilities of the available personnel. When personnel changes occur a redistribution of duties is often necessary. Sometimes an employee is outstanding in the performance of certain activities and deficient in others. Occasionally this situation elicits a change in organization.

Structure and Role of the Recreational Service Organization

The manner in which a recreational service agency is formally structured will have tremendous significance for its potential effectiveness and efficiency. The formal organization is best perceived as comprising the roles that are assigned to employees of the system. This really means that each person within the organization is responsible for carrying out certain functions. Accountability for required activities may therefore be fixed. Additionally, the administrator is able to identify lines of communication between individuals as well as to identify the employee's organizational status. The administrator has the tasks of staffing, training, supervising, and evaluating the performance of all those employed by the system. Evaluation is necessary to ensure that the objectives of the agency are being achieved and to obtain improvement in organizational outcomes as well as worker performance.

While each person brings his or her intellect, interests, talents, and skills to the organizational matrix, the various levels of experience and knowledge will affect each person's perceptions of agency aims. In many instances discrepencies between the employee's perception and the administrator's understanding of the roles which each should play in the greater scheme of the organization produce friction and dissatisfaction. Sometimes the unsatisfactory condition occurs because "square pegs" are forced into "round holes." Often a communications gap produces a hostile atmosphere that is conducive to clashes of personalities. The administrator's responsibility is to coordinate the objectives of the organization and the means selected to attain these goals with employee needs. When these elements are logically integrated and compatible, there is greater opportunity for harmonious behavior.

The structure of any recreational service organization has direct relationship to the objectives for which it is responsible. To execute the assignments and be held accountable within the system, individuals must be employed and organized. The development of a formal organizational structure permits the recreational service to combine and arrange its resources so that the essential goals of the agency can be realized. The structuring of an organization will probably define the degree to which it is productive and effective. Organizational structure, in order to optimize recreational opportunities and create an employment environment capable of eliciting rational behavioral patterns, needs to be based upon agency objectives, fundamental work activities, the situation in which the organization is established, and external pressures impinging upon the agency's ability to perform.

Objectives and Aims

Objectives are the final destination towards which a recreational service system channels its energies and resources. The *aims* of an agency are generally statements that provide orientation; the *objectives* are more precise and provide a sequence of intermediate steps attainable by certain dates. Moreover, objectives can be numbered, counted, and evaluated. How an agency derives its aims and objectives depends on the mission of the agency. If the mission is to provide the agency's constituency, with the latest, most comprehensive recreational opportunities then the aims of the agency will be projected in that general direction while the objectives, on the other hand, will guide the daily operations of the organization. Organizational structure mirrors the aims and objectives, while retaining the flexibility to react to external influences. These may be political, economic, social, jurisdictional, or any other pressure to which the agency is forced to respond.

Fundamental Work Activities

All recreational service agencies are concerned with several elemental functions. These activities involve planning, organizing, staffing, development, coordination, financing, recording, and educating. These functions may be further refined as being part of administration insofar as the management and coordination of personnel, materials, and money are required. In addition, the essential responsibility for programming of the establishment of recreational opportunities is the *sine qua non* of every recreational service organization. Finally, the distribution of recreational services refers not only to the points and methods of delivery, but also to the technique of education through public relations and other information means. In this way, the mission of the agency is carried out.

Situational Milieu

The changing conditions in which the organization finds itself are significant to agency structure. Rapidly moving events cause radical short- and long-term shifts in the environment. The agency's ability to respond to rising expectations on the part of its patrons, or its sensitivity to the needs of increasing numbers of minority groups requires a structure that permits ease of communication, quick response to realistic demands, and the ability to develop and supply activities and facilities that will more readily meet the needs of population shifts.

Immigration or emigration may produce conditions that require new approaches by the agency. Different ethnic groups with cultural traditions and aspirations that may be quite different from customary populations require that the agency be cognizant of such increments or decrements and act accordingly. Demographic factors must be well understood by recreationists. Wherever there are good health delivery services, there is a concomitant rise in the number of older adults in the population. While older adults have the same recreational needs as any other segment of the population, their needs are different in degree and interest patterns, and these differences must be taken into account in programming. Better education also produces a population that is impatient with the slow bureaucratic style of many established institutions.

External Influences

Changing Attitudes. Prevailing religious and moral beliefs have always influenced people's attitudes toward leisure activities and recreational services. Sharp divisions in religious practices are now apparent in every country where there are orthodox and reformed elements. Of course, those who practice no religion or profess no faith must also be considered in the provision of recreational services. This latter group is increasing, albeit more slowly than those who adhere to some organized practice. The agency must be prepared to accommodate and arrange for the kinds of activities which will serve both temporal and secular orientations.

Technological Changes. Industrial changes can produce rapid shifts in population, requiring that the agency be able to reallocate resources swiftly to keep pace with the population's recreational needs. Better means of transportation can also influence the agency's programming function. When mass transportation is readily available, city dwellers are freer to travel greater distances for recreational experiences. This underscores the need for planning and construction of recreational places that can supply the kinds of opportunities for which people travel. Improvement in communication, furthermore, means that people are exposed to new ideas about what the good life is. With more sophisticated information about activities comes a desire to attempt fulfillment through creative, self-expressive, and invigorating recreational formats. The agency's structure must have the flexibility to change with changing times.

Economic Pressures. Economics does much to expand or restrict services. The agency must be structured so as to be able to exploit a rich endowment or conversely, to continue to offer recreational opportunities despite financial retrenchment. During times of expansion when there is a great deal of financial support, some recreational agencies simply augment staff positions without any thought as to whether more personnel is really needed. Moreover, additional workers may strain the agency's chain of command by placing more emphasis on bureaucratic controls than on actual services. During times of inflation when financial support falls off, cutbacks are made in personnel as well as in services. Where the structure of the agency is sound, the agency can withstand shifting economic fortunes and still maintain its capacity to perform. Nevertheless, economic changes cause profound shocks to the system.

Political Pressure. Single object pressure groups can cause a variety of problems for the recreational service department. These pressure groups really wield enormous influence beyond the immediate numbers of their involved members. Particularly is this so if they gain support from political figures and their demonstrations and confrontations are picked up and publicized by the mass media. The consequences of these attacks can be a loss of support for the agency. On the other hand, the agency may be able to enlist the assistance of pressure groups as supportive elements for the expansion of recreational facilities, spaces, and activities. Again agency structure will have to bear the burden of accommodating expanding or contracting programs.

Demographic Changes. Demographic changes also play an influential role in terms of how the system will respond to and accommodate new demands for service or can create demands for new services. This has been alluded to in the discussion of the situational milieu and does not require repetition. Of course, there are countless environmental variables that put pressure on the agency's ability to continue its major task. Vandalism, crimes against recreational participants, drug and alcohol abuse at recreational facilities, safety practices and unsafe patron behavior, accessibility of recreational facilities for physically disabled persons, air pollution, water shortages, all play a part in determining the manner in which the organization shall be structured and how it can execute its mission. There are too many variables to list conveniently, and each locale may have its own set of conditions which defy any generalization. However, it is not wrong to state that there is a model organizational structure which can be applied everywhere, depending only upon the ability of its government and its population to support the enterprise. Despite all of the variables mentioned in this section, a structure can be developed which, notwithstanding local traditions, procedures, and expediency can be thought of as an idealized plan. Naturally, this plan is subject to modifications, but the fundamental principles which govern its existence will not change.

Community Organization for Recreational Service

Fig. 1 shows how an independent public recreational service department is integrated within the total community recreational service system. This plan centralizes the control of areas specifically intended for recreational purposes, and the program to be conducted thereon, in a recreational service system. There is no organic connection of this department with any other public agency except that which is raised by formalized contract or through associations which adroit administrators attempt to initiate and maintain for the good of the community. Additionally, contact can be maintained through whatever governmental authority controls the jurisdiction in which the agencies are situated and to whom all are responsible. All governmental agencies having anything to contribute to the health, education, and welfare of the community would be expected to cooperate.

This plan has the advantage of placing community recreational services under the auspice of an independent agency charged with that responsibility and no other. Specializing on the single mission is generally successful in securing greater attention to the provision of recreational opportunities from the governmental jurisdiction and from the citizens, including more adequate budgets, customs, practices, and politics.

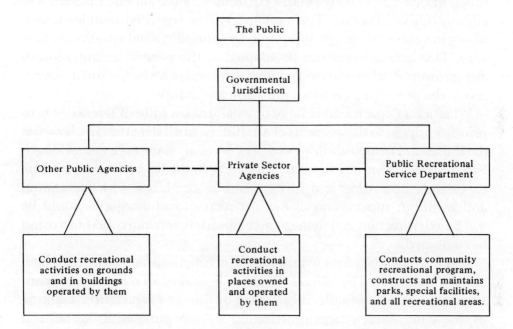

Fig. 1. Community integration of the independent public recreational service department.

The department's employed staff is more likely to be selected on the basis of professional and technical competence in dealing with recreational matters. By controlling its own facilities, the system is better able to organize its program more comprehensively and efficiently than if it depended upon other agencies for the use of land and buildings.

Although the recreational service agency has the mandated responsibility to provide recreational opportunities to the community, it does not lose sight of the fact that no single agency has sufficient personnel, areas, and facilities to be the sole provider of all recreational services. The agency is simply the last resort of the people to public recreational service. Under the plan all other public agencies are invited to contribute their expertise and material resources to the performance of this function. There is little question that recreational service is a large enough undertaking to engage the attention of more than one agency, and that organic connections are not necessary as long as cooperation between them exists and is fostered.

Internal Structure of a Recreational Service System

A model organization of a recreational service department is illustrated in Chart 2. This chart takes cognizance of the general principles of administrative structure. The model should be regarded as an ideal plan of organization, although local or other jurisdictional conditions may vary. This arrangement can be adapted to the general organization of any governmental operation and may still remain a viable format regardless of the prevailing customs, practices, and politics.

Whether a department is large or small makes little difference. These principles apply to departments of all sizes. In small departments, however, the duties and responsibilities would of necessity have to be consolidated. For example, some of the staff functions could be performed by line executives. Recording and filing could be combined with accounting and auditing; supervision of distinct recreational categories could be combined; direction and management of widely separated facilities could be combined.

It is not unknown for governmental jurisdictions to have certain staff functions performed by officers who serve several or all other departments. Legal counsel, for example, is furnished by the chief legal officer, auditing by the chief fiscal officer, purchasing by the purchasing agent, and personnel administration sometimes by a civil service department. Notwithstanding this centralization of staff functions for the entire jurisdiction in question, the several staff officers usually have their counterparts in each department; for someone in each department must regularly prepare and account for financial records, requisitions and stores, personnel records and management functions, and account for funds. While construction, including design and engineering, is sometimes assigned to the department of public works or to its chief officer, it is frequently put out to bid with private firms. Even under those circumstances, it is not unusual for landscape design and construction to remain within the province of the recreational service department—if it is large enough to have such a division.

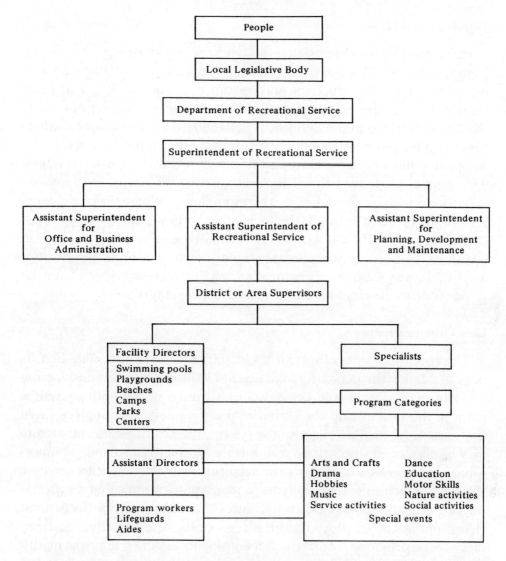

Fig. 2. Schematic of a model public department of recreational service.

In Fig. 2, *line* responsibilities and relationships are indicated by vertical connecting lines and *staff* responsibilities by horizontal connecting lines. It must be obvious that the chart illustrates a large department in which all recreational service functions of a jurisdiction are incorporated and consolidated in one agency. As always, the degree of ramification in organization and specialization in particular administrative and executive duties increases with the size of the department.

Legislative Functions

Fig. 2 shows a local legislative body at the top deriving its mandate from the public. This is a policy making group, but no attempt is made here to spell out the functions and operation of such bodies. It is sufficient to state that the legislative body may be the local governing authority, the highest elected public official, or some board or commission authorized to act for the government. In many instances an individual directly assigned to the legislative body and responsible only to it is the secretary. This person keeps the official records, certifies official resolutions and other documents, and handles the correspondence. Where the recreational service department is small, the legislative body would not be justified in employing a full-time secretary, but might assign secretarial duties to one of its members or to a clerical employee who performs other duties as well. In any case the person employed as secretary should not be responsible to the chief executive officer of the department.

Line Organization.

The chief executive officer of the department, or superintendent, is responsible for the general management of the department and for the efficient maintenance and operation of all units of the entire physical plant of the system, and the activities programmed. If enough of these units are developed throughout the system, intermediate administrators may be employed who will be accountable for the performance of subordinate employees assigned to the facilities and the activities in their charge. For example, there may be so many playgrounds that a supervisor of playgrounds may be called for. That person will be in general charge of the staff employed on all playgrounds. Additionally, assistance may also be provided by certain staff employees assigned to no particular area or facility but related to the promotion and conduct of activities at all centers.

The supervisors of all distinguishable facilities, e.g., playgrounds, beaches, swimming pools, camps, centers, etc., may report directly to the superintendent, but if the department is large enough this relationship may be exercised through an intermediary executive in charge of all activities, with the title of assistant superintendent of recreational service.

Sometimes the department has responsibility over so large a region that the area is geographically divided into two or more districts. Each district has an intermediate executive who answers to the superintendent and is in charge of all facets of the recreational services administered. Under this kind of organization, the geographic assistants control all areas, facilities, and services together with their respective personnel within that district.

Staff Organization

In addition to the line organization just described, there are certain staff duties related to the entire plan of operation which should be explained. These are illustrated in Fig. 3. In Fig. 2 the vertical line flowing from the chief executive (superintendent) office to the administrator in charge of recreational services contains all of the line positions in the agency. In Chart 3, the divisions of the department are shown to explain the various duties and responsibilities that staff personnel perform. All functions connected by a horizontal line immediately below the superintendent and which flank the line functions are staff positions. Staff duties are related to the entire organization. Personnel in these divisions provide whatever technical or service information and expertise is necessary to assist the line people in carrying out their functions and making them more competent to do so.

Among the staff positions will be those filled by central office personnel under the supervision of a business manager or some such appellation. These several functions are centralized in a general office where they are accessible to all who need them. If the office or clerical functions are sufficiently numerous and differentiated, as would be likely in a large system, then each subsection of the division would be headed by a supervisor who was a specialist in that particular occupation. The several staff functions are as follows:

1. **Secretarial Services (Dictation, Typing, Filing, etc.).** These functions are shared by all departmental elements. Modern office practice tends to centralize these duties whenever it is practical to do so. For example, rather than assigning a stenographer to each employee who dictates, the stenographers are pooled and their services are on call when needed. Dictation machines are also utilized, and the tapes or belts are merely sent to the stenography office for transcription.

2. **Purchasing and Supplies.** Many jurisdictions adopt plans for the centralized purchasing of necessary items whereby the services of the jurisdictional purchasing agent are available to all departments. However, someone is still required to prepare and follow through on the numerous requests which the single department submits to the purchasing agent

and to interpret the requisitions in terms of the exact needs of the department. Someone would also be necessary to consolidate requests for materials to be bought so that the advantages of quantity buying may be obtained. Additionally, any recreational service department will probably have a store of supplies which must be accounted for and distributed. Any large department would undoubtedly have a large storeroom with several employees and facilities for delivery. Under such circumstances one employee would have to function as a purchasing agent.

3. **Personnel Records.** Personnel management is infinitely benefitted when reports and records of employees are maintained for current and future reference. The keeping of such records and reports has ramifications throughout the entire system. Such records, particularly for payroll purposes, but also for assignment and other management allocations are important for agency operation.

4. **Financial Records Management.** All accounting procedures are undertaken by this section. This refers to the detailed recording of information concerning the monies received and expended and the relation between the several accounts maintained by the department. This data will be compiled in the form of records and reports for the guidance of administrators. The function of auditing may also be performed by members of this staff, but an official audit will probably be conducted by the controller's office, and, perhaps, by a non-jurisdictional auditing firm. Auditing assures the correctness of the records and accounts. It also determines whether the money allocated to specific accounts has actually been used for that purpose.

5. **Public Relations and Education.** Every recreational service department needs publicity to keep the public informed about its various services including where, when, and for how much. This is a distinct staff function related to all the facilities and areas operated by the department. Public relations is also used to gain public support. Therefore, whoever heads this section should be cognizant of the chief executive's philosophy and policy as well as the rules and regulations of the department. Moreover, the public relations head must have ready access to the several operating units of the system so that educational programs will have maximum exposure and impact.

This section also serves as a general information service to the public, answering the countless questions that are asked of the recreational service department. This relieves the administration and other central office workers of many annoyances and interruptions. The information

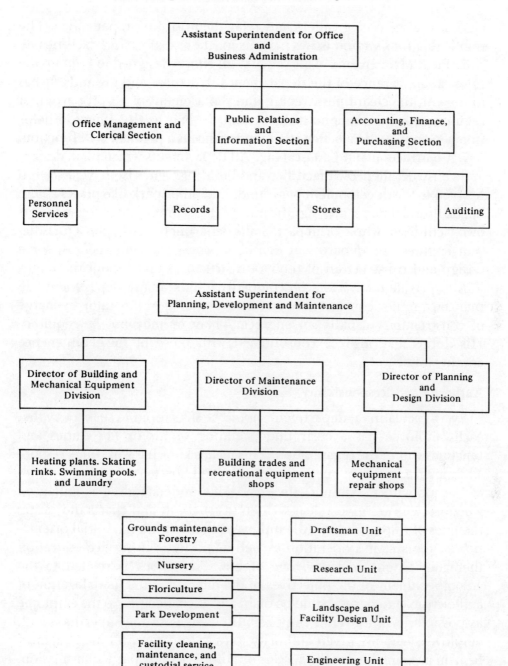

Fig. 3. Staff functions.

clerk can also receive callers and refer them to the proper office. The public relations section issues permits for the use of various facilities.

6. **Plant Maintenance.** This refers to all efforts designed to keep up the physical appearance of the department's structures and grounds. It has to do with the cleanliness, repair, and replacement of all property that requires upkeep throughout the system. Insofar as this function helps line personnel to do a better job, maintenance is a primary staff function.

7. **Construction and Landscaping.** All departments which plan, design, and construct their own facilities and buildings will also have a section devoted to the development of grounds and other park-like places where horticultural effects are significant. A department may construct its own facilities in whole or in part. Some departments call upon a jurisdiction engineer or department of public works for construction; some design and construct all of their own structures and let out the larger jobs to private contractors on competitive bids; many departments do their own minor construction. In any event, an administrator in charge of construction—usually an engineer—may or may not be required. His duties may also be consolidated with those of the maintenance administrator.

Authority and Responsibility

Every recreational department should be structured in such a way that each employee has a clear understanding of his or her duties and functions within the organization. This means knowing what one's responsibilities are, to whom one is responsible, and how to carry out the duties of the job with maximum efficiency. This understanding is enhanced when workers are given clear written instructions and charts indicating the lines of responsibility. All employees should undergo initial orientation to the system's operation as well as periodic in-service education thereafter to ensure knowledge of how their work is related to the accomplishment of the objectives of the department. The delegation of authority to employees should be plain and as challenging to the employee as possible. While overall responsibility rests with the superintendent, employees who are given authority to carry out certain functions must be held accountable for the success or failure of their particular mission.

Department Coordination

In a large system in which functions are internalized through the various sections and divisions of the organization, there is always a danger that coordination between divisions may be lacking or deficient. This tendency is compounded when the work of the agency is conducted at widely separated geographical areas. Joint projects in which all segments of the agency must cooperate, such as a departmental pagaent, exhibition, or field day, greatly assist to integrate the several parts. Departmental meetings and an in-house organ (newspaper or bulletin) regularly covering departmental affairs and social occasions can do much to improve intradepartmental relations and to promote understanding of employees' problems.

Decentralizing the Executive Establishment

Every organization tends to overcentralize the executive functions. It's very human to want to hold the reins. In an efficient system the executive delegates control and authority for making decisions as far down the line of organization as is consistent with effective work completion. This practice helps not only in relation to specific issues but it also reduces executive overhead and encourages subordinates to develop a personal sense of responsibility. In all respects the delegation of authority and decentralization of executive functions leads to broader experimentation, provides opportunity for adaption to local conditions, and saves time, money, and effort. When employees come to realize that decision making is reflected down the chain of command and is a function in which they take part, they respond with increased loyalty to the department and identify more with the goals of the system.

The inclination to overcentralize the executive functions is widely associated with the disposition to build up an unnecessarily large central executive staff. A major concern of the executive should be to put as many employees on the line as is possible, consistent with the efficient executive control of the work to be performed. The relation between the number of administrators and office workers in a central office as compared with the number of recreationists at the places where the essential function of the agency is performed should be continually evaluated. Very often employees are brought to the central office for special work, and reassignment back to the field is delayed or permanently stopped. Assessment of the work being performed at the central office often reveals that some of it is no longer necessary, may well be a sinecure, and can well be dispensed with. Some chief executives are under the wrong impression that a large central office is a reflection of the executive's brilliance or ability to command an impressive work force. This is a grave error that more nearly mirrors a lack of sound judgment.

Selecting the Executive Staff

The appointing authority should be very careful, when filling executive staff positions, to employ individuals who can complement each other in abilities, knowledge and interests. All executives need not be cut from the same cloth. Needed in centralized offices are people with enthusiasm, imagination, and promotional verve. Another requirement is an abiding concern about social problems, and a desire for the improvement of the social order. (The conservative, business-minded executive with a logical mind, sense of proportion and understanding of economics brings a much needed point of view to the department. The sympathetic and approachable executive who has the ability to develop good rapport with employees is also needed.) It may indeed be difficult to find an executive with all of these diverse capacities, so it is all the more important to seek a balance between executive and staff that can achieve the best combination of attributes.

Similarly, the selection of the staff should also consider the contacts which have to be made with different elements of the population; religious, ethnic, racial, and socioeconomic. Contacts with various private, quasi-public, and governmental agencies are also necessary. The department is in a very favorable position if its executive staff includes suitable persons for cultivating all of these contacts and relationships. Apart from these considerations, all executive positions should be open to both sexes and should be filled only on the bases of merit.

Chapter 8

THE ADMINISTRATION
OF RECREATIONAL SERVICE

In one of the classic statements concerning public administration, Luther Gulick wrote:

> Administration has to do with getting things done; with the accomplishment of defined objectives. The science of administration is thus the system of knowledge whereby men may understand the relationships, predict results, and influence outcomes in any situation where men are organized to work together for a common purpose.[1]

From this statement, it may be understood that recreational service administration has to do with combining disparate elements, that is, personnel resources, physical resources, and financial resources, in order to carry out some foreseeable goal. The goal is the public or private provision of recreational services. Administration deals with the arrangement of routine operations on a daily basis so that recreationists are enabled to fulfill their professional functions. By facilitating the performance of recreationists, administrators smooth out the complexities that most human enterprises contain and make more services possible in the most efficient and effective manner. This really means that administration is concerned with the dovetailing of highly diverse factors which comprise the agency so that the work of the department will proceed with maximal effectiveness, minimal waste, and optimal recreational services delivered to the people of the community which the department serves.

Of all the modern social agencies, few have wider dealings with the tremendous range of human interests and deeds than does the community recreational service department. Its essential purpose is to provide a comprehensive program to all residents of the community during their respective leisure. In accomplishing this purpose the recreational agency

---

[1]L. Gulick and L. Urwick, Eds., *Papers on the Science of Administration* (New York: Institute of Public Administration, 1937), p. 191.

must focus the knowledge and techniques available to it from business, law, planning, and those appropriate aspects of scientific management by which the agency is made more capable in undertaking the responsibilities mandated by its establishment. In addition, the department must recruit highly skilled and technically competent individuals who are professionally prepared to operate the department, together with ancillary personnel, including volunteers, who can more nearly supplement and complement the recreationist. Moreover, the added precaution of economic utilization of people, materials, and money in ways that will produce efficient, systematic, and effective services of a recreational nature is required.

Only through organization can optimal service without duplication of effort and waste of material and fiscal resources be produced. No small detail should be overlooked, and every individual employed or enrolled within the personnel aspect of the agency should have clearly defined duties. Departments in which every employee is always ready to think and act promptly and effectively will have the regular functions, authority, and responsibilities of each carefully assigned. Authority will be centralized, responsibility designated, coordination utilized, and relationships definitely fixed. Organization should be looked upon as the structural facet, or form-giving element, of the agency; whereas administration is the planning, directing, and controlling of the operation of the organization through coordination. Organization is a part of administration concerned with the arrangement of all elements pertaining to the agency in such a way that appropriate service will be engendered.

Organizational Concepts

Too often, recreational service agencies have no real plan of organization or, at best a superficial one. Many agencies have simply reacted to changing times, the organization being structured about whatever personnel was available and with no thought to any logical plan. Any modifications made in these agencies have been largely ones of expediency brought about by emergency conditions. Typically, community recreational service departments start off as summer programs which, after having proved successful in attracting whatever clientele there is, become accepted by the local government as a part of an existing agency or are established as a separate member of the municipal family. Initially, the department may have been built around one person, usually the individual in charge. In time, with the accumulation of additional duties as a result of being made a full-time department, or having incurred responsibilities as a subordinate branch of a larger enterprise, the agency has to broaden the scope of its activities. When it is finally learned that the agency cannot carry out its functions with the existing personnel, other individuals are hired. Unfortunately, if the agency's program has been geared to the skills of the individual worker rather than to the recreational needs of people living in the community to be served, there is bound to be a noticeable weakness in the structure of the organization. Often, the program is unbalanced, with too much emphasis on one phase and not enough on others. A constricted view of the work to be done, rather than an orientation embracing the fundamental principles of recreational service in the community, determines the direction of the agency's activities. Attention is focused on petty details, while the larger problems of balance, scope, variety, and progression of activities within the program are unresolved. In this instance, concepts of coordination and cooperation are of distant concern.

Organizational Planning

When the organization is based upon logical methods, inefficient conditions cannot become entrenched. Organization has as its rationale the idea that only through cooperation and coordination will there develop maximum output with minimum expense and effort. Specialization and the desire to meet the needs of the total population are outgrowths of modern professional interest in recreational service. Increased size adds to the problems of control through increased numbers of participating personnel and greater complexity of the system. Specialization concentrates expert attention on activities and limits the possibility of error. However, specialization strengthens the requirement for coordinated effort and for ways of widening the concepts of these specialists by having them look beyond their specific interests to the needs of the agency as a whole. A soundly planned organization is the structure upon which administration depends for essential cooperation, direction, control, and coordination.

Examination of the large recreational service departments indicates the multiplicity of functions undertaken and executed. In some instances, thousands of persons may be employed. There are specialists in a variety of recreational activities, construction and maintenance, business administration, public relations, personnel management, and an extended list of other areas. Each individual spends their vocational life in the preparation and practice of a specific area, being particularly able to perform certain endeavors or to give expert technical guidance in one area. Through organization, functions are identified and categorized. This allows specialists to be employed to take responsibility for those functions which should culminate in a coordinated effort permitting each specialization to function effectively, while all specialties are combined to produce a common goal—recreational service. On every level of the agency hierarchy the supervisor coordinates the work of subordinates; in turn, this work and that of others of equal rank are coordinated by a superior until the executive of the agency finally coordinates all activities being carried on within the system. One of the required functions of any administrator is to effect coordination within the area of authority, whether that sphere be the department or some division of the agency. The more extensive the department, the more desirable is coordination and, therefore, the greater is the need for an organization developed to facilitate the efforts of the executive and subordinates in obtaining unity of purpose and harmony.

There is hardly an ideal organization for every recreational agency. Nonetheless, certain principles and standards can be followed in the development of an organizational procedure which can be valuable for each agency. The standard should constantly be kept uppermost in the mind of the executive and should be varied from only with exceptional reason; on the other hand, the structural pattern should not be maintained regardless of changing needs and other modifying pressures. The study of standards of organization will offer reasonable choices for the development of a logical organizational plan. However, environmental as well as internal influence may necessitate deviation from what might be considered an ideal organizational plan. Political machinations, available professional personnel, financial support, community traditions, and other factors, all play an important part in any structural arrangement.

Basic Organizational Standards

As each recreational service agency has conditioning factors peculiar to itself in areas such as region, finance, authorization, legal establishment, operating and volunteer personnel available to it, public support, participant demand, pressure groups involved, financial resources available, natural and artificial resources available, a unique statement of rules and prescriptions cannot be formulated which might be applicable to the organization of all agencies. However, certain fundamental standards can be provided by which actions can be guided and from which levels of attainment may be judged. Details of application may differ as a result of unique conditions, but the following standards are valuable as underlying bases for logical organization.

Classification. A comprehensive examination of the entire range of activities, operations, and services to be produced must be made so that each facet of the agency and its units can be identified and assigned relative responsibilities. There is little question that anyone with a good knowledge of recreational service would attempt to establish a department unless all requirements for that department, in a specified locale, were analyzed. Recreational service agencies are organized chiefly to provide experiences of a recreational nature to all persons in a given community, if the agency is of the municipal family, or for a particular clientele. It would therefore be decidedly foolish to establish the agency without first determining whether the public wants or is ready to accept the provision of public recreational service, whether such an agency can employ professional personnel, and whether adequate financial support will be available to permit a comprehensive and varied program at a price which the community is willing to pay. Unless the answers to these questions are positive, additional public education and dissemination of information relating to individual need for recreational experiences must be made the first order of business.

Simplification. All activities that are not essential to the production of recreational services should be eliminated, and those activities that are continued should be managed in the simplest and most efficient way.

Functional Orientation. The organization should be structured on the primary purpose of the agency and not around personnel. The nature of recreational service determines the chief functions of the agency, and thus, of itself, offers the correct foundation for organization. Functions, or activities, have no limitation; individuals are restricted in what they can do and to what extent they may develop. Functional orientation distributes work and responsibilities. Similar or complementary functions should be grouped so as to form the several major divisions of the system. For example, all requisite activities concerning business administration should be classified in one major group. All necessary activities relating to the maintenance of the physical plant of the agency should be placed in another major class, and all activities relating to the direct provision of recreational experiences should be put into a third category, and so on. Each of these groups will then be the foundation for a major division of the system. This provides a sound structure which prevents overlapping, duplication, and omission of functions to the detriment of the department as a whole. When a system is developed around clearly identified functions and those responsible for them are liable for specific outcomes, the result is one of flexibility, growth, capability, and adjustability to whatever changing environmental situations bring. When major divisions are established to care for the respective groups of like and complementary functions, then responsibility can be fixed, valid costs of operations known, department budgets accurately estimated and prepared, and the necessary personnel employed.

Authority and Responsibility. Centralization of responsibility and wide delegation of authority in order to fix the former and render the latter most effective in the production of recreational services are necessary. An individual does best and accomplishes the greatest result when given a definite job to be completed in a specified time, the work being of a nature for which the individual is physically and emotionally suited and competently prepared to carry out. Assignments should be of a difficulty sufficient to demand the highest quality of effort that the person has to offer. Individual effectiveness is increased through in-service education and improved working conditions. Carefully instructed personnel know to whom and for what they are responsible; they have a better understanding of the purpose of the agency; and they are enabled to perform most efficiently, quickly, and economically those things they were employed to do. Similarly, improved working conditions develop morale, loyalty to the system, and dedication to the field.

Scientific formulation of work responsibilities leads to specialization of effort and develops experts in some particular activity, with resultant advantages derived from concentrated attention. Care should be exercised, however, not to narrow the scope of work to such an extent that the individual can be confident and/or competent only in one minute form of activity. A certain amount of versatility is not only desirable but vital, if the recreational service agency is to offer the most comprehensive program possible. Recreationists should be expert in several program categories, but should also have a wide acquaintance with and knowledge of all program categories and resource possibilities.

An individual exercising authority should be held responsible for the execution of all activities within the limit of that authority. Conversely, no individual should be held responsible for the proper execution of operations that do not fall under his or her jurisdiction. Ultimately, of course, all responsibility rests with the departmental executive, for example, the superintendent of recreational service. Although it has been stated that an executive may delegate authority, responsibility may not be delegated. To a certain extent this is true. Nevertheless, some responsibility does fall upon the individual who has been given authority to carry out a specific operation. Failure to perform adequately when proper authority to control a given operation has been received reflects unfavorably upon the delegator as well as the recipient. When authority is delegated, it should be clearly defined. There should be no overlapping of authority nor any question about with whom responsibility lies.

Standardized executive control through the delegation of authority and acceptance of responsibility requires establishment of clearly defined lines of supervision and an insistence upon a chain of command from the executive downward. This provides a basis for discipline and coordination of all work to be accomplished. In addition, it stresses the probable lines for advancement within the agency's hierarchy, and teaches leadership techniques and other operational knowledge to personnel who understudy their superiors.

Standardization. The substitution of standard operating procedures, in the routine of daily affairs of the agency, for policy statements concerning individual activities should be made. Particular techniques of best practice, carefully determined, should be adopted and applied throughout the agency.

Whenever feasible, certain standards of practice, expressed in terms of definite qualitative and quantitative units or patterns of behavior, should be made the model by which all performance and productivity may be evaluated. Standards of performance provide administrators with specific terms by which to measure efficiency, evaluate leadership, appraise program content, and estimate future planning. Unless standards are introduced into the daily operations of the agency, there is no basis for comparison and no sure method for understanding whether or not the agency's efforts approximate the objectives for which the agency was established. Standardization permits better control and affords a greater degree of accuracy in analyzing the system's productive capacity for the rendition of recreational service. Properly instituted standards furnish incentive to personnel to achieve a level of competency which they can clearly perceive, rather than personnel being dependent upon some nebulous ideal about which there are no means of determination.

Planning. The satisfactory accomplishment of the agency's purpose can be attained only when there is a logical plan by which all the system's personnel and all its interests and functions are guided. Therefore, intelligible, sharp, and comprehensive plans are essential to effective administration.

Planning assists achievement of objectives. It defines the real interests of the system, the goals to be reached, and specifically details the priority, personnel, facilities, space, material, and money to be used in their accomplishment. The goals provide a basis for action, setting up primary objectives, and the means and techniques to be utilized in arriving at these objectives. They are not arbitrary rules or regulations, but highly practical and elastic guides which take into consideration the present environment and shifting conditions and/or needs of the community or clientele to be served. With planning, the arrangement of work, the delegation of authority, and the fixing of responsibility are decided upon, decisions are made as to what should be done, who will do it, how it will be performed, and when and where it should be carried out. Because recreational service deals with people, the offering is constantly changing as people's needs are continuously being modified. For these reasons, planning is of utmost significance if the agency is to satisfy demand.

Charting the System

After a department has been established, it is often difficult to picture it in its entirety to determine whether a logical plan of organization has been created. To ascertain the strengths and weaknesses in the structure and a sound basis for agency operation, an organizational chart should be drawn. The chart graphically indicates the direct relationship of functions and existence of lines of authority and responsibility, as well as the interrelationships between line and staff personnel and divisions. The charting procedure is an excellent test of logic and structural soundness, inasmuch as any organizational relationship that cannot be diagrammed easily is often poorly planned and unintelligible to the organization's personnel. There are distinct advantages for the use of organization charts, particularly for the largest agencies where so many employees are involved in agency operations. However, charting is also applicable and of benefit to smaller departments as well. An organizational chart indicates major divisions of a recreational service system (Fig. 1).

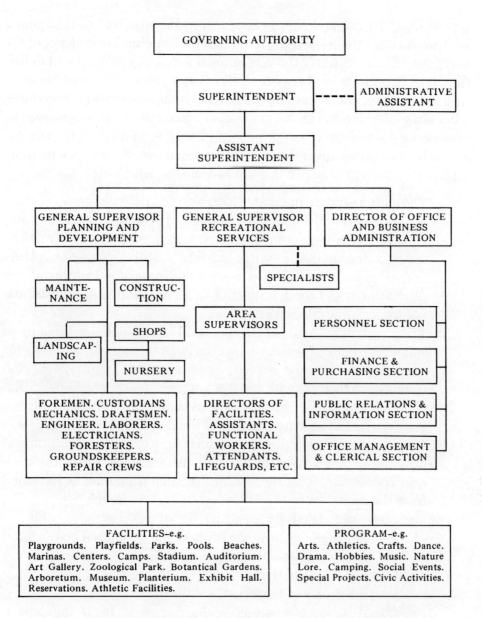

Fig. 1. Organizational chart for a hypothetical recreational service department.

Recording the System

Organizational charts that clearly identify lines of authority, responsibility, and specialization are one step in making each employee cognizant of his functions and significance within the structure of the agency. In order to offer the most comprehensive and intelligible concept of the organization and its work, the recreational service agency should define the general policies of the system, detail the rules and regulations by which it operates, and attempt to standardize routine operating procedures. This vital information can be made easily available to all employees by publishing a set of directives or an administrative manual of the agency. Actually, there are several types of manuals which the recreational service department may put to good use, among which are:

1. The administrative manual, which contains policy statements relating to the functions of the agency; operating procedures and fundamentals; personnel practices; public relations information; the organization of the system as a whole, with a detailed explanation of general duties and responsibilities; a definition of the subdivisions and their respective activities; and general information concerning the whole system.

2. The program manual, which covers all phases of a comprehensive and well-balanced series of appropriate recreational activities for the population to be served; provides rules, regulations, and instructions dealing with the teaching, guidance, and supervision of recreational experiences; suggests types of activities; and lists a great variety of activity possibilities and resource material.

3. The divisional manual, which applies only to a given division and provides detailed specifications for the activities which the division carries out. The significance of such a manual is indicated from the inclusion of the following topics and items:

   a. Name of the activity for which the division is responsible.
   b. Precise statement or description of the divisional activity and the range of functions covered.
   c. General duties of the division.
   d. Specific duties of personnel within the division.
   e. Coordination maintained with other divisions of the department.
   f. An organizational chart of each section of the division.
   g. Complete specifications for each section of the division.

The value to be derived from procedural manuals depends to a great extent upon the opinion of those who are most concerned with the consequences revealed by records. The manual must undergo periodic revision and consistent modification. It is, therefore, subject to additions and deletions to ensure that it reflects the organization's current conditions and requirements. The worker is thus enabled to evaluate better past activities and to assist in the formulation of new recreational experiences and practices. Such records are vital if standard work methods and operating procedures are to be common.

In large recreational service systems the various manuals may be voluminous and in extreme detail, with a careful elaboration of the rules, regulations, policies, and procedures by which the agency is governed. Such detail is necessary if every routine phase of operation is to be covered adequately. Standard operating procedures are the result of compiled records and reports of the department over a long period of time and tend to reflect the common occurrences, behavior, functions, requirements, and control necessary for effective administration. "Going by the book" does not hinder the ingenuity and innate creativeness of the recreationist. On the contrary, it frees him or her from the problem of making inaccurate appraisals or using poor judgment in delicate personal contacts with the general public.

The manual serves as a standard for personnel conduct of activities as well as a quick reference to establish correct practices. The manual provides a ready source of information on a wide variety of routine problems which often confront recreationists in their dealings with the public. These published expectations of professional responsibilities for employed personnel, as well as for the conduct of participants do much to offset petty annoyances and occasional personality conflicts that may arise. The manual is not the *last word* by any means, but it does offer an easy device whereby the typical problems of scheduling personnel, working attire, facility responsibility, custodial operations, plant maintenance, holidays, salary increments, routing schedules, club management, supervisory factors, liability, and the minutiae of daily on-the-job practice are reduced to an easily handled and systemized routine. By clearing away some of the clutter that usually hampers the recreationist in his practice, the manual of procedures generally permits the professional more time to experiment and develop new program ideas. Creativity is one product of standardizing operating procedures in manual form. Manuals are developed over extended periods wherein administrators and other personnel, by way of exposure to recurrent and in some cases repetitive activities, realize that much time and effort can be saved in handling the day-to-day business of the agency.

The administrative manual usually covers the following work and personnel policies:

1. Personnel Management

a. Any Change of Address. Currently employed personnel should have their home address and telephone number on file with the central office (if a small agency) or with the facility office.

b. Uniform Dress Requirements. Regulations are in effect and notice is given of correct attire for all staff personnel assigned to various divisions and/or activities of the department. If the department requires that a specific uniform be worn by its employees, it must provide a uniform clothing allowance and indicate where such garments and other accessories may be purchased. Otherwise, it must issue a standard uniform. The dress of professional staff personnel should be appropriate to the occasion and conform to whatever detailed dress descriptions the department deems necessary. The department may also require some badge or emblem to be worn as a distinguishing insignia indicating the status of the employee.

c. Substitutions. Employees are remunerated for work performed. All employees are hired by an authorized office and compensated on the system payroll as local jurisdiction demands. Under no condition can an employee be absent from job responsibilities and substitute another person.

d. Employment Schedules. Regular hours of work for all personnel of the department are fixed according to departmental requirements. Specific assignments normally run a full 8-hour day, not to exceed 40 hours per week. Depending upon the need of the program, day and night work schedules are made up in conference with divisional and/or district superiors, depending upon the organization of the system. Because the department operates a 7-day per week program, starting in the morning and continuing through the evening hours, a regular two or three personnel shift is required in order to meet the supervisory needs of the program. Such aspects of scheduling as meeting day and night needs, compensating for overtime, and assigning night duty on a regular basis must be taken into consideration. Any compensatory time must be taken within a specified period and may be saved and added to the normal vacation time allowed.

e. Emergency Leaves and Sick Time. As a standard operating procedure, each employee who must be absent from his job because of illness must notify his immediate supervisor as soon as he is able on the first day of illness. In the event that an employee becomes ill on the job, the immediate supervisor must be notified in order to cover the assignment. In the event of an emergency or acute sickness requiring an extended period off the job, sick leave allowances are in operation, and time off with full or partial pay as enumerated in the work schedule will be in effect. The department will set a limit on the amount of sick leave that can be accumulated during any one year with full compensation. Other incidents requiring time off, such as being called to jury duty, will be worked out individually.

f. Annual Leaves and Vacations. The municipality will generally have some policy for vacations. Usually, employees are allowed a specified time with full pay after having successfully completed one year of service. The annual leave is increased after continuous employment with the community. Increments in annual leave may be noted after 5, 10, 15, or more years, with appropriate increases in leave time. Specific forms for leave requests are devised by the department, and upon written application, vacations may be arranged. Vacations shall be arranged to interfere least with the program needs of the agency.

g. Remuneration. All pay rates are established in conformity with unicipal policy and are subject to special provisions which reflect professional, technical, and other pay categories. The department usually has some form of pay schedule and increment plan by which continuous satisfactory employment in the department is rewarded. Step increments may be annual and at one or more steps per year depending upon worker competency and performance. It is usual to raise more highly proficient workers or those who in the opinion of their supervisors merit such increments. Such evaluations are made by immediate supervisors and passed upon by whatever administrative staff the department employs.

h. Staff Conferences and In-Service Education. All employees of the department are expected to attend regularly scheduled in-service educational programs, institutes, workshops, demonstrations, or lectures. Such meetings are designed to improve employee competency and efficiency as well as for professional development. Regularly scheduled conferences for staff personnel dealing with work schedules, job assignments, program ideas, daily operations, or any other matters will be attended by all appropriate employees.

i. Program Participation by Departmental Employees. Under no circumstances will professional personnel of the department participate in any departmentally sponsored or operated recreational activities. Non-participation, in this instance, means as an active player or competitor. It in no way terminates the professional obligations which employees have as leaders, supervisors, or instructors.

j. Conflict of Interest. Employees may belong to whatever organizations they wish for their professional development, social enjoyment, or other reasons. However, such affiliations should not be the cause of conflicts of interest between the employee and the department.

k. Professional Education. All employees are encouraged to take advantage of any university or college professional educational courses. However, the department will stipulate the number of hours and/or courses which any employee may take while working full time in the system.

l. Functions of Personnel. The job specification identifies the requirements of each position. It establishes the conditions of work which will result in an optimal contribution of the recreationist to the success of the agency as a whole. It provides the worker with a clear understanding of his duties and obligations within the system and his relationship with others. Further, it defines responsibilities of the position and the authority which it carries. The individual is therefore in the situation of best appreciating what is expected of him within these lines. Each position specification should contain the following information about a particular job:

(1) General responsibilities.
(2) Principal objectives.
(3) Primary functions.
(4) Limits of authority.
(5) For whom responsible.
(6) To whom responsible.

2. Public Behavior

a. Intoxicating or Alcoholic Beverages. No person shall be allowed to possess or consume alcoholic beverages in or on departmental properties. Usually, there is a municipal ordinance prohibiting the use of such beverages in public places.

b. Profane And/Or Obscene Language. The use of such language is considered to be offensive to public taste and as such cannot be allowed. However, the constitutional provision of free speech may prohibit real enforcement.

c. Public Health and Safety. In order to maintain the health, welfare, and safety of those who utilize public recreational spaces and facilities, the following regulations may be applied. No person shall be allowed to:

1) Vandalize or otherwise deface or destroy public property.
2) Carry or discharge firearms or fireworks, slings, or other weapons.
3) Remove any public property from the allotted area.
4) Pollute or otherwise wrongfully utilize any water facility.
5) Kindle fires except in properly designated places.
6) Gamble.
7) Behave indecently, insofar as community standards are concerned.
8) Ride or drive any animal or vehicle except in places expressly designated for such activity.
9) Engage in riotous, threatening, or indecent conduct.
10) Conduct any business without the express permission of proper departmental officials.
11) Deposit any refuse of any kind except in proper receptacles as are provided.
12) Have animals, except cats and dogs on a leash of suitable length and strength.
13) Campaign politically, transmit handbills or posters, hold religious services, parade, or otherwise disrupt the normal function of the recreational facility unless such activity is officially sponsored by and part of the recreational service program.
14) Use narcotics or other illegal or harmful drugs or chemical substances which render rational behavior unlikely.

d. Volunteers. All recreationists should attempt to recruit and utilize layment as instructors, escorts, guides, and in other capacities as volunteers in order to supplement and expand the offerings of the recreational program. There are many opportunities for the provision of recreational experience that cannot be taken advantage of because of a lack of staff personnel. Volunteers make additional activities possible. The initiative of skilled, enthusiastic, and dedicated laymen should be made an integral part of every recreational service program. Volunteers can be of extreme significance in the enhancement and attractiveness of a planned program.

3. Administrative Operating Procedures

a. Accidents. Usually, only minor injuries shall be treated by departmental employees, unless a physician is a departmental employee (by contract). If an injured person requires immediate medical attention, proper authorities must be notified. First aid procedures should be instituted at once to prevent more serious injury to the individual.

b. Accident Reports. Accident report forms will be utilized whenever a patron is injured or personal property is damaged by departmental equipment at any departmental facility. Reports of injuries or property damage are filed in accordance with municipal regulations.

1) Every effort shall be made to complete all parts of the accident report, including the names, addresses, and statements of all witnesses.
2) In the event of serious injuries, including the death of a participant or spectator, the supervisor of the facility shall make an immediate verbal report to his immediate superior and file a complete written report within 24 hours.
3) Departmental employees will not utilize their own vehicles to transport injured persons, unless unusual circumstances force such transportation to be used, but will request police or hospital department ambulances to render assistance.
4) Departmental employees will render whatever first aid is required, request medical assistance if necessary, report all facts, and in no way make commitments on behalf of the department.
5) In all cases of serious injury to participants, where the proximate cause appears to result from faulty equipment or a hazardous area, the departmental employee supervising the facility shall request a police photographer to photograph the area. The employee immediately concerned with the situation shall be prepared to indicate the possible causes of the accident in order to guide the policeman in the subject or angle of the picture. In the event that a police photographer fails to respond, the recreational service worker should telephone his immediate supervisor and apprise him of the fact that he was unable to arrange for a photograph to be taken of the suspected area, facility, or piece of equipment.

c. Participations. Attendance should be counted during the hours the facility is in operation. The count is recorded on an official form provided for that purpose. There are several formulae utilized for taking an attendance count during the day. Any one of these may be used to determine the number of visits to the facility. The attendance count is the total number of all persons visiting the facility. Such a count shall be made each day and recorded on the weekly report for submission to the central office.

d. Daily Log. Entries in this journal record the activities conducted at the facility under immediate supervision of the local staff. Its purpose is to reflect an accurate picture of all organized activities sponsored, promoted, and supervised by the staff of the facility.

e. Closing Hours. Usually, regular activities at any recreational facility cease at 10:00 p.m. However, on special occasions activities may be scheduled until a later time. The approval of superiors should be secured in advance. If advance approval cannot be obtained, the circumstances should be reported immediately after the working day on which this deviation of schedule takes place.

f. Opening Hours. All personnel should arrive at their respective facilities not less than 15 minutes prior to the officially designated time for opening. Upon arrival, employees should follow this standard procedure:

(1) Open all entrances and rest room doors.
(2) Raise the colors.
(3) Set out any special equipment.
(4) Check over all supplies.
(5) Inspect all apparatus.
(6) Designate any unsafe equipment for removal.
(7) Make entries in proper ledgers concerning any faulty equipment.

g. Inspection of Facilities, Equipment, and Areas. It is the responsibility of the facility supervisor to make a complete daily safety check of all equipment in order to ensure hazard-free utility for participants. Furthermore, each employee has the obligation of surveying all recreational areas, facilities, and equipment and reporting inadequacies and/or deficiencies. All hazardous situations should be reported immediately to the central office for correction. The employee must follow up by continual check until the condition is corrected.

h. Transportation. If the department has a contract for the use of buses for recreational center groups, the following procedures should be initiated: Each center is authorized to conduct a specific number of bus trips throughout the year. In addition, the department may furnish transportation to certain city-wide and special events. In order to maximize the use of buses, recreational supervisors are requested to coordinate activities requiring transportation with nearby centers, within their district, if possible.

i. Facility Improvement. A supervisor of a facility may initiate a request for improvement of the facility on a form specifically designed for that purpose. The request may concern remodelling, renovating, or adding to the facility which would result in substantial modifications of the existing facility. The individual initiating the request for improvement should provide full details of the proposed modifications, including estimates of the probable cost of the project, sketches, line drawings, and the reasons for the proposed improvement. If the request is approved, complete plans and specifications are drawn up and action is taken upon the modification.

j. Requisition for Supplies, Materials, and Equipment. It is the responsibility of the supervisor of a facility to anticipate the needs of the program and to request an adequate supply of material to carry out program operations. All requisitions are transmitted to the proper storeroom at a date fixed by local need.

k. Criticisms and Complaints by the Public. On occasion, justifiable criticisms and complaints are received by departmental personnel. All such complaints must receive careful consideration and be reported to the proper supervisors. Where a situation appears to warrant immediate action, the proper supervisor is notified by telephone, so that the matter can be attended to without delay. In reporting complaints, care should be taken to give full details concerning time, place, individuals involved, and the situations about which the complaint is made. Courtesy and intelligence may be the best way to handle many of the complaints and tend to build up good public relations.

l. Fires. Should a department facility sustain a fire from which any damage results, a telephone report must be made immediately to the proper supervisor. Such a report should be followed by a written report to the central office. The report should contain the name of the facility, the date of the fire, the hour at which the fire occurred, how it was discovered, where it took place within the facility, the extent of damage, a list of property destroyed, the cause or suspected cause of the fire, any other pertinent information which can assist in fixing responsibility, and precautions or regulations that can be taken to prevent similar occurrences.

m. Disturbances or Unusual Situations. Whenever any unusual condition occurs at any recreational facility, the supervisor is required to notify his immediate superior. A written report is to be made at the earliest practicable time thereafter.

n. Referral Problems. Occasionally, problems of a nature not consistent with the work of the department will come to the attention of workers. These should be referred to the proper authorities and/or other municipal agencies organized to provide assistance in the area of social welfare cases. Nevertheless, the recreationist should be knowledgeable about, and have pertinent information of, other agencies specifically concerned with social welfare problems.

o. Vandalism. In addition to the problem of maintaining the facility in a clean and attractive manner, all employees should be alert to detect any markings on any interior or exterior surfaces. Such offensive markings mar the facility and must be removed as soon as possible after detection.

p. Utilization of Equipment. All employees must be aware of the hazards which exist if equipment is utilized improperly. Employees should always insist that equipment and other apparatus be used in a manner consistent with the safety of the participant.

q. Care of Equipment and Supplies. Each facility will have one employee responsible for the condition and maintenance of all equipment, supplies, and materials charged to the specific facility.

r. Loan of Equipment. Depending upon departmental policy and philosophy, the lending of equipment, supplies, or providing material assistance to other agencies within the community, but not a part of the department, may or may not be permitted. If such lending is permitted, it is usually done on a priority basis, with all departmental needs having precedence over all recipients. The policy may require the posting of a bond or payment of some fee which is held in escrow until said material is returned in the same status as when borrowed.

s. Storage and Maintenance of Equipment and Supplies. All material should be stored neatly for easy accessibility. The storage area should be locked when the supplies are not in use. Keep a perpetual inventory of all material in storage. Label all dangerous materials and store them in accordance with their respective instructions. Use good housekeeping procedures when dealing with combustible materials.

t. Repair and Salvage Operations. All damaged or worn equipment, supplies, and materials may be salvaged and repaired or renovated to the extent that they become serviceable. All such items which cannot be repaired or used at the local center should be collected and transported to the central repair shop of the agency. In order to secure correct distribution and credit, all such items should be clearly marked with the name of the center.

u. Care and Use of Floors. The multipurpose use of floors makes them of great importance in the maintenance of the facility. All employees can perform an excellent service by careful supervision of participants in order to avoid abuse of wooden floors. Specific rules for the care and maintenance of all floors, whether of wood, asphalt, tile, or some other material, conform to the best preventive maintenance in practice.

v. Keys to Departmental Facilities. Issuance of keys to all departmental facilities is limited to those employees requiring keys to specific facilities or centers. No unauthorized person shall have a key to a department facility. All keys are issued and accounted for by receipt. When personnel who have custody of department keys are transferred, resign, retire, or are otherwise terminated, all keys that have been issued are accounted for prior to clearance. No employee shall have duplicate keys made for any facility. If an employee loses a key through negligence the cost of replacement will be charged to that person. Any loss of keys to departmental facilities must be reported immediately to the employee's supervisor.

w. Furnishings and Decorations. At particular recreational facilities, live Christmas trees may be used. Only electric lights will be used for decorative purposes and these shall be installed by electricians employed by the department. Artificial Christmas trees are fireproofed by the department and almost any decoration may be used upon them. However, all decorations must conform to fire department regulations.

1) When installing decorations for parties or dances, care must be taken to see that such effects do not interfere with the usual program in the center. All sponsored groups using their own furnishings and decorations shall install and remove same, subject to the approval of the facility supervisor.
2) All decorations must be installed in such ways that they will not mar the surface to which they are attached. Such decorations will conform to fire department regulations.
3) All flammable materials shall be fireproofed.

Much could be written about recording all manifestations of the agency's program and operations, but the ramifications would be overpowering.

It is enough simply to indicate the previously mentioned possible classifications of duties, functions, and responsibilities without spelling out
the multiple details that constitute administrative procedure for any
single agency. Large departments will, of necessity, have to submit to
greater detail and variety in systematically recording standard activities
undertaken on a daily basis. Nevertheless, every agency, regardless of
size, should have a procedural manual to which staff members can refer.
Its size and type will reflect upon the size of the department staff and all
the operating considerations which together make up the entire agency.

Significantly, administrative and other divisional manuals indicate
the degree of control and influence the department has upon public
confidence and conduct, inasmuch as the largest segments of the manual
are supportive of routine acts. These routine operations are a direct
measure of public esteem, because where the public has continually
utilized the agency's program and become accustomed to agency policy it
tends to accept the department as a necessary service. Thus, routine
activities require standardized procedures because of the volume of
requests, suggestions, and criticisms received and the number of participants. Departmental sponsorship and organization make possible
the speedy translation of recreational requests to standard operating
procedures. This does not remove the department's responsibility to
be creative. On the contrary, it requires the agency's staff to be constantly
creative in supplying new recreational concepts and activities to a public
that continually demands new and broadening experiences. Routinization
must not mean stagnation. Reducing many or most contingent factors to
a basic routine merely saves time and effort by not having to look for
answers which by the very volume of demand require standardizing.
Routine quantifies particular facts, classifies them, and promotes a rapid
system whereby repetitive activities may be processed more readily.
Administration is the process which attempts to coordinate and facilitate
a variety of functions performed by diverse personnel in order that the
most comprehensive and effective program of recreational activities will
result. To this end, all phases of planning, organizing, supervising, and
directing the utilization of financial support, physical plant, property,
and personnel are undertaken. Proper administration is vital if organized recreational services are to be valuable to the public. Administration of recreational services has only one outcome and that is the
production of high-quality organized recreational experiences. The development and operation of recreational activities for people is the only

reason for justifying administration. The chief purpose of all administration is the improvement, extension, and provision of high-quality planned recreational opportunities in an optimal environment.

To effect a harmonious relationship between professional personnel and the normal daily requirement of public participation within the program, a detailed system of administrative procedures which often minimizes friction in handling routine matters is helpful. Such procedures, in the form of manuals, should not be interpreted as confining professional activities nor reducing professional functions to mere paperwork managers. The manual is designed to alleviate purely routine reporting and will never restrict the recreationist in the performance of his professional responsibilities. All rules and regulations that are necessary and developed over a long period of time, while the department is in operation, record particular behavioral controls which assist in departmental success. These standardized procedures should never become the last word in personnel management, but are useful as guides in meeting the countless questions and problems that may have arisen over a period of years. It is important to emphasize that all recreationists employed by the department should be concerned with and participate in the development of operating manuals.

The administrative process is necessarily elastic because it deals with people and changing conditions or situations. Adroit administration strikes a nice balance between the individual needs and interests of recreationists and the smooth operation of the department. Professionalization will more than compensate for the latitude given to the recreationist in the conduct of recreational affairs. Rigidity of structure and circumscribing policies and regulations will do more to hinder the competent worker than almost any other procedure, except, perhaps, poor supervision. Large departments with numerous personnel are forced to enact systematized methods for working with personnel. In some instances, this proves beneficial to all concerned. However, the best administration is that which allows the highly competent and professional worker to do the job and carry out its responsibilities with a minimum of direct regulation and a maximal respect for personal integrity and desire to do the best job possible. Administration exists to facilitate worker needs in performing the only justifiable reason for employment, the production of a comprehensive, worthwhile, and satisfying recreational program.

Chapter 9

FINANCING PUBLIC RECREATIONAL SERVICE

I f recreational service on the municipal level is a distinctive governmental function, why do so many community recreational service
departments experience budgetary problems? The municipal, county,
state, or federal recreational service agency should be accorded the same
place in the governmental hierarchy as are other long-established
departments. No other department is expected to return a profit or to
underwrite its own support, yet municipal departments of recreational
service are enjoined, even demanded, to return money to the general
fund of the community. This is inequitable, dangerous, and indefensible.

Noted authorities in law, urban planning, public administration,
sociology, and education have long and repeatedly stated that municipal
recreational service must be treated as an essential governmental function and not as a reducible frill. Many experts spell out in detail the
advisability of providing a firm tax base to support the program and
necessary facilities for the operation and maintenance of public recreational
services. Why, then, do public recreational service agencies continue to
depend on sources other than taxes for their developed activities? Should
public or governmentally operated recreational service agencies be denied
adequate tax support? Why do so many communities assess fees and
charges for activities which are supposed to be free to the general public?
How can public recreational service departments justify returning excessive amounts of money to the municipal general fund? Is there something wrong with the modern municipal concept of operating local
public recreational service departments? On what basis should fees be
charged, or is there ever any activity or facility which should require
attached user fees? These questions constitute some of the most serious
and complicated problems confronting public recreational service agencies throughout the country.

Every legitimate and legal precedent points unalterably to the fact
that public recreational service is, indeed, a governmental function. If
the use of the term *public* has any meaning whatsoever, it connotes

201

accessibility by people to the services of a governmental agency without additional fees or charges. It certainly means open to the public, free of charge, and supported *"in toto"* by taxes. Whenever public agencies begin to assess fees and tack on charges to services that are supposed to be paid for by an appropriation from the general municipal fund, there is complete nullification of the principle of public recreational service. Such practices fly in the face of the concept of governmental function and public agency. Obviously, this is an extremely common practice. There is little possibility that any public recreational service agency exists in this country today which does not in some way supplement its tax appropriation with fees and charges. Does this mean that such practice is either good or right? Most administrators of departments defend the user fee on the basis that they require additional money to perpetuate the operation of the agency or that those who utilize the service should pay for it directly. Is this a true statement? Let us look at the facts.

Almost all revenue collected by municipal departments of recreational service is turned over to the general fund. Few agencies have special or earmarked funds designed to set aside revenues for the specific purpose of extending public recreational services. The simple truth is that most municipalities use the funds returned to it from fees and charges, posted by recreational service departments, for other municipal functions. Such monies may be utilized to build new public buildings, augment personnel on the police and fire departments, purchase new city vehicles, maintain streets, lights, sewers, and other public works; but rarely are they employed to provide additional public recreational service. The department must still fight for its appropriation from the general fund along with all other municipal agencies.

Legitimate Sources of Recreational Funds

The impetus to place public recreational service on the same level with other local departments of the municipality has progressed despite, rather than as a result of, community sentiment. Average citizens would much rather spend money, whatever the price, for those things from which they benefit personally than pay a slightly higher tax rate for those services that will benefit the entire community. Human nature being what it is, selfishness and personal aggrandizement are more readily apparent and consistent than the larger view of community welfare and social betterment. The fact that more than 10 billion dollars is spent each year in the United States on personal consumption of liquor, and that school, park, and recreational land and facility acquisition are so often turned down in public referenda surely bears out this view. Nevertheless, it is only on the basis of tax support that public recreational service departments can or should operate.

Donations and Grants. The public agency has the right to and should accept all gifts, bequests, endowments, awards, donations, and grants of real or personal property and money or other articles of value, insofar as such gifts do not involve the corporate entity in litigation or where the acceptance of such articles, items, or objects would cost more to maintain or operate than they are worth. Philanthropic organizations are more than welcome to provide financial support for experimental or continuing activities which the department can organize and administer. Subventions from the state, bond issues (which involve voluntary taxation), federal grants, rebates, and allowances are all legally constituted methods of supporting public recreational services of various types. Wherein is the rub? With all of these sources, the fundamental program of balanced activities may not be supported adequately, and the cost of capital improvements are almost never carried by a general fund appropriation.

Fees and Charges. Fees, charges, and/or concession operations are possible sources of money for the public recreational service department. Because public recreational service is a genuine function of government and not a proprietary or profit-making effort, the idea of charging for the very services that are supposed to be free appears to negate the premise on which the public sector of the field stands. The public agency is not in *business,* nor can it afford to compete with private enterprise. It cannot sell commodities, goods, or services that are obtainable through purchase in the private sector of the community. To do so would invite massive retaliation by commercial organizations who could justifiably charge that the public agency is taking unfair advantage of its position. Yet there is a defensible position for the public agency to take in the question of assessments or user fees and concession charges.

A legitimate instance of user fee assessment would be those activities in which a small group of persons receives intense personal instruction in an activity which normally would not employ personnel for such a particular object. Instruction is an essential part of the recreational program. No one should have to pay for it because it is an integral part of the ongoing series of activities administered by the department. However, if it is some esoteric instruction in yoga, flying, conversational foreign language, or short-hand lessons, where the skills involved are not necessarily those which the typical recreationist would possess, the department could and should attach a fee for instructional services. If the activity gained such popularity that it requires the department, in the interest of extending recreational possibilities, to employ a full-time instructor to handle this activity, the fee should be withdrawn and an appropriate budgetary line item substituted to support this activity. For experimental activities, in which there is no background of how popular it will become or to what extent it will attract potential participants to the agency, the fee is attached. As soon as the activity proves itself and becomes a routine part of the departmental offering, all fees should be withdrawn. This, for all practical intents and purposes, is another part of the fundamental program of activities. When the activity, under such circumstances, is assumed by the department as a routine item and later loses its popularity, or interest disappears, then either the activity is dropped or, for those few who still want to participate, the fee is reestablished.

Maintenance of buildings, grounds, and facilities should not require user fees. Maintenance is a legitimate ongoing overhead expense which the agency will have whether people participate in a given activity or not. The golf course will still have to be watered, mowed, cultivated, rolled, and so on, whether 10, 100, or 100,000 persons utilize it. The same thing holds true for swimming pools, beaches, community centers, parks, playgrounds, boating facilities, tennis courts, fields, game courts, and other equally important areas. Fees should not be demanded for use of these places. They have been acquired, constructed, and developed as the base upon which all, or almost all, the programmed recreational activities of the agency stand. Without them there would hardly be a program, at least not a very attractive program. Then how are these facilities to be financed? The typical answer is pay-as-you-go revenue bonds. This may, in fact, be a logical answer, but one vital aspect is being ignored in the rush to capitalize on the modern physical plant—a tax appropriation to cover the capital investment, or borrowing.

A few experts insist upon segregating capital from routine budget items. They maintain that any commercial enterprise would not note as an expenditure a sum disbursed to construct a storage tank, let us say, but would carry it as an asset and would establish for it a plan for depreciation and amortization. A community center, swimming pool, golf course, or park, if paid for prior to obsolescence, should be viewed as an asset. It is also true that capital expenditures in local jurisdictions do not run evenly. The financing of a swimming pool might be disastrous if it had to be paid for in one year.

The chief hazard of the separated capital budget is the concomitant inclination to rest completely on borrowed money. All bankers relish the thought of governmental indebtedness, but the taxpayer should demand that such practice be halted. It is no rarity for municipalities to have 25 per cent of their tax funds absolutely tied to the debt service and 50 per cent of the commitment awarded to interest, and the other half for retirement of the principal sum. It has been stated that the larger and more affluent the jurisdiction, the less defense there is for debt. As Charlesworth states:

> After a society has become stabilized, however, it has no routine phases; the rounded and mixed character of its make-up gives it a constant statistical average. It is not the *nature* or the *size* of the project that determines whether bonds should be issued or assessments increased; it is the *indivisible character* of the project that is controlling. If the project is big and also indivisible, and the jurisdiction is small, borrowing must be resorted to; in all other cases the improvement should be handled in stride.[1]

There are situations where the community is so affluent that not one of its citizens would be financially hurt if fees were assessed for various services. For example, if an individual can afford a boat, he or she can afford the charge for mooring it at a public dock or marina. If an individual's taste runs to horseback riding, he or she can afford the fee for the hour's ride, particularly if this occurs in the urban center. In a community where affluence is average the individual may wish to join the public golf course association and pay a yearly fee, instead of belonging to a private country club where the dues are presumably much higher. This may be permissible. However, what of the not-so-affluent individual residing in the same community? Perhaps the person, too, wants to play golf (the game is no longer a rich person's sport), but cannot afford the yearly fee. The individual must either save money for the fee, play only intermittently, or not at all. Is this fair? In this society an individual must learn to differentiate between what is personally valuable and what is not so valuable. If playing golf is more valuable than another activity, which may cost nothing, then the individual is obligated to save until the game of choice can be afforded. Does this void

---

[1]J. C. Charlesworth, *Governmental Administration* (New York: Harper and Row, Publishers, 1951), p. 327.

the idea of public agency service? Does it defeat the very purpose for which the agency was established?

Where every individual in the community is solvent enough to have a boat and boats are an accepted recreational activity, then community marinas should be supported by tax monies. However, where the community follows the usual economic levels from wealth to poverty and boating is not considered an ongoing recreational activity for all, it would be most discriminatory for the not so affluent to have to help support, by tax monies, the free use of mooring facilities. In such instances, fees for such use should be fixed. Yachting, motorboating, aeroplane piloting and ownership, polo, riding to the hounds, are still not considered ongoing activities of the routine recreational program. These experiences require individual wealth that is beyond the capability of most persons. Under these conditions, riding stables maintained by the municipality, the community airport, marina, community polo field, should all be maintained and supported by user fees. Should the time ever come when such activities are participated in by everyone, or where each individual expects to be able to participate in activities of this type, then they should be made part of the basic recreational program and supported by tax funds.

Concessions. Another possible source of revenue is available to the public recreational service department, that of profits from operating concessions. Concessions are all those operations dispensing goods and services not offered by the department, but farmed out on a bid and morals basis to businesses which guarantee to return money to the agency. In fact, concessions have come to be looked upon, in certain quarters, as political patronage plums. Unscrupulous politicians have sometimes helped themselves to a profit at the public's expense by requiring personally owned commercial enterprises, or those with whom they have some business connection, to operate in the areas controlled or operated by the public department. If this is not the case, there are other disadvantages in having commercial operators selling commodities. The public facility, whether beach, park, center, or some other structure, has been financed from tax monies. It is illogical and not in the best interests of the citizens of the community to have private commercial enterprises operating businesses and making a profit from the taxes invested in public facilities. There is, however, a clear and purposeful step which recreational service agencies may take. Instead of backing away from the responsibility of operating snack bars, restaurants, and other amenity service shops and stands, the departments should actually have a complete division or bureau that does nothing but operate such enterprises.

The goods and services that can be sold in public places or at public facilities are those that make the patron's visit to the facility more enjoyable. They may be food or items for use at picnics, outings, for games, sports, or bird-watching. The only stipulation concerning the public agency's operation is that there be no excessive profit attached to the selling. Goods and services must be provided at the lowest possible cost and should cover the expense of providing the personnel, overhead, and cost of the commodity. Sale of space, as for the parking of cars, should be nominal to help defray the cost of constructing the parking lot and the salaries of employees, and any surplus should be applied to offset the cost of activities. Revenues from the sale of locker space, checking clothing, or vending machines can be applied to personnel wages and construction and maintenance of additional facilities which would not be considered a budgetary item for recreational service. Amenity items and services are justified on a proprietary basis, in that they are a convenience for the patron and not a necessity for the production of satisfying experiences.

Sponsorship. A public department may attempt to finance specific activities or underwrite the development of certain physical facilities by appealing to the generosity of national or international corporations. Some communities have been successful in obtaining corporate gifts which sponsor camp scholarships for inner-city youth, tournaments, and trips, pay for advertising through mass media, refurbish a community center, establish a park or bank of tennis courts. Of course, the sponsoring agency receives excellent publicity and goodwill in return. The money expended by the company can become a tax write-off as well. Other local business enterprises may sponsor particular activities or donate equipment, supplies, or materials in return for having the company mentioned in any news release given or program notice printed. Money for the support of public recreational service is usually generated from a number of contributors. By far the greatest source of money is derived through taxation. Additionally, funding may also be enhanced by obtaining money from bonds, grants-in-aid, and non-tax income from fees, charges, concessions, business enterprises, and gifts. Most of the revenues received by local governments for operating recreational services are produced through a general property tax. Additional monetary resources may also come from central government grants-in-aid to municipalities or other local jurisdictions, i.e., special recreational service districts, for the development of specific recreational facilities or programs. Earnings, chiefly from public service enterprises, business taxes, personal income taxes, license fees, franchises, fines, forfeits, donations, fees collected, and charges levied for special services rendered or amenities and material provided, account for the rest of the revenues.

Taxes

Typically, the funding of public recreational service is directly obtained from local tax revenues. Taxes used for these purposes constitute four major categories: general, special, millage, and special assessment.

The general tax is levied upon real and personal property. Each year an assessed value is made on all such property by the appropriate governmental official who is usually designated as the assessor. The total assessed value of all taxable property is divided into the amount of revenue that will be needed so that the tax rate can be determined. The general real estate tax normally provides support for most local services. For this very reason community recreational service has not been adequately financed. Functions of local governments have greatly increased in cost and number in recent years. In the face of rising tax rates and its position within government, public recreational service suffers by comparison to public safety, health, and welfare services. Recreational service finds it difficult to justify its existence in a world that is growing more mechanized, congested, and expensive. Just at a time when people's leisure has begun to increase at an unprecedented rate, when the need for community recreational services has increased proportionately, there has also been rapid swings from boom to recession with concomitant decreases in the real value of what money can purchase. Under these circumstances, all governments have found it extraordinarily difficult to appropriate funds which could satisfy the demands made for public recreational service.

In various places, reliance upon a general property tax is being supplemented or actually superseded by the imposition of income taxes on residents and nonresidents who work within the municipality. However, this does not constitute a major source of revenue on the local level, as yet. Naturally any personal tax on income would have to represent the chief source of revenue for the central government. In recent years, the state has found itself in the position of supplying a wide variety of resources to local legal subdivisions. There are more subventions (direct grants for special purposes) than before as well as direct financial support to cities and towns for recreational services. During recessions, however, state support diminishes to negligible proportions with cuts in local services as a direct result.

Special Taxes. Whenever a special recreational service district has been initiated, special taxes may be used to support public recreational service. Imposts on a broad range of items, including liquor, admissions, motorboat fuel, sport and game supplies, may be given directly to the support of district services. Of course, where the state organizes special recreational service districts, it can be a direct supplier of finances simply utilizing the district organization as an immediate conduit for the promotion of local recreational functions by the central government.

Millage Taxes. A millage tax, denoted in mills (a mill is one-tenth of a cent), is usually levied against the assessed valuation of residential or industrial assets. The amount obtained is given to the local recreational service department in the form of a fund solely for that purpose. The advantage of having a distinct tax of this type is that residents are taxed directly for the support of recreational services. If the service is viewed as being valuable to the people they will continue to support it.

Special Assessment Taxes. In some localities it is generally accepted that taxes will accrue to those few residents who benefit directly from a specific service performed by the municipality. In some instances special assessment taxes are used to finance the development and construction of recreational facilities and parks emplaced in pre-selected neighborhoods and designed to supply services to residents of only that section of the community.

Allocation of Tax Monies

Almost everywhere, the financial needs of the recreational service department are considered by the authorizing bodies prior to the beginning of the fiscal year. Appropriations are then made in the budget to provide for the needs with equitable consideration also for the capacity of the locale to meet them. The claims of public recreational service must be judged in comparison with the claims of many other governmental functions.

In this day, governmental functions which are not readily perceived as necessary to the security of the people or mandated, as is education, is somewhat at a disadvantage in this procedure. There is an inevitable tendency to accommodate the more established, and by implication the more important, functions first and then reluctantly to squeeze out small appropriations to those departments whose functions are only dimly recognized as being significant to the people served. With the ever present unwillingness to increase the tax rate, relatively new functions do poorly unless there is an unmistakable and broadly based public demand in their favor. Recreational service is one of these newer governmental functions, and has not yet achieved sufficient general recognition to warrant compelling public support.

Recreational services are extremely important for the public's well being and quality of life, but the necessity of providing for them rarely seems pressing. The attitude among members of governing bodies appears to be that these needs may be deferred while more urgent needs are taken care of first.

It is likely that the future support of public recreational service will depend in great measure on the ability of the appropriate government to commit itself to the financing of purely local recreational services as well as those services which account for more regional and/or general populations. The aid rendered by the government through establishment of special districts can be replicated in metropolitan districts and other population centers as well. Permanent federal financing of a function which heretofore has been considered purely local could occur as the state becomes the only viable source of funds through income taxes. Of course, cost sharing between local and central government may become the surest method for the support of this function.

Financing Major Property Acquisitions and Improvements

Financing land acquisitions and improvement for community recreational service is often more difficult than obtaining budgetary allocations for the maintenance and operation of recreational facilities after they have been installed. Once facilities have been acquired the necessity for maintaining and operating them is obvious; moreover, once an allowance has been made in the municipal budget for maintenance and operation, there is a disposition to continue it year after year unless there is a sharp curtailment of the general fund. Unfortunately, financial resources of many of today's communities have been so stretched that even operational allocations weaken or stop with a consequent closure of some facilities.

The continuation of the established municipal services is a primary obligation upon the revenue of the municipal government. When these have been estimated, accretions and installations to municipal holdings are then considered. Land costs rise annually, as do the expenses for offering many city functions. This is partially explained by union demands for employees, economic cycles, and the natural expectation of workers to obtain higher wages and salaries. Thus, it is increasingly difficult to finance additions to land and improvements from the current revenues derived from the general property tax and other similar sources. Other methods must be found and used.

Pay-As-You-Go. The pay-as-you-go plan requires that all additions and improvements of a capital nature will be made annually, to the extent that the government has the financial resources to pay for them. While all cities should try to use this procedure, the tremendous variety of improvements required drains the funds available from current revenues. Generally, comparatively inexpensive projects of a recreational type have been benefited by this method.

Financing by Bond Issues. Bonding represents a second major financial source for municipal recreational service property acquisition and improvements. Bond issues with few exceptions require submission of the definite proposition to the electors at a general or special election called for the purpose. Usually a two-thirds majority in favor of the issue is needed before it can be made. After approval, the retirement of the bonds and interest on them are a charge against the assessable real property of the taxpayers, although the tax rate therefore is separately computed and listed on the individual tax bill. Legislation limits the amount of bonds that a city can issue for general governmental purposes, including recreational service.

Cities have been more inclined to vote bonds for the acquisition and improvement of large regional parks and for parkways than for neighborhood recreational places. However, as public recreational service becomes better understood and residents are aware of their own need for recreational experiences it is likely that city bond issues will include acquisitions and improvements of neighborhood and completely local recreational areas and facilities.

The scarcity of neighborhood recreational centers in nearly all cities presents a problem of finance which municipalities will increasingly have to face in the future. The rate of progress in acquiring these facilities through annual appropriations from current tax funds is absolutely unsatisfactory. It appears reasonable to assume that as old bond issues voted in days of relative prosperity are retired, cities will be able and more willing to adopt comprehensive plans for land acquisition and improvement which is based upon the concept that every residential neighborhood must have its community recreational center, adequate in size and appointments to be efficient in its service and a credit to its neighborhood. This is a goal which will not be attained easily. It is especially true in the light of the need to rebuild or re-plan cities. The areas that will be required are in many cases in neighborhoods already congested and in which there is no vacant land. The acquisition of a suitable property with sufficient acreage in such neighborhoods will require the condemnation and purchase of many developed lots in each instance; unless, of course, school buildings are used for these purposes after the school day.

Bonds represent a method of deferred payment by which the cost of procuring property and its subsequent development can be made. There are a variety of bond forms, which vary according to the method of payment or the way in which funds are collected for the debt service. Among the common types of bonds are term, callable, serial, general obligation, revenue, and assessment bonds. Description of these bonds is beyond the scope of this text.

Financial Earnings of Recreational Service Departments

Although public recreational service is universally thought to be a free public service supported by taxation, there is a certain tendency to procure some financial support from the collection of fees and the imposition of charges for a variety of services and commodities.

Perhaps the most often cited reason for fees and charges is that special services enjoyed by a few should not be a charge upon all of the tax-payers and should be paid directly by those who enjoy the special benefit. It is, therefore, the special nature of the service or privilege offered which provides substantiation for the imposition of fees and charges. No one advocates that all community recreational service should be self-sustaining, nor that the ability to support itself should be the deciding factor as to whether or not a given function will be supplied in the program. To do so would be equivalent to stating that public recreational service should not be a governmental concern since it can be rendered on a commercial basis.

Positions for and Against Fees and Charges

Those who oppose the levying of fees and charges do so from the standpoint that those who commercialize the service forget its recreational and educational intent and judge the success purely by the profits realized. The attitude thus taken is that any activity is successful to the degree it produces revenue sufficient to be self-supporting or, of even more importance, to turn a profit for the agency. With this attitude foremost there is a decided inclination to select personnel to operate the department in a manner consistent with business rather than recreational standards.

Another major consideration against imposition of fees and charges is that if additional fees are to be levied or charges are to be assessed, those who most require recreational services in their lives will be least able to afford it. Public recreational service is the last recourse of those community residents who cannot afford anything else or whose economic status is such that they cannot pay private commercial establishments for the recreational services which government has come to accept as its own province.

Those who argue for fees and charges state that the practice of charging for recreational service affects favorably the behavior of those who participate. This point of view may well be questioned. It is more probable that when fees are levied or charges made, more effective measures of control of the public are established. This is self-fulfilling because such control is expected by those who have paid for the service, and the desire to collect added revenue has made the control measure necessary. It is also likely that fees and charges may select a class of patronage which is more amenable to control.

Perhaps the chief proposal for the imposition of fees and charges comes in terms of having those who use facilities and engage in activities actually pay for them, instead of spreading the cost equally among all residents. It is also stated that the use of additional fees and charges is the major means by which departments can continue to supply quality programs and maintain facilities; without such revenues programs would be greatly limited. Finally, proponents of fees and charges maintain that the willingness of the public to pay for special activities or any activities is a valuable guide for the planning of installations and the development of the program.

Earning Sources

Earnings of recreational service departments obtained from fees and charges are of three different kinds; first, charges for recreational service; second, charges for commodities or amenities which are incidental to participation in recreational activities; and third, earnings from services rendered of a nonrecreational nature and which have no direct relation to the public recreational program. The policies which need to be adopted by a recreational service department should be different with respect to each of the three sources of earnings.

Contemporary Practices Concerning Fees and Charges

For services of a purely recreational character, fees and charges are levied for participant use of recreational areas and facilities and for receiving instruction. Fees levied include the following:

1. Entrance fees to swimming pools, beaches, golf courses, tennis courts, stadiums, auditoriums, zoological parks, museums, and night-lighted facilities.
2. Entry fees are typically collected for use by participants at golf driving ranges, archery ranges, skeet shooting facilities, and rifle and pistol ranges. Fees are by the hour or by the unit of equipment used, e.g., number of golf balls issued for practice drives, etc.
3. Winter sport facilities may charge for participation, particularly where tow or aerial lift must be operated. Indoor ice-skating rinks also have entrance fees.
4. A fee for individual and small group instruction is generally charged for lessons in golf, swimming, gymnastics, art, crafts, music, dance, drama, tennis, foreign languages, horseback riding, mountain climbing, scuba diving, sailing, and other specialized instruction.

Fees are also charged for the administration of athletic leagues and tournaments. Because of increased popularity of organized athletic events, and a concomitant demand on the part of the participating and spectator public for highly qualified officiating, as well as excellent facilities, there needs to be some form of payment made to cover operations. Charges are imposed to cover the organization of teams into leagues; the drawing and publishing of schedules for play; services of qualified officials such as referees, umpires, linemen, and others; any extrinsic awards given to winners; and incidental expenses connected with highly involved competitive athletics. Moreover, a forfeiture fee to guarantee the appearance of teams and registration fees for individual athletes may also be levied.

Establishing Fees and Charges

Only a maladroit administrator would exploit the public by presuming that fees and charges should be in amounts that will finance the department. When fees are charged they must be determined with the best interest of the public in mind and should never be what the traffic can bear. This would defeat the very purpose of public recreational service. If it is to be considered a commercial venture only, then the proper administration of it would be the private sector. Since this is patently not the case, then a judicious blend of discrimination and real costs will determine the amounts of fees and charges to be levied.

In general, recreationists agree that recreational services in the public sector should be delivered without charges if adequate funds from other sources can be obtained to make the policy feasible. If it becomes necessary to levy fees and charges for recreational and nonrecreational service or for commodities offered and rendered, the need for policy to guide this action is advisable.

The paramount problem associated with fees and charges is that they tend to deprive the poor and other persons with special needs from obtaining recreational experiences which are considered to be valuable to all people. Even when charges are moderate, they are usually too high for families who are poor, particularly when the expense of transportation is added. To deprive those most in need of the values of access to public recreational service is indefensible. Therefore, provision must be made for service to those of low economic means. Facilities or activities that normally have an admissions fee or charge can be made available for certain sessions during the week without charge. Facilities in poorer neighborhoods may operate without fees and charges. Special arrangements may be made to permit poor people to participate without out-of-pocket cost to them.

Dangers of Revenue-Producing Resources

Rather than offer a detailed statement on dangers inherent in the development of fees, charges, and excessive concession profits, a listing of questionable practices and outcomes should suffice.

1. The practice of assessing fees and charges to ongoing recreational activities under public agency sponsorship negates the concept of tax support and generic governmental function.
2. There is a hazard that unenlightened political or managerial authorities will use the recreational service department for the production of monies to subsidize municipal government.
3. Fees and charges attached to programmed activities defeat the purpose for which the agency was originally established.
4. One specific danger lies in the municipality's attempt to employ individuals who are not career recreationists to administer the department for business purposes rather than for public services.
5. Political patronage for past favors may result in the establishment of party cronies as executives, with fees and charges being used to "pay off" politically incurred debts.
6. Charging whatever the traffic will bear commercializes a public function of government, usurps the prerogatives of the private sector, restricts participation to those who can afford to pay, sets up the climate for double taxation, and places unlimited temptation upon the administrator to ignore the preemptive aspect of recreational service orientation in favor of simply making profits.
7. If fees and charges are permanently affixed to the municipal function of recreational service provision, it is likely that the body politic will begin to wonder why they have to continue to pay taxes to support an operation for which they have to pay an additional user fee. Enlightened taxpayers will seek to determine why an apparent public agency requires fees and charges in order to function at all. With such questioning comes a breakdown in public trust and support of the recreational service department.
8. No other municipal agency, for example, police, fire, health, or public works, charges fees for performance of the service for which they were established. No other municipal agency is expected to furnish a steady source of revenue which will apply to the general fund. Continued charges for services which in theory are supposed to be supported by taxes will undermine the agency's governmental status and revert it to a quasi-public or proprietary function.
9. The individuals who require the public recreational service most— children, older adults, out-of-school youngsters, and others who are on the fringes of an affluent society—will be adversely affected by a pay-as-you-use agency. The very people the agency should be

attempting to reach and satisfy are the ones who will be most discriminated against by fees and charges.

10. It may be that activities will be programmed only on the basis of profits generated. There are some activities, which because of mass appeal, can be organized with charges assessed for entrance. It would be unfortunate, indeed, if only those activities which stimulated great spectator interest would be offered as a consequence of being able to produce revenue for the municipality. There are agencies, at this time, whose policy for the selection of recreational activities is based on revenue production.

Some general standards apply to the financing of public recreational service. The following concepts are thought to be of a practical and ethical approach.

1. Because society identifies recreational experience as a significant aspect of human life and has accepted responsibility for the provision of recreational services through governmental jurisdictions in the public sector, it must furnish basic recreational activities and the financial resources needed to support such activities.

2. In order to carry out the mandate set by the body politic, governments are established to satisfy welfare needs of society. The increasing demand for public recreational facilities, spaces, and programming indicates an explicit approval of the expenditure of tax resources for such recreational service.

3. Although there is no scientifically established standard for the determination of per capita expenditures for recreational services, other municipal functions may be studied to provide some estimation of what the costs are for financing public recreational activities. It must be understood that finances are necessary not only for spaces, facilities, and personnel salaries, but for the continually expanding variety of activities being programmed by creative recreationists. Items are now being included in budget requests which were not in existence 10 years ago.

4. Appropriated funds should be used in a discriminating manner. Although it is true that there are no special recreational neighborhoods in communities, for example, where a low-end socioeconomic neighborhood receives the largest center, outdoor facilities, or increased leadership personnel and higher income neighborhoods receive little, the examination of neighborhoods within the

community will tend to reveal the recreational habits and consumption of recreational resources and activities by residents. Where there is a lower social and economic level prevalent in a neighborhood, the likelihood does exist that a larger percentage of appropriated tax funds should be spent there. The rationale for such a statement is the economic rule of diminishing returns. Where individuals are thoroughly capable of determining their own recreational pursuits on a private basis, they will probably seek facilities other than public ones for their experiences. Lower income groups, on the other hand, do not have the financial resource necessary to engage in many non-publicly sponsored recreational activities and therefore rely upon them to a greater degree than do the more affluent. Tax money should be expended where the need is greatest and where the return for such expenditures will bring optimal fulfillment and satisfaction.

5. Wherever there are recreational user fees for public agency programs, there is a question of whether the agency is adhering to basic concepts and principles of governmental function. Essentially, all recreational activities for which there is an expected participation should be free of all costs. In rare and special circumstances, such as experimental or special service experiences, fees may be attached. Such charges, however should not be used to support other phases of the program. They should be at cost and be utilized specifically to offset nonbudgeted monetary needs. Such fees must be reasonable and apply only until such time as the activity is either integrated into the ongoing comprehensive program or dropped from the scheduled activities.

6. Budgeted appropriations must be scrupulously earmarked for the purpose of funding the department of recreational service. Unless tax funds are so allocated they may be used for functions other than those originally intended.

7. In general, recreational activities that are universal in appeal and which satisfy a common need must be offered free of charge.

8. Fees or charges may be justified on the basis of providing a special facility or activity to a small group when there is a lack of appeal for the activity to the general public.

9. When participation in an activity is closed to the general public and limited to a private membership exclusively, a fee for the provision of the faculty, activity, or other resource services may be

charged. Such exclusive activities, if provided at all, on public property should be operated at the expense of those benefiting from such services.

10. When the service is received by nonresidents who are not taxpayers in the jurisdiction where the service is rendered, a fee may be charged. The justification for such fees comes from prohibiting outsiders from utilizing such services or for making the nonresident share in bearing the cost of operation. If there were such a thing as reciprocal taxation, where municipalities prorated payments on the basis of their residents using other cities' recreational facilities and activities, there would be no justification for assessing nonresidents. However, this is not practical nor is there any precedent for it. It is equitable that those who do not bear the burden of supporting local agencies through taxation should share the cost of providing services based upon tax support.

Other Forms of Financial Support

Many communities have neighborhood associations, citizens' group "friends-of-the-park" societies, ethnic and cultural organizations, etc. These groups often donate time, money, and effort in support of public recreational facilities and activities. Sometimes this takes the form of sponsoring special events. Usually the support is developed as a main channel or coordinating body, which solicits and obtains financial assistance from the business community, and citizens generally, and foundations or other philanthropic groups that continue to the support of the department's program, facilities, or individual activity.

Chapter 10

PLANNING RECREATIONAL SERVICES

Proper planning is the only logical method to forestall chaotic measures and appalling expenditures resulting from the growth of population, attrition of natural resources, expansion of metropolises, and modification of conditions arising from technology and scientific advances.

There is no more important movement for the enhancement of urban areas than city planning. American cities, with few notable exceptions, have been allowed to grow without accounting for long-time needs and the essential coordination of the various parts which go to make up the whole city. This is true whether the community in question is urban or rural. The historic right of the private property owners to put their land to whatever use they decided, without concern for the effect of such use upon adjacent properties and its influence on the community welfare, had been maintained beyond reason. The result, in large cities, has been oppressive congestion, strangulation of industry, paralysis of traffic movement, blighted areas, unspeakable living conditions, delinquency, crime, poor health, and a host of other ills. The need for urban renewal to meet changing conditions and requirements caused enormous expenditures which might have been saved if consideration had been given to planning and the development of comprehensive or master plans.

Public planning is based on the longtime and continuous logical study of the needs of any community and the appropriate control of current and forecastable growth concomitant with the needs. It inquires into the sociological, economic, political, geographic, ethnic, and other demographic factors that contribute to the mosaic of community life. It deals with such factors as land use and the control of such use in relation to present and future population; transportation needs; business and industrial developmental facilities and structures; educational and recreational needs.

Public planning has its remedial and developmental applications. It concerns itself with the relocation of traffic arteries, the widening of streets, and removal of unsightly structures, suitable dwellings substituted for slums, and the reconstruction of blighted areas which characteristically surround the older business districts of large cities as well as of small ones. It also regulates the growth of new outlying areas in order to avoid the errors of the past.

Aspects of Planning

Planning is a continuous process that attempts to preserve the best features of the community while forecasting future needs. Planning for recreational service is the study of human needs and the scientific examination of contemporary resources, demographic growth, and urban expansion. It analyzes the related problems of land usage and the management of such use by correctional and developmental application. It is concerned and related to the orderly control of the physical development of the community, although it cannot be separated from program planning. Programming invariably influences the direction that physical planning takes.

The chief function of planning is to collect and make available the technical data and expertise necessary to ensure that more adequate, harmonious, and accessible recreational spaces and facilities are developed according to need and on a sound priority basis. Planning is really an attempt to prevent waste while resolving a host of problems concerning area beautification, traffic congestion, and population redistribution. Planning also is concerned with the proper distribution of recreational spaces and the proposals for construction of the varied facilities required to provide the indoor and outdoor activities which make up the balanced program. One purpose of planning is to promote, extend, and make available the necessary areas and physical plants for a more perfect administration of public recreational service.

All phases of planning have some influence upon the recreational interests of the people of any city, but certain characteristics of public planning have immediate impact upon the function of public recreational centers in already built-up residential areas with no vacant space. Sufficient areas must be preserved for public use in sections not entirely developed. District recreational facilities need to be sited. New subdivisions must be controlled so that open space for future recreational needs can be preserved. Regional park and wilderness areas in the outlying districts need to be reserved before development encroaches upon them and land becomes prohibitively expensive.

Planners counsel the meticulous devising of a master plan for land use against which all proposed new development of industries, transportation, subdivisions, and properties for public use are monitored. Such plans must be legal instruments, which would make adherence to them compulsory, and proper discretionary power in regard to their modification must be assigned to an appropriate governmental agency. Decisions by the Supreme Court of the United States recognizing the legality of zoning ordinances have made this possible. Some states authorize the adoption, by legally organized planning bodies, of authoritative master plans. Many cities have adopted master plans.

Planning is the exploration of all possibilities for the development of those spaces and structures which will enhance recreational services to the people of the community. Planning involves the collection and examination of pertinent information, so that some basis for issuing policies and executing programs may be carried out in relationship to the design and development of physical properties.

Information gathered for use in planning contains unrefined date pertaining to the community. It serves as a guide for future substantive actions and operations involving the recreational agency's physical growth. Problems are identified, information is obtained, and procedures are undertaken so that duplication, inefficiency, and economic waste will be avoided.

When raw data are accumulated, they must be refined, analyzed, and categorized for easy comprehension. The projection of alternatives and the appraisal of the consequences of such actions must be examined. Recreational planning concerns the broad makeup of the community in order to determine the most effective placement of physical recreational facilities to meet potential population movements, the recreational needs of present users, and the recreational needs of future patrons. Planning is a coordinated enterprise, entailing factors dealing with other physical properties of the community, such as school system, police, fire, health, transportation, and other public facilities. Elements for consideration in planning are:

1. The growth rate of the community—the chief impacts which influence community expansion.
2. The economic base of the community—the essential activities

which produce wealth within the community and upon which the economy of the city is founded.

3. Demographic studies—all facts relating to the distribution of people within the community according to age, gender, ethnicity, religion, education, social, cultural, vocational, and racial characteristics. Such studies indicate population densities, needs, and movements within the community, as well as traditions, mores, and personal attitudes about the city.

4. Geopolitical boundaries indicate local, regional, and district relationships, topographic features, natural resources, and gateways and barriers to the future growth of the community.

5. Land use surveys portray how land is utilized within a given community, and list the physical resources of the city for map projection. This information is particularly useful in locating transportation and communication facilities, residential, commercial, industrial, and public land use zones.

6. Financial factors incorporate studies of tax bases and rates, property value, outstanding bond issues, community revenues, and the ability of the community to pay for a comprehensive recreational system.

All the foregoing topics are systematically investigated so that precise actions can be taken in the orderly acquisition of space and the designing and construction of physical facilities for recreational service.

Planning Considerations

1. Space should be acquired according to community growth trends. It should be consistent with a scientifically conceived plan and be acquired before obvious need for such properties develop.

2. Properties for recreational service use in fully developed areas should be acquired as opportunity permits.

3. Lands for park purposes should be held in perpetuity for public park use only.

4. All recreational properties should be situated in a manner that citizens may have the opportunity to enjoy them.

5. All recreational facilities should be designed and constructed for appropriateness and attractiveness. The design should provide whatever rooms are necessary and suitable to the requirements of the public recreational program produced therein.

6. Facilities should be sited for the most efficient use of land and convenience of the age group or groups for which they are planned, safety of users, and effectiveness of supervision.
7. Recreational structures must be properly maintained and should provide the essential public conveniences.
8. Buildings and grounds of the public school system should be designed for multipurpose utilization and made available for use by the community groups. The facilities of public recreational service areas and structures should be made available to the public school system under mutually beneficial agreements.
9. Recreational areas may be developed adjoining public school property.
10. In neighborhoods devoid of schools, recreational spaces may best be developed to serve the needs of residents.
11. Duplication of areas and facilities may be avoided where public school buildings and grounds can be utilized in the provision of the recreational service program.
12. The use of recreational facilities should not be limited to daylight hours only. Efficient illumination will permit more timely use of these recreational areas, thereby increasing the services to be provided by the same expenditure. Lighting must be suitable to encourage active participation rather than mere observation.

Planning Procedures

The most important part of any planning program is the preparation of a comprehensive plan dealing with a particular problem, in this case that of a recreational service. Because planning objectives are based upon logical decisions and alternatives in order to meet current and future needs the plan is essentially a compilation of information about the physical, demographic, political, and economic resources in the development of the community. All planning procedures are usually predicated upon the completion of surveys to gather information about the community, the collation of such information, and the development and implementation of a master plan.

Collection of Data

Initially, a survey must be undertaken to assess the community. At this stage all physical qualities of the community are noted and listed. Included in this study would be data on open spaces, forest and water resources, topographic features, residential areas, commercial areas, industrial areas, transportation methods, streets and other traffic carriers, all public buildings and structures, sewage lines, dams, reservoirs, and parks or reservations located adjacent to or near the community. The second phase of the survey would be to indicate the community's potential. Any suggestion for renewal, renovation, or correction should be indicated in proposals for the continued development of the community along recreational lines.

All community estimates and appraisals are made in terms of historical background information and research concerning the community and its growth. Of extreme significance would be the demographic aspects of the community: the growth, distribution, density, composition, and movements of population in the community, as well as such social manifestations as schools, churches, health facilities, all recreational agencies, protective agencies, and financial and economic trends observable in the community. Because the purpose of obtaining factual information is to aid in the preparation of a master plan, attention must be focused on assembling only those data of significance to the development of the plan.

Master Plan

Fundamentally, the master plan is a guide for the long-time development of the community. In preparing the master plan, the first objective is to indicate the outstanding community features in correct relation. For purposes of recreational planning, the location and form of land uses, the features and sites of proposed open spaces, the transportation systems and traffic patterns, the location of public buildings, and the distribution and types of public utilities, together with specific proposals for their development and extension, are necessary. Other projects which will affect the plan, although not particularly related to these factors, are concerned with urban renewal, greater efficiency of transit systems alleviation of traffic congestion, and other long-term public improvements. The recreational service master plan attempts to forecast the development of the community in terms of 25-year periods. For this reason, a detailed and accurate diagnosis of current activities and reliable information pertaining to projected growth is basic to any decision making predicated on the plan.

A contemporary trend in residential planning has been to identify areas in terms of neighborhood units. In many communities, neighborhood patterns have developed spontaneously around suburban or newly constructed outlying shopping centers. However, there are some well-planned neighborhoods. The local or neighborhood unit concept is a recent innovation promoted by urban planners which has, as a main object, the development of easily defined intrinsic neighborhoods arranged around a local recreational center or complex having at least one school within the area. Generally, these publicly planned neighborhood units are delimited by natural barriers, such as major traffic arteries, railroads, waterways, cultivated green spaces, or wooded areas which serve as buffer zones.

Typically, the neighborhood is planned to provide residential housing for the population, an elementary school to serve that population, and recreational facilities suitably designed and adequate to meet the requirements of local residents. Amenity agencies are frequently mapped out for development on the rim of the unit, specifically at traffic junctions, and contiguous to districts of a similar nature in adjacent neighborhoods. The street system and traffic load capabilities must be given significant consideration. The vehicular arteries and pedestrian streets must be designed to facilitate traffic movement but prevent use by through traffic. In order for the neighborhood unit to function most effectively, vehicular traffic cannot be allowed to discourage the cross movement of people. Major traffic carriers can act as well as any natural physical feature as a distinct barrier to pedestrian use in an area. Attention must also be focused upon the protective services of the community and the structures needed for the maintenance of effective police, fire, and health departments.

Public Land Use for Recreational Services

In almost every community, but particularly the large urban center, sections of land are reserved for public and quasi-public utilization. These uses are chiefly concerned with the provision of services to the entire community or some part of it. In this classification are lands reserved for streets, public utilities, buildings, buffer zones, schools, and all types of recreational facilities. The policies under which these various land uses operate cannot be segregated from the agency responsibilities to which they relate. Therefore, it is necessary to omit additional mention of these services of government and concentrate on the one function of primary interest—recreational service.

Land and spaces categorized as recreational cover a wide variety of uses including playgrounds, parks, reservation, playfields, community centers, beaches, campgrounds, swimming pools, outdoor theaters, golf courses, riding trails, bicycle paths, tennis courts, auditoriums, gymnasiums, band shells, aboretums, zoological and botanical gardens, museums, scenic vistas, historical sites, waterways forests, and other open spaces. Recreational areas and spaces include quasi-public and privately owned lands and facilities which are available for public utilization.

The amount of space segregated for recreational purposes in any given community varies greatly with the local conception of providing for public recreational service. If the community feels that recreational experience is a vital governmental function designed to meet the changing needs of people, the likelihood exists that a greater-than-normal proportion of the available land will be devoted to recreational uses. Where a community does not accord value to recreational experience, the amount of land made available for recreational purposes decreases. Recreational spaces differ significantly from community to community and within different neighborhoods of a single community. The space necessary for recreational uses depends a great deal upon the physical situation of the community, as well as upon the interests, age groups, occupations, and educational, social, and economic levels characteristic of its people. At this time, there are only educated estimates as to the space requirements for recreational use in the community. Such estimates may run anywhere from 5 to 10 per cent of all the community land available, to one acre per every hundred persons residing in the community. The basic error of such figures is that they do not consider population mobility, density, or need.

Site location and variety of utilization are probably of greater importance than is the total allotment of space set aside for recreational uses. Recreational facilities and areas must consider all people residing in the community as well as transient populations. The chief factor concerning amount of space devoted to recreational objectives is its accessibility to the population which most requires it. Facilities designed to meet the recreational needs of the local neighborhood have to be located within one-quarter mile of almost every resident. The facilities must be easily accessible without hazard from vehicular traffic and must not be barred by any natural or man-made physical objects. On the other hand, regional parks and camping and picnic facilities need not be closely situated to the local population. They may be located on the outskirts of the community, or in distinct, but accessible, sections of the community without regard to distance. Such outlying or peripheral facilities are intended for a mobile population which will travel some distance to reach the site.

Recreational site planning requires scrupulous attention to the acquisition of open space for future population needs. Careful consideration must also be given to present residential districts, population composition, population trends and movement, population distribution and density, future population composition, distribution, and density, as well as other governmental services essential to the health, education, welfare, and safety of the population. Other factors which affect long-term recreational site planning will be concerned with street plans, present and future school sites, and other public building construction.

In the selection of sites for recreational purposes, every effort must be taken to make basic use of areas which, for all other practical intents and purposes, would prove to be uneconomical, unfeasible, or otherwise undesirable. Such areas are prime spots for scenic views, hiking trails, and nature paths, and have program value. Thus, steep hillsides may be converted to winter sleighing, skiing, or tobogganing areas. In the summer the hillside might serve as an observatory, beginner's hill for novice mountain climbers, as part of a cross country or steeple chase run, and so on. Deep gorges, ravines, rocky promontories, so-called submarginal lands, swamps, bogs, and other land equally unsuitable for commercial or industrial development may well be excellent for recreational purposes. These various areas may be easily incorporated into the program by making use of them as passive or active recreational spaces. Bird-watching, hunting, geological explorations, collecting minerals, studying the ecological process of a given environment, are all potentially worthwhile recreational experiences. However, these lands should not be bought, leased, or accepted for recreational use unless they are situated in suitable locations. A deep ravine, for example does not have to be accessible to the general public if it can be reached by an interested climber. In fact, accessibility may not be the only standard for selection. Availability for the purposes for which such areas are intended may make them desirable recreational areas if for no other reason. When the space is to be utilized for a tot-lot or neighborhood playground, it must be of adequate size and situated within the neighborhood where it will be convenient to those whom it will serve.

Standardized Recreational Facilities and Their Placement

Every community should have a variety of basic recreational facilities in which all of its people may find a balanced series of recreational experiences. Ideally, a small playground or tot-lot, with minimal equipment, should be situated at the center of every 100 children under six years of age. This area can be 10,000 square feet or less in size and located in such a site that children could have access to it without crossing any street. The play lot can be fenced in, contain a large sand pile and a few pieces of ceramic tile or concrete forms, gaily painted, and have benches set in on all sides. Parents would thus be the means of supervision, and the typical sandbox and building block play of early childhood could be satisfied.

The neighborhood playground should be exactly what its designation implies. Every neighborhood within the community should have a playground. The playground is designed essentially, although not exclusively, for children between the ages of 6 and 15 years. The neighborhood playground may have from 3 to 10 acres, contain multipurpose areas, a shelter, toilet facilities, quiet games area, court games area, and sufficient space to conduct a comprehensive and balanced program for the individuals who attend. In many instances, the playground can be lighted and thereby serve an older age group during the evening. It is not uncommon to find tennis courts, volleyball courts, handball courts, boccie, and basketball layouts as well as the aforementioned facilities on playgrounds. The neighborhood playground should be adjacent or in close proximity to the local elementary school, thereby taking full advantage of any availability of the school for recreational purposes. The neighborhood served by the local playground will have a radius of not less than one-quarter mile. The park-school concept, which incorporates this plan, has been implemented in several cities. In the park-school concept, school buildings are constructed either on or adjacent to park sites so that the combined facility can be used for both educational and recreational purposes.

The district recreational center is an indoor facility containing the space and equipment necessary for the ongoing year-round production of a highly effective and diversified program of recreational activities. It should serve all age groups and be open from morning until late at night to meet its primary obligations. It should be adjacent to an intown park of not less than 25 or more than 40 acres, and should contain a variety of passive and active areas, including at least one fully equipped and staffed playground, walking paths, a variety of playingfields, courts, appropriate plantings, and picnic spots. The district center should be able to serve the needs of people from an area within a radius of between one-half and three-quarters mile.

The regional recreational complex is a tract of land not less than 100 acres, ranging to 2000 acres. It contains a highly diversified series of terrains, has facilities of many types, and also may be planned to house the community's zoological and/or botanical exhibit. It may be located near a museum of natural history, art museum, or other educational center. There is every likelihood that the complex may have a field house constructed upon it for a variety of sports and game activities, at least one outdoor theater and band shell, a relatively large lake, with facilities for boating in summer and iceskating in winter. It may have an outdoor stadium, as well as golf courses and one or two swimming pools or other aquatic areas. If the regional complex is located close to a major waterway, such as river, sound, bay, ocean, gulf, or great inland lake, it will probably have marina and beach facilities. Generally, there will be well-designed spaces for almost every recreational taste. Walks, bridle paths, bicycle paths, and observatory, bird sanctuary, scenic vistas, fountain displays, reflecting pools, and picnic and camping areas may well be part of such a regional center. This may be considered to be the chief recreational plant of the community, and, depending upon the density of the population, may well be able to care for all the people. Except in the largest urban centers, one such regional center is all that is necessary. As many as 10 to 20 of this type of complex may be required to administer to the citizens of the great metropolitan cities. It is a necessary correlate that only with easy accessibility by major transit systems or by a series of highspeed traffic arteries will these regional complexes serve the purpose for which they were created. The ability to attract patrons to these centers depends, to a significant extent, upon the mobility of the population and the available transportation systems, both public and private.

No community can be considered fully prepared to promote the most comprehensive coverage of recreational services unless it has, within a short distance from its borders, a noncity-owned recreational reservation. Such a facility is usually operated by a county, state, or federal government and can be within two hours' drive, by express highway, from the city limits. The reservation may be part of the county park system, a state park or forest, or a national park, forest, or monument. Any of these facilities will have special features of natural phenomena or manmade attractions which draw attendance. Panoramic views from promontories, spectacular waterfalls, mountains, gorges, fall foliage, trees, ocean views, geologic remains, scientific curiosities, quiet glades, and an abundance of natural and artificially created areas on which a wide diversity of recreational activities may occur will be expected of the reservation. It may not be within the power of the community to provide this facility. However, with increasing federal and state awareness of the need for acquisition of open space and the development of these areas for recreational purposes, there is every reason to believe that the community can request such governments to plan for the acquisition and development of such facilities. Because the city itself will have no jurisdiction, it must join with other communities and request planning and development assistance from county or state government, with funds from the federal government to supplement and underwrite the costs. If communities work together for these additions, they may find higher jurisdictions more receptive to such needs. There has long been a movement to develop parks every 100 miles in some states.[1] With the present availability of federal funds for some purposes, this movement may remain a wish. Although farsighted men realized the need for the acquisition and preservation of scenic areas and the development of permanently established parks which would help to conserve our natural resources, even now after 50 years, with an emergency of our own making, in terms of destroyed resources, little of positive value is being done.

Without really opening a Pandora's box of confusing statements, reiteration of a chief consideration cannot be made too often. The community should be able to rely upon the city school system for utilization of every school building within the public domain. Each school, with its central location and abundant rooms and facilities, may serve admirably as a local neighborhood recreational center if an elementary school, as a

---

[1]B. Moore, *A State Park Every Hundred Miles, Bulletin, National Conference on State Parks,* (Washington, D.C., 1921), pp. 4–7.

district center if a junior high school, and as a regional center if a senior high school. The tremendous expenditures of tax funds for the design, construction, and maintenance of these school buildings make it mandatory that they be used to a maximal extent. No city can afford to allow the schools to stand vacant when there are so many people to be served. The school buildings are a valuable recreational facility and should be so employed. The other alternative is, of course, the major construction of purely recreational buildings and centers. The cost of these additional facilities, when schools are so well suited for this role, indicates a complete abdication of responsible behavior on the part of those who have jurisdiction over the school system. Every effort must be made to incorporate a school building and its entire surrounding physical plant into the municipal recreational service system. That this idea has not received greater impetus and effect is due to a lack of knowledge of governing politicians and the resultant crises which may be perpetuated if there were a strong municipal movement to take over the operation of the city school system.

The traditional employment of boards of education is fast being outmoded. While it is not the intent of this book to deal in prophecy, it may happen that, in the future, there may well be a decided move against local school districts and the school boards which operate them in favor of districts which are congruent with the municipal limit and a municipal agency to operate the school system. There certainly appears to be no trend toward municipal government taking over operation of the school system, but we may yet see the day. School systems no longer need the protective benefit of nonpolitical school boards (if such were ever of value), and the day is fast approaching when municipal governments will operate school systems just as they operate other protective and promotional agencies. When this happens, as it most surely will, school buildings will become an organic part of the community recreational system, and their utilization for recreational purposes will enable them to be employed at a greater economical rate in proportion to their original cost of construction. Whether or not school systems remain under the operational jurisdictions to which they are now attached has little to do with the case. School buildings and the abutting grounds must be made available for public recreational purposes. The sooner school authorities permit such use on a daily basis throughout the year, particularly on weekends, during holiday periods, and over the summer months, the better the community will be because its recreational capacity to serve its constituents will be increased.

Recreational Planning Survey

In order for the municipality or other local subdivision to prepare a priority schedule for the selection of sites, acquire lands, develop properties, and institute a program, a careful survey of the community must first be undertaken to gauge the present and future need. In outline form, the following subjects are included in any recreational survey performed in the community:

1. Historical Factors

    a. Establishment of the community
    b. Neighborhood development
    c. Traditions

2. Physiographic and Other Features

    a. Land and water areas involved
    b. Topography
    c. Elevation above sea level
    d. Streams, rivers, lakes, and other waterways
    e. Average monthly temperatures and precipitation
    f. Scenic, scientific, historical, and other cultural features
    g. Geopolitical boundaries

3. Legislation

    a. State enabling acts and statutes
    b. Municipal ordinances and codes
    c. Zoning laws and restrictions
    d. Building codes

4. Population Data

    a. Estimated or actual present population
    b. Population distribution, density, and composition
    c. Ethnic groups
    d. Racial groups
    e. Population migration (trends and movements)

    f. Occupational distribution

    g. Age groups

5. Housing Data

    a. Rental values by neighborhoods

    b. Existing housing projects and their populations

    c. Proposed housing and subdivisional developments

    d. Character of homes by neighborhoods

6. Community Organization

    a. Governmental Organizations

    b. Protective agencies (police, fire, civil defense)

    c. Promotional agencies (health and sanitation departments)

    d. Promotional agencies (school system, libraries, conservation)

    e. Welfare agencies

    f. Private organizations

      Churches

      Youth-serving agencies

      Social, civic, and fraternal groups

      Business and professional groups

      Philanthropic agencies

    g. Coordinating agencies and councils

    h. Special interest groups

7. Recent Municipal Studies and Surveys

    a. U.S. Census

    b. Master plan or city plan studies

    c. Urban renewal projects

    d. Land use maps

    e. Streets and traffic pattern surveys

    f. Neighborhood layouts and patterns

    g. Drainage and sewer systems

    h. Priority schedules for municipal construction

The Region and Planning

Among the general and specific factors influencing the programming of recreational services in any community will be the region and those aspects which compose it. The term *region* is used in its typical sense to convey the idea of a homogeneous geographic area. In a broader sense, region may be defined as any contiguous areas with common geographical characteristics, joined as the result of extensive interdependent factors (for example, economic activity, population, and geographic segregation), or with common problems as a result of shared resources (for example, water pollution, mass transportation difficulties, labor market, trade centers, and industrial facilities). Regions may be of an intrastate or interstate variety. A single state may be apportioned into distinct segments called regions. These regions are based upon the same characteristics as would qualify regions of an interstate type. They are distinguished by geographic proximity or contiguity, share common problems, or are related as a result of economic development. The grouping of regions for purposes of programming recreational experiences may be made best on an intrastate basis. However, there are several groupings of regions which might be applied to continental United States in terms of regional government or even federal governmental programs of recreational service. In each instance, the designated region has been employed in order to reveal more thoroughly those factors which might influence programming. Among the most common regional groups are:

1. The Triad: the Northeast, the Southeast, and the West
2. Nine Multistate Regions: New England, Middle Atlantic, Great Lakes, Old Confederate, Plains, Southwest, Rocky Mountain, Pacific Northwest, and Western
3. Modified and Multistate Regions: Atlantic Coast, Gulf Coast, Ohio Valley, Tennessee Valley, Northern Plains, and so on
4. The Individual States
5. Intrastate Categories
6. Metropolitan Regions

Climate. Each region, except those of the intrastate categories, will have climatic variations that have a direct and significant influence on programming recreational services—seasonal changes, mean temperatures, and the rain cycle. Moderate and severe weather conditions will invariably affect the type and kind of recreational activities which can be produced successfully within a given region. For example, in certain sections of the country, outdoor recreational facilities and activities can be offered 11 months of the year; in other regions less than 4 months may be profitably spent outdoors. These climatic extremes will find reflection in the type of facilities that have to be constructed and maintained and in the form of activities which predominate programs. The amount and intensity of rainfall, the length of days, and the duration of twilight or evenings will have a marked influence on whether recreational activities are experienced in buildings or open spaces.

Topography. Topography refers to features of the terrain of a region and includes such things as land elevation, flatness, ruggedness, hills, mountains, gorges, valleys, canyons, sloping land, coastlines, contours, and other prominences which can be useful or a hindrance to certain aspects of any recreational program. Mountain climbing, spelunking, collecting, viewing, conservation are all suitable for a planned program of outdoor recreational activities. Flat uninteresting vistas, little or no contour lines, or sparse vegetation may not provide resources for the already named activities, but they can lend themselves to other equally enjoyable experiences, for example, fields for sports and games, quarter horse racing, drag strip racing, cultivation, soil erosion abatement, and other forms of recreational activity. Each region of the country, even the plains, offers some recreational opportunity insofar as topographic features are concerned. However, where the lack of rugged or interesting terrain provides little in the way of nature-oriented activities, man-made construction may be one solution to recompense for the natural deficiency.

Natural and Man-Made Resources. Among the natural resources that could be employed for recreational purposes in any community program would be those contained in regions where large tracts of wilderness and open space still exist in spite of creeping urbanization. Forests, caverns, coastlines, estuaries, gulfs, bays, ocean, lakes, rivers, streams, swamps, marshlands, tidal reaches, geologic formations, and fish, game, and wildfowl refuges and preserves constitute the regional resources of a natural type which can be programmed for a planned series of organized recreational experiences by departments whose jurisdiction encompasses such an environment.

Metropolitan areas, on the other hand, offer the variety of the urban center. Such facilities as zoological and botanical parks and gardens, museums of art, science, and natural history, concert halls, tall buildings, world famous historical sites, churches, tombs, bridges, harbors, and port facilities are but a few of the fascinating resources which can be incorporated in a series of planned recreational activities. Urban-based departments have at their command the vast city as a facility which can be used for guided tours, entertainment, education, and achievement in all phases of recreational experiences. The city readily lends itself to every aspect of the balanced program. Whereas it is valid to state that man can construct nothing to equal nature's variety of color, beauty, and design, it is also reasonable to know that man is capable of compensating for the lack of natural abundance by creating artificial projects which offer enjoyment and opportunity of a different sort. Although the city does not afford the vistas of a mountain, desert, or forest region, it does provide a fascinating setting of its own. Man has gathered together a complex of resources and facilities to satisfy every sense and need within the confines of an urban region. The goods and services available within the city and the city, taken *in toto,* can be a remarkable recreational resource.

Essentially, planning is concerned with the selecting of possible ways of providing recreational service. It is a procedure that involves a careful examination of the community in terms of populations, natural resources, traditions, economic capability to sustain and support the agency and its program, and a supply of competent staff personnel to carry out plans once they have been settled. No aspect of community life can be overlooked in planning for recreational activities. Every possible source of disaffection must be considered and all resources, whether personal or physical, should be included. The community is a complexity made up of complexities. Communities are people and people contribute the greatest difficulties in resolving problems dealing with recreational service. It is a fundamental rule, therefore, that the problems of people, their uniqueness as individuals, and the additional conflicts engendered as a result of social intercourse require carefully planned and systematically analyzed ideas. Planning is the method by which research procedures are applied in an attempt to offer better recreational services immediately as well as at some future point in time.

Chapter 11

PROGRAMMING RECREATIONAL ACTIVITIES

The public recreational service department's primary responsibility is the development of a program of activities that can meet the diverse needs of people. The organization and mobilization of all the community's resources, both physical and personal, in order to produce a balanced, comprehensive, and varied series of recreational activities are necessary if programming is to be performed logically.

The essence of all recreational service is the program. It is the only justification for a recreational service department. Programming consists of planning, scheduling, and implementing an organized series of sponsored recreational experiences through the utilization of all community resources in such a way as to offer routine, special, passive, active, varied, and graduated activities. Community programming requires an inclusive plan of action under the auspices of a central agency, such as a public recreational service department. All activities sponsored, administered, and supervised by the system combine to form the program. Everything that the department does, whether employing personnel, constructing facilities, recruiting volunteers, or managing paperwork, finds outlet in one culminating goal—the program. To this end, all the energies, intelligence, talent, and skill of qualified personnel are organized to provide the most comprehensive program possible in order to meet the various needs of the people living in the community. The basis for programming lies in the concept that each individual in the community must be given the *opportunity* to participate in at least one departmentally sponsored recreational activity. There should be something for everybody in the way of recreational experiences. Since the department is charged with the responsibility for providing total community recreational service, it must offer planned experiences which may be undertaken by all persons residing in the community. Fundamentally, all persons must be served during their leisure.

239

Identification and Classification of Recreational Activities

The balanced recreational program is composed of 12 equal categories, within which many varieties of activities are defined. These categories are coequal insofar as they contribute satisfaction, enjoyment, and other recreational values to individual participants. These 12 categories cover almost every possible recreational activity which can be planned, programmed, or scheduled and offer a diverseness which is as broad in scope as the human mind is able to determine. With few, if any, exceptions, nearly every recreational experience may be included in this classification system. The 12 categories are art, crafts, dance, dramatics, education, hobbies, motor performance, music, outdoor education, service activities, social activities, and special projects.

Art

Art may be defined as any personalized expression of a graphic or plastic nature representing or symbolizing some concept. It is part of the process of communication. Essentially, it is a method of self-expression through visual factors arranged to satisfy the needs of the person who creates them. It may be that only the artist can explain his work, but the explanation is neither important nor required. More importantly, art in any of its many forms is a visual means of conveying ideas, moods, or personal feelings. The art category may be divided into several easily distinguished parts, which readily lend themselves to incorporation in a recreational program. Among these parts are:

GRAPHIC ART	PLASTIC ART
oil painting	stone sculpture
water color painting	metal sculpture
wash drawing	clay sculpture
pen and ink drawing	glass etching
finger painting	ivory carving
charcoal sketching	wood carving
pastel drawing	precious metal smithing
photography	lapidary
dry point etching	tapestry making
silk screen painting	mosaic tile making
crayon drawing	glass blowing
	mobiles

Ramifications. All age groups may participate in art activities. Whether the child draws in crayon or the skilled artist creates in oil, each person is enabled to find expression. Art may be programmed on an instructional basis, that is, graded classes to develop skill, technique, and ability. There are always beginners. Primarily, the youngest age generally falls into this class. However, many older children, youth, and adults are also beginners. They need the stimulation and confidence found among a group of people who come together to learn a new skill. As with all skills, other participants will have had some prior experience and may be classified as intermediates. They are not highly skilled, but have basic knowledge of materials and media, and have some technique. The third class is made up of highly skilled individuals who wish to continue in an instructional session, perhaps studying under a well-known artist. All these skill levels must be considered in developing the category of art.

The noninstructional phase of art is for those persons who have the skill, talent, and knowledge to create, but lack a place in which to participate. The agency, through its schedule, can offer an art room in which people may perform without instruction. Another facet of art is appreciation of it. There are those individuals who cannot or do not want to draw, paint, or sculpt. However, they may have a desire to learn about art. Art appreciation classes organized to develop aesthetic interests and an understanding of what art is may assuredly be incorporated in the art activity.

Art classes are scheduled according to ability. For young children, short instructional sessions are programmed, for adults, longer sessions. Experience and exploration of community interests, needs, and requests will assist in the determination of the number of art classes, lessons, equipment spaces, and instructional leadership necessary.

Crafts

The fabrication of any material or ornamental, utilitarian, or manipulative purposes from animal, vegetable, or mineral substances may be termed a *craft.* It is a creative process of intrinsic value to those who seek satisfaction through the shaping, molding, and modification of materials. Although the line of demarcation between an art and a craft is thin, it is distinguishable, and the two should not be confused or placed in the same classification. Although they are or can be intimately related, they are two separate categories and should be treated as such for programming purposes. Craft activities may be differentiated in the following manner: substance (animal, vegetable, and mineral) and function (industrial, nature, and marine).

Substance

ANIMAL
leather craft
shell craft
bone carving
horn carving
taxidermy

MINERAL
metal craft
clay modeling
glass making
bead craft
ceramics
plastic lacing
plaster of paris
jewelry making
pottery making
sand sculpture
stone craft
soap carving
chemical crafts
snow sculpture
ice sculpture
coral craft

VEGETABLE
weaving
sewing
crocheting
needlepoint
embroidery
basketry
block printing
knitting
paper sculpture
raffia work
appliqueing
cardboard sculpture
wood carving
crepe paper craft
papier-mache craft
dyeing
woodworking
candle making
whittling
hooking
braiding

Function

INDUSTRIAL CRAFTS
electrical shop
masonry
smithing
mechanical arts
plumbing
cabinet making
tool and dye making
furniture refinishing
fur coat remodeling
hat designing
dress designing
gift wrapping
tinkering
bookbinding
woodworking
clock making
glass grinding
printing/book making

MARINE CRAFTS
knot tying
rope making
sail making
boat repairing
surfboard shaping

AUTOMOTIVE CRAFTS
building automobiles
repairing automobiles
motor tuning
boat designing
plane constructing
bicycle making
model making
glider building
motorcycle repairs

NATURE CRAFTS
fly tying
lashing
canoe repairing
shelter building
fire making
implement making
net making
cooking
specimen mounting
driftwood craft
stenciling
spatter painting
vegetable printing
potato puppetry
Indian craft

Ramifications. Craft activities invade nearly every part of the recreational program and tend to enhance other categories. Crafts of and by themselves are extremely satisfying to the individual whether it is a small child playing with miniature hammer, nails, and saw or a highly skilled craftsman tooling an electric motor. Within these two extremes lies a multitude of experiences pleasing and expressive of individual wants, needs, and capacities. Crafts can be done in a solitary manner, but usually the craft activity organized at a recreational center is a social experience carried on in a group setting. A craft is such an individualized medium that almost anyone can find outlet through this experience. Like art, it may be organized in graded classes in which instruction and supervision are maintained. Noninstructional crafts may be organized wherein skilled persons congregate to tinker, shape, carve, mold, hammer, or make other changes in wood, metal, or leather materials. Many individuals, particularly adults, find a hobby which lasts them a lifetime, as a result of attendance in a crafts activity.

Instructional leadership is of primary importance in programming crafts. Unless there is a competent worker who understands the use of media, tools, and space requirements, the activity is likely to meet with little success. Leadership, either professional or volunteer, and essential tools, work spaces, and materials are vital to crafts. Certainly, there are simple craft activities which do not need extensive tools and equipment or expensive materials. However, such activities are more likely to appeal to young children than to the majority of adults who wish to participate. The ingenuity of professional leadership is apparent from the production of many craft activities without expensively procured supplies and materials. Salvaged materials sometimes afford the greatest satisfaction. There is a good deal of pleasure in designing and fabricating something useful, ornamental, or manipulative from a piece of junk or scrap. With competent leadership almost any craft project is possible.

Dance

Any rhythmic movement, gross or fine, which is sustained by a regular tempo, beat, or music, may be termed *dance*. Dance has been conceived as a method of nonverbal communication, as kinetic movement to relieve tension, and as a means of social and individual self-expression. The dance category may, for ease in programming, be classified as follows:

FOLK DANCE	SOCIAL DANCE
square	waltz
round	rumba
ethnic	tango
	fox-trot
	fad

CHOREOGRAPHED DANCE	RHYTHMICS
ballet	free exercise
modern	games
concert	tap
interpretive	clog

Ramifications. Like all skills, dance must be learned. One of the most popular recreational activities, dance has found almost universal expression in every culture. A dance may reflect traditions or a general contemporary feeling. Many dances are outgrowths of religious rites or of ethnic backgrounds and depict the celebrations and mores of different cultures. Dancing is a graceful rhythmic motor skill which can be enjoyed by spectators and participants alike. As an outlet for self-expression, dancing may be solo, dual, or group. Dancing fosters socialization and allows people to satisfy a basic urge to respond to a pleasing tempo.

Although social dancing still attracts the greatest number of persons, square and folk dances have come to be extremely popular, and interest in these forms of the activity is growing. The criteria for selecting specific types of dance forms are influenced by the age, sex, prior experience, degree of skill, and the size of the group involved. Instructional phases of dance may be divided into the familiar beginner, intermediate, and advanced classifications.

Of primary importance is the presence of qualified leaders to conduct instructional activities and provide competent guidance for the inclusion of all who seek enjoyment through this medium. The various forms of dance enable almost everybody to achieve a sense of satisfaction and release of tension. The techniques involved and the objectives to which people aspire vary greatly, thus offering opportunity for individuals to experience emotional outlets. Through instructional classes for the development of needed skills, in sharing the vicarious stimulation of watching the dance as a spectator, this activity proves of immense value as a socializing mechanism and contributes to the cohesion of any group so involved.

Dramatics

Communication through aural and visual means, whereby an individual can emote and express himself or reproduce the expression of others by interpretation, mimicry, symbolism, or spontaneous activity, may be defined as *dramatics.* The element of performance, whether in front of an audience or not, is incorporated. The scope of dramatics is extremely broad and includes many activities, among which are:

MANIPULATIVE PERFORMANCE	CREATIVE DRAMA
marionettes	pantomime
puppets	improvisation
shadow plays	games
juggling	charades
prestidigitation	psychodrama
(sleight of hand)	sociodrama
FORENSIC PERFORMANCE	THEATER
monologues	blackouts
dialogues	plays
debate	dramatizations
public speaking	demonstrations
story reading	operas
storytelling	operettas
impersonation	tableaux
choral speech	skits
radio plays	stunts
	clowning

Ramifications. The constructive utilization of a story, in either plays, pantomimes, role-playing, or spontaneous re-creation, allows participants to express themselves in terms of their needs and interests. Dramatics and its various forms, using a medium of reality, fantasy, and wish-fulfillment, make the individual aware of himself and cause him to empathize with others. Every age group enjoys some aspect of dramatics.

Children love to tell and to hear stories, to play dramatic games, to act out fairy tales. Adults enjoy a good story as does the teller.

Dramatics also includes games, improvisations, plays, and other forms which convey ideas by means of speech, action, or both. Essentially, the dramatic performance is the most highly personalized of all the categories. It is the individual on whom all attention is focused, and it is the individual who must interpret the idea or character about which the story is written. In creative dramatics there is no story line, and the role-taker must act out ideas spontaneously, as the mood or action dictates. For a formal play, the actor has lines to memorize and must reproduce the character prescribed by the author.

As in all planned recreational activity, a prime requisite is qualified leadership to serve in a directorial capacity, to act as a resource, or to supervise the entire presentation. Dramatics classes, appreciation of drama in its different forms, and actual performance upon the stage all require expert guidance. Dramatic presentation may be of the workshop variety in which the participants learn by doing. On the other hand, when the play is performance oriented, many weeks must be taken for rehearsal, sets must be designed, lighting and other equipment must be accumulated, and all details of presentation must be planned. In many instances, performers gain confidence through participation and are able to overcome any emotional barriers that prevent them from taking part. Drama is valuable to the individual as a medium for self-expression through representations of characters and roles which may be the creation of another person.

Education

Any instructional activity wherein the primary reason for participation is the enhancement of knowledge or the learning of a new skill, idea, or subject may be termed *education*. Formal or classroom instruction of subject matter and informal learning experiences programmed specifically to teach a skill are part of this category. Although almost all recreational activity may be defined as educational, it is not the place of the recreational service department to teach subjects which might better be left to the school system. Certain educational objectives may be planned and noted in an organized program, but the atmosphere and the emphasis are quite different from those of the school classroom. The activities which typically form the educational category are:

ADULT EDUCATION
citizenship
civics
first aid
curriculum subjects
grammar
mathematics
history
geography
science
current events
industrial arts
etiquette
floral designs
horticultural arrangements
home gardening
maternity and child care
accounting
bookkeeping
typing
stenography

LINGUISTIC ACTIVITIES
foreign language groups
debating
public speaking
choral recitations
conversation
discussion groups
forums
quizzes
storytelling
storyreading
lectures
liturgical groups
panel presentations
seminars
symposia

LITERARY ACTIVITIES
book clubs
book review groups
short story writing
library cataloguing
play writing
technical writing
poetry reading
poetry writing
Bible reading
letter writing

Ramifications. Nothing enhances enjoyment as much as having knowledge about a given subject and being able to bring that knowledge to bear when a situation demands it. Knowledge opens many doors to quiet satisfaction. It extends the promise of awareness, recognition, and appreciation to any subject. The category of education lends itself most particularly to the recreational setting because learning is enjoyable, especially when the information gained is learned during one's leisure. Subject matter of formal curricula as taught by the school places emphasis upon progress toward a specific goal, with so many units learned and examinations taken. The recreational orientation of education stresses satisfaction on the part of the learner without examinations and the pressure to achieve a specific grade. Classes in recreational education are designed to help people improve this knowledge, to increase skill, to share in social occasions, and to develop physically, emotionally, and intellectually. Generally, all programmed instruction emphasizes the activity or subject to be learned. The individual's interest dictates the speed and progress that will be made.

Education during leisure has tended toward a variety of skill learning of curriculum subjects, such as typing, first aid, driver safety, letter writing, short story writing, and civics. However, any subject may be offered. When literary, linguistic, or commercial courses are offered in the program, they are there because a demand has been created and interested people desire them. Formal subjects are offered in the hope that exposure to the information will prompt additional study and provide incentive for improvement.

Competent leaders are required for the presentation of most educational subjects. Volunteers may be utilized for such skills as fur coat remodeling, furniture refinishing, or the like, but in general, qualified instructors must be employed. The educational category offers opportunities for personal exposure to information about which some confusion exists. Political debate, local government in action, open forums, current events, book clubs, and other sources that stimulate the individual's thinking are valuable contributions effected in these activities.

Other forms of education are quizzes, puzzles, and mental games. These activities have received scant notice from practitioners, even though they are quite enjoyable to participants. It must be remembered that the education category rests entirely upon the mental capacity, willingness to learn, and basic interest of potential participants. It has been found that nearly everyone can learn if the material presented is stimulating and beneficial, or if the individual is motivated to acquire the information. On these bases, education may afford the best hope in the provision of recreational experiences.

Hobbies

Hobbies are highly personalized interests having to do with the acquisition, knowledge, appreciation, manipulation, fabrication, or design of some thing, subject, or concept. So diverse and peculiar are hobbies that any listing, no matter how extensive, would only begin to indicate the variety of human interests that can be classified as hobbies. It is probably easier to indicate the activities that are not hobbies. All activities requiring performance, such as dramatics and music, or participation in sports and games may be thought by some to be hobbies, but they are not. An interest ceases to be a hobby when performance becomes a part of the experience. For example, music appreciation, collecting music, knowledge of music, and writing music may be considered hobbies. However, when the individual performs music, that is, sings or reproduces music on an instrument, the activity cannot be considered a hobby. If a hobby can be any activity, anything and everything may be identified as a hobby. There is no basis for a definition. Definitions differentiate and set apart. If everything is accounted for under one topic, there is no difference in activities. Performance is clearly different from collection, knowledge, or manipulation. It is a unique factor which permits classification within other categories.

Ramifications. There are some persons to whom all activities of the balanced program mean little or nothing. By temperament, emotional capacity, or for other personal reasons, they do not want to participate. They do not want any part of the program. For these individuals, there is always one outlet the recreational agency can offer. The highly personalized and individual hobby enables each person to select at least one area of interest. There need be no others for participation. The hobby category is organized quite differently from the other 11 classifications. There are no classes of instruction by which a person may learn a hobby. There is no extrinsic motivation the recreationist can bring to bear which might stimulate participation in a hobby. The recreationist may, however, organize interest groups or clubs when a hobbyist requests it.

The function of the recreationist in attempting to engage an individual's attention for hobby purposes may well come in terms of exposure. Some individuals are compelled to attempt one form of hobby or another as a result of personal observation, casual conversation, attendance at a hobby show where various displays and exhibits were demonstrated, or simply by chance encounter. However people are initiated into the mysteries of the hobby, this activity becomes an absorbing and long-time pursuit. All hobbyists are fanatics concerning their particular hobby. Nothing is more pleasing to the hobbyist than to be called upon to demonstrate or explain an interest. This is one way by which hobbies are spread. The enthusiasm which the hobbyist exhibits is contagious and usually infects an entire audience of spectators or listeners.

The recreationist has a chance to assist in the spread of hobbies by locating hobbyists of various types and scheduling clubs that promote the exchange of information, by displays, lectures, and other media, for the transmission of knowledge. If hobby clubs are already in existence, then the recreationist can encourage hobbyists to utilize recreational facilities throughout the community for meetings as well as for the scheduling of hobby shows. Continual exposure of people to hobbyists and to the interests from which hobbies are developed may be the best method which the recreationist has at his/her disposal. Providing space and facilities for hobbyists can be fruitful in widely disseminating hobby possibilities. In the long run, most stress is placed upon the individual's capacity to be interested in a worthwhile pursuit and to develop personal skills in undertaking total responsibility for maintaining the activity.

Motor Performance

All activities requiring gross and/or fine muscle control which may be devised for physiological development, extension of capacity to endure, or for competitive purposes are called motor performance. Sports, games, and conditioning experiences are one means of classifying and identifying motor performance. Sports are all recreational pursuits that are not restricted by time, rules, or to a distinct or specifically delimited, universally known area. Games, on the other hand, have special rules and codes to which all players must adhere. Games are conducted in carefully defined and distinguishable spaces, segregated from all other activities, and are usually relegated to a selected portion of time or by units in which the games must be completed. Sports, when so regulated, may be modified to become games. Games can never be sports. Motor performance can be identified in several ways and contain the following activities:

INDIVIDUAL
ACTIVITIES
swimming
gymnastics
tumbling
track events
field events
riflery
pistolry
archery
equitation
rowing
bowling
fishing
surfing
diving
golf
sledding
skiing
ice-skating
roller-skating
skeet shooting
walking
sailing
fly casting
weight lifting
bicycling
hang gliding

DUAL
ACTIVITIES
fencing
wrestling
handball
squash
tennis
table tennis
badminton
aerial darts
horseshoe pitching
shuffleboard
synchronized swimming
two-man sculling
billiards
paddleball
climbing
racquetball

TEAM ACTIVITIES
baseball
basketball
cricket
field hockey
football
ice hockey
lacrosse
rugby
soccer
volleyball

GROUP ACTIVITIES
calisthenics
weight training
circuit training
drills
tug-of-war
relays
tag games
ball games
dodgeball
pass ball

water polo
polo
softball
crew sculling
curling

circle games
beater goes round
slap jack
apparatus play
hiding games
boccie
croquet
goal-hi
stunts
self-testing

Ramifications. It is unfortunate that many recreational programs are so heavily larded with motor performance activities and little else. Sports and games are rather easily scheduled within any program and have almost universal acceptance. Motor performance is no more important in the balanced recreational program than are any of the other categories. Nevertheless, sports and games have received an inordinate amount of emphasis. Motor performance can be appealing to all age groups and to both sexes, and the other cultural factors may not affect its popularity. Motor performance is a part of living from the time a child expresses itself in random kinetic movement until, as a mature individual, he or she takes his last evening constitutional. Every waking moment has some facet of motor performance in it.

Traditionally, young men and boys are attracted to and participate in a variety of motor skills. Young women and girls also appreciate elementary games and rhythmical movement. With maturity, however, most females' interest in sports and physical games decreases. This is also true of adult males' active participation in team sports, although they may become the more fanatic of the passive spectators who follow team sports. With the popularization of sports and game competition, a result, in great part, of the recent worldwide coverage of the last three Olympic Games by the mass media and, in part, of the increasing attention given to the physical fitness level of all Americans, participation increased dramatically. Public relations selling by commercial establishments has changed the image of many games. Because of the advertising of bowling centers, more women are bowling now than ever before. The same holds true for golf, tennis, swimming, track, gymnastics, and dance. Popularization of any sport or game by television has been matched by an upsurge in participation. Where previously females might have considered sports and game participation unfeminine, they now realize that the women participants in swimming, skiing, ice-skating, ballet, modern dance, tennis, golf, gymnastics, horseback riding, water skiing, and track not only possess beautiful figures, but are extremely feminine as well. No longer does the woman look with distaste upon motor performance. Another basic reason lies with the public school system, which promotes physical education activities from the elementary level through the college level. Physical education, has done much to foster carry-over for recreational participation long after the individual has left school.

The recreationist has the responsibility of programming all forms of motor performance throughout the year. Plans must be made to meet the needs, skills, and experiences of all people in the community. The standard for selection of motor activities into the program is not how many will be spectators but rather how many will be participants. The schedule of physical recreational experiences should include both highly organized formal activities and self-directed, informal, and free play activities. Within this format there should be some motor performance that has an appeal for each individual according to his own skills, proficiency, experience, and prior exposure. There must be instruction for each level of ability, through clinics, workshops, and both individual and group practice. Competition is valuable in motor performance, but emphasis upon extrinsic awards and winning at any price must be avoided. The justification for participation should be the enjoyment and satisfaction an individual derives from playing the game and taking part in the sport.

Whenever there is serious thought given to competition, a place should be established for all those who wish to participate. The highly skilled performer certainly has a place in the recreational games program, but so does the individual with little ability and no experience. The intramural program, with its intention of allowing every interested person to play the game, may be the best method available in meeting the needs of people. Intramural teams should not be confused with specialist teams. Intramural activities are designed to offer equal opportunity for participants to compete against those of average skill. The intramural program consists of competition among those persons who frequent one recreational facility. It may consist of double or single elimination tournaments, ladder or pyramid contests, or round robin tournaments. It may be a coed program, which might promote greater interest at one age and deter interest at another. In any case, the recreationist will be in the best position to organize such an activity.

Intermurals are those competitive activities organized between two or three neighborhood recreational facilities, for example, centers or playgrounds, and are conducted on the same basis as intramurals are. The difference here is that an off-facility event can be scheduled and additional interest may be secured. Extramural activities are those highly competitive events scheduled on an interdistrict and city-wide basis, with great emphasis upon skills. They serve to focus attention upon the individual or single team and are useful in meeting the needs of those who have great ability, skill, and experience.

In whatever way the various forms of motor performance are programmed, they have a natural appeal. There are motor skills for the physically fit or unfit, for the strong or the weak, for those who have endurance, and for those who have little stamina. There are activities which demand poise, balance, flexibility, agility, speed, and grace. Other activities require hand-eye coordination. Sports have many values, not the least of which is to offer the participant the opportunity of belonging to a team, receiving personal satisfaction in attaining some objective, or simply enjoying the exhilarating effects of whatever game is being played.

Music

Any activity which produces vocal or instrumental tonal or atonal sounds having some form of syncopation or tempo is music. Music may be thought of as being either vocally or instrumentally produced, a combination of these forms, the act of creating music, and an appreciation of performance. Music is a means of expression and can motivate action, evoke personal response, and elicit mood changes by appealing to and stimulating emotional reactions. Music may be classified into several component parts, among these are:

VOCAL ACTIVITIES	INSTRUMENTAL ACTIVITIES	
community singing	solos	quintets
barbershop quartets	duets	septets
solos	trios	octets
glee club	quartets	
a cappella choirs	bands	
choruses	rhythm bands	

ensembles
madrigal singing
round singing
singing games
chorales

MUSIC APPRECIATION
concerts
recordings
radio
television
musicology

orchestras
symphony bands

COMBINATION
ACTIVITIES
operas
operettas
musicals
variety and talent shows
parades
pageants
festivals
circus

Ramifications. Music has an appeal for all ages, both sexes, and in some of its various forms may be performed, listened to, or appreciated by receptive people. Singing by oneself, in groups, formally, or spontaneously, participating in ensembles for instruments, composing music, writing lyrics, learning to appreciate the techniques of a virtuoso, or just listening to any recorded music has a significant place within most recreational programs. The ability to enjoy music is acquired easily, for there is a particular type of music for every taste. Musical activities may be offered in graded instruction for individuals or groups, appreciation classes, programmed background music to coincide with other activities, musical shows, talent shows, choral presentations during religious ceremonies or holidays, and community sings.

Some musical activities may be arranged in contests whereby performers attempt to create the most perfect type of the music they prefer. These contests should not be confused with talent shows or other contests of this kind. Illustrative of talent contests are the barbershop quartet, marching band, fife and drum corps, and other musical groups which, although practicing for their own pleasure and satisfaction, are brought together once each year to perform en masse or as contestants.

Recreationists may be able to stimulate interest in the establishment of small ensembles whose members may never want to perform in public, but who utilize the recreational facility as a place for practice sessions. The development of brass choirs, string quartets, vocal groups, rhythm bands, jazz combinations, and string bands can arise from such organization.

The recreational service agency should act as a musical clearinghouse for the community by maintaining an adequate library from which records, tapes, and books on music could be borrowed. At every opportunity the department should sponsor community concerts, music under the stars, band exhibitions, glee clubs, a cappella choirs, and other music groups which may interest people and allow them to find a satisfying and creative outlet through music.

Outdoor Education

All nature-oriented activities based upon the physical and natural sciences expressed by the living in, collecting specimens of, acquiring knowledge about, and finding appreciation in the outdoor environment may be considered as outdoor education. Outdoor education may be represented by the following:

BIOLOGICAL SCIENCE
agriculture
agronomy
biology
bacteriology
botany
floriculture
horticulture
ichthyology
ornithology
entomology
silviculture
pomology
genetics
zoology

PHYSICAL SCIENCE
chemistry
physics
astronomy
geology
mineralogy
oceanography
geography
topography
speleology
spectroscopy
meteorology
lapidary
ecology

NATURAL HISTORY
anthropology
ecology
paleontology
archaeology
mythology
nature lore

OUTDOOR LIVING
camping
hiking
climbing
cave trips
excursions
tours

Indian lore	hunting
folk lore	fishing
conservation.	

Ramifications. Broadly stated, outdoor education embraces all the learning activities that deal directly with the wise utilization and appreciation of the environment. It consists of learning by actual performance in the natural laboratory of all outdoors.

The degree to which the aims of outdoor education are achieved will nearly always be the effect of the leadership provided. The leader of outdoor education, which includes all activities carried on under this category, requires more than skill or technique in nature study, conservation, camping, or other specialities. Important as highly developed teaching skills are, they do not compensate for high quality leadership. When soundly planned and administered, outdoor education provides the best features of schooling, camping, recreational experiences, and skill development of the individual. Within the natural setting the individual has the opportunity of being himself. This necessarily suggests, without temporizing, an optimal situation in terms of environment, facilities, program, and leadership. In order to obtain high quality experience, the environment must be attractive, safe, stimulating, and developmental. It requires good leadership, programs, facilities, and resources, which can provide opportunities for physical fitness (with all it implies), promotion of sound health habits, and concern for others.

Outdoor education, particularly camping, offers excellent modalities and experiences for the development of participants who might otherwise be stifled in a less permissive atmosphere. Here the individual is, for a little while, taken away from his normal routine of school, home, or business, and placed in a dynamic situation under the guidance of professionally prepared personnel. This type of organized activity may eventuate in the individual's own appreciation for an indulgence in outdoor educational activities on his/her own at a later time.

In an outdoor environment the individual is able to be self-expressing most freely. There are no distractions, such as noisome cities, densely populated neighborhoods, or the loneliness of isolation from one's peers, unless isolation is what the individual seeks. Here the needs of the individual are satisfied. The child or adult has an opportunity to live in proximity to nature. Whatever value there is in looking upward to the sky on a spectacularly starry night, seeing a clear moonrise, watching ribbons of light stream across the face of earth at dawn, catching the first drops of a summer shower, standing in appreciation of magnificent autumnal coloring, or gazing at the panoramic view after a long climb is fully realized. Living close to nature teaches each person something of how best to appreciate the resources of the land. The therapeutic value of outdoor education comes from simply being in the outdoors, living at an unhurried and unharried pace, learning whatever new skills one is capable of performing, and experiencing an entirely new series of activities or relearning valuable skills which have been forgotten through disuse.

The recreationist has an ethical obligation to help preserve and conserve natural resources. At every season of the year there is some aspect of outdoor education which can be incorporated into the program. Through the instillation of awareness of natural resources, participants may become a highly vocal and mobilized group to argue for the preservation of open space, wilderness areas, and other natural phenomena necessary for outdoor activities. By teaching people to appreciate the value and beauty of the outdoors, converts may be won. Those who are most vociferous for the maintenance of natural places in the face of entrenched opposition have had some chance to camp, climb, hike, or birdwatch. The organization of nature interest clubs, gardening clubs, astronomy clubs, nature craft activities, wilderness tours, and other stimulating experiences of this kind is an essential aspect of the comprehensive and balanced recreational program. The department should take advantage of any open space, stream, waterway, forest, game refuge, or park in which to inculcate and dramatically present, to active and potential participants, the inherent values of recreational activities in the outdoor setting.

Service Activities

All activities voluntarily engaged in by persons who wish to assist others in learning, appreciation, skill development, or making the community a better place in which to live as a result of their interest, talent, and sense of responsibility may be termed *service activities*. It is the selfless giving of time, energy, and sometimes money purely for the satisfaction derived from helping another person or an entire community. Perhaps more than any other activity, service to others may be considered as the most rewarding. It is just as enjoyable as any of the other activity categories, requires the same sense in an even greater or more intense emotional response of well-being and warmth, as the recipient of the service succeeds in the undertaking where assistance was given. Watching an individual develop skill, knowledge, emotional maturity, or an appreciation of a variety of subjects as a direct consequence of one's own instruction, guidance, or support provides the donor with a feeling of achievement and a sense of self-esteem for being able to help when another individual depended upon it. Service to others may be attained even when the volunteer does not work directly with other people. By offering time, skill, or technical knowledge, a person may gain a valuable recreational experience. Service activity is as broad as the entire field of recreational service. However, for simplification, services may be organized around these classes:

COMMITTEE WORK
membership on:
  boards
  councils
  interest groups
  resource groups
  committees

DIRECT ACTIVITY
art
crafts
dance
drama
education
service activities
social activities
special projects
Nonleadership Work
stage lighting
clerical work
registering contestants
receptionists
decorators
fund raisers
transportation
ushers

LEADERSHIP
hobbies
music
outdoor education
motor performance

Ramifications. Every community has the potential personal resource of special skills and an infinite variety of talents waiting to be discovered. It is the responsibility of the recreationist to ensure a balanced program by investigating the possibility of incorporating the service phase of recreational experience into the program. To whatever extent an individual possesses some talent or ability, it may be useful to others and therefore a viable contribution to the community at large.

Lifelong skills acquired as a result of occupation, hobbies, education, or living within one community may be the basis for providing voluntary services to others. There is no phase of the program that may not be made more valuable to participants as a result of some volunteer's experiences and donation of time or effort.

Of necessity, volunteers must be recruited. This is best done by a survey of the community performed by staff members of the recreational service department. Some volunteers simply walk into the agency and ask to be allowed to help in any way. However, for the most part, volunteers must be sought. The department should maintain a list of possible volunteer positions needed in the conduct of the program, in the operation of the agency, or in enlisting support for the department. With these slots in mind, people may be recruited. Many people would like to help, but feel that they do not have special talent or do not realize that they do not have to be skilled in program in order to be useful and make a valuable contribution. Unfortunately, too, some administrators do not recruit nor do they want volunteers assisting in the program, because they feel that volunteers require more time than is worthwhile to give them. Such an attitude on the administrator's part not only is bred of ignorance, but is completely out of keeping with the idea that volunteer service is an integral part of the recreational program.

Recruitment of volunteers may be facilitated if relevant sources are determined before any drive is carried on. Retired individuals, high school-aged youngsters, hobbyists, fraternal organization members, and others are prime targets as recruits. The same fervor utilized for developing good public relations with the public should also merit consideration for developing a corps of volunteers for the department. Once individuals have been recruited, a screening process must be instituted to indicate those who can be placed within the various voluntary classifications. Individuals with a high degree of program skills should be placed in a related sector, those who have administrative or clerical experience in the appropriate sector, and those who can perform significant work for the department in other areas should be used in these areas. An experienced interviewer should be employed by the department to screen the volunteers, and the potential volunteers should write statements clarifying their aims and primary sense of purpose in offering their time.

After the initial recruitment and screening, the volunteers should be given a basic orientation to the agency's philosophy, functions, and goals. In this way, the would-be volunteer can be made to recognize what the agency is attempting to do, why it performs the way that it does, and the contribution that it makes to community welfare. After the orientation, there should be a period of in-service education to prepare the volunteers for service in any facet of agency operation. For those who will work with recreationists at a variety of facilities, scheduled observations and tours should be made, as well as a brushup of skills and methods of instruction and supervision. For those who will be administrative assistants, office management techniques should be thoroughly explained and demonstrated. There is room in the daily operation of program to include all who want to lend their time and energy.

There are certain drawbacks to the utilization of volunteers, but their positive benefits to the program far outweigh any undesirable characteristics. It is true that volunteers may not be as reliable as paid employees and that they will not owe first allegiance to the agency. However, the agency should do everything in its power to stimulate loyalty and dedication in the volunteer just as it does in the employed individual. Moreover, the dependable volunteer frees the professional worker to do a more extensive and inclusive job of programming than might be allowable without additional help.

For all the negative reasons listed as to why volunteers should not be assigned or utilized, there is one overriding fact for their incorporation— service is a recreational activity and it must be considered if the recreational program is to be balanced with something for each person's taste and satisfaction. Recreationists have the mandatory obligation to serve people, and they can do this in one respect by offering opportunities for providing service to others through volunteer efforts. The benefit which volunteers contribute is so great that no program may be considered successful without them. The value received from a dedicated and skilled volunteer is incalculable to the agency. No program should be without as many volunteers as can be recruited.

Social Activities

All experiences of a recreational nature wherein two or more people come into close contact, and where there is some direct relationship so that communication exists, are social. With the exception of solitary recreational activities, all situations of a recreational nature are intensely social. Communication, in this sense, does not have to be verbal. It is enough if individuals can satisfy their need to belong to a group by merely being present at an activity in which the group is involved. Communication can be verbal or nonverbal. Close proximity, coincidental participation in the activity, and common interests often open avenues of receptivity and acceptance which are essential to sociability. Because social activities are generic to every category of the recreational program, only a sampling of these experiences is listed. Social activities may be grouped as follows:

FORMAL ACTIVITIES	INFORMAL ACTIVITIES
parties	games
banquets	active
ceremonials	mental
programmed dances	musical
concerts	party
dinners	table
balls	community singing
teas	social dancing
festivals	conservation
holiday celebrations	koffee klatches
commencement	drop ins
	pot-luck suppers

Special Projects

Out-of-the-ordinary activities conducted at intermittent intervals, requiring extra effort, and adding variety and spice to the otherwise routine daily experiences of the program come under the heading of special projects. Such activities may involve participants who might not be attracted to the standard recreational activities. Special projects may be conducted throughout the year, but each special project is unique and is programmed only once in any given year. These feature presentations are complex and take strenuous effort at all stages, whether planning or actual operation, if they are to be successful. They must be colorful and exciting in order to draw active participants and spectators. Almost any idea or theme will serve as the vehicle for a special project. However, most projects are classified in the following manner:

EXHIBITIONS
art show
craft show
animal show
hobby show
gymnastic exhibition
horticultural show
tableaux
nature exhibit
FESTIVALS
fair
circus
field day
carnival
block party
community picnic
holiday celebrations
yacht regatta
MUSICALS
band day contests
parade
opera
operetta
pageant
symphony concert
talent show

Ramifications. Special projects spotlight, correlate, and include many if not all of the other program categories. The special event may be looked upon as a culminating activity for a season, a month, or a unique occasion. The special must be coordinated with other phases of the program and maintain the balance between routine and the change of pace which such an activity provides. Special projects are those events calculated to stimulate the individual who participates in the daily activities offered by the department as well as the "stay-away" person. It affords the once-in-a-while excitement necessary to attract new participants and to sustain those who do the daily work.

Key events which trigger the special project should be built around midyear and year-end periods. The summer festival, Christmas carnival, or winter frolic requires, perhaps, six months to one year of planning and preparation for success. For this reason, the special project cannot be programmed on a routine basis. It would surely sap the energies and creative expression of those required to do the work. Special projects that take place too frequently lose their speciality and become commonplace. The recreationist must know when to inject the special into the program. There is a natural progression of events which leads directly to a culminating activity inclusive of all the other recreational experiences that have gone before. In the normal course of events, every three-month segment of a program may terminate with a modified special event, every six-month segment, with a major special project. Within these time periods other special events may be programmed, but they cannot be of the magnitude of the semiannual projects. Holidays make excellent themes around which a special event can take shape. But there is no single month within the year that does not contain a holiday or commemorative date of some note. Therefore, recreationists in charge of programming special projects would do well to limit such activities. The less there are in any given year, the greater the anticipation and satisfaction when they occur.

Chapter 12

SUPERVISION AND RECREATIONAL SERVICE

The supervisor enjoys a unique position as a mediating force between management and program level employees. The supervisor has a triple role: 1) translation of administrative policy into action; 2) serve as the channel by which employees' grievances become known to top officials; and 3) carrying out a primary leadership function—facilitation of the production of services for which the organization was established. In recreational service it means obtaining the cooperation of all subordinate workers, whether line or staff, so that qualitative and efficient activities of a recreational nature are supplied to the constituency of the agency.

Supervision effects the optimum recreational service possible through the enhancement of recreationist competence, primarily by reinforcing professional development, and by promoting scientific methods of analyzing functions for improved working procedures. Supervision in any field of endeavor is an attempt to improve worker competencies so that ultimately the most effective good or service will be provided. In the field of recreational service this is no less true. The final result of supervision should be the production of all of those conditions that make the rendering of recreational services most effective. Many of the problems which affect human behavior and environmental situations, and which interfere with a high rate of capacity for the accomplishment of all recreational services involve supervision.

Cooperation Versus Compulsion

The supervisor is chiefly concerned with people not with areas, programs, or things. Capable of offering technical advice and guidance for improved performance of subordinates; the supervisor must also appraise and evaluate personal techniques so that the supervisory process may be made more effective; as well as exercise leadership. The latter aspect of the supervisor's role may just be the single most important aspect of supervision. The entire process of supervision should be one of leadership. The duties and responsibilities of the supervisory position may differentiate it from other job levels insofar as descriptions are concerned, but the fundamental manner in which supervision is carried out is through leadership.

The supervisor needs to obtain the cooperative efforts of everyone with whom contact is made, in order to produce recreational services for the public good. Cooperation is really a voluntary commitment of energy. One cannot demand cooperation. If it is not given freely, only the threat of reprisal, including dismissal, will elicit work from subordinate personnel. Individuals may perform their assignments under duress, but it will be merely in terms of the written job description—and then grudgingly. Under such conditions the program of recreational service will deteriorate. Subordinate personnel who are neither satisfied nor happy in their work will not perform optimally. Whatever the cause of nonperformance, poor morale, working conditions, mistrust, lack of motivation, administrative neglect, incompetency, lack of internal communications, worker apathy, or management's inability to create a democratic environment within the department, the supervisor's function is to overcome such detrimental conditions and coordinate, stimulate, and assist the professional growth of all employees of the agency. This cannot be done by issuing directives and enforcing assignments by threat. Of course, the supervisor always has the authority to coerce subordinate workers into job performance, but this can only lead to the same or worse situation in not producing an effective recreational service for the public. It is the fact of coercive authority which may diminish the effectiveness of the supervisor. The initial suspicion and anxiety which subordinates manifest for the supervisor must be overcome if a leadership role is to eventuate.

The Nature of Supervision

Supervision is leadership. In the most valid sense of the term, the complete supervisory process is intimately associated with all the interrelations and interpersonal connections with which leadership is defined. It cannot be otherwise. If supervision is thought of as simply the oversight of subordinate workers, or merely the inculcation of technical knowledge to obtain more competent performance, it is not supervision. Such a narrow construction of the supervisory process leaves too much to be desired and may be thought of in terms of directing workers without their having any input into the planning or policy development by which the agency operates.

If we construe recreational service as a field employing professionals to provide the basic services which people have come to appreciate, then it is necessary to understand that professionals are educated to the point where they will not willingly forego what they conceive to be a part of their prerogative, that is, the shaping of policies for the agency and a representation in the decision making which will eventually affect them. Supervisors and administrators may offer an environment which is not conducive to democratic participation or may not concern themselves with initiating personnel procedures based upon sound human relations, but they will reap what they have sown. Subordinate employees charged with conducting recreational activities will be of inferior quality, less competent to perform the responsibilities for which they have been employed, and surely less motivated and dedicated in carrying out the various assignments vital to the effective program. The reason is obvious. Professionals do not care to work in situations where their professionalism is taken lightly, where they cannot exercise their ingenuity, discretion, and intelligence. Individuals who fall for the lockstep routine of the assembly line probably do not care enough to question policies, procedures, or the activities which they are enjoined to execute. Under these circumstances it would hardly seem possible that recreationists would submit themselves to such a threatening environment. Those who would acquiesce are those who could not feel comfortable in exercising their own initiative or who appear to function best in authoritarian climates. Such individuals are happiest when taking orders and carrying out assignments without question. They need not think nor actually be concerned with what they are doing.

Professionals, by their very nature, will rebel at having passively to accept orders handed down without being provided with logical and factual explanations for them. Professionals pride themselves on their individuality, talent, skill, experience, and knowledge. They believe that they can perform their jobs as well as anybody and better than most. For this reason, they will feel mistreated and unnecessary if they are just ordered about. Hence, recreationists would leave the agency's employment rather than continue to submit to undemocratic practices and less-than-professional relationships. The residue of employees will be those of inferior capability, intelligence, and responsiveness. The agency will be saddled with those who constantly require close instruction in carrying out their job responsibilities and, in all probability, will attempt to do as little as possible in fulfilling their assignments. This result will necessitate even more watchfulness on the part of supervisors, and they will not be getting the return for their own efforts. The provision of recreational service will deteriorate, and all the negative effects of poor personnel practices and procedures will rapidly and readily become apparent.

Supervision by directives will stimulate an exodus of highly motivated and competent recreationists, who will seek jobs elsewhere. Professionals can never be retained where an atmosphere of supervisory threat pervades the agency. Anxiety should be alleviated if workers are to give their best efforts. This means that all positive practices should be made operational as quickly as possible and that those employees who have the capacity, maturity, and interest should be enabled to participate in the development of program, policies, and conditions which will, sooner or later, have an effect upon them. Thus, supervision should be conducive to the production of an environment in which workers will want to cooperate because they believe in what the agency is doing and they have a sense of belonging to a group to which they are devoted. Such a situation will develop as supervisors employ the techniques and processes of leadership and are themselves seen as leaders and not simply as heads who must be obeyed.

Supervision incorporates all aspects of human development, such as participant satisfaction within the scope of agency activities, employee competence in the guidance, direction, or instruction of activities, program development and organization, and evaluation. It includes all those involved in the provision of recreational services and all efforts to assist people to obtain and exercise innovative concepts. To this end leadership is uppermost. Supervision, then, may be defined in terms of the objectives for which it is used, aims which give meaning to the methods applied, and as a positive force in developing interpersonal relations. Finally, it is used to free the talents and intellect of all those who come within its purview.

The Supervisory or Mediating Level

In recreational service, the position classification between program, or functional, worker and administrators has been termed supervisory. Within the hierarchy of the department, the supervisor stands as the mediating member of the agency. He is the heart of the organization. Just as the program and administrative levels may be described as the extremities and the head, respectively, the supervisor performs the vital work without which the agency cannot begin to operate effectively. The competent supervisor literally pumps the life blood of expertness and encouragement into the channels of departmental function.

Supervisors execute decisions made by administrative personnel, interpret agency philosophy, policy, practices, and scope to subordinate workers in functional positions, and act as advocates and buffer between the program workers and administrators. The latter aspects of the supervisory function serve to bring the program personnel a better understanding of administrative practice. The supervisor allies himself neither with the administrator nor with the functional workers, but serves as the counselor to both. Just as he interprets decisions downward through the chain of command, he also explains the needs and objectives of workers to the administrators. It is the function of the supervisor to offer such expert technical assistance, both to the administrator and the functional workers, that success in various spheres of work assigned to them is more likely to be reached.[1]

The process of obtaining cooperation from groups or individuals and of coordinating such activity toward established, desirable objectives is supervision. This aspect of leadership arises in the formulation of recreational policies, in the planning and evaluation of the program, in the selection and education of workers, and in the community organization and operation. It has been generally considered that the focus of supervision is on the improvement of instructional and educative processes for the production of more effective, efficient, and competent recreational personnel through the development of their capacities and abilities. However, supervision as a leadership process in recreational service is the exclusive property neither of supervisory personnel nor of any level within the recreational service system. As a process whereby expert technique is used to provide the best possible arrangement of facilities and experiences for public benefit, supervision may be performed on every level where valid leadership is found. The functional worker supervises the recreational activities of participants and on occasion of co-workers, just as the executive or administrator may also exercise

---

[1]W.H. Burton and L.J. Bruechner, *Supervision: A Social Process,* 3rd ed. (New York: Appleton-Century-Crofts, 1955), p. 11.

supervision in the performance of responsibilities. No one position has sole claim on the ability to supervise or on the use of supervision in the daily fulfillment of on-the-job living. It may be that each worker is their own best supervisor, because only when the individual is able to supervise personal functions will there be development as a professional person.

Supervision in recreational service is characterized by the following functions:

1. The exercise of leadership and the awareness of leadership ability in others, with attendant stimulation of that capacity whenever it is discovered.
2. The study and improvement of the activities presented in the recreational program, the materials, supplies, and equipment utilized in the program, leadership methods, and group processes developed as a result of agency initiation.
3. The interpretation of recreational and agency objectives within the system as well as to the community at large. Internally, this may be considered as the guidance and instruction of recreational personnel and volunteers. Externally, it is part of the public relations function utilized to explain the purpose and operation of the agency.
4. The determination of the individual worker's ability and inclination for learning new methods of activity presentation and for accepting work suggestions or advice.
5. The assistance of workers in their professional development, the instilling of objective reactions toward the work situation and the problems which may confront the worker, and the analysis and instruction of professional objectives and the stimulation of dedication toward this service.
6. The in-service education of recreational workers and improvement of their personal work habits. This may take the form of individual or staff conferences; observation of better prepared workers; utilization of a professional library; prescribed attendance at clinics, workshops, conferences, or other learning situations; or any additional techniques which may be imparted to the worker.
7. The field observation of program operation and personal interview of staff personnel for aiding in the improvement of worker technique and for recommending desirable changes in the pro-

gram related to the findings. This function is carried out through the analysis of records and reports as well as through inspection and examination of the leadership methods in use by workers.

8. The education and improvement of supervisory personnel and the evaluation of the technical efficiency of supervision with recommendations for needed modifications. This latter aspect of supervision is urgently required if the supervisor is to be current in knowledge and techniques. Thus, there is an implication of supervision of self as well as the need for consistent objective appraisal of supervisory tasks and expertness.

Effective supervision is based upon consideration of changing conditions within the community or agency and of the basic aims and policies of the department or system. It is built upon collected primary information in the evaluation and execution of methods and techniques. Supervision, to be effective, must include recognition of the fact that individuals differ. Not only are there personality, mental, and physical differences, but educational, experiential, and motivational differences which influence and apply to skills and technical presentation. The awareness of these individual traits helps the supervisor to realize that there is a need for a variety of techniques and that there is no one *best* way to lead, instruct, guide, or function in an activity presentation. Basic differences in individual personality will require separate techniques, some of which may be adapted to fit specific personality patterns, but the techniques utilized by each worker can be analyzed and improved.

Rapport Develops Cooperation

Rapport between individuals must be built and maintained to develop cooperation in the work. The result of cooperative enterprise should lead to the growth of each worker's fullest capacities through the process of leadership rather than through subservience to official authority. Any narrow or biased individual placed in a position of authority can force a worker to comply to specific acts because of the implied threat of dismissal which the former has. However, this type of relationship will never lead to productive worker participation and will probably result in malingering wherever and whenever possible. Even in professionally minded persons, the resentment which accrues as a consequence of harsh imposition of authority without logical explanation for arbitrariness gives rise to performance inadequacies despite professional intent. Supervision must shape the agency and community environment in an effort to encourage any creativity and productivity inherent within supervised personnel.

Both the program recreationist and the supervisor must be consistently aware of the objectives toward which they are striving. Supervisory leadership should be such that it generates admiration and provides direction for the worker instead of achieving agency aims through arbitrary autocracy. It is more important for the supervisor to create an atmosphere in which subordinate workers are stimulated to offer suggestions, carry on arguments in order to influence outcomes, and participate in innovational activities designed to better their service, then it is to demand unquestioned adherence to formal methods. In this way, a democratic attitude is fostered, and the worker is more likely to contribute his best efforts on behalf of the agency.

Supervision as a process may be facilitated through careful selection and assignment of recreationists, that is, by the placement of the right worker in the right job at the right place and time. This may be accomplished through the provision of adequate recruitment procedures, inservice educational practices, orientation of workers to the agency and to their assigned tasks, and continuous interpretation of agency aims, needs and principles of work. Supervision is made easy by the consistency and evenness in operation of agency routine, the chain-of-command organization of line and staff functions, and the use of records, reports, guidelines for work practices, paperwork management, and standard operating procedures which all personnel recognize and which call for maximum output with the least amount of friction between personalities.

To assure the reduction of aggravating conditions and the continuance of smooth operating procedures, the supervisor must observe the forces at work affecting the productivity and efficiency of program personnel. Irritating environmental factors, whether of a personal or material nature, should be removed either by transfer or by amelioration in order that supervision may be facilitated. Where friction between workers, for any reason, causes a loss in service to the public, measures must be taken to eliminate these annoyances. Generally, transfer of workers to different locations in the system will resolve such problems, although extreme situations may require dismissal as the only solution. Where environmental conditions, such as poor working atmosphere, excessive noise, dirt, danger, or other factors are observed, steps should be taken to eradicate them.

Professional attitudes toward the agency and the entire field of recreational service, including such intangibles as loyalty, discretion, dependability, initiative, and dedication, must be stimulated in all departmental personnel for better employee-supervisor relations, as well as incentive for higher productivity and greater creativity. Finally, the supervisor should encourage self-evaluation among professional and voluntary workers, since it is only when the individual actually wants to improve, thinks there is just reason, or realizes the necessity for improvement that any success in this direction will occur. Regardless of the hints or threats utilized in any method of supervision, in the last analysis it is up to the individual worker to better techniques and relationships with co-workers and participants who are served.

Supervision is provided by giving help at each point of personal contact in the recreational program of the agency. These varied offerings include such elements as individual, group, and staff conferences, reliability of the supervisor for keeping appointments at definitely stated times, and a constant, stable, and mature attitude on the supervisor's part to give objective attention to individual problems, of either a personal or a professional nature. Basic to supervisory accomplishment is the function of interpretation of new recreational policy throughout the organization, field observation among workers for constructive improvement and for worker appraisal, and critical self-analysis and evaluation as a supervisor.[2]

Supervision as a leadership process not only inspires workers to become receptive to the assistance it can give, but it also provides impetus for self-criticism and evaluation of personal effort. To the degree to which these supervisor-worker relations are attained, the results will be rewarding to the supervisor, the worker, the agency, and the receiving public. Supervision democratically, systematically, logically, and objectively administered can do much to spur morale among personnel so that the agency becomes the recipient of cooperative and coordinated work. The success of supervision can be measured in terms of worker improvement and program effectiveness. Supervision must be impartial, firmly grounded in scientific analysis, universally applied throughout the agency, and creative in its efforts.

---

[2]*Ibid.* p. 85.

Problems in Supervision

Perhaps the single most fundamental issue which supervisors feel they have to face is the problem of increasing anarchy within the organization. This is more commonly referred to as the loss of position prerogatives among supervisors when they inaugurate what is anxiously looked upon as democracy. The supervisor who sees himself as a victim of lost authority with less and less ability to order subordinates in their respective tasks is afflicted by human relations in organization.[3]

Among the internal questions which supervisors inevitably pose are those which deal with getting work out of recalcitrant employees, that is, those who question the necessity for having to do the work. "Won't employees tend to question every assignment and won't they feel free to do as they please if we do not have the ability to threaten them with retaliatory consequences for failure, insubordination, or a host of other punishable offenses?" The fact that supervisors ask these plaintive questions is an indication that such individuals have no conception of supervision nor are they able to lead. No supervisor worth anything should ever be afraid that subordinates will not work unless the threat of punishment hangs over them. No real supervisor needs to utilize position, with all of the implied power at work, to get high level performance from subordinates. The question of discipline need never arise if the supervisor is a real leader. But is this last statement really valid? No matter how competent a supervisor might be and regardless of leadership capacity, there could be individuals who are employed, through various methods of entree, who either cannot function within a democratic milieu or who exploit the situation to get away with as much as possible. Under these circumstances, the supervisory leader should apply such appropriate disciplinary methods as are necessary. Such methods may be no more anxiety provoking than technical instruction to the worker so that accomplishment of assignments can be made or at the other extreme a recommendation for discharge of the worker for cause. Between these possibilities lies an array of creative techniques and routine instructional procedures which may obviate the need for any disciplinary activity. The whole question boils down to the establishment of rapport between the supervisor and subordinates and ability to employ the leadership process with all the concomitant meanings and effects that this can have on others.

---

[3]W.R. Land, R.G. Corwin, and W.G. Monahan, *Foundations of Educational Administration: A Behavioral Analysis* (New York: The Macmillan Company, 1967), p. 295.

From the beginning of the appointment the supervisor has a sensitive problem to face in any attempt to deal with a number of procedural problems concerning relationships. Of paramount significance is the way in which subordinate employees see the supervisor. They may well look upon the supervisor with initial distrust because of the authority, not only to discipline them, but to deny them economic security. It is this potential threat to their livelihood which causes so much consternation, anxiety, mistrust, and conformity by employees.

> The supervisor always has a difficult function in any case. He must try to motivate the worker to perform most effectively. Yet, the supervisor is faced with an immediate negative factor that he must fight to overcome. All workers are initially fearful or suspicious of supervisors—a natural enough feeling, because it stems from the superior—subordinate relationship of the hierarchy. Such a relationship carries the overt or implied threat of punishment for noncompliance with directives, procedures, or supervisory "suggestions". Almost every worker faces a new supervisor with some hesitation. The supervisor has real power over the subordinate, or the worker feels that the supervisor has such power whether the authority exists or is simply a myth. Whatever the job situation, the worker approaches the supervisor with the idea, if not the knowledge, that the supervisor has the power to economically punish him if the worker does not subscribe to orders. There can be no real leadership under these conditions.[4]

When an incompetent person is appointed to a supervisory position there may be a valid basis for subordinates' anxiety. Such an individual is capable of capricious actions which might lead to employee discharge, demotions, admonitions on the record, or other penalties for almost any behavior which, in the eyes of the supervisor, is offensive, even if it is not. This is where the balance of terror really begins, not knowing how the incompetent supervisor will view innocent questions or inquiries which are desirable if a better program of activities is to be produced. When supervisors feel threatened by subordinates, because of their greater competency, they become defensive and hostile. Under such circumstances almost any retaliatory response, with neither rhyme nor reason, is possible. The supervisor holds forth because of the position within the organization, not because of any actual knowledge possessed.

---

[4]G. Hjelte and J.S. Shivers, *Public Administration of Recreational Services* (Philadelphia: Lea and Febiger, 1972), p. 209.

Supervisory Ploys and Negativism

As an indication of the negative aspects of supervisory authority and an illustration of the deterioration of positive human relations in conjunction with an inferior individual assuming the supervisory position in any recreational agency, the following ploys have been selected. They are designed for the person who is incompetent to perform the duties of office because of a lack of intelligence, poor preparation, weak character, or other perfidious and insidious personality defects.

There are countless ways to hinder progress, frustrate the well-intentioned employee, and negate pertinent and logically constructed ideas related to the recreational program, its personnel, and the practices incidental to them. The really poor supervisor, however, has been able to make a fine art of the practice of subterfuge and escape from decision-making while giving every appearance of being sincere, conscientious, and considerate in all dealings with subordinates, superiors, and the laymen who participate in the agency's program. It is this supreme mediocrity which will be under examination. The techniques herein listed may be applied anywhere, particularly when the supervisor is insecure in the position because of personal incompetence, partiality, pride, and lack of professionalism.

1. When presented with any document which needs your consideration or approval and you do not understand what is necessary or required, rattle the paper and clear your throat several times. This will inform the individual who presented you with the paper that you are giving the missive your utmost attention and earnest appraisal, although you have no idea what is going on.

2. When presented with a well-detailed plan of operation showing much thought and effort, do not immediately read any part of the presentation. Weigh the material in your hand; if it seems heavy, put it on your desk. Inform the individual who performed the work that "it looks good" and that you will look it over carefully later on when you have enough time to give it the attention it deserves.

3. No matter what proposal is made to you concerning the operational aspects of personnel use or program content, always complain that "things are moving too fast" and that "we've got to slow down in order to consider properly what we are doing." This will, in effect, allow you to do nothing.

4. Appoint an advisory council or committee to "help formulate plans, policies, and activities". Disregard all suggestions the group makes. This will serve to frustrate even the most ardent agency supporter. The resulting demoralization will more than offset any good concepts which might be developed by the group.

5. Give any and all your subordinates meaningless titles, for example, supervisor, director, manager, or specialist; this will cause them to work harder, but it will save operational costs, since no salary increases can be given merely for titles. Keep all authority in your own hands while delegating responsibility, so that every problem must be brought to you for resolution. This will enhance your reputation as a Solomon.

6. Play politics. This is better known as "checker-moving." It consists of finding ways to do little things for others who in turn may be utilized to assist you in attaining your objectives. Of course, these favors may not be returned when you need them most because of other considerations, for example, self-aggrandizement or preservation. Even when you can be more effective and perform your functions with less expense, overlook these possibilities. Make sure that the recipients of your largesse are properly indebted to you and realize that the flow of "goodies" can be stopped any time they do not reciprocate. There are some who might frown upon this activity and might even stoop to using descriptive terms such as rebates, kickbacks, or graft, but these persons have little or no influence and are quite narrow-minded.

7. When asked a question which you cannot answer because of your inadequacy, look surprised, pained, and then condescendingly, at the questioner. These tactics should imply to the person who questioned you that the query is so simple it should not have been asked in the first place. This act tends to embarrass not only the questioner but also any would-be interrogators who might like to question you because they might be placed in the same stupid position.

8. Whenever you convene a staff or group conference and some argument arises, do not attempt to settle the difference immediately. Appoint a committee. The question may never be solved if you select the right people for the committee.

9. Whenever sensitive social problems are brought up for discussion by your board, your staff, or interested laymen, state that such a

problem is generic to the entire society. Nobody will know what you mean, they will be embarrassed to ask what it means, and they may drop the matter.

10. If a specific subject is discussed in any meeting and the participants look to you for some kind of declaratory statement, either say that the problem is part of a vicious cycle which cannot be attacked until a more remote part is first resolved, or use vague phrases or meaningless jargon in answering the question. This technique can be utilized indefinitely, will serve to confuse everyone, and will probably result in no action at all.

11. If the same situation as in technique 10 occurs, another subversive device is to utilize the "tangent approach." Simply seize upon a word which sounds familiar to you and begin a discussion concerning it. Although your discussion will have absolutely nothing to do with the original point which needs examination, it will serve to camouflage your own stupidity, ultimately confuse all of the discussants, and allow you to escape the task of attempting to explain what you do not understand. You will never have to say "I don't know" to anybody when this technique is applied.

12. Make grand statements about the future of your agency. Reinforce these statements by quoting some statistic, any statistic, to impress your listener. Say that you never made any such statement, if the listener proves you wrong.

13. Whenever there is an outcry by some persons against any member of your staff, do not bother to investigate the claims. Simply assume that the public is always right and your worker is always wrong, and either chastise or discharge. This is particularly effective in regions where extreme veneration of the past is a form of worship.

14. Never back away from a stand previously taken. Even when you realize that the position which you have taken is completely false and that you are battling from weakness, pretend that the facts are nonexistent and keep up the fight. You will take on the luster of heroism to mediocrities like yourself. At least you can always tell yourself that you conducted yourself with dignity after your position has been defeated.

15. Jealously guard your position. Never employ anyone who appears to have bright promise, a better education, or more skill, or who may disagree with you. This will serve three purposes: (1) you will

remain as chief mediocrity in your agency; (2) no one will ever disagree with you; and (3) you will never have to suffer odious comparisons between yourself and a competent individual.

16. If by some unpredictable lapse you have employed an individual who is skilled, competent, well prepared, and dedicated to recreational service, obstruct every effort. Place that person in the most untenable positions. Frustrate all needs, and goad him or her into some rash statement or action so that you may charge insubordination, thereby ridding yourself of a troublesome gadfly.

17. If by some unforeseen chain of circumstances one of your subordinates gains some prominence in a particular specialty, get yourself appointed chairman of a committee working on that specialization, assign specific work relating to the specialty to your subordinate, and then take the credit for the work which was performed.

18. Do not read any articles or current books pertinent to your field. Rely upon outdated materials for your information. After all, you went to school, and what was good enough for your father is good enough for you. This will have an excellent effect upon your staff, because some of them will never have read anything and they will believe that you, at least, are keeping up-to-date.

19. Name-drop. Whenever you are part of a discussion, always include the name of one or more outstanding persons working in the same field or closely related to it. Such a tactic will imply to your listeners that you are close to them and are therefore just as important, and that perhaps they should not bother such a personage with their problems.

20. Always shift the blame to someone else. It does not make any difference concerning the nature of the mistake, injury, or wrong suffered as long as you do not have to bear the onus of guilt. Just make sure that you can "pass the buck" to some scapegoat.

21. Always assume a negative attitude. It is easier to say "no" than "yes." Be sure that you look for the adverse possibilities involving any matter; then, when you say "no", there will, at least be some justification. Better still, say "It will never work." Do not elucidate. Leave the proposer with the feeling that you have actually tried the idea before and have conclusive evidence that the proposal is ridiculous. If that is too obvious, say "we have been doing it for years."

22. Have a pet cliche to spring upon anybody who comes to you with

an idea. "I'm with you a thousand per cent." This will indicate to the proposer that you really believe in this concept. After the person leaves, promptly forget anything that was said. This device will make all parties happy.

23. Never take a risk. Never try anything which has not been made stale or safe by overuse. Never attempt to progress. In fact, if you can possibly work it out, do absolutely nothing. If you do not do any work at all, no one can ever accuse you of doing anything wrong, and your record will be clean. You may even get promotions, and you will certainly retain your job when others are being discharged for wilful or logical thinking.

24. When somebody disagrees with one of your pet projects, run, do not walk, to the nearest yes-man and lay your project before him. He will agree with you—1000 per cent. This will suffice to show the individual who disagrees with you that he or she is in a minority and does not know on which side their bread is buttered.

25. Call weekly staff meetings and imply that you are flexible and openminded and will objectively consider any ideas or suggestions which any staff member develops. Upon receiving staff suggestions or opinions, criticize them, find fault with anything you can. Make sure to ask for petty details to justify the suggestion. This will cure anybody else from making proposals and being placed "on-the-spot."

26. When you call staff meetings or preside at board hearings, ostensibly to receive suggestions and proposals, come with your plans already drawn and preconceived notions set. Allow everybody to make some sort of contribution. When the discussion begins to break down, introduce your own plans and ram them through. In order to make certain that your project is going to be carried, ask for a show of hands or a voice vote. Your subordinates will be afraid to object, and your board members will not object because they do not wish to appear stupid.

27. Play favorites among your staff members. Be sure to join at least one office clique, or form one of your own. Those who belong are your own kind; the others will never get the plums. Suspicions may spring up, but you may be rewarded by having troublemakers resign rather than having to work under such intolerable conditions.

28. Say that *the* answer is unavailable. This tactic allows you to forget that a question was ever asked and requires no response.

29. When a point is brought up to which you have no logical reply, say that any discussion of the problem is subject to misrepresentation by outsiders and request that because of its supersensitivity the question be tabled for a closed-door session. Strongly imply that anybody who would ask a question of that nature is a communist, a fascist, or member of whatever the current negative ideology happens to be.

30. Imply that anyone who disagrees with you or who is dissatisfied with the agency, the program, or your stupid practices is either sick, or one who has such abnormal personality problems that whatever transferred frustration is felt is to that of the agency. Then all your cohorts can make bad jokes and laugh at the person's expense.

31. Be sure to ask for an explanation of any question which arises. Hope that the explanation is long enough so that there will not be enough time for a reply. If there is time for a reply, utilize the tangent approach (see technique 11).

32. Criticize your subordinates regardless of their competency. Be sure to find something about which you can be critical or caustic. Never offer instructional ideas or explain how weaknesses of method or presentation may be overcome. This will probably result in personal insecurity among your staff personnel and ultimately give them ulcers, or at least a spastic duodenum.

33. Plagiarize. Steal the work of others whenever you can. Uninformed people will think that you are creative, and providentially, it is extremely difficult to prove that you have really stolen another's work. Your reputation will grow with each successful raid.

34. Say "this discussion has been interesting and informative," even if nothing has been accomplished and the opposite is true. This device serves two purposes: all participants will feel as though they either contributed something or received something from the meeting, and each person will recognize your superior talents as a parliamentarian and coordinator.

By following these techniques, a new low in human relations and personnel practices may be attained. For those on any organizational level who are of mediocre caliber, these methods may provide the knowledge required to avoid awkwardness in dissembling and duplicity of action. Mediocrities should unite in this endeavor (if only to save themselves from being found out). The perfect motto for those who are bovine in thought and deed might be "downward and backward toward stagnation" or "it is better to take two steps backward than to go forward with some risk." Diligent study and application of these methods will make the practitioner nimble in avoiding decisions. The reverse of these practices is required of the supervisory leader and leadership on all levels.

Appointment of Incompetents

Where individuals are appointed to supervisory positions and pervert the meaning of supervision they do irreparable damage to employee morale and integrity. In fact, the better subordinates will soon decamp to other agencies rather than put up with the dictatorial arrogance and mindless formulations of the incompetent. Of course, some competent persons will stay on the job despite harassment because of any number of personal or economic reasons. But what of the others who will remain? Those who are of questionable value to the organization insofar as technical competence is concerned will probably stay. Since they do not threaten the supervisor, they cannot be all that good. Others remaining will be those who really do not care about the service or what they do as long as they maintain their jobs. Such individuals eagerly conform to the dictates of the supervisor, despite the possibility and probability of deteriorated service to the public, because the syncophant has learned that this is the easiest road to promotions and raises.

How does an incompetent person obtain appointment to a supervisory slot? The ill-prepared person obtains preferment in the same way that any incompetent receives choice assignments. Either the department is absolutely wasting time, money, and effort because of hopeless incompetence from top to bottom, or political maneuvering has succeeded in placing the individual in the position. Political machinations are still prevalent in both small and large agencies throughout the United States. There are still time servers who have risen from the ranks to become supervisors or administrators, not on their recreational service ability, but because of whom they know in the political party in power, through nepotism, personal friendship, or ways designed to get around the appointment of persons to positions on the basis of their ability to perform the job. Surely, this cannot come as a complete surprise to anyone.

Thus, poor supervisors provide a haven for poor workers and generate an increasing rate of departure among highly regarded employees. It is Gresham's law at work among people; poor (incompetent) people drive out good (competent) people. There can be no resolution of the problem until poor supervisors are discharged, political patronage is discouraged, and appointments at any level are based upon open competition, with qualifications for the position well known, criteria of professional preparation firmly established, pertinent experience gained, and standard tests administered. So-called crash programs, wherein minority group members are employed because they are minority group members, should be discouraged in the same way that employment in consequence of political affiliation, friendship, family, or favoritism should be abolished.

Recreational service is only as good as the least of those employed to provide the service. Any incompetence cheapens the department and casts some taint on all operating personnel. Incompetents must either be summarily dismissed or be offered opportunities to raise their efficiency and effectiveness through inservice education and formalized study. Every individual who is employed within the department should have the chance to improve performance. However, if the employee rejects the opportunity or cannot reach an acceptable level of practice, the department has no recourse other than to discharge the individual. It is a fallacy to believe that every person either is capable of or has the personality, skill, or talent to be a recreationist. Although some insist that any reasonable individual can function in the role of recreationist, the idea is not true. Without proper professional education before practice there is every likelihood of failure in one or more functional areas. A competent supervisor has the responsibility, among other functions, to weed out the incompetent and to assign technically proficient individuals to job responsibilities where, because of their skills, knowledge, interests, and experience, they will best be able to serve the public.

Supervision in a Democratic Environment

Even with competent supervisors, subordinates still suspect that unless they conform to requests or suggestions they will be punished. The supervisory leader must overcome this handicap from the first meeting held with co-workers by being democratic. Subordinates should be asked for suggestions, ideas, and counsel. Furthermore, this type of meeting requires a planned atmosphere of openness where each person can contribute as much or as little as is necessary. There should never be any attempt to criticize ideas merely for the sake of criticism. All suggestions should receive proper consideration by the entire group. Where feasible, ideas will be adopted; where not, they will be rejected with thanks. At no time should the employee ever feel patronized, condescended to, or ignored. In such an environment there seems a greater likelihood that sound working relations will be developed, employees will come to have confidence in their supervisor, rapport will be established, and the basis for mutual trust and support will have been firmly grounded.

When subordinates realize that the supervisor plays no favorites, has high expectations of work performance, respects them as professional peers, asks them to participate in the decision-making processes which give them a say in the shaping of policies that will guide the operation of the agency, then they will reciprocate. Mutual trust and confidence have to be earned; they cannot be ordered simply through rank or position within the organization. If rapport can be established, many of the disciplinary actions which seem to plague organizations will tend to disappear. The behaviors that require admonishment or more severe penalties will disappear, as employees are encouraged, taught, supported, and rewarded for diligence. Where employment is stimulating and the employees look forward to being on the job, many of the petty aspects, such as tardiness, slovenly appearance, poor preparation for an activity, discourtesy, and other irritating tendencies, are nonexistent. This change does not occur overnight. It requires patience, understanding, insight, and an appreciation for the other person's point of view. More importantly, it really needs leadership because modification of behavior will have to be obtained.

Will democratic organization lead to a breakdown in worker efficiency? Can the supervisor exercise any authority and still maintain the democratic environment? Employment practices should be of such a nature as to recruit individuals who are highly qualified for the recreationist position by educational preparation, commitment to the field, and enthusiasm for the job. At this point, the agency has the best of all possible worlds. It has recruited, inducted, and assigned a reasonably competent person to fill a vacancy within the department. Now it becomes the agency's responsibility to retain that worker for as long as possible, insofar as the worker fulfills obligations to the department. This is where the supervisory effort should be directed.

A competent supervisor will channel all efforts toward maintaining the employee's morale, building ego, and establishing rapport with the employee in order to sustain sound personal relations between the employee and the agency. Under such circumstances it is only *by* democratic procedures that any employee will increase loyalty to the agency, attempt to broaden skills and knowledge for greater service to the community, and feel that he or she is an integral and valued member of the agency team. By binding the worker closer to the organization the supervisor stimulates dedicated efforts and devotion to the agency. Under these conditions the worker will be more efficient and effective. The typical malingerer's attitude will be absent, because the working environment permits the program recreationist open expression without hesitation, and without fear of retaliation. This climate should be sufficient to retain the competent and ensure the continued productive effectiveness of the recreationist. Naturally, the supervisor plays a key role in the creation of this democratic environment and the initiation of relationships which support morale and the desire to continue association with the agency.

But what of those occasions when workers infringe upon the established policies or rules of the agency, let us say by displaying conduct that is detrimental to the service or that can lead to friction among other employees. In such instances the democratic climate still prevails. However, such an atmosphere need not come into conflict with the necessity to exercise authority and punishment when negative behavior warrants it. The supervisor is never a sloppy sentimentalist because of beliefs in and practice of warm human relations. Rapport does not break down objectivity. On the contrary, it probably provides the practitioner with a greater insight into the immediate and long-term needs of others and makes the perception of strengths and weaknesses keener. Emotionalism should never be permitted to interfere with objectivity. Lack of emotionalism does not mean lack of human feelings or emotions. Not at all. It signifies that the supervisor does not permit emotionalism to cloud the issues which have to be resolved, particularly when they directly concern employee behavior.

Certainly, minor infractions can be discussed privately with the perpetrator, but they cannot be tolerated for long. If they are, other employees will begin to believe that favoritism is being shown to the one who continues with faulty practices without concomitant punishment. Initial warnings may be given in private interviews concerning why such behavior is occurring. Perhaps discussion of the matter will resolve it. It may be that personal problems are hampering the employee's work, emotional problems may be interfering with judgment, or any number of other extenuating circumstances could be the cause. Punishment without ascertaining the facts or reasons behind undesirable behavior can lead only to further recrimination, hostility, and finally, an abrupt break with the agency. Everybody loses from such action. The supervisor can never be percipitant in actions or prejudge without determining all of the facts in each instance. Gathering facts is a slow process, but it may keep a competent worker from leaving and save the agency time, effort, money, and reduced service while it searches for a replacement. The facts may indicate a matter as simple as the employee feeling that he or she is being taken for granted and that agency representatives neither care about nor really notice what is being done. This problem sounds trivial, but the vagaries of human nature may conceivably cause such a reaction. Merely attempting to find out what the problem is may negate punative action.

The supervisor should be able to view each employee as an individual with certain needs and drives, assist that person whenever help is required, ask for help in return when necessary (without embarrassment or anxiety), and expect the employee to carry out duties and obligations, for which pay is received without worrying that the employee will feel hostile or "put upon" because performance is required. The supervisor should never feel apologetic to subordinates for asking them to do the work they were employed to do.

More to the point, if the employee feels that personal appearance or manner does not affect the public's regard for the department, he/she is misinformed and should be corrected in no uncertain terms. While the garb of contemporary society is absolutely permissive, there is no reason to assume that those who work in the public service should not be neat and clean and appropriately dressed as the occasion demands. The image of the agency is related directly to how the public views each employee. Therefore, unless they are on some detached assignment which would preclude their dressing in some way, recreational service employees should dress in a conservative style. Insofar as private agency employees are concerned, they will have to conform to whatever their agency requires.

Authority and Democracy

A particular source of confusion for some supervisors is the role of authority within the democratic milieu. Some supervisors tend to contrast authority with democracy. They conceive the word *authority* as synonymous with the term *dictatorial* and the word *authoritative* with the term *authoritarian.* Unless supervisors understand the differences between these concepts, they will continue to have difficulty in resolving problems among peers and subordinates. The significance of authority in democratic supervision is the recognition of the need for some kind of control vested in those responsible for a group. This authority should be understood to be synonymous with official appointment and the execution of specific duties and responsibilities. Scrutiny of group behavior shows that a good deal of authoritative leadership is consonant with cooperation in almost every kind of commonly espoused effort. Laws, policies, responsibility, and well-defined channels of action are a fundamental part of democratic life. Democratic cooperation replaces the selfishness of authority with the selflessness of group control without displacing authority. For any joint enterprise there will always be a need for authority, whether it is legal in nature, based upon knowledge or expertise, assigned by some institution, or given official designation. Whatever the source, it is a genuine component of democratic cooperation.

Participation and Democratic Supervision

The single most important criterion of democratic cooperation is the quality and quantity of participation achieved by every member of a group in the planning and operation of activities for and by the group. This is no less valid for employees working in an agency and the part that they can play in defining and administering program, objectives, policy, and choices of the agency. To the extent that every agency employee is enabled to experience satisfaction in determining possible avenues of action, the inducement to remain with the agency is strengthened and working relationships are established more firmly. The democratic trend in supervision is really the increased role played by those employees on the line who are not officially designated as supervisory or managerial staff. Supervision is increasingly participatory and cooperative. Policies and programs affecting the working environment and human interrelationships should be developed through open discussion and total participation. Despite the apparent limitations which might be imposed on a group in which everybody participates, in order to reach policy and program formats which will be beneficial and effective, all supervisory efforts should be directed toward this end. Under the presumption that competent recreationists have been employed by the agency, each person should be able to contribute some idea or experience which can prove practical, worthwhile, and generally satisfying to all concerned.

There can be little antagonism to the concept that everyone who is vitally concerned or directly affected should have a voice in determining plans, policies, programs, and be a part of the decision-making process. The best supervisory practice limits participation to those who are immediately concerned with the problems or questions in which their knowledge and experience will enable a rational solution. When supervisors begin to employ the technique of participatory involvement, with concomitant responsibility for the consequences, then employees feel that they are being considered as human beings, not as mere cogs in a wheel, and reciprocate with loyalty, dedication, and productive effort.

Supervisory Techniques for Cooperation

The supervisor who is concerned for the increased technical capacity of subordinates, who wants to establish rapport with peers, who desires to retain competent personnel for the longest time should be prepared to implement the following concepts: (1) All decision-making functions should grow out of the needs of the group insofar as such needs are directly related to organizational problems, programming, clientele satisfaction, or working conditions. (2) The physical environment should be conducive to maximum group productivity. Conferences should be held periodically at a convenient time and in a place that is adequate in size, well-lighted, well-ventilated to prevent drowziness, and designed to facilitate sound human relations. The conferees should be able to see and hear one another without straining. (3) Whatever decisions are made should be equitable in apportioning a fair share of responsibility to all group members. In the last analysis, a group can act efficiently only through its members. Responsibility for action should be shared in terms of individual interests, capacity to perform, and experience. (4) Sufficient time should be alloted to ensure that current problems will receive adequate attention and so that some reasonable solution can be developed for substantive action. (5) The supervisor should be vitally involved with consideration for subordinates. One of the most important factors on which potential followers view a leader is from the aspect of considerateness. This degree of reflection regarding circumstances or observation of the feelings of others can do much to support the establishment of trust and confidence in the supervisor by the subordinates. When the group has such trust reflected back to it, then rapport is a reality. Consideration is another way of stating concern for the welfare of subordinate employees. (6) The correct selection of candidates for appointment to recreational positions, the placement of them in situations designed to promote their functional effectiveness for themselves and the recreational service system, the schedule of compensation, the provision of relative security based upon competent work, the recognition of outstanding service, and the day-to-day competent functioning of the line recreationist are concerns of the supervisor. The most productive effort the supervisor can make comes from the consideration shown to subordinates. (7) The supervisor should inaugurate a program for encouraging employees' creativity by activating a working situation where the employees feel free to express themselves on any matter pertinent to the organization. There must be continuous stimulation of experimentation with new ideas and activities. No person should be stifled or downgraded during an attempt to innovate. With supervisory assistance, but better without, each recreationist should be invited to submit new ideas, to make suggestions for overall agency and program improvement. In such circumstances, program recreationists will gain self-confidence as well as the ability to evaluate their own proposal. (8) The supervisor should have the flexibility to adapt to individual differences in education, experience, ability, and interest which the employees of the agency will display. Attention will have to be given, as is necessary, to those who require it without making them so dependent upon assistance that it becomes a crutch. To some the supervisor will act as a resource, to others guidance will be given, and to still others instruction. Time to satisfy the needs of those who comprise the staff has to be made. Appointments scheduled should *always* be kept. The calendar is available to schedule meetings and conferences with the staff. All other functions are secondary to this essential one.

The Supervisor's Obligations

The supervisor in recreational service is probably the most important individual in achieving the aim of effective utilization of people. By directing, supervising, guiding, and otherwise managing the energies of those individuals for whom the responsibility is vested, the obligation for actually performing the normal aspects of personnel administration is the supervisor's. Obtaining maximized efficiency and effectiveness from program recreationists while maintaining a satisfied work group is the supervisor's job. Additionally, there is also the burden of sustaining the agency's public image.

The supervisor represents the administration to subordinates, because the methods, attitudes, and behaviors employed reflect those of the department. The individual employee of a large department has little or no opportunity to see the executives; contact with them is through the

supervisor. Therefore, the philosophy, attitude, knowledge, and equa-
nimity of the supervisor in dealing with subordinates will do much to
develop their loyalty to the agency, confidence in the administration,
and enhanced efforts with the satisfactions derived therefrom. Having a
dual responsibility both to subordinates and superiors places the supervisor in the difficult role of mediator.

Immediacy of Supervision

For some time now the relationship between the extent of supervision
and its effects upon employee attitudes and productivity has been well
known. Broad spans of control and few levels of authority seem to result
in a more effective organizational structure and produce a large number
of highly competent employees. Concomitantly, there are heightened
morale and output. Conversely, where supervisory proximity to workers
results in close supervision, there is a drop in morale and productivity.
Close supervision is defined here as controlling how workers perform
and what they do on the job. In a study conducted by Day and others, it
was shown that close supervision adversely affects workers' desire and
capacity to perform.[5]

Some writers and theorists focus on the either/or aspect of supervision
and neglect personal motivation for effective performance. Supervision is
concerned exclusively neither with subordinates nor with management.
Real supervision is most effective when it fulfills the program demands
of the organization, which should equally satisfy the needs of the workers.
Both facets of organizational life, that is, agency demands and employee
needs, are quite consistent and complementary. Supervision as a leadership function probably agrees with the research findings of Fiedler that
production-oriented supervisors may be likened to task leaders and
personnel-oriented supervisors are analogous to socioemotional leaders.
Each has a place in setting the tone of the group's environment. Under
certain conditions, production needs receive greater emphasis. As the
situation changes and morale factors require encouragement, the supervisor becomes employee centered.

There are indications that when the supervisor wants to meet the
objectives of the agency, the degree to which subordinates are satisfied
with their supervisor's supportive behavior in reference to them facili-

---

[5]R.C. Day and R.L. Hamblin, *"Some Effects of Close and Punitive Styles of Supervision,"* *American Journal of Sociology,* Vol. 69, No. 5 (March, 1964), pp. 499–510.

tates task performance.[6] Naturally, there is a difference between loyalty to a person and loyalty to the ideals and purposes of the agency. However, employees must perceive that their supervisors support them and are willing and able to represent them, whenever necessary. In addition, the degree to which functional workers and their immediate superiors exert influence on agency policy and, therefore, operations is correlated to high performance and productivity. When either productivity or effectiveness is utilized to appraise job performance, there is a well-defined and direct relationship between such criteria and supervisory control.

Supervisor's Role in Improving Performance

Communication is one of the chief methods utilized by supervisors in carrying out their respective assignments and in gaining the kinds of cooperation necessary for highly effective work performance. It is one of the fundamental aspects of leadership and, yet, often is also one of the most neglected. The communicative process makes possible transmitting instructions, executing instructions, and influencing attitudes, beliefs, and work. It is a primary way by which ideas are exchanged and through which people are motivated to behave.

In general, the purposes of communication are to inform, assist in the resolution of problems, to instruct and educate, to offer opportunity for participation and recognition, and to distill the innovative forces and concepts of agency workers.[7] For these reasons, communication is used to transmit rules, regulations, and policy (as well as administrative philosophy) throughout the agency; to obtain the ideas and suggestions from all functional workers; and to secure the best internal relationships possible so that maximal cooperation and coordination develop.

Communication is the associative link between all facets of the organization and serves to connect plans and action from inception to execution. More often than not, it is a cost-saving technique as well as an instrument for determining the quality of performance. The environment of the agency is reflected in communication insofar as transmission and reception are concerned. The ability of any supervisor to gain response from subordinate staff and willingness to perform their several

---

[6]R.C. Miljus, "Effective Leadership and Motivation of Human Resources," *Personnel Journal,* Vol. 49, No. 1 (January, 1970), pp. 36–40.

[7]P. Ash, "The Many Functions of Discussion," *Supervisory Management,* Vol. 16, No. 3 (March, 1971), pp. 21–24.

functions effectively depends, in large measure, upon the quality of communication.[8]

Communication will be most effective when the following environment is created:

1. Recreationists must receive complete and honest supervisory appraisals on all matters which pertain to them and their conditions of work.
2. Recreationists must receive a rationale or justification for the policy statements issued by administrators.
3. Recreationists must receive clear explanations of the problems that affect the ability of the agency to conduct its operations.
4. Supervisors must develop an environment in which communication flows freely throughout the agency.
5. Supervisors should elicit the functional recreationist's ideas, suggestions, comments, and opinions in developing improvements in operations, policies, plans, programs, and general services.
6. Wherever possible, supervisors should be able to provide prompt answers to inquiries and render appropriate decisions on matters of immediate concern to employees and to the function of the agency.
7. Supervisors should attempt, by every means possible, to clarify ideas prior to committing them to the communication channels.
8. Supervisors should examine the real objectives of each communication.
9. Supervisors should take into consideration the entire physical and social milieu concerning the impact that the message has on the receiver whenever there is a need for communication.
10. Whenever feasible and appropriate, consultation with others may be most beneficial in preparing communications.
11. Supervisors should always understand that messages frequently carry overtones and meanings which may not be desirable. The fundamental content of the message should be studied to eliminate incorrect or negative nuances.
12. Supervisors should always make sure that communications are useful to those who receive them.
13. Supervisors must learn to initiate follow-ups on their communications and not assume that receivers will always understand the

---

[8]"To Do Their Best Work Everyone Must Communicate," *Industrial Research* (July, 1970), p. 77.

message, even though the supervisor is sure that he or she has communicated clearly.

14. Supervisors should always utilize the communications process as a developer of sound personal relations as well as an informational network.
15. Supervisors should always strive for consistency. This means that supervisory behavior should not be the "Do as I say and not as I do" type.
16. Supervisors must understand that communication is a two-way process. Its success depends upon transmission and reception.

Advice and Guidance

Another technique for gaining supervisory effectiveness is the provision of counseling and guidance for functional recreationists. Almost any personal problems can affect a worker's performance. Often the supervisor must become involved in providing guidance and counseling to some degree. Whenever an employee's personal problems begin to have a negative effect upon the capacity to perform or causes conflict between workers, the supervisor has the responsibility for intervening.

The essence of supervisory counseling is to assist subordinates to be more effective in their work and to provide them with an accurate appraisal of their status in the organization. Counseling offers an opportunity for employees to understand their relationships with their peers and superiors. Counseling occurs during the course of conversation between the supervisor and the counselee only—no other parties are involved. Counseling, when appropriate and provided competently, offers opportunities for cooperative endeavor, because during the counseling process empathetic relationships are formed, rapport is established, and situations, misunderstandings, and uncertainty are cleared up. Obscure meanings, which tend to confuse people, are eliminated during counseling.

A subordinate employee may be offered a sense of personal direction during counseling and thereby immensely profit from it. In some instances, anxiety-provoking conditions which hamper worker effectiveness can be completely expunged if guidance is given.

A supervisor may be able to detect certain qualities or latent talents of the subordinate which might never have been suspected prior to counseling. When these capacities are brought into the open, the individual may be able to develop these abilities and, with this as a new starting point, be encouraged to go on to greater effectiveness and higher productivity.

In the same way, negative characteristics which tend to hamper interpersonal relations are drawn to the worker's attention through calm, constructive means. Without embarrassing or belittling the subordinate in any way, unpleasant behaviors or hostile mannerisms can be inspected, analyzed, and finally terminated, to the benefit of all concerned.

The counseling procedure can promote personal growth reciprocally. The worker will mature as perception of strengths and weaknesses are gained. Enhanced capability, and status within the organization, may result from this developmental process. The supervisor also will experience some personal growth, as increased self-confidence and personal satisfaction, which comes from rendering assistance to others, is obtained. The supervisor will come to learn that each subordinate is unique, that each has particular strengths and weaknesses, and that each has something to contribute to the overall welfare of the department if encouraged to do so. Counseling stimulates individual respect for those who are able to carry out their responsibilities. It also permits the supervisor to exercise leadership and gain insight and empathy for those with whom the work is shared.

Motivation

Motives are the internal drives which stimulate the individual's actions. Incentives are those extra-personal rewards which excite the motive. They start or stop, promote or demote, and arouse or deter human activities. Thus, incentives are the conditions which inspire dynamic forces within the worker or the intrinsic qualities of the job which are utilized to influence or modify the behavior of the worker. The supervisor should have any number of incentives designed to appeal to subordinates. Understanding the needs and desires of those with whom he or she works well equips the supervisor to offer the appropriate catalyst which should spur the functional recreationist to greater productivity and effectiveness.

The stimulant selected by the supervisor should directly appeal to the motive which is salient in the individuals concerned. If the inducement has widespread appeal, the outcome is likely to be that much more effective than if the appeal is directed toward only one motive. When incentives have been properly chosen in consideration of employee needs, the result will be observed in an increased effort and value on the part of the worker. Of all incentives, the ones with greatest potential for assuring worker receptivity and increased capacity will be of a nonmaterial nature. Such incentives deal with ego and self-actualization needs. Since these needs can never be satisfied, they perpetually incite the worker to perform at maximum in order to obtain personal feelings of accomplishment. The achievement motive is significant because it helps to satisfy the individual's self-actualization needs. The more the individual succeeds, the more ego satisfaction is derived. Therefore, promotion is an effective incentive that the supervisor has to recommend because it represents some fulfillment of ego needs. Additionally, there are material awards which coincide with increased status and prestige. Other incentives which nominally grow out of ego needs are those aspects of ego satisfaction that stem directly from obtaining recognition for work performed.

Both material and nonmaterial incentives can be used specifically to enhance worker effectiveness or induce modification of behavior. Neither type of incentive should be used to the exclusion of the other. Each can reinforce the other. However, the greatest opportunity for increasing efficiency and production among workers will come from nonmaterial incentives based upon ego needs, if material benefits are adequate to accommodate basic physical and social needs.

Incentives can take form as rewards or punishments. Rewards accrue for performing in those ways which are deemed of value to the agency; punishment is the outcome of performing in ways that are detrimental to the agency. Supervisors have two methods to utilize: one approach will consist of leadership acts that encourage, stimulate, or influence workers to reach higher goals; the other will employ threats of many kinds which compel output. Fear, in fact, may goad an employee to perform at a higher level of production or effectiveness than he or she might ordinarily sustain, but it is questionable as to how long the threat of reprisal can hang over an individual before a point is reached where either greater threat must be used or the individual leaves the agency. For the kind of people which recreationists are, namely, professionals, the use of fear is not only counterproductive, but hopelessly outdated. If a supervisor has to force recreationists to perform, they either do not belong in the field or there is something radically wrong with the kinds of jobs they are being asked to do.

Fundamentally, the objective of motivation is to create a sense of possession and pride in previous accomplishments on the job and anticipation of greater satisfaction for future achievements which will cause the employee to continue with the agency and sustain maximal performance. It is the supervisor's responsibility to develop an environment in which those factors that stimulate worker achievement can be organized into a sustained force that will coordinate individual aims with organizational goals. The particular incentives selected by the supervisor must appeal to the motives which are currently pronounced in the workers. An incentive which is attractive because it serves several motives is of greater effectiveness than one which concerns only one. If the choice of incentive is found to be inadequate to produce the desired ends, the supervisor has the opportunity to attempt to modify the worker's appreciation of the value of the incentive or to utilize another stimulus.

No matter what specific incentives are employed to enhance worker productivity and effectiveness, they must be integrated with all other employment factors. Motivation to improve performance is one method supervisors can use if other elements are consistent with employee satisfaction. The supervisor can assist the functional recreationist to succeed and find personal satisfaction on the job, thereby retaining that person for the agency, by working with the employee to develop performance goals against which performance may be checked. Incentives of various kinds are offered to the extent to which the goal was reached or surpassed. In this way, the employee has the option for setting a personal level of achievement consistent with those of the agency's overall objectives. The supervisor can provide the proper incentives for inducing subordinates to perform at high levels. The supervisor will be able to establish lines of communication and appropriate relationships, and to give guidance and counsel as necessary. Under these conditions, leadership will be felt and workers will be retained by the agency for the duration of their effective professional lives.

The person who is responsible for the supervision of functional personnel involved in the activities program of a recreational agency should have a purposive and wide knowledge of recreational service; generally open to suggestions, but also possessing special education concerning many methods and techniques. Awareness of the fact that not all workers can utilize the same procedures with the same degree of success, because there is more to being a recreationist than the mere use of standardized methods. The supervisor must be impartial and exhibit integrity at all times. Nothing ruins morale faster than favoritism toward some while ignoring the efforts of others. The supervisor must recognize superior methods. Continually encouraging personnel, to the extent to which they are capable, to modify their methods where necessary, the supervisor's educational preparation must be richer than that of those who are supervised. Experiences must be broader in content and scope.

Supervisors must be responsible for the achievement of the recreational program in the system. Historically, this responsibility devolved upon the functional recreationist, and failure in achievement was placed upon the worker's inability to perform. This concept should be corrected, for in most cases, *as the supervisor is, so is the program.* This inference can support a foundation for evaluating the effectiveness of supervision in recreational service. The competent supervisor is a creative person. By originating criteria for the agency and stimulating close cooperation and coordination among all individuals and groups who work *with* him or her; dedicated leadership serves as the stimulus which encourages concentrated effort and maximal output in reaching the recreational goals for which the agency was organized.

Chapter 13

PUBLIC EDUCATION AND PUBLIC RELATIONS

I t is a professional mandate that the public be exposed to the variety and diversity of recreational opportunity available through planned and organized recreational activities. All persons need to be educated to recognize the facts and nature of recreational service.

Public education relevant to recreational service may be defined as a basic instructional plan of cooperatively utilizing every available ethical means of informing all citizens of the values to be derived from its public recreational systems, in order that understanding and appreciation may be engendered and fostered. In this way, awareness of opportunities and attitudes of receptivity can be developed so that better personal relations between the agency and the public will be encouraged. The necessity for public goodwill is indispensable if the people for whom recreational services are organized and administered are to receive benefits and take advantage of the satisfying experiences offered to them. Essentially, however, goodwill is an outgrowth of recognition, and recognition is dependent upon comprehension.

Public Education as Necessity

For too long, people have been ignorant of the truth concerning public recreational service. To some extent, this has been the fault of recreationists themselves. Too few recreational agencies have undertaken the arduous task of enlightening the public about the real story of the field or about the functions and role the agency plays in community life. The public simply does not realize that the public recreational service department is the best single agency for securing satisfying, enjoyable, safe, and planned experiences specifically designed for the happiness of the participants. As a public service organization the recreational service system is required to provide facts about the operation, administration, and the results generated therefrom. Individuals who have little or no knowledge of public recreational service, or of the departments operating in the field, cannot be reasonably expected to appreciate the offerings. In fact, it would be surprising if, without knowing of the availability or understanding the nature of recreational opportunities, any persons were to take full advantage of the services provided.

Recreationists have tended to find fault with the public for its apparent apathy and nonsupport of public departments. The fault does not lie with the public, but in large measure it is a problem caused by the systems themselves. Recreationists have taken small pains to clear up misunderstandings, smooth conflicts, or provide explanations of the department's functions, responsibilities, and services to the public. Whatever misconception has arisen comes from a basic lack of effort on the part of recreationists to extend the agency's usefulness through the development of good public relations. It is quite comprehensible, therefore, to accept the reasons why the humanitarian feature of recreational service has not received its fair share of appreciation and why the public has allowed the recreationist to work in relative obscurity. As education enhances knowledge and awareness of the field, and status for recreationists, there will be a concomitant development of goodwill toward public recreational agencies, which is essential for them to accomplish most effectively the fundamental promise of providing recreational opportunities for all the people all the time.

Chiefly, two considerations make it necessary for the public to know about recreational service and the public agencies which carry on the work: that the entire community may profitably avail itself of the services offered; and that the recreational systems may properly be empowered to extend their utility. In rendering services recreational departments must perform several functions: programming recreational activities; employment and professional development of competent staff; planning, design, construction, and maintenance of physical plants and facilities; and administration. It is apparent that public education is focused on the best interests of the community, but there is reciprocity in that the department enjoys considerable benefit as well. Until recreational agencies can attract greater support through participation, they will not be enabled to offer a comprehensive series of activities, make more adequate recreational places and facilities, employ the best prepared and most competent leadership, nor effectively administer the complex facets of agency operation. Public education through the provision of greater identification and discovery of significant value to the community is of specific benefit to the recreational service department. Offering authoritative, timely, and interesting information will attract favorable attention and advance the interests of the field as a whole and the agency in particular.

Outcomes of Public Education

The objectives of public education must be clearly understood, worthwhile, in good taste, and reachable. The objectives should be easily definable and basic to the nature of the agency. There is a need for identification of the public to which the campaign of education is directed. Every public relations program must be appropriate for what it is attempting to accomplish. The fundamental idea being promoted must be socially sound and have general appeal and value for the public. A public relations program must have desirable goals and should support only that which is in good taste. The whole concept of ethical practice revolves around this point. Consideration must be given to current public opinion. This is particularly important where the agency is attempting to educate persons of all positions and status and specifically if the idea to be disseminated is new, different, or likely to encounter objections. Unless it can be related to accepted beliefs, the idea is likely to be dismissed without much thought. The larger goal of public education must be attainable. This can be realized through careful planning. It is true that coincidental situations, facts, or conditions may be highly publicized and gain attention and success. However, the procedure of public education should not rest upon the startling news event or fortuitous circumstances. There must be a definite, intelligent, and carefully devised plan with scrupulous attention given to all details.

A careful well-organized plan of public education should:

1. Develop public appreciation of recreational service.
2. Expose people to a wider variety of possible recreational experiences.
3. Disseminate information about the recreational system and develop knowledge and understanding of department functions.
4. Encourage genuine good public relations between the citizens and their department.
5. Modify negative attitudes and opinions which adversely affect the department.
6. Suggest a more precise survey and analysis of the community in

order to determine needs and resources wherein the recreational agency can assume a more vital and rightful role.

7. Cooperate and coordinate activities with all other recreational organizations within the community to provide total community service.

8. Foster a definite desire on the part of employed personnel to understand the work of the department and effect better relations and closer contact with the public.

9. Clearly define the economic support necessary if the public system is to be enabled to carry out its ethical mandate.

10. Justify the necessity for the construction and maintenance of additional recreational facilities and areas in order to meet community needs.

11. Stimulate participation of citizens in utilizing existing facilities and areas and in taking part in planned recreational activities.

12. Remove political patronage from the public department.

13. Clarify and explain professional personnel standards in terms of more effective recreational offerings promoted in the safest manner.

14. Publicly explain the position of the recreational service system as the chief source of skilled and continuous provision of recreational experiences so that it may be widely understood that this service is available to the community.

15. Encourage volunteers to offer their time, talents, and skill in broadening recreational opportunities.

16. Avoid competition for the same participants among all agencies offering recreational opportunities in the community.

17. Promote voluntary contributions, endowments, gifts, and bequests.

18. Discover and list every segment of the public which may be of significance in shaping opinion favorable to the agency.

19. Encourage private citizens to consult the agency for information and program resources in seeking personal nonprogrammed recreational experiences.

20. Improve the relations between agency and mass media for a more valid and sympathetic presentation of departmental practices and policies.

All these outcomes are developed through a sound, carefully organized plan of public education; in order that these benefits may be effected, a complete analysis of the appeals and content of the program is essential. There must be a detailed and systematic plan for initiating and sustaining a successful program of public education.

Planning Public Education

Before the public recreational service department can undertake the necessary action of educating its community, it must develop a plan that will systematically utilize every possible means of a comprehensive and unified campaign. Countless opportunities throughout the year lend themselves to effective and colorful use in educating the public. These situations and occasions should be coordinated into the campaign, and every advantage must be taken of them. However, the public education program cannot be an intermittent affair of hit and miss, trial and error. There must be a sound and logical procedure by which each facet of the campaign is fitted into a complete and intelligible picture. The campaign, like the recreational program itself, is on a distinct schedule of pre-determined events. A successful public education program is the culmination of a regularly released series of items which have continuity and thereby build interest. A schedule of events should be released to all mass media in a prearranged sequence on a periodic and routine basis in order to awaken public anticipation which may eventuate in support. Every item released at definitely spaced intervals is concentrated on increasing the education of the public.

A successful effort will be made only with a clear understanding of the recreational service department which is to be the beneficiary of the educational campaign. Every facet of the department should be carefully researched to make certain that all the facts are known before the campaign is initiated. Questions that must be answered concern the history of the department, how, when, and why it was established, and information about its development, functions, policies, and personnel. It is particularly desirable in the case of policies to know why they came into existence. How does the department benefit the community? Who has guided the development and operation of the agency? What is the department's position in the municipal government? in the life of the community? Has it been progressive in meeting changing conditions as well as in planning for future situations? What are the advantages that will accrue if the department is given community support? What are the opportunities and resources available which will have a positive effect upon the community and its citizens? These questions answered with the truth will do much to educate the public and engender public commitment and support for the recreational system.

Analysis of the Public

The chief fact to be provided concerns the public to which the appeal is to be made. What does the public already know about and how do they react toward the public recreational service department? Reasonably accurate answers to many questions may be found through the use of the well-established statistical sampling method. A carefully selected sample of a fraction of the public may be surveyed to determine answers for the entire aggregate. Sampling surveys may be conducted by personal interview, by mail, by telephone, or through a panel of permanent or periodically selected individuals. After the questions have been asked of the persons making up the sample, the responses must be analyzed, evaluated, and verified if they are to be utilized as guides for a public educational program.

Staff Requirements

Employed personnel of the recreational service department are all the staff that a public education program usually requires or has. However, some large departments may be fortunate to be able to employ one or more public relations specialists who will be responsible for the technical dissemination of material that serves to educate the public. The number of staff personnel needed to operate a continuous public education program will depend, in large measure, upon 1) the quantity of material to be collected and studied; 2) the amount of writing to be performed; 3) the media to be utilized; 4) the coordination necessary for centralized and decentralized phases of the program; and 5) the mechanical and routine work which can be done by nontechnical personnel. The smaller and one-person departments will have to rely upon the recreationist to get the job done or will need to recruit volunteers who can offer assistance. The larger and more efficient metropolitan departments will undoubtedly have a specialist who has the function of public relations only. Many successful education staffs consist of a supervisor, sometimes a writer or an editor, secretaries, and clerks.

The permanent staff of the largest urban systems may consist of a director or supervisor in charge, an assistant, several interviewers, at least one analyst, one or more writers, an editor, a photographer, clerks, typists, and secretaries. The effectiveness of the public education program will be contingent upon the competency of the director and his assistants. It is also dependent upon the degree of centralization of authority, and upon a clear line of demarcation of duties and functions. The director of public relations should have an important voice in the formulation of policies concerned with the management of public education. This means that technical counsel should be observed in order for the person to carry out the assignment and details of the program in the way that will best serve the interests and needs of the department and the community.

The employment of a public relations director, on either a full-time or part-time basis, realistically assists the realization of a workable procedure of public education. The public relations director must be a specialist in mass communications and should be thoroughly familiar with recreational service. Such a person will know best how to gain attention and sustain public interest. He/she must have enthusiasm and a good imagination. Such characteristics are indispensable to one who must stimulate support with new ideas and initiate action. The director is the best qualified person to advise on the methods of public education.

Standards of Practice

Unlike commercial operations and other business ventures, the public recreational service department must conduct its public relations in strict accordance with a professional code of ethics. The public agency cannot be ruled by the competitive element, but must function in a way that is most beneficial for the community and its citizens. A program of public education must utilize every possible ethical means of providing the truth about the agency and its operation to all persons. Furthermore, information about the entire field of recreational service and its attendant parts must be offered. Publicity is not the answer. A soundly developed plan of factual content interestingly presented and disseminated in the best manner for attractiveness and impact requires attention to the smallest detail. Exaggeration, personal aggrandizement, and statements that distort the real objective of the agency must be shunned.

The Educational Program

Prior to the initiation of any educational program of public relations, research is necessary to disclose points of conflict and other areas of misapprehension between the public and the recreational service system. Whenever public apathy, nonsupport, or unfavorable opinions as a consequence of certain policies which the agency follows are discovered, a planned series of explanations and procedures to remedy unfriendly attitudes must be undertaken. More specifically, some citizens may have developed erroneous ideas concerning the fees and charges which the department sets or about its budgeted expenditures because of their inability or unwillingness to analyze the public record. Much progress has been made in recent years in making annual reports containing financial earnings and expenditures intelligible to laymen. The presentation of interesting, attractive, and simple reports, which are widely disseminated, may be one of the more significant features of departmental relations. Other citizens may have developed a dislike for the department because of a poor first impression, which they gathered when meeting with an employee who was discourteous, indifferent, or ignorant. Misrepresentations in scheduling activities, errors in the program which occur frequently, and a parochial or competitive view of other agencies in the community may inspire public irritation and ultimate rejection of the agency. Such attitudes are dangerous. One disenchanted individual may be the beginning of a movement to abolish the department because it is an unnecessary frill and a waste of the taxpayer's money. Whatever the cause of ill will, it must be corrected and the facts of correction appropriately publicized.

A program of public education needs to employ every form of media which can be effective in widely publicizing the true nature of the department and its functions. Five specific avenues are available to recreational service systems for the attainment of this objective; oral presentations, literary presentations, graphic presentations, a combination of these means, and the organization itself.

Oral Presentations

Education may be greatly promoted by word of mouth. However, such education may be positive or negative, depending upon the information obtained. True statements concerning the public recreational service department can be beneficial, but slanderous, dishonest, or biased statements can do much to hurt the system. Surprisingly, but unfortunately, some departmental personnel become either disaffected or disloyal, or through ignorance speak of the agency in terms that can best be described as detrimental. Upon the superintendent, therefore, lies the responsibility of providing such personnel with the correct information and taking steps to dissuade those staff persons from their negative opinions. All personnel of the department have an important role to play in public education. Professionals, most particularly, should be so well informed about the responsibilities, functions, and operation of the agency that they are ready, willing, and able to discuss the department intelligently and explain its workings to all who wish or need to know.

Participants. Probably the most effective means of educating the public with respect to the recreational institution is through the program participant who has achieved satisfaction or enjoyment in a given activity.

Unless the department can offer a program geared to meet the recreational needs of all people in the community, it should not undertake a plan of public education; in fact, it has not lived up to the reason for its establishment and should be abolished. Unless the public recreational service department is prepared to offer a comprehensive program of great variety and diversity under the guidance and direction of competent recreationists, it is not representative of the ethical practice which makes recreational service a great humanitarian field of endeavor. By providing the type of program which will generally meet the needs of people, a public department of recreational service will best publicize itself ethically. The satisfied participant who has enjoyed an activity and who feels achievement in some way can do more to educate and gain public support for the agency than can any other medium. This is the essential reason for the existence of the agency—to satisfy participants. A satisfied participant will do more than any other method to counteract adverse opinion, because as a member of the public direct experience with the system has occurred.

Staff Personnel. Employed personnel are especially influential in gaining satisfied participants, and their words as well as performance are a vital asset in public education. Staff personnel, whether professional, technical, or ancillary, are in constant contact with members of the public. The first contact that an individual may have with the department will probably be with an employee. If the employee takes an interest in the person, attempts to answer whatever question is asked, knows about the program offerings, facilities, and schedules, and displays courtesy, the likelihood is that the department will reap great benefits. Conversely, ignorance, rudeness, curtness, and affectation can do much to ruin any image which the agency must maintain.

Personnel employed by recreational agencies invariably talk about their work. They relate incidents that occur daily. It is of the utmost importance that all personnel be encouraged to give a true picture of the department and what it stands for. Personnel management procedures afford excellent opportunities to recruit carefully, to screen, and to induct intelligent and competent individuals. The scientific management of personnel offers many techniques to prevent employee discontent and promote loyalty. In order to preclude disaffection, the recreational service department must treat its personnel with consideration. Every staff member must be made to understand the intrinsic role he/she plays in contributing to the overall effectiveness of the agency. Each employee must be made to believe that the image of the system rests with him or her. In a sense this is the truth, for all employed personnel contribute to the operating efficiency, the adequacy of program opportunities, and the maintenance of the agency. Regardless of the position of the employee, there should be indoctrination with the idea that whatever is done contributes in no small way to the production of recreational services for the entire community. If the employee really feels that the work is important and recognition is received for doing a good job, the usual reaction will be sincere interest, dedicated loyalty, and satisfaction which, in consequence, will produce favorable public education. Devotion to duty, however, is not enough. All employees must be taught the basic facts about the agency, its respective policies, and this must be reinforced periodically through in-service education. It is apparent that public recreational service departments will be handsomely repaid by treating their employees in such a manner.

Speakers Bureau. The recreational service department should recruit staff members to represent it at a variety of meetings whenever speakers are in demand. A roster of speakers should be developed so that every phase of agency operation or specialization can be explained. A well-selected speaker with a prepared talk presented to any community club, association, or organization does much to encourage interest and foster learning about the agency. Staff employees who are selected for the bureau should be good public speakers, be able to deliver an interesting statement, and must be well acquainted with the agency and its operations. They must be capable of fielding questions on agency policy and be able to answer any questions concerning programming, facilities, or other general facts of operation. Questions dealing with specific administrative detail should be referred to the proper authorities. The function of educating the public can be promoted by seizing every opportunity to reach as many organizations as possible with appropriate talks.

Advisory Councils and Committees. Every public recreational service agency should establish a lay advisory council or committee to assist in planning the program as well as in offering an indication of public interest. Such associations should be formed on a neighborhood basis, for individual playgrounds, centers, and for specific age groups, for example, youth, older adults and parents, as well as for the community as a whole. These groups of elected or selected representatives become the cadre from which word-of-mouth information spreads. Usually, members of these groups have numerous contacts, or they occupy strategic social positions in their respective neighborhoods. Each member of a committee or council is thereby able to speak with other people concerning these aspects of the public recreational service department about which they are familiar.

In order to give impetus to the work of public education, it is absolutely essential to educate committee and council members themselves. All these individuals will be willing to give of their time and energy for the benefit of the department. Significantly, this is considered to be a satisfying recreational experience for those who participate, and they are participating on a voluntary basis in any case. To begin with, they have assumed a certain responsibility by becoming members of committees and councils. However, their energies must be channeled correctly so that what they have to say will be factual and contributory to the good of the agency and the community. Periodically, members of these groups should be given an indoctrinating talk regarding the department. To improve their knowledge of the agency and stimulate their enthusiasm, a visit to all centers of operation can be arranged for them.

Radio. Radio is a natural channel for public education. To contact a mass audience, perhaps radio is one of the best media. Broadcasters are generally willing to utilize ideas and material with news value or human interest and popular appeal. One of the finest avenues available for the formation of positive public opinion and, incidentally for the education of the public, is through radio commentators, who usually have quite a following. Spot Announcements, as well as news or special features, can be made. However, arrangements with broadcasting stations must be made well in advance, script or other materials must be submitted for clearance, and the program itself must be carefully prepared so that its presentation will be as perfect as possible.

Telephone. The telephone can be a striking means for quickly informing the public about specific activities, changes in plans, or answering inquiries. Most important is the way in which the telephone is used. The person answering a telephone for the agency should maintain a pleasant tone of voice and be able to respond, efficiently and in a courteous manner. It must be remembered that the telephone is intrusive; therefore it should be used only at times when it will not disturb the person called, and never at the dinner hour. One of the ways in which telephone communications can be established is the chain phone call. If departmental volunteers can form a telephone link, information about any number of departmental problems, activities, facilities, or necessary support can be dispatched swiftly. The chain call simply asks that the first person telephone two friends, who in turn call two friends, and so on. It may be that particular groups will have a telephone corps wherein each member has a selected list of members to phone. In this way, all members are quickly contacted and informed about any modifications of schedule or provided with whatever data are necessary. Chain telephone calls have proved extremely effective in political campaigns, and there is no reason to suspect that they cannot be just as significant when used correctly by local recreational service departments.

Sectarian Agencies. Much factual information can be disseminated to the public by way of the pulpit. By obtaining the cooperation of the local council of churches or the ministerial association, it is possible to gain the undivided attention of those who might not, in the ordinary course of events, be swayed or contacted by other means. One Sabbath each month could be set aside by clergymen for a discussion of the public recreational service department. A tie-in can be offered between such an address and almost any of the biblical passages concerning work, leisure, the Sabbath itself and the meanings that this has for each individual. The minister may give the address or it may be delivered by a selected speaker. If the minister decides to speak, he or she should be provided with informative material concerning the agency, so that sufficient preparation is available to offer enlightening concepts to the congregation.

Schools. Schools constitute one of the most important fields for dissemination of public recreational service information. They at once provide a captive audience and a fertile area for the implantation of facts that will well serve the community immediately and in the future. Arrangements can be made with school superintendents and principals of each school for providing regular talks by qualified speakers on recreational service and the specific department of the community. Not only can interesting information about the department and its program be offered, speakers who appear at career guidance assemblies, which most high schools arrange, can do much to assist in the recruitment of volunteer, part-time, and potential full-time employees. Many extracurricular groups are oriented toward recreational participation. The activities, sponsored by the school, can become an excellent avenue whereby a qualified representative of the department can appear as part of the club or organizational program for one or more meetings. A definite message can therefore be communicated to young and developing minds.

Clubs, Societies, Associations. A staff representative who can deliver a stimulating and informative talk dealing with departmental plans, programs, or operational practices will be in demand at various social, civic, business, professional, and other interest groups of the community. Hard-pressed program chairpersons of these organizations are always seeking appropriate topics with which to enhance members' participation. The well-selected speaker with a prepared talk can do much to further the work of educating the public through the spoken word.

Literary Presentations

The written word of an intelligent recreationist capable of stating an idea can shape public opinion. Recreational service departments have utilized the printed statement for a long time but, unhappily, the type of writing they generally produced was formal, dogmatic, dull, full of statistics, and contained information not designed to be highly readable by the public. The public recreational service department must publish reports and keep records because it is accountable to the people for what it does. Furthermore, citizens want to read and understand what is reported to them. Legal discourses, financial statements, and long, dry, uninteresting literature cannot educate because the reader's attention and interest will be lost after the first insipid page. If the public recreational service agency really desires to educate the public by literary means, it must supply information that is interesting as well as informative. In small departments the responsibility for compiling this material rests with the executive, with another staff person, or rarely, with a volunteer.

The employment of a specialist on a full-time or part-time basis to write and edit such material is vastly superior to any other method. The literary output of the agency can be disseminated to the public in many ways. Every form of written information can be utilized and fitted into the planned program of education.

Periodicals. Daily newspapers and weekly or monthly magazines are effective methods of placing the achievements and goals of the public department before the general public. The necessity for current events and timely news is obvious. News must be interesting and, when possible, entertaining. It must attract attention, sustain reader interest, create favorable attitudes, and gain support. Literary efforts should be presented as dramatically as possible, for dramatic presentation is often more convincing than straight copy. It makes the underlying reason for the copy not only interesting, but easy to remember. Human interest features, a novel combination of familiar subjects, a question asked in dramatic form, or an offer of service may become dramatic and stimulating methods for presenting material. Every news item should be clearly pointed. Care must be taken to create the impression desired. No written effort should ever be issued if it cannot be fully substantiated by the facts.

Good reporting is based upon the news of the department. The person in charge of developing educational material can begin by compiling sources that can be used in news releases, among which are:

Significant events

Appointment of advisory council members

Meetings of the council, neighborhood councils, committees

Anniversary of establishment of the department

State or national occasions which can be tied into the agency's activities.

Annual banquets, dinners, celebrations

Annual national conference

Annual state conference

Annual district or regional conference

Local pageants, commemorations, or traditional events

Tournaments and program contests

Awards of merit to employees

Opening of an exhibition

Construction of a new or improved facility or area

Program demonstrations

National holidays, festivals, patriotic occasions

Special weeks, days, or months, e.g., Recreation Month
Reports on special studies
  Reports on community recreational conditions
  Reports on community surveys and master plans
  Reports on construction
  Reports on land acquisition
  Reports on federal grants
  Reports on institutes, workshops, and staff development program
Personalities
  Visits by dignitaries
  Personal accomplishments of participants
  Visits by interested community groups
  Winner of leagues, tournaments, games, contests
  Employee advancement within the department
  Interviews by departmental employers
  Contributions to the community made by employees outside of
  the agency
  Recognition and awards to individuals for voluntary service
  Endorsements of the department by local officials and prominent
  citizens
Departmental policies
  New rules and regulations governing certain events or facilities
  New employment policies
  Public conduct policies
  Policies regarding hours of facility operation

Newspapers are the chief published medium of both news and educational information. Indeed, they have come to be known as the great national university. It is in newspapers that the true story of the public recreational service department may be told. Because the extent to which news, feature, and human interest items are used is subject to the attitudes of the newspapers, it is necessary to know something about the way in which they are organized. The individuals who make up the editorial board, the various departments and specializations of the newspaper should be well known to the recreational service employee who is directly concerned with placing information with the newspapers. Because each editor generally supervises and determines the nature of all material to be used as news which will appear in the paper, it is desirable to cultivate that person assiduously. The maintenance of friendly relations with city, managing, and departmental editors is extremely important. Among the general rules that can be followed when working with editors are:

1. Omit trivialities.
2. Plan the educational program before presentation.
3. Keep personal calls brief and never place them just before a deadline.
4. Try to accommodate an editor at every opportunity.
5. Do not conceal any facts.
6. Make the releases interesting and timely.
7. If doubtful about the benefit of any story to the department, trust the editor's judgment.

In many communities, the public recreational service department may become a good source of news for newspapers. If the department can generate enough news, it may become important for newspapers to assign a reporter to cover the agency and bring in departmental stories. There is no sound reason why the public department should not accord special privileges to newspapers. The situation is one of mutual appreciation. If the department expects to have its stories printed in the newspaper, reporters must have free access to the department. The resulting newspaper publicity is of several specific types: straight news stories, feature articles, editorials, departmental column, society columns, news pictures.

Standard Practice for Typed News Releases. Educational information intended for newspapers and magazines should generally be prepared so as to conform to commonly recognized standards of practice. For example:

1. Copy should be on white paper, standard size (8½ inches by 11 inches).
2. Releases should be typed clearly, double- or triple-spaced, and on one side of the paper only.
3. The release date should appear in the upper right-hand corner of the first page.
4. There should be an indication of whether it is for morning or afternoon release.
5. The source of the release should appear in the upper left-hand corner of the first page.
6. Copy should begin not less than one third down the first page and there should be ample margins of not less than one inch on either side.
7. No headings should appear on the story.

8. All pages should conform to the style of the prospective user.
9. Each paragraph should be self-contained and not carried over from one page to another.
10. The word *more* should appear at the bottom of the page if additional copy appears on the next page.
11. The release should be folded so that the copy shows on the outside.
12. Duplicate copies should not be sent to competing media.
13. Editorializing should be avoided.
14. Finish should be indicated by an end mark, e.g., "30" or #.

These standards relating to copy in the preparation of news releases are the result of experiences with many magazine and newspaper offices. Other media have special rules in addition to these, and they also must be respected if the educational program is to go forward. In the preparation of a feature story, special care must be given to the lead or topic sentence. This is a brief introductory statement. It should tell, in 30 words, the answers to who, what, when, where, why, and sometimes how. The lead must be so written that if it is the only sentence that the reader actually digests, the essential elements of the story will be obtained. The reader may not have all the details but at least the basic facts will have been read. The story itself should be so constructed that it may be cut at any point and still be coherent and informative. If at all possible, the story should be limited to one page.

Contests and School Papers. The department of recreational service may well sponsor elementary through college essay contests, especially at a time traditionally oriented to recreational activities. Many subjects dealing with public recreational services may be utilized in such compositions. English teachers are usually willing to cooperate in learning endeavors such as these, inasmuch as they stimulate the regular classroom work.

The school or college paper may be an effective medium to publicize the department effectively. If the department organizes activities which include the student body, in part or whole, there is great likelihood that the paper will carry features, facts, perhaps a regular column, and an editorial concerning departmental offerings, the need for public support or other helpful statements which win friends for the department. The utilization of clip sheets, which are printed to look like miniature newspaper pages or galley proofs, may be useful to the department in keeping school periodicals regularly informed of programmed activities and other information.

Magazines and Sunday Supplements. Magazines offer a channel for certain kinds of public education. However, it is generally not possible to obtain space in the same way or on the same subjects as it is in the newspapers. Nevertheless, it is possible to get magazines to run excellently prepared stories of great detail and length which may add to the educational program. It is difficult, but not impossible, for a writer to reach the editors of magazines because of the nature and requirements of the publications. Material submitted to them must conform to their required patterns. Several publications in the recreational service field are rendering invaluable assistance. However, these serve mainly to educate those who are already employed in the field, rather than the lay public. Among the magazines which carry articles dealing with the field are *Reader's Digest, Saturday Evening Post, Good Housekeeping, Family Circle, House and Garden, Better Homes and Gardens, and House Beautiful.* The news magazines such as *Time* and *Newsweek* have special sections devoted to leisure and recreational activity. The business magazines such as *Fortune* and the trade, technical, or professional magazines provide a fertile and relatively easy access for gaining acceptance. All these magazines should be sought by recreational service departments as a means of educating the public. There are many possibilities—factual articles, descriptive essays, and pictures with news value.

Departmental Bulletins. Mimeographed or printed bulletins should be distributed by every recreational service agency. They may contain a feature story, specific facts about the agency (for example, number of employed personnel, activities offered, facilities, up-coming events), or they can be devoted to the publication of current policies and contain action pictures of sponsored recreational activities. Bulletins may be useful in mailings and also may be placed in the lounges of recreational centers and other public buildings for general distribution.

Pamphlets and Directories. A small comprehensive booklet about the public department can be of inestimable help in educating the public to the organization, administration, and operation of the agency. The purpose of the departmental pamphlet is to help explain the services of the department in language that is interesting and understandable. The use of a pamphlet of this type is effective, particularly when complemented by other media. Directories are indexes of services, facilities, activities, special or current events offered, and names of supervisors and other employees, and also may list supplies, materials, and equipment as well as literary resources. An alphabetical listing of all recreational agencies within the community, supplemented by commercial agencies of various types, completes the directory.

Departmental or House Organ. Mention has been previously made of the necessity for maintaining goodwill among employees and educating them so that they can speak with factual authority of the many services and facets of the department in their respective contacts with the public. The departmental or house organ is an internal magazine written and edited for, and sometimes by, employees rather than by the administrative staff. It is published by the agency for distribution and free circulation solely among the members of the operating staff of the department. It may also be distributed to volunteers and the auxiliary personnel who contribute time and effort toward departmental success. It is a publication which can be issued once each month and constitutes one of the most effective means for securing the interest of all workers. Needless to say, the departmental organ can be produced only in the largest agencies having numerous employees.

The departmental magazine may run from a single sheet of mimeographed or letterpress periodical to the more nearly complete journal containing 4 to 35 pages. House organs generally cover the following subjects:

Agency information—pay schedules, work schedules, appointments of new supervisors, construction of new facilities, advancements, availability of higher positions, expansion of the program, contests, line and staff arrangements, personnel policies, and official announcements.

Employee information—awards for special service, recognition for superior job performance, commendations, promotions, new employees, retirements, obituaries, staff meetings, conference participation, employee interviews, and service anniversaries.

Efforts to increase effectiveness—reduction in waste, staff development programs, safety, health, suggestions and criticisms, technical articles, resources available, editorials, and letters to the editor.

General interest items—articles by members of the staff, book reviews, current events, classified ads, personal improvement articles, recipes, fashion notes, interior decoration, hobbies, quotations, family news, and personals.

To be effective the departmental organ must be highly readable. It must have a pleasing format, neat printing, and attractive illustrations or pictures. Such a periodical should be geared to meet the needs of its readers. It should, as a matter of course, represent the mutual interest of the department and the staff. Although a great deal of the information printed in the journal may be informative, it needs to reflect the reciprocal feeling of respect which the administration has for the staff. The internal journal assists in orienting employees' attitudes. It serves as one medium by which the agency can build mutual trust and confidence between itself and its operating personnel. It offers an outstanding opportunity for the department to win the interest and influence the actions of those who should know the agency best—the employed staff. Public education, like charity, begins at home.

Annual Reports. Annual reports may become an effective instrument for informing the public about the organization and administration of the public recreational service department. Chief among the reasons for publishing an annual report are (1) to conform with legal requirements of public accountability; (2) to establish a permanent record of the accomplishments, operations, and financial disbursements of the agency; (3) to familiarize people with the program of activities, facilities available, and professional personnel who conduct and supervise activities; (4) to recognize all those who have contributed to the rendering of public recreational service within the community; and (5) to stimulate interest, provoke attention, and encourage participation in the program. The annual report must be something more than a statistical accounting of how many people participated or how much money was spent for the maintenance of buildings, grounds, tools, and equipment. It must be readable, thought-provoking, attractive, and informative. This means that bone-dry profit-and-loss statements, meaningless numbers, and percentages that offer calculated misrepresentations must be omitted. There are ways to present financial statements, participation statistics, and factual information that are interesting, bright, and attention getting.

Pictures constitute an important part of any annual report. Photographs of special events, of the standard operating activities, and of highlights during the year should be selected to give a sound understanding of the opportunities provided by the departmental program. Graphic art work, carefully inserted, can do much to alleviate the tedium of going through a set of figures. Comprehensive summaries of fiscal facts can be profitably included, along with a statement of budget needs and projected plans. The annual report may be an excellent selling device in gaining additional support for anticipated needs. If it is well prepared, it serves as a significant educational medium.

Letter Writing. All letters should be personal and informal, unless they are required to be formalized by the nature of an inquiry or in requesting information from a specific resource. Many agencies make the mistake of not replying immediately to questions or criticisms. All replies should be mailed within three days of their receipt. Nothing infuriates an individual so much as not having a mailed inquiry answered or having to wait weeks or months for an answer. All letters should be written with the following concepts in mind:

1. What is the basic objective of the letter?
2. What facts, opinions, or impressions are to be conveyed?
3. Does the opening sentence capture the idea to be transmitted?
4. Does the tone of the letter approach the subject from the recipient's orientation?
5. Does the letter contain a worthwhile idea?
6. Is it positive?
7. Is it integrated around one primary idea?
8. Does it include any inconsequential material that detracts from the ruling idea?
9. Does it omit any essential points?
10. Are all facts and ideas in logical sequence and intelligible?
11. Is it cordial?
12. Does it express confidence?
13. Does it fully answer any questions which the correspondent asked?
14. Is it typed neatly?

Many recreational departments have found it good practice to send a brief, informal letter to new residents. If the community is small enough so that all new arrivals are known by some central agency, for example, a realtor's clearinghouse, new residents can be contacted easily. During the start of a new playground operation, the opening of a new center, or other recreational facility, a list of participants can be made and letters can be sent to them encouraging their suggestions for improvement of the activities or offerings. Letters such as these can be extremely effective in promoting goodwill and, incidentally, in calling attention to new activities, facilities, or other innovations which the department sponsors.

Graphic Presentations

Visual presentations are a valuable method for public education. Stimuli received through the visual sense are normally lasting and impressive.

People appear to understand a great deal more if they are shown something, rather than told about it. Graphic presentations seem to promote great comprehension and long-lasting remembrances of any given subject.

Exhibits. Every recreational service department should direct that each permanent recreational facility have an exhibit in a particular place for inspection at all times. An outstanding idea is for the various facilities to set up exhibits depicting the operations and recreational activities chiefly performed at the facility. For example, a swimming pool might display a collection of action photographs of water shows and/or competitive events; a playground might offer a permanent exhibit of art, crafts, hobby, or nature-oriented activities; a recreational center might set up an exhibit of a model or a proposed new center, or feature a bound scrapbook indicating the highlights of the variety of activities carried on there; a golf course might display a schematic diagram of the links with the various flora that are utilized and the watering system to maintain the greens and fairways; a neighborhood or community park could have a scale model of the park with all of the trails, playing areas, picnic spots, activity places, and aesthetic views or outstanding natural phenomena specifically marked; the central office of the department might carry an instructive permanent exhibit of model records and reports. In every division, unit exhibits of this nature might be available for the edification of visitors touring the agency. Permanent exhibits can usually be kept up to date by replacing, whenever necessary, obsolete items with those of more immediate interest.

Posters and Bulletin Boards. The strategic placement of striking posters and bulletin boards is valuable in the promotion of neighborhood and city-wide recreational services. Posters should be artistically contrived and be able to tell a story in a well-designed format. Posters may be large or small, irregularly or regularly shaped, and placed almost anywhere. They should be used where people congregate: in windows or on counters of banks and food stores, in the lobby of the local motion picture theater, at entrance to recreational facilities, or on supporting columns or posts. Attractively created and colorful posters can serve as one exciting medium for the enlightenment of the public.

The utilization of bulletin boards can do much in publicizing the department's schedule of activities. Bulletin boards are always regular in shape, although they may be of any size. They must be installed at points where they can be seen immediately, or situated where the volume of traffic is heaviest. Pictures and notices placed on the board should be kept current. The board itself should never appear too cluttered, but should be kept neat and so designed as to produce the most pleasing effect. Bulletin boards may be open or have glass coverings. In either instance, they can be enhanced by artfully concealed lighting, direct or indirect, which can do much to draw attention to a specific spot on the board.

Combined Presentations

There are many opportunities to educate the public through a combination of media. Some of them are:

Motion Pictures. Many progressive departments have filmed and produced motion pictures describing the work and the activities of the department, which are available free for use by selected agency employees in assisting in public education. Most recreational service departments usually cannot afford to produce motion pictures for public distribution. However, several excellent films are available for showing by recreational agencies. This means of education is particularly invaluable inasmuch as the public is educated and entertained simultaneously. Many phases of recreational service may be shown to the public through the medium of motion pictures. There is little question that recreational service can be vividly portrayed by this means. The public has always accorded much interest in films and this can be advantageously exploited by departments with imaginative administrators.

Television. Television is an exciting medium that has received less attention than it should because it attracts viewers in every locale. The simple fact that there are now more than 300 million receivers in the United States is an indication of the vast potential which this means has to offer. Perhaps television has superseded all other media in its ability to instantaneously transmit significant news in a visual manner. Then too, well-known commentators have developed an extremely large following and do much to shape public opinion as well as to report information. Telecasting costs are so phenomenal that paid advertisements are calculated in the thousands of dollars for announcements that take seconds to deliver. It is unlikely that recreational service departments could ever budget enough money to sponsor a telecast. However, through the good graces of television stations, time is often given for a variety of local current events features. Stations continually seek out sources which either make news or are concerned with human interest stories. For this reason, departments can make arrangements to televise a series of regularly scheduled telecasts dealing with the operation of the agency in its manifold categories.

To be fully effective, telecasts must occur at stated periodic intervals so that they may be scheduled for viewing release at a time when the public is prepared to see them. The telecast should become an established routine and not an intermittent, hit or miss, program. If arrangements can be made wherein the telecasts occur once each week, each program will be part of a series developing one central theme. Whatever the presentation is, it should be concerned with recreational services in the community, with the public department in particular, should never be longer than 15 minutes, should be precise and interesting, and should always emphasize the relationship between individual achievement and satisfaction, and the recreational opportunities available through the departmental operation. It is sound judgment to reinforce the telecast with a printed pamphlet for distribution to interested parties or for general distribution at recreational centers.

The television program or, if time does not permit, the message must be carefully prepared so that its presentation will be as compelling as possible. Photographs or videotapes of activities currently offered by the department might be included. In addition, some entertainment by the participants in the music, dance, art, or drama activities of the program might be offered, if it is of good quality. One public recreational service department has for years been able to select different groups from various centers and playgrounds throughout its community who do live presentations in the studio. Such performances have earned the department an outstanding reputation. A typical television announcement may be helpful in procuring time from local stations (Fig. 1.).

Tours. A most useful way of gaining goodwill for the department is by conducting guided tours of the agency. Visitors may see the department and its various operations by one of three types of tour.

Individuals may be guided through the department almost every day. Persons of local influence who indicate a desire to see the agency at work should be taken on an intelligently guided tour throughout the system. It is important to remember that each department must be shown in actual operation. Only in this way can the visitor best gain an understanding of what competent recreational service really means. At the conclusion of the tour the individual may be presented with one of several brochures, pamphlets, or even a copy of the annual report, which will help to reinforce what he has observed.

Groups may be taken throughout the recreational system. Arrangements should be made to accommodate as many local community organizations as possible. However, specific days should be set aside on a routine basis, and standard invitations to tour the department should be given to civic bodies. School groups of all grades may be indoctrinated effectively by the group tour method. Close alliance must be maintained with the local school system for this reason. Among the groups whose influence upon community life will be significant if the members are favorably impressed by the tour will be parent-teacher associations, business and professional women's associations, service clubs, church groups, taxpayers' alliance, and other civic-minded organizations.

TELEVISION CONTINUITY FROM X-RECREATIONAL SERVICE DEPARTMENT

Time: 25 seconds

Words: 54

Video	Audio
Slide #_____ (Photograph of activity group)	Public recreational service needs you. It is your local avenue to personal enjoyment, satisfaction, and fun. Your participation in any of these offered activities will give you a sense of achievement--art, crafts, music, drama, sports, hobbies, or outdoor education.
Slide #_____ (Phamphlet offer with X department name and address)	Learn more about your recreational service department Write today for this free pamphlet.

Fig. 1. A typical television announcement.

The public should be invited to a general open house at the department at least twice during the year. National Recreation Month and December present excellent opportunities for inviting the public to visit and see the system. The itinerary for such tours must be well planned and conducted. Features of unusual interest can be called to the attention of the visitors, and items of special significance can be selected for demonstration so that the visitors acquire a better appreciation of the services available from the department. It is necessary that, insofar as possible, the normal course of activities can be presented for visitor's observation. Each division of the system can then be exhibited in its routine functions, that is, performing those activities and providing the facilities, personnel, and recreational experiences which have come to be expected in the usual skilled manner.

Special Media. All items used to remind the public about recreational service and the local department can be included in this phase of public relations. Such items as decals, stickers, inserts, tickets, postage meter messages, lapel buttons, hats, and other novelties can be utilized to carry a particular statement. Such messages may be a few words, for example, "Conserve Parks," "Public Recreational Service," "Volunteers for Service," and so on, to one page statements for insert under car window wipers, in telephone directories, or into shopping bags at local food markets. Each of these items, alone or in combination, can do much to publicize the recreational services offered by the local system. The real effectiveness of such media comes in terms of perpetually reminding the public that the department exists to serve and that the facts of availability are equally accessible.

Slides and Illustrated Lectures. Photographic slides, line drawings, and other illustrations can be used in furthering the education of the public. They can be employed in augmenting talks and lectures about the public department of recreational service and for stressing the numerous activities offered by the system. Although slides can be made without color, those in color are striking. A series of slides or filmstrips showing all phases of producing a pageant, parade, drama, circus, or field event—from inception to completion—may prove stimulating to the public. Added enjoyment and comprehension of the scope of recreational experiences available to the total community can be furnished by a series of pertinent scenes taken at various sites throughout the agency. Good photography and coloring will do much to heighten such scenes. Simultaneous records, tape recordings, or a speaker provides additional emphasis where necessary. Use of minicams offers an inexpensive and dramatic means for making such presentation.

The Department

If the recreational service department wishes to gain the goodwill of its community, it must enter into the life of the community. Departmental personnel should participate in all projects which have to do with the encouragement of education, the improvement of health and welfare, and the furtherance of economic prosperity. Staff personnel, acting as good citizens, should become involved with and take an active part in such civic bodies as the League of Women Voters and the school board, and join whatever social or political association they so desire. Through such interest and contact the public department has ample opportunity to present its own cause and, specifically, to stress the contributory part it plays in the life of the community.

Organization. Departmental structure will play an important part in assisting in public education. How the department is arranged for the promotion and operation of recreational services will do much to influence public opinion for or against the department. If the structure is limited or ineffectual, particularly is this true of one-man departments, the reception afforded the department by the community will be reflected therein. It should be quite apparent that the basic organization of the public department is an accurate indicator of its impact upon the community. If the community has little regard for the agency, it will block steady development in terms of additional personnel, facilities, financial support, and other indices of status. However, where the department is provided with an internal structure designed to meet the multitudinous recreational needs of the community, there is a positive indication that the agency is highly regarded or that over a period of time it has been allowed to develop and receives public support. All large agencies were not established at current size. They have had to justify their existence through many valuable services to the community over many years. When recreational service is thought to be a frill, an unnecessary device for padding the city payroll, or a function which can be cut at the first sign of economic retrenchment, then it may validly be stated that the public department has not enlightened the citizens of the community concerning its significance.

Another facet of organization comes in terms of professional practitioners or recreationists employed by the department. If the department is heavily loaded with technicians, maintenance personnel, custodians, and groundskeepers, there is every reason to believe that the public will not be educated in understanding agency functions. Such personnel maintain facilities and wait for orders from the agency hierarchy; they do not plan, neither do they program. This is not surprising, for they are not equipped to deal with the problems of organizing and administering a complex program of varied and extensive activities of a recreational nature. They are not educationally prepared to handle the human problems and situations that continually confront the recreationist. Professional education, if not extensive field experience, is the major difference which sets the professional apart from the technician. It is this difference that allows the recreationist to understand the reason why, as well as how, recreational activities are initiated and carried on. An entire philosophical orientation is provided to the professional person which is wholly absent from the less educated. It is for these reasons that a department heavily staffed with technical and maintenance personnel may not be able to communicate clearly with and educate the public. Technicians may be able to instruct an activity competently, under supervision, but they are not as capable nor as likely to function as planners. Not being able to visualize the need for public education completely, they are more likely to forget it. The recreationist, on the other hand, is constantly under obligation to educate the public to understand their own recreational needs, both personally and collectively, as an outgrowth of professional principles. The recreationist has learned that careful attention to public needs and desires is as much a part of programming as skill and knowledge of activities. The employment of recreationists, therefore, will generally produce a public relations and education program.

Facilities. Universally, the first impression to be received by the potential recreational participant, casual visitor, or critical observer is the state of the recreational facility. An effective means of forming a good opinion of the agency is through a well-maintained and attractive facility. The center, park, swimming pool, or playground does not have to be expensively appointed nor does it have to be of the most modern design but it must present a neat and clean exterior, painted where paint needs to be applied, metalwork polished, woodwork and masonry in a good state of repair, walks swept, grounds without litter, plantings pruned or in a physical state of obvious upkeep, to make a good impression. The facility should be appropriate for the site on which it is situated. It should be of a size adequate to meet the demands of participants and spectators in the neighborhood; it should be attractive and inviting. There should never be a stale odor pervading its atmosphere. It should be well lighted, well ventilated, and colorful and carefully decorated to make the visitor want to examine it and perhaps find a place for him/her in some activity being offered there.

A dingy looking facility, painted battleship gray or olive drab, has a demoralizing effect upon those who might want to utilize it. Unfortunately, many aquatic facilities utilize these colors, fail to keep the locker areas free from excess moisture and noxious smells, and are poorly ventilated and/or lighted. Poor maintenance practices reduce the effective utilization of the facility by people who do not care for such a fetid environment. Recreational centers should always be bright and cheerful, with recessed lighting, well-placed bulletin boards and posters, and a comfortable lounge area. All equipment and areas necessary for the provision of a comprehensive indoor recreational program should be available and scrupulously inspected each day for signs of wear. Crafts rooms should be separated from other recreational activities because of noise, odors from chemical reagents, or the type of materials employed. All facilities should be checked regularly for safety factors, fire-fighting equipment, and control of noise, dirt, or any negative features. Not only will such a care and maintenance program do much to earn respect for the agency, such practices will also lengthen the life of the facility and the equipment utilized within. Preventive maintenance, coupled with well-designed and competently supervised facilities, can be a most effective method for the development of good public attitudes about the agency and a positive first impression so vital to the encouragement of public support of the system.

Program. The primary reason for the establishment of any recreational service department is the operation of a comprehensive and varied program of recreational activities. This above all is the chief educational device for developing public appreciation of and respect for the department. A soundly administered program which provides opportunities for participation in activities from which people gain enjoyment and satisfaction is a public relations medium of incomparable value. The program itself can provide all of the elements which will cause word of mouth dissemination of positive opinions about agency performance. As was indicated earlier in this chapter, a participant or spectator who enjoys himself is already sold on the importance of the department and will probably support recommendations calling for additional financial support for facilities, leadership, and program. Conversely, all the readily available means for disseminating information for public education come to nothing if the final proof for the existence of the department is a mediocre program at best. Unless the department can produce a program which can, in some way, reach almost every individual living in the community with at least one recreational experience in which that person will find self-realization, skill, confidence, achievement, satisfaction, creativity, or just plain fun, it is not functioning in the manner for which it was organized. A balanced program offers the best hope of any recreational service department to influence the community on its behalf. It is an educational device that can expose potential participants to experiences of a recreational nature to which they may have never given thought. The program can assist in the development of new skills and the continued use of acquired skills, and raise the aspirations of those who have never considered themselves to have any skills at all. A well-planned, competently supervised and led activity can search out latent talents, inspire reticent individuals to attempt to learn something about which they may have thought but never dared try, and assist in the growth and recreational development of every person it contacts. In such an idealized setting, the positive nature of the experience must inevitably lead to the recognition and appreciation of the department's role in community affairs.

An Example of Events in a One-year Program of Public Education

January

    1 Release of annual report

    7 Radiobroadcast. Local Station 11:00 a.m. "Your Recreational Service Department."

   14 Newspaper release. Feature story. "Public Recreational Service and the Community."

   21 Talk before the Junior League Club. Luncheon meeting. "The Need for Recreational Service."

   28 Group tour of public recreational system for Junior League. Afternoon.

February

    1 Open forum at X–Recreational Center. 8–9:30 p.m. "Volunteering as a Recreational Activity."

    8 Radiobroadcast. Local station 11:00 a.m. "Recreational Service and the Conservation of Natural Resources."

   15 Newspaper release. Feature story. "Encroachment on Our Parks."

   22 Talk before the Civitan. Luncheon meeting. "The Function of the Public Recreational Service Department."

   28 Group tour of public recreational service system for Civitan. Afternoon.

March

   1 Newspaper release. Announcement of district conference on professional preparation.

   7 Talk before Junior Chamber of Commerce. Luncheon meeting. "The Financial Value of a Community Recreational Service Agency."

  14 Group tour of public recreational service system for Junior Chamber of Commerce. Afternoon.

  21 District conference on professional preparation.

  28 Radiobroadcast. Local station 11:00 a.m. "The Need for Professional Practitioners."

April

   1 Newspaper release. Announcement of essay contest dealing with relation of recreational service department to community.

   2 Junior high school talk. Assembly period. "Junior Leaders of Playgrounds."

   2 High school talk. Assembly period. "Your Future in Recreational Service."

   9 Radiobroadcast. Local station 11:00 a.m. "The Recreational Service Master Plan."

  16 Group tour of public recreational system by high school students. Afternoon.

  18 Newspaper release. Announcement of Playground Leaders Institute.

  23 Dissemination of pamphlets throughout community concerning, "Fees and charges—How They Can Be Eliminated."

  30 Telecast. Local station 12:00 a.m. "Humanitarianism and Public Recreational Service."

  30 Group tour of public recreational system by junior high school students.

May

   1 Newspaper release. Announcement of winner of essay contest.

   8 Radiobroadcast. Local station 11:00 a.m. "The Role of the Department of Recreational Service in Human Achievement."

  15 Talk before League of Women Voters. Luncheon meeting. "Pollution of Our Waterways—Steps to Abatement."

  22 Telecast. Local station 12:00 a.m. "Therapeutic Recreational Service and the Homebound Disabled."

25 Talk before Business and Professional Women's group. Luncheon meeting. "Coordination for Total Recreational Service."

31 Newspaper release. Feature story. "Regional Recreational Complex Development."

31 Group tour of public recreational system by League of Women Voters. Afternoon.

31 Newspaper release. Announcement of program for Playground Leaders Institute.

June

1 Newspaper release. Announcement of National Recreational Service Month.

7 Radiobroadcast. Local station 11:00 a.m. "Leisure Arts and Skills."

14 Open house at all recreational facilities throughout system. 2–5 p.m.

21 Talk before Lions Club. Luncheon meeting at X Recreational Center. Talk: "The Public Recreational Service Department Operation," followed by group tour of center.

23 Newspaper release. Feature story. "Needed—A Federal Recreational Service."

25 Career Guidance Day at high school. Assembly period. "Recreational Service—Field of the Future."

30 Magazine article. "Public Access to Public Facilities."

30 Newspaper release. Announcement of Summer Festival. July 4th celebration.

July

1 Talk before Grange group. Dinner meeting. Talk: "Rural Recreational Opportunities."

2 Newspaper release. Summer festival schedule of activities culminating in pyrotechnical display on Fourth of July.

7 Talk before city manager's group. Luncheon meeting. Talk: "Public Recreational Service as a Governmental Function." Tour of system for group.

14 Radiobroadcast. Local station 11:00 a.m. "Guides to Camping Out."

21 Newspaper release. Feature story. "Federal Funds for Local Recreational Development."

28 Talk before Associated Women's Clubs. Luncheon meeting. Talk: The Need for Neighborhood Recreational Advisory Councils."

30 Talk before Exchange Club. Dinner meeting. Talk: Coordinating Councils in the Community."

31 Telecast. Local station 12:00 a.m. "Departmental Policies in the Operation of Parks and Playgrounds."

August

1 Newspaper release. Announcement of Carnival.

8 Talk before local Bar Association. Luncheon meeting. Talk: Liability and Public Recreational Service."

15 Radiobroadcast. Local station 11:00 a.m. "Teenage Councils."

22 Newspaper release. Feature story. "Teenage Leaders in Volunteer Assignments."

29 Talk before local labor organization. Dinner meeting. Talk: The Problem of Supervision."

31 Newspaper release. Announcement of Carnival schedule of events.

September

1 Newspaper release. Announcement of National Recreational Congress and departmental participants.

3 Talk before veterans' group. Luncheon meeting. Talk: "Special Services in the Community," followed by tour of agency.

8 Talk before Parent-Teacher Association. Dinner meeting. Talk: "Recreational Services and the Schools."

15 Talk before the Daughters of the American Revolution. Luncheon meeting. Talk: "The Constitutionality of Public Recreational Service," followed by tour of agency.

22 High school talk. Assembly period. "Horizons Unlimited."

23 Radiobroadcast. Local station 11:00 a.m. "Hobbies and Their Value."

30 Newspaper release. Feature Story. "It's Your Program."

October

1 Talk before sectarian group. Dinner meeting. Talk: "The Church and Public Recreational Service."

8 Newspaper release. Announcement of Halloween party and program.

15 Radiobroadcast. Local station 11:00 a.m. "Music Appreciation."

18 Newspaper release. Feature story. "The Establishment of Community Theater."

23 Talk before junior high school. Assembly period. "So You Want to Volunteer."

30 Telecast. Local station 12:00 a.m. "Swimming, A Year Round Sport."

31 Newspaper release. Announcement of aquatics classes in swimming, boating, and lifesaving.

November

1 Newspaper release. Announcement of Thanksgiving Day ceremonial observance.

10 Newspaper release. Announcement of Veteran's Day program.

14 Radiobroadcast. Local station 11:00 a.m. "Each One Teach One."

21 Newspaper release. Feature story. "Physical Fitness and Recreational Activities."

24 Newspaper release. Announcement of Pilgrims Progress as special event.

30 Talk before Chamber of Commerce. Luncheon meeting. Talk: "Land Values and Good Park Planning."

December

1 Newspaper release. Announcement of Christmas pageant and open house at all facilities throughout the system.

5 Talk before local realtors' association. Luncheon meeting. Talk: "Land Dedication in Real Estate Subdivisions."

10 Radiobroadcast. Local station 11:00 a.m. "Something for Everyone— the Principle of Recreational Service."

15 Newspaper release. Feature story. "Christmas and Recreational Service."

21 Telecast. Local station 12:00 a.m. "Christmas Music by the Recreational Service Department Concert Band."

24 Public hearing on land acquisition and new facility construction.

It stands to reason that the foregoing schedule of appearance and messages disseminated through a variety of media does not list the only things that can be done. They are merely some suggestions of what can be utilized. It is apparent that each day throughout the year can be heavily invested with public relations devices to assist in the education of people living in the community which the public recreational department serves. The ideas previously listed barely touch the wellspring of information and facts that can be so readily offered for the development of goodwill and favorable opinion. For example, the well-planned program of public education also has daily information schedules of activities. Advantage should be taken of every facet that can be exploited for instructional purposes.

PART III
EXTERNAL INFLUENCES
ON RECREATIONAL SERVICE

Chapter 14

EVALUATING RECREATIONAL SERVICES

E valuation of public recreational service is an ongoing process. It is the study, assessment, and enhancement of every facet of the recreational service system in the community. Fundamentally, this process should be performed by all personnel concerned with any phase of program or its supportive features. From the information obtained by appropriate evaluative means, decisions can be made as to the quality of the comprehensive recreational program and the effectiveness with which it satisfies public needs and demands for such service. The faults and successes of the program and the departmental operation are thereby revealed and plans for resolving any problems can be developed. Procedures with the greatest probability of achieving a more efficient departmental operation may then be planned and undertaken. More effective programming and a total system most nearly satisfying the leisure requirements of people in the community are probable.

The most rewarding starting place for evaluating a public recreational service system is to examine its philosophical orientation, its expressed aims and objectives, the nature of its clientele, the requirements of the community, and the social, economic, and political context in which it operates.

All public recreational service departments are instrumentalities for providing recreational opportunities to the people they serve, thereby improving the quality of life of those who participate or who appreciate the offerings. Still, there is no one way by which the major purpose may be executed. The responsibility of providing recreational opportunities to all people in the community during their respective leisure is the mandate of the department. There is doubt that any public recreational service system can carry out such a mandate. Nevertheless, the ideal is a projection against which all efforts are measured. When the endeavors of the department begin to approximate the primary goal, it may be said that the system is effective. The closer to the ideal actual performance comes, the more intensive the effort and the greater the comprehensive coverage will be. The truth of the matter is that, although for establishment and evaluative purposes the goal of the public recreational service system is stated in terms of complete responsibility for recreational opportunities, the system can never deliver this promise. No system of this type will every fulfill or satisfy the demands placed on it.

The reasons for noncompliance are simply not enough men or women, materials, or money to perform the task mandated to the public system. Other competing needs force continual reassessment of priorities, financial support, and allocation of limited resources for the public recreational service department. At a time when land prices are soaring, manpower needs rising, facility construction being outraced by a mushrooming population, and other agencies demanding a slice of the economic, political, and social pie, there seems little hope of the public recreational service system carrying out its function. Thus, noncompliance results more from frustration of administrators than from a desire to circumvent the responsibilities laid on the department.

However, evaluation can determine how closely the system does come to serving the public and details the gap between available opportunities and those which could be made available. It can show how many positions should be established and filled, the types, sizes, and units of physical places that should be acquired, developed, or maintained, and the necessary supplies, materials and equipment that should be provided for the balanced program. Additionally, the entire program can be evaluated for comprehensiveness and variety. There may not be one best way by which the separate public recreational service systems throughout the country may attempt to achieve the ideal. Each system, therefore, must be free to define its own recreational guidelines and programs for achieving the goals that originally gave rise to this American movement.

Measurement, Evaluation, and Appraisal

Measurement, evaluation, and appraisal are sometimes used synonymously. Unfortunately, the words do not mean the same thing. Measurement is the procedure used to determine the quantity of a given item or subject. It indicates how much of a thing, item, or phenomenon is actually present. Evaluation, on the other hand, is concerned with the qualitative aspects of phenomena. It is a process which attempts to generate pertinent information about a given subject so that decisions as to what it is worth can be made. Essentially, evaluation finds out how close a specific behavior, activity, or service comes to a presumed goal. Appraisal may be a means of assigning value to an item or subjects, but the assignment of value is performed concomitantly with the activity to be appraised. It may be likened to concurrent auditing wherein the objective is to compare what is being done, when it is being performed, against a known standard. Thus, appraisal is concerned with how adequately a particular thing compares with a known value.

Evaluation and Appraisal of Recreational Service

Evaluation is a process that requires information to be collected and analyzed in order to determine whether or not a recreational service agency within the community is meeting the objectives for which the agency was created. Goals have been defined and every attempt must be made to reach them. Evaluation is the method by which inadequacies, once discovered, are corrected. It is both process and product analysis utilized to determine whether the services provided by the agency actually are those which were originally formulated for the agency. Evaluation is never a finite activity. It is concerned with an ongoing recreational program, not with one that has ceased to function.

Planning for evaluation must be carefully arranged so that each facet of agency operation is carefully investigated. A system of standards must be set up so that outcomes may be measured against them. In evaluating any recreational service department, the community in which the agency is situated must also be appraised. No department, however well staffed and administratively productive, can overcome the deficits of an apathetic population, poor natural resources, or a governmental organization which is unsympathetic to the aims of the agency. For this reason, community attitudes, organization, and resources must be examined in order for a true evaluation of services to be recorded. The evaluation of recreational service departments will manifest interest in the production of efforts designed to meet the recreational needs of the community's populace as well as in all of those educational factors involved in stimulating public participation. Each sequence of evaluative planning focuses attention on what was produced and achieved in terms of what should have been attained.

Appraisal is a procedure whereby current activities are observed and measured for sufficiency, competency, and effectiveness. The primary concerns of appraisal are methods utilized and adequacy of items brought under investigation. It is a preoperative and concurrent operational procedure designed to determine how activities are carried out while they are being performed. It serves as the basis on which evaluation is made. Appraisals conducted prior to action will be chiefly about spaces, facilities, property, and equipment. Appraisals that are concurrent are devoted to personnel and activity procedures. The methods used for appraising any aspect of the department are observation, examination, and inspection.

Why Evaluation is Necessary

One of the most important purposes of evaluation is to accommodate the recreational service offerings to meet the differing needs of individuals within the community. The program is not some concrete form into which people are pushed. It is an adaptation of many activities and experiences which fulfill and satisfy the recreational desires of people. Individuals are not expected to conform to some rigid program structure. The program is adjusted to fit people. Evaluation assists in identifying the specific needs people have. It reveals the strengths and weaknesses of the recreational agency and its program. It provides the bases upon which to compare one department's program with another's. It makes feasible a study of the progress of a program between different dates, the development of standards, and the need for possible improvement. Generally, the evaluation process is continued for the following reasons:

1. To ensure that the recreational program meets the stated needs and desires of the people in the community it serves. Of major concern is the validity of the program. Does the program actually perform the functions it purports to perform?
2. To promote professional growth and education among the staff members of the recreational service system. An evaluation of personnel practices in terms of efforts made and effects produced in the way of professional competency during time on the job should be undertaken.
3. To ascertain the flexibility of policies within the system. Have rigid specifications which preclude modification in the face of changing times and conditions been adopted? Are the aims of the public agency consistent with the public's expectation in the community? There must be a definite concern for new ideas, concepts, methods, and activities, as well as the opportunity for professional growth and

expression. *Status quo* should not be maintained insofar as personnel relationships are involved. The day of regimented thinking has long since passed, and evaluative procedures may more nearly democratize most administrative activities. Whether or not people verbally express themselves in terms of personal needs being met by the activities of the program, their thoughts, advice, suggestions, and intellectual participation in the formulation of agency policies should be taken into consideration.

4. To appraise personnel quality and qualification in relation to specific functions within the system.

5. To develop firmer foundations of agency philosophy so that a logical frame of reference is developed. The philosophy of the agency involves principles of practice, ethical and moral conduct, and the orientation from which all departmental operations stem. There is also a concern for an understanding of the historical function of the agency and the reasons for its establishment. Where necessary, current practices must be updated inasmuch as the achievement of ideal ends require practical techniques.

6. To effectively gauge public sentiment, attitude, and awareness of the public recreational service system. To judge whether or not an effective public relations presentation and interpretation of facts of the system are being made to the community.

7. To increase knowledge gained through practice and to test current practice as to applicability in the public recreational setting. Comparisons must be made between what is being done on a standard basis and what the department is doing. There is a necessity to ascertain the strengths and weaknesses of all departmental practices by contrasting them to what is conceived as a national norm for communities of the same size and type. To compare what similar agencies are producing, the techniques being utilized, and the product which is being developed in relationship to the system.

8. To appraise existing facilities, physical property, and plant as to their adequacy, accessibility, safety features, attractiveness, appropriateness, availability, and utilization.

9. To seek out and eliminate any detrimental features within the program or the agency.

10. To add any feasible and constructive devices, methods, and experiences to the system in order to provide the most efficient and effective service to the people of the community.

11. To promote recognition of the agency and recreational service as a whole on the part of the citizens of the community.
12. To replace outmoded concepts and invalid ideas which the public may have concerning the recreational agency.
13. To promote, insofar as is possible, the professionalization of the agency personnel and the services provided.
14. To avoid unnecessary expenditure of public monies because of inadequate coordination of community agencies in the provision of recreational services.
15. To ensure the agency and its personnel against political upheaval and partisan politics.
16. To ensure that adequate provision of spaces, areas, and facilities will be safeguarded against any encroachment, by establishing protection in perpetuity through dedication of all physical property for public recreational purposes only.
17. To improve the services offered by the department.

Major Areas to be Evaluated

1. Space, physical plant, and equipment
   a. Adequacy
   b. Safety
   c. Availability
   d. Attractiveness
   e. Appropriateness
   f. Multiple use
   g. Accessibility
   h. Cleanliness
   i. Good repair
   j. Good design
2. Programming
   a. Program content:
   Is the program comprehensive, balanced, and flexible?
   Are community resources utilized maximally?
   Does the program reflect the purpose and policies of the agency?
   Is every effort made to involve lay participation in the organization of activities?
   Are all segments of the population considered?
   Does the program meet the recreational needs of people living in the community?

3. Program meaning:
   Is there carry-over value for individuals in activities of the program?
   Does the individual obtain a sense of achievement, self-expression, satisfaction, and enjoyment from participation?
   Does the individual attain a sense of belonging to some group; does he/she identify with a group as a result of participation in programmed activities?
   Are individual differences in skill, maturity, intellect, prior experience, age, and sex taken into consideration?
   Is there opportunity for creativity?
   Is there opportunity for socialization?
   Does the activity promote goodwill?
   Are artificial barriers to activity eliminated?
4. Staff
   a. Qualifications:
      Educational preparation
      Prior experiences in a professional setting
      Personality factors
      Leadership ability
      Intelligence
5. Technique:
   Are their skills and knowledge adequate to fulfill professional duties and responsibilities?
   Do they have leadership ability?
   Do they have instructional ability?
6. Sufficiency:
   Is there adequate professional personnel for staffing program and agency needs?
   Is there effective supervisory leadership?
   Is there an effective in-service educational program?
   Are there opportunities for professional advancement?
   Are material aids and devices utilized to encourage continuous professional development on the job, such as professional books, journals, audiovisual aides, pamphlets?
   Are there personal resources available for professional development?
7. Administration
   Are administrative processes handled in the most efficient way?
   Is management by objectives an established process?
   Is work processed as rapidly as possible?

Is there effective coordination between the public agency and all other agencies?

Are records and reports maintained so that past performances can be analyzed?

Are policies established to provide guidelines for all applicable operations in which the department is concerned?

Methods of Evaluation

Of vital consideration, if evaluation is to proceed, is the selection of suitable methods and the construction of easily understood and appropriate instruments of evaluation. Those methods and instruments that are most compatible and economical in providing valid information for the particular purposes established will be utilized. Selecting or constructing instruments of evaluation is essentially a two-part procedure: identification of what is to be evaluated and acquisition or development of an instrument that will do the most accurate and valid assessment.

All phases of recreational experience simply cannot be evaluated. The public will probably not allow itself to be tested, either individually or en masse, because it will undoubtedly feel such a program is time consuming and unnecessary. There are no rating scales to measure the genuine satisfaction engendered in the performance of an activity or the enjoyment generated through participation in countless experiences of a recreational nature. Attitudes, interests, and personality aspects can be tested validly, but only in terms of a small random sample of the total public. In all likelihood, evaluation of public attitude and understanding of public recreational service will have to be learned through public relations and educational devices rather than through tests.

However, certain obvious participations can be measured easily, if this is an objective which the agency desires. Quantitative measurements are rather easily contrived. They represent the "how much" or "how many" and are useful in identifying the use to which various facilities and activities are put. With such quantitative factors, an accurate measurement of how popular a given activity within the program is and of how intensely a particular facility, center, or area is used. Such information may prove useful when planning for additional areas, facilities, and activities. There are many standards and norms set for measuring physical activities, such as how fast, how far, how high. There are few applicable instruments which can provide a qualitative measurement in satisfaction received, pleasure attained, aesthetic interest stimulated, or attitude modified. Assuredly, there are tests that will indicate this information, but they are expensive to run, require a great deal of time, and an inordinate amount of cooperation from those who are tested. The question arises, are they readily applicable? Only where there is an extreme desire on the part of the layman to subordinate personal interests to the rather dubious satisfaction of assisting a public agency in the performance of one of its functions can these measurements be made. Does this mean that no evaluation can be made? The only reasonable answer is no. Evaluation can and must be made, but its basis should be oriented to those topics and subjects that are determined easily. The facilitation of the process is in no small way a significant factor in concluding whether any evaluation can be made profitably.

Determining Attitudes and Related Concepts

The attitudes, interests, values, motives, and appreciations of the individual who is a potential participant within the recreational program are important to recreationists in several ways. Chiefly, they affect the things of which the person is aware, and second, modification in them often is a particular objective of public relations devices. The terms indicated previously apparently refer to feelings stimulated by the social milieu in which the person is surrounded.

Attitudes must be defined as positive, negative, or neutral learned responses relating to a given subject or thing which can affect behavior. They are usually based upon emotional or psychological feelings rather than upon logic and systematic reasoning about the given object. Interests, on the other hand, are those subjects or things to which an individual is attracted positively. There is a definite pleasantness related to interests. Values refer to those things considered by the individual to be most significant or worthy. Essentially, values denote the individual's basic choices as to ends and means. Appreciation may be resolved into an emotional response toward an appealing object or thing. It connotes awareness, recognition, and an aesthetic fulfillment or satisfaction from seeing, hearing, or having contact with a given subject. Motives reflect an immediate need for fulfillment. They are drives to action. Motives indicate an unsatisfied condition or tension within the organism. When tension is diminished as a result of specific action taken, then the organism has regained balance and satisfaction results. Satisfaction and equilibrium within the organism are a consequence of successful reduction of tension by virtues of some behavioral manifestation.

Dimensions of Personality

Attitudes have various dimensions. All the dimensions, or degrees of intensity, are matters of inference. They can be measured to determine how any individual reacts to particular stimuli, in this instance, the recreational service agency and the activities produced by the agency.

Protagonism. Protagonism is the dimension usually considered and measured. It is the degree to which an individual shows favoritism for a specific attitude object.

Pitch. Pitch is the degree of feeling the individual has toward a given attitude object.

Readiness. Readiness is the rapidity with which an attitude can be stimulated in an individual's mind. It is concerned with the primary thoughts that immediately come to the person upon direct confrontation with any provocative stimulus.

Constancy. Constancy is reflected in the variety of attitude objects toward which an individual maintains the same attitude. Thus, persons may be spoken of as being "radical," "liberal," "reactionary," or "conservative," because they have a single constant attitude toward a broad range of objects.

Measuring Attitudes and Related Concepts

Techniques for evaluating and measuring attitudes are numerous and vary widely. Although attitudes can be inferred from observable behavior (attendance at activities, efforts to provide voluntary service by instruction, monetary donations, or technical assistance), a great deal of the methodology concerning attitudes has been instrumented by verbal indexes.

Self-Testing. These measuring devices are guided response items used to determine attitudes and interests through self-reporting. By randomly selecting a public which will cooperate in responding to such tests, the department may ascertain attitudes towards phases of agency program, activities, and facilities. However, these results could be biased simply because the sample included cooperative individuals.

Scales. A variety of scaling instruments can be utilized to determine attitudes towards a given object. A scale is constructed by arranging statements relating to a particular subject under investigation. The subject being tested simply checks the statement within a given range (from highly favorable to decidedly unfavorable or hostile to) so that the attitude object is indicated.[1]

Interest Inventories. Interest inventories are measured by standardized instruments that require an individual to select subjects in which he manifests interests from a large number of activities. Generally, interest inventories are based on knowledge that successful achievers in vocational fields have similar interests, and that the interests of persons in one field differ significantly from those of individuals in another occupation.[2]

Sociometric Tests. The sociometric test procedure requires each member of a group, such as a typical recreational group, to choose one or more members for a given purpose. Sociometric data may be useful in improving a person's social adjustment and indicate the individual's degree of social acceptability by one's peers.[3]

Projective Testing. Projective techniques present the subject with an ambiguous stimulus which calls for a response that can be interpreted so as to gain insight into the personality of the subject.[4]

Application of Techniques. It must be emphasized that all such attitudinal, interest inventory, and projective techniques may well be applied to professional personnel of the departmental staff in order to evaluate their suitability and compatibility for the responsibilities which recreationists undertake. As in all evaluation programs, measuring the effectiveness of staff personnel is essential if professional development and worker efficiency and effectiveness are to be encouraged and, even more important, improved.

The traditional utilization of measurement and evaluation has been to gauge dimensions of attitude, interests, motives, and values, as well as to determine the variables of personality structure. There has also been a direct concern for the quantitative rather than the qualitative aspects of recreational service because such items were relatively easy to program and measure. Recreationists have normally been oriented toward how many individuals participated in a given event at a specific facility

---

[1]T.D. TenBrink, *Evaluation: A Practical Guide for Teachers.* (New York: McGraw-Hill Book Company, 1974), pp. 273–292.

[2]D.P. Campbell, *Manual for the Strong Vocational Interest Blank.* (Stanford, California: Stanford University Press, 1966).

[3]P.N. Middlebrook, *Social Psychology and Modern Life.* (New York: Alfred A. Knopf, 1974). pp. 486–491.

[4]*Psychology Today: An Introduction* (Del Mar, Calif.: CRM Books, 1970), pp. 449–459.

rather than with the intensity of satisfaction received by each individual who participated or looked on. The difficulties of obtaining information revealing the quality of participation are not insurmountable and, with better measuring devices and more easily administered tests, satisfaction as well as attitude, motive, and values will become known.

For attitudes, interests, values, and motives, the most accurate and reliable measuring instruments are observations, self-reporting devices, rating scales, and inventories based upon successful achievers. Peer evaluation also may be helpful in determining the social acceptability of the individual within a group to which he or she belongs.

Evaluation is the process in which the quality or worth of anything is discovered. Generally, this involves the generation of information so that a comparison of the status of the item or subject in question with a standard suitable to a determination of its worth can be made. Before recreational service outcomes may be ascertained, they must be understood so as to be disposed to measurement. Thus, nonpersonality phenomena can be measured solely in relation to their dimensions, properties, or attributes. Dimensions must be chosen for measurement in terms of the nature of the phenomenon, the object of the measurement, the accuracy required, and the standard to be used in evaluation. The general dimensions usual to most phenomena of recreational interest are identity, number, and organization of segments, time, rate, place, intensity, and activity.

One Approach to Evaluation

The most appropriate approach to evaluation is one that uses a problem-solving technique and that is logically consistent with the scientific method. The techniques utilized may be those that have been developed for handling any problem:

1. Realizing that some dissatisfaction, requirement, or difficulty exists.
2. Precisely identifying the problem.
3. Establishing measures for handling the problem and alternatives predicated on previous experience and technology.
4. Dealing with the problem.
   a. Retrieving information.
   b. Fixing the requirement for additional data.
   c. Determining and choosing potential sources of data.
   d. Developing procedures to obtain information.

    e. Obtaining and classifying information.

    f. Studying and explaining the results of investigation.

5. Making assessments

    a. Judging possible outcomes.

    b. Defining the outcomes most likely to succeed.

    c. Making moral judgments.

    d. Coming to a decision.

6. Executing a program resulting from the decisions.

7. Studying the outcomes of the program and modifying it as situations arise that make such changes advisable.

Evaluation is a process of making value judgments based on relevant information dealing with all facets of the recreational service system. The fundamental ideas undergirding this orientation are that judgments concerning the elements influencing the values and satisfactions to be gained by participating clientele must be made in terms of the agreed-upon purposes and objectives. The accuracy of any judgment dealing with the outcomes of the recreational service program is certain to be augmented if it is founded on specific unequivocal information that rationally explains and determines the conflict or problem confronted, and on the frame of which practical assessments may be developed of what must be done.

The evaluation of any particular array of data may be made from estimates and aims, from objective criteria, or by utilization of other measures developed by professionals or those interested in or concerned with the investigation and solution of related problems.

In formulating the procedures to be undertaken to make improvements, alternatives must be selected that, in the judgment of the problem solvers, will result in the best outcome. Access to extant information pertinent to the potency of the proposed program or to steps taken to achieve desired modifications in comparative situations will be valuable.

Additionally, the procedures instituted to improve the program must be evaluated by making value judgments about the changes that have occurred and the satisfaction and/or enjoyment that has been achieved by the clients.

Fundamental Procedures in the Evaluative Process

Specific steps are vital in effectuating evaluation:

1. The chief aims and purposes of the recreational program must be defined and agreed upon. They mirror the goals and needs of the community.
2. Evaluation should be founded on a logical study of individual and community needs. It should be distinct and established in terms of conduct expected of individuals and groups involved.
3. Facts must be obtained about the satisfaction and enjoyment or enhancement of life that the formulated objectives may have produced. Analysis should reveal whether qualitative changes have occurred from recreational participation.
4. An investigation of the recreational environment and the practices established to attain the aims, incorporating the behavior of potential participants within and outside of the organized program, must be made.
5. Analysis and explanation of all results dealing with personal satisfaction, enjoyment, and participation are terminal procedures, introducing whatever new definitions of aims and values are necessary to establish new purposes and objectives. Additionally, improved methods and techniques to achieve the modified goals and unprecedented goals must also be developed.
6. The necessary cooperation of all persons involved with the provision of community recreational service must be gained in evaluating the total opportunity available to clients and in the planning for improvements.

Range of Evaluation

Evaluation involves the progress made in attaining agency purposes as determined by the approximation of present practices and programming with the original goals set from community need. It is employed to define whether or not certain values and objectives are being met, whether programming satisfies the felt needs of citizens and improves their lives. The scope of evaluation must be comprehensive by covering every factor that might influence the effectiveness of the program offerings, such as political philosophy, ability to support the recreational service department, and the desire to finance the department on a sound fiscal basis. Evaluation is a continuous self-searching process.

The entire process of evaluation is closely related to research methods because of the information generated by scientifically applied techniques. The amassing of evidence, supportive or critical, of operational methods indicates the discontinuance, retention, or reinforcement of some program activities and current administrative procedures. Evaluation suggests the promotion of some recreationists, the reassignment of others, the employment of new practitioners, and the separation of others from the agency. This information comes from the continuous analysis of the goals and values of the department, the competency of personnel, and the community fabric.

It is by appropriate procedures that evaluation may most validly serve to improve the program. Such activity is ongoing, and information about every aspect of the system and its direction are proper subjects for thorough analysis and interpretation. Only when the department is placed under scrutiny by objective personnel is the evaluative process optimized. Scientific method, critical techniques, and administrative desire to improve the departmental product are the three elements on which valid qualitative and quantitative measurements and judgments are made.

Evaluation of Recreational Services

Cities are extremely interested in evaluating their recreational services in relation to generally applied standards. In public health work, for example, standards have been published by the American Public Health Association, and cities are scored periodically in relation to the standards accepted by the Association, which enables a city to detect the probable weaknesses in its public health provisions and stimulates improvement. Public recreational service has now reached the stage where some authoritative standards are being established. Information concerning recreational service is being gathered continuously and directed toward the creation of procedures of evaluation. Among such studies should be:

1. Establishment of a public recreational service system with proper allocation of funds to competently staff the agency, provide for operations and capital improvements, and effectively conduct public programs.
2. Granting to an autonomous department functioning within the local jurisdiction the full authorization to make policy, create positions, and otherwise maintain and administer the system.
3. Initiation of planning procedures to guide the development of the public recreational service system to enhance the functions and to avoid waste, inadequacies, duplication, and deficiencies.

4. Devise personnel standards of such a nature that only those individuals who can demonstrate their theoretical and practical knowledge and skill will be employed permanently. Minimal standards for induction into the system require graduation from accredited institutions of higher education with major in recreational service education and other experience depending on the level of position.

5. Development of program standards containing balance, comprehensiveness, and variety so that opportunities of a social, cultural, educational, physical, and ethical nature may be provided to all who participate.

6. Establishment of planning procedures for land acquisition and the design and development of all recreational places, structures, and facilities to serve as functional recreational centers wherever required.

7. Initiation of a standard procedure whereby coordination of the disparate agencies of the community can be brought together so that total community recreational services can be offered under optimal conditions.

With these concepts on which to base subsequent action, an effective evaluating tool may be devised to assess the practical outcomes of the operating system in respect to the original goals and values guiding the system's administration.

Selected Reference

Bloom, B.S., and others: *Handbook on Formative and Summative Evaluation of Learning* (New York: McGraw-Hill Book Company, 1971.

Chapter 15

POLITICAL FORCES AND POLICY

Political reality concerns all the interacting behaviors necessary to carry out public recreational service despite political patronage, economic retrenchment, pressure group tactics, civil service deterioration, and other external or internal conditions which tend to frustrate a community recreational service department. Realism, in this instance, is the face-to-face situation developed without regard for public recreational service and is typically beyond the scope of the department. It is sometimes a ploy to force attention to facts and unrelated issues. In such circumstances the highly visible and relatively powerless department simply becomes a pawn in confrontations between community groups and elected officialdom.

Political realism is the effort undertaken to work out problems which arise during the normal course of departmental operations. Almost always, these are questions of relations with the community at large. To some practitioners it may mean stop-gap measures offered only to survive or remove pressure from the individual in charge. More intelligently, it is the application of knowledge to a stressful situation which arises because of certain unmet needs. The solutions to such problems should never be met expediently, but should be investigated to determine what underlying reasons caused the problems to develop.

To fully comprehend the impact that politics has upon the field of public and even private recreational service, one must understand the meaning of politics in the American system. Politics has sometimes been called the art of the possible. It is that, on occasion, but it is also the various alliances, intrigues, maneuverings, and development of the kinds of constituencies which permit election to office and/or control of the legal levers of power. This chapter provides the necessary background for the reader to better recognize the contradictory elements which constitute the political process and, incidentally, influence the size, shape, and scope of public recreational service. Indeed, so pervasive are political forces that no social sector is immune from their domination. Politicians are creatures of expediency. They like to call themselves pragmatists, but in actuality they will do whatever it takes to gain re-election without regard to ethics or what may be a remote good. The exchange of favors, payments made at the right time to the appreciative person, employment obtained, parks cleaned, playgrounds installed, contracts given are all components of the political process. Each plays a part in the complex scheme of who will wield power on the political scene. People must be made aware of how politics affects their daily lives—particularly that which we normally think of as our own personal discretionary activities taking place during leisure.

The name of the game in politics is to get elected, be re-elected, and control the power that usually flows from the office. Individuals can be elected to office on the basis of the platform they publicize, their personal charm or charisma, or if the voters are disenchanted with the current office holders and desire a change. Once in office, however, the task of self-perpetuation becomes the paramount function of the politician. Politicians must perform in a manner calculated to win the confidence and support of whatever constituency will return them to office. This requires a certain sensitivity to the needs, wants, and demands of the electorate. For example, an individual of a specific race, ethnic group, or religious affiliation is appointed to an important recreational department position, despite the fact that the person may not be qualified and capable of performing, so that the current administration can point to that appointment as being one of the ways the political party is responsive to minority needs. Staying in office also requires an ability to know how to balance the various factions, representing a variety of special interest groups, with the integrity of the office and resources available to carry out the task.

The term *political* is used here to indicate the kinds of arrangements which have to be devised in order to obtain reasonable objectives. It is a process of accommodation and it involves compromise, tact, and discussion. The entire procedure is based upon an understanding of human needs and the methods employed to gain benefits by the parties participating in negotiations. Recreationists must recognize the fact that if they are employed by public recreational service departments they will be within the political sphere of influence and need to understand how the system operates so that they may best be able to cope with the typical interferences or infringements which some political operators attempt.

The Nature of Politics in Society

The development of individuals is conditioned not only by direct personal encounters of the primary kind, but also by participation in more encompassing social groupings. Among these larger arenas of social association are those designated by the term *political affiliation.* In the sense of its use here, political matters do not concern the individual as a unique person, but as a member of the social order. The relationships are founded upon the social role and structure rather than upon particular personal attributes. Political life is impersonal, despite the fact that its functions have an immediate or delayed effect upon the lives of all who are subject to the rules, regulations, and legislation which govern the social organization.

Human beings are political animals. This is illustrated by the way people inherently drive to establish broader and more complex social systems. The human imagination continues to seek new ways to formulate corporate existence. People tend to transform their environment to suit their own purposes and they also develop new patterns of social organization. The political life of human beings enables them to satisfy their objectives more efficiently than could be expected if each simply followed his or her own dictates and performed separately. The ability of the community to accomplish all of the enterprises which need to be performed can only be achieved with some kind of organizational combination. We have long since learned that specialization and the division of labor is a necessity for the human community. The political arrangement multiplies the power and effectiveness of diverse strengths and coordinates all actions into a reciprocally/supportive entity.

The basis for the establishment of social organization is division of labor. Everybody does not perform the same task. Each concentrates along those lines for which some proficiency or inclination is apparent. In this way specialization occurs. The nature of modern society is such that there must be a distribution of goods and services. This is where political organization and facilitation comes in—acting as a means for the coordination of specialized functions and exchange of materials and services.

One problem that arises in any study of politics is power. The realism of politics is established through the exercise of power. Power is the ability to do or perform. It has to do with that which is possible in human affairs. Thus, the need for compromise permits certain arrangements to be carried out. On this basis functions are enacted, influence is felt, and possibilities are turned into actualities.

Political Organization and Government

The political system of any jurisdiction is expressed through the governmental machinery, which is a traditional enterprise of the body politic, i.e., the public, and also the party apparatus, the informal means by which the governing authority is motivated. The political system is composed of two facets; one is the formal and visible bureaucracy and the other is the informal, behind-the-scenes manipulators who probably control the sources of power. Sometimes the elected official is also the political boss of the system. In some instances the elected official is merely a front for the real bosses, who are not elected but control the finances, appointments, and enough of the voters to ensure election or re-election for the party's choices.

American political history is replete with the names of elected bosses and political party bosses who have run the system as their own personal domain. In many instances the citizens were ill served. In some cases, citizens were satisfied that their government was the best—but rarely. The names of William Tweed of Tammany Hall fame in New York City, Frank Hague of Jersey City, Thomas Pendergast in Kansas City, James Curley in Boston, William Thompson of Chicago, James J. Walker in New York City, and more recently Richard J. Daley of Chicago come immediately to mind in terms of the questionable or outright corrupt practices that were perpetuated in the name of government upon the citizens of the various communities.

Nor have county, state, and federal levels of government been immune to political officials who have corrupted their office and prostituted themselves in exchange for money, influence, or other considerations. The Watergate scandal of the Nixon Administration, the ABSCAM exposures of federal lawmakers, the jailing of Reagan appointees for corrupt practices, governors found guilty of bribery, fraud, or other illegalities, the awarding of contracts for kickbacks and other government abuses are nothing new. However, it is appalling to realize that in this day and age there are both elected and appointed political figures who are perfectly willing and able to engage in illegal, immoral, and contemptible activities at the expense of those who placed them in positions of trust.[1]

The Political Machine. The social structure of any jurisdiction is a vast complex of human associations, living in competitive conditions, cooperating to maintain a precarious balance between various nationalities, religions, races, and standards of behavior. It is the interactions between these different groupings and the contrary interests of millions of people bound together in a cultural mixture that identifies the urban region. Equilibrium is maintained through organized government. How a modern city attempts to find its way through the provocations, conflicts, and antagonisms for the right political solutions that will lead to higher levels of social control is little short of amazing. Contemporary politics is played out against the backdrop of discord, rivalry, and enmity caused by ignorance and suspicion as well as from close contact between different cultural representatives, ethnicities, and races. Instead of election campaigns in which basic principles and issues are raised, there are too often vicious attacks on personalities and demagogic appeals to the prejudices and bigotry of the electorate. Instead of a government which emphasizes highly qualified and competent specialists, there is usually a government by vested interests.

Despite all the corruption and graft, and all the positioning to subvert the uses of the public trust, the fact remains that government exists and that in many instances it is efficient. In the face of some corruption and inefficiency, governmental enterprises are operated effectively, with integrity, and live up to the responsibilities which have been given into their care. Surely there will always be scoundrels who sell themselves for whatever their office will bring. But there are more people of integrity; and just as surely they will prevail. How did this all come about and to what extent does it affect the provision of recreational services?

Party Politics. Organization is the underlying support of politics. In this country a two-party system developed and, to a remarkable extent, the two major parties have continued to exert profound influence on the political process. The loyal party worker is organized at the grass roots level. Whether we discuss city, county, state, or national politics, organization is the watchword. From the precinct level, through ward, to city,

---

[1]Topics of the Times, *The New York Times* (Feb. 27, 1992), p. A24. Also Clifford Krauss, "House Scandals Prompt Call for an Administrator" *The New York Times*, (March 9, 1992), p. A15.

county, and finally state levels, the political machine is at work: currying favor with the voters in various ways, playing upon the needs and interests of the citizens, and attempting to deliver the vote at election time. For example, a city councilor makes a direct request that certain parks or playgrounds in his or her district be cleaned immediately. This political pressure on the department may mean that some other recreational facility will not be so well maintained; meanwhile the councilor can show the constituency how rapidly their requests get translated into action. If it works, the party becomes ascendent. Once in office, party officials control the levers of power, and this tends to perpetuate them and their minions in office.

The Constitution does not provide for political parties, so in a sense the political party has no legal foundation. A party is an association of like-minded individuals who are brought together because of their overriding special interest. The political party, or machine, is a service organization. It tries to meet the needs of its constituency. Whether in or out of power the party machine operates on a daily basis. It is set up to perform those activities which will foster good will among the voters as well as placing them in some obligatory position to support the machine's candidates at the right time. Sometimes, of course, votes are bought. In the past, party workers carried out welfare type activities. More recently, however, these activities have been less noticeable in the face of other efforts which take form at local levels, such as:

1. Securing physical improvement for the neighborhood.
2. Finding jobs for unemployed individuals.
3. Assisting individuals who run afoul of the law.
4. Assisting individuals to secure loans.
5. Speeding routine procedures so that construction can begin.
6. Providing advice concerning family relations.
7. Obtaining better facilities for recreational purposes.
8. Obtaining traffic signals at the behest of concerned citizens.
9. Obtaining better housing for constituents.
10. Assisting individuals to enter the country or procure citizenship.

It is understood that these are just *some* of the services offered by the political machine. Persons who seek favors from the political boss, at the precinct, or national level, also obligate themselves to vote for the party's choice or perform the party's bidding. That is the deal. Personal benefits immediately conferred may have a very costly long run effect, but the instant or relatively immediate gratification of need seems to offset the more remote concept of selling one's vote, contributing to the party coffers, or actually working for the party.

Patronage. Perhaps the most damaging aspect of party politics, aside from plundering the public treasury, is the employment of incompetent or unqualified persons in patronage positions, in what is known as the spoils system. ("To the victor belong the spoils.") Thus, to reward party faithfulness and support, the political boss obtains paid posts for party adherents and cronies. This often means that the public is cheated twice: Public taxes pay the salaries of incompetents, and the responsibilities for performing efficiently are not fulfilled.

The Patronage Problem

Where the patronage system exists, its operation may be explained in terms of what occurs in a typical recreational service department. The entrenched political party has finally suffered a defeat, and the new party has appointed a new superintendent for the department. Recreational service is invariably looked upon as a political plumb, because there are many low-level ground maintenance, lifeguard, and playground positions, particularly in the summer, which are available for filling by party affiliates. Two kinds of patronage programs are possible. One holds sway over all appointments owing to the lack of a civil service or open competitive examination system; the other is concerned only with jobs during the summer. It is to the former that this discussion now turns.

Where political appointments are rampant after an election, the new superintendent, if he/she has any intelligence, calls all employees together and states that no one is to be replaced at once, if at all, and that all personnel are expected to perform their respective duties and responsibilities as usual. The superintendent then tries to determine during the subsequent weeks which workers are essential to the operation of the department, who are competent, and who are replaceable. By identifying key personnel, and learning that the most effective workers do not always have administrative or supervisory positions, the administrator is in a better position to protect essential workers. Even before the appraisal is concluded, a representative of the party committee comes and says that the party wants a half dozen positions. The superintendent acquiesces and notifies six of the most inefficient employees that they will be dismissed.

No one really objects to the political system at this time since (1) the superintendent has simply gotten rid of six pieces of deadwood and does not expect to employ any who could possibly be worse; (2) the party man has six jobs and is not concerned that they may be low level appointments because of concern for vote-getting and many times one modest job will produce a larger number of votes from friends and relatives; (3) the deadwood knew that they would be dismissed and have been busy looking for work elsewhere instead of working. The party bosses allocate the jobs among the party faithful.

Shortly, the appointed party workers present themselves to the superintendent and indicate who their sponsor is. They owe allegiance to the party and not to the department or the superintendent. The superintendent is delighted to have them and assigns them work which it is his or her hope they will be able to perform. If it is learned that the newly appointed workers are indifferent to department authority, are unwilling to work, or precipitate a morale problem within the agency, an appeal to his/her own sponsor (if he/she is relatively unknown to the troublemakers' sponsors) and requests that a substitution be made. Most politicians will not shrink from such a request because there is still a job to be filled and additional votes to be garnered. After all, if an incompetent or lazy person has to be removed, the onus is not on the politician. Naturally, the political sponsor will reject any attempt to remove the job from his/her personal allocation if it is sensed that the request for substitution was made with intent to embarrass.

During this time the first consignees have been inducted into the agency. The party representative again appears and requests that additional vacancies be made. Now the superintendent, who has by this time found the initial draft none too capable in operating the department, starts to hedge. The party man is asked how effective and efficient services for the community are to be provided when the party is placing incompetent personnel in the department. Nevertheless, as a party follower the executive will bow to the party's wishes. Then the question of whether it is good politics to debilitate the effectiveness of an agency which comes into direct contact with so many of the voters of the community. The party man, who is familiar with such responses, will compromise and reduce the request by one third; this has been prepared for under any circumstances of intractability. The superintendent must now choose those who are to be eliminated for the party's benefit.

This procedure is followed until party demands for employee positions reach the vital segment of essential persons without whom the department will surely flounder. The superintendent refuses to accept any more of the party's loyalists, and the party representative is forced to desist as soon as it is realized that the superintendent will be supported by his/her superiors.

In the second instance, the political party may be faced with an entrenched civil service procedure which cannot be tampered with. Then, the only patronage positions available will be during the summer months when non-civil service employees may be hired to supplement a burgeoning program. Typically, the party representative will request the department to supply the party with at least 50 percent, perhaps more, of the vacancies which are expected to accrue. The party will then fill them with their own people in the same manner and under the same conditions as they would without civil service. However, the summer positions are at such a low level that they are merely irritants to the efficiency of agency's performance and will not do irreparable damage. Particularly is this true where the work is of a technical type or requires specific competencies. Lifeguards, for example, must be able to swim and rescue others. It would not be good politics if it was revealed the public beach lifeguards had permitted someone to drown because of their own incompetence. As it is in many public recreational service departments where the community is ridden by patronage placement, a core of professional employees maintains the operational effectiveness of the agency. It resists removal by changing administrations and exists, usually, at the supervisory or middle management level.

Wherever professional personnel are employed at the chief executive level within a patronage system, they must be guarded in their attempts to resist political intrusion. Recreationists in executive positions may have to trade-off low-level positions in order to retain key positions for other professionals whose competence is required to sustain agency effectiveness. Adroit recreationists in executive positions may be able to overcome patronage ploys, even where civil service procedures are not available, by establishing open competitive examinations, both written and practical, as well as well-publicized job descriptions. The rigors of testing and publicity can do much to discourage even the most intrusive political hack from too much interference with the ongoing workings of the department. Another method is best described by Charlesworth, who writes:

> The best tactic for the administrator faced with obtrusive politicians is to pretend that he knows nothing of their intentions. Bland astonishment is a better defense than is up-stage lecturing on political morals. The worst device

of all is to try to outmaneuver the professional politician; the well-meaning public servant should not try to beat an expert at his own game and should remember the last line of the old limerick about the smile on the face of the tiger.[2]

Despite the U.S. Supreme Court decisions to abolish the time-honored procedures of patronage, which permits the newly empowered political party to dismiss adherents of the former party from incumbencies, at least insofar as low-level functionaries are concerned, political satraps will find the means to circumvent legalities. There are any number of hoary practices which can be brought to bear against unreconstructed governmental employees. Among the routines which can be practiced against those who are reluctant to embrace the new ideology or are holdovers from a former regime are demanding compliance to a schedule which is unreasonable, performances which are unattainable, or conditions of work which are so demeaning that the incumbent is either forced to become insubordinate or grows weary of an untenable position and resigns, retires, or seeks employment elsewhere. Naturally, such practices will be subjected to further scrutiny and, perhaps, redress by the courts. However, it seems little likely that those whose rights are infringed upon by political patronage maneuvers will have the resources to take their cases to court and plead for their cause. In most instances, court machinery is so cumbersome and of such interminable duration that the plaintiff will long since have been both financially and physically exhausted.

The Supreme Court's latest ruling on patronage requirements did not touch the issue of decision-making positions, and this area is still open to the machinations of those who utilize political office to reward the party faithful. Low-level governmental employees may no longer be regarded as prime targets for removal simply because they belong to or were appointed by the other party. Although this is a step in the right direction, it does not prevent the most prevalent abuses of the patronage system which can fill a line agency's vacancies with those who are merely on the public payroll in consequence of who rather than what they know. Surely, this can mar the performance of any line agency and particularly that of a public recreational service department. Armed with the knowledge that the courts will take a dim view of forcing employees to resign because of political credentials, the recreationist in an administrative

---

[2]J.C. Charlesworth, *Governmental Administration* (Westport, CT: Greenwood Press) 1972, p. 175.

position may be in a better position to combat the attempted takeover by political bosses of the hiring function. It remains to be seen how well and how wisely executives are going to use this court decision to avoid burdening their departments with sinecures or simple incompetents.

Where the machine has control, there will be patronage positions to fill. Those departments which must operate to serve the public are hampered by having unprepared individuals assigned to the jobs and are thereby unable to carry out their mandates. This persists until incompetence reaches epidemic proportions. By then, the public becomes so disenchanted with the way its money is being misused that it sweeps out the party in the next elections and votes a new set into office. Now the stage is set for the same performance, except by the opposite party.

This cycle is broken when elected officials carry out their mandate on behalf of their constituencies rather than in the service of the machine. Where conscientious officials are in office, there is greater likelihood that a merit system of some kind will be operating, so that the most qualified will obtain employment. This does not always occur, of course, but it happens more frequently than not and this is one of the best ways to reduce political chicanery and manipulation. Since the party machine is fueled by the money it gets from those it places in positions, as well as from graft, required donations, and other forms of political blackmail, a great deal of its financial "clout" is lost under a civil service or merit system.

Civic reform and the implementation of the merit system are no guarantee that the political machine will be killed off. Constant vigilance on the part of all citizens coupled with the investigative reporting of the mass media can do much to keep the public treasury from the clutches of those who have voracious and illegal appetites.[3]

As political candidates begin to realize that their hope of re-election depends on the positive services they have rendered to the public, they will acknowledge that they must have specialists and other experts who can handle the highly technical functions which the jurisdiction normally provides to its citizens. Thus, the government assumes the functions of both regulatory and service organization. When this reasonable idea is accepted, patronage will no longer be the preferred method of rewarding the party faithful.

---

[3]Selwyn Roab, "Housing Agency Contractor Named in Fraud Indictment," *The NY Times* (Feb. 28, 1992), p. B3.

There will always be political influences wherever citizens reside and where there are differences in opinions, attitudes, or experiences. However, the political reality will be to achieve a balance that can enable the jurisdiction to maintain itself while providing the kinds of services which are necessary if people's lives are to be enhanced. For example, a leading unionist asks the director of recreational service for a summer job for his son. In many instances the summer job results in lessened union pressure or, perhaps, a greater productivity demand upon union members in the department. The appointment will directly contribute to increased recreational services because of the favor owed.

Political Concepts

Fundamentally, political resources are means whereby one person within the hierarchy of a policy-making organization can influence the behavior of others. Political impact may be generated from the authority of position within the organization, expertness (specialization), leadership, position within the communications network, party affiliation, or buying power.

Political factors may develop in terms of the agency's ability to deal with environmental contingencies. Such contingencies may be the capacity of the department to perform its mandated duties, the degree to which the department's activities are not replaceable, and the degree to which the effective operation of the department is of paramount importance to the overhead political structure of the community. To the extent that the department can cope with the uncertainty of human behavior by providing satisfying experiences for its various constituents, to the degree that political forces recognize the importance that effective recreational service has upon the voting public, and to the extent that departmental practices are carried out effectively so that they become nonsubstitutable insofar as other community departments are concerned, the greater will be the department's political foundation.

A variety of political tactics may be employed in the process of policy formulation. Such tactics may fly in the face of integrity, openness, and democratic procedures. However, they are the tactics of political realism and are, unfortunately, constantly used by individuals or groups to gain their own ends. While political realism necessitates the description of the hypocritical use of power to gain ends which may or may not be consistent with departmental missions, realities rather than naivete or optimism dictate the need to illustrate political methods. Thus, a partial listing of political tactics might be to:

1. Channel, withhold, and present information only as necessary. The policymaker gains in influence and power to the extent that information is current, reliable, and applicable.
2. Always maintain options for maneuvering. Never decide anything which might be used to establish some promised goal, reward, or action.
3. Seek information only from designated sources. Do not accept information from conflicting sources or there may be pressure to recognize other inputs, thereby opening the way toward internal dissension.
4. Develop protective alliances. Determine what superiors consider to be of significance and assist them by responding. At peer and subordinate levels, enhance the status of allies with recognition, monetary rewards, titles and prerogatives.
5. Compromise on trivial matters to give at least the appearance of willing negotiation.
6. Confuse the issues, that is, bring in irrelevancies to obscure the situation.
7. Always assume the role of expert. This gives the appearance of confidence and of knowing what must be done.
8. Never permit familiarity. Social distance is required if power is to be maintained.
9. Utilize delaying tactics if confronted by unfavorable proposals.
10. Whenever a reverse is inevitable, give in to the proposal. Such action may lead to a more favorable trade-off later on.

Of course, most knowledgable individuals realize that these tactics are employed. Obscurantism, cronyism, falsification, postponement, and failure to confide or report accurately so that effective action may be taken in time are favorite methods used by those who are in power and wish to magnify or retain it. The fact that these methods seldom lead to operational effectiveness and may, in fact, cause a deterioration in performance, personnel morale, and eventually public support does not seem to have penetrated the minds of those who make use of these political measures. Policy must therefore be established which can erase such techniques and provide a stage where openness, leadership, competence, and integrity have a chance to flourish.

Development of Problem-Solving Strategies

The objective of understanding political realities within the special fabric of the community is designed to provide a framework for information collection, analysis of considerations which produce problems, and the formulation of alternative courses of action for probable solutions. For these reasons it is necessary to recognize:

1. pertinent claims, threats, and opportunities prevalent in the agency's environment,
2. the need to define missions and objectives,
3. the necessary tactics to satisfy objectives,
4. the resources required to fulfill agency plans,
5. that evaluation is a continuing process which must be accomplished if agency performance is to be of a quality necessary to satisfy the varied constituencies of the department, and
6. that internalities and externalities must be understood if the aims of the agency are to be achieved.

In analyzing the complexities of political reality, it is relatively simple to become inundated by the amount of inputs that require simultaneous consideration, for example, patronage factors, political machinery, economics, lobbies, organizational factors. When these complexities exist, some strategy which can facilitate the easing of potential conflicts from within and from outside the agency needs to be developed. Additionally, such procedures should enable the agency to provide its services to the community without excessive hindrances from those environmental forces which, by virtue of their respective vested interests, can forestall or diminish recreational service effectiveness.

Initiating the kinds of policy necessary to permit agency adjustment or accommodation to a variety of confrontations within the social milieu requires the development of knowledge and skill in analysis concerning specific situations. The recreationist must gain an understanding of the political realities, involvements, and sometimes conflicting responsibilities which accrue to any community-based agency attempting to serve diverse publics. It will be essential to scrutinize the organization's structure, environment, and policy-making process so that approaches can be taken which will assist in overcoming agency stagnation in the face of subtle and not-so-subtle opposition. The conceptualization of policy formation and the development of administrative skills in presenting and implementing solutions to problems are required. Searching analyses concerning the agency and its relationship to and within the community must be performed if comprehension of its functions is to be attained. Furthermore, only when the recreationist completely understands the roles which the agency plays within the community and the impact which internal and external forces impose upon the agency can there by any semblance of policy formulated to assure the continuing capacity of the agency to perform in ways that are beneficial to the community while preventing organizational atrophy or misuse.

Problem Solving and Policy Formation

Policy formation involves decision making and all efforts which affect the agency's operations over the longest period of time, and employ vital resources toward opportunities of value which can significantly aid the agency in carrying out its mission. Policy itself is an intellectually based statement conceived to guide agency performance and human behavior, either as a reaction to a perceived problem or in anticipation of conflict. The function of policy is to foresee incongruencies, challenges, or conflicting interests and implement counterproposals that successfully disarm potential stressful conditions before they become critical. Policy, in the latter instance, provides alternatives relating to basic mission, organizational goals, and strategies for accomplishing them. In the former function, policy is contingency based; that is, it is protective of the agency and defensive in nature, designed as a holding action rather than as the basis for directional decisions over an extended period of time. Reactive policy is analogous to the knee. jerk. Any response is a gut reaction rather than an intelligent appreciation of the facts, because the policy-making process has been short-circuited or is nonexistent.

Policy should not be thought of in terms of short intervals. This is mere expediency and consists of almost any plausible action to ameliorate whatever current pressure is being generated for whatever reasons by some organizational group or external derivative. Such emergency measures may work as a cosmetic or superficial solution, but they do not resolve the underlying causes nor apply the resources necessary to come to grips with central issues that are the source of conflicts. Expediency is not the appropriate measure for handling human problems. Allocation of vital resources, such as personnel, finances, and material, requires a continuing process of evaluation and clarification, so that viable choices can be made upon the conflict, with a high probability of successful resolution. This is neither a one-time-only program or something that can be developed on short notice. Such emergency thinking is useful only to submerge the real issues which face the agency and the community at large. It may buy time, but it does nothing to provide the services which the community should expect. Defensive policy is implemented after the fact. It is much like the bandage applied after an injury.

Anticipatory policy, on the other hand, is not only more effective than defensive policy, it is a continuing process that seeks out root causes for dissatisfaction and provides alternative proposals from a well-thought-out position. It consists of information gathering, analysis, projection of alternatives, and decision making based upon inputs from many different sources, so that the needs of the community can be satisfied with the greatest possible benefit to all concerned. Of course, there may be the necessity of placating certain interest groups while trying to find the most satisfactory choice. But even here, the agency has anticipated problems and tried to reconcile differences or provide efforts which will meet outstanding needs as it struggles to bring the full impact of its resources to bear. Foreseeability is a responsibility of the community recreational service agency. It should be prepared to allocate its specific resources so that stress-producing conditions cannot make headway. Unless the agency has a process by which it formulates policy on a continual basis, it will always be in the unenviable position of having to react to situations over which it has little or no control. To the extent that any agency develops reactive policy it confronts issues from a position of weakness. Policy formation should be viewed as a continuing, changing social process whereby behavioral manifestations are guided as situations or conditions undergo transformation within the agency or in the agency's environment.

An understanding of the basic mission of the agency is always required so that tangential issues do not become confused with the major task of the department. Too often, a "tree" syndrome develops as a result of unclear statements of mission which should be the department's first priority. This occurrence means that objectives are formulated as leaves and branches, because the trunk is obscured as heavy overgrowth. The same effect is observed in public recreational service departments. There are so many pressure groups whose prime concern is with their own particular brand of activity or interest that the departmental mission is lost in the clamor for service to high profile or peripheral targets.

Any formation of policy will necessarily have to be concerned with limited resources and the choices that can be made on the basis of fortuitous opportunities in a shifting social environment. Thus, if the mission of the agency is clearly defined and, therefore, becomes the foundation on which the agency's philosophy is based, there is a good probability that the agency will remain on proper course despite threats to its integrity. The mission of the department may be defined as the overall goal toward which the agency directs its efforts in providing the essential services for which it was established. It circumscribes the scope of operations necessary insofar as services to the constituency are concerned.

Once the mission has been determined, organizational aims may be designated. Aims are the immediate or long-range objectives toward which the agency aspires in achieving its mission. Aims may be developed in consequence of comprehensive analyses of both internal and external environments, or they may be directed by the intuitive grasp of the agency executive or other persons of influence within the hierarchy of the department. Aims also may be derived from the intricate play of forces within the organization. However, if the agency mission is, in fact, accepted and esteemed, the aims must be supportive of the mission's achievement.

Methods by which aims are attained are tactics. Tactics are specific actions undertaken which have as their goal the accomplishment of the stated aims. Tactical decisions might include such diverse elements as 1) selecting a particular segment of the community for the reception of needed recreational services on the basis of the department's capabilities to perform, 2) focusing effort on obtaining additional support from sectors other than the public in order to fulfill agency responsibility, 3) deploying resources so that the likelihood of success is greater, and 4) designating certain personnel as having the authority as well as responsibility for the oversight of the operation in order to ensure achievement. Tactics, then, are the patterns of actions or decisions made with the end in view of satisfying the mission which the agency has defined as its *raison d'etre*.

Among the tactics undertaken to assure compliance with the stated mission are various assessment and developmental activities employed to monitor quality of programming, resource allocation, clientele satisfaction, personnel performance, facility attractiveness and capacity. Such tactics are implemented through periodic status reports, data analysis, interviews, questionnaires, and supervisory inservice procedures. Each person employed within the organization is furnished with a description of responsibilities and position requirements. An unstated, although implied aspect of the job is the pattern of behavior which the agency expects and the functions, duties, and authority assigned to the incumbent. The role that each recreationist assumes within the agency is directly related to that person's perception of the agency and a niche within the hierarchy of the organization. It is this perception which tends to stimulate patterns of behavior and motivates the individual insofar as professional performance is concerned. Thus, the worker's understanding of functions and personal professional preparation, if such has been obtained, should provide a basis for quality performance. However, how the worker actually behaves also will be an outgrowth of treatment by the system and other interpersonal relationships developed in the course of normal working conditions. The agency's attempts to instill loyalty, dedication, and ego-involvement in the employee will have much to do with its ability to retain outstanding workers and accomplish the task for which it is responsible.

The mission, therefore, defines the objectives, or aims, of the agency which reflects the capacity of the organization to achieve based upon the environment in which it operates. Recognition of aims produces the tactics, which are the specific methods for reaching the goals toward which the department is oriented. Both the operational environment and the organizational aims provide circumscriptions on the possible alternatives available to the agency. The commitment of resources, whether monetary, material, or personnel, represents the initiation of a comprehensive plan designed to achieve results consistent with the aims originally suggested. This activity imposes upon and affects the environment, both internally and externally. Environmental modifications have tremendous impact upon agency capability and therefore upon the outcome of reaching particular objectives. Under altered environmental conditions, the ability of the agency to perform may be seriously impaired. This impairment may arise from any number of political inputs which require tactical revisions. The entire process is cyclical, and every action has some consequence of an environmental nature which, in turn, influences the agency's output or ability to serve.

The key to this process is the executive or policy formulator. Positioned in the center of the environment, assessing the situation, in order to propose an optimal program for satisfying the agency's clientele, meeting environmental constraints, correctly allocating resources, and achieving the fundamental mission which is the organization's function, is a primary responsibility. How the manager operates to devise methods for combating negative environmental forces is based upon problem-solving methods from which decisions flow. Decisions are never made in a vacuum. Eventually, commitments must be made for a particular tactic. Utilizing problem-solving methods, the administrator, while taking certain risks, may reduce the factor of chance. Relying upon rational analysis and a knowledge of the situation to formulate policy can effectively fulfill the agency's responsibility to the people it is designed to serve. Thus, the administrator sorts out various alternatives based upon logical analysis. Yet there are obvious risks because the work occurs in a dynamic social situation where people's motives and the vagaries of human nature are operating. Keeping those variables in mind, executives must allocate their agency's resources despite the fact that there may be conflicting sets of interests involved. Policy making is best viewed as a mediating influence in which certain trade-offs may be necessary so that equilibrium is achieved and support for the present and future of the agency is maintained.

The bases for reaching decisions and solving the problems which confront the agency are chosen from the support received from the publics which the department is attempting to serve, as well as from subordinates with appropriate competence and enthusiasm. Support for certain decisions may come from whatever board or commission legally operates the department or, perhaps, from the elected officials of the local government or their appointed representatives. Modifications in such environmental components as the economy, popular culture, technology, employee competence, pressure groups, interest groups, and employee organizations also provide input data upon which decisions will have to be reached. Assessment and forecasting environmental changes are significant aspects for informed decision making in the solution of problems.

Two other variables also are part of the problem-solving pattern. First, the departmental output is either accepted or rejected by the environment in which it operates. If outcomes are unacceptable, the environment will simply abolish the organization. For example, when programming capacity is aimed at one segment of the population without regard for the recreational needs of other citizens, there is bound to be an increasing dissatisfaction with the agency. The greater the dissatisfaction, the more likely it is that the department will suffer reverses in its attempts to gain an operating budget. In instances when public dissatisfaction has reached enormous proportions, the political officials respond by eliminating the agency or curtailing its ability to function. Of course, the economic factor is a constant threat to agency ability to perform. Thus, during periods of economic retrenchment, vociferous insistence by the more conservative elements of the population might demand the cutting of budget allocations to the recreational service department. This would be consistent with the philosophy either that public recreational service is a frill of government or that the individual should find the means for personal satisfaction of recreational needs without recourse to governmental assistance. In economically depressed periods, officials may be swayed strongly by such arguments. Under these circumstances the departmental mission is jeopardized or, at the very least, badly impaired. Recognizing the situation and acknowledging the presence of such unsympathetic views, which probably exist at all times regardless of the economic conditions, the policymaker must understand the need to marshal those forces favorable to the continuation of public recreational service and appeal to them as part of the constituency of the department for support in times of economic crisis. Although there may be the probability of a diminished financial allocation to the department, there is less of a chance that the operation will be undercut and so damaged that it cannot perform its functions in any way. There are typical economies which might be instituted, certain maintenance functions which could be delayed, greater utilization of volunteers, reliance upon free or inexpensive materials with which to conduct a program rather than the purchase of the more expensive supplies. All these possibilities may be utilized to offset actual cuts in monetary appropriations to the department. Even under these circumstances, the executive has been able to sustain his department in the face of environmental pressures which seek to abolish or so cripple the department that it might as well be disestablished. But such confrontations and their solutions can be performed only when the executive understands the forces that play a role in the environment in which the agency is situated.

The second concept concerns elements composing the organization's environment. There can be no idea that the environment is made up of independent variables which have neither association nor impact upon each other. All environmental factors are interdependent. This means that changes in any one element has some influence on some or all other elements and that such changes that occur will alter others to a certain degree. For example, governmentally initiated legislative changes in race relations in the United States has led to a number of alterations in the attitude of people toward racial questions. In some instances, the effects of such legislation have been to exacerbate rather than to heal. Nevertheless, the law mandates certain actions to be taken in regard to racial discrimination, or other forms of discrimination for that matter. Such legislative activity has resulted in changes in traditional mores of society. Simultaneously, features of the cultural environment have had impact upon the government to enact legislation. In consequence of these legislative enactments, personnel policies and practices have been affected and these are part of the agency output which has been altered as a requirement of law. Many other examples of environmental change, both internal and external, could be given.

Organizational Reactions to Problems

Policy formulation requires the selection of alternatives among competing sets of values. A medium for controlling such conflict lies within the structure of the organization. Thus, how individuals perceive themselves as an integral part of the organization, in terms of interacting to roles expected by position, does much to define reactions to pressure. Individuals have certain expectations concerning their behavior in particular positions within the agency hierarchy. Even if the individual is confident of the capacity to perform there are other considerations which might give pause when confronted with conflicting value sets. The first refers to the person's attitude toward the inconsistent or contrary expectations that are understood as contemplated in the confrontation. The second refers to a personal view of the consequences for any infraction of the competing expectations. For example, the administrator, may have been told to develop certain high-risk, innovative programs for a particularly vocal group that arouses much sympathy from the general public. At the same time, however, the remembrance of those who have taken high profile stances and do not succeed, learn to their regret that any future career to which they aspire is endangered. It appears to be a well-known axiom in public service fields that well-publicized efforts, regardless of their ingenious qualities or noble aims, must succeed or else one's career falters or becomes jeopardized. This is probably why many career administrators are hesitant about being entrepreneurial and/or innovative. Their perceptions indicate that they cannot afford visible errors. Their superiors may quickly utilize such "failures" for supporting a scapegoat movement, or a fickle public led by local news media may leap upon the hapless administrator and judge that person incompetent on superficial investigation or no investigation at all. When the administrator knows that legitimate evaluation will be made on the error-free image created, there are sufficient grounds to feel that this has a profound, if not decisive, effect on behavior, the roles which are played within the organization, and the policies which are chosen.

Although other considerations have a great deal of influence on the way an administrator will function in dealing with problems or in establishing policy to ameliorate problem-causing situations, the personal perception of the individual insofar as role conflict is concerned may explain why some administrators do nothing, thereby raising no question about personal competency, intelligence, ambition, knowledge, or adroitness, rather than trying to accomplish something, which may be met with possible failure, ridicule, and the termination of the positions they hold. Paralyzed with the fear of confrontation between role expectations and role conflicts, they may decide that no effort or the maintenance of the *status quo* is the best possible escape. Of course, some administrators have reached "the level of their own incompetence."[4] They do not have the skill, intelligence, or talent to perform, but merely take up space in the organization. They could not innovate even if they were moved to do so. They have no conflicts because they are incapable of understanding. To this group of so-called administrators, anonymity is their greatest protection. They neither seek highly visible programs nor desire publicity. They desire only routine activities which require little of them and are content to "serve time" until retirement. This section does not apply to them, because they are anomalies of the field and should not be equated with the majority of professional personnel working under difficult conditions. It is necessary, however, to recognize incompetents for what they are and to indicate that not all administrators are professionally endowed, ethically practice their calling, are dedicated to recreational service, nor attuned to the risks of a public career.

Personal Interest

Personal interest may have a great influence upon the policymaking process and the decisions reached prior to adopting policy. Self-interest is developed variously. Among these are the ways in which the individual perceives the world, those things or ideas which have value, and

---

[4]L.J. Peter and R. Hull, *The Peter Principle* (New York: Bantam Books, 1969), p. 7.

those conditions which seem best suited for personal advancement, optimal satisfaction, or material gain.

There is no such thing as the unswerving goal and logical decision making. There is a variety of significant influences upon the judgment of any individual in a policymaking position. Certain preferences, attitudes, information received, new technologies developed, pressure from significant others (peers or superiors), may lead to a re-evaluation of goals, the rejection of previously held opinion, a redefinition or alteration of both individual inclination and organizational aims. This pattern may be observed as a continuing process of screening and feedback by which the individual shapes his interests and judges his effectiveness. The sources of information received and the perceived aspects of self-interest thereby become guides to the behavior of policymakers.

Subjected to conflicting expectations because of the hierarchical position held, the administrator may be unable to resolve the competition between personal and others' satisfaction. Under such circumstances, the administrator may seize the initiative and perform the task with the objective of achieving the agency's mission. This may, in effect, produce strength insofar as personal interests are concerned, if the professional aspirations coincide with the mission of the agency, as they should. Even where the administrator conspicuously fails, the fact that attempts were made in the face of overwhelming odds should have a mitigating influence. Although there is a certain propensity for political figures to distribute blame, thereby escaping the consequences of citizens' wrath, there is also a concomitant protection being established by the administrator's willingness to do what is known to be both ethical and professionally correct in carrying out the mandate of the agency. The nature of the field is to have many successes in small things, build constituencies which become defensive and protective of their enabler, and thereby provide a cushion from the punishment of dismissal or other threat in the face of highly visible failures.

With the tenor of the times, that is, the economic instability, political intrigue, interest group pressures, and other important variables, all impinging upon the ability of the policymaker to reach decisions that will result in success, it is not indefensible for the administrator to attempt trade-offs. Where there are contradicting indicators, the administrator must thread a cautious way in improving the lot of those who have come to trust and depend upon him or her. Investigation and discarding any number of choices to determine the greatest good for the greatest number must be tried. Surely there will be disappointments and, perhaps, disaffections. However, to the extent that the administrator has attempted to fulfill the professional obligations which will maximize benefits to the constituency of the department, the record will be clear. Political authorities may tend to exploit the situation and, in the short term, they may succeed in driving out the recreationist, but the news media and other interested citizens' groups will demand satisfaction, so that the long-run effect will reinforce the administrator's position and policy decision.

Of course there are risks. Recreationists in public service cannot shut their eyes to the potential danger which lurks as assigned responsibilities are performed. Conflicting values and competing interests are part of the hazard of the field. Unless the administrator is simply incompetent or becomes paralyzed by overt threats that is, economic retaliation, job loss, litigation, grievance procedures, lack of cooperation, personal self-interest should be complementary to and, indeed, grow out of the agency's mission. If such were not the case, there would be little of compelling interest to keep that person within the field. The inherent satisfaction from making attempts to reach the goal by which the agency measures itself serves as the stimulus that motivates the administrator's efforts.

A variety of methods is employed by policymakers attempting to ameliorate conflict situations. Certain values may be derived from competing interests. Prevention of breakdowns in the ability of the agency to serve the community while retaining the stimulation and generation of ideas for mission accomplishment and program enhancement is of value to all concerned. Competition may be justified to the extent that the most worthwhile and justifiable program can emerge. Conflict is not all negative. Values and constructive ideas probably develop and can flourish in the climate of necessary justification, if one or the other interest is to be adopted by the department. The most feasible, attractive, and factually prepared position should manifest itself under the searching focus of resolving conflicts. Methods for such resolution are the following:

Explicitness and Legitimacy of Roles. Lucid and precisely expected patterns of behavior can assist policymakers to become more independent and thereby reduce or eliminate jurisdictional disputes. If the position assignments are clearly understood and accepted, they are likely to provide the foundation for one influential factor in minimizing conflicts.

Position Coordination. A much utilized technique in resolving conflicts is to rely upon legitimate authority or the organizational responsibility to wield power. The chief advantage for such reliance is that more decisive and faster action is gained. However, there may be a concomitant loss in elasticity as well as the possibility of lack of acceptance of the decision. Authority provides the capability of negotiation and accommodation which offsets counterforces of a political type. Thus, rational positions may be attained despite initial hesitation or unacceptance. The important element of compromise is available and permits conflict resolution.

Organizational Correlation. Several organizational arrangements may be used to combat potential conflicts. Good internal communications may be one device by which objectives and resource allocations can be harmonized. Individuals may be designated as coordinators with the function of gaining cooperation from disparate divisions of the organization. One difficulty which arises is that coordinators may forget their function and merely represent their own self-interest, with concomitant diminishment of collaboration. Naturally, if agency success and reward structure are made congruent, then coordination will probably occur and this problem alleviated.

Ego-Involvement and Shared Values. Where the aims of the agency are developed with input from as many employed personnel as possible, there is the likelihood of ego-involvement with a desire to see that agency success is attained. Under these circumstances, the probability exists that dysfunctional operations and self-defeating competition may be abjured for the coordination necessary to accomplish designated tasks and assure departmental achievement. Wherever objectives cannot be reached, unless cooperation is forthcoming from the various organizational elements, then joint operations are mandated and coordination rather than conflict becomes apparent. The introduction of shared values through ego-identification should be produced to foster cohesiveness. Projects should be initiated whereby all divisions of a department can be integrated, resources and effort joined, and goals clearly identified with the interests and values of those concerned.

Negotiation. Negotiation can be an effective device for coordination where there are common or complementary interests. In order to accommodate the interests of those who make up the diverse sections of the organization, there may be the need to solve problems jointly. When individuals can see that the solutions offered are beneficial and do not result in significant losses, that is, one section's gain is accompanied by an equivalent loss to another, then the potential for joint problem solving exists. Negotiation can be an effective force when competing interests set about working out differences through the study of issues before adopting any tactical plans of action.

Coordinating Conferences. A joint problem-solving technique involves conferences between potential or actually competing parties, so that honest discussion of issues and policies can be made. Such meetings are designed to open lines of communication and to establish methods by which personal and group commitment to improved organizational functioning is the outcome. The development of rapport between competing interests is the surest way for obtaining the kind of behavior and cooperation necessary, so that problems can be dealt with constructively. An important technique is to find the common elements upon which the parties can agree and thereby establish a basis for effective interaction. Out of such interchange can grow recognition of problems, barriers, priorities, and plans of action on which subsequent policy may be recommended.

All these procedures are born of the desire to achieve the mission of the agency. Objectives are those steps by which the mission is to be accomplished. Role performance indicates the real patterns of behavior exhibited by personnel employed by the organization. Role performance would be composed of analysis, initiation, and acceptance of policy so that operational effectiveness could be reached. The outcomes that might be produced in light of these strategic concepts for mitigating conflict and arousing coordination would incorporate such performance measures as comprehensive programming, the satisfaction of the many publics which make up the constituency of the department, flexibility, stability, responsiveness, physical plant attractiveness, and personnel output through effective interaction.

Politics and Recreational Service

But what has politics to do with the field of recreational service? To the extent that politicians write the laws which govern society, they can influence many of our actions and activities. The law is a pervasive element in our society. It regulates the daily lives of people, companies, corporations, and governmental functions. In the public sector, politics of the bureaucratic and the party type are intimately connected with the organization, operation, and administration of the public department of recreational service. In the same way, recreational agencies of the private sector, whether of the commercial or voluntary kind, are regulated by a variety of laws and must comply with many different political demands. These latter may range from the demands or requirements of influential members, patrons, or special interest groups whose views have to be taken into account before any decision can be made concerning the continuing operation of the agency.

All recreational agencies have constituencies who have needs and who make demands upon the agency. Overlaid on the constituencies are the political aspirations and impingements of elected and party office holders. These people have enormous power in controlling resource allocation for public agencies and their legislative dominance affects the laws that control and regulate the ability of the private sector agencies to perform. In all of the sectors, there are political forces at work which tend to restrict or expand the objectives of the agencies which are the focus of attention.

Depending upon the political philosophy of the elected local officials, the public recreational service department's mandate to provide comprehensive recreational opportunities may be curtailed or expanded. Thus, a conservative mayor, city manager, or municipal councilor for example, may perceive public recreational service as an infringement upon private enterprise, as an outgrowth of the public welfare system; or may view the public agency with such disfavor that they will do everything possible to throttle, dismantle, or eliminate the recreational service department. In the conservative view, tax monies should not be used to pay for public recreational service. Since the conservative sees private enterprise as the means by which people can best employ their respective leisure, tax resources need not be allocated for such use. Moreover a conservative administration will attempt to disestablish the public recreational service as one way of showing the taxpayers that money can be saved.

Simultaneously, those who are directly affected by such political views will be marshalling their own forces to obtain better treatment, more resources for the continuation of the agency, and financial support that will mean more comprehensive programs, adequate facilities, and a chance to satisfy the need of the agency's users. This clash of interests is intensely political. On the one hand, elected or appointed officials who actually govern the community see their function in a particular way. Those who oppose them, whether they are an embattled bureaucracy, the people whom that bureaucracy serves, or other persuasive voices— either within the political party in power or from the influential segment

of the community—will attempt to counteract such actions. In all likelihood some compromise will be reached. This is part of the art of the
possible which is a fundamental feature of political life.

Since all politicians want to be re-elected, party voices advising a less
stringent attitude toward the public agency will probably be heard. After
all, the elected officials must have some record to run on. If they alienate
a large enough segment of the voting population by abolishing a popular governmental function, voters may even the score by not returning
them to office or by unseating the entire political party. Political manipulators must always be able to read the pulse of the voters. They are
constantly receiving information about how people feel concerning any
action or proposal which elected officials try to impose. On sensitive
issues of any kind, proposed action may take months in preparation
as the political party in power tries to propagandize the public into
accepting the scheme. In many instances, such an educational campaign
is successful, and the politician gets what he or she wants. Conversely,
campaigns fail or countermeasures are swiftly and successfully mounted
against the politician's plans. The give-and-take of political machinations are acted out on the open stage of the mass media, although there
are closed door sessions where proposals are thrashed out away from the
clamor and pressure of those who are waiting to report to a waiting
public.

Voter Apathy

What helps officials most to get away with abuses of power is voter
apathy—the "I-don't care" attitude. When the voters are too lazy or
indifferent to monitor the actions of their elected officials and hold them
responsible for poor management or corruption, they leave themselves
open to graft and other criminal and damaging practices. The voting
public has a notoriously poor memory; it soon forgets the incompetence,
negligence, or fraudulence of elected officials. Many politicians are
returned to office again and again despite revelations of terrible records
regarding public service. Either voters conveniently forget to vote or
they cynically believe that it is "better to deal with the Devil you know,
then one you don't know." Voter apathy simply provides the unscrupulous person in political office with a license to steal or to use the power of
office to hurt or destroy political enemies. It all comes down to the same
common denominator. The use of millions of dollars to buy one's way to
power is now apparent. This is the legacy of voter apathy. For example, a

real estate developer obtains a large tract of land. Because he contributed heavily to the mayor's election campaign he becomes the most favored land owner to sell property to the city park department, whether or not the land parcel is most appropriate for the city to own for recreational purposes. Only through enlightened, active vigilance can voters prevent weak, dishonest government from undermining public recreational service administration.

Pressure Groups

No community is without its special interest groups. These pleaders may have sufficient numbers to swing the balance of an election for or against a candidate. Pressure groups run the gamut of special interests. In the field of recreational service such groups may be concerned with city beautification or with park or other recreational facility emplacement in a given neighborhood. They may seek the delivery of services to various minorities, disabled populations, or the use of outdoor spaces for recreational experiences. All of these issues and many more can be taken up by special interest groups who lobby for favored status, for the enactment of proposals in support of their demands, and for—or against— the provision of specified services according to what is considered to be in their best interest.

For example, the deputy director of the department obtains 1,100 signatures on a petition demanding that he be named director upon the resignation of the present director. The city manager does not want to employ the deputy in the top position. Faced with this situation, the city manager may well permit the deputy to take the written examination for the director's position even though the deputy does not have the necessary educational qualifications. In this way the city manager recognizes and assuages the political pressures of the petitioners without appointing the deputy to the job. If the deputy should fail the written examination, which is a prerequisite for the oral examination, the city manager can show that the director was at least given a fair chance to compete for the position.

Special interest groups need not be large to exert an impact on the general public, especially if their cause is one that generates sympathy. Thus, disabled populations, such as the mentally retarded, physically disabled, and others, have the ability to arouse public indignation and/or concern far beyond the actual numbers of potential voters which these people represent. This places great pressure on the recreationist who is confronted by demands, which may or may not be met due to resource allocation for the agency. Only the elected official or city manager can satisfy resource allocation problems. Special interest groups know that they can place a public administrator at a disadvantage and create unfavorable publicity which puts that administration in a bad light. That is why many recreationists and elected officials are quite careful about how they treat special interest groups.

Among the political ploys that pressure groups use are:

1. Public relations
2. Propaganda
3. Confrontation tactics or harassment
4. Mass demonstrations
5. Mob action which may become a riot

Each of these methods has its strengths and weaknesses, but they all serve the same purpose—to intimidate. The underlying threat issuing from the use of these tactics is that they convey the idea that many more people are involved in the group's concerns than perhaps there really are. If the threat is directed toward the recreationist administrator, it may be intimated that his or her superiors will be contacted unless specific demands are carried out. These can range from a demand for direct recreational services, accessibility to facilities, employment of personnel from the special interest group or directly from the neighborhood which the agency intends to serve. Any and all of these demands are subject to the concerns of pressure groups. The ultimate threat, of course, is the suggestion that so many people are involved with the special interest that they will be able to command sufficient votes to obtain their desires. This is something that gives pause to every politician.

Private Sector Involvement

To some extent, political pressure can also be brought to bear on private organizations. For example, to stall the construction of a facility permits may be denied, lost, or subjected to so many procedures that the company involved loses its commercial advantage of time and place. Even such private sector agencies as voluntary organizations may be subjected to political harassment if they are not willing to comply with requests for cooperation on some issue or project. What is more, such harassment can be perfectly legal and done with such adroitness that the voting public will be made to believe that whatever tactics are being used are for the public good. Thus, a restaurant owner may be subjected to repeated inspection of the premises by the public health agency, fire department, public works, building inspectors, and the like, to the point where the owner is either driven out of business or complies with the request. Of course, graft payments on the same basis are not unknown. However, there are certain situations where political officials might want some cooperation and use this method to pressure the business person to conform. When buildings and structures are involved, particularly where customers or patrons may be exposed to crowding, fire, food poisoning, and other hazards, there is an area for leverage to be applied in obtaining the form of accord that political figures want.

Naturally, the same tactics that special interest groups use in the public sector can also be used in the private sector—and for the same reasons. Neither public agencies nor private organizations are defenseless against special interest groups and political influence. Although elected officials may have the authority to govern, it is a day-to-day operation of the various departments, supplying many functions and services to the constituency, upon which the official builds a record for the next election. No public official can afford to rest upon a substandard record. Therefore, elected officials are beginning to understand the need to employ the most highly qualified persons to administer and operate the various departments under their control. This means that the old patronage system tends to break down under the pressure of having to stand for something beneficial to the citizens routinely.

Moreover, public recreational agencies have developed constituencies of their own. They serve the entire community with whatever resources they have, perform a wide variety of tasks that are looked upon with favor by many members of the special interest groups within the community, and may mobilize these forces when excessive political influence or constraint threatens the ability of the department to perform competently. It is quite normal for people who feel very strongly about the development of recreational facilities, the employment opportunities for sons or daughters in the community's department, or the comprehensiveness of recreational services made possible by budgetary allocations, to defend the department vociferously against political encroachment and reductions of financial support.

Private sector operations also have constituencies—those whom they serve—or they may band together in a better business organization which attempts to influence those political forces arrayed against them or which are trying to gain compliance to certain restrictions, ordinances, or other regulations. Since the private sector organizations do not depend upon taxes for their operations, they are relatively more independent of political interference with their operations. They may be able to combine in such ways that they will have the means to ward off political threats. They may do this by litigation against political officials, by advertisement, by buying political power, by mobilizing public opinion against the party in power, or by any pressure group methods.

Voluntary agencies are usually not prey to political officials because their constituency is neither large nor significant at election time. Most of these agencies are benign and their operations have little or no effect on the amount of taxes raised and collected. Additionally, they do not fall under a merit, civil service, or patronage system, so they cannot serve as a job bank for the party faithful. For these reasons, voluntary agencies are almost never involved in the political arena, except as special pleaders for their own cause.

Political Exploitation of Recreational Services

It is not unusual for governments or private individuals to use recreational activity or organized services to promote a particular ideology. We have all been exposed to political candidates who employ entertainment of various kinds to enhance themselves in the eyes of potential voters. Some politicians bring in bands, ensembles, singers, instrumentalists, or entire shows to entertain those who are listening to the speeches of the candidate. Sometimes television broadcasts are utilized to display the political wares of the would-be office seeker. Since television is looked upon as an entertainment medium, the entire political program tries to present the candidate's views in the guise of enjoyable experience.

Although the use of entertainment has had a long history, dating back to the bread and circuses of ancient Rome to the current attempts at "cooling" the superheated atmosphere of summer's discontents in the big cities, the exploitation of recreational activity for such purposes is well known—if not appreciated. Some of this activity appears to be relatively innocent. However, there is an underlying element that arouses suspicion of the motives. Is it possible that recreational activity is used in this way to attract an audience and simultaneously distract the electorate's attention from what the candidate really stands for? Too often, the entertainment provided sends the audience away with the notion that the candidate is a wonderful person—after all, the session was enjoyable, what with one-liner jokes, musical interludes, and the like. Recreational activity, used in this way, may polish a candidate's image, but it can also mask superficial ideas and questionable attitudes.

The utilization of recreational services to defuse potentially dangerous situations brought about by disaffection with the dominant system is a political device calculated to appease a vociferous or threatening group. Examples of this maneuver is the city's use of high profile recreational events during the summer to placate inner-city residents or to show opposition groups that the political party in office is sensitive and responsive to the needs of certain special interests. This is exploitative to the extent that the basic needs and issues go unanswered or unresolved; recreational activities are employed as a bandaid while deep wounds are permitted to fester.

Special Pleading

Because all individuals and groups are in thrall to the powers of government, it is sometimes necessary to remind politicians and their minions that government ideally is supposed to benefit the constituency and not the insatiable power-hungry thrusts of officeholders and bureaucrats. Well-organized interest groups have a variety of techniques which they use at their own discretion in bringing about desired changes in the laws which they do not like, in interpreting administrative regulation which affects them, or in gaining some advantage which will necessarily provide the recipient with more wealth, greater service, exploitative rights, or some other attribute deemed to be valuable. Thus, the chief tactics used by interest groups are negotiation, intimidation, seduction, propaganda, public protesting, and public confrontation.

There are as many special interest groups as there are groups. Each individual is not above utilizing the group as a base for gaining advantages which might not otherwise be acquired without the unity of the group. Of course, many groups fail in achieving anything at all, and some fail to obtain their desired ends for any period of time. It is not necessary to list all of the special interest groups. It will suffice to indicate merely a representative categorization of groups into which many smaller aggregates will be classified. Thus there are conservation/ecological groups, preservationists, racial, ethnic, and religious groups, groups representing the disabled, aged, youth, girl, or woman. Some groups are business-oriented, others are social, civic, or service-oriented, some represent geographical locations, and not a few are combinations of all those mentioned, with the additional thrust of having a single overriding interest from which the group receives impetus.

The methods employed by interest or pressure groups to influence administrative policy are as diverse as the groups themselves. The actions of the groups are a reflection of the aims, intelligence, competency, knowledge, numbers, and financing which the groups have at their respective disposal. Some special interest groups tend to feather their own nests by subverting the objectives of organizations through membership on the policymaking body of the organization. Thus, it is not unheard of that certain special interest groups fight to have so-called lay representation, since in this way they may infiltrate legitimately and attempt to influence policy. The demand for direct representation of specific interests on administrative board, commissions, committees, or other legislative bodies is a device that has been used to great effect by many groups seeking to control the benefits of a recreational service department for their own purposes. Such purposes do not have to be nefarious. They may, in fact, be highly beneficial to the general community. However the intent, the element of special interest manipulation, still operates. The following special interest techniques and the possible countermeasures which recreationist administrators may take are:

Negotiation. Some pressure groups try to gain their own way by failing to comply with administrative policy or regulations and then negotiating with the agency either to escape penalty, if there is one, or to soften or modify the agency's demands. Negotiations may be accomplished through legal maneuvers including litigation, or at least the threat of litigation; face-to-face meetings with the agency executive in hopes of obtaining surcease from the offending rule or regulation; a promise to accede to the policy in question if certain other considerations are offered or met. Finally, there is simply the delaying tactic, designed to prolong the time in which the policy is flouted before actually complying. In the latter instance, there may be many meetings between the group and various of the agency hierarchy before a final executive order is enforced. In any event, the group probably decided to comply with the policy but simply wanted a test situation to determine how long the agency would be kept from taking substantive action against them. Negotiations have a peculiarly reasonable air about them, and even under the most trying circumstances there is a facade of good will, as if to say, "We are all well-intentioned and rational human beings and this discussion is conducted in a spirit of friendship." Pressure groups do not apply pressure for enjoyment. They are striving to effect some change, usually to their advantage. The executive must understand the ground rules before exercising authority or resolves whatever differences there are. Every feature of administrative policy is going to be examined by pressure groups in order to gain the greatest advantage. Knowing this, the recreationist will be better prepared to meet the negotiators in a serious and informed manner.

Essentially, negotiation is a process of persuading groups to perform in certain ways without resorting to duress to which they might normally be subjected. Negotiation may be employed routinely when it facilitates the initiation or application of departmental policy, for example, in dealing with concessionaires who must conform to established standards; or independently when it is used to mediate between interest groups in confrontation with departmental administrative procedures. When in the course of normal activity the public department has to be unpleasant to particularly intractable groups, negotiation makes a commendable substitute for litigation.

Some prescriptions can be followed in any negotiating procedure. The more spontaneous the negotiation appears, the more likely it will be effective. The basis of all negotiation is leadership. If the recreationist involved will utilize knowledge of interpersonal relationships in attempting to influence the confronting special interest group, there is great likelihood of successful persuasion. It is a grave error to attempt to negotiate from a position of irrevocable demands. It is better to enter a bargaining session with some margin not already known. Finally, it is most effective if a third party can be introduced into the negotiating meeting. A neutral third party with sufficient status and unquestioned integrity may do more to reconcile seeming incompatible positions. Where there is an interested third party, and the antagonists can agree on some compromise position, they may safely report back to their constituencies that it was the intervention of the third party which prevented them from achieving their irreducible demands. All sides will be satisfied—usually. Neither side will have lost face, and each may claim to have upheld whatever principles were in question. The most important issue will have been settled to the benefit of all concerned. In this way, negotiation may gain compliance with administrative policy or regulation which otherwise might never have been settled or might have led to disaffection from the recreational service department. The recreationist administrator must understand when and how to employ negotiations in dealing with vociferous and concerned interest groups.

Intimidation. Pressure is sometimes applied when the interest group takes its case directly to the recreational service agency's political superior. Here, there is an attempt to influence the appropriate political figure in terms of potential votes to be garnered if the politician can either direct or persuade the administrator to repeal or modify whatever agency policies or regulations have aroused the special group's ire. Some political officeholders feel that they have a responsibility to all citizens in the community which they govern or represent and will not support blatant attempts to subvert or coerce public policy. Other officials, more concerned with their personal need to maintain office, will bow to any demand for special preferment and press for any and all demands made by a voting block.

Another form of attack, although of an indirect nature, may still be characterized by intimidation when the special interest group appeals to the administrator's direct superiors by heaping abuse and making several complaints simultaneously. Under such circumstances, the superior may support the subordinate, but then probably begins to wonder whether it would not be better if someone with less flare for generating conflict were in charge. Continuation of these methods can do much to lessen the effectiveness of any administrator, particularly when nominal or immediate superiors begin to think of the person under attack as a liability.

It is not unknown for letter-writing campaigns to be started by pressure groups in hopes of arousing political support for their objectives or objections. When political officeholders receive large mailings concerning any subject to which they can offer redress they usually seek ways to placate the supposed dissatisfied voters. Another use of mail is to send threatening letters. These letters are often looked upon as crank mail, but in some cases, the individual on the receiving end is so intimidated by the contents that the specific interest object is served. The recipient either complies with the interest group's demand, resigns rather than take further abuse, or softens the position which gave rise to the objections in the first place.

Seduction. Another tactic, not unheard of in the arsenal of pressure groups, is to invite the administrator to attend conferences, workshops, or institutes held by the special interest groups. The administrator who is invited to present a keynote address or participate in some equally important public discussion is typically familiar with the goals and philosophy of the host organization. The attendant politeness which usually accompanies such host-guest relationships requires that the administrator says something amenable, and the typical desire to be agreeable often leads the speaker to commit on departmental policy matters which can be detrimental to one's position. In the objective frame of reference of home precincts he or she would never have stated such ideas. However, ego needs sometimes get in the way of administrative common sense. Unless administrators recognize the danger when accepting invitations from groups antagonistic to the policies of the agency, they can be too expansive and affable and wind up in the embarrassing position of publically retracting statements or conforming to ideas fundamentally opposed to agency policy.

The best defense against such imposition and possible embarrassment is good common sense. Administrators should never permit themselves to become enmeshed in a situation in which a public speaking engagement for an organization, with diametrically opposed philosophies, requires the voicing of niceties which can either jeopardize or render their real position suspect. There is no reason to refuse speaking assignments if the administrator recognizes the hazards accompanying such public exhibitions, knows what will be said, and does not become involved in ego-building experiences which bring applause immediately, but regret later. The approach to blandishments made by special interest groups should be one of courtesy, objectivity, and a forthright statement of intent corresponding to the agency's known policies or principles. Under these circumstances, either the special interest group will withdraw the invitation or administrators will be able to make their case without further expectations or potential co-option.

Propaganda. The mass media are frequently utilized by special interest groups to generate counteractions against repressive or aggressively innovative agencies. For the most part, mass media attempt to maintain neutrality, but where they have editorial policies opposed to the agency's direction, they will generate issues and statements critical of the agency. Anything that helps to sell newspapers or provides a higher listener or viewer rating for radio and television will be carried. Op ed columns, letters to the editor, broadcast or telecast editorials and their rebuttals, are all part of the propaganda picture which special interest groups can employ either to discredit or to halt a program or policy which they oppose.

An expedient often used is the direct mail campaign. This may consist of a form letter, placed in a newspaper, which the supporter simply cuts out and signs. The letter is directed to the agency, political official, or legislative body of which redress or change is being asked. Sometimes petitions are gathered in response to some issue or problem, and the results are tabulated and sent to the responsible agency or the political superiors. Not infrequently, the special interest group writes individual letters, variations of which are copied, and sent to the respective agencies or political bodies from which a response is expected. This prevents the administrative disclaimer that only a few persons are involved and that they are sending a pattern-letter or telegram. Letter writing campaigns can be tremendously effective if directed to the right recipient. The recreationist on the receiving end of a letter-writing effort must make every effort to discern whether there is a legitimate reason for the correspondence or whether the letters are merely another ruse by special pleaders to gain some particular advantage which they probably should not receive. Whenever letters begin to take on a pattern quality, that is, have the same key phrases, it may be assumed that some group is attempting to influence an administrative procedure. When concerned individuals are motivated to write to officials or agencies, they do so with a distinctiveness that cannot be mistaken. Special interest groups tend to be rather heavy handed in their efforts. Critical observation of all correspondence is required to determine the source and the reasons for mail on particular issues.

Public Protesting. In recent years, a dramatic and a sometimes dangerous appeal has been made through mass demonstrations, marches, sit-ins, slowdowns, invasions, or riots. During the 1960's, mass protests were organized and highly publicized in attempts to gain civil rights. Some of the confrontations led to violence; others obtained what the groups demanded. The United States' participation in the Viet Nam conflict brought massive waves of protest, rallies, meetings, and other demonstrations which sometimes erupted into episodes of violence, rioting, and looting. When recreational agencies have not been able to supply mandated services, facilities, or leadership, they have invariably come under attack by the special interest group most adversely affected. These legitimate cases need to be ameliorated as quickly as public policy and fiscal support can make amends. However, some special interest groups have a limited concern, and their attempt at administrative intimidation involves the tempering of policies, rules, or regulations which apply to them only. Youth gangs, for example, have resorted to mass demonstrations in an effort to coerce certain benefits from recreational service agencies.

In many instances, recreational administrators have authority to regulate the issuance of permits for the holding of parades, public meetings, large commercial gatherings, for example, rock concerts and the like. Under such circumstances, the recreationist should investigate the conditions and applicability of the demand for these gatherings insofar as the public interest is concerned. Whatever public gatherings can be sanctioned, they should be. However, when such gatherings have as their sole purpose the stirring up of senseless emotions which can develop into dangerous excesses involving interference with the public safety, the gatherings must be surrounded with every precaution. It is every citizen's right to seek out public assembly, obtain redress for loss or wrongs against him or her, but it is not legally defensible to participate in mass protests which infringe upon the rights of others and end up by being public nuisances, riots, or overt acts of aggression against persons.

Public Confrontation. One of the most effective means for gaining and holding public attention, as well as obtaining ventilation through the mass media, is the direct presentation of facts or opinions at an administrative hearing. It is not uncommon for recreational service administrators to hold public hearings on controversial issues in order to determine how citizens feel about them. Here is an opportunity for any interested person to stand up and state an opinion, present views, plead a cause, attempt to obstruct or obscure plans and programs, or try to have specific operations enhanced. Public hearings may be requested by aggrieved citizens to decide upon some significant policy. Additionally, special interest groups may request and receive permission to come before elected or appointed officials to state their objectives or call for responses to real or imagined grievances. It is not unheard of to have a special interest group descend upon a hapless official without any prior arrangements and make demands. Sometimes such sessions become unruly, but people must feel very strongly about an idea or a plan before they will call in a body and harass an official.

Public hearings have attracted a good deal of attention, particularly those on issues that arouse intense emotions. Every individual has some vested interest in where a highway, golf course, park, zoo, or beach is going to be located. Sometimes citizens, who hold a single idea in common, band together and become a special interest group. These groups are eager to be heard in public assembly. They have a point of view to get across.

Press conferences may be called in order to force a policy statement from an official who is not prepared to present such a statement. In such instances, this line of attack can cause only embarrassment for the official and the agency which he represents. Untimely utterences, wrong answers, or even the classic "No comment" may be construed in ways which are detrimental to the future performance of the agency and its integrity. Among the techniques utilized to create confusion or to gain a selected objective is to barrage the official with a series of questions building up in significance. A single indicative question may then be presented which, even when turned aside, reveals the agency's position. Mass media stories may then be used to lever the agency so that it accedes to the wishes of the special interest group.

Recreationists must remember that special interest groups are supremely interested in one area only. They bend every effort to secure their position and will not be content with anything less than success. They either win concessions from the administrator or attack, making the position untenable. Consequently, the recreationist must have the courage of his or her convictions. If he or she kowtows to every special interest that pleads for preferment, then the performance is unprofessional and the incumbent will soon be used as a doormat by any group which knows it can intimidate. If, on the other hand, the recreationist proclaims independence of political roles and proceeds to carry out the official mandate regardless of potential political attack or other tactics that will be employed, there will be a fight to remain viable, but it will be a good fight.

Chapter 16

SOCIAL INFLUENCES
ON RECREATIONAL PROGRAMMING

The analysis of cultural factors which directly influence the provision of recreational service is necessary if social pressures are to be understood and balanced by essential recreational opportunities. Recreational experiences are universally desired as having personal value contributing to the common good. Any activity recognized as encompassing such values will, of necessity, be of significant concern to almost every type of social institution. Agencies that attempt to teach about the constructive use of leisure are confronted by numerous and sometimes conflicting community standards. The organization of human leisure and the operating practices for the development of soundly planned and conducted recreational activities face an increasing number of friction-producing pressures, as social values become modified and human institutions undergo startling metamorphoses.

Contemporary society is in the midst of a social revolution, one that is rapidly disassociating itself from a passive and controlled philosophical discussion to a highly verbal and aggressively active movement. As with all revolutions some violence to people, institutions, and ideas is bound to occur. The impact of the social revolution has focused attention upon inequalities in many areas of human contact. In the wake of abdication by state and local governments to administer fairly and see that justice is done, the federal government has had to take some drastic measures. New legislation, aimed at the immorality of social injustice, discriminatory practices, and disenfranchisement of a large block of legally constituted voters, and an upsurge in what might be termed social disintegration have caused new problems and require new methods on the part of recreationists attempting to meet their professional obligation.

Greater mobility, automation, cybernetics, massive leisure, problems arising from the possession of leisure without the skills to utilize it correctly, greater per capita wealth, larger numbers of people possessing a higher level of education, less illiteracy among relatively long residing citizens, but greater illiteracy among immigrants, greater distribution of more information through the mass media, and other related factors that have a tendency to sweep away former standards of behavior have left a residue of guilt, fear, hostility, frustration, anarchical situations thinly veiled by a veneer of obedience to legal authority. In this social milieu, every aspect of the community must be examined because so many impingements upon the wise use of leisure are apparent. The community must be carefully analyzed in terms of its people, its natural resources, its existing facilities, the probability of acquiring additional spaces and facilities, problems which result from encroachment, pollution, waste, inefficiency, and inadequate personnel.

An expanding world market, a larger proportion of people being educated at the college level, a larger work force, the desertion of certain moral and ethical behaviors in the face of an uneasy world situation, a tendency toward materialism, all have produced a restless and searching type of behavior. Into this charged atmosphere the recreational service agency must come to do the work for which society initially established it. Social status, sex, age, vocation, education, migration, and the continued destruction of great natural resources combine to bring about a serious threat against the programming of recreational activities that can meet the divergent needs of people. Nevertheless, the recreationist must bend all effort to produce a balanced series of activities which can attract individuals and enable them to take advantage of opportunities that are presented. To this end, community examination is undertaken. By considering all of the possible factors which might influence the planned recreational program, the recreationist assumes the most efficacious position possible in formulating the type and scope of the different activities necessary in developing the comprehensive program.

Traditions. Specific regions of the country have, and are noted for, traditional activities. The tidewater region of Virginia is noted for fox hunting, the lake region of Minnesota is known for fishing, the Rocky Mountain region in Colorado is noted for skiing, as are the Green and White Mountains of Vermont and New Hampshire. Sailing and boating are particularly fancied along the Atlantic and Pacific coasts, but nowhere is there more enthusiasm for this traditional activity than in the New England region. The South has a tradition of cotillion dances, and racoon and opossum hunts, and the Southwest is noted for the rodeo. Basketball has been a Midwestern activity and horseracing is well known in Kentucky. Regions within the states of Ohio and Pennsylvania support Amish, Mennonite, and Dunker communities whose traditions are still quite puritanical. The blue laws of New England and some parts of the South also affect forms of recreational and leisure activity. The Plains region has the tradition of state fairs, community festivals, and agriculturally based recreational experiences. Heavily forested regions associated with the lumbering industry gave rise to the traditional activities associated with logging camps, such as woodchopping contests, tree climbing, logrolling, timber topping, and so on.

Regional differences in climate, history, settlement, economy, natural resources, and trade, industries, transportation, media, or communication centers have helped to shape the form of recreational activity that is generally considered to be characteristic of particular regions. These traditions are so ingrained and expected that they must be integrated into all planning for community-based recreational service programs. To ignore traditional activities is to weaken the total effectiveness of the balanced program. Many potential participants can be lost if a well-known or customary recreational experience is omitted. In any program setting, it is better to work from the familiar to the less well-known activities in order to fulfill the instructional responsibility of making additional opportunities available to people.

Demographic Factors

Demography, the study of human population, is one of the most crucial factors that can influence considerations of programming recreational services in any community. The number of persons in the population of a specific geographical area and their density or dispersion with reference to the unit area and resources are the chief components of demography. Knowledge of the size and distribution of population for any area is most rewarding to the recreationist researcher who attempts to objectively identify and classify population statistics. These two aspects are the easiest to obtain and are subject to quite accurate and reliable measurement. Size and distribution of population, however, are only two of several conditions affecting the type and variety of recreational services needed in a given area. Other factors modifying and having direct consequences on programming include social, economic, and vocational status, educational level, previous recreational experience, residence, migration, ethnic groupings, religious affiliation, sex, race, age, and political association. The direction and intensity of the effect on programming of any alteration of these factors as well as in the size of population are apparent. The variety, magnitude, and gradation of activities actually realized by people stem from the correlation of all of these features.

Residence. In determining the composition of the population of a given community, it is first necessary to classify the nature of the area. Any region may be divided into rural and urban categories. In recent years the phenomenon of a growing suburban population has also been classified. Residential environment, including peer pressure, living conditions, socioeconomic status, and family life, tends to mold personal development. Within the restrictions controlled by genetic inheritance, residence is one of the most important existing forces shaping the particular personality traits which any individual will acquire. How an individual looks at potential recreational activities may be strongly influenced by residence.

Rural society offers a distinct contrast to urban society. Agriculture is still the predominant occupation of the rural dweller. Sparsity of population, a high degree of ethnic and cultural homogeneity, and a considerable vocational, social, and territorial permanency characterize the rural area. Nature orientation is the outstanding feature in the life of the rural population. Restricted social and political contact within a limited geographical region produces a more conservative outlook. In almost every way the urban dweller is dissimilar from his or her rural counterpart. Ethnic and racial diversity, greater expectation of governmentally provided services, occupation, economic level, and social involvement are some of these differences. Even with mass media providing greater informational dissemination, news reporting, and diversity of opinion, the influences on the country person and the city person are profoundly different.

There is, however, a third residential basis on which to classify population—suburban. This is the current phenomenon of population migration from the urban to a more rural setting without the accompanying characteristic of an agrarian economy. The suburban resident is an urban worker who generally resides in a community which depends for its economic base upon providing amenities. It is, in fact, a satellite of the urban center, located anywhere from 10 to 50 miles from the central core of the city, but with umbilical attachment to the central city by means of one or more express highways or other transport systems. Suburbia represents a new classification of residency for population analysis.

Neither rural nor urban, the suburban area has a few characteristics of both. It is a completely gray area that defies general categorization. There are many divergent natural and man-made environments that impinge upon the individual living in suburbia, with the result that specific traits which distinguish rural and urban populations are difficult to type. Depending on many variables, such as socio-economic status, mobility, educational level, attitudes, etc., the suburbanite is a composite of rural and urban traditions, mores, and economics. The homogeneous factors that can be discerned within rural populations also may be seen in suburban residents. The heterogeneous facets that mark the urban population also are to be found in the suburban population.

What continually confounds the whole idea of urban-suburban-rural categories are the criteria to be utilized in any classification system. If the basis for classification is strictly number, then the size of the community may segregate rural from urban. If, however, it is a question of incorporation, economics, occupations, or density, then rigid classification becomes more difficult to apprehend. Nevertheless, these factors are utilized in order to reflect more accurately the various degrees of suburbanization or urbanization from the most rural areas.

The effect of population density on recreational programming is considerable. Urban centers rely much more than rural areas upon man-made facilities and structure and there is a greater need for such structures to accommodate a larger population. A greater variety of structures exist and a more diverse and comprehensive program is available to the urbanite than to the rural dweller. There is more probability that the city will have a large and efficient department of recreational service offering many specialists and ancillary personnel who are prepared to program a comprehensive and continuing series of recreational experiences. In rural areas where sparsity of population is usual, together with the fact that more than one million farm families are leaving rural areas for urban centers each year, the likelihood is that no agency program exists, or, if there is one, it depends upon natural resources for a greater proportion of recreational activities. There are exceptions to this generalization. In the main, however, rural programs of recreational activity are characterized by poor facilities, small departments in terms of the number of personnel employed, and reliance upon routine and time-honored activities.

Ethnic Groups. Only population density and the rural-urban dichotomy take precedence over the classification of ethnic background or land of national origin. The extreme importance that ethnic background has for programming recreational activities may be better understood from the significant differences between the cultural backgrounds and economic status of native and foreign born. Ethnic patterns and the heritage and traditions brought to this country from other cultures have tremendous impact upon programming. Each ethnic group, whether foreign born, first or fifth generation, looks with a certain amount of pride upon its nativity. Even after a high degree of assimilation, foreign-born persons still have a feeling of affiliation to the traditions and cultural displays that have been developed over centuries of social intercourse. For these pertinent reasons, recreational service departments must determine the size and variety of ethnic groups residing within the given community and attempt to involve these citizens through activities that are representative of national origin. Typical of ethnic group heritage and tradition are those activities which have gained national flavor and support. St. Patrick's Day parades, Columbus Day ceremonies, and observances honoring such national heroes as Baron von Steuben, Count Casimir Pulaski, Kosciusko, Garibaldi, Layfayette, and others comprise certain activities of an ethnic origin. The Mardi Gras of New Orleans, the Chinese New Year celebrated in New York's and San Francisco's Chinatowns, and Pilgrims Progress in Plymouth, Massachusetts, are all examples of ethnic activities which have become part of the folkways of America.

The force that ethnic factors exert upon recreational programming is so clear that the exclusion of ethnic celebrations from the organized program makes reasonable a suspicion that a less-than-professional job is being performed. Ancestral heritage colors and offers many opportunities for a variety of wholesome and interesting experiences to be included in the program. Ethnic dances, such as the hora, kazatsky, schottische, flamenco, tarantella, and so on, can be of significant interest for their respective programming. Foods of foreign lands may be emphasized during a fair, festival, or cooking class. Cooking *aficionados,* as well as those who would be attracted to a cooking class sponsored by the public recreational department, would delight in learning to make shish kabab, lasagna, goulash, sukiyaki, or any of the countless ethnic foods. Cooking and baking contests, cookouts, celebrations, and special events can always be made more enjoyable when food with an ethnic flavor is introduced.

Ethnic sports and games have had a great influence upon typically American leisure activities. The Italian game of boccie, the American Indian game of lacrosse, the Scandinavian gymnastic or Turnverein societies, the Middle European game of soccer, the English sport of punting or rowing, the Scandinavian sport of skiing, the Dutch sport of ice-skating, the Swiss sport of mountain climbing, the French sport of bicycle racing, the Central European sport of distance running, and many other recreational activities, including archery, wrestling, fencing, judo, kendo, bowling, handball, golf, tennis, animal breeding and showing, volleyball, polo, mahjongg, whist, chess, pinochle, and cribbage, are all of ethnic import. Thematic materials for hundreds of activities utilizing immigrant backgrounds can do much to involve people in traditional or new and exciting recreational experiences.

Race. Racial characteristics condition the acceptance and involvement of some recreational activities, but for the most part racial factors have a social, political, and regional connotation. All races have the same needs. However, it is in the social sphere that problems occur. Legislation has been introduced to prevent discrimination on the basis of race or minority status, but recreational activities are performed at a level on which no amount of punitive or restrictive legislation will have any effect. Social intercourse, association, affiliation, and membership are all social matters and as such are psychologically or emotionally motivated. Although the public recreational service department has an obligation to offer a program for all persons residing in a given community, there is little likelihood that any degree of racial integration on a social basis will be attained until racial prejudice is eliminated.

Mass spectator and a few individual activities may be programmed without regard to race. This will also be valid for instructional classes and most of the program categories. However, intensely social activities, such as dances, parties, club associations, and perhaps dramatics, will tend toward segregation because of racial factors. Nevertheless, the public department must organize activities wherever residents live, regardless of race. The department must provide opportunities for all forms of recreational experience in spite of racial imbalance and ignorance. Because there is *de facto* segregation of races in terms of residency, the problem of integration becomes less important concerning neighborhood activities. However, where neighborhoods are changing as a result of minorities moving in and Caucasians moving out, the problem reaches severe proportions. In a few enlightened communities, racial factors do not play an essential role in influencing the type and kinds of recreational activities that can be programmed. Most communities find that only certain forms of recreational activities can be scheduled because of race problems.

Integration and involvement in recreational activities will always be an individual affair. Participation in planned recreational activities that are racially integrated will invariably be subject to ambivalent emotions. Real or fancied slights can provide fuel to an already explosive situation.

Nevertheless, recreational opportunities should be made available to all who may want to participate. Such participation, being a highly individualistic prerogative, must be as attractive and enjoyable as possible to counter bigotry and ignorance.

Age. One of the more important facts pertaining to population is the age of the people in a given community. It is not an overstatement to say that data concerning the age and sex of the population are among the most valuable to the recreationist. The professional practitioner requires information concerning the number and sex of the population of particular ages and their proportion to the population of the total community. Data concerning age and sex distribution are invaluable in planning for facilities and specific activities of the recreational program. The recreationist realizes that there are age group characteristics which will have a marked effect on the kind and gradation of organized recreational experiences which can be offered by the public department. In order to plan the recreational program logically, the recreationist must be well acquainted with age group characteristics and make every effort to satisfy those that are generalized as well as those that are displayed by individuals.

Social Status. As in nearly all other cultures and societies, there is a social class system in the United States. This system of social status is closely connected to economic level, residence, family background, education, and other factors. Some individuals have been so indoctrinated with the idea of social class that they can identify only with whomever is also clearly affiliated with or an integral member of the same class. It is not uncommon for such individuals to consider attending a specific school and no other, entering a specific occupation and no other, or attending a specific function or functions at a particular place or places and no others. All people are influenced by the standards and values of their environment. Social situations are sufficiently strong to shape attitudes and opinions, and selection of companions.

Social status is the degree of influence possessed by an individual in any community, based upon sharply defined, recognized criteria. Among these criteria are family affiliation, economic worth, occupation, religion, race, residence, and the residue of all these interrelated components that form the power structure of the community. Each person brings to any group a complex of values, opinions, behaviors, skills, and experience which in turn affect, in various ways, the objectives, size, cohesiveness, variety of activities, and affiliations. Each person is molded by environmental and social forces that originate in the customs and codes of the social class from which the individual comes. As a result of previous and concomitant social experiences, one person may be highly skilled in group living, whereas another may be unable to identify himself with any particular group. Not everybody is fortunate enough to become a part of a group. Even with association, not all individuals are capable of seizing the opportunities of relating and performing well the functions assigned in a group situation. The significance of social experience makes obvious the need for considering the placement of individuals within the program. Persons who have experienced satisfaction in social living are better able to function in involved group situations and can achieve their objectives. The social background of individuals prepares them for the assumption of different roles in a variety of groups. Those who are not well prepared either need more intense professional assistance or fail in their specific goals and gain little satisfaction.

Social status has another affect on political participants within any recreational program. Some people feel that they cannot participate if the "wrong" people are also in attendance. There are those who look down upon what they call "the lower class." Such bias prohibits these persons from joining any group, regardless of the interest they have for it, when those whom they consider socially inferior are also participating. With upward mobility and greater opportunity for the attainment of more education and better occupations increasingly prevalent in this society, this aspect of social life is slowly dying. Nevertheless, it is still a factor that requires attention by the recreationist who plans a program.

Educational Level. Although educational level is relatively unimportant to children, it begins to take on greater significance as the individual matures. With other children, and particularly young adults, varying educational levels and intellectual experiences create a diversity of interest, ability, and skill which can be a divisive force. Educational differences may be so pronounced that individuals who might have come from the same social environment find that they have little in common, or if they have one thing that brings them together, they find that they have no idiom for mutual understanding and contact. Almost all recreational service departments bring many people together to form groups of varying interests. It is in the artificially contrived groupings, prevalent and necessary for recreational agencies, that educational levels are so far ranging. Where such groups are brought into being as a consequence of some overriding civic problem, a recreational activity of common interest, or some other shared experience, the inherent conflicts originating from differences in educational background can be transcended for a short time. Only with the assistance of a skilled recreationist, to surmount the wide variance of knowledge and maintain the group in spite of differences of this sort, will there be any value to participants. The programmer must carefully analyze educational background and intellectual attainment of potential participants when planning recreational activities.

Occupational Range. There is little question that vocational position merits serious thought in programming for public recreational agencies. Occupational identity frequently serves as a major basis for establishing groups when organizing recreational activities. Employment in a particular occupation does not necessarily mean that the individual associates only with those who are similarly employed. However, social involvement with others who are employed in the same capacity, on the same level economically, or especially within the same firm is observed continually and seems to be a natural outcome of employment. Except in urban-based employment, where workers have to commute to their place of business, the likelihood of social relationships developing beyond those with whom one shares a working environment is quite slim. Even today, distinct lines are drawn between those employed in the trades or in factories and those in the professions. Lawyers, bankers, physicians, scientists, and engineers are probably in the same economic bracket, receive about the same social approbation or community recognition, and usually maintain the same area of residence. For these reasons, they are more likely to belong to the same social, political, civic, or religious associations. They will typically move in the circle of relationships closed to others. In like manner, people who are employed in the same factory, or horizontally in the same industry, will tend to find their social acquaintances and outlets at this level. There are some tradesmen who, by virtue of tremendously increased wages, have been able to afford greatly improved residences, and for this reason may be accorded a social status previously denied them. A materialistic culture still places extreme importance on the economic worth of the individual, and, money derived from employment assists in the upward climb.

Whether or not vocational position is a basis for the formation of recreational groups, and this is questionable because so many other factors are involved, the recreationist should realize the significance of occupational identity in programming. It is simply one more conditioning facet which represents population composition.

Religious Affiliation. In a country of complete religious heterogeneity, religious affiliation can never mean church domination of the cultural life of the people, as it does in countries where an established church is supported with state funds. However, church and sectarian associations still influence many social customs and contribute a great deal to the colorful ceremonies, ritual, taboos, and moral values of those who participate. To a considerable extent, religious denomination plays a large role in establishing specific recreational experiences associated with sectarian affiliation. Many nationally recognized holidays, and more particularly regional observances, are of an essentially religious nature. Christmas, Easter, Yom Kippur, Rosh Hashanah, Purim, Hanukkah, St. Patrick's Day, St. Valentine's Day, Thanksgiving Day, Saint's feast days, Halloween, Mardi Gras, and many other events celebrated during the year are basically religious occasions, which through many generations have been modified to meet the social and cultural demands of modern society. Nevertheless, to orthodox, conservative, and even reformed individuals of many faiths, these holidays still carry predominantly religious overtones. Perhaps the Sabbath has the deepest religious meaning for most sectarian practitioners and colors the recreational program in terms of what and when activities can be scheduled.

In some instances, it is helpful to know the religious affiliation of potential participants when planning a program of activities. Some sectarian groups in the United States discriminate against a variety of recreational activities and in some instances against anything that may be termed recreational. The South, for example, is well known as a "Baptist or Bible Belt." Although the Southern Baptist Convention, based in Nashville, Tennessee, has long been an initiator of church recreational programs, there are other Baptist congregations which strictly frown upon dancing, card playing, and other recreational activities. Depending upon the region and which sectarian form has the plurality, the recreationist will be wise to heed local religious customs and make the most of religious holidays, festivals, and other ritualistic events by utilizing them as program themes or structuring an entire activity or series of activities with the religious observance as the keynote.

Migration. An equally important factor for consideration in programming recreational services is the movement of people. People immigrate to a place, community, or region, or they emigrate from some place. The movement of people, whether to, from, or within a given location, is of tremendous social significance. Migration directly affects the social structure and has a powerful influence upon the personalities of individuals. Through migration, the individual dissolves almost all personal social obligations and sheds the ties of group association and the positions which gave status in them. Cut adrift from all former primary and special interest groups, separated from class identification, the individual must attain a role and find a place within the social structure of his residential neighborhood. The migrant sheds the role of indigenous person and assumes that of foreigner. The whole process of becoming accepted and finding a position within the class structure of the new community may be slow and painful.

Whenever population movement becomes a question of radical change in the shifting of residence or state of allegiance, the dislocation that follows may be passed along for several generations. Particularly is this true when a new language must be learned and different customs assimilated. Many of the millions of migrants who came to the United States during the late nineteenth and early twentieth centuries never completely adjusted to the new society. The ethnic dislocation was so severe that it necessitated a ghetto-like existence for the new immigrant. This is somewhat valid today, as different racial groups migrate from southern communities to northern and far western metropolitan areas. That such radically different groupings and cultures have caused painful environmental pressures can be clearly observed in the rash of race riots which erupted across the country during the late 1960s. The outbreak of lawless rioting in the Watts district of Los Angeles in the summer of 1965, followed by similar clashes in Natchez, Mississippi, Springfield, Massachusetts, and Chicago, Illinois have all been linked in some way to migration.

Migrants, whether from different regions of the country or from foreign countries, face a long assimilation process which is typically slow and difficult. As long as they live, in some cases, they are marked by some distinguishing physical or social characteristic of the stranger. They are never fully at ease, nor completely able to comprehend their social environment. Foreign-born migrants may continue to live in the cultural existence of their previous homeland. More often than not, there is a second generation carry-over, especially when the original language spoken at home is not the vernacular tongue. The older generation finds protection and status in the cultural patterns of the Old World. The children try to break away, obliterate all traces of their foreign heritage, and seek acceptance and total assimilation with the new customs of contemporary society. These situations can lead to family conflict and tend to color the view which the migrant has of the community.

Three types of migration typically affect the recreationist's concept of programming. For analytical purposes migration may be identified as a population movement out of a community, into a community, and internal movement. This facet of migration has a great deal to do with the density and distribution of the population. Forecasting population movement, for example, noting internal trends, is important for the development and construction of recreational spaces and facilities. Land acquisition, prior to the buildup of the size of the population in one section of a community, is a valuable consequence of such forecasts. The analysis of population by region of origin, and occupational, educational, economic, and social level will mean much in terms of programming. Recreationists must not only account for permanent residents, but also plan for transient populations upon which the community may depend. The tourist trade has become a most lucrative economic base for more than one city. But urban growth and a spreading population in one or more directions remain the biggest problems for prognosticating internal migration by recreationists. Planning the program to accommodate present and future area residents will influence the kind of activities and necessary facilities to be employed.

Recreational Experience. Although all persons have the right to participate in public recreational activities and share equally in the services offered, all do not have the same capacity to receive value from such opportunities. The factor of previous recreational experience and the concomitant skills developed by such experiences must be recognized by the recreationist and taken into consideration as attempts to program recreational activities are made. There is no standard description of how prior experience in a recreational situation will affect the skill and practice of an individual. It is well known that certain individuals never become skilled in specific activities regardless of how long they practice. This is readily observed in many motor skill activities. However, these individuals feel comfortable and knowledgeable in the activity of their choice even when they do not achieve great skill. Much the same can be indicated for a variety of other recreational categories.

Age, intellect, and natural ability play important roles as to whether an individual will be able to engage, with a high degree of skill, in recreational activities. Young children without any previous knowledge or experience in activities require a good deal of direct supervision and guidance in learning activity skills, as will those individuals who for medical or social reasons need constant direct supervision if they are to benefit from therapeutic, educational, or rehabilitative programs, are not in sufficient contact with reality, or whose pathological behavior prevents them from abiding by socially accepted norms. As individuals become more familiar with activities through practice, they are better able to use their personal resources to greater advantage and to find increasing success in what they do.

With a history of previous recreational experiences and the related development of skills, people require less direct supervisory assistance and can effectively achieve satisfaction independently. Initially, persons may need total assistance in instruction, planning, organization, and operation. With continued performance, however, this need diminishes until the recreationist may be employed minimally as a resource, for some technical problem which skill alone cannot solve, or in an advisory capacity. Programming then comes under the influence of precious experiences, as it concerns the degree of skill which the individual had developed and his ability to take complete advantage of opportunities afforded by agency operation. The more familiar and confident people are within the setting of recreational activities, the more likely they will require a broader spectrum of activities from which to choose. Familiarity, in this instance, requires a comprehensive and dynamic program.

Agency Structure

The essential aspect of agency structure comes in terms of a sufficient number of recreationists able to offer a well-balanced program. The department should have one division that is totally concerned with programming. The root of agency structure is determined by an adequate number of personnel equipped to perform in a competent manner. Division of labor into specialties and a complete description of duties and responsibilities for these line personnel are basic in order to provide comprehensive recreational services. All activities of the program are performed at a variety of facilities, and these areas and structures should be manned to a degree sufficient to carry out the primary function of the agency.

The most desirable facility arrangement will correspond closely to the number of neighborhoods situated within the community. In small communities (under 5,000 population) there may be only one recreational center with an attached playground. This may be supplemented by school department facilities. In the largest urban centers, however, there will be not less than one playground in each neighborhood, and these will be augmented by various spaces and specialized structures on a district, community, and metropolitan basis. In any event, the personnel requirement will change the size of the facility and the needs of the participants at the facility. There may be small playgrounds, relatively isolated, in some large urban areas which because of size will not admit an attendance that necessitates more than one worker during each eight-hour segment of operation. However, the usual personnel commitment for a neighborhood playground is two recreationists per session during the morning, afternoon, and evening. If attendance warrants, more workers should be deployed at these recreational facilities.

Recreational centers usually contain club rooms, auditorium, sometimes a gymnasium, multi-purpose room, art and craft room, lounge area, office and supply rooms, and other specialized areas for the continuous programming of many recreational experiences. The larger and more complex the center, the more it will be necessary to secure an adequate staff for its operation. The typical center usually employs one full-time director and an assistant director, complemented by one or more full-time program workers, and as many specialists as are needed to offer a diversified program of instruction, game, social, and other self-directed activities. The utilization of part-time workers and volunteers to complement career employees is also a valuable and integral part of the program.

Employment Practices

A large urban department of recreational service employs a permanent corps of career recreationists to perform the operational responsibilities of the program. The employees function as directors, functional or program workers, and specialists (program skills). These are line personnel specifically qualified and held directly responsible for the production and effectiveness of the program. They are subordinate to a district supervisor in charge of a geographic area or of specified facilities who in turn coordinates program events, such as city-wide sports, special events, dramatics, and so on, with the assistance of supervisors in these specialties. There may be four or more district supervisors, depending upon the size of the city and the districts into which it can be divided for most efficient operation. Typically two but less than five neighborhoods constitute a district. In a major metropolitan area, the department may divide the city into three basic categories and have line supervisory personnel in charge of all recreational programming for their respective areas. Thus, the common denominator of the city will be the neighbor-hood. Two or more neighborhoods comprise a district, two or more districts make up a community, and two or more communities equal a city. The district supervisor is responsible to a community supervisor who reports to a general supervisor or other designated administrator. In charting such an organizational plan, the largest agency is taken as an example in order to illustrate more clearly the major employment cate-gories and the typical lines of authority and responsibility. The ramified structure of a large department more nearly indicates the responsibili-ties of various workers, whereas it is difficult to illustrate employment practices with smaller agencies. Small departments simply reduce all overhead personnel, have fewer program workers, and capitalize on part-time and seasonal employees. Small communities almost never employ any full-time specialists. Rather, the specialist is hired on a *per diem* basis for a specific activity session or is employed at a particular time of the year.

Every department organizes its program staff in a way that will prove most effective to meet the conditions and needs of the local situation. Although there is no one best plan, there are organizational procedures that appear to be more valuable in fixing authority for functions and delegating responsibility for operations. Fig. 1 is such a plan.

Fig. 2, although introducing functional supervisory aspects of com-munity-wide services, does away with line personnel control of special-ists and places coordinating functions with the executive in charge of the program division. This may appear to be an effective method for ensuring proper coordination and program planning, but it also places a crushing burden on the program supervisor because that person is the administra-tor responsible for the total recreational service program for the city. By inverting the functional and district supervisory positions, additional personnel must be employed when there are a sufficient number of distinguishable facilities to warrant a supervisor. In medium-size depart-ments, these city-wide functional supervisors may report directly to the superintendent. When, however, the department is large enough, there will be another executive interposed. Although these supervisors are responsible for the performance of two or more definable functions, for example, program and maintenance, they will remain responsible to the executive in charge of the program division. All other divisions of the system, that is, business administration and engineering, are consid-ered to be staff functions and are coordinated at the divisional level.

Again, these charts illustrate the organization of a large metropolitan recreational service system. In smaller agencies the same aspects of departmental structure and organization apply, but the duties and functions of personnel are telescoped considerably and either consolidated or eliminated. In small departments there will be no intermediate supervisory level, and it is probable that directors of facilities will report directly to the chief executive of the organization. Such consolidation may make for ease in personnel management, but it leaves a great deal to be desired in providing effective recreational services for the total community.

Financial Considerations. Perhaps the fundamental necessity influencing all programming within the agency is the factor of money. The chief ingredient for the production of the program may be personnel, but unless financial support is available there cannot be the paid professional leadership so vital to programming. Programming can still be provided and a well-balanced series of recreational experiences can be offered if recreationists are employed. The highly qualified professional can, by ingenious methods, perform prodigious feats by turning junk into salvageable crafts material, converting vacant lots into playgrounds, and old loft buildings into teenage club rooms. By utilizing existing public structures and facilities, competent leadership can provide opportunities for a stimulating, comprehensive, and balanced recreational program. However, the time spent in searching for these properties, volunteers, and materials may more profitably be expended in bettering the program, giving expert technical assistance and instruction to participants, and organizing the community for recreational services. This latter function can be fruitfully attained when there is sufficient monetary support to supply the diverse structural, space, and equipment needs of a well-rounded recreational program.

There are certain facilities which the most highly competent recreationist cannot provide. One cannot teach swimming if there is no aquatic facility available. Some art, craft, sport, and music activities cannot be included with the recreational opportunities afforded by a community simply because they do not exist there. The financial factor is one that exercises indomitable influence on what can be programmed, where the activity takes place, who provides the guidance, instruction, supervision, or leadership for the experience, and whether or not it will be open to all community residents or only a paying few. Recognition of financial need governs, to a large extent, the size of the agency, the ability of the department to meet the diverse needs of people, the inclusion of staff specialists, and even the mundane responsibilities of having the necessary filing cabinets to maintain the reports and paperwork detail of the program. Of course, computer use still requires serious funding for hardware and software.

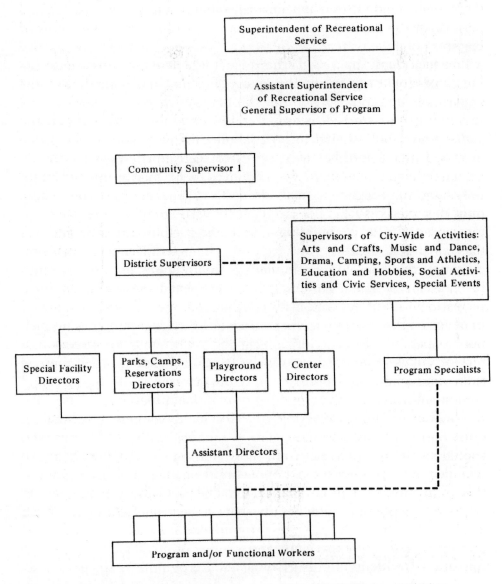

Fig. 1. Hypothetical organization of recreational program division by community.

Administrative Procedures. Certain standard administrative practices have direct influence on the program. Unless these operating procedures are utilized, the possibility of having an ineffective, and therefore, a dissatisfying program offering is distinctly probable. These administrative techniques are concerned with the maintenance of good public relations (see chap. 14), the development of sound personnel policies and practices;[1] the efficient recording of daily occurrences throughout the system,[2] and continual appraisal and evaluation of departmental performance (see Chap. 21). Even more important and having greater impetus upon the recreational opportunities programmed by the agency will be the commitment of the administrator toward the system, meaning the professional career administrators' view of their obligation to the department, the community, and the field.

Administrative techniques must make logical use of current research and any new applicable methods for more valuable presentations. There must be constant emphasis upon the employment and development of professional personnel and all environmental factors that encourage career workers to improve their own techniques. The community continually must be surveyed so that population analysis and trends can be made and recognized. The administrator must feel the need to call the attention of the proper authorities to any deficiencies that can affect the provision of maximal and balanced recreational service to the community. This may be in terms of water pollution and waste, land encroachment upon recreational spaces for other governmental functions, inequitable salary standards, interference with departmental operations by other municipal agencies, unfair reporting or misleading statements reported in mass media, and other political or social pressures which can wreak havoc and cause dissension and dissatisfaction among the staff of the department.

First and last, the administrators must be professionals with total personal commitment to recreational service. They must insist that all other positions calling for professionals are filled with recreationists and specialists competent to carry out those functions assigned to them. All administrative procedures should have but one end and justification — the production of a program of recreational experiences designed to satisfy all people in the community. This is the ideal situation for which

---

[1]J.S. Shivers, *Introduction to Recreational Service Administration*, (Philadelphia: Lea and Febiger, 1989, pp. 137–154.

[2]*Ibid*, pp. 97–116.

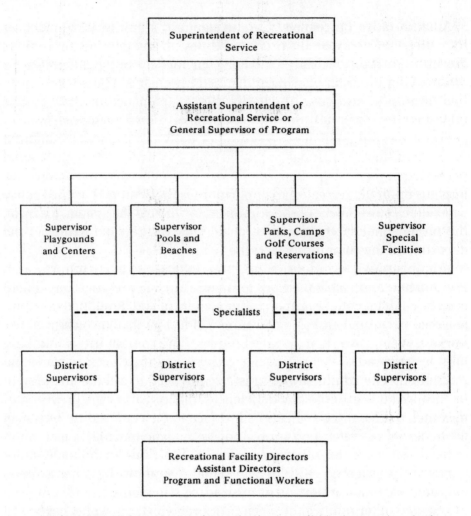

Fig. 2. Hypothetical organization of recreational program division by supervisory level.

administrative techniques are geared. This goal may never be realized, but it is the standard by which all facets of the program and, in a larger sense, the department are compared.

Departmental Jurisdiction

The department with cognizance over the recreational service provision for any community has a great deal to do with how that service will be programmed. When there is a separate and autonomous agency primarily responsible for the direct provision of community recreational services, all efforts will be focused upon that chief goal. There will be no stinting of monetary resources, personnel, facilities, or equipment for the fulfillment of that function to the extent that they exist. When, however, other overhead agencies become the administrative unit for undertaking the recreational service function, along with whatever primary function the agency was established to perform, then recreational service in the community suffers from being a subordinate objective.

When the municipality has seen fit to consolidate two separate but related agencies, such as the park department and the recreational department, the recreational service function will deteriorate unless the executive in charge of the consolidated department is a recreationist. Too often, in consolidation moves, the municipal government places the former superintendent of parks in the position of departmental chief executive. In most instances, the former park executive is schooled in forestry, horticulture, engineering, or landscape architecture and does not appreciate or understand the nature of programming recreational activities. Hence, the budgetary allotment for programming and leadership becomes progressively smaller, and funds for ground maintenance, landscaping, facility construction, and other park-oriented objectives take precedence.

The recreationist, in the consolidated position, considers the park to be part of the total recreational spaces and facilities to be utilized under the unified department. There is an allocation for the maintenance of areas and facilities, with emphasis on planning, design, and construction of needed new projects. However, the essential nature of the department is given its proper due, that is, the provision of a balanced, comprehensive, and competently supervised recreational program.

In other situations when the overhead agency has a primary function of education, welfare, health, public works, conservation, police, or fire fighting, recreational programming usually deteriorates. When the recreational service function becomes secondary to the main job for which the agency was created, the secondary function is relegated to an orphan class and is systematically downgraded. Most administrators, who have not been professionally prepared as career recreationists, simply do not have the understanding or necessary background and skill to focus attention on this vital community service. They are content to administer their first calling, and sometimes delegate sinecures, supernumeraries, or other questionable personnel to the job of programming.

When the primary function of the agency bears little relation to that of recreational service, but recreational activity is considered a necessary facet, or it contributes in some way to the welfare of agency constituents, then recreational activity is oriented toward some end other than that usually associated with public recreational service departments. Military service organizations, for example, program recreational activities for service personnel in an effort to promote morale, keep their personnel on the base, and enhance community relationships. School institutions program recreational activities which are basically educational in content, closely tied to the formal curriculum. Church agencies offer recreational activities to their members as a direct outgrowth of moral teaching and in an attempt to cultivate spiritual values. Youth-serving and social agencies often provide recreational services in order to develop good character in youth and community-oriented behavior among the groups which they serve. Treatment centers and penal institutions administer recreational activities as having direct value in maintaining patient or inmate morale, in teaching new skills, in the process of social or physical rehabilitation, and in the production of new ideas, habits, and attitudes which will assist the individual to live a better and more wholesome life after leaving the institution. Every agency has a primary mission to perform. In the course of achieving its chief aim, the agency may introduce recreational activities to stimulate interest or attract additional support. In any event, the programming of recreational activities on an organized basis is performed for some motive aside from individual enjoyment and satisfaction. Recreational activities are used as means to achieve a different end. They are utilized to promote the orientation of the agency.

Community Viewpoint

One other important factor which influences programming outcomes is the support the agency receives from the government of the community in which it is situated. There are many autonomous departments unable to do the most effective job of programming because the local government, while giving lip-service support, does not really feel the need for monetary expenditures which could increase staff positions and offer a more comprehensive program. Even if the citizens in a community want the service, they may face a recalcitrant board of finance, mayor, city manager, or other local governing body which overrides their petitions. This latter action is done at the elected officials' own risk, although voters seldom remember either campaign promises or the vagaries of the incumbent.

If the community is unwilling to support a public recreational service department, if it is not ready to assume the financial burden of taxation necessary for the operation of the agency, then it may always turn to quasi-public or private agencies. In these circumstances, programming becomes a tentative thing. The quasi-public agency requires a great deal of private contribution for its support, although it does have a small appropriation from tax funds. Generally, quasi-public agencies that perform the recreational function are attached to some municipal department, for example, the police athletic or fire athletic league. United Givers or Community Chest funds invariably support one or more agencies which provide recreational services. Unfortunately, such agencies do not operate on a full-time basis. When they do operate full time, they usually restrict their services to a select clientele. When private agencies are the only means for providing recreational services to the community, the entire population can never be served. Private agencies always restrict their clientele to those individuals who are members of the organization, thus effectively screening out all who are not members.

Planning Factors in Programming

The recreational program is not a series of individual activities strung together without any cohesive factors. It is a carefully integrated and planned combination of many activities selected on the basis of individual and group interests, related ideas, and themes organized to achieve particular aims. Among these aims are the realization of personal fulfillment, satisfaction, enjoyment, physical and mental health, and the development of positive social relationships. Essentially, programming is the balanced correlation of leadership personnel, required space, facility, or equipment, a specified activity, and a participant at a time and place, both convenient and attractive, for some performance to occur. Presumably, the client's joining in an activity of a recreational nature, either as a passive spectator or as an active participant, will result in certain satisfactions.

Participant Planning

One of the basic concepts of programming is to involve as many potential participants as possible during the planning stage. Programming cannot be carried on without the support of those who will ultimately benefit from activities and voluntary association with organized recreational experiences. The recreationist may not simply dictate to the community at large the content of the program and expect instant acceptance and large attendance. There will always be some people who need to be told what to do and when to do it, with each phase carefully scheduled and arranged for their convenience. However, there is no guarantee that even those who require such assistance will participate. More likely, the recreationist must work with representatives of neighborhoods or with specific groups as a whole. The professional function is to enable them to operate and develop a program which is consistent with their interests and needs. When individual workers are assigned to small groups, each group may have a recreational program of its own, based upon the skills, knowledge, interest, and needs of the membership. When, however, the recreationist functions at the community level, as is most often the case, he or she must work with a small sample of the citizens in the community. If the department organizes neighborhood advisory councils and utilizes them in planning the program, the recreationist acts as a transmitter and catalytic agent. By serving as a guide, advisor, and resource person, or taking a more active part in formulation, the ability to offer selected choices which are practical, stimulating, and capable of meeting the needs of the recipients is strengthened.

Whether planning the program for one center, one playground, or another neighborhood facility, the recreationist should constantly seek out individuals who appear to be leaders or those who indicate a desire to assist in the production of a program. In order to involve as many different people as possible in any given neighborhood, committees should be set up for each facet of the program. Additional committees may be organized for administrative and nonleadership purposes. These local committees can meet weekly, provide ideas for activities for the following week, and serve as part of the public relations medium in disseminating information about the program. One member of each committee may be elected to participate in an overall steering or coordinating council for the neighborhood. In this manner potential participants can be attracted to the program in the valid assumption that they have had a significant part in developing it. Participation is almost completely assured and support will invariably be generated when people feel that they have contributed their own energy and talent in planning activities. Ego involvement with some phase of the program will induce those very persons to ensure the success of the presentation. Participant planning plays another important role in programming: it is in itself part of the recreational program and can be a most enjoyable and satisfying experience because it is one aspect of the service category. Participation in behind-the-scenes negotiations, devising activities for others to encounter, and generally performing a useful and necessary task in planning sessions is just as recreational as are the activities normally thought of in that respect.

Individual Need

The planning of an activity and the experience itself must be kept within the bounds of practicality and reality insofar as the potential participant is concerned. Successful accomplishment of any given recreational act, even the desire to perform in such an activity, is predicated upon the individual's capacity, ability, and limitations. The mental equipment possessed by individuals will enable them to accept certain responsibilities and facilitate their performances. With individuals of limited mental ability, the recreationist is required to protect them from situations where failure and resulting frustration and unhappiness are inevitable. However, the professional has the obligation of stimulating participation in those areas where they are capable. Individuals without any physical, mental, or emotional dysfunction are limited only by lack of knowledge, experience, and practice. A limitation may also be imposed as a result of a lack of interest, but the competent leader will attempt to overcome this lack by exposure of the individual to stimulating and attractive situations. In any event, nondisabled people may achieve to whatever extent their capacity will allow. For those potential participants with some disability, the recreationist must develop modified activities in which they may attain success.

As in all planning, individual welfare and satisfaction are uppermost. Although recreationists usually work with large numbers of people, the individual, rather than the aggregate, is the ultimate determinant of success or failure in programming. The recreationist can never forget that all activities must contribute something of value to the individual. Programming mass or spectator events can be justified solely in relationship to the value derived by the participating individuals. This does not militate against programming mass activities, but emphasis should not be laid on how many attended a given activity. What the participation has done for the individual, what has been achieved, whether or not anything has been learned, or the person developed socially, emotionally, physically, or mentally are the criteria upon which any recreational experience should be evaluated. It is to individual need and interest that programming must be oriented.

Time

Time is the basis on which the recreational program operates. Leisure is the free time which people have to participate in recreational experiences. The work of the recreational service department finds its rationale for establishment in the leisure which people have to spend. At almost any time during each day of each week there will be those in the community who have free time. One of the elemental procedures necessary, if the public agency is to serve its constituents well, is to determine who has leisure and when. On this foundation the program structure will be built.

Program content will be made more interesting if it is related to current events, incidents, occurrences, or historical and traditional situations. The timeliness of activities assists in arousing and maintaining interest and participation in planned activities. Time is significant in planning the program because it involves all persons residing in the community. Of necessity, surveys must be made to find out what age group and which gender are free to participate. Planning the playground or center program will rely upon these two factors. While the adult age group will remain stable, except in communities with a high population of "shift" workers in local industry, the free time components of children and adolescents change. If the program includes preschool age children, activities must be planned for them when they can attend. Consideration must be made for parents if their presence is required. School-age children will not be available to the program during school hours throughout the academic year. Working adults will usually participate only during evening hours and on the weekends. These time elements are therefore of extreme importance in the development of the program.

Time can be segmented into the following components for utilization in programming: hourly, daily, weekly, monthly, seasonally, and annually. The entire program hinges on time and the proper scheduling of leadership, facilities, equipment, and activities.

Hourly Segment. Dividing the recreational day into hourly segments is of assistance in programming for children whose attention span is short and who may be expected to be restless if activities are prolonged. Typically, each hour is indicated in terms of the commencement of particular activities as well as by half-hour segments for the younger age groups.

Daily Schedule. A daily listing of all activities to be offered by the recreational facility on an hourly basis is desirable. The daily program is designed to meet the needs of the facility and the neighborhood it is intended to serve. Unless each neighborhood has the same population composition and the facility and staff positions are duplicated, each daily program will be different. The differences will be determined by the population to be served, the leadership employed, the facility and space available, and other administrative factors. Among the considerations which influence the daily program will be the age, occupational status, and skill of people living within the neighborhood. In designing the daily program to meet the needs of the population, the recreationist should be aware of when activities at the facility will be practical. For example, preschool-age children will probably make use of the recreational facility during the morning hours, from 9:00 a.m. until 11:00 a.m. The department should also be prepared with some activity for the parents of these children.

Some time before noon, older retired adults may make use of the facility and an appropriate series of activities must be planned. Out-of-school youths tend to frequent the facility in the early afternoon, as do the preschoolers. After three o'clock in the afternoon, children of elementary school age begin to utilize the facility. Although some of the children under 11 years will probably leave for supper and not return, children between the ages of 12 and 14 may come back to the facility until 8:00 p.m. The senior high school age group begins drifting into the facility sometime after 7:00 p.m. and will generally stay until closing. Older adults rarely remain after 10:00 p.m. Young adults may be expected to arrive after 8:00 p.m. and remain until closing. If the facility is open during weekends, as it should be, there will be a noticeable shift in usage by children. The elementary school age child will arrive earlier and remain later than on weekdays. This is not true for the adolescent or older adult. Their arrivals and departures tend to be constant.

Weekly Schedule. A weekly program assists the recreationist in planning for recurrent and instructional activities. It provides a feeling of continuity and allows participants a chance for selecting specific activities in advance and makes them aware of the times at which the activities begin. The weekly schedule enables the recreationist to enhance the program by adopting his activities and materials to appropriate themes.

Themes add color to the routine activities and provide a carry-over from one day's activities to the next, with a culminating event at the end of each week. The variety of interests and the diversity of activity offerings prohibit the scheduling of all such experiences during any one day. Weekly scheduling facilitates the incorporation of diversity and variety for recurrent, intermittent, and unique recreational activities to be programmed.

Monthly Schedule. Of chief consideration in planning a monthly program is the inclusion of sequential and graduated activities which culminate in a special project, usually based on some theme, that demonstrates many of the activities carried on at the recreational facility. Such an event presents the opportunity of correlating activities in order to enhance each one. By combining the different categories into one month special event, many more participants can perform. City-wide tournaments, various leagues, and those activities which require not less than two or three weeks of preparation before they can be introduced should be included in the monthly plan. Among the activities for which additional time is needed are formal plays, double elimination tournaments, some craft projects, certain art objects, and innumerable exhibits, displays, and shows. The month-to-month schedule of activities may be quite applicable in neighborhoods where the recreational program has been newly established. Because the recreationist responsible for the neighborhood facility must have time to become acquainted with the special character of the neighborhood, it is unlikely that programs will be scheduled for periods longer than one month in advance. Only after prolonged contact has been made with the neighborhood, and those variable factors which can influence the program have been determined to some extent, will there be an attempt to program for periods longer than one month.

Seasonal Schedule. The changing seasons offer countless opportunities for the construction of an interesting and comprehensive recreational program. Seasonal programming tends to follow the traditional activities which have been utilized by many locales throughout the country. Except in regions where there are extremes, the four seasons provide a natural setting for the development of various and highly diversified experiences. With seasonal shifts, different themes and culminating special events may be brought into the program. Seasonal programming offers the chance for planning three months in advance. It is reasonably assumed that where the recreational service department is well established, long-range planning of recreational activities on a neighborhood, district, and community-wide basis follows. The content of the seasonal program is not merely the proliferation of daily, weekly, and monthly programs. A seasonal program is operated on the basis of special projects which may be profitably introduced only once, at a specific time of the year, and for that reason requires scrupulous attention to many planning details. The nature of the event is such that it may take many weeks and even months for plans to materialize and for the prior preparation necessary to ensure success. Invitational contests, tournaments, and meets usually require at least three months of intensive preparation. A holiday celebration with parades, exhibits, demonstrations, and other planned events may require six months of planning before it is ready for production.

Seasonal planning considers the nature of the activity to be offered, the community factors operating to influence participation, the time such an activity requires for successful presentation, local traditions and expectations, and the adequacy of the departmental staff to stimulate interest and attract attention. Typically, the themes under which the seasonal program operates are essentially related to the conditions that prevail during any given three-month period. For example, the summer season of June, July, and August will allow a larger number of children to participate in outdoor activities than at any other time of year. The winter season of December, January, and February offers opportunities for a special winter carnival or festival that can occur at no other time.

Annual Schedules. The recreational program for the entire year is developed from all of the preceding time segments. However, there are some facets of the yearly program that should be emphasized. There is no period during the year when the public recreational service should not be operating at maximal capacity. It is unrealistic for any recreationist to assume that people have no interest in recreational activities at certain times of the year. Such an assumption is pure nonsense. As Hutchinson states:

> The interests people have for leisure activity do not wane as the days become shorter during the year. An examination of the shift in emphasis of the commercial amusement attractions during the winter shows very little differences in the desires people have for activity. The differences lie in *where* the activities take place rather than *when* they take place.[3]

---

[3]J.L. Hutchinson, *Principles of Recreation* (New York: A.S. Barnes and Company, 1949), p. 187.

Public recreational service agencies are established to serve people during their leisure. Leisure is increasing for many, although decreasing for a few. Particularly is this true among various occupational groups whose work hours have remarkably decreased in the past five years. Elderly adults, after retirement, have almost unlimited leisure. Better working conditions, increased fringe benefits, vacation periods, longer weekends, and holidays are the times around which public recreational service agencies should concentrate their programming function. These are the times in which people are free to participate. The recreational service day should begin at 9:00 a.m. and continue to 11:00 p.m. during the week. On weekends, the number of hours may be increased. Inasmuch as there are always people in the community who have free time at all hours of the day and evening, the public program must consider scheduling activities all the time. Public agencies cannot afford to exist on a part-time basis. They have been established as full-time operations and have the responsibility for offering services whenever people have the leisure to utilize them. Leisure has become almost universal in this country. For these reasons, public recreational agencies must remain open and operating each and every day of the year, subject only to staffing requirements. There is no such idea that recreational services are only needed at specific times. People seek recreational activities all the time. The public department is obliged, therefore, to operate all of the time.

Themes

One of the ways in which activities can be made more attractive and stimulating to the potential participant is the organization of recreational experiences around some central idea. In this way, every activity that is planned and organized by the department focuses attention on a single concept and contributes to its presentation. Themes are topical ideas that lend a common element to every activity which can be scheduled within the program. They provide a basic aim that lends color and effect to the most routine activities. Essentially, themes offer natural opportunities for the integration of various categories of activities into a combined presentation. Such combination actually increases the satisfaction of participation, as the different parts are joined together in one symmetrical event. An example of the utilization of a theme which integrates many activities might be a winter carnival or summer festival. Depending upon the overall activity, let us say a musical in this instance, many features of the program could be exhibited. The categories of art, crafts, dance, drama, music, motor skills, service, social activity, and special events could be combined. Artists would be called upon to paint appropriate sets and scenes; craftsmen would be brought into play for the construction and design of sets, stage, lighting, and properties; music and dramatics are part of such activity; all dramatics is intensely social. Participants in the service category would enlist the assistance of volunteers to act as ushers, stage hands, lighting technicians, coaches, makeup designers, grips, sound technicians, publicity agents, and so on. Motor performance might be included if the musical featured any aspect of gymnastic, fencing, or other physical skill. There is little question that the entire performance would be a special event. The theme of festival or carnival would be the point of departure for the entire program.

To a lesser extent, themes can play an important part in making program activities more enjoyable during every week of the year. Each week can be devoted to one theme. Each month and season also may be appropriately concerned with themes. The progressive nature of instructional activities invites thematic concepts. As the individual develops greater skill in whatever activity interests him, a variety of themes can serve as incentives for additional practice and ultimate presentation or exhibition. Themes may be organized around the following events:

holidays (national)	seasonal
traditions (local, regional)	religious
ethnic and cultural	commemorative
patriotic	miscellaneous

Gradation

Every category, except hobbies, service, and special projects, will offer opportunities for instruction to be given. A program that is free from the taint of stagnation must be progressive in scope. Progress is best maintained when individuals are enabled to develop proficiency in the activities that interest them. Gradation of activities requires a tripling of program activities, meaning that each skill taught at the recreational facility may be offered at the beginning level, intermediate level, or advanced level. Beyond this requirement is the differentiation of age groups into which classes are divided. In crafts, for example, there are projects designed to familiarize the individual with tools, material, equipment and the finished product. At each age, there will be crafts appropriate to the needs of the group. With maturity and responsibility, more complicated and intricate crafts may be introduced. At the youngest age level simplified and easily understood projects are included. But even at the youngest ages there will be those who show precocity or unusual advancement. Such individuals should not be held back and deprived of more advanced techniques, for they will tend to drop out of the program if their interest cannot be maintained. Graded instructional courses prevent, in most instances, the withdrawal of participants because of boredom, possession of a high degree of skill, or association with individuals who are not capable of handling tools and materials. It is possible through this instructional sequence to maintain contact with program participants from earliest childhood through old age. The graded aspect of programming facilitates modification of activities to meet mental, physical, or maturational limitations. Gradation is necessary in the program because it allows people to acquire skills and interests that will have carry-over value for them.

Balance

The recreational program must serve all interests, needs, personalities, and levels of skill. For these reasons it must contain a variety of activities in which all people may seek satisfaction. Balanced programming has to do with the inclusion of many activities within all categories in order to attract participation. There should be something for everyone in a public recreational service program. Each individual should be able to find something of interest if the program is correctly balanced. There will be a compelling program which can stimulate interest and desire to learn among all citizens in the community. Balance is particularly important in providing equal opportunity for participation. Because the categories must cover all, or nearly all, recreational experiences in which people show interest, there should be enough variety to offset emphasis on any single category.

Balance indicates diversity. It means consideration for skill levels attained by individuals as well as organizational forms by which the activity is programmed. There must be opportunity for both active participation and passive appreciation, for solitary as well as group experiences, for performance as well as looking on, for motor skills as well as mental skills, for giving service as well as receiving service. Progressive aspects of the activity are also considered in terms of individual development and proficiency achieved. In the balanced program there is a place for the beginner, the individual who has some knowledge or skill, and the advanced or highly skilled and resourceful person. There is, in short, equilibrium among the component parts of the program.

Flexibility

The ability to meet any contingency or condition as a result of changing interests, weather, population, or for circumstances beyond the control of the recreationist is termed *flexibility*. Alternate courses of action planned in the event of unexpected conditions damaging or destroying primary plans must be handled with the same judgment and concern as are scheduled activities. Reserve plans should be prepared in the event of sudden rainstorm, snowfall, illness, damage to a vital facility, or other emergency situation. Modification of the site, and adaptability of the activity to meet the needs of potential participants, are always part of the sound program plan. The alternate activity includes professional personnel, facility determination, transportation requirements, planned activities, and method of ready communication to publicize whatever changes have to be made.

Foreseeability, that is, the recognition that there always exists a possibility of disruption or curtailment, places the burden of detailed secondary planning in the hands of the recreationist. The alternative activity may be a duplicate of the scheduled activity with the exception of location and/or facility. A primary example of alternative planning and flexibility is illustrated by the understudy role in any play. Featured players always have back-up actors in the event that some emergency renders them unable to go on with a performance. An open-air concert, art exhibit, or hobby show should not be cancelled because of rain. Plans should be made to move the performance indoors. Even rain or snow days contribute to flexibility. If all those concerned, either as performers, exhibitors, or spectators, know that an alternate date has been made in the event of inclement weather, then cancellation of an activity on a given day will not ruin the effort which has gone into its production. At worst, only a few potential participants may be lost. Wherever possible, however, the activity should be held at the same time on the same day, but at an indoor facility. In this way, those who are prepared to attend will not be disappointed and none will be lost to the activity.

Leadership

In programming recreational activities, an essential element that influences the success or failure of the activity to meet its stated objective is leadership. In developing plans for the inclusion of all recreational categories, serious consideration must be given to the adequacy of staff requirements necessary to achieve proper instruction, supervision, and guidance. The one ingredient without which public recreational service loses much, if not all, impact is the quality of professional leadership available. Every one of the categories is predicated upon sufficient professional personnel available to conduct activities and offer leadership resources. Community-wide programming necessitates full-time employed personnel to give continuity, comprehensive planning, and daily attention to the operational functions of the agency. Volunteers or part-time employees may assist in the development of program and broaden opportunities, but they cannot replace professional leaders. The program is only as valuable as an adequate personnel force can make it.

Spaces, Structures, and Facilities

The development of an adequate program of recreational service depends upon the design, construction, and maintenance of indoor and outdoor areas appropriate to the conduct of program. Requirements range from quiet corners in a playground or park to immense spaces in which camping, hunting, fishing, mountain climbing, or other outdoor activities may be programmed. Many recreational activities simply cannot be organized with an expectation of success unless specific facilities are available and accessible to participants. The public recreational service department is required to acquire, to design, sometimes to construct, and always to maintain physical plants and properties of a size and type sufficient for all phases of the program. However, acting in coordination and conjunction with other sectors of the community, including churches, youth-serving agencies, other municipal buildings, and schools, such properties may also be considered as potential recreational resources.

The modification, renovation, or reconstruction of existing buildings may result in additional useful space, which can make the facility a better place in which to conduct the program. The wise utilization of all possible available areas, as well as modern design for multiple use of formerly restricted spaces, allows for the inclusion of additional activities. Successful programming is concerned with availability and accessibility of recreational facilities for public use. Space requirements for activities to be included necessitate the development of a well-balanced series of structures and outdoor places which are suitable in size, situation, and attractiveness. Suitability also means placement of rooms within a building, ease of supervision by personnel, traffic flow, building design, color scheme, cleanliness, comfort, and interior decor. Many activities also require special equipment, materials, and instruments if they are to be programmed.

The recreational program is the single most important function with which the recreational service agency concerns itself. Every conceivable means and effort must be taken to ensure the well-balanced, comprehensive, and varied program. Programming represents all the directed energy which the agency has at its disposal to effect the most valuable, satisfying, and attractive program possible. Programming is influenced by many far-reaching factors, including community fabric and milieu; individual need, interest, and capacity; social, economic, and educational levels; previous experiences; occupation; and many other aspects of the culture of which it is a part.

All recreational programs are justifiable under the principle of providing something for each person in the community at all times. Success in recreational programming depends upon logical planning, standards of activity selection and development, and techniques for their implementation. Programming is a complicated process requiring professional leadership and support. Ultimately, programming is effected by an arrangement of competent leadership, interesting activities, and recreational places at which performance occurs. Detailed planning, based upon certain knowledge of the community and its people, resources, and potential, is of inestimable value in establishing a sound program in which all people may attain satisfaction, enjoyment and a feeling of personal well-being.

Chapter 17

RISKS AND SAFETY CONSIDERATIONS

Severe, crippling, and sometimes fatal injuries are increasing on public and privately operated recreational facilities. These unfortunate accidents are the direct result of inappropriate behavior of participants, incompetence of organizational employees, negligence by operators, or a combination of these factors. Personal injury almost invariably gives rise to a lawsuit against the agency. People are much more likely to sue for punitive and other costs when they are injured while watching or taking part in leisure experiences at places operated for recreational purposes. A changing social climate, greater liberality of legislative intent, judicial interpretations and decisions that no one should suffer irredeemable harm from the negligence of others have contributed to the anxiety of business executives and public officials. Their occupation constantly exposes them to the stress of litigation and all of the negative effects accompanying the pre-trial depositions, investigations, court appearances, and eroding public confidence and support.

Questions of competence, professional practice, degree of care, elements of risk, negligence, and incautious behavior all stem from a fundamental lack of safety principles, policy, standards, and procedures. These are vital for the protection of the patron of recreational services as well as for the agency which promotes recreational functions. Until a well-established safety education program is an actuality, there will continue to be a condition of jeopardy for all concerned. To be sure, the individual may have contributed to the injury; but a comprehensive safety program together with widely disseminated information dealing with unsafe situations can predictably reduce both the casualty rate and the likelihood of successful lawsuits against those delivering recreational services.

The Basis of Recreational Safety

Risk is inherent in nearly all recreational activities of a physical type. Even such activities as crafts, not normally considered a risk activity, can become dangerous to participants under certain conditions. Accidents happen in the delivery of recreational services, and the potential for injuries to persons and damage to property cannot be minimized. Nevertheless, the reduction of accidents and the prevention of behavior that can lead to serious injury can be accomplished. Without eliminating the element of risk from recreational experience, which is one of the motives for engaging in such activities, there is still much that can be done by intelligent administrators and competent workers.

Policy Establishment

Of necessity, two functions must be undertaken if accident prevention is to become an established policy. What safety is and a commitment to its moral and legal responsibility must be developed. Environmental factors can be controlled so that the probability of accidents will be reduced or eliminated. This means that a comprehensive safety program must be initiated and become the fundamental element which professionals recognize as their own obligation. The program will be based upon both environmental safety practices and an intellectual premise to educate all those whose recreational participation requires a positive attitude toward personal safety. Recreators must recognize that they have a contribution to make in maintaining their own security by not behaving in ways that can lead to accidental injury or worse.

The Safety Program

Any safety program must be formulated to establish safe conditions for recreational experiences of all kinds in varying situations, to demonstrate safe working conditions within the physical plant, and to promote safe practices and behavior on the part of all those who are patrons of any recreational enterprise. Safety planning may be inaugurated by executive order, but its successful execution cannot be assured until all parties are educated to it and actively assist in its planning. This means that employees of the agency as well as active recreators and spectators should have some input into what a safety program contains and how it will be carried out.

All recreational service safety programs require approval by whatever authority governs the organization. Whether this is a private board of directors, commission, elected or appointed official, there must be a commitment to more than sporadic safety campaigns or slogans. Safety measures and procedures may require the authorization of construction, maintenance practices, sound and pertinent policies and their publication, in-service staff education, and public education. To become educationally effective the safety program is the ultimate responsibility of the executive. Moreover, such a program will be founded upon psychological factors, probability, and injury prevention. Individual attitude toward safety for others as well as for one's self is the essence of accident prevention. To be sure, wise principles of organization, management, and supervision must be brought into play. Research designed to ferret out accident experiences by those either served by or delivering recreational services will form a basic knowledge upon which effective safety practices can be grounded. From the outset, recognition of supervision as a key element in the success of the program must be assured. As is necessary for the desired objective, the evaluation process will be invaluable for determining the effectiveness of any safety program.

The Safety Officer

Recreational safety can be attained through a comprehensive plan that includes the elimination of physical dangers from the property. The inculcation of policies and practices that are clearly identified, comprehensible, and employed on a daily basis in order to maintain a safe environment is vital. It will be required that one individual be assigned the task of organizing the safety program and seeing to its effective execution. One reasonable objective is that all users and purveyors of recreational service should be responsible for their own safe conduct insofar as they have the maturity and intelligence for that assumption. An informational program emphasizing safety skills, knowledge, and positive attitudes must be designed to insure safe living. Any rational plan will include preparation for emergencies. All personnel will have training in first aid and, wherever feasible, in paramedical techniques.

Accident Prevention

Personnel engaged in accident prevention recognize that certain behaviors either cause accidents or prevent them. Indeed, it is specific behavioral forms as well as environmental hazards which produce high accident rates and result in serious injury. Accidents which typically occur at recreational sites probably can be avoided. In order to develop an accident prevention program investigation must be made to determine the causes so that remedial methods may be found. Not all accidents are caused by human factors. On occasion, pure chance or forces beyond the control of human ability will have been operating. Accidents caused by natural forces probably cannot be controlled. For the most part, however, it is human behavior that is a determining factor in nearly all accidents. Given the "correct mix" of human behavior and environment, an accident is likely to occur.

> A man attended a swimming meet to which the public was invited. Seats were arranged around the swimming pool and loudspeakers were placed so that spectators could hear announcements. Several speakers were placed on the slanted roof of the locker room building. During the meet a gust of high wind blew one of the speakers off the roof onto the head of the man seated below. The spectator suffered a minor concussion, had vision impairment, and was taken to a hospital. The public department was subsequently sued and charged with negligence for failing to foresee the probability of such injuries stemming from the conditions that prevailed. The pool operator was liable for redress to the injured party for all damages that resulted from failure to exercise the reasonable and prudent care required.[1]

Because of the nature of recreational activity and the part which probability plays, the outcome may vary from absolutely no injury or damage to death. Nevertheless, no one may discount the potential for accidents and as long as such potential exists, the most significant area of concern will be with environmental conditions that are suspect, human behavior which is questionable, and other psychological and social conditions which may have an impact upon accident causation.

> Three children, all male, went into a neighborhood school playground one Sunday morning and began to play hardball. The youngest child was seated on an emplaced bench along the third base line. A pitched ball was hit by the child's brother and struck the boy beneath the left eye. He suffered an orbital fracture and some minor eye injury. In a court ordered settlement, the operat-

---

[1]George Hjelte and Jay S. Shivers, *Public Administration of Recreational Service*, 2nd ed. (Philadelphia: Lea and Febiger, 1978), p. 165.

ing authorities were adjudged to have been negligent in permitting the placement of a bench so close to the third base line, for not having provided adequate protection for spectators, for not preventing access to the ball field at inappropriate times. The operating authorities acknowledged their own negligence. The case was settled for $6,000.[2]

Planning for Safety

In planning facilities and areas, the physical environment must be investigated so as to lessen the probability of substandard behavior as well as eliminate obvious hazards. Planning to eliminate dangers that could be built in because of poor design or to restrict some act of faulty judgment or potential human error may reduce the occurrence of unacceptable behavior.

Instruction. Instruction is the transmission of knowledge, skills, values, and a sense of personal responsibility. It is certainly the most far-reaching and behavior modifying of all measures available to recreationists for reducing injuries and accidents among practitioners and patrons. Instruction is concerned with human motivation, attitudinal change, perception, psycho-social factors, and performance ability. Attitudinal orientation requires a diverse application of methods for development or change. Such programs or directed learning may be offered through publications, lectures, educational courses, group dynamics, and other appropriate techniques as the individual comes in contact with recreational service agencies of all kinds.

Observance. Observance deals with the compliance to rules, regulations, policy statements, and local, state, and federal legislative enactments which are pertinent to recreational safety. For example, ordinances which underlie certain rules and regulations governing use of specific facilities should be upheld and enforced whenever and wherever they apply. Unless individuals are made to realize that noncompliance will lead to immediate or inevitable punishment (with all of the anxiety which that word implies), the rule breakers will feel free to continue in their thoughtless disregard for the rights of others and for their own or others' safety. Observance of all regulations relating to recreational performance should have an immediate remedial effect. In one respect observance becomes a social control in that it sets limits on the conduct of individuals. Effective

---

[2]Jay S. Shivers, *Recreational Safety the Standard of Care.* (Fairleigh: Dickenson University Press, 1986), p. 173.

observation will have the salutory result of causing individuals (who are at the age of discretion or above) to reflect on the consequences of unsafe behavior and may prevent subsequent accidents which arise out of rule-breaking activity.

Accident Sources in Recreational Service

Before any program of accident prevention is put into operation, the sources of the problem must be examined from all angles. Human behavior and environmental dangers may be only the surface explanations for accidents. There are many other variables that influence human behavior and they can have serious repercussions on the safety of recreators.

Insufficient Information. The lack of sufficient or appropriate information can give people a false sense of security that may lead to disaster. People must be alerted to all possible dangers before an accident occurs. The poorly informed person is much more likely to take risks that the well advised individual would shun. It is incredible how many people will dive into water of unknown depth where they cannot see bottom and don't know if any obstructions are present.

A young man of 23 years was injured when he, while in the company of three friends, dove into Seeley's Pond located within the Watchung Reservation operated by the then Union County Park Commission. The young man struck his head on an underwater obstruction. On the day in question, the water level was high and after seeing one of his companions dive into the water and stand in neck high water, he dove into the same general vicinity with disastrous results. He sustained a fracture of the neck as well as other injuries. The young man is now a quadriplegic with no hope of recovery of the use of his upper and lower extremities. The operating authorities were determined to have been negligent in not posting warning signs, in failing to clear the stream bed of debris, and in not properly policing the pond area which was locally known as a "swimming hole" during and over a forty year period. The young man was awarded $280,000 plus an annual annuity in an out-of-court settlement.[3]

Inappropriate Behavior and Disposition. Accidents can often be attributed to carelessness, foolishness, laziness, procrastination, and similar inappropriate behavior. Under certain circumstances people sometimes respond in ways that are inappropriate for the situation; they take chances which can end in tragedy. Taking that one last downhill plunge even though one is fatigued, bouncing on a trampoline without spotters present, or failing to use protective landing mats or crash pads in a

---

[3]130 New Jersey Superior Court Reports, p. 540, October 11, 1974.

gymnastics class, even when they are available, are examples of this kind of attitude.

There are some situations in which one has to take risks. But when one is engaged in recreational activity, it is unwise to take chances that are *unnecessary* and often dangerous. Practitioners are sometimes faulted for not taking the necessary correcting actions when a dangerous condition has been brought to their attention. This may be reflected in sloppy work habits, laziness, or procrastination. Any one of these unsafe practices may result in jeopardy to life or limb. Perhaps entrance doors to a community recreational center have been designed for maximum visibility by the installation of glass doors and adjacent glass panels. The danger is that individuals may collide with the glass partitions, especially if they are in a hurry. The recreationist can solve this problem by having the glass etched in an attention-getting manner, or by substituting panels of glass brick or translucent plastic, or even simply by attaching decals or strips to reduce or eliminate the hazard. What happens instead is that the practitioner will put off having the glass entrance altered even though he or she realizes that an accident may occur. The procrastination usually continues until someone is hurt or property is damaged.

Poor Maintenance Practices. One of the more insidious forms of danger stems from poorly carried out maintenance: the cleaning and repairing of physical facilities and grounds. The recreator assumes that the recreational place is safe; the participants assume that ball fields, running surfaces, waterways, or beaches are free of debris and hazardous material. To a great extent this is a valid assumption, but in some instances maintenance practices are shoddy or so incomplete that a dangerous condition exists. Even when departmental procedures specify that certain places must be cleared of debris, that chuck holes be filled in, grass mowed, and other routine maintenance be carried out, the procedures are not undertaken. As a result, a participant is injured. The following case illustrates the point:

A young man cut himself when he fell on broken glass while running on the local playground's ball field. His parents brought suit against the department, the playground supervisor, and the superintendent of the department for negligence. The lower court supported the department's defense of governmental immunity and extended it to the other defendants because they were acting in a supervisory capacity. The case was appealed to the state Supreme Court which reversed the judgment of the lower court. The plaintiff argued that the defendants had a duty to inspect the premises and be assured that they were maintained in the proper condition. Failure to do so would lead to accidents and injuries. The case was ordered back for re-trial. A similar case was heard against a school board in Virginia. (Short v. Griffitts, 255 S.E. 2d 479 (Va. 1979).[4]

Dangerous Behavior. Improper behavior in relation to environmental conditions produces at least 90 percent of all accidents that occur at recreational places. Some people have gone from the relatively controlled violence of handball to the greater risk sports of racquet-ball, squash, or jai alai, in which the hand and arm have high-powered extensions that propel the ball many times faster. Despite the increased danger, many people persist in playing at close quarters without proper protective equipment such as safety glasses and helmets. Injuries to vulnerable parts of the body have been sustained by hard hit balls, and skull fractures, blindness, and other injuries have been recorded in court game environments. Although the nature of the game has changed, the player's response to increased danger appears not to acknowledge potentially severe accidents.

Scuba diving alone, careless use of mechanical devices or dangerous chemicals, starting down a slide before the one in front is off, placing fingers under a seesaw, ice skating fast in a crowded space are all examples of potentially dangerous behavior that shows a lack of proper precaution. The key to good safeguards is to anticipate and be alert to what may happen.

Limited Performance Skills. Accidents often happen because individuals test their abilities to perform before they have mastered the necessary skills. Many injuries accompany attempts to perform gymnastic or tumbling stunts when the novice attempts a maneuver before being fully trained for it. Drowning victims are likely to be poor swimmers who have attempted something dangerous or too hard for them, such as trying to cross a riptide or getting caught in an undertow without the proper knowledge, stamina, and aquatic skills. Novice skiers, divers, bicycle riders, skaters, and others with insufficient skill may attempt to perform at levels far beyond their present ability.

Aside from lack of skill, other factors may intrude upon an individual's ability to perform. Fatigue, illness, loss of emotional control, or the use of drugs and chemicals can drastically reduce one's ability and judgment. Under the influence of alcohol, drugs, or emotional stress an individual can lose all sense of proportion and take foolhardy chances. Thus some

---

[4]Smith v. Village of Pine River, 232 W.W. 2d 241 (Minn. 1975).

people might perform on a dare or try to show off by attempting a spectacular stunt with unfortunate results.

Environmental Perils. The great outdoors is full of natural hazards which cannot be overlooked, especially since the natural setting attracts millions of people each year in activities such as mountain climbing, caving, white-water canoeing, kyaking, camping, and others. To natural hazards are added artificial dangers from open mine shafts, wells, land that has been stripped of its ground cover or earth-retaining propensity as a result of heavy logging so that land slippage can occur, and other man-made perils that lure some people into participation.

In spite of natural hazards, there is greater likelihood of injury because recreators do not pay attention to their surroundings and behave in ways that are inconsistent with safety. To the natural dangers of noxious weed poisoning, animal mauling, bee stings,[5] snake bites, falling off precipices, drowning in flash floods, and so forth, business persons and recreational planners have added their own devices for luring the potential recreator to the recreational site. Thus, artificial mounds are developed on ski slopes, unfenced walkways are constructed up to the edge of boiling natural springs, the development of ocean beaches may change the pattern of tidal currents so that artificially contrived undertows or riptides are produced. All of these human impingements on nature add to environmental perils.

> A case in point is that of an eight year old child, whose tobogganing mishap occurred when she struck the lower portion of a split-rail fence which had been used to divide a snow hill. One half was used for skiing and the other was used for coasting (both sledding and tobogganing). Although there was gross incompetence and negligence displayed by the county department operating the recreational facility—night lights were turned off while the child was still tobogganing down the hill—the severe injuries might never have happened if the barrier separating the two sliding areas had been composed of something other than rigid fence posts and rails. The net result was that the child was nearly decapitated, suffered monumental neck and head injuries, and is, today, blind, deaf, and paralyzed from the neck down. An award of $5.3 million was made in this case.[6]

It is only when tragedy strikes, and then under the pressure of adverse publicity or an unrelenting avenger (usually a parent), that man-imposed

---

[5]James C. Kozlowski, "Insect Sting and Bite Liability: a Limited Duty for Landowners," *Parks and Recreation* (October, 1990), pp. 24–19.

[6]*Newark Star Ledger* (February 2, 1978).

barriers or hazards are eliminated. With sound educational preparation such as would be found in a well-thought-out safety program, many hazardous conditions in the natural environment can be overcome. When accidents do occur, however, they are directly related to the fact that most people fail to behave appropriately or act in ways that will increase the danger of accident.

Certainly, accidents can be anticipated in uncontrolled environments, specifically where participants may not have an appreciation for the hazards to be encountered and, perhaps, insufficient skill to counter any threats which the natural surroundings may have for them. But humans have the capacity to manage the conditions which tend to affect them, thereby diminishing the possibility for accidents to happen. Proper planning can make certain that safety features are designed into a recreational site, instruction can prepare the individual to perform at a skill level which is well within the range of his or her ability, and compliance with common sense as well as with regulations enacted to prevent misfortune from striking can be a preventative force which promotes safe exercise for recreational satisfactions. In all of these circumstances, one must learn how to avoid both incautious behavior as well as environmental dangers.

Variable Sources of Accidents. Very frequently accidents result from not one but multiple causes. In many instances the victims could have prevented the accident by exercising a little effort. Many reasons may be offered in explanation. The following fictional report sketches the details and dramatizes the variables involved.

> Mr. Smith, a home craftsman, had a well-equipped workshop in the basement of his house. The metallic guard for his electric bench saw became disconnected from its base and had to be removed. Mr. Smith intended to replace the hand guard, but failed to do so. One evening as he was cutting lengths of wood, he inadvertently placed his hand on the spinning blade. His hand was immediately severed and he died from loss of blood and shock.

Although this accident could have been prevented, Mr. Smith's death cannot be attributed solely to his failure to replace the hand guard. It goes far beyond that single cause. Smith must have realized that he was placing himself in jeopardy every time he used the saw without the guard. Perhaps Smith decided to take the chance because he had "gotten by" on previous occasions. Possibly Smith was inattentive on the fatal evening because he had something on his mind. He could have been worrying about any number of problems and therefore incapable of taking the proper precautions. Perhaps the fatality was caused by a combination of factors: procrastination, poor work habits, ignorance, emotional stress, preoccupation, or laziness, to name a few of the many possibilities.

Lack of Supervision. Despite educational programs, there are a variety of situations where the absence of supervision may be the cause of accidents. For some activities close supervision is absolutely necessary during the initial stages if risks of injury are to be avoided. With attainment of greater skills and more knowledge about safe living, the degree of supervision can be reduced. However, there are certain activity forms which will always require supervision of a direct and immediate type regardless of performer proficiency and knowledge. Failure to offer this kind of supervision is negligence on the part of operators.

Negligence. The failure to exercise the degree of care for the safety and well-being of others or oneself that a reasonable and prudent person would have exercised under similar circumstances is negligence. Note that not only the authorities but the individual who is injured may be guilty of negligence. Unless individuals are forced to assume personal responsibility for incautious or dangerous behavior on their part, even the best safety program will be undermined.

Poor attitudes, unsafe habits, lack of skill or knowledge, poor judgment, may all contribute to negligent conduct. Individuals who do not habitually take risks with their own life and safety are less likely to perform activities that require skill levels far above their present capacity, nor would they operate with inadequate information about the degree of danger accompanying certain activities. Because there are inherent risks in many recreational activities, only the well-informed person can make a valid judgment regarding his or her ability to assume such risk.

While it is not always possible to identify the specific attitudinal error, skill ineptitude, or personality trait answerable for a particular accident, every conceivable tendency should be explored in order to determine the characteristics that tend to aggravate personal susceptibility to accidents. Rehabilitative efforts may then be developed toward assisting people to become aware of and master the shortcomings that imperil them.

Foundations for Recreational Safety

The practice of safe living by no means suggests the elimination of all activities that offer potential hazard. The urge to perform under some risk must be considered as a motivating factor for the performance of many experiences. Even a cursory glance at the causes of accidents infers the technique to be employed in preventing their occurrence. The approach that will best fulfill the requirements in contemporary life is that of persuading people to change their habitual ways of doing things. It also means educating people so that they can acquire the information, skill, and understanding necessary for corresponding attitudinal modification. Once knowledge about safe living is presented and acquired, people will be more apt to function in an effective manner despite the presence of environmental dangers and the inherent risk to be encountered in recreational experiences.

Safety Education

It must be the function of recreational service agencies to develop safety education programs which can benefit all who come into contact with the agency and its offerings. It is useless merely to present information without any attempt to make sure that such knowledge is assimilated and practiced. Unless people are motivated to develop and practice resistive skills, until they acquire the custom of scrupulously conforming to universal as well as particular safety principles, they will not have learned to live safely. The safety education program should establish in every person the appetite and the capacity to protect himself from potential danger in all situations containing both familiar and unfamiliar hazards.

Personal Responsibility. Of course, a safety program is beset by one obvious disadvantage. It is attempting to do remedial work with mature individuals whose personality traits and emotional needs were set long before. Trying to change the habits and attitudes of these individuals is a monumental task and may not always be successful. Nevertheless, the recreational service agency must make the effort. The optimum place to begin safety instruction is with young children. Caught at an early age when emotional need and personality are still relatively plastic, the instructional methods may be oriented to achieve the goals of safe living. The young need the kind of clear, direct information with which to acquire self-understanding, self-control, and outlets for acceptable self-expression. It is of some importance that safety education use a group model as the means for assimilating values found to be desirable. Any aspect of personal adjustment will more nearly be acceptable to the individual when the peer group shows itself to be highly favorable to safety practices and condemns behaviors that are perilous.

Young people typically gain their greatest satisfaction from the admiration of their peers, probably more so than from parents or other adults. If the safety program can teach a sense of responsibility in young people, these attitudes, habits, and knowledge will pervade all of their contacts and may prevent the formation of negative traits or daredevil behaviors that might end in injury or death. There seems little reason to believe that any safety education program will be able to compensate for or overcome inappropriate attitudes and poor performance habits. It is possible that some individuals might be helped to recognize their vulnerability and proneness to accidents. However, this is a long, drawn-out process which requires a great deal of time and trouble. The safety education program must, nevertheless, work with all people who come into contact with the recreational service agency. Through diligent effort it may be possible to assist individuals in learning how to handle themselves defensively so that they are not unnecessarily exposed to environmental hazards or to their own innate propensity for judgmental errors in performance.

Safety education cannot simply be the dissemination of rules and regulations concerned with "right" conduct. Soundly conceived, it will offer a complete program of defining and determining environmental hazards, pointing them out to all concerned, stimulating proper behavior for optimized enjoyment and personal satisfaction while establishing the kinds of performance habits and attitudes in those with whom it works. Recreational safety should be a basic function of all organizations that have anything whatsoever to do with the provision of recreational service delivery. It can only serve to help the agency and those who seek its benefits through participation or observation.

Behavioral Patterns

Individuals differ widely in physical and mental ability. Intelligence should play some role in the avoidance of accidents. Superior physical endowment such as coordination, flexibility, and speed should enable those who are so blessed to experience accidents less frequently than those who are not as strong, quick, or so well-conditioned. Yet, it can be shown that physical condition is not the complete answer for the prevention of accidents. Personal motivation is probably the most significant factor for the individual. Although intelligence and good physical condition can affect the severity and number of accidents a person has, other behavioral responses tend to influence how and whether an individual will be vulnerable to environmental hazards and personal adjustment to critical situations which call for speed of reaction if injury is to be avoided.

Concentration. Attention to a particular set of circumstances and the perception of some potential danger do much to assist in the reduction of accidents and the likelihood of severe injury even if one occurs. The ability to concentrate upon an event or part of an incident which becomes a predicament makes the individual more highly conscious of the factors involved and lessens reaction time to any critical stage. Any interference with the ability to concentrate on the prevailing conditions, e.g., fatigue, emotional stress, preoccupation, or some other restrictions ordinarily become the bases for consequences which are unfavorable. Safety in most recreational activity depends upon the concentration/attention factor.

Perception. Awareness of the physical environment is important because it permits the individual to recognize potential hazards. Awareness of one's surroundings plays a significant role in developing a sure feel for both safe and unsafe situations, and acting accordingly. Lifeguards, for example, have the responsibility for observing the way in which swimmers and divers behave. Lifeguards with developed perceptions can usually anticipate, by their actions, those persons who are likely to come to grief in the water. By calling these individuals' attention to their behavior the lifeguard may prevent accidents from happening. Expertness in any recreational activity permits the recreator to recognize or perceive certain actual or likely hazards and therefore allows time to avoid them.

Motivation. Safety in recreational situations can be taught and learned. Generally, interest may be stimulated and sustained through evoking one or more of the fundamental motives that move people to action: a) an appeal to survival; b) reward or recognition for positive behavior; c) use of peer pressure; d) an appeal to reason; e) appeal to basic fears or anxieties; and f) ego-involvement.

Recreational Safety Instruction

The problem of modifying behavior, so that the number of unsafe acts and violations of common sense practices will be diminished, is a most significant condition. While children are subject to parental teaching in the home and may learn a considerable amount of the do's and don'ts of safe living, the instruction of safety is the primary responsibility of those organizations which are established to offer recreational experiences of various kinds. Unless the recreational service agency is prepared to undertake this important instructional contingency, a disproportionate number of unsafe activities at recreational places will become commonplace.

Instruction should begin with the very youngest children who frequent the different activities sponsored by recreational agencies. Whether these are school operated functions, private or sectarian organizations, or the administration of public recreational service systems, the responsibility for inculcating safe habits is one which lies with the agency. As the individual becomes older, there should be direct teaching of skills, knowledge, and attitudes. Children must learn about unsafe practices such as jumping on and off moving swings, following one another too closely down a sliding board, or diving or jumping into water about which little is known. Similarly, high school age youth must learn about safety practices, rules, regulations, and policies, as well as skills. Undergirding all of this information is the development of good attitudes. Education for recreational living in safety demands expert guidance and teaching.

It has never been sufficient merely to transmit information about safe practices or behavior. For too long recreational agencies have simply played a defensive role by passively warning people. That has proved to be inconsistent with the responsibility which recreational service agencies have in contemporary society. Recreational safety requires an aggressive posture, one that thrusts itself into the vision and attention of those who want to participate in any way. Therefore, transmission of information only is not considered standard operating practice. Rather, the function of fostering safe conduct at recreational places necessitates active involvement in the direct instruction and supervision of people who make up the patrons of the system.

Recreational service agencies face an immediate challenge to fulfill certain responsibilities which have been laid upon them by legislators and the public. Recreationists must do everything within their power to supply impetus for acquainting people with safety attitudes and practices. If the recreators assimilate knowledge and change their behavior from foolhardy to wholesome, everybody will have benefited. To the extent that accidents are reduced and injuries lessened or eliminated the safety program will have been successful. Eternal vigilance to environmental dangers and to substandard behaviors is the best method for combatting tragic accidents and ensuring greater safety in the recreational service field.

Chapter 18

ENVIRONMENTAL IMPACTS

Recreationists should turn some of their attention to the pressing need for public instruction dealing with the environment. The time is ripe for professionals to expound on the deleterious effects that unrestricted growth, abuse, and misuse of natural areas can have on a precious resource. Environmental problems are of current concern. People are ready to listen and learn. They must be warned and prepared to oppose environmental degradation. Of course there will be a *quid pro quo*. Such education that is provided requires time away from programming as well as raising the costs of offering direct recreational services. Plans that may be devised to save ecosystems when made operational, will be expensive. Nevertheless, professionals are required to help educate the public so that the "greenhouse effect" may be ameliorated, the ozone layer replenished, acid rain stopped, and other destructive factors proscribed.

Americans must vigilantly guard their outdoor resources. Negligence can make them easy prey to those who would commercialize and exploit such resources without regard to detrimental environmental consequences.[1]

For the past few years, there has been an upsurge in the development of recreational facilities of the amusement and resort type, whose prototypes are Disney Land in California and Disney World in Florida. With the economic success of these parks, many imitators have attempted to buy up otherwise marginal land and develop it for amusement purposes. All the negative features so far enumerated are part of such development. Even the Disney company, not satisfied with its corner of the market, attempted to develop a wilderness fastness in the High Sierras and was stopped only when environmentalists brought legal action to halt a governmental plan to permit the construction on more than 50,000 acres of mountain wilderness. This area would have been turned into another

---

[1] *The Economist* "Greenhouse Economics," (July 7, 1990), pg. 21–24.

vast resort and amusement park, with concomitant traffic problems, scarification, animal disposal, and other environmental degradation.

All the aforementioned impacts have a debilitating effect on the environment, because such efforts create imbalances and bring pollution and spoilation to regions which have never felt the blight of human hands. Despite all of these invasions, there is a place for the construction and development of recreational areas and facilities which can be beneficial to people. Sound planning practices must be instituted to prevent undue and overextended development of spaces that probably should be left undisturbed. Recreational facility development is important if individuals are to enjoy a variety of experiences which require use of natural resources. For the most part, however, recreational development should be implemented where people already cluster—in cities. Natural resources can be enjoyed and used, if they are not misused or abused indiscriminately.

The Threat of Exploitation

People's greed has probably done more harm to the natural wealth than any other single destructive force. Not content to take what is needed for survival and profit, people have wantonly destroyed naturally endowed areas simply for pleasure and because they ignored the fact that natural resources are not inexhaustible. But there are those who see in a variety of natural resources the glitter of monetary return far in excess of what has to be invested. These individuals and corporate agencies would deface and spoil natural areas and mineral resources to reap a greater profit. In some instances, corporate investments can be coincidental with the preservation of natural resources, but too often, profit blinds, and conservational methods that should be taken are not or are done in half measure, with a resultant pollution or complete demolition of the resource.[2]

A typical act of exploitation was attempted in the state of New York, where a utility company tried to situate a power plant at one of the lovliest scenic views along the Hudson River in the highlands. The question under consideration was whether aesthetic values are worth anything when they come in conflict with corporate needs. The Consolidated Edison Company of New York requested the Federal Power Commission (FPC) to grant a license that would allow the firm to build a

---

[2]Michael Satchell, "The Boston Harbor Press," *U.S. News and World Report* (September 29, 1990), pp. 58–50.

$160-million hydroelectric power installation at Cornwall, New York. The company stated that under the law the FPC has no right to take aesthetic values into account in rendering a decision. The Scenic Hudson Preservation Conference, which led the conservation fight against the installation, insisted that the FPC not only had the right but was obliged to consider these values as the basis for making a decision.

At one time, Consolidated Edison planned to demolish the north front of Storm King Mountain by blasting and gouging out of the rock wall enough room for a giant power plant supplied by water from a huge storage reservoir to be located high above the plant in the Hudson Highlands. Water would be pumped from the river into the reservoir during the day to generate power as required for capacity periods of New York City's never-ending electrical demands. The current would have been transmitted across the Hudson by submarine cables, then sent mainly by overhead high-tension lines to New York City. These high-tension lines would have required a pathway not less than 150 feet wide for the distance between the plant and the city and would thus take additional woodland and recreational space out of accessibility. Aside from the acquisition of public domain for corporate uses, the entire concept of spoiling a scenic wonder for millions of people was casually shunted out of the way by a company whose only thought was a favorable profit statement. Certainly, this attempted blatant exploitation of the public domain for economic gain at the expense of natural beauty and those who are yet unborn would positively earn money for the corporation, but cost the people an asset which no amount of money could buy.[3]

California is another state with commercial interests gnawing at its priceless heritage from the Mesozoic period of evolution. For many years commercial timber companies have acquired vast stretches of the public domain where the giant redwoods grow. These companies have systematically logged the trees until, at present, there are some areas where one can travel for miles and not see a single tree—only stumps, a visual reminder of the graveyard of vanishing forests. After a lapse of 56 years, the federal government is again showing interest in preserving a dwindling species of tree.

In 1908, Theodore Roosevelt established Muir Woods National Monument, thus putting the federal government on record as obliged to preserve California's mammoth coastal redwood trees. Since that presi-

---

[3]"The Hudson," *The New Yorker,* Vol. XLI, No. 30 (Sept. 11, 1965), pp. 41–43.

dential proclamation, and despite state and private acquisition of redwood stands for parks, the number of acres of redwoods has been reduced from 2 million to 750,000. Of 300,000 acres of virgin redwoods still in existence, only 50,000 remain safe from being cut over by lumber companies.

Because further delay in acquiring these virgin stands might forever end the once vast resource of redwood forests, the federal government has considered appropriate action to safeguard these trees for the benefit of the public. In a report released on October 8, 1964, the National Park Service recommended the federal purchase of up to 53,000 acres of additional redwood forest for national parks. The report advanced two points: the redwoods represent a priceless asset, and preservation of these trees would provide an economic boom for northern California. In the first instance, public interest in these trees has been evidenced over many years, particularly by visits from persons from all over the world and the United States. These interested people have been willing to contribute substantial amounts of money for the purchase, dedication, and preservation of groves of redwoods. Since 1902, private citizens have poured more than $10 million into efforts to preserve the redwoods. Much of this money has been directed through the "Save-the-Redwoods League," a group founded in 1918 that carried on a nationwide fund-raising campaign and information program. Californians have spent another $9 million in taxes to create the state's 28 existing redwood parks. Another good reason for saving these trees is the fact that they grow nowhere else on earth.

The strongest opposition to expansion of redwood parks has come from the logging concerns and their employees, who view conversion of privately owned forests into parks as a threat to northern California's economy. Within days after the National Park Service report, the Redwood Empire Association, representing the major lumber companies and other northern California *commercial interests,* criticized the plan as economically disastrous. The Park Service disagreed, because its report estimated that within 5 years after the establishment of the new redwood parks, some one million visitors annually could be expected to visit the three counties containing these trees. Within 15 years, the number of tourists increased to 2 million annually. Within 5 years, tourists spent approximately $3.6 million annually on food, lodging, gasoline, and souvenirs. The expanded parks generated $11.2 million worth of business within 15 years.

The lumbering concerns are not so worried about the economy of the area as they are about making additional profit by cutting the extremely valuable trees. In spite of vital public interest in the redwoods, and the undoubted fact that these giants are priceless, the exploiters want to disregard public need in order to capitalize on a rapidly dwindling part of America's natural resource.

Even state agencies, whose normal responsibility is to protect the general interests of the public, succumb to the easy money to be gained by exploiting the natural resources at the expense of the very people they are charged by law to protect. More specifically, the National Wilderness Preservation System provides that the wilderness areas shall remain open for prospecting for at least 20 years. That ended on December 31, 1983. Conservationists and recreationists who battled for the passage of this act wanted more restrictive legislation on wilderness areas, so that such loopholes in the law could not be used for the advantage of a few to the discomfort of all. Yet, this has been allowed to occur. The wilderness act was a compromise between dedicated conservationists and some influential members of the Congress who would not support the bill because it contained restrictions on new mining claims upon passage. The congressmen represent mining and other vested interests. Nevertheless, the law was enacted with the compromise feature built into the bill as an open invitation for individuals to exploit these regions. While a few Forest Service employees believed that the mining provision was not an open invitation for would-be prospectors, Forest Service officials actually believed the opposite to be true. Apprehensions were apparent in the obvious attempts being made, under the appearance of mining claims, to circumvent the letter of the law in order to obtain individual preserves, literally estates, in the wilderness areas, much like private domains with all the rights of hunting and fishing.

Some Forest Service officials in Washington pointed out as examples of state exploitation the advertisements published in western states which proclaimed good fishing and hunting on small mining claims at prices of $2,000 to $5,000 each. Officials believe that some individuals received the impression that they would not have to do any mining and would be safe in using the land as a vacation resort. How unfortunate that state governments were more interested in obtaining revenue from such doubtful sources than in protecting the rights of the public by adhering to the spirit, as well as the letter, of the law.

The Threat of Encroachment

Lands that have already been dedicated and set aside for recreational purposes, such as parks, playgrounds, preserves, wilderness areas, beaches, nature trails, and other outdoor areas, are under constant threat of encroachment by other public agencies seeking land upon which to construct vitally needed facilities. There is no question that communities need schools, streets, police and fire stations, hospitals, and low rent housing, among other of the more essential buildings, but communities also need parks and recreational areas easily accessible and available for people. When recreational places are taken for buildings of various types, they are seldom if ever replaced. The land, once it has been torn up, cemented over, and built upon, is lost forever to people as a recreational site. As Murphy has so eloquently written:

> Once land has been taken from forest, parks, farm, wet land, beach, or other use for city expansion, it is nearly impossible to reclaim it from the urban expanse. Given the increasing trend to city living, the expansion of urban-industrial civilization with its rise in demands and expectations, the growth in population, and in the more affluent countries, the urge toward recreation away from the city, it is not hard to see a crisis in the making. Ignoring it and hoping it will depart of its own accord scarcely seems the better course.[4]

Public agencies are under the mistaken impression that land so taken is economical for the city. Such recreational lands, like parks, do not have buildings or other structures already developed on them, the land is already owned by the city, and it is easier to build a road through a park or to build a hospital or school on park property than it is to acquire comparable property on the open market and demolish any buildings situated on the site.

Misunderstanding of the economics of this form of encroachment is predominant among shortsighted politicians, who view the immediate savings to the city by acquiring park property for building purposes without realizing that it will eventually cost the city many times the amount that was "saved" to purchase new property in replacement. For example, the construction of a hospital upon park property will simply cost the community the total sum of actual construction. Inasmuch as the city owns the land, the property is merely transferred to the proper department. However, as demand for more recreational spaces grows, because of an increased population, and particularly because such a

---

[4]E.F. Murphy, *Man and His Environment: Law* (New York: Harper and Row, Publisher, 1971), p. 156.

population is more aware of the need for recreational areas as a result of better education and communication, the city will have to acquire new sites to satisfy its residents. The acquisition of new property within the modern city is unusually expensive. The additional expense develops because land values rise along with the growth of the city, and because urbanization generally means that the land has been used for buildings or other structures that will have to be demolished before the site can be utilized as a recreational facility. All this adds to the expenditure caused by short-term thinking.

Property required for the location of vital community needs other than recreational experiences should be purchased regardless of immediate cost. Neighborhoods slated for urban renewal projects are the sites which should be used for police stations, access roads, garbage disposal plants, water works, sanitation garages, and hospitals. If these structures are not situated where they will do the community the most good, then other buildings should be condemned and razed. Recreational facilities, specifically parks, that are allowed to be destroyed to make way for streets and other public utilities can never be replaced in their natural state. If the community has to wait to acquire such areas, the cost of this acquisition will be many times the original price of the property that was encroached upon, and probably will cost much more than the entire development which replaced the original park. Parks situated within the crowded neighborhoods and the core of cities are almost impossible to replace once they have been taken for uses other than recreational ones. The city and its population are much the poorer when there are no park areas in the central section of the community.

Typical of the narrow views prevalent are the incidents which occurred in several cities throughout the United States in 1964. In New York City three separate proposals to divert parks for purposes other than parks were made. During February, the Board of Estimate of the city overrode the objections of its own Planning Commission and approved the conversion of a 1.35-acre section of Morningside Park from park use to a site for a new public school. Although this is one of the most congested neighborhoods in the city of New York, the Board of Estimate nonetheless transferred the land to the Board of Education for construction, and stated that New York had more park land than any other city in the United States, and besides, the area in question was rocky. The fact that there are more persons living in the city of New York than in any other city of the United States apparently did not impress the Board of Estimate sufficiently for it to leave the park intact. In July, the Commissioner of the Department of Real Estate for the city proposed that public housing be constructed in the northern section of Central Park as well as in other New York parks. The Commissioner of Parks had this to say:

> This is a continuation of a short-sighted tendency to attempt to use park properties to resolve problems in sites for schools and other park buildings. This proposal to use park lands for the construction of apartment houses is nothing new. Similar proposals have been defeated in the past because they would deprive the public of park facilities for an interminable length of time while other land was cleared and new facilities constructed and would violate the inalienability of park land.... If this proposal is in any way encouraged, it will mean that park lands are no longer inalienable, and that the rights of the majority of citizens and their children through the enjoyment of the irreplaceable natural features of park landscapes can be sacrificed at temporary expediency.[5]

In September, a proposal of the Sanitation Department to build a garage on an undeveloped portion of Alley Pond Park in Queens was attacked by the chairman of the City Planning Commission, who is reputed to have stated that park lands should not be diverted to other uses, however worthy. This stand foreshadowed a sharp conflict between the Planning Commission and the city's Site Selection Board. The Planning Commission opposed the proposal because the use of the park for a garage would eliminate nearly four acres of park land, would result in a steady flow of sanitation trucks through the park, and would make it impossible to provide for a suitably planned development of surrounding park areas.

Historic Bushnell Park in Hartford, Connecticut, was all but dealt a death blow by the State Highway Commission, when that body approved plans for extending a new interstate access road through part of the park. Much park land is already taken up by the State House of the Legislature, and this latest move would have effectively destroyed any further park use of this once beautiful and truly historic city park, situated in the center of the community. Cooler heads prevailed; the state highway department was prevented from running an overpass through one section of the park.

During the summer of 1964, the stand of trees along the Charles River Drive in Boston was threatened by the Boston Public Works Department which wanted to remove the trees in order to widen the parkway. A

---

[5]Letter from Newbold Morris, Commissioner, Department of Parks, New York, New York, December 2, 1964.

determined group of citizens opposed the move, took their case to court, and obtained an injunction against any action being taken to destroy the trees. Only an alert and concerned citizenry can effectively halt these encroachments.

Even when laws are passed to preserve specific lands, for example, the Wilderness bill, there are examples of public pressure against the wilderness found within the act and elsewhere. Illustrations of this are ascertained by examining provisions in the bill. The Gore Range-Eagle Nest Primitive Area of Colorado is made up of rugged rock-climbing peaks and spectacular ridges. Forest Service officials had tentatively decided that an undetermined amount of land at the southern tip of this area, but not exceeding 7,000 acres, should be made available for Interstate Highway 70. Now, the Secretary of the Department of Agriculture is authorized by the law to remove the acres, if he determines that the action is in the best public interest. This would be done when the Secretary reviews whether the primitive area should be included in the wilderness system. He also may recommend the addition of other lands, not now within the area, to replace the 7,000 acres that may be cut.

These incidents are typical of what happened with greater frequency throughout the country. With increasing demands being made upon land for many purposes, recreational service agencies are in direct competition to acquire new lands and even to retain what they now hold. A sharp look needs to be taken at the present and future needs of the population, if confusion and conflict are not to make chaotic the proper designation of land use patterns. But even more vital is the necessity to prevent continued encroachment upon park and other recreational areas.

Typical Outdoor Recreational Areas Furnished by Conservation

Either as a necessity or a general good, society believes that outdoor recreational pursuits are important to its health, welfare, and happiness. For this reason, municipal, county, and state, and federal parks, forests, and other facilities have been established at great tax expenditure. They range in scope and kind from the neighborhood playground to the great preserves of wilderness to be found in national forests, as well as the scenic beauty of the magnificent national parks. One of the most significant uses of our outdoor areas is for recreational purposes. With increasing leisure, money, and information, and the nearly universal use of private cars and other methods of transportation, as well as the construction of highway facilities into the most attractive regions of the country, tens of millions of persons are now utilizing natural areas in place of the hundreds of thousands of a few years ago.

Among the facilities which can be provided only if proper conservation procedures are taken are:

Roadside Rests. A large proportion of those who travel by automobile to reach the outlying recreational facilities must spend not less than six hours driving. They do not generally plan to utilize facilities that are closer to their homes, but seek a distant site for their final destination. They are chiefly interested in picnicking and resting in attractive locations along the main highways, of which there are now over 5 million miles in the United States. All public areas should be situated in suitable locations and not the typical uninteresting, nonscenic, gouged-out spot at the side of the road that one usually finds. Even where commercial forestry is practiced, roadside stops, particularly along streams, glens near waterfalls, overlooks, and other attractive sites should be retained for recreational development.

Campgrounds. Many vacationers, especially those traveling by automobile, with or without trailers, plan to spend their leisure in campsites. This requires recreational planning and landscaping of high quality. The camping areas must be located away from roadsides and main trails so that complete freedom from noise and the dust stirred by automobiles may be enjoyed. The segregation of particular areas for camping purposes offers an effective method for the control and guidance of individuals in their utilization of the outdoors. Facilitating participant use without a great many restrictions provides access to attractive settings while maintaining these sites. Conservation methods have to be observed if camping areas are not to be misused. When campgrounds are insufficient to accommodate the number of users, certain destructive tendencies are observed. Soil becomes impacted by overuse, vegetation is destroyed, and the fertility of the area is seriously affected. In some instances, careless or ignorant users vandalize trees and bushes in their search for fuel. At times, the novice camper may hammer nails into living trees on which to hang clotheslines, bedding, and other paraphernalia. Trees may be scraped, scarred, and even knocked over by automobiles. As Brockman states so well:

> Proper planning and development of campgrounds are vital to the best use of recreational areas. Good planning not only preserves recreational interests for use by future generations but also ensures everyone of an equal opportunity

for enjoyment, provides the maximum number of camp spaces consistent with the character of a given area, and fosters maximum efficiency and economy of operation as well as public safety.[6]

Parkways. Many individuals enjoy viewing an attractive scene rather than being a part of it. For this reason, and because the individuals may also like continual change, travel along routes that have deliberately been selected for unusual geologic formations, relatively primitive areas, heavily forested regions, or unique scenic or historic sites affords a recreational experience. The parkway is easily accessible to metropolitan areas. Through the acquisition of sufficient land to allow the development of the property as a continuing belt of heavily wooded land, a reasonable degree of rough terrain often supplies an impression of solitude and remoteness. Space, water, ground cover, and whatever animal life may be found along the parkway play an important role in the preservation of such a resource. Unless plant and animal life are conserved, the constant stream of traffic will soon obliterate the natural environment.

Picnic Areas: Picnic areas may be set aside in almost any park where adequate planning has been arranged for these facilities. Typically, the picnic site can consist of a table, a low stone, brick, or cast-steel fireplace with a secured grate, a nearby freshwater outlet, and toilet facilities. Certain sanitary precautions must be observed in order that the site does not quickly deteriorate as a result of indiscriminate refuse disposal. Toilet and drinking facilities should conform to modern health standards and practices. Conservation practices which will ensure the preservation of the area must provide protection of trees and shrubs from damage, trampling of soil, and the resultant destruction of grassed areas. Control can be gained by rotation of the sites as well as by the emplacement of equipment which cannot be moved to other locations. Specific parking places also will lessen the damage that can accrue from unrestricted parking.

Reserved Timbered Areas. Within recent years special areas having unusual scenic values have been set aside for use and enjoyment. These are categorized as exceptional lands that are of such interest and uniqueness that they must be preserved. Examples of such areas are the redwood groves of California and the white pine areas of New York, Pennsylvania,

---

[6]C.F. Brockman, *Recreational Use of Wild Lands* (New York: McGraw-Hill Book Company, 1959), pp. 234–235.

and New Hampshire. These sections have been set aside for their scenic, scientific, or historic interest and as wilderness areas intended to preserve large tracts of remote virgin timberland without encouraging permanent dwellings or the extension or construction of highways.

Wilderness Lands. Considerable popular sentiment has been developing for the preservation of primitive or remote lands that contain few if any permanent inhabitants, provide no essential means of transportation, and are of sufficient size so that individuals may travel for several days or even a week and not retrace or cross their line of travel. Visitors to these outlying areas are expected to provide their own means of travel by either walking or horseback, and the primitive features of the region are to be protected and preserved. Accessibility, even by helicopter, is limited, and only those willing to carry their own gear and sturdy enough to explore these vast spaces are afforded an unsurpassed opportunity to see lands of superlative views and awe-inspiring majesty. All roads, settlements, commercial operations, and most power reclamation projects are or should be prohibited. Some trails and temporary shelters may be provided.

Wilderness areas are generally situated in regions of high altitude, in remote places where commercial values are low, and scenic and esthetic values are high. These areas do not lend themselves readily for timber production because of the slow growth rate of the trees, the areas' inaccessibility, and their low-quality forests. About 200,000 acres, or 300 square miles, of this type of forest is considered adequate minimal size for a wilderness area. It is expected that those attracted to these wilderness areas must travel on foot or use pack and saddle horses, boats, or canoes as a means of traversing these areas. Those primarily interested in camping, mountain climbing, and hiking in remote and solitary regions will enjoy such recreational experiences at minimal expense.

State Parks. Nearly every state has some land set aside for a state park system. These areas are situated some distance from metropolitan regions, although they may be reached by excellent state highways. They contain some wilderness areas, camping and aquatic facilities, and sometimes sports and game areas. They may be heavily or lightly utilized, depending upon their approximation to large urban centers.

Even when they are densely populated and heavily used by those who reside in nearby cities, the character of the parks is maintained because these persons do not penetrate far into the interior of the parks. The visitors are content to utilize the fringe picnic and other amenity facilities which are located along the edges of the area. Thus, one of the conservation problems in state parks is that of distributing use so that certain areas are not permanently damaged or destroyed.

National Parks. The most impressive of the outdoor resources dedicated primarily to recreational experience may be said to be the national parks.

> At best the national parks present the scenic masterpieces of this country, with a spatial setting appropriate to much presentation, and indeed a part of it. Considered in this way, such intangibles as beauty, majesty, and grandeur of the scene become natural resources subject, unless conserved, to marring and in some instances, if pressures for commercial use are not constantly resisted, to utter destruction.[7]

National Monuments. The national monuments are areas set aside less for unique scenic interest than for historic, scientific, or cultural value. Most of the monuments have been established by presidential proclamation. A few have been established by Acts of the Congress. Although the more scenic monuments may be found in the western part of the United States and the historic sites in the East, there is a fair distribution of national monuments throughout the country, and they provide a series of highly enjoyable recreational experiences. In a few instances, monuments may become national parks, as has been the case of Grand Canyon, Zion, and Olympic national parks, which were first reserved as monuments. The national monuments range in size from one acre to 2½ million acres.

> The most significant difference between a national park and a national monument is found in the comparative value and quality of the natural resources to be preserved, each park being supreme in its special scenic or scientific field. Fortunately no conflict exists; a national monument that is found to possess the outstanding qualities required can, with the approval of Congress, be transferred to the status of a national park.[8]

National Forests. National forests are located largely in the Rocky Mountains and Pacific Coast states where almost three quarters of the total acreage of forests of this type is found. This was the original development, since most of them were established from the public domain. The gross acreage of national forests approximates 190,000,000

---

[7]S.W. Allen, *Conserving Natural Resources: Principles and Practices in a Democracy,* 2nd ed. (New York: McGraw-Hill Book Company, 1959), p. 196.

[8]A.F. Gustafson, C.H. Guise, W.J. Hamilton, Jr. and H. Ries, *Conservation in the United States* (Ithaca, N.Y.: Comstock Publishing Associates, 1949), p. 307.

acres. The lands are largely of second-growth and cutover timber in the East and virgin timber in the West. However, a good portion of the forests is situated in high altitude regions, which make them less valuable for commercial exploitation because of poor quality timber or inaccessibility. The forests themselves are extremely valuable for watershed, forage, and recreational purposes, as well as for timber production. These areas are extremely attractive, an indication of which may be observed from the 9.1 million acres recently withdrawn from the national forests for the wilderness preserves. They are now more generously distributed throughout the country as a result of recent purchases of forest lands by the federal government. Fishing, camping, hiking, hunting, trapping, and the construction of temporary summer homes by permit are some activities enjoyed in national forests.

Protection and preservation of the natural resources offer inherent recreational values which would otherwise be marred or completely demolished. Unless competent plans are put forward, the damage to recreational lands will be of such proportion that their continued use will be negligible. Basically, conservation of the outdoor properties for availability by the public will stand as the best method of preserving such facilities over the longest period of time.

Incompatibility of Recreational Use and Conservation

There is an inconsistency between conservation and the utilization of natural resources for recreational purposes. The two appear to be inimical. On one side there is an almost fanatic concern on the part of conservationists to *preserve* the natural places without any alteration and to stop whatever imbalances man-made inroads have made on the ecological processes. To this objective the avowed intent of certain conservationists seems to be to keep all the outdoors just as though population pressures and economic incentives did not exist, that is, leave primitive areas as if contemporary civilization had never come to the United States. This means that the great outdoors cannot be used.

The paradox of use versus nonuse is best exemplified in the various reports and statements sent out by federal and state governments, which list an increasing number of conveniences and amenity services, thus almost removing the reasons for going away from the normal routines of modern living. New roads providing greater access to the wilderness are constructed, electric outlets, flush toilets, modern restaurants, lodges, swimming pools, and all devices which can so readily be found in urban living are being included as part of the governmental development of outdoor recreational places. At the same time, these agencies are also decrying the tremendous influx of persons clamoring to get to wilderness, as well as to park lands, in order to find whatever they conceive to be their personal recreational satisfactions. The simultaneous objectives of use and preservation are mutually exclusive.

Examples of the statements issued by governmental agencies showing their concern for both conservation and use includes:

__ to acquire typical portions of the original domain of the state which will be accessible to all of the people . . . conserve these natural values for all time; administer the development, use and maintenance of these lands and render such public service in so doing, in such manner as to enable the people of Florida and visitors to enjoy these values without depleting them.[9]

To preserve large forested areas and marginal lands along rivers, small water courses, and lakes for recreational use different from that given by the typical city park, and so that these tracts may remain unchanged by civilization, so far as possible, and be kept for future generations.[10]

The chief function of this Division is to conserve for all time for the use and enjoyment of the people of Indiana certain areas of typical Hoosier scenery in its original state . . . it should protect and preserve such areas and in so doing provide access to them, provide means for their fullest and most complete enjoyment by the people . . . [11]

First, that the national parks must be maintained in absolutely unimpaired form for the use of future generations as well as those of our own time; second that they are set apart for the use, . . . and pleasure of the people; . . . [12]

The twin purposes of the establishment of such an area as a national park are its enjoyment and use by the present generation, with its preservation unspoiled for the future; to conserve the scenery, . . . by such means as will insure that their present use leaves them unimpaired . . . [13]

Every one of these laudable statements is, in fact, a contradiction in terms of meaning. There are statements indicating that the original or primitive aspects of acquired lands will be preserved in perpetuity. On

---

[9]Florida State Senate: "The Collins bill," Senate Bill 441, 1949.

[10]G.W. Williams, "Wise Laws Gave Impetus to Illinois Park System," Revised Statutes (1963), Vol. 2, Chap. 105, Sec. 466(3).

[11]Indiana Department of Conservation, Division of State Parks, Lands and Waters: "Description of Properties and Facilities," n.d. (mimeographed).

[12]J. Cameron, "The National Park Service: Its History, Activities, and Organization," *Service Monographs of the U.S. Government,* No. 11, Institute for Government Research (New York: Appleton-Century-Crofts, 1922).

[13]U.S. Department of the Interior, National Park Service: "Annual Report of the Director of the National Park Service to the Secretary of the Interior for the Fiscal Year Ended June 30, 1932," Washington, 1932.

the other hand, there are statements that these very same lands are to be made highly accessible to the public for its use and enjoyment. There cannot be preservation and utilization at one and the same time. If people are continually encouraged and educated to enjoy the natural setting, there will, if for no other reason, be less of the natural environment for the present population, and much less for future populations, to enjoy.

With an increasing population and competition for land by an expanding urbanization, the wilderness will eventually disappear. Humans are by nature extractors and exploiters, and for this reason their presence in areas that were once primitive has destroyed much of the natural regions. Land acquisition for recreational and primitive areas will never be able to be maintained with a continuously expanding population. Modern Americans have committed themselves to an urban existence that does not look with favor upon life in the primitive outdoors. As Green has written:

> Except for use and consumption, the outdoors actually receives little attention. In part to serve his own comfort and convenience, the hypothetical average American prefers a "human scale" in his natural setting. He is not a "lover of nature in all her moods," whether that man-made personification be romantic or classic. What the nature poet may describe as sublime and awesome, or static and calm, fails to stir his imagination . . . [14]

Contemporary existence indicates that most people's leisure be spent in an urbanized environment. For this reason there is little knowledge engendered about the outdoors. Understanding of and familiarity with the natural environment produce an attitude toward the preservation of scenic settings and unspoiled areas; lack of knowledge and the skill to participate in activities that require competence in the outdoors promotes difficulties and makes enjoyment almost impossible. Unfamiliarity and ignorance encourage behavior that lessens the value of an area. Acts of vandalism, littering, and deposits of refuse in formerly beautiful locations are yet another indication of the human presence in and damage to natural lands. The recreational worth of wilderness is adversely affected by and in conflict with most of civilization's influence.

A tremendous increase in tourist travel has occurred since the National Park Service was established in 1916. During that year more than 300,000 visitors took advantage of opportunities to visit the parks. In 1965, the

---

[14]A.W. Green, *Recreation, Leisure, and Politics* (New York: McGraw-Hill Book Company, 1964), p. 13.

number of users of the national parks amounted to well over 90 million, and the federally owned forests attracted in excess of 120 million visitors. The projections of visitor use in the 1990's are awesome.[15] With governmental agencies' systematic exhortation to the public to enjoy themselves at these various facilities, a continually greater number of campers, hikers, viewers, tourists, and other vacationers will descend upon the parks and forests. There is little doubt, then, that these recreational consumers must eventually overrun the wilderness and obliterate it. In order that the public may enjoy the phenomena provided by a bountiful nature, observe wildlife in its natural environment, and live, however briefly, in primitive areas, governmental agencies have highly developed the recreational feature of these wild regions.

> Accommodations for visitors at hotels, lodges, and camps are provided to meet the needs or desires of every class of tourist. Facilities are available for those who wish to pitch their own tents . . .

> Excellent road systems give access to the more important centers. Trails for walking and horseback travel are generally available for those who wish to penetrate even the most remote sections. By using these trails the visitor really gets to know the parks.[16]

However, a great deal of conflict has been stirred up by the methods in which parks are being opened. Many believe that the wilderness cannot be maintained under such conditions, and that the very features which make it wilderness must be impaired by these developments. Serious questions can be raised in relation to the terms *use* and *preservation.* Additional queries may be made about what constitutes need and what is the greatest good to be obtained for the largest number of persons or even whether the greatest good for the majority is ethically consistent if it denies or infringes upon the rights of minorities. These questions are not simply theoretical semantics, but have practical application to problems confronting recreationists at this time.

Compatibility of Recreational Use and Conservation

If conservation is seen as the regulated use and management of depletable natural resources so that their durability is prolonged for the longest period of utilization, if it means the careful management of resources

---

[15]J.B. Albright, "U.S. Parks: Ever More Popular," *The New York Times Travel,* (March 15, 1992), p. 3.

[16]A.F. Gustafson et al, *Conservation in the United States op.cit.* p. 304.

that can be replenished to afford continual utilization without obliteration, permanent damage, or destruction, then there is no polarity between recreational use and conservation. These aspects of conservation can and should be carried out by recreationists and those who have direct interest in the development and maintenance of natural phenomena.

The meaning, importance, and goals of conservation have greatly expanded within recent years. Conservation is chiefly a local problem, although its results have regional and sometimes national implications. It must fit the local social and economic requirements. Although the immediate objectives differ from region to region and state to state, the ultimate aims are fairly consistent. For example, in some areas conservation attempts have the utilitarian objective of preserving water for irrigation, power, or drinking purposes. In some states an adequate supply of cover is necessary for the forage of animals. The development of the most attractive scenic and aesthetic effects can be accomplished only if growing forests are maintained. Soil conservation to prevent the washing of soils into streams, lakes, and rivers is of tremendous significance in certain regions. Conservation of natural resources is of importance in every part of the country. Conserved forests are the habitats of fish and game. Outdoor recreational areas would be less valuable if there were no trees, grass, or flora. Thus, multipurpose conservation has been given wide status.

One of the most important uses of natural resources is for recreational purposes. It would, for example, be almost impossible for most persons to use their leisure for any sport or game, for receiving a sense of awe and a feeling of adventure, if they did not have access to the outdoor environment. Rolling land, rugged terrain, hills, mountains, panoramic vistas, forests, waterways, wildlife, a variety of flora, all make a significant contribution to the recreational experiences of people everywhere. The satisfaction to be obtained from participating in high-quality recreational activity in the outdoors requires space, unique terrain, cover, and in specific situations, recreational experience must be the chief use of these natural resources.

In terms of this discussion, the recreational facilities usually found in municipalities that permit outdoor activities are mentioned, because land, which is the essence of designated recreational space, is part of the natural resources. However, dominant attention will be given to those areas that generally constitute the reservoir of natural resources in the outdoors: wilderness, water, fish, game, and forests. These natural resources may be used for many purposes, alternately, simultaneously, or exclusively for and dedicated to recreational use. The varied recreational resources, such as favorable climate at different times of the year, diversified terrain, topographical features that are scenically, scientifically, or historically interesting, are unequally distributed throughout the country, which probably accounts for the spasmodic utilization of land and the differences in the kind and extent of outdoor recreational experiences.

The scattering and uneven arrangement of physical resources stress the need for well-conceived plans in relation to immediate and potential utilization of natural areas. There is not merely the requirement of additional space to be set aside, withdrawn from the public domain, particularly for a variety of recreational activities, but it seems obvious that many types of outdoor recreational experiences are in harmony with other forms of land utilization. When such compatibility is feasible, methods must be worked out so that the most effective diversified land use can be developed. Ultimately, only intelligent coordination and scientific management of the land will encourage the most beneficial recreational use by the greatest number of people, in accordance with the continuity of all essential land values. In any event, natural resources can be diminished or obliterated. The perpetuation of recreational values obtained from the outdoors will occur only if conservation practices are performed.

To the degree that natural resources, specifically land, are diversely affected by nearly all man's activities, the whole concept of conservation is consistent with recreational use. If not for conservation, that is, the deliberate and directed maintenance of natural resources, then soil depletion in the face of accelerated erosion would continue unabated. Waters, cleaned in defiance of pollution caused by industrial development and the expansion of metropolitan areas, would be useless. Scenic, historic, or archaeological areas preserved in opposition to the flooding of these resources, as a result of the erection of dams and the formation of artificial lakes, would be lost forever. Prevention of the destruction of forested regions, grazing lands, promiscuous drainage of swamps and marshes, all of which affect the natural cover, habitat, and ecological balance of fish, game, and wildfowl, makes their preservation possible. The perpetuation of wilderness areas provides experiences to be gained in no other setting. But without conservation, the values to be received from passive or active participation in outdoor recreational environments would be impossible, or at best so reduced that only those lands in private ownership, which adhered to conservation practices—if such lands had the features described previously—would provide valuable recreational experiences, and then only for the select few.

Basic Objectives of Recreational Conservation

The need for recreational space increases with the consequent increment of population. With expanding leisure opportunities and both the economic capability and mobility to utilize free time recreationally, there is a concomitant necessity for providing a wide variety of recreational places for people. Such provision requires the use of all resources, whether they be situated in urban centers or in remote wilderness areas. This means a dedication to the principles of conservation so that land availability is consistent with population needs and the various uses to which land may be put made accessible to users in many different forms. Furthermore, recreationists will have to examine potential participants' needs, interests, and perceptions so that recreational places can be designed which more nearly satisfy the diverse requirements they have.

Centers of population should be explored to determine whether and how the entire community may be utilized as a recreational resource. This may mean the acquisition of additional land within the city and the development of both neighborhood, district, and regional facilities of many types. This must not be construed as limiting such planning to active recreational facilities only, but should include those recreational spaces which lend themselves to camping, geological, naturalist, and conservation forms of recreational activity. Thus, zoological, botanical, agricultural, arboretum, nature conservancy, aquatic, park, reservation, and other natural areas should be incorporated into any comprehensive recreational service system.

Certainly, outlying areas can also become potential recreational places if the means for transportation is found. However, as previously noted, there has been a tendency to overcrowd, congest, and construct without thought to the values which soon disappear under such onslaught. Highway construction, unrestricted land use for industry or commerce, cannot long remain without some ecological dislocation and consequent irreversible damage to man's environment. If wilderness areas are to be conserved, they must be protected from unconstrained use. Less, not more, comfortable routes to such natural places should be available to those who wish such experiences. The public in general should be educated to the values which many wild or developed places can have for them. A rational plan for rationing the well-known national parks, monuments, and other popular places should be undertaken while there is still time to save them from being loved to extinction.[17] New national parks, historic sites, and other outdoor areas should be opened to meet the growing demand for recreational experiences which occur in natural settings, but sound policies governing their use must be employed to protect them from abuse.[18]

The maintenance of a balanced environment which preserves the ecology, minimizes despoilation, eliminates pollution, and provides appropriate recreational space for urban, suburban, and rural dwellers is a demonstrable obligation of the recreationist. Leisure needs which find outlet in recreational activity are satisfied when a balance exists between many kinds of outdoor recreational resources and the development and practice of logical ecological and conservation efforts which materially assist in producing environments that are aesthetically pleasing and scaled to human needs.

Among the activities that should be encouraged by recreational service authorities, whether in urban centers or the hinterlands, are:

1. The sponsorship of recreational activities which receive stimulation from being associated either directly or indirectly with environmental concerns. Antilitter campaigns, pollution abatement programs, camping with its ramifications, agricultural experiences, waste recycling, conservation practices, nature lore and study, botany, biology, astronomy, geology, mineralogy, meteorology, animal husbandry, orienteering, hiking, climbing, speleology, and many other recreational encounters which are enhanced by occurring in or through association with natural places.

2. The acquisition, maintenance, and management of open spaces with special emphasis on the protection and preservation of park lands, wildlife sanctuaries, water resources, inland wetlands, forest areas, and other natural and scenic places which encourage an appreciation for the environment simply because it is there.

3. The sponsorship of concerned persons who are interested in the passage of legislation directed toward the protection and preservation of open space, wetlands, tidal flats, and other endangered

---

[17]R. Kraus, *Urban Parks and Recreation: Challenge of the 1970's* (New York, 1972), p. 37.

[18]J.F. Murphy, J.G. Williams, E.W. Neipoth, and P.D. Brown, *Leisure Service Delivery System: A Modern Prospective* (Philadelphia: Lea and Febiger, 1973), p. 54.

areas from encroachment by highways, industrial construction, oil spills, atomic or other chemical and domestic contaminants, as well as the establishment of some state agency directly responsible for environmental protection.

4. The development of programs which do not demand the use of motorized vehicles.

5. The closure of parks and recreational places to motorized vehicles of whatever type, except by controlled access through some form of mass transportation, preferably by self-contained electric power.

6. The closure of parkways to automobiles and motorcycles, so that hikers, horseback riders, bicyclists, joggers, and pedestrians may use them.

7. The development of linear recreational facilities abutting parkways or appropriate highways to take advantage of public accessibility and the right-of-way which are often overlooked for such purposes.

8. The acquisition of disused railroad rights-of-way for a variety of recreational uses in season. Such former trackage could be utilized for hikers, bikers, snowmobiles, cross country skiing, trails, and the like.

9. The direct education of individuals to the use for which open space may be employed for recreational purposes. Attempts should be made to reduce the use of the off-the-road motorized vehicles through ecologically fragile areas which can rapidly deteriorate under the impact of motorbikes, dune buggies, and snowmobiles during the winter. Concurrently, some attempt must be made to provide reasonable facilities and spaces for those whose recreational interests dictate the need for motorized vehicles.

10. The sponsorship, through public schools, libraries, religious, civic, and service organizations within the community, of programs that discuss dramatically the impact that people have upon the ecology when they maliciously or unwittingly pollute the water, air, or leach out soils through chemical seepage and spillage. Cinematography, slides, books, magazines, and perhaps stage presentations could be employed to persuade potential users to assist in the conservation of environmental properties which can do much to enhance their daily lives.

Citizens must be kept ever vigilant and be ready to oppose crass waste and improper use of the national heritage of natural resources whenever they occur. Constant scrutiny of governmental functions and responsibilities is required if timeless benefits are to accrue to all persons. Such instances in which public demand restricts governmental interference, waste, or destruction of the public domain prove that the people's voice can be heard, and that an aware citizenry can make their demands felt and satisfied. However, eternal preparedness to cry out against infringement of any person's right to the great natural preserves of this country is the price that must be paid.

The protection of important recreational lands is of infinite significance, because these lands are particularly subject to damage as a consequence of overexposure to an irresponsible public. Specifically, careful attention must be given to the extent and method of the development of such land, as well as to the type of activities conducted thereon. Although the public may not fully realize the notable recreational features available unless sufficient means for their inspection and investigation are provided, it must be recognized that construction of any sort interposes contrived and affected components that destroy the natural values for which interest was originally aroused. For this reason, continued physical development of outstanding outdoor recreational places should be held to a strict plan. Amenity facilities may be included in plans for the utilization of outdoor areas, but they should be minimized and never viewed as being more valuable than the natural resources themselves. Perhaps it is better to sacrifice *some* consumer comfort and convenience than to destroy, forever, natural areas with artificial elements and compound the conflict with population wrought impaction.

Selected References

Brockman, C.F., and L.C. Merriam, Jr.: *Recreational Use of Wildlands,* 2d ed. (New York: McGraw-Hill Book Company, 1973).

Brubaker, S.: *In Command of Tomorrow: Resource and Environmental Strategies for Americans* (Baltimore: Johns Hopkins University Press, 1975).

Chapter 19

RECREATIONAL SERVICE FOR PERSONS WITH DISABILITIES

One of the supreme ironies of life in modern American society is that the general public is almost always ready to give sympathy or pity to those who are physically disabled or mentally ill or retarded, but is constitutionally unable to accept them as fellow participants in recreational activities. There seems to be a collective guilt complex based upon "there but for the grace of God go I" which enlists aid for segregated facilities and opportunities, but denies a place to the disabled person in normalized situations. Of course, the attitude of the population is reflected in its recreational representative—the public recreational service department. It is only in the past 20 years that disabled persons have had an impact upon the consciousness of the American people and their appointed officials. It is only within the past 15 years that public recreational service agencies have begun to plan and develop both the facilities and conditions conducive to allowing disabled persons their justifiable opportunities for recreational service.

Now, of course, Public Law 101-336 enacted on July 26, 1990, prohibits discrimination on the basis of disability. More importantly, it specifically includes accessibility to public and private recreational facilities, as well as denoting a mandate for appropriate participation in such services.

The prevailing attitude toward disabled populations has had a long history. For some, affliction is the manifest condemnation of an angry God for sins committed. There are still individuals who believe such errant nonsense. Others cannot control their aversion toward anyone who is not whole in mind or body. Still others are so certain that physical loss of limbs or organs makes life not worth living that they cannot escape projecting their inability to understand and cope with the loss onto the person who has sustained it. They are so full of pity for the affliction that they cannot see the person who is afflicted. Then there are those who are sure that impairment is shameful. These individuals have

471

been in the forefront of shutting away all mentally ill, retarded, or chronically ill persons in institutions that are far enough from the mainstream of life that they are forgotten. And finally, there are those who are simply afraid of the unknown, as we all are about some things with which we are unfamiliar. Disfiguring diseases, deteriorating physical conditions, mental illness, mental retardation, and a host of other degenerative afflictions seem to strike with a capriciousness that is demoralizing. Laymen are constantly bombarded with the idea that they are potential medical cases with little to be done for them. Disease has always been an unknown quality for any culture. Superstitions and myths have grown up about the causes and appearance of various diseases. Hidden in the subconscious of many persons is the idea that if they have as little contact as possible with sickness or disability, they will escape the probable consequences. Of course, this is fallacious, but it is as good a reason as any for denying some people their fair share in obtaining an enjoyable life style. There are an additional few who seem to enjoy the idea that there are others who are afflicted in some way. To add insult to injury, there has almost been a conspiracy to prevent disabled persons from becoming involved in recreational activities even if they have the ability to do so. Some public authorities have devised regulations which restrict a physically disabled, mentally retarded, or neurologically impaired person from taking part in public recreational activities. For too long artificial barriers have been erected which prevent entrance to public facilities by those in wheelchairs or with other limitations which preclude their climbing stairs. Now we are seeing an end to this unthinking mismanagement. Both the people and their representatives have become more aware of the difficulties which have been created for the disabled persons or those of limited ability, and as a result great improvements are being made.

Adaptation of Recreational Conditions

Adaptation is the method by which any recreational experience, facility, space, rule, piece of equipment, or situation can be modified to provide the disabled person an opportunity to participate. Game times may be shortened, if fatigue prevents the individual from taking part in an activity, so that the person can perform without fear of having to withdraw. Rules or regulations covering certain activities can be simplified so that the individual may be given instruction, without fear of failure or concern that errors will accrue because of misunderstanding the complexities of the activity. A course, field, court, or event can be shortened. It could require the development of lighter weight pieces of equipment so that an individual could participate, for example, lightweight horseshoes for pitching, less pull on a bow for archery. It can mean the utilization of more or fewer players on a team or the modification of the method of play, such as allowing unlimited hits until the ball goes over the net in balloon volleyball or regular volleyball. Ramps may have to be installed so that certain physically disabled persons could gain access to a variety of recreational facilities. Rails, textured surfaces, or other guide devices might have to be placed so that blind persons would be able to orient themselves and thus be able to participate in whatever recreational event was being offered. It certainly would require modification of tools, implements, or other material necessary for the effective performance of some art, craft, or musical activity.

Normalization

For the most part, adaptation is required if the concept of mainstreaming is to be placed into effect. Perhaps the most important and exciting trend affecting recreational service today is normalization. Normalization refers to the total integration of the disabled person into society. The practice of normalization was developed in Scandinavian countries and has been transplanted to the United States, where it has played a great part in changing the nature of institutions for specific impairments as well as for influencing public recreational service.

Normalization, as employed in the United States, is a process of preparing the disabled individual who has been placed in an institution for return to the community. It includes the placement of a person and provision of continuing supervision and supportive services if needed. Institutions utilizing the practice include prisons, mental hospitals, and schools for the mentally retarded. The last mentioned places make the most extensive use of normalization. The retardates return either to their homes, to halfway houses, or group homes, which are dwellings where several former residents of an institution may live together with or without supervisory personnel. Those who live in halfway houses have been assisted in job placement either in the private business sector or in sheltered workshops. The typical job may be of a repetitious nature or one involving simple skills. The sheltered workshop may be operated by either the institution or some other organization. Recreational services are provided to the homes with the objective of helping residents to take part in the community recreational program and so facilitate their integration into society.

As a consequence of the normalization trend, so many mild and moderate retardates have been placed in the community that institutions for the mentally retarded no longer house a significant number of them. The residents at such institutions are now largely those who are severely and profoundly retarded, emotionally disturbed, or multiply impaired, and even these are being placed in smaller facilities. Normalization has also brought change to community recreational services, because retarded persons and emotionally disturbed persons returning to the community need special consideration in recreational programs. Many communities not previously providing special services are now shifting their priorities to meet the need.

Mainstreaming

Normalization has been largely responsible for the development of a procedure described as mainstreaming, which is the integration of the disabled person into the regular and routine activities conducted by community recreational service departments. It is not difficult to understand why normalization influenced the development of mainstreaming. If a disabled person who has returned to the community from an institution is provided only with services that isolate him or her, that person again becomes segregated in much the same way as in an institution. The solution, manifestly, was the individual's integration into the regular program—mainstreaming.

Mainstreaming is not a new concept. In the early 1960s work was initiated by several community-based agencies in the United States in developing recreational activities for disabled persons (chiefly physically disabled, since mentally retarded and emotionally disturbed persons were not then in the public recreational programs). The desirability of providing segregated recreational activities for such persons as opposed to integrating them with normal persons in regular activities was much discussed, with effective arguments being presented by proponents of both. In consequence of these discussions and the then prevailing public opinion, guidelines were developed with which participating agencies agreed. When disabled persons cannot participate to their advantage in regular activity, the department should provide a special activity if it is able to do so. Thus, dualism was initiated. Regular participation in recreational activities will be contraindicated if it endangers the individual, or does not promote self-satisfaction, improvement of skills, attitudes, or physical capacity to perform.

It is often difficult to determine just when an individual can participate in the integrated activity safely and successfully. Also, it is quite likely that the individual might be able to participate in some aspects of the regular offerings and not in others. For the most part, it is apparent that participation in routine physical activities of a vigorous and strenuous nature provides the most difficulty, and that the other major recreational categories can be adapted more easily to meet whatever limitations impairment places upon the disabled. To resolve these vexing problems, a type of programming called the dual program is a single activity divided into two sections. One section offers the regular activity and everyone participates in it at some time or other. The dual section presents activities adapted for and appropriate for those who cannot participate in the activity being offered in the regular program at any given time. Disabled persons move in and out of the special section, depending upon their ability to participate.

Dual scheduling was frequently utilized during the early 1960s by agencies that had adapted programs. However, few departments had them. Programs that did exist served chiefly physically disabled persons. Several departments offered specialized activities in the individual's home. These were conducted by recreational service departments for the homebound individual and were never thought to be transitional forms for later mainstreaming. Such programs were operated by a few enlightened departments. For the most part, however, disabled persons residing in the community were often ignored and not served recreationally. When mentally retarded and emotionally disturbed persons began to be moved from the institutional setting back to the community, there was the usual outcry by some anxious laymen that property values would fall or that crime would increase, but these fears proved unfounded and the procedure moved forward. First there was dualism, then mainstreaming.

The arguments for mainstreaming, as opposed to segregated activities for disabled persons, point out that segregation isolates the individual from the rest of the world. It is emphasized that freely mixing people of all sorts presents a realistic environment in which the disabled person, with current capacity to perform, can best learn what he or she is able and not able to do. The presence of a disabled person is helpful to all, because everybody can develop understanding of the limitations and the potentialities of the disabled without becoming contemptuous or over-solicitous. It is reasonable to expect that by bringing people together there will be greater opportunity for the development of appreciation for one's own abilities and limitations, and appreciation for those of others. This does not occur automatically. It requires careful considera-tion and planning to guide individuals toward acceptance of others for their true worth.

There are specific situations in which it is absolutely necessary to place individuals in a special activity for instruction and/or services. The severely impaired or disabled person whose needs cannot be ade-quately served in the regular program requires segregation. Also, there are times when an individual could participate in a routine activity, but who would have to be offered another opportunity when such activities proved to be counterindicated. Thus, for example, an individual with rheumatic fever may be able to participate in a regular activity when a volleyball unit is offered but must be removed from the regular activity and placed in a special unit when basketball is offered, in order to protect them from the possibility of dangerous overexertion.

It is a high time to overhaul the dual choice system and place it at the service of the disabled with all types of impairments. To make the dual system more effective, the special section could be geared to assisting the individual to participate in the regular activities wherever possible. Even individuals with severe limitations could be placed in the regular program if arrangements could be made for them to receive support from the recreationist while they are in the regular program. This might necessitate the presence of a professional person educated in therapeutic recreational service, but even this is not likely. There is no reason to believe that recreationists would not be prepared to work with disabled individuals and be able to adapt activities to meet whatever limitations are imposed by impairments. No special preparation is required, only the willingness to perform and the ingenuity to modify when necessary.

Staffing Patterns

Many public recreational service departments have been unwilling to provide for disabled persons because they say that they are not ade-quately prepared to employ a recreational specialist who would be able to offer a variety of activities. The arguments against such provision for disabled persons range from anxiety about liability in the event of injury to fear of condemnation by citizens who do not want to be associated with impaired persons. These are quite valid fears. Much precaution should be taken when providing recreational activities for disabled persons but with few exceptions not any more so than would be taken in the provision of routine recreational activities. The degree of responsibility taken by the public recreationist is based upon common sense and good judgment. Standard safety formats, written policy concerning the use of areas and equipment, and competent supervision are the keys by which accident, injuries, and concomitant litigation to recover damages will be avoided. Insofar as anxiety raised by citizens of the community who decry their being subjected to the presence of disabled persons, the recreationist must act professionally. It is the recreationist's responsibility to provide recreational services to all the people living in the community, not merely to the "normal" population. Furthermore, it is the recreationist's responsibility to overcome whatever opposition is raised through an educational program. Surely, many examples are given for not providing disabled persons with recreational services. There is only one justification for doing so. It is the mandated function of community recreationist's to serve all people. If this is not done, then there is professional failure.

The chief drawback for such provision seems to be that one would have to have special preparation for working with the disabled. In short, one would have to be a therapeutic recreationist in order to know the disabling conditions and provide the kinds of activities which would be most appropriate for involved persons. It may be an excellent idea to employ a therapeutic recreationist to guide the overall development of recreational activities for disabled persons, but this is not necessarily required. Any community recreationist can be prepared to work with the disabled client. For the most part, such work will deal with adaptation and the removal of mobility barriers for participation. When an impairment is so severe as to preclude participation without infringing on the enjoyment of others, then a dual program should be initiated.

The need for a specialist should not be the excuse used to deny needed services. All that is necessary is the assignment of a recreationist to that part of the program devoted to the needs of the disabled. If departments assign workers to assist with the production of activities, schedules, and the allocation of equipment, together with recommendations for the elimination of architectural barriers and other limiting conditions, either environmental or personal, then the provision of recreational service to such persons will be assured. Instead of finding excuses for preventing disabled people from regular recreational participation, recreationists must assume an advocacy role and educate both the public and those who are impaired that they have a significant role to play in community recreational offerings, and can do much to alleviate some of the discrepancies which now exist. The entire population must learn that disability of whatever kind does not have to become a hindrance in finding fulfillment through recreational experiences.

Of great importance is the need for staffing; it must be remembered that much more staff time will be expended in planning and preparation of activities for disabled persons than will time spent for actual participation. This is because adaptations must be made where necessary, individualized instruction and assistance requires preparation, and some modification of tools, equipment, layout, or other changes must be developed. The desirability of volunteer assistance is underscored. The well-prepared volunteer can do much to extend personalized assistance which might otherwise not be available. Furthermore, when five or six disabled persons are in a group, it is generally advisable to have a volunteer to provide them with some form of instruction, assistance, or intensive personalized help so that they do not have to wait for one recreationist to get around to all group members. Volunteers may also come from the ranks of disabled individuals. There are many physically disabled persons with high degrees of skill in a variety of activities. They may utilize their talents and skills to enable other persons to participate in recreational activities.

Some physically disabled persons may be able to teach physical activity. Others may be able to direct musical or theater groups. Still others have artistic talent and knowledge and may serve as instructors in any of the graphic or plastic arts. One example of how disabled persons may be assistive is the following situation:

> A recreational department developed a day camp facility for disabled persons. One of the activities was swimming in Long Island Sound. Persons in wheelchairs had to travel several hundred feet in order to reach the beach area and found the going difficult in the sand. The blind clients volunteered to push the wheelchairs, and in this manner, with the sighted wheelchair persons providing directions and the blind individuals supplying the muscle, both groups were able to participate at the seashore.

Surely, there are many instances in which disabled persons, depending upon their abilities and limitations, can be volunteers and augment the professional staff to the same extent as can nondisabled persons. Recreational service departments should attempt to enlist the aid of diverse community residents for volunteer services, because this is a significant recreational category in itself. There is as much enjoyment and personal satisfaction engendered from volunteering as is obtained from any other form of recreational activity. Under certain conditions the degree of satisfaction achieved by the volunteer may be even greater than that which could be gained from other forms of recreational participation.

Program Opportunities

Many recreational programs can satisfy disabled individuals through the acceptance of most or almost any category of recreational activity. Except for the most strenuous physical activity (even this is open to question), there is almost nothing which should be prohibited to a disabled person. Limitations on activity will depend upon individual motivation, skill, previous experience, desire, appreciation, or the availability of skilled instruction. There are countless examples of blind skiers, runners, and swimmers. The Para-olympics, first initiated at Stoke-Mandeville in England under the instigation of Sir Ludwig Guttman, and the Special Olympic Games, under the auspice of the Kennedy Foundation, indicate that many of the disabled population have long been overlooked and discounted before they were given the opportunity to participate. There is good reason to believe that some of the impaired clients can participate with nonimpaired individuals and not only give a good account of themselves, but compete and win.

One example is the Israeli para-olympic volleyball team, whose membership is composed of arm and leg amputees. This team regularly competes with teams of physically nondisabled persons and wins. In fact, except for their prosthetic attachments, it would be difficult for the layman to discern the almost imperceptible hesitation in gait which members of this team have. A double-leg amputee is a regular team member and performs in an outstanding manner. Typical movements require diving, rolling, falling, jumping, stopping short, and all of the other kinetics associated with competitive volleyball. This is but one instance of how physically disabled persons might be mainstreamed. The sight of a person in a wheelchair competing in an archery tournament, playing billiards, participating in art, craft, music, or drama activity no longer raises the least concern. One-armed golfers, baseball players, tennis players, painters, and musicians abound. Even double-arm amputees have learned to play a variety of musical instruments, including the piano, when fitted with utility hooks. Some persons who have had arms and legs amputated as a result of accident or disease have learned to ski, sail, scuba dive, and swim skillfully. Blind individuals perform in a variety of recreational activities, including long-distance running, ski-joring, bowling, table tennis, and other experiences once thought impossible. The list of activities in which the disabled individual can participate is literally inexhaustible. All that is really needed is public education, personnel willing to work with them, and an enlightened administration dedicated to removing artificial barriers and prejudices which prevent disabled clients from receiving the kinds of services which the community is ethically mandated to supply.

In the area of the performing arts, little must be done to make opportunities available for the disabled. Minor adaption is required for appearance on a stage, in a musical activity, or even in dance. Even the paraplegic in a wheel chair can participate in a variety of dances. Participation in art, music, drama, social activities, intellectual activities, excursions, sports, and games might need little modification of the basic activity for mainstreaming to occur. More importantly, it is the acceptance of the disabled person's right to receive recreational services provided by the community that is a question. To the extent that the community does not restrict entrance into community centers, playgrounds, stadia, swimming facilities, or access to the various program opportunities which its public department presents, then disabled persons will be well served. Through adaptation, many limitations imposed upon the disabled may be overcome. Through education, the disabled may become just another participant within the community program. Whether by mainstreaming or dualism, such persons must be served. Not to provide these services flies in the face of the basic principle of equal opportunity to all and is contrary to antidiscrimination laws. Recreationists should be vitally concerned with the abilities and not the disabilities of individuals. Their abilities will enable them to participate in the full range of recreational experiences while their disabilities will be a personal reminder that some activities should not be attempted.

Of course, certain disabilities prove so formidable that mainstreaming is either limited or counterproductive. In some instances of mental retardation, for example, the tolerance level of a non-retarded person for the retarded is low and neither party benefits from close association. However, there are many instances where educable retarded persons have been well accepted within the community group and contribute both to their own satisfaction and to the comprehensiveness of the program. Except when the disabling condition is so severe as to prevent participation without specialized instructional assistance, guidance, or the necessary assignment of one staff member to the disabled person, it is probably appropriate to include disabled individuals within the overall program planning effort. Simply blocking people out because they have some disability or impairment, without really attempting to determine whether their residual abilities are sufficient to enable them to participate in the public recreational offering, is contrary to the basic principle of recreational service to all in the public sector.

Disadvantages of Specialized Agencies

Not infrequently, disabled persons are prevented from participation in community-operated or-sponsored recreational activities because of the misguided belief that their recreational needs are being met satisfactorily by specialized agencies operating within the community or the region. In other cases, some persons are dissuaded from utilizing public facilities or requesting admission to a public program, because of these same deficient understandings. There can be no faulting the tremendous help which the different specializing agencies provide to the disabled. All those agencies which have taken a particular disability, disease, or other impairing condition as their own and provide comprehensive assistance in a wide variety of living situations perform heroically. Some organizations serve blind, deaf, retarded, or physically disabled persons, or those with heart disease, muscular dystrophy, diabetes, leukemia, cerebral palsy, arthritis, and so on. The list of agencies providing information, financial support, medical assistance, food supplements, education, work, family assistance, and comprehensive recreational services, including facilities, leadership, and programs, is at least as extensive as the various diseases, impairments, or defects which produce the disabled.

These agencies are needed. They should receive the financial support necessary to carry on their vital work. For the most part, they do superior work in their efforts to help. The single most important drawback is the fact that they have been most successful in gaining public support and selling the public on the comprehensiveness of their programs. They have done this so well that there is some truth to the oft-noted contention that public recreational service departments do not have to provide recreational services for disabled individuals because they are taken care of by the specialized agency. This is nonsense. No matter how well specialized agencies perform, they cannot reach all community-based disabled persons. A specialized agency may be a regional body, rather than a local one, with the consequent need for disabled clients to be conveyed to the regional center if they are to receive services. When transportation is unavailable, so are the services. More often than not, disabled persons are not well served by the regional agency because they cannot reach it.

Every community does not have a specialized agency which provides for this population. Moreover, even where there is one specialized agency its operational policy may preclude working with disabled persons whose disability or affliction does not fall within the accepted category of persons for whom the agency was designed to work. For example, an agency working with the blind may be disinclined to work with a person with cerebral palsy. An organization that deals with the mentally retarded may not be capable of working with paraplegics or quadraplegics. To state that all specialized agencies are willing and able to work with any disabled individual is an error.

Compounding the error is the public agency's abdication of service to disabled persons because the public agency believes that a specialized agency is capable of providing recreational experiences to a specific portion of the population. Much remains to be done by public recreational service departments in the way of coordination, augmentation, and cosponsorship of recreational activities, facilities, and leadership in conjunction with specialized regional or local agencies. When this occurs, much of the gap between what should be available and what is actually supplied will be diminished or abolished. Furthermore, the public recreational agency will merely be living up to its own announced principle of coordinating its function with other organizations based within the community so that the greatest population will be served without exception.

Under such circumstances, the recreational environment for disabled clients will be improved immeasurably. Coordination of effort really means that specialized agencies can perform their services for particular populations in a segregated situation. It also means that the specialized knowledge which such agencies have about specific disabilities or impairments can be put to good use in combining efforts with the public recreational service department and other community organizations. As more cooperation exists and better coordination is brought about, the influence of normalization will be more readily felt and mainstreaming will be the outcome. Simultaneously, dual programs can be operated with the assistance of the specialized agencies.

However, unless public recreational agencies are willing to assume responsibility for disabled persons residing in the community—and this requires a change in attitude and policy on the part of recreationists—there is little that will be accomplished. As long as public recreational service departments are incapable of looking beyond the immediate need to offer programs to the unimpaired segment of the population and insist upon the fallacy that specialized agencies can handle all recreational problems of the disabled, this attitudinal change cannot occur. Relying upon the myth of specialized agency omnipotence will not help gain the advantages of inclusion within the public recreational program.

Guidelines for Comprehensive, Recreational Service for the Disabled

In order to effect the best possible recreational services to people with disabilities, public recreational service departments should adopt philosophical orientations which would encompass views of furthering individual self-actualization, expression, and satisfaction through opportunities engaged in during leisure. Parochial orientations should have no part in such a philosophy. Public recreational service departments should be willing and have the ability to provide the broadest spectrum of recreational experiences to disabled persons, which can enhance their lives and make the community a better place in which to live.

1. Every community/public recreational service department should be responsible for implementing a coordinating committee which would become the chief investigative arm of the community for seeing that recreational opportunities are provided to the disabled. This committee would be charged with planning for, contacting recreational agencies or organizations with recreational potential, coordinating facilities, spaces, leadership, and materials to supply disabled persons with the most effective and efficient provision of recreational services possible.

2. Every public recreational service department should make a commitment toward discovering who the disabled individuals are within the community and making sure that there are opportunities for recreational experiences on a demand basis. Additionally,

the department should be prepared to offer both normalized and mainstreaming opportunities based upon personal abilities to perform. Dual programs may be offered by the department to augment special agencies within the private sector or provided when disabilities are so extreme that it will not be advantageous to the disabled individual to participate within the regular program.

3. It must be recognized that disabled individuals may move in and out of the mainstream program at will. Therefore, dual activities must be offered. Particularly is this valid if there are no specialized agencies within the community, regional special agencies, or one special agency whose program and facilities can be coordinated with the public department's efforts.

4. The utilization of volunteers from segments of the population is necessary in order to promote maximized recreational experiences for the recipients of voluntary efforts and the volunteers.

5. The dual program should be carefully planned so that specialized recreational services are provided to disabled persons based upon their particular needs and not upon some stereotyped concept.

6. Recreational activities for the disabled should offer opportunities which provide for active and passive experiences with emphasis upon group-centered situations.

7. The recreational program should offer activities which have a strong carry-over value and lifetime interest. Even though some persons may have limited home opportunities, there should be extensive experiences which afford multiple choices that can sustain the individual.

8. Transportation to recreational facilities or activities should be a concern of public authorities. The disabled person's need for transportation, to take advantage of the department's provision of recreational service, probably hinges upon the ability to get to a public recreational center or other facility. For this reason, every effort must be made to arrange for economical transportation or to supply recreational services to the disabled person by bringing the program to the neighborhood or, perhaps, to the individual. Mobile recreational facilities may be one of the means by which such service can be given.

9. No disabled person should be prevented from participation within the public recreational service offering because of inability to pay fees or charges imposed. In fact, the public recreational service

department is the last resort for any person residing in the community to obtain free recreational opportunities.

10. All architectural or mobility barriers should be removed from public recreational places or facilities. Easily identifiable doors to sanitary facilities, exits, ramps, elevators, construction of toilets, drinking fountains, and other amenity or functional space must be planned with disabling conditions in mind.

11. Operation of dual and mainstreamed activities should be provided on a daily basis, as is the regular recreational program. Disabled persons should not be restricted to some specific time or day or week when they may participate in routine or special recreational activities. Frequency of attendance and daily program schedules should be determined by the needs of participants in relation to the resources of the department and its primary purpose.

12. Policies and programs should be developed which reflect a philosophy that public recreational service is mandated to provide recreational services to all people residing in the community. Each person is entitled to the opportunities provided, based upon his citizenship and not upon his physical, emotional, or mental conditions. To the extent that the public department can offer recreational opportunities to people consistent with their personal needs, it will be fulfilling its professional obligation.

Chapter 20

MOBILITY BARRIERS AND ACCESS

Attitudinal barriers which once discriminated against the disabled individual's right to engage actively in contemporary society have fallen. There is increased awareness of the vitality of this general population within our communities, and advances are being made in alerting the public to the persons with disabilities rights in pursuing a normal life. People are generally more tolerant and receptive of the mainstreaming which integrates the disabled person into community programs. For this to take place, however, other barriers of a more concrete nature must come down. This chapter examines the problems of mobility barriers and their impact on the delivery of recreational services to the disabled.

Types of Disabilities

There are millions of variously disabled persons in the United States. It is unfortunate that only individuals confined to wheelchairs are designated as disabled. This segment of our population has a high visibility because of problems of restricted mobility due to architectural barriers. This group represents a minority of the estimated 50 million Americans with a permanent or temporary disability. Architectural barriers are a constant reminder that society has designed many areas and facilities without thought for the disabled population.

As a humanely oriented profession, recreational service must recognize its obligation to make its resources available to the total population. In most communities the needs of the disabled are often overlooked when it comes to recreational activities. The American Standards Association lists the following basic categories of physical impairments:

1. Nonambulatory disabilities which confine individuals to wheelchairs.
2. Semi-ambulatory disabilities which cause individuals to walk with difficulty. Examples include those with cardiac and pulmonary

problems, and those who require the use of braces, crutches, or canes.

3. Noncoordination disabilities which are due to brain or peripheral nerve injuries.
4. Disabilities associated with the aging process that significantly reduce mobility, flexibility, coordination, and perception.
5. Visual disabilities ranging from total blindness to some impairment of sight which expose individuals to danger.
6. Hearing impairments which might make an individual insecure in public areas because he or she is unable to communicate or hear warning signals.

These broad categories include differing degrees of impairment resulting in temporary or permanent disability.

Mobility Barriers and Federal Law

The moral issue of barriers has been hard fought during the last decade. Advocacy groups have been successful in gaining the enactment of new laws protecting the rights of the disabled. The Architectural Barriers Act of 1968, PL 90-480, was passed to ensure that "any building, or facility, constructed in whole or in part by federal funds must be made accessible to and usable by the physically handicapped." The law proved ineffective until Congress passed the Rehabilitation Act of 1973, PL 93-112, Section 504 established the Architectural and Transportation Barriers Compliance Board in order to insure that federally funded facilities complied with federal law. The Board's task was to "investigate and examine alternative approaches to barriers confronting handicapped individuals particularly with respect to public buildings and monuments, parks and parklands, and so on." Unfortunately, because of reductions in federal aid, this board has not been very effective in bringing noncon-forming buildings into compliance with the law. The Compliance Board has very few inspectors, and investigation into the enormous number of violations is virtually impossible. It has been estimated that the board has potential jurisdiction over some 399,000 federally owned and 52,000 federally leased facilities. Only when a suit is filed by an individual or advocacy group does legal action occur with respect to the existing laws.

In 1975, Public Law 94-142, Education of All Handicapped Children Act, was passed to ensure the rights and educational opportunities for all disabled children. Included in this mandate was a clause stating that recreational activity, as a related service, could not exclude children from wholesome leisure opportunities. The presence of architectural barriers constitutes exclusion from activity for the disabled. (Recreational service professionals must use PL 94-142 and PL 101-336 as a wedge in broadening the impact of the constructive use of leisure by enlarging the scope of programs offered for the disabled in a barrier-free environment.) Attempts to circumvent laws designed to protect the rights of the disabled should not be tolerated by recreationists. Now with PL 106-336, the "Americans with Disabilities Act of 1990," Congress has established a clear and comprehensive prohibition of discrimination on the basis of disability.

Legal Interpretations of Public Laws

Three recent interpretations of PL 94-142 and Section 504 of PL 93-112 illustrate the impact of this legislation on recreational services for the handicapped. They are summarized below.

The first case clarifies the actions to be taken in providing a recreational experience for a child in an appropriate manner without infringing on his or her civil rights:

> *May an individual be carried physically into a swimming pool for instructional or recreational aquatic activities?* An official policy statement from the Office of Civil Rights extending rules and regulations for Section 504 *prohibits* physically carrying or lifting individuals so that they can participate in activities. Carrying an individual is considered circumventing basic requirements of Section 504—i.e., facility and program accessibility. Carrying also compromises the personal dignity of an individual and fosters greater dependence rather than independence.
>
> Prior to the full implementation date for Section 504—June 2, 1980—more lenient interpretations and applications of carrying were permitted during the three year transition period. In some instances carrying still *may* not be a violation—this depends upon the individual and severity of his/her condition. If a condition is so severe that the individual must be carried in a majority of activities, carrying may also be permitted to get him/her in and out of a swimming pool. However, persons responsible for such programs must explore the many ways in which swimming facilities can be made accessible for even the most severely handicapped persons. Involve program participants in decisions that so intimately affect them—they have practical and functional ways of resolving many of the most difficult problems.[1]

---

[1]PL 94-142: Questions and Answers," UPDATE (March 1981), p. 7.

The second case concerns the application of PL 94-142 and the responsibility of teachers to accept disabled children in their classes. This example parallels the problem faced by many public recreational agencies in providing leisure opportunities for disabled persons within the community setting. In the past the issue was ignored and any attempts to integrate disabled persons into regularly scheduled programs were discouraged. Limited use of facilities would be permitted if the disabled individuals would arrive as a group and had supervision accompanying them from an outside sponsoring agency.

The time has come for recreational administrators to stop using the argument that they are not equipped, prepared, or financially capable of implementing programs for the disabled. It is only a matter of time before similar court cases will test the recreationist's position on any resistance in providing accessibility to recreational opportunities. The comparative educational case follows:

> *Should a teacher be forced to accept a student with a disabling condition if the teacher feels unprepared and/or incapable of teaching and reaching such a student?* Basic responsibilities for guaranteeing a free appropriate education to every child with a disabling condition rest with local education agencies; state education agencies also have specific responsibilities in this process. Provisions clearly enunciated in PL 94-142 to assist teachers in accepting and teaching students with disabling conditions include: (1) *comprehensive systems of personnel development* — engaging inservice programs and activities; and (2) *support* for teachers — including such things as resource assistance from various specialists; needed materials, equipment, and devices for students; and appropriate professional materials.
>
> Too often inservice programs and activities have been nonexistent or one-shot affairs; few state and local education agencies have provided the support intended by and included in PL 94-142. In situations where such professional activities have been integral parts of programs, great strides have been made with teachers having little reticence about accepting and teaching students with disabling conditions. Physical educators have been among educational personnel most ready to accept students with disabling conditions into their programs and activities; trends in physical education lend themselves to meeting individual differences among all students, including those with disabling conditions.[2]

The third interpretation deals with the argument that equal treatment in some cases may be discriminatory. During the summer months when

---

[2]"PL 94-142: Questions and Answers," UPDATE (March 1981), p. 7.

beaches become crowded flotation devices are often banned from use in the water. Is this ban discriminatory in its effect?

A ruling by a state recreational and park authority prohibits use of flotation devices in any of its swimming facilities. Many individuals with disabilities are able to take part in swimming activities only if they use flotation devices. Does this make the prohibition against flotation devices discriminatory? This appears to be a Section 504 violation, since the ruling makes swimming activities in these facilities inaccessible and is contrary to program accessibility requirements. Individuals are not only excluded from swimming activities, but are denied benefits from such participation, discriminated against because of disabling conditions, and not provided equal opportunities for participation—equal treatment can, in and of itself, be discriminatory. Flotation devices can make swimming programs accessible and are types of accommodations required by Section 504.

Concern has been expressed about permitting flotation devices for individuals with disabling conditions but not for able-bodied persons. Although this could be viewed as reverse discrimination, such a ruling is perfectly legal and within prerogatives of the state recreation and park authority. Another approach might require only U.S. Coast Guard approved flotation devices for able-bodied persons and whatever type necessary and appropriate for individuals with disabling conditions. Individuals with disabling conditions could be required to alert facility managers and/or life guards on duty about their needs for and uses of flotation devices. this is warranted for safety purposes—both for the individuals using the devices and the other people using the facility.[3]

State Legislation and Mobility Barriers

State legislation has supported federal laws to serve the rights of the disabled in all state financed facilities. Financial hardship is not a reasonable cause for a community to be exempt from making necessary renovations to existing facilities. The law is clear: comply or face the consequences of litigation and extensive negative publicity. It is the responsibility of the recreationist to recognize the recreational needs of all community residents and know how architectural barriers can deny leisure opportunities to disabled persons.

Having examined some of the legal aspects of the problem, we turn now to a detailed discussion of the architectural barriers which prevent the disabled from participating in recreational opportunities. These hindrances will be discussed in three categories: accessibility, design, and safety.

---

[3]William Servedio, "Eliminating Mobility Barriers in Recreational Areas and Facilities," *Parks and Recreation* (November 1979), p. 71.k.

Accessibility

In a research study released by the American Mutual Insurance Alliance, the following advantages of accessible facilities were given:

1. Fewer accidents in buildings reduces losses and rates under health insurance.
2. Wide doors and ramps permit rapid evacuation since standards recommended for aiding disabled persons also meet highest fire prevention standards.
3. Since buildings with aids for disabled individuals have fewer hazards that result in accidents and liability claims, insurance rate reductions may be obtained on public liability policies when architectural barriers are removed.
4. Elimination of barriers reduces chances of work-related accidents so that employers benefit through reduction in compensation insurance premiums.

Significant accessibilty resulting from interior building modifications is not the total solution to increased participation by the disabled in recreational programming. Recreational service departments must attempt to identify areas which restrict participants from entering recreational facilities. The modifications of areas and facilities for recreational use should use the same national standards as those implemented in hospitals, schools, and some public buildings in conjunction with the Architectural Barriers Act of 1968.[4]

Fig. 1. International symbol of access.

Programming. Programming and accessibility go together if success is to be achieved. Elaborate recreational offerings for the disabled population are of no value unless facilities have been properly modified to allow freedom of movement from the adjoining parking lot to the building or recreational area. Unfortunately, while public buildings often display the international symbol of access (Fig. 1), they fail to provide other amenities deemed necessary for full participation in any recreational program. More detailed examples of these other areas will be discussed in the section on design.

---

[4]William Servedio, "Eliminating Mobility Barriers in Recreational Areas and Facilities." *Parks and Recreation,* (November 1979), p. 71.

Accessibility must include all parts of the community if provisions are made to involve disabled individuals with those in regular programming. Getting the different special populations to facilities may be of prime importance in obtaining participation. The extent of offerings is significant, but if these people cannot gain access to the centers, then the activities and the normalization process is worthless.

Transportation. Transportation is the first hurdle that must be surmounted before the more obvious problem of inaccessible buildings. Community recreational agencies have determined that two major problems compound difficulties when providing programs for the disabled. The first is the unwillingness of individuals to be identified as disabled and, therefore, different from the rest of society. This is an issue beyond the scope of this chapter. The second factor is getting those who are aware of the normalization process to and from agency sponsored programs. The recreationist must lead in integrating different populations in activities that are realistic in terms of the abilities of all those who participate at any time.

Mass transportation could solve some of the mobility problems for the disabled if vehicles were modified to accept individuals with some disabilities. In many cities the new kneeling buses and those equipped with a hydraulic lift have been a great help for persons in wheelchairs. It is important to situate recreational facilities in the most centralized area of the community in order to decrease travel time and make it available to the greater number. Unfortunately, most communities do not have very sophisticated transit systems. The recreationist should investigate modes of transportation used by other social service agencies or civic groups in the community. Dial-a-ride may be one answer to inadequate public transportation for the disabled. It may be necessary to convince the community to purchase its own van or perhaps have a local automotive dealer provide one on a lend or lease basis. Elaborate programs and new facilities designed to meet state and federal legislation for accessibility are of no use if the individual cannot get to the location. The first step in the removal of barriers is the provision of reliable transportation for the disabled.

Design

Recreational service agencies receive federal and state assistance which obligates them to make their facilities accessible to the disabled. Extensive renovation of existing recreational facilities is usually not necessary. Slight modifications can enhance the disabled person's opportunities to engage in activities in surroundings that differ little from those used by their peers. Changes do not have to be extensive and costs can be as low as one half of one percent if modifications are included in the original building design.

Preferential Parking. Consideration should be given to the exterior environment immediately surrounding a building or facility. Parking accommodations and their location abutting the main entrance is most important. It is necessary to provide preferential parking spaces in order to avoid the long and arduous trip from the lot to the entry point. Parking areas for the disabled should be reserved only for those who feel that their disability warrants such use. These spaces should be a minimum of 9 feet, with a 4-foot allowance for a wheelchair transfer area provided between every two spaces. Parking spaces for the disabled should be designed so that they are parallel to adjacent spaces.

Signs. Proper placement of signs to inform the general public and the disabled of parking and other accessibility provisions is very important. Simply display the international symbol of access composed of two elements—the wheel chair figure and either a square background or a square border. Provision should also be made to route the disabled over the most accessible and safest path to the building entrance by means of strategically placed signs along the route. The area and direction of pedestrian and vehicular traffic should be clearly delineated to prevent accidents.

Ramps

The accepted method of enabling persons in wheelchairs to mount the curb of the sidewalk leading to a building is by means of curb ramps. Recommended specifications for curb ramps call for a minimum width of 3 feet, with flared sides, and flush with the street level. The curb cut should have a textured surface by means of a raised or abrasive strips to decrease the potential for slipping, but not hinder wheelchair movement. In addition, tactile and visual aids should be provided along ramps to warn visually impaired as well as sighted pedestrians that they are approaching a change in surface elevation. The surface of the ramp should be coated with a bright, iridescent color to warn bicyclists, pedestrians, and motorists that they are approaching an intersection. Low vision users would also benefit from a high contrast between the ramp and the surrounding pavement. This coloration would improve visibility and reduce the possibility of twisting an ankle or tripping on the edge of the ramp.[5]

Max. gradient 17%

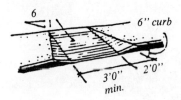

Note:
*avoid "lip" greater than
½" wherever ramp meets
adjacent paving at top or
bottom.*

Fig. 2. A Flared cut curb ramp. *Source:* U.S. Department of Housing and Urban Development. *Barrier Free Site Design* (April 1975).

Inept attempts to comply with the American National Standards Institute (ANSI) specifications may cause more harm than good. A little compliance is like a little knowledge; both can be dangerous if not skillfully employed. Inexperience in construction, design, and maintenance of acceptable modifications in ramp installation is usually obvious in those instances where in-house work crews have completed the work. If workmen do not have the proper instructions concerning ramp specifications, the precision instruments for measuring angles, and the supervisory inspection of the ramp for compliance with the guidelines, then the project's effectiveness is questionable.[6]

Park and Playground

Ramping can be designed into different types of recreational areas and facilities. Proper placement of ramps in a park can open use of facilities not usually available to the disabled allowing ease of access. In most cases, the changes would be welcomed by the general public. The construction of ramps is not an attempt to eliminate all steps in the recreational area. Ramps simply provide an alternative to those individ-

[5]William Servedio and William McLeod, "Problems of Accessibility," *Journal of Physical Education and Recreation* (June 1980), p. 36.

[6]Ibid., pp. 37 and 38.

uals who have difficulty climbing steps. The designs should allow for ramps and steps to be built alongside each other (Fig. 3).

and should follow the accompanying construction guidelines.

MAX. LENGTH 30 FEET BETWEEN LANDINGS

18"

MAX. GRADIENT 8.33%

12

Figure 3. Outdoor Ramps. *Source:* U.S. Department of Housing and Urban Development *Barrier Free Site Design* (April 1975).

Guidelines for Construction of Outdoor Ramps

1. Plant materials should be located so that shadows do not prevent sun from melting snow and ice on ramp surfaces.
2. Provide minimum average of 5 footcandles light at all ramp and stair locations.
3. Ramp widths vary according to design situations. Preferred minimums are:
   One-way ramp: 3 feet minimum width
   Two-way ramp: 6 feet minimum width

4. Maximum length between upper and lower landings should be 30 feet. (Fig. 4 illustrates four types of ramping systems that can be used in parks and playgrounds.)
5. Handrails should extend a minimum of 18 inches beyond top and bottom of ramp.
6. Maximum gradient (slope) should be 3.33 percent.
7. Maintain 5 feet minimum clear space at both top and bottom of ramp.

The use of circulation patterns, ramped bridges, raised sand areas, climbing timbers, and rocking bridges are some of the innovative ideas that can be incorporated into existing play areas. This type of design would also be helpful to mothers pushing baby carriages and to youngsters pulling a wagon or riding a tricycle.

Swimming Access

Lack of accessibility to swimming areas, a problem long ignored, has denied the disabled the opportunity of cooling off during hot summer days. Swimming can be a very pleasurable experience for this population because of the sense of freedom found in the fluid environment, especially with the aid of flotation devices. The enjoyment can be heightened if the pool water is slightly heated. The warmth of the water adds a sense of security to those venturing into a pool for the first time.

Pools. Fig. 5 shows a pool designed for the disabled which allows entrance by either a ramp or steps. Since the wheelchairs are constructed of plastic material the individual can be wheeled right into the pool without the need of a mechanical lift or physical assistance by another person. Once in the pool the wheelchair can be removed if the individual transfers to the underwater bench or uses a flotation device for support. Handrailings are obviously an important part of ramp design and should always be included. A design eliminating the typical wall ladder and replacing it with ramps and steps would be most beneficial for the elderly, the obese, the temporarily disabled, and others. Fig. 4 illustrates four types of ramping systems that can be used in parks and playgrounds.

Guidelines for Pools

1. Floats and pavement markings should clearly warn swimmers of water of increasing depth.

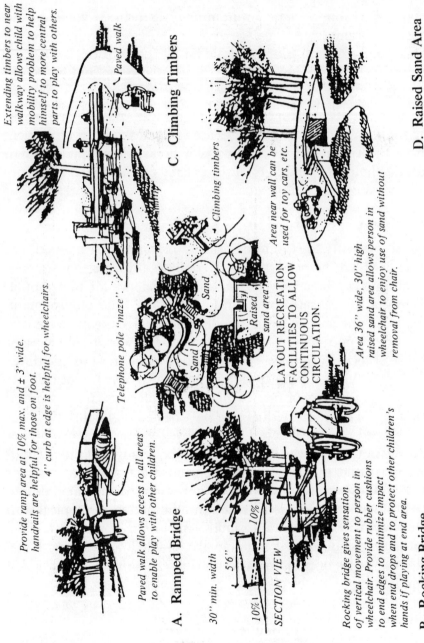

Extending timbers to near walkway allows child with mobility problem to help himself to more central parts to play with others.

Paved walk

C. **Climbing Timbers**

Climbing timbers

Area near wall can be used for toy cars, etc.

D. **Raised Sand Area**

Provide ramp area at 10% max. and ± 3' wide. handrails are helpful for those on foot.

4'' curb at edge is helpful for wheelchairs.

Telephone pole "maze"

Paved walk allows access to all areas to enable play with other children.

Sand

Sand

Raised sand area

LAYOUT RECREATION FACILITIES TO ALLOW CONTINUOUS CIRCULATION.

A. **Ramped Bridge**

Area 36'' wide, 30'' high raised sand area allows person in wheelchair to enjoy use of sand without removal from chair.

30'' min. width

5'6''

10%

10%

SECTION VIEW

Rocking bridge gives sensation of vertical movement to person in wheelchair. Provide rubber cushions to end edges to minimize impact when end drops and to protect other children's hands if playing at end area.

B. **Rocking Bridge**

Fig. 4. Types of ramping systems. *Source:* U.S. Department of Housing and Urban Development, *Barrier Free Site Design* (April 1975).

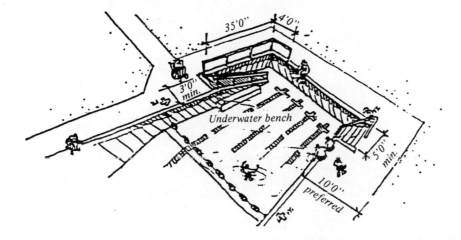

Fig. 5. Recommended pool design. *Source:* U.S. Department of Housing and Urban Development. *Barrier Free Site Design* (April 1975).

2. All paving should be nonslip and nonabrasive to bare feet.
3. Provide ramp entrance for disabled to enter pool. Ramp should be at maximum 10 percent gradient. Surface should be nonslip and have a curb at edge. Handrails should be provided on both sides at 36 inches height.
4. Provide stairs wherever possible rather than a ladder. Stairs are more easily negotiated and can be used to sit upon if wide enough.
5. Provide underwater bench for resting upon. Location should prohibit other swimmers from jumping from above. Use rounded edges throughout.

Fig. 6 illustrates the construction of an outdoor recreational swim area suitable for lakes. Accessibility from bathhouse or parking lot is achieved by constructing a paved walkway to the lake edge and beyond. The platform at the end of the path allows the disabled person to remain in the wheelchair in a half-submerged position, thereby affording maximum participation in the water. Safety precautions have been designed into the facility to prevent individuals in wheelchairs from rolling off the ramps.

In designing ramps for any facility, the maximum gradient for an extended length should not exceed 1:12. That means that for every twelve feet covered, there should be only a one foot increase in elevation. Ramps utilizing this ratio should not exceed 30 feet in length (see Fig. 7). Additional specifications for making buildings and facilities accessible

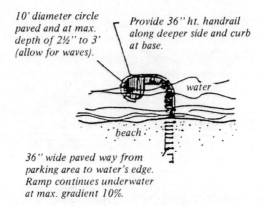

10' diameter circle
paved and at max.
depth of 2½" to 3'
(allow for waves).

Provide 36" ht. handrail
along deeper side and curb
at base.

water

beach

36" wide paved way from
parking area to water's edge.
Ramp continues underwater
at max. gradient 10%.

Fig. 6. Design of an outdoor swim area. *Source:* U.S. Department of Housing and Urban Development. *Barrier Free Site Design* (April 1975).

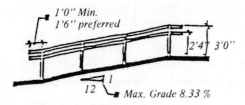

Note:
Length of ramped walk should be
adjusted to slope of particular lake
profile. (10% max. gradient) and should
consider size of anticipated waves.

1'0" Min.
1'6" preferred

2'4" 3'0"

1
12
Max. Grade 8.33 %

Fig. 7. *Source:* U.S. Department of Housing and Urban Development. *Barrier Free Site Design* (April 1975).

can be obtained from the American National Standards Institute, Inc., 1430 Broadway, New York, N.Y., 10018.

Signs and Signals

Signs must be designed with care. People with vision impairment may have trouble identifying storage, offices, toilet facilities, or recreational spaces unless readable signs are provided. Elderly people often have difficulty distinguishing bluish-green, blue, and violet colors due to the lens gradually yellowing and filtering out these colors. Similarly, a reddish filter may be encountered as cataracts develop. People with forms of color blindness may have difficulty distinguishing certain shapes if colors are not chosen with care. Red, bluish-green, and reddish-purple create visual problems for people with color discrimination deficiency.

The proper placement of signs can improve traffic flow and decrease unnecessary time and effort in finding the most accessible route to a particular program or facility. Figure 8 depicts some of the signs used to indicate various amenities for the disabled. Signs should also inform the general public as well as disabled persons of any potential hazards. The following general guidelines are suggested by the U.S. Department of the Interior for readable signs for recreational areas.[7]

1. Place signs within easy range of vision and reach.
2. Keep signs free of obstructing branches and buildings.
3. Place signs at a height comfortable for children and seated/standing adults. Use consistent mounting height and location.
4. Greatest readability is achieved through the use of light-colored characters or symbols on a dark background.
5. Raised characters should be at least 5/8 in. (16mm) high but no higher than 2 in. (50mm) and raised at least 1/32 in. (0.8mm) off the background to be "legible" to blind or partially sighted persons. Symbols or pictographs on signs should be raised at least 1/32 in. (0.8mm).

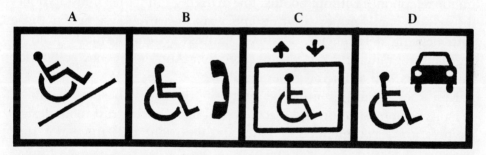

Fig. 8. Standard signs indicating accessibility to facilities for the physically handicapped. (A) Ramp. (B) Telephone. (C) Elevator. (D) Parking.

6. Raised characters should use standard alphabet and arabic numerals; the majority of people with severe visual impairments do not read Braille.
7. Use a precise and clear message.

---

[7]*A Guide to Designing Accessible Outdoor Recreation Facilities,* U.S. Department of Interior, Washington, D.C. (January 1980), p. 51.

Doors and Entrances

The purpose of door hardware is to enable the user to open the door with minimum effort. Frequently, disabled persons are unable to apply strong mechanical leverage because of the height at which the door handle is placed. Designing the handle to accommodate extremes in the reach of users is important in a properly planned facility. This may require multiple handles, longer vertical handles, or some other variation.

A primary entrance to buildings or facilities must be suitable for use by the disabled. Directing handicapped persons to the service entrance or freight elevator can no longer be tolerated. The entryway should be a minimum of 34 inches and preferably 40 inches in width to allow unobstructed passage of wheelchairs. A level platform starting approximately five feet in front of the entrance and extending into the building will assist persons in wheelchairs to open the door without difficulty. Electronically operated doors that swing or slide open are desirable, but installation is expensive. Thresholds should be flush with floor to avoid obstructing wheelchairs.

Interior Facilities

Basic factors to be incorporated into the interior of a building are low public telephones without booths; low drinking fountains; nonskid floors throughout; and proper lighting and visual warning systems for those with hearing deficiencies. A public address system normally used in regular programming can also become a backup emergency system for the blind as well as for the general public.

Rest room facilities must be properly designed to spare disabled persons from frustration and discomfort. The following rest room design features are recommended: First, it is important that the toilet stall measure at least 3 by 5 feet and have a door with a 34-inch clearance. Second, the door must swing outward to allow entry and sufficient turning radius for a wheelchair once inside the stall. Third, grab bars should be mounted on both sides of the stall. These are minor modifications which can be easily made in most public rest rooms.

Other interior adaptations are also required. Especially important is the problem faced by the disabled person confined to a wheelchair who attempts to participate in regular programming. The location of the activity will dictate to what degree that person will function within the program. In a wheelchair an individual's height is decreased by

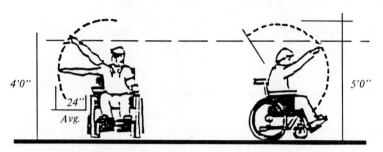

Fig. 9. Average reach limits for adults in wheelchairs. *Source.* U.S. Department of Housing and Urban Development. *Barrier Free Site Design* (April 1975).

approximately one-third while the girth is doubled. This reduces the average reach limits for adults in wheelchairs to those shown in Fig. 9. Note that the maximum reach is 5 feet, but the actual grasping reach for objects to one side of the wheelchair is only 24 inches. This means that the maximum height for switches, levers, handles, etc. must not exceed 4 feet.

Before scheduling an activity with a wheelchair participant the recreationist must consider, among other things, where switches and plugs are located, whether a work table may be too high or recreational materials may be stored out of reach. The necessary adaptations can usually be made at very low cost to the recreational agency.

Spectator Seating

Increased numbers of disabled persons are attending spectator events in public and private facilities. Day trips for institutional residents have become very popular. Clients are taken to various athletic and cultural events in local arenas. For safety and mobility, appropriate space should be provided for wheelchair clients in an area that is level and free from obstruction. The general viewing audience should not be hampered by the location of the wheelchair clients.

Aisles must be kept clear to meet local fire codes, but disabled persons must also have speedy access to exits in the event of an emergency. They cannot be asked to give up their mechanical mobility aids during a performance in order to use the regular seats. If an emergency should occur, it would be very likely that these individuals would be left stranded in their seats. At stadiums and arenas, where there are many aisles and exits, it is important to explain a designated exit route to the disabled spectator before the event begins. Fig. 10 shows wheelchair seating section and access ramp.

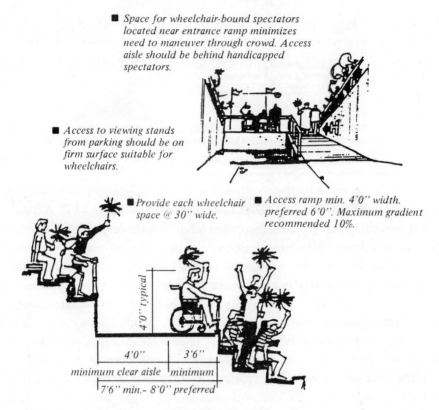

Fig. 10. Wheelchair seating section and access ramp. *Source:* U.S. Department of Housing and Urban Development. *Barrier Free Site Design* (April 1975).

Wherever possible the seating area or space should be sheltered from rain and sun. Long exposure to the sun can be especially dangerous to the disabled client, and the recreationist should be aware of this.

The Department of Housing and Urban Development suggests the following guidelines for seating for the disabled:

1. In seating areas with an excess of 75 seats, a minimum of one seat or 2 percent of the total seating (whichever is greater) should be allowed for wheelchairs.

2. Likewise one seat or 1 percent of the total seating should be designed to accommodate people on crutches or people using walkers.

The recreationist should check facilities for accessibility before taking disabled clientele to large spectator events. Preplanning will avoid the embarrassment of having disabled persons denied entrance because a facility is improperly designed or unsafe. A cooperative effort between the recreational department and the operators of the facility could result in eventual modification and accommodation for disabled persons.

Safety

Safety is an important concern for all participants who use facilities and participate in recreational programs. The recreationist should be aware of what minor design changes to the interior of the facilities can improve safety and help prevent accidents.

Of prime concern are floor surfaces. Whenever possible, nonskid materials should be used in hallways, activity areas, showers, bathrooms, and especially on ramps. The use of carpeting is not always a good solution to the problem of slippery floors. The carpet fiber must be short enough to allow ease of movement by wheelchairs without impeding individuals using crutches, braces, or canes. Shag or long-napped carpeting is not recommended in public buildings having able and disabled users.

Other factors to be considered when planning programs for the disabled are steps, walls, fences, gates, lighting, site furniture, vegetation, walks, intersections, and basic physiological needs. All of these matters must be taken into account when designing new recreational facilities or renovating the old. The improvements made to assist the disabled will prove valuable not only for them but for everyone.

The following guidelines by the Architectural and Transportation Barriers Compliance Board suggest specific ways to initiate and carry on a mobility barriers project in the community. The public recreational service department should be guided by these ideas when initiating a program or correcting existing mobility problems.

Check to see if a committee on barriers exists in the community. If not, run a classified ad in the local newspaper asking interested persons to contact the department in order to form such a committee.

Contact local or area organizations already working with disabled citizens (like the Easter Seal Society) for help.

Ask local civic groups (such as the Lions Club, which has a guide dog project) about sponsoring a drive in the community to make citizens aware of barriers.

Survey the community, from parks to shopping centers, for barriers; encourage local media to publicize your findings.

Plan an access guide to the community as a project of the barrier-free committee and/or a service to the community; the local chamber of commerce may help underwrite its printing and distribution.

Encourage candidates at all levels to openly support a barrier-free environment.

Invite disabled citizens to serve on the committee and to appear on local "speak-out" programs.

Recruit local architects and engineers to help the group monitor local construction to see if access if being considered.

Encourage local administrators, architects, bankers, builders, contractors, developers and educators to work with the department and the committee toward a safer, freer, more accessible community.

Learn about state and local building codes and laws concerning access for disabled citizens.

Try to install a ramp or curb cut at a public building; get local shopping centers to designate more parking areas for disabled persons (many local ordinances require this).

In undertaking to solve the critical problem of accessibility the recreational professional must enlist the aid of the entire community. With the help of many resources within the community as well as assistance from the state and federal government the task can be accomplished.

Chapter 21

VOLUNTARY RECREATIONAL SERVICES

Voluntary organizations are those agencies within the private sector whose primary purpose may be nonrecreational but which nevertheless offer social contacts, facilities, amenities, and services that fill the leisure of people and are, indeed, recreational. It is by selective association through membership that voluntary organizations derive their main strength. The significance of the free association of individuals for engagement in commonly held interests, which have recreational overtones or direct recreational outcomes, cannot be overstated. Almost everyone is a member of at least one voluntary organization of some sort—a congregation, trade union, benevolent association, or interest club. These collectives intensify the potential for recreational pursuit, provide opportunities for social relationships, for contrasts, for contents, for formal and informal instruction, for the development and establishment of standards, and for the encouragement of greater interest, appreciation, and participation. Their derivatives contribute in no small way toward socialization, formation of public opinion, and the spread of information. This kind of voluntary diverse organization around the leisure patterns of people probably encompasses the single most pervasive influence of American social existence.

Voluntary agencies may best be described as being nongovernmental in establishment or affiliation, and financially supported by private contributions (fees, charges, tithes, dues, assessments, philanthropic donations, or solicitations through fund drives). Such agencies are organized under laws which control private enterprise, and they may very well be companies or corporations of a secular or sectarian nature. Their membership is drawn from those persons who are attracted by similar interests, ideas, values, or needs, and who can pay the cost of membership.

Voluntary agencies within the private sector should not be confused with quasi-public agencies, although the latter provide similar services. The quasi-public agency is usually affiliated with some governmental arm, either by direct sponsorship and organization—as a police athletic

507

league, or by being chartered by government—as the American Red Cross. Quasi-public agencies almost always derive their financial support from public giving or other philanthropic donations, but they may receive "seed" money from tax funds for undertaking certain programs which are desired by a governmental agency. Finally, the clientele toward whom the quasi-public agency aims its work is specialized. Technically speaking, anyone may participate in the offerings of a quasi-public agency, but in actuality participants will have been determined from a pre-selected segment of the population and targeted for receiving service. This designated clientele is chosen on the basis of geographic location, economic status, emergency need, or perhaps as a consequence of the accumulation of social or environmental deprivation which the agency is trying to correct.

A college student union is really open to anyone. However, since the facility is situated at the college campus, in actual fact anyone who wants to use the facility must be at the campus. Thus, use is automatically restricted to those who are geographically accessible to the campus. The American Red Cross systematically provides emergency services to victims of disasters. They also serve armed forces personnel. Some of their first aid, water safety, and aquatic programs are open to anybody who can attend. Nevertheless, only those few persons who require such skill development or renewal of certificates attend these courses.

Private agencies, to the contrary, have no affiliation with any public or governmental agencies and do not receive any tax funds for general support (they are a profit-motivated business enterprise), although they may undertake contractual agreements with government for the performance of special programs. This, of course, merely serves to enhance their balance sheets at the end of the year. For the most part, funds are obtained through the imposition of various fees and charges. The clientele to be served is the membership.

Community Based Agencies

Among the community based agencies organized to meet social needs of general concern are those which offer a variety of services of which recreational activities may be incidental, coincidental or intentional. The recreational services that are developed are typically looked upon as the means to some larger end. There are agencies primarily interested in character building, adult education, control of drug and alcohol abuse, ethnicity, religion, social welfare, housing, health care delivery, agriculture, or some other special interest. The range of reasons for the establishment of voluntary associations is as varied as the groups and individuals that compose them. One thing is certain: people band together because they feel that problems specific to themselves may be solved in this manner, or because common interests motivate their association and satisfy personal needs.

Youth Serving Agencies

Youth serving agencies are as varied as individual needs and interests dictate. However, they may be identified as having primary concern for the health, safety, and welfare of young persons by contributing to the development of character, promotion of religious affiliation and values, inculcation of occupational skills, and other positive attributes.

There are nationally recognized organizations which have local outlets, units, branches, or chapters. Some are loosely federated with an umbrella or parent body; others are completely autonomous at the local level while maintaining tenuous ties to a national headquarters as well as utilizing the identifying name.

Whatever general purpose these organizations profess, there is a strong recreational element involved. Whether the program is produced as a nature-oriented skill developer, for physical fitness outcomes, to sharpen social skills and provide instruction, guidance, counseling in the arts, crafts, homemaking, sports and games, or to teach sound safety practices and first aid, recreational activities are a major attraction for drawing membership and participants.

Nonsectarian Agencies

The Boy Scouts of America, Girl Scouts of the U.S.A., Boys' Clubs of America, Girls' Clubs of America, Camp Fire Girls, Future Farmers of America, 4-H Clubs, Police and Fire Department Athletic Leagues, American Youth Hostels, and Future Homemakers of America are all examples of nonsectarian youth serving agencies. Each of these organizations has a specific purpose for being and each has been described in detail through handbooks, annual reports, and other pertinent literature published by the agencies. Abundant information as to their history, philosophy, program, structure, etc. may be obtained from any standard almanac or encyclopedia of social agencies, or by writing directly to the national headquarters of the organization.

Sectarian Agencies

Affiliation or expression of ethical and religious articles of faith with the particular name of the organized institution in the title generally indicates the predilection of this type of voluntary agency. Agencies may be identified with Christian teachings, Roman Catholic doctrine, Jewish concepts, Islamic practices, or with other sects.

The better known sectarian affiliates of the major denominations are the YMCA and YWCA, Catholic Youth Organization, Young Men's and Young Women's Hebrew Association, and the Salvation Army Youth Programs. Countless local denominational churches, temples, and synagogues all supply widely diversified recreational programs for congregants and members based upon need, interest, and financial support. The scope of activities may run from intercultural activities with a religious base to day camping, residential camping, extensive indoor social and recreational facilities for the conduct of classes in the performing arts, art, craft, hobbies, sports and games, physical fitness activities, health promotion, education, and all sorts of interesting and absorbing leisure pursuits. In all, the sectarian agencies offer a broad spectrum of activities designed to enhance personal growth and enrich human relationships.

Special Interest Groups

These are agencies organized around a particular idea or vested interest. They promote activities and enlist the aid and support of a membership body as well as propagandizing the general population through their own publications or sponsored broadcasts and telecasts; additionally, they provide releases to the mass media designed to obtain favorable legislation, public opinion, or financial support. In the course of their operations they may also become the legitimate focus of news.

The special interest lends itself to recreational experience. Millions of people participate in, enjoy, and work for specific interests during leisure. Such activities may include environmental and wildlife concerns, hobbies, athletics, special populations, the fine arts, and performing arts, and literally anything else that can capture the imagination, attract attention, and gain sufficient adherents who will want to initiate a formal structure to represent, promote, and popularize the interest. Special interest organizations have developed around the protection, promotion, or popularization of ethnic heritage (Italo-American, Franco-American,

Polish-American, Spanish-American, German-American, etc.); physical activities such as archery, badminton, baseball, softball, football, bowling, boating, pistol and rifle shooting, golf, tennis, fishing, birding, caving, snowmobiling, hang gliding, railroading, bridge, chess, stamp collecting, book collecting, and collecting of all kinds; disease prevention, and literally the full array of interests which the human mind is capable of conceiving.

The following examples are among the special interest organizations which promote aspects of recreational service or single experiences. Appalachian Mountain Club, U.S. Coast Guard Auxiliary, the Outdoor Boating Club of America, the National Campers and Hikers Association, the National Rifle Association, the Sierra Club, American Camping Association, American Cerebral Palsy Association, Easter Seal Society, National Association for Retarded Children, the Nature Conservancy, the Joseph P. Kennedy Jr. Foundation, Junior Achievement (a business-oriented program for youth), the New York Philharmonic Society, the National Federation of Music Clubs, the National Council of State Garden Clubs, Science Clubs of America, Little League Baseball, Biddy Basketball, the U.S. Lawn Tennis Association. Many special interest groups have counterparts in nearly every country of the world. These voluntary associations foster cultural, social, physical, and intellectual interests which are intensely recreational in content and expectation.

Another kind of voluntary organization which generates delivery of recreational services is the neighborhood, community, or settlement house. These are social group work agencies whose history began with the formation of the Neighborhood guild of New York City in 1886 and Hull House in Chicago in 1889. The early objectives of these organizations were to assist in the assimilation of immigrants, to help the victim of poverty, and to instruct in various social and civic skills. Today, the historical descendants of these institutions have such diverse programs and purposes as providing mental health counseling, education, preventative health services, referral services for many problems, personal enrichment, and recreational services. Aside from neighborhood and settlement houses there are also the Fresh Air Fund (essentially a residential camping network for deprived children from the inner city), and the Children's Aid Society.

Social welfare agencies attempt to satisfy the leisure needs of those persons who reside within the radius of service which the agency is able to cover. Typically, these agencies cater to those living in a poorer socioeconomic area of an urban center. Some 250 such agencies exist throughout the United States in major cities. While not facility bound — there are many outreach programs available — the agencies' greatest impact comes through in-house recreational programs which can take advantage of available facilities.

Benevolent, Protective, Fraternal, and Civic Organizations

Private organizations of these types enroll an aggregate membership in the multimillions. Apart from their specific aims and goals, these associations promote the welfare of their members as well as that of the community at large. This general regard makes their respective contributions of recreational opportunity so important to the national leisure scenario.

Private associations provide all forms of recreational experiences ranging from the simple and informal poker game to secret ritual initiations, meetings, rites, and highly involved and complex tournaments, parades, festivals, fairs, or shows. Such groups may meet in the basement of a church, in an arranged for and scheduled public school room, or in elaborate buildings and centers which they own. The variety of private groups, clubs, and societies runs the gamut of personal involvement. A great deal of time, money, and effort may be spent in belonging to such organizations, or they may merely represent superficial relationships with little meaning beyond an infrequent meeting for continuing social intercourse.

Among the well-known benevolent societies are the Elks, Moose, Eagles, Masons, and Daughters of the Eastern Star. Civic organizations include the Rotary clubs, Lions, Kiwanis, Jaycees (Junior Chamber of Commerce), Federations of Women's Clubs, Civitan, League of Women Voters, Daughters of the American Revolution, Association for Business and Professional Women, the Exchange Club, and many, many more. In addition, there are countless ethnic, historical, and educational collectives whose output of a recreational nature is truly phenomenal.

Employee Recreational Services

Employee recreational services have come to be recognized by management and unions alike as necessary to employee health, morale, and productivity. Depending upon orientation, either corporate or worker point of view, organized recreational services could be used to gain employee loyalty, higher quality performance, enhanced morale, a feeling that someone in the company hierarchy is concerned, and retention within the work force.

From the union aspect, recreational services are provided to show the membership that their union association cares for their off-the-job living needs. Moreover, the union supplies and delivers recreational facilities, various activities, and organizational leadership designed to gain further adherence by the workers to the union cause.

Employee recreational service may be developed by management through the personnel department; by trade unions through their local units; by employees who attempt to organize recreational activities independently of either union or management; and by the establishment of cooperative entities which have representatives of management, unions, or, if a union is not involved, employees who contribute to the administration of any program that ensues.

Whoever provides the organization and administration of employee recreational services, whether management, union, or employee association, there is great similarity of recreational activities offered. The major differences come in terms of facilities and philosophy. Generally, size of firm and centralization of work force have a great deal to do with the kinds of recreational areas or places that will be available. Typically, plant type operations or concentrated employee work location, as at a home office or major office of a company, may be sufficient for management to construct a separate on-site recreational facility. Some of these are quite large with many rooms or expandable spaces for a variety of simultaneously held activities. Facilities may range from a small storage room inside or a horseshoe pitching pit outside to a well-appointed recreational building with meeting rooms, craft shop, auditorium, gymnasium, swimming pool, exercise or health room, and other specialized indoor facilities that would be the envy of most community recreational service departments. Outdoor areas can include court game areas, baseball/softball diamonds, tennis courts, archery and shooting ranges, as well as night illumination for tournament play and practice sessions.

In some instances, a combination of management and employee financial support has resulted in the development of an array of recreational areas that serve the broadest spectrum of leisure requirements. It is not unusual for these arrangements to outfit facilities with equipment, apparatus, supplies, materials, and other contrivances which permit a wide variety of opportunities for employee recreational participation.

Unions, too, provide extensive recreational areas and facilities for their members. During the construction of the Alaska oil pipeline, the Teamsters Union built a number of recreational facilities containing bowling lanes, swimming pools, and other necessary spaces for use by members when they came off the line. Other unions, such as the United Auto Workers, have had a tradition of supplying extensive off-plant recreational centers for their membership.

Recreational Activities

Competitive physical activities have been a mainstay of employee recreational services since the first athletic associations were formed in the late nineteenth century. It is not uncommon for a company of whatever size to field a team in some ball game. Intramural events as well as intercompany games invariably attract participants and spectators. Recently, women's softball teams have been organized and travel far and wide to play in leagues for national championships.

Travel activities for employees is a service that has a long tradition. From the earliest excursions by horse-drawn cart, train, or steamer to today's package deals, employees may obtain group and cut-rate fares to domestic and foreign tourist destinations. Domestic company travel programs criss-cross the country from Disney World to the Golden Gate. Honeywell of Minneapolis, for example, has an extensive travel program for its employees, with special package trips to Russia or Japan among the itinerary choices offered. Hundreds of other companies plan and carry out travel programs costing over $100 million each year. Of course, employees pay for these services, but discounts, group rates, and other merchandising benefits make the prospects extremely attractive and less expensive than could be obtained elsewhere.

The Bayer Aspirin Company of West Germany is another example of the kind of leisure experience open to employees. This firm has an all-employee symphony orchestra that travels throughout Europe giving concerts. Its membership offers expert musicianship, but is drawn from the company. Many Japanese firms offer calisthenic exercises at their places of business to keep their workers fit.

In fact, the entire concept of health maintenance has received intensive scrutiny by insurance companies who offer their own employees cardio-vascular exercise fitness programs in order to prevent heart attacks and maintain worker productivity. The Travelers Insurance Company of Hartford, Connecticut has a variety of such activities and continues to promote its "Older Americans Program" designed to prevent premature deterioration and to maintain individual autonomy. Recreational activity plays a significant role in this project.

Hobby clubs, educational activities, social activities, arts, crafts, music, dances, picnics, theater parties, and a host of other opportunities are available to employees whose company is organized to provide recreational services. Lunch time recreational activities can be short or long depending upon the length of time taken for the noon break. Anything from checkers and chess to handball, horseshoe pitching, volleyball, basketball, or other dual and team games may occupy the leisure of the work force.

Putting out an in-house newspaper may be as much a recreational activity as are other more typical experiences. The reportorial staff can be drawn from among employees. The newspaper may be mimeographed, photostated, or printed. It can run from several to forty pages and may appear daily, weekly, or monthly. A newspaper relies upon the enthusiasm of its staff as well as upon the avidity of its readers. Most company newspapers are weeklies and are lovingly composed of everything that appeals to staff and readership. This may mean editorials, agony columns, recipes, travel notes, promotions, transfers, anniversaries, retirements, marriages, births, deaths, poetry, short stories, anticipated activities, personal profiles, sports events, and so forth.

Organization and Administration

The most convenient recreational arrangement will occur at the place of employment. However, many recreational activities organized for employees can take advantage of whatever community based resources are available. Thus, a local recreational service department may set up an industrial league; and county, state, and federal facilities may be scheduled and used for a number of periodic company activities. Sectarian and voluntary agencies may be contacted for use of their facilities.

Insofar as financial support is concerned, programs and facilities may be underwritten totally by management; by employees through fees, charges, or other assessments; by unions; or by some combination of these possibilities. Furthermore concessions by vending machines or in-plant refrectories may net the employees association a handsome profit, thereby permitting more extensive support for comprehensive programming.

There is no doubt that employee recreational services will continue to expand as the economy begins to recover. It is expected that management will consider human relations an important part of their dealings with employees, and will therefore offer considerable support services to earn the loyalty and productive efforts of the work force. Enlightened management must concern itself with the work environment as well as with off-the-job potentials for employees. Yet they must perform in ways that remove any hint of paternalism.

In some circumstances, employers view recreational services as a public relations ploy aimed at its own work force. Others see such services as improving the company's image within the community, which can result in a more favorable legislation or taxation position.

In not a few cases, trade unions may bargain for the provision of employee recreational services with concomitant facility construction. Sometimes competition for employee loyalty will arise between management and the union. Regardless of the stimulus, the likelihood of expanding recreational services for employees is probable, particularly in large companies with a centralized work force. Moreover, most executives believe that such services contribute significantly to the mosaic of the entrepreneurial system.

PART IV
THE MAKING OF THE
RECREATIONAL SERVICE PROFESSION

Chapter 22

PROFESSIONS AND THEIR IMITATORS

The rendition of the most competent objectively performed skills at the command of the recreationist, with the concept of enhanced individual worth uppermost, is the primary function of the professional practitioner. Self-appraisal and a willingness to learn new techniques when applicable contribute to the professionalization process. The personal desire to develop and maintain contact with advances in the field is an essential characteristic of the professional person. All ethical acts, which devolve upon the recreationist, relating to best practice, applied knowledge, educational pursuit, and humanitarian ideal are the result of the attainment of professionalism. Professionalism is the manner in which certain practices are carried out and the steps taken to ensure that specific standards are being met. It stems from practice within a field which is considered to be a profession or is attaining professional status.

Recreational service can be a significant social force with possible influence upon all persons. Public institutions that render services of a recreational nature, no less than private organizations with historic traditions of service, are outstanding among the long-lived agencies of culture. Nearly every person is touched in some way by the enterprise of the practitioners and students engaged in recreational service. In an endeavor as potentially vast and important to the well-being of people, it is necessary that considerable attention and purposeful thought be given to the occupation and status of those who are recreationists. The effectiveness of service to all people primarily rests upon these professional practitioners. The examination of professionalism in its ramifications and the criteria upon which a profession may be established constitute the main problem to be settled in support of the field.

Recreational Service as a Profession

Any category of practitioners who become concerned about their role and position in society has recourse to seek recognition as a professional group. The more intensive their realization of their social function and obligation, the greater is the aspiration to become a professional. Frequently, leaders of recreational service demand higher standard of personnel and increased professionalization, for they are conscious of the fact that this avenue is the most direct means of securing improvement in the status of recreationists, in their conditions of work, and in the kinds of services offered by the variety of agencies which employ them.

Perhaps the most frustrating question asked is whether or not recreationists are professionals. In order to clarify the position of the practitioner and answer the question, the definition of what a profession is must be offered. If the practice of the recreationist fits the standard by which profession is defined, then the answer is obvious. If for one or more reasons the work of the recreationist does not meet the qualitative criteria, then modification of practice and education would normally be required.

The term *profession* clearly symbolizes a complex of indicators. The recognized professions manifest all or almost all of these factors: they are acknowledged in their preeminence, and are surrounded by other vocations displaying one, some, or few of these features. The vocations that occupy the position of centrality and are thus termed *professions* have certain characteristics that distinguish them from all other types of occupation. The essence of professionalism is intellectual insight applied to the ordinary course of human events, obtained as the consequence of prolonged and particularized education in the acquirement of a specialized technique.

As Carr-Saunders and Wilson have stated so explicitly:

> The practitioners, by virtue of prolonged and specialized intellectual training, have acquired a technique which enables them to render a specialized service to the community. . . . They develop a sense of responsibility for the technique which they manifest in their concern for the competence and honour of the practitioners as a whole—a concern which is sometimes shared by the state. They build up associations, upon which they erect, . . . machinery for imposing tests of competence and enforcing the observance of certain standards of conduct.[1]

---

[1] A.M. Carr-Saunders and P.A. Wilson, *The Professions.* (Oxford: The Clarendon Press, 1933), p. 284.

Characteristics of a Profession

Responsibility. What most singularly distinguishes the profession from other occupations is the concept of responsibility. Responsibility here is defined as the rendition of services in such a manner as to combine good judgment with humanitarian effort and ethical conduct. All professions work with people. The closer an occupation comes to providing services to people directly and the further it remains from working with things, the more it may be likened to the centrality of profession. Thus, humanitarianism becomes the key trait by which the profession is recognized. On one hand, vocations such as engineering or architecture may appear as professions because of the theoretical knowledge and prolonged study necessary to gain proficiency. However, on closer inspection, these fields, although scientifically based and aesthetically formulated, tend to work with the applications of the science to things rather than to persons. They are more concerned with material constructs than with human needs. Law, which is founded upon the study of human institutions and is not scientific *per se,* is basically involved with the problems of individuals and the variety of individual needs which social pressures produce.[2]

Competency. Another mark of the acknowledged professions is the formation of associations, the main objective of which is to appraise and test for the specialized competence necessary in the technique of the field. In the development of the technique that is unique to the field and the responsibility that accompanies the possession of an intellectual competence, there also exists a concomitant need for the maintenance of an ethical code. The association initiated by the professional group has, among its chief aims, the obligation to safeguard the general public and the practitioners through the institution of a register of qualified persons. The register is a minimal set of standards set up and administered by professional personnel of the field. It is the least qualitative measurement of whether or not an individual is competent to function as a member of the profession. More usually than not, it is a quantitative device relating to the educational preparation and experiential background of the individual who wishes to practice.

Ethics. The professional code of ethics, always developed from an association of professional personnel, provides specific behaviors by

---

[2]S.B. Stein, "The Business of Law Need Not Replace the Profession of Law," *The Baltimore Evening Sun* (October 8, 1990), p..

which the professional is guided in practice and enforces the observance of particular standards of conduct. Such a code may delimit acts that are detrimental to the profession, to society, and to practitioners. It may govern a range of actions, from the acceptance of fees for service to the concept of privileged communication between client and professional. In whatever way it is observed and administered, the code of ethics is part of the humanitarian principle that segregates a profession from other occupations.

If a definition of the term *profession* is necessary, then it may be conceived as a vocation in which an affirmed knowledge of some specialized field of learning or science is applied to the ordinary course of human events or to the practice of an art based upon it.

Education

To prepare a person for effective practice, the assimilation and deliberate utilization of special knowledge, not readily accessible to laymen, is necessary. Only by way of a particular series of educational experiences does the recreationist begin to understand the fundamental premises that make up professional responsibility. In these basic assumptions and hypotheses are contained the insights of method and technique. But beyond the surface promise of *how* an effective performance is derived are the reasons *why* specific functions are instituted and maintained. In many instances, nonprofessional persons, skilled and competent volunteers for example, can perform effectively for the benefit of those participating in the program. They may have skill or talent in any of the activities on which the total program is constructed. These same individuals can make up a cast for a play, paint or draw a picture, repair a faulty gadget, or serve in many utilitarian ways. They may perform effectively without recognizing the sequences of actions taken nor having any grasp of why they do the things that they do. The recreationist, on the other hand, needs to know certain skills that will be used within the program and the related needs of human beings upon whose satisfaction these procedures are based. The professional practitioner must be more than routinely competent. Understanding the underlying principles and the foundations of the necessary standards and skills of performance is essential.

Thus, it follows that a practitioner who knows only methods or techniques of application without understanding the rationale for the practices merely follows a trade and is not engaged in a profession. The practitioner who has little to recommend but experience without education may know many techniques that allow achievement of objectives with tremendous results, and still have no concept of what has been done to achieve the desired consequences. The recreationist not only has the ability to perform successfully, but also has a profound knowledge of subject matter pertaining to the nature of individual differences and human personality, social values, personal growth and development, mass communication and the learning process, human ecology, and an unqualified comprehension of the foundational concepts and theoretical insights that are used to formulate organization and administration of agency services.

The recreationist is not professional merely by reason of knowing specific methods for programming, leading activities, or organizing group experiences. The professional practitioner must have conceptual insight concerning the essential facts and philosophy on which the accomplished techniques and standards for action are based. Conceptual understanding is not simply an abstraction without practicality. It is vital to the practitioner on eminently utilitarian grounds. Theory provides the foundation for improved practice and for handling extraordinary situations. Standard operating procedure may suffice for routine assignments, but in extreme conditions or when exceptional instances demand resolution, only the insight gained by intellectual command of fundamental assumptions allows enough impetus and facility to change outdated or unreliable techniques and innovate. Thus, conceptual insight makes possible the type of practice in which unusual and exceptional circumstances are met by creativity and experimentation. The practitioner who only memorizes rules instead of learning to understand the guiding theoretical concepts on which the rules are founded runs the risk of becoming rigid and static. Routine skills and standard techniques do not always offer the correct methods or answers, particularly when new conditions require new methods and answers. As Phenix has so aptly stated:

> Dynamic and flexible practice is possible only when the guiding theoretical framework is comprehensive enough to include unusual and novel circumstances and to suggest promising avenues for experimentation. The educator who has merely learned to follow the rules is lost in cases where there are no rules or where they give the wrong results. Only the professional who has sufficient theoretical understanding to modify old procedures and create new

ones is in a position to turn such emergencies into opportunities rather than failures.[3]

If such an assumption is correct, and there is no reason to disbelieve it, then it also must be valid that the professional education of recreationists cannot be considered satisfactory when the preparation deals only with program techniques and management practices. To be fully effective a mandatory inclusion of studies that offer basic instruction in the behavioral sciences, learning process, and social milieu must be provided. Of particular significance is knowledge of the primary historical, social, and cultural facts pertaining to recreational service, and of psychology, philosophy, and those inter-disciplinary studies which can offer theoretical fundamentals in the applied sciences. To these prerequisites the critical aspects of professional education for recreationists must contain the following essentials: (1) a high degree of knowledge and demonstrable skill in several areas of program activities; (2) a thorough understanding of recreational service, its philosophical rationale, ability to analyze the component concepts upon which it is based, and ability to interpret intelligently and relate recreational concepts to other spheres of human endeavor; (3) the development of the ability to communicate, to transmit as well as to receive ideas for the furtherance of human effectiveness through recreational achievement; and (4) the mastery of the theoretical foundations and validated facts upon which standards of practice are built and through which the advancement of improved recreational service may be effected.

Humanitarianism

As America has, in the modern era, progressed within the democratic political frame of reference, it has also continued to move toward an interdependence which is intrinsic in urbanized culture. The goal of society has, therefore, been focused increasingly on the provision of individual development and utilization of personal capacities which can contribute to the entire community and society as a whole. Today's professions are chiefly concerned with development of the individual rather than with functions that merely promise survival. It is recognized that the development of the individual and all humanity grows out of knowledge of people. In order to serve society, the profession must serve each person. Logically, recreational service, which is directly committed to the well-

---

[3]P.H. Phenix, *Philosophy of Education* (New York: Holt, Rinehart and Winston, 1958), p. 159.

being of people, has begun to focus attention upon highly skilled services as well as to show a concern for the individual being served. Ethical obligation, applied intelligence, and professional assistance are oriented to the individual within a given environment in terms of what the person needs and what he or she wants.

The professions are established primarily to serve humanity through the organization and administration of services to advance individual welfare. They all deal with people, serving them as individuals, in relation to human well-being. The professional practitioner is required by laymen, because of specialized competence essential to the needs of the recipients. Thus, in providing services to people, the practitioner does things with and for them. In receiving these services, the layman reacts in relation to personal values, and how he or she feels about the professional. Historically, the professional practitioner has been vitally interested in offering services in valuable ways, thus enabling the recipient to profit physically, mentally, socially, intellectually, and culturally from the elements received.

In addition, the practitioner is sought after because the individual has specific problems for which personal resolution is impossible. The professional, with technical skill and competence, is able to offer a solution to the person who may not have the knowledge required or the personal adequacy to mitigate difficulty. The professionals normally specialize in working with persons under these circumstances. The rendition of professional functions is predicated on the basis of support for the recipient. No service can ever be made which tends to subvert the individual's ability to make personal decisions. If through the provision of professional acts the individual's capacity for self-management is diminished, then these acts lose their effectiveness and assume a threatening guise. As Towle has written:

> Furthermore, respect for the total person in every profession implies that concern for one area of his welfare must not ignore his general welfare. Respect for the integrity of the individual implies that, in administering to his physical health, we take into account his mental and emotional needs and responses and that, in administering to his intellectual needs, we do not ignore the physical or social self. Respect for the integrity of the person implies also that his rights to self-determination within social limits be regarded, that individual differences be appreciated — in short, that the professional relationship be oriented at all times to his identity as a person with rights as well as obligations.[4]

---

[4]C. Towle, *The Learner in Education for the Professions As Seen in Education for Social Work* (Chicago: The University of Chicago Press, 1954). p. 4.

Nonpredictability

A subcriterion which marks a profession is the factor of nonpredictability. To the extent that the practitioner cannot predict, with any accuracy, the outcome of the confronting problem while working with people, the closer the approximation to professional vocation. The more confused and dimly perceived the consequence of the service offered by the practitioner, the surer it is that he/she belongs to a profession. Why is this true? Fundamentally, this proposition stems from the humanitarian concept, which is the single most important segregational standard between a profession and any other vocation. Other occupations may approach the centrality of a profession through prolonged education, codes of ethics, or organization, but the real professions, from the ancient ones of law and medicine to the youngest ones of education, social work, and recreational service, have these in common, plus the responsibility of working with people.

It may be seen that members of occupations that work with things (any of the trades, sales personnel, advertising personnel, engineers) may provide a service to people by offering them food, clothing, shelter, transportation facilities, and amenities. However, to render these functions, things rather than people become significant and uppermost in the view of these venders. Tradesmen (carpenters, masons, plumbers, electricians, repairmen) work with things; sales and advertising personnel sell things or promote things; amenities personnel offer tangible services which may be listed as things. Even architects or engineers work with things. The same is true for chemists, pharmacists, and military personnel. All members of these occupations work with material, equipment, facilities, or formulae whose consequences can be predicted with certainty. They do not work with unknown factors, they deal with something, the results of which can be predicted with mathematical precision. Unquestionably, some of these fields are going to be involved with problems that baffle the mind, but only for a brief moment, and then merely because additional knowledge has not been added to the archives of the field. When knowledge is acquired, complete predictability results. There is no confusion; there is less concern with unknown factors. Every act is seen with clarity and understanding. The technique is faultless. Step by step the work goes forward until a finished object or performance has been accomplished. Recent genome mapping and the breaking of the DNA code are a case in point. Such is not the situation with those fields primarily working with human beings. Each individual brings a separate problem or group of problems. Each person, because of individuality, is unique in the universe, and has an infinite capability to react in ways that cannot be predicted with any degree of accuracy. No one can ever say with certainty what any human being will do under any given set of circumstances in any given environment. Thus, it may be stated that the nearer to absolute predictability one gets in a vocation, the further one is from employment in a profession.

This idea may engender some protest from occupations that wish to be considered as professions, but if one assumes that humanitarianism is the chief characteristic of a profession, then nonpredictability follows. It also may be said that the typical profession exhibits certain distinct factors, and that other occupations approximate this condition of complex characteristics more or less intensely, because they have some of the same factors in common with the acknowledged professions. Nevertheless, the denominator of humanitarianism indicates how closely each field approaches professionalization, owing to the possession of these traits in complete or fragmented form.

Variability

In much the same manner as the factor of nonpredictability testifies to the remoteness or approximation of a vocation to the central tendency of a profession, so too does the feature of variability. In this sense, variability has to do with the variety of problems which confront the practitioner during service delivery. Those occupations dealing with finite objects or material goods have comparatively less variables to contend with in solving problems, whereas those occupations confronted by a great range of variable factors come closer to the infinite variety faced by the professions in dealing with the human factor.

Machinists, for example, have few variables in their work. They are basically concerned with the issues of stress, tolerance, malleability, rigidity, fissility, tensile strength, and other structural facets. These factors are readily accounted for, and whatever compensation is necessary can be adequately measured for a completed product to take form. Recreationists, on the other hand, have an infinite array of endless problems which they must face as they deal with people. The needs, desires, wants, and problems of persons coupled with the unknown of human behavior evoke an unlimited set of variables. There are no sequential steps that will solve a similar problem in one or more persons each time. What may work well for one individual may fail with the next under identical conditions. The technique utilized may be faultless, but there can never be a guarantee that it will succeed even though it has been successful at a prior time. No formulae have yet been created which can determine exactly the reactions of human beings.

In all probability, those occupations that tend to few variables have a lesser proximity to professions, which have an infinite complex of variables with which to operate. The more scientifically oriented and less personalized the occupation, the further it is from true professional status. Vocations that are dehumanized to the extent that inanimate objects are their sole concern or in which only a science is applied have less of the profession in their calling. Vocations based upon scientific knowledge which is specifically applied to the every day lives of people or where knowledge is founded upon human institutions and then made responsible to the service of humanity are, in all likelihood, professions.

Technique

It has developed that technique or special competence, obtained as the result of intellectual preparation, is one of the chief distinguishing factors of professions. The possession of a technique gives the practitioner a knowledge denied to most other people, or endows him or her with skills which the average individual does not own. Does the recreationist possess some special competence? Do they have a particular technique or knowledge which the average person does not have? Opinions diverge quite sharply on this point. From one point of view, the recreationist not only does not need special competence, but does not have any. Any person can perform the functions of recreationists, it is said. Volunteers have many skills that are used in a great variety of activities within the recreational service program, and they are not specifically prepared in professional curricula. Therefore, the recreationist cannot pretend to possess any exceptional skills, competencies, or knowledge which the average intelligent individual does not have.

The supposition on which this non-professional concept of recreational service rests is that recreational service is made up of activities which are so natural that it requires nothing more than ordinary good sense to organize and administer them. The commonly held fallacy that it is not necessary to teach a child to play because it is instinctive is part of this antiprofessional tendency. Those who oppose professional preparation and deny a specialized technique do so on grounds that anyone who is of at least average intelligence, by daily association with the problems and responsibilities of the recreationist position, will automatically learn all functions and solutions by observation and trial and error.

In contrast, the assumption upon which the professional view of recreational service is based is that specific knowledge and special skill are vital in order for the recreationist to be competent. Simple association and intelligence are not sufficient for the organization and administration of recreational services. The orientation and philosophy to which the student is exposed in professional education programs develop feelings and attitudes that will make it possible to think and function appropriately and effectively. Disciplined thinking, increased capacity to perform competently, objective service to people, understanding those with and for whom one works, a high degree of skills, and the knowledge to organize and operate a comprehensive program of recreational services do not take place in any way but by deliberate design. The best environment for obtaining technique is not a matter of common knowledge, and the average individual has neither the time nor the guidance to master the knowledge or functions of the recreationist.

The affirmation of recreationists to special knowledge and technique can be validated through the generally accepted, reliable, and thoroughly tested department of learning of applied social science which makes up professional preparation. The consequences of utilizing professional leadership as opposed to non-professionals in practice should amply substantiate superior achievement. Special competence through professional education invariably produced a categorically superior practice to that accomplished by persons without this particular technique and knowledge.

Professional Association

To this point, attention has been focused upon the factors on which professions are founded. But a special competence may be an actuality and individuals may practice it, and still there is no profession. A profession can exist only when a technique is practiced in common and a relationship is developed between the practitioners. These ties of commonality can be structured in only one way—that of a definitive association.

The professional society has a fourfold function. The first is the testing of professional competence. This is not to be construed as professional education. Far from educating the future practitioner, a profession, through its various committees within the society, has inaugurated an examination mechanism to evaluate what the higher institutions of education have taken responsibility for, that is, technique as a consequence of prolonged intellectual preparation. Usually, the professional group studies, evaluates, and then imposes certain minimal standards for competence which would-be practitioners must attain. Tests of competence have generally been of the written, oral, and in some instances, the practical type, presided over by practitioners.

Examinations are the accepted method of testing for special competence and theoretical insight. True professions rarely admit unexamined individuals to membership. However, on occasion, special dispensation is granted to a particularly outstanding practitioner who has not had the advantage of technical study. This rear door approach to membership in a professional association is one that can be used infrequently at best, and then only with the highest discretion.

The second function of association is one of discrimination. Any exclusiveness attached to a profession is practiced with the sole idea of shutting out the incompetent. For no reason other than to expose those individuals who cannot measure up to minimal standards for qualification as practitioners can exclusiveness be justified. When an individual is incompetent, it is primarily up to the professional society either to bring pressure to bear upon those persons so that they may not inflict their incompetency upon a trusting public, or to cause whatever legal action is required to disallow that individual from continuing in the profession. Recreational service has never proceeded to this action, probably because it has no power to prohibit local jurisdictions and private agencies from employing incompetents. Beyond this, there is an added factor of lack of licensing by state bodies which would force would-be practitioners to meet minimal standards for practice in the field. Only therapeutic recreational service has begun to impose national testing on would-be practitioners for certification purposes. This should eventuate in formal licensings.

Professions regulate membership conduct and practice through a procedure called registration and certification. The register, then, becomes a statutory governing body for the profession, empowered by the membership and the executive to draw up certain standards of practice, education, ethics, and personal behavior to which all practitioners must adhere. Initially, registration makes no distinction between those who came on it because of their achievements, both educational and experiential, and those who are accepted by virtue of being practicing workers.

However, once a specific period of time has elapsed after the register is in effect, only those individuals who can demonstrate reasonable attainment through educational preparation, practice, and testing are accepted and certified.

Recreational service has attempted to promote registration of qualified persons as an initial action prior to more stringent regulations being effected. At first, registration is an association's private means of indicating acceptable and qualified practitioners. However, registration is a forerunner of national certification and eventual state licensing procedures. Registration implies certification, or the authentication, of the recipient's assertion of special competence. With special competence to perform, there is also the suggestion of a grant of privilege to those who are registered. Privilege carries with it certain immunities and responsibilities. Recreationists must perform at the highest level of competence to safeguard patrons from injury or damage to property. When recreationists function in the most responsible manner in a given situation, concomitant rights should be accorded. By granting these privileges, the state should rightly expect recreationists to assume full responsibility for their activities as professional persons. In order to protect its constituents from misfeasance or malpractice by persons operating in recreational service without competence to practice, the state can institute licensing procedures. Thus, a licensing system developed by state government would necessarily have to turn to the professional association for criteria on which to base the minimal standards applicable for the competent performance of the recreationist.

Some suggest that certification and licensing merely lead to mediocre performance because such procedures rely upon having the "right" credentials. Credentials, meaning an appropriate education, with all that such experiences imply. Those who feel that the certifying process is designed to create a monopoly of the average, by screening out potentially great practitioners, view exclusion as the means whereby ability rather than practice is the standard. Personally, I view all certification processes as the way to prevent unqualified persons from practice. If skilled practice only required a warm and empathetic personality, the entire credentialing procedure could be abolished. Everyone with a penchant for working with others would do so. But professional practice requires more than a willingness to serve and have a pleasing personality. It requires, also, a knowledge base and the acquisition of relevent skills by which the service is delivered. The process of certification presumes that individuals have the character traits necessary to serve others and tests the knowledge that has been acquired to determine pertinent skills and theory. It serves as the floor, not the ceiling, by which practitioners will be selected. Far from acclaiming mediocrity, professionalization sets the bases for future practice by excluding those who are not educated. The premise rests on the ideal of covering in those who have mastered the facts, skills, and philosophy of the field and paves the way for a standard of practice below which no licensed person may go. This is to raise the level of practice not to lower it to a regressive mean.

But who shall say whether or not an individual is competent to practice in the field? What are the minimal standards which any potential recreationist should obtain prior to presentation for induction into the field? Actually, the professional association is in the best possible position to ascertain the adequacy or readiness of a practitioner to meet any licensing requirements which a state body would administer. It can establish criteria of performance by which the potential practitioner can be measured. However, this is, at best, only a partial answer for creating acceptable standards to which the potential recreationist must conform. The key to competency lies with professional preparation in recognized institutions of higher education. To the extent that the professional preparation offered by universities and colleges is the same in terms of studies and content, the licensing agency as well as the registering body may find that education can be made to perform an initial screening function in determining practitioner competency.

Whatever examinations may be utilized to evaluate competency, the association's certification board may require certain educational qualifications before allowing the would-be practitioner to advance to any other practical demonstration of competence. The board could, of course, exempt the recipient of a baccalaureate degree with a major in recreational service education from some of the examinations. Nevertheless, the association would have to delegate some of its authority to the pertinent faculties of universities where professional curricula exist. A council whose representatives are selected from accredited institutions would then be able to formulate national criteria by which professional programs could be standardized. In this way, the board would be assured that insofar as intellectual insight and theoretical knowledge were concerned, each would-be practitioner who held an appropriate degree from a recognized college must have the same minimal educational background and could then be tested fairly with all other applicants for induction into the field.

As of November, 1990, the first national test for certification of therapeutic recreationists was initiated. It stands to reason, therefore, that weak programs of recreational service education undermine the reputations of all colleges and universities. A profession of recreational service with poor admission and scholastic standards critically reduces the effectiveness and quality of professional preparation at all levels. Lack of explicit accreditation standards for recreational service education permits any institution to engage in the preparation of potential practitioners. Local loyalties and political considerations being what they are, it is almost impossible to control the quality of educational preparation for recreational service except through a nationwide system of voluntary accreditation, which gives support to high quality institutions and calls attention to those which have either paper curricula or fail to come up to standard. Only in this way can evaluating bodies be assured of some common learning technique to be equitably distributed among those who seek employment in recreational service. Without the basis of professional education as a fundamental premise for further testing, the entire concept of professionalism must be abandoned.

Professional Access. To offset the possibility of poor preparation, the council for accreditation would surely sanction only those institutions offering professional courses conducted by qualified faculty as well as offering research, library, affiliated, and other necessary resources for the complete education of future recreationists.

The primary function of a registration certification is to control access into the profession, on the presumption, of course, that employing bodies want to hire individuals who are certified as competent to perform the duties for which they are paid. To administer this function the board of registry must have the authority to maintain the register and the right to enroll, or to refuse to enroll, a name upon it. With this authority, its supervision over entry would be final. It must be understood, however, that the board of registry would ultimately be responsible to the executive body of the professional association. In establishing criteria for entry, the recognition of diplomas from accredited universities as admission to the register, after an initial period of practical experience has been achieved, would form the chief means of induction.

The essential responsibility of the registration authority is to ensure the effectiveness of licensing procedures. The wherewithal to encourage institutions of higher education to broaden the preparatory program so that the disadvantages of early specialization could be overcome would also be made the province of this authority. This might be elicited by testing for a high standard of general education in any examination process to be given. Beyond this, it could stimulate the extension of both theoretical and practical education within the university itself and promote practical field work as part of the professional curriculum.

Licensing. When the state finally recognizes the value of contributions made by certain professions and occupations as being necessary to the general health, education, or welfare of its constituents, then it moves to safeguard the public by requiring that specific standards be maintained. In some instances, the state requires licensing procedures as a simple means for taxing purposes or in order to be better able to police the dispensation of goods and/or services which might be harmful to the public. However, when the state becomes aware of a field's service to people, it may require that certification be established to ensure a minimal standard of competence among those who practice. If this step is taken, and licensing procedures are initiated, the state automatically confers prestige upon the field and provides special privileges to it, for example, exclusive use of occupational name and practitioner title. The process of licensing is the best method by which the status of an occupation and its practitioners can be raised. Because the grant of privilege and prestige attaches to the field so endowed, the state also acts to supervise professional preparation to ensure competent functioning. Licensing to ensure professional competence means common recognition by the state, the general population, and other professional peer groups. Through this procedure, the field with licensed practitioners obtains many rights, among which are sole utilization of a professional title or designation, privileged communication, and so on.

Certification. But certification itself, rather than licensing, is the prerogative of the professional association. Not only the public is hurt when incompetents attempt to function in a profession, but the recreationist and the entire field of recreational service are penalized in terms of loss of public confidence and a downgrading of status. Thus, it is vital that admission to professional prestige and recognition be policed by the professional society itself as it is concerned with the potential practitioner's capability. In fact, only professionals are really competent to determine whether or not an individual is qualified to practice in their field. A system of accreditation for institutions offering professional preparation in recreational service education, an internship program for those who successfully pass the curricula, and some form of rigid induction examination prior to registration and employment should be the standardized procedure in order to produce certified recreationists.

Codes of Conduct. The third important responsibility of the professional body is the establishment of a distinctive code of ethics, meaning a salient ideal of conduct, expressed in several different rules, and prescribed, no doubt, by varied authorizations, but founded upon two broad principles which pervade the professional realm. The first principle is the protection and probity of the profession itself. The second principle is the ideal of objectivity in service.

When an individual becomes a member of a profession, there is undertaken a responsibility to perform honorably and faithfully. An obligation to serve the interests of the public assumed. The responsibility of the professional to perform to the best of his or her ability, without prejudice against the recipient, is generally conceded in all professions. The only question here is what is in the best interest of the recipient. All other factors are subordinate to this paramount issue. Thus, the recreationist must employ all personal skills and knowledge to provide the best possible service to those who would partake of them. Recreational service will gain the confidence of the public which it serves when its members abide by the faithful performance of their special skills and collectively administer whatever censuring and regulatory machinery may be required to ensure compliance. Incompetents must not be allowed to practice nor can the profession allow its membership to become lax in the attainment of high standards of skilled performance. This concept is basically one of self-preservation. Without it, the public would soon consider the recreationists with contempt. In order to gain public esteem and achieve status, the principle of internal security should be operable in the association. It is largely a professional society's task to maintain an assured standard of ethical practice. Sanctioning conduct of recreationists is necessary if only for the advantage which accrues to the field as a whole.

Objectivity. Professional objectivity is the other foundational factor upon which rests the determination of ethical practice. The professional person has an essential obligation toward the agency's clientele or to the employer. It is an attitude of dedication to the field heralded by an overwhelming sense of responsibility; it is characterized by the self-respect engendered through service given rather than of attention to or interest in self-aggrandizement. The professional person who gave a lower standard of service to people who, in his or her opinion, "did not count", whose status might not be enhanced in the eyes of governmental authorities, would be regarded as a dishonorable individual by professional peers. Some practitioners might restrict their service to political figures, the very wealthy, or the famous personality in an attempt to surround their practice with an aura of status not granted when providing service to "ordinary" people. The prestige thus acquired might endow practitioners with higher status within the organization for which they work, but would lower them in the eyes of fellow practitioners. The very fact that the phrase *professional quality* is in common usage assuredly suggests that an ethical code demands behavior which primarily considers the needs of the individual to be served and the quality of the work performed. As Phenix has written:

> The second foundation is the ideal of disinterested service. According to this ideal, the true professional does not engage in practice solely for personal satisfactions or financial rewards, nor does he do his work faithfully merely for the honor of the profession, but he is motivated by the pure ideal of rendering service. He finds intrinsic value and a sense of fulfillment in making available his special ability for the welfare of others. The vocation of the professional at its highest is one of service rather than of gain for individual or group. The professional is a trustee to whom has been given the stewardship of gifts which are for the good of all. It is this spirit of disinterestedness which gives to a profession such nobility, elevation, and honor as it may deserve.[5]

The professional person has one mandatory role to observe in all dealings with people after acceptance in a field devoted to humanitarian service—the obligation to serve the interests of the public. The professional must provide all those techniques and services which are at his or her command and place them at the behest of whosoever requires them. There can never be personal bias or whimsical discrimination permitted to influence the best judgment or skill in practice. For the professional, every person must receive whatever technique or resource is required for that individual to attain equality of opportunity.

Finally, professional associations must necessarily have some judicial machinery for implementing whatever code of ethics is established for the field. Each profession has the power to exclude from its association those who do not observe specific rules of conduct and conform to certain standards of behavior. Exclusion and other disciplinary measures

---

[5]P.H. Phenix, *Philosophy of Education* (New York: Holt, Rinehart and Winston, 1958). p. 169.

have generally been deemed necessary to offset the poorly qualified worker whose intrusions upon the public are often ill-advised and harmful.

The existence of disciplinary power within the professional association is required for two chief reasons: the maintenance of a high standard of technical competence, and the fulfillment of a moral standard. The concept of technical proficiency may be construed to mean all those practices in effect throughout the field which are generally considered to be of such type that their inclusion will lead to the most beneficial contribution for the public which the agency serves. Moral standards are considered to be related to the prohibition, by professional peers of high reputation and competency, of any disreputable, infamous, or reasonably disgraceful conduct. Exclusion from membership should rest primarily on moral grounds rather than on technical competence, because technique necessitates the utilization of judgment rather than mere routine, and each practitioner must have some leeway in exercising intelligence in the service of the public. If, however, the recreationist is confronted with litigation as a result of negligence (which, it would seem, can arise only from ignorance and incompetence) and is found guilty of the charge, then the association should also undertake to remove that person from the register of the association and any certification concomitant with it. If such action could bring about the prohibition of that person from ever practicing recreational service, so much the better for the field and the public. Publication of the name of any person against whom such action is taken might have a most salutary effect on potential misfeasants, inasmuch as no employing authority of any consequence would want to take the chance of hiring a person whose moral or technical competence was questionable. Such drastic action would follow only, if in the eyes of professional peers, the transgression was quite outrageous or of such turpitude as to warrant it. The distinctive feature of a valid profession, as that appellation is generally construed, is not simply the profession of disciplinary powers, but the ultimate purpose for which they are used.

In a professional association some sort of executive council provides for the examination of practitioners for actions that are detrimental to the reputation and interest of the field. This adjudicating body, or tribunal, is specifically convened for hearing any charges or pleas. The membership of the tribunal must always be composed of professional practitioners. It cannot be stated too strongly that professional conduct has been, in the main, created by professional thinking, and the maintenance of such standards should be left to the enforcement of professional practitioners.

Fundamentals of equity demand that any hearing, which could imperil a practitioner's status on a professional register or demean a reputation in a professional association, must be held before a properly constituted adjudicating board, or tribunal, specifically authorized to hear such preferments. Every member of the tribunal must receive prior notice of the proceeding at which a charge is to be reviewed, although the hearing is not nullified or impaired in any way if every member does not attend. However, not less than two thirds of the tribunal so appointed should appear at any hearing in which a charge is to be heard. The accused must receive all specifications of charges alleged, and shall be heard in any defense of same if desired. The functions of adjudicator and prosecutor cannot be performed by the same person. For that reason, any member of the tribunal who may have been active in bringing charges against the accused must disqualify himself or herself from sitting in judgement. These are only minimal requirements in order to ensure equal justice for the accused. It is not the intent of this section to prescribe the legal niceties or hearing procedures to be observed. Suffice to say that in circumstances in which the professional society initiates judicial machinery to maintain its ethical code, the tribunal may and usually does imitate the proceedings of law courts.

One warning is necessary. Frivolous charges may sometimes be made against a practitioner on grounds of technical incompetence because that person does not follow the usual line of reasoning or the accepted philosophy which a majority profess. The hazard in subjecting an individual to a tribunal of peers without the possibility of appeal is horrendous. In this instance, the danger would perhaps be grounded not in too great an affirmation upon the maintenance of a standard operating procedure, but in the ease it would provide for witch-hunting. The divergencies of theory and concept of recreational service, and even of the terminology used, among educators and practitioners in recreational service are widespread. Equally infamous is the enmity shown by the protagonists of one philosophy or orthodoxy towards the advocates of another, and the *empressement* of each faction to enjoin a pet theory upon the rest of the profession. Human nature being what it is, the fear of allegations, either true or false, against upholders of a heretical point of view is always present. The temptation to use the authority which a professional society provides to its judicial tribunal as a means of punishing those who adopt or do not adopt the practice of any given philosophy or theory is a clear and present danger. It cannot be reiterated too often that offenses having to do with morality rather than with technical competence should fall to the province of the association's tribunal, although where negligence has been or can be shown, in fact, the society should act to rid itself of an incompetent member.

Professionalization of Recreational Service

To the extent that recreational service exhibits the central characteristics which validate any profession, it is approaching the social status usually reserved only for the traditional vocations of law, medicine, and theology. However, on the basis of the central tendencies which distinguish the professions from quasi-professions and other occupations, then recreational service falls somewhat short. Figure 1 best illustrates this concept. The horizontal line represents all occupations. Each successive increment toward the angle represents the vocations that require a higher degree of skill or technique. The points close to the angle represent all

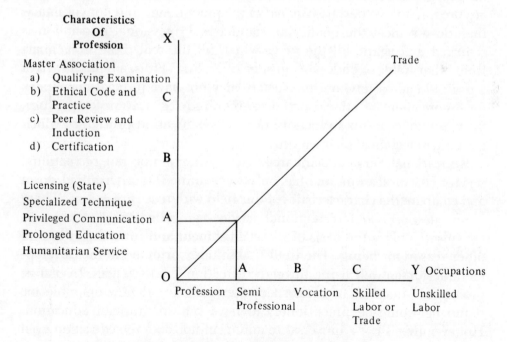

Figure 1. Societal format from trade to profession.

fields that require prolonged education for proficiency as well as technique. Only those points falling within the A box stand for vocations that are dedicated to humanitarian service and have prolonged education for specialized technique, established associations for the transmission of knowledge within the field, and the institution of an ethical code for practice. The apex of the angle stands for the validated professions that possess all of the traits that act as criteria, for example, prolonged education, specialized technique, humanitarian dedication, a master association with complete authority over qualifying examinations for induction into the field, a code of ethics, judicial machinery for the enforcement of moral behavior and ethical practice, and the registry of practitioners or other certification procedures.

The closer a field approximates the conditions of apex, the more acceptable it becomes as a profession. Some vocations may appear to have all of the qualifications necessary, but upon close examination they are found to be deficient in one or more criteria. The further from the angle a field moves, the more evidently it is a trade or non-skilled labor. Because humanitarian service and prolonged education are the distinguishing features of a profession, the neglect of either one of these hallmarks precludes recognition as a profession. Even when these traits are present unless they are *required* of the practitioner, and not voluntary, they do not meet the qualifying standards. Professional association is required, but again, all the items which set the real professions apart from other fields of endeavor must be operating. Thus, a field may have a professional society, but the society may not have judicial machinery for enforcement of ethical practices, required registration for practice, peer examination for induction, nor the certification procedure which guarantees technical competence.

Recreational Service Compared. As to whether or not recreational service is a profession, one has only to examine the criteria laid down and compare the characteristics of this field with true professions. There is no question about recreational service being dedicated to humanitarianism. This is the basis of its establishment and function. It has no other reason for being. The field is absolutely oriented to the development of human well being through recreational experiences. Insofar as prolonged education is concerned, there is a trend now operable for requiring would-be practitioners to have certain minimal education. However, this is not a universal requirement nor does the education even have to be professional. There is still considerable political appointment operating to the detriment of the field, because patronage positions do not require educational qualification or other professional endowment. It will take some time before a prolonged professional educational sequence is absolutely required of individuals who wish to practice in recreational service. Today, this is still a voluntary process, left up to the individual and not a part of the obligation required for induction. Nevertheless, as more communities face the leisure challenge, and as more information is disseminated concerning the field, today's apathetic public may become aroused and concerned enough to demand well-qualified and professionally prepared practitioners. When that time arrives, recreational service will move inexorably closer to professional status.

Finally, there is a question relating to professional association. However, there are still splinter and other professional specialty organizations which may remain outside of the greater body. Under these conditions, the idea of peer examination, registration, certification, ethical codes, and other association practices are less meaningful and, in most instances, nonexistent. Although the aspiration toward professional status is apparent and much effort is being made to promote professionalism among practitioners, recreational service has neither reached a point where this can be brought about immediately, nor will it achieve its goal until all mandatory requirements are met. At best, it may be said that recreational service is a quasi-profession attempting to approximate the standards of the true profession.

A Professionalizing Program

In order that recreational service as a vocational experience can acquire the features which professions have, an eight-point program is here defined. By adhering to the conditions described, professional status may be achieved.

1. A broad educational program directed at the general public must be initiated at the earliest moment. By improving the image of the recreationist, the entire field can be strengthened. Opportunities must be found for the dissemination of information through a variety of media which tend to raise the status and promote the image of the recreationist. The establishment of television and radio programs depicting the recreationist in practice must be suggested to major networks.

2. The provision of increased understanding and support of recreational service must be engendered. Individual practitioners and state societies should prepare an information service to individuals and groups. Such a service would provide speakers before lay groups, make better use of mass media, and distribute a selected list of films, books, feature stories, and other audiovisual materials to lay groups through the offices of the professional society. A direct line of communication must be maintained with community leaders, and local, state, and federal legislators, particularly in relationship to current developments in recreational service. The field must obtain cooperation from other interested groups for the adequate support of recreational services and sponsor a continual series of lay and professional conferences on recreational service problems of wide significance on the local and state level.

3. Promotion and dissemination of research applied to recreational service should be an integral part of association practice. The attention of all practitioners and educators should be called to the outstanding publications and studies being made in the field. Worthy new texts, master's theses and doctoral dissertation, applicable journals, and current experimentation must be widely known.

4. The development of more highly competent practitioners through required professional education programs should be made obligatory. The entire process of recruitment, focusing attention upon capable and willing young people in preparing for leadership roles in recreational service, should be undertaken. Scholarships and other financial benefits to students should be encouraged. The establishment of administrative internships should become part of the joint responsibility of educators and practitioners. The sponsorship of workshops, conferences, studies, and projects devoted to the development of leadership skills can be augmented.

5. Practitioners acting through state societies can do much to promote the needed legislation for the stringent licensing of recreationists. The procedure of registration, exclusion, ethical codification, examination, and accreditation in the field cannot be underestimated in the movement toward professionalism. Thus, a national registry board, practitioner certification, the ethical code, judicial enforcement, examination for induction, and cooperation with institutions of higher education for their accreditation would be the probable outcome.

6. The involvement of state legislative bodies for the licensing of recreationists as well as for the establishment of state offices, commissions, or departments of public recreational service can be implemented through individual state associations. The writing and enactment of laws implementing licensing procedures which would require minimal obligatory professional education and a specified standard of practice would do much to extend the influence of professionalization. Through such licensing, many communities and agencies not now cognizant of the field and its practitioners might be made aware. Beyond that, improved status, salary policies and practices, and enhanced positions within agencies might be effected. From such legislation might also come the employment of only registered and certified recreationists, commanding a level of recognition consummate with the high degree of competence earned through prolonged education and intellectual insight.

7. The extension of professional practice throughout the field and the observance of and conformity to a published code of ethical practices must be maintained. Practitioners should attempt to identify problems of legislation, recreationist supply, and community awareness and recognition affecting the field. The development of proper programs to resolve or alleviate these problems must be achieved. Agency policies which recognize and reward the special contribution made by career recreationists as distinguished from part-time volunteers or workers must be developed.

8. The academic community can do much to enhance the stature of the field by developing a disciplined study which gives more detailed and in-depth examination to historical and political matters than it currently does. Academics need to disengage from overly simplistic ideas prevalent and encourage systematic and deeply probing analyses of philosophical concepts, administrative techniques, leadership theories, and other operational procedures which impinge upon and influence the provision of recreational service.

The Recreationist-Professional Practitioner

The term *recreationist* is defined as professional practitioner in recreational service. But what does professional really denote. The true professional is unique among persons because of special technique demonstration, has attained an intellectual insight and a logical theoretical basis for the vocation, and has developed high standards by which ethical practices in the vocation are maintained. At the same time, the dedication to the service of humanity make the professional truly representative of all people. The recreationist, to be professional must adhere to the regimen of prolonged education, objective and ethical conduct in practice, and a continual search for that which is true.

Howard G. Danford has succinctly characterized the recreationist in the following terms:

> The professional leader is motivated primarily by ideals of service rather than money.... He believes that people, not activities or facilities, are the most important thing in the world and that the basic purpose of recreation is to enrich the lives of people. ... Since people are the most important thing in the world, the professional man respects all human beings and is interested in their welfare.[6]

There are many ways in which the specific professional characteristics can be observed and expressed. However, the three chief premises upon which all recreationists should base their practice and conduct are fundamental for professional responsibility.

Preoccupation with Public Welfare

The primary concern of the recreationist is always to act for the best interest and welfare of the participant. Because recreational service seeks the total development of the individual through experiences which are recreational in nature, no practitioner can correctly be considered a professional unless there is unquestionable dedication to that objective. For a practitioner to behave in such a way so as to reap self-benefit, either of status, economic means, or psychological preferment, by disregarding the needs of clients, is to disobey the principles of professionalism. The individual participant expects to receive qualified and ethical service from the recreationist. It is, therefore, obligatory for the recreationist to abide by the belief through provision of experiences which will enhance the participant's skill, mental acuity, and personal satisfactions. The practitioner who violates this concept has no right to the claim of being a professional.

---

[6]H.G. Danford, *Creative Leadership in Recreation* (Boston: Allyn and Bacon, 1964), pp. 100–101.

Continual Search for Truth

A second fundamental factor determining the professionalism of the practitioner is a concern for and pronouncement of the truth. The recreationist must never have a closed mind to alternative points of view. The professional should always be willing to challenge misrepresentation and demagoguery wherever they are found, with whatever the true facts indicate. The two common opposites of truth are ignorance and misconception. Ignorance is a complete lack of knowledge about any given subject which precludes an understanding or recognition of the truth. Misconception, on the other hand, is undeniable error having its basis in faulty reasoning, biased opinion, or deviation from true facts. The practitioner can never allow the error of expediency or conforming with majority pressure which is prejudiced in favor of any individual or group. Professional objectivity and the courage of personal convictions to withstand faulty reasoning, even if such is the attitude of many, is mandatory. The recreationist needs to develop moral intelligence.

Moral intelligence may be defined as the ability to discern what is right or true, regardless of social pressure or mass opinion to the contrary. It is, perhaps, the one quality of intelligence which can be taught and learned by diligent search. Moral intelligence is, in fact, "good character." sists of behavior which excludes immorality, both from thought and action. Lip service, sanctimonious platitudes and hypocrisy are foreign to this quality.

The recreationist must stand prepared to justify actions convincingly on the basis of true facts. To mislead or deliberately falsify information, because it might lead to the request for more than mediocre performance, is an act that is unworthy of a professional person and one that is unethical. The recreationist must bend full intellect to the collection and analysis of all pertinent facts regarding the provision of recreational services. Sincerity and devotion to the cause of truth dismisses pretentiousness. Through the intelligent assimilation of knowledge concerning the field, particularly of performance, the professional recognizes personal limitations as well as competencies; weighing various ideas carefully, keeping an open mind to all considerations, unless there is neither merit or application, and maintaining a reasonable attitude.

The leader constantly searches for additional knowledge which can be useful. He is always intent upon discovering faster, better, stronger, more adequate, more productive, and less expensive and time consuming processes.... The restless mind is one which is not satisfied with just getting an answer. It wants to know the reasons why. The inquiring mind is never content to wear blinders or follow the well-rutted path without determining if there are other paths to follow or if there is a wide world beyond the blinders.[7]

Dedication to Ethical Practice

The differentiation between a mediocrity and a professional person is, essentially, in terms of expressed attitude toward one's vocation, peers, and self. Dedication is one form of loyalty. It is perseverence, constancy, and integrity of purpose against all odds. The principal condition is complete selflessness. The dedicated person creates high standards of practice and then lives up to them. As Brubacher has written:

> The professional person knows so vastly more than the layman that the latter is almost completely at a disadvantage in determining whether the professional service he is receiving is to his best interest or not. Consequently the professional person must take extra precaution to assure his public that he is not confusing his own personal interests with theirs. The only way he can unmistakably do this is to put their interests unequivocally ahead of his.[8]

The chief method by which the recreationist can assure the public of dedication to ethical practice occurs in the high regard in which professional competence and technical skill are held, in the way in which responsibilities and obligations are carried out. Sensitive to and totally devoted to those professional activities which ethical considerations make mandatory, the recreationist must naturally offer expert knowledge and technique chiefly for the public's service. Monetary reward, although necessary and significant in any person's life, is definitely of lesser importance than the concept of public service and social welfare.

If recreational service and its practitioners wish to achieve professional status in this society, a completely different approach from the methods currently in use is necessary. In this day, when technological advancement and an increasingly enlightened public demand highly competent, proficient, and effective recreational workers, we no longer can tolerate unprofessionalism. Of necessity, practitioners must set their

---

[7]Ibid., p. 466.

[8]J.S. Brubacher, *Modern Philosophies of Education,* 3rd ed. (New York: McGraw-Hill Book Company, 1950), p. 115.

house in order. They must accept the criteria that govern the long-established professions and adopt the methods, principles, and standards that differentiate professions from other occupations. The closer recreational service approximates the conditions which the older professions have already achieved, the sooner will it be recognized by these same professions and society in general.

Among the criteria commonly assumed to endow an occupation with professional characteristics are humanitarianism, objectiveness, research, prolonged esoteric education, common technique, association of peers, and an ethical code of practices. Subordinate standards supportive of these essential factors are concerned with induction into the field, peer examination, reciprocal accreditation, standardized nomenclature, state sanction through professional licensure, association, registration, certification, judicial procedures to remove incompetent or unethical practitioners, and a national education program designed to inform the public about recreational service and its practitioners, thereby ensuring future material for recruitment into the field.

What the Future Holds. In an age of cybernetics, automation, thermonuclear power, and space exploration, it is no small supposition to foresee a time when all decision-making functions will belong to those who have become professionals, or who are at least under professional persuasion. With the rise of specialized technique to keep pace with increased knowledge and technology, there will be a concomitant increase in personnel engaged in intellectual occupations. This will be most valid for recreational service and its incumbent practitioners. Opportunities for specialized and prolonged education are gradually being extended and required. It is probable that the future will belong to those who have the education and talent to seek careers as recreationists. To the extent that more highly competent individuals are being professionally prepared for careers in recreational service, a more efficient provision of services should be engendered. Even more significant is the consequence of such education upon the field in general, in which the aspiration to see professional technique completely and capably used would furnish a selfless motive. Professional education, particularly those courses dealing with ethics and objective practice, will imbue the would-be practitioner with the idea, ideal, and desire of humanitarian service rather than self-aggrandizement. The education of the professional person is as much an indoctrination program as a preparation for future practice. Professional pride and quality in the effective offering of recreational services would become a compelling force.

Chapter 23

PROFESSIONAL PREPARATION
FOR THE RECREATIONIST

Only recently has any specific attention been focused upon the kind of person a recreationist must be. Even now there is some question as to whether an individual who is skilled in one or more activities is better suited to perform the various functions of a recreational worker than one who brings to the organization an ability to get along with or influence others. Many people are not sure what the preparation for the profession should entail, or even if a professional education is necessary. There are some who are convinced that any college graduate, regardless of major emphasis, but preferably one with a general humanities or liberal arts background, may be sufficiently qualified to handle the responsibilities of the recreational worker. And of course there are those who feel that no specialized education is required, but that on-the-job experience is all that really matters.

These views have always been popular with individuals who did not have professional educational preparation, and they will continue to be popular until recreational service achieves more of the professionalized aspects which the recognized professions already claim. The field is still in a transitional phase, and the old order dies slowly. The established practitioners who have "gotten by" for years with inadequate programs are usually the first to raise alarm at any plan that espouses a preparatory course for induction into the field. However, as the functions of recreational service administration and programming become more complex, there will be an increasing demand for executives and lower-level recreationists who have the knowledge for directing and managing personnel, materials, and money in the provision of recreational service to whatever clientele is pertinent. To this end, therefore, professional preparation will have to be based upon an adequate and well-rounded educational program.

There is general agreement among the most concerned practitioners and educators that the recreationist should be an individual worthy of emulation, an exemplar of what a well-educated person should be, a worthwhile and effective citizen of the community, and one whose actions, whether professional or personal, are above reproach. It has only been approximately forty years that programs of professional preparation have been inaugurated to include college curriculum patterns directed toward educating potential recreationists. Today, a well-rounded educational program exists in many institutions of higher education where both bachelor and graduate degrees, with specialization in one of the options of the field, may be attained.

General Education

General education refers to the first two years of undergraduate study. This period is devoted to basic courses in the humanities, the natural sciences, and the social studies. The aim of these studies—what is usually called a liberal education—is to prepare the individual most effectively for future intellectual achievement, civic responsibility, a sense of "fitting in" to a pattern of living and learning on the collegiate level, and better appreciation of the cultural milieu.

The Liberal Studies

Recreational Service as a study considers that the human organism is a product of external environment, physiological stimuli, and the effects which both of these factors have on the physical and mental state of the individual. As a behavioral discipline, recreational service can no longer be thought of only in terms of physical activities, regardless of how active or passive they may be; it must be considered in terms of all human behavior. The discipline will derive its effect from a logical progression of intellectual activities in the first two years, culminating in the practical application of theory to actual field conditions. Professional preparatory curricula will build on the foundations of Western philosophy, from its early beginning in Greece to present-day theory and criticism. When a philosophy of recreation is spoken of, it will be in terms of all philosophy as it relates to behavior in order for the student to obtain a complete grasp of how human beings have been viewed in this society and in past societies.

Applied to the philosophical structures will be biological, sociological, physiological, and psychological theories and criticisms, which are directly interrelated with recreation and recreational experience. After mastering the theoretical knowledge of how human beings develop, learn, and behave under various conditions, the potential recreationist will be in a better position to understand and work with people and to lead or enable them to attain fruitful experiences.

A broad general education must be the basis upon which specialized and technical studies will be imposed. Without the humanities, sciences, and social studies, the person is little more than a trained specialist, poorly equipped to face the numerous situations where a thorough knowledge of the human environment is necessary for efficient professional service.

The graduate of a college or university preparatory curriculum should have a complete knowledge of philosophies of recreation, the nature of recreation, and definitive frame of reference for its use, and should understand the differentiation between the field of recreational service, recreational experience, and recreation for wide application. A thorough background in history is important, as are language skills, for understanding and communication.

The recreationist must be versed in the processes of human motivation and learning in order to apply this knowledge most effectively. Among the social sciences, there should be basic courses in introductory psychology, and when this is mastered, intermediate and advanced courses in social, applied, and educational psychology. Depending upon expected specialization there will probably also be some phases of abnormal psychology; beyond this, there should be a profound knowledge of human institutions and their origins, and of society in general. Social problems, particularly of a rural and urban nature, will be part of this preparation. The entire question of community guidance and aspects of deviant behavior also belongs to this phase of learning.

In the natural sciences learning should include the fundamentals of earth sciences and the biological development of life on earth; the understanding of space and the natural forces which impinge upon the earth as a point in space and time; the sweep of natural history as it relates to the many elements of nature as a given segment of the human's environment, i.e., ecological studies. These are the bases of an education which will enable the potential recreationist to understand and cope with the diverse needs of people.

The liberal studies are instituted as foundational courses designed to increase the individual's capacity for broadening appreciations and therefore living a fuller and richer life. A primary concern of the liberal studies is the discovery of potential and latent talents and skills, and the development of the individual toward his or her potential. Attention should be focused upon the individual's cultural heritage, overlaying that with the knowledge necessary for participation in the institutions, interrelationships, and dynamic interchange of society.

Values of General Education

Effective communication, the transmission and interpretation of ideas, is one of the inherent values of general education. It exposes the student to literature, composition, forensics, and logic, all of which are useful for articulateness, comprehension of language usage, and critical thinking. Studies in history, government, law, and sociology provide the student with some knowledge of social values, i.e., discrimination between ethical and unethical choices. They enable the individual to make decisions based upon sound principles of behavior and conduct and to make value judgments. The study of history, through which we learn of the errors of prior social orders, can do much to prevent the mistakes of the past from being repeated.

A proper general education not only prepares the individual for intellectual achievement and civic performance, but it also effectively integrates all education so that specific areas of knowledge are well related to each other. Thus natural phenomena will be better understood in terms of the impact which each has upon human ecology. Technical skills for later life will depend upon such knowledge, and rational and aesthetic activities will also benefit. The latter are of vital concern for the effect which they will have upon the individual's participatory capacity in the cultural experiences produced in community patterns of life. Effective liberal education enhances the aesthetic and emotional aspects of life. It incorporates a thorough initiation into the fine arts and perhaps offers such development in one art that an individual may participate as a creator rather than as a consumer without any vocational overtones. Effective liberal education supplies the student with interests and skills that can ensure a life enriching experience through the continued reading of good literature. In short, it develops many-faceted individuals who have self-understanding and an awareness of their place in the universe.

Professional Education

The primary purpose at the next level, professional education, is the preparation of selected students for leadership in the field of recreational service. Instructors of the professional curriculum try to expose students to a wide range of specialized subjects, each providing some basic method and knowledge of one aspect of the entire spectrum of the well-rounded recreational program. To this are added those courses designed to integrate various experiences and combine them inseparably so that their values and relationships are dependent upon each being utilized. Thus the future recreationist will be more than a mere specialist. The professional will be equipped with a thorough knowledge of humans, the environment, and those skills with which to organize as completely as is possible a program to serve the recreational needs of the population.

This professional training will produce generalists, rather than specialists, able to obtain an overview of the total variety of individual activities which may enhance the recreational value of the program. Such a curriculum will, in effect, turn out through a sound educational process an individual who is an organizer and administrator, able to supervise a wide variety of experiences and combine them into a greater whole. Such a person would not be bogged down in one narrow activity skill, but would have a knowledge of many skills, as many as there are individual categories of activities within the comprehensive recreational program.

It is true that the student would be expected to have activity skills, but this will not preclude the one all-pervasive skill, i.e., the ability to organize and administer a full-range recreational activities program for people. The saleable skill and educational goal of such preparation is to produce a generalist. The skills of organization, coordination, supervision, and management normally belong to the leader. Hence, the prerequisites of the professional program center around the study of leadership.

Each activity skill to which the student is exposed places emphasis, not upon the product of the activity—although this is important—but upon leading people in the activity. The establishment of human relationships and the influence of conduct, wherever possible, coupled with attempts to ingrain the value of understanding people as unique individuals, is the function of all recreational skills or methods courses within the professional curriculum. It is not enough to work with things and do it well; one must also work with people, and work insightfully. The professional course does not produce leaders; it produces individuals who have been exposed to the methods and principles of leadership. Such a program cannot teach leadership, but it does indicate how a diligent student may become a leader.

The recommended courses in the professional curriculum, to be discussed hereunder, would include the following:

1. History and Principles
2. Organization and Programming
3. Recreational Skills
4. The Recreational Laboratory
5. Planning Spaces and Facilities
6. Introduction to Administration
7. Leadership Principles and Methods
8. Field-Work Experience

History and Principles Course

A history and principles course is required if the student is to be acquainted with a conceptualization of the field of recreational service. The sweep of historical perspective allows the student to understand more fully the development of recreational service as a field of study and as a practicing function of public, quasi-public, and private service.

Such a course is designed to present a better understanding of principles and practices by which recreational service function and upon which varying philosophies of this field are built. Thus, the prospective recreationist will be afforded an opportunity to develop concepts concerning the field, personal understanding of professionalism, the meaning of recreational service and recreation, socio-economic-religious movements affecting the growth and development of this field, the economic importance of recreational activity, human resources for recreational experiences, the social institutions providing recreational services, and the initial development of professional responsibility.

This type of course will further provide an acquaintance with essential factors of recreational living and with resources of an environmental and personal nature. Normally, a course in the history and principles of recreational service will include information pertaining to the field in Western civilization. With such an introduction the student would be on solid ground for the several other professional courses that are an intrinsic part of a major core sequence. History, of course, indicates the direction from which the field has come. Principles should conform to the ethical practice which must be applied if the field is to develop into a great humanitarian service.

Organization and Programming

Courses in organizational theory and practice are necessary to ensure understanding of how the recreational service is established and how it operates in its various settings. With techniques for problem solving, the situations pertinent to organizational structure which appear difficult can be worked out. There is a great body of knowledge which can be brought to bear on any of the problems that arise in the implementation, organization, and operation of recreational services.

A knowledge of programming is necessary if progressively attractive activities are to be presented. Programming avoids duplication and concentrates effort where it is needed. It is the ethical responsibility of public and private recreational agencies or systems to orient the individual participant toward socially acceptable mental and physical health patterns that will enable that person to work and serve to the best of his or her abilities. The policy of the agency must not be inclined toward gross statistical representations, but must include within its goals and ideals the concept of teaching social acceptance in conduct, respect for individual rights, good fellowship, and mutual appreciation. Activities allowing for recognition of individual dignity, skill, affection, status, and enjoyment are all part of the over-all policy presented by the agency which is translated into programming.

The recreational program and the techniques that guide programming for recreational agencies are never static. The program must develop and grow out of the needs of people. Through programming, a constant evaluation of activities provided for recreational service is maintained, and the department may then offer better opportunities for its constituent public to satisfy itself. Through programming the department finds both the leadership and the means to allow participants to discover new recreational experiences. Continuous experimentation with new ideas may provide enriched experiences to those participating within the program.

Recreational Skills Courses

Program skills which the student should obtain for future use in the practicing field include music, art, crafts, camping, dramatics, motor skills, social skills, and the instructional techniques to transmit such skills. Each of these program specialities requires a separate course or courses, depending upon the degree of skill which the student wishes to obtain. Basically, however, the student is provided with essential skills and the methodology for instructing the various experiences.

The program skills are not offered with the idea of producing specialists or experts. They are offered to give the student an opportunity to learn the variety of values inherent in any of them so that the possibility of combining them into an interdependent program or utilizing two or more units in combination to produce a more worthwhile effect may be recognized. Thus, a theater production could combine music, art, crafts, certain motor activities such as dance and rhythmics, aspects of speech, and the industrial arts. Pageantry also requires many of the same skills. Camping combines leadership aspects with almost all of the program skills. Physical activity, including as it does sports, games, and other motor action, is utilized throughout the well-rounded recreational program. There is little within the broad scope of recreational programming which cannot be included in the skills necessary to the recreationist.

The student is exposed to the varied presentations to gain some degree of skill which may later be useful in practice. Individuals may also have some talent in one or more basic skills that they wish to develop, not only for program purposes but for their own recreational satisfaction. Wherever such talent is discernible, the individual is encouraged to enhance that skill to the desirable degree. Of course, such intensive work must not preclude exposure to other activity skills nor tend to narrow the scope of learning to which the students are subjected. All activity skills are offered as parts of an overall program which should make use of all skills if our aim is to satisfy every person who comes to the recreational agency, in whatever setting.

The Recreational Laboratory

The recreational laboratory provides much-needed practical experiences that are ordinarily not available in the regular courses. Opportunities are given for planning and preparation of materials and activities in recreational programming, so that students can perform the varied functions in which they are to engage. The laboratory gives the real contact with the problems involved and a chance to experience the relationship of various types of practice which may be applied in an overall recreational service program.

The laboratory course usually includes experience in the following:

1. Social recreational activities—mixers, parties, dances, games, stunts, skits, other organized activities.
2. Recreational materials; place and scope of literary activities in the recreational program; sources of materials for recreational service in any setting; the development of resource files for a variety of activities, with decorations, food, social activities, dance, music, rules and regulations for games, arts and crafts, drama, discussion groups, nature study, facilities, etc.
3. Introductory outdoor education and conservation.
4. Audio-visual materials, sound systems, graphic arts, movie projectors, tape recorders, public relations techniques.
5. Organizing clubs and special interest groups.
6. Organizing a workshop or a clinic.
7. Operating a league or tournament play.

Planning Recreational Spaces and Facilities

The design and construction of recreational spaces and facilities belong to experts in the fields of architecture and construction, but these experts must seek the advice and assistance of those who have knowledge concerning the utilization to which certain land and water areas, physical plants, and facilities will be put. Many so-called recreational structures simply become landmarks to the builder's incompetency because recreationists are not invited to advise the architect of practical program needs during the planning phase.

Functional use of space and functional planning of physical facilities is a concern of recreationists. There is a distinct need for students to learn about the design and construction of functional recreational structures. The trend toward providing separate courses concerned with the planning, design, and construction of recreational spaces and facilities has nearly become a pattern in institutions of higher education where professional education is offered.

Usually, courses dealing with planning include design, construction, and investigatory methods for appraisal and evaluation of the setting in which the recreational department is situated and the concomitant recreational needs. Provision for most of the following subject matter normally made:

1. Master and long-range plans.
2. Short-range and emergency plans.

3. Physiography and other corollary features.
4. Legislation.
5. Demography.
6. Community organization and housing data.
7. Standards for recreational spaces and facilities (tentative).
8. Land acquisition and usage.
9. Specialized facilities and other physical structures.
10. Park planning and design.
11. Accessibility and mobility barrier abolition.
12. Maintenance.

The student then receives applicable information based upon sound principles and factual research so that he or she is able to function more effectively as a professional person and supply whatever resource is necessary for the operation of a more inclusive recreational system.

Introduction to Recreational Service Administration

The undergraduate professional curriculum must offer the student some opportunity to learn administrative problems and the techniques for handling them. While most recent graduates of professional curricula do not immediately become administrators, usually entering the field as functional workers or in some cases supervisors, there are those who begin their careers as assistant administrators, or even administrators. Because administrative aspects are found at every level within the recreational organization, it is necessary that the student be prepared to some extent for understanding and solving administrative problems.

The introductory course normally contains information relating to the legality of public recreational service system operations, and, perhaps, that pertaining to private and/or commercial operations. An understanding of the function of the agency is also provided, including a comprehension of the law of liability. Almost always the course covers phases of personnel management, budget-making procedures, planning concepts, program development and control, inservice education, maintenance, and record keeping.

Leadership in Recreational Service

The major methods course in every undergraduate professional program should be on the principles and methods of leadership. This course is vital to students, for it attempts to teach an individual how to attain leadership within the recreational setting. Basically, leadership application in the field of recreational service is concerned with self-comprehension, understanding the feelings and needs of others, practical knowledge of the social group situation sources, and types of influence within some organizational framework, and the principles necessary for effective leadership.

Leadership orientation to recreational service is primarily related to the future recreationist's ability to adjust to a variety of complex situations, to develop a personality which allows for maximum facility in getting along with others, and to establish a set of objectives based upon ethical philosophy for providing recreational services.

The need for a leadership course is apparent if students are to gain knowledge of others. A good deal of basic research has been done relating to human dynamics, leader ability, and the identification of the types of groups. There must be some kind of integrated learning process to pull together elements of social psychology, group work, levels of leadership, effects of leadership, and motivation for leadership. Such information provides the student with some reference as to why, where, and how leadership develops. Typically, the leadership course deals with the foundations, fallacies, techniques, and methods by which the leader in the field of recreational service attains, stabilizes and retains influence with others.

Field-Work Experience

Field-work experience is an introduction to the various duties and responsibilities which the recreationist encounters on the job. It is during this phase of professional education that the student has the opportunity to try out his or her understanding of people, apply knowledge of the field, and determine an approach which may enable him to satisfy people's recreational needs. This is the students' first-hand experience with those to whom they may provide service in the future. Thus the student has an opportunity to ascertain whether the recreational field meets career expectations.

The field-work experience, to be most effective, is planned so that the student can assume some direct responsibility for the initiation, preparation, operation, and direction of recreational activities in a variety of settings. Such practice permits the student to put into practice the theories, techniques, and skills which have been assimilated during the professional education period.

Throughout the field-work experience students will be given such direct leadership responsibility as will be most meaningful to them, and also the opportunity to observe immediate supervisors and other personnel of the field agency's professional staff, from time to time, in the performance of their obligations.

Educational Degrees and Professional Employment

Among the goals of professional education are equipping students to secure positions in the field. Post-secondary schools attempt to develop the necessary skills and knowledge which will enable the future recreationist to function effectively at a level which time, experience, and capability dictate. Institutions of higher education have programs to assist graduates in finding a place in the agency of their choice. The different degrees awarded at various levels entitle their holders to anticipate different levels of professional employment. Specific career opportunities are discussed in Chapters 24 and 25.

Junior Colleges. The two-year colleges offering an associate arts degree have generally been beneficial to students who are preparing for some specialty among the major program categories. Students who graduate from two-year colleges do so with the idea that they may eventually continue at a four-year institution or take terminal degrees and work in the field at the program or face-to-face level. In some instances, an individual with a two-year degree may obtain promotion and become a supervisor, administrator, or executive of an agency or department. For the most part, however, associate art degree holders are often viewed as technicians and specialists at the program level of leadership.

Four-Year Institutions. The four-year college or university degree holder may enter the field as a program or functional worker. However, it is more likely that the bachelor's degree, plus the usual part- or full-time work experiences which the student may have obtained while working toward the degree earns a higher entry level position. Such an individual may expect to qualify for a center director's position, a supervisory position, or occasionally, an administrative position. The most likely proposition is for the graduate of a four-year undergraduate curriculum to be inducted into the field in some supervisory capacity and work up from there.

Graduate Programs. Graduate programs produce a number of special options which enable master's degree holders to expect administrative and executive positions in large departments within the field of recreational service. It is quite likely that graduate degree holders will obtain supervisory and middle-management positions. With several years of experience, such individuals can expect to gain admittance to managerial rank and attain eventual executive status in an agency or department.

More and more in recent years, communities have recognized the advantage of employing individuals with greater depth to their professional education. For this reason, career-oriented students should think in terms of advanced degrees. While it is true two-year college graduates *may* obtain administrative positions, graduate degree holders are much more likely to be employed and retained at higher supervisory and administrative levels.

Chapter 24

ROLES, FUNCTIONS AND RESPONSIBILITIES
IN RECREATIONAL SERVICE

This chapter is concerned with leadership. Since the process of leadership may be found in all kinds of organizations offering recreational services, the same levels will be discovered although titles may vary. By examining these levels it will be possible to classify descriptive facts relating to the categories of recreational service leadership. Leadership may be classified by four distinct levels: functional, supervisory, administrative, and executive. This chapter will consider each of these ranks in turn, examining the typical functions of recreationists at each level.

The Functional Level

The functional level of leadership in the field of recreational service is also known as the program, operational, or basic level within agencies performing services of a recreational nature in communities. This simply means that professional employees of the agency perform their functions on a face-to-face basis with those who participate in activities organized, operated, or sponsored by the recreational agency. Employees on the functional level are typically concerned with carrying out a schedule of various activities, including a wide variety of recreational experiences for participants or spectators. Such work will generally take form as the organizing, promoting, or directing of group games, sports, or aesthetic activities; service features; minor aspects of public relations; answering questions posed by individuals coming to the recreational centers, playgrounds, or other facilities in which such personnel are employed; instructing individuals in various skills; guiding, coaching, assisting, or enabling those who participate within the agency-operated program to achieve a certain measure of satisfaction and, perhaps, competence in an activity of their choice. Table 1 exemplifies the kinds of duties which program level recreationists perform.

Table 1. Program Level Duties

1. Carries out activity assignments organized for a particular facility (center, playground, park, camp, etc.), under supervision.

2. Organizes, promotes, and conducts various recreational activities at an assigned place.

3. Helps to plan the daily schedule for facility activities.

4. Keeps records of activity program.

5. Inspects supplies, materials, and equipment for appropriateness and safety.

6. Distributes and monitors supplies and equipment.

7. Encourages groups and individuals to participate in the facility program.

8. May serve as a counselor in a day-camp operation.

9. Performs all of those functions which are useful to the promotion and enhancement of recreational activities in the facility to which he or she is assigned.

The recreationist in the position of functional leadership has a professional obligation to carry out the duties and responsibilities that the assignment requires. This may be construed as organizing, planning, guiding, directing, or instructing in specialized recreational activities. These duties are usually performed within the confines of a recreational center, park, playground, or other specialized facility being used to provide recreational services. The recreationist may either direct or assist in the direction of a seasonal operation on the playground or have complete or temporary responsibility of a center.

Depending upon experience in conjunction with professional preparation, the functional worker may be assigned increasingly more difficult and complex responsibilities. Initially, the recreationist does simple activities, with primary emphasis on the leadership of groups of whoever the clientele of the agency is. In this capacity the recreationist assists the next higher level of functional leadership and works under supervision until he or she is thoroughly acquainted with the techniques and operations of the agency. The instructions for work, i.e., specific methods and procedures, are received in detail and the work is subject to periodic observation, inspection, and appraisal. Such performances are required to meet minimum specifications established by the agency.

The variety of duties performed by the functional worker on a somewhat higher level may best be seen from the following listing of normal activities: assists in the issuance and collection of supplies, materials, and equipment utilized for specific activities within the recreational program; helps to organize various activities, such as games, groups, dramatics, singing, dances, athletics, art, crafts, and social activities; gives instruction, guidance, or coaching in several activities, which may include rules of playing certain games or athletics; assists in the establishment of league play, tournaments, or other competitive activities; sees that necessary precautions are observed to insure the health, safety, and welfare of participants and spectators; provides preliminary first aid in the event of a minor injury; performs routine inspections for equipment in order to maintain their effective operating capacity and to secure the safety of users; performs minor custodial functions of a routine nature.

When the recreationist gains experience on the job, he or she may be promoted to carry out the functions of a more responsible position. In this instance there would be performance of skilled and technical duties which require directing a great many recreational activities at a designated facility. The recreationist would be immediately responsible for the planning, coordination, and direction of activities at a specific facility or for assisting in the direction of a wide variety of activities at a recreational center. Supervision is received from an immediate superior, generally an area supervisor, through observation, work review, field records, and staff meetings. Recreationists may also supervise the activities of subordinate recreationists and lay volunteers.

The kinds of duties performed by the more experienced recreationists may be seen from the following partial listing: helps to administer the recreational program at a center or directs a recreational program at an assigned facility; performs such public relations work as is necessary to stimulate and maintain the interest of potential and actual participants in the recreational activities of the facility; organizes, guides, conducts, and directs many recreational experiences, including competitive and noncompetitive sports, games, contests, hobbies, special interests, youth, children's, and adult groups; has custody of and issues supplies, materials, and equipment and recommends needed repairs or replacements; keeps records and reports of the operation of the facility; assists in formulating recommendations or makes recommendations concerning the place the facility has in the overall community recreational system; or helps in analyzing citizen interest and support of the recreational system.

In large agencies the recreationist may attain yet another step up on the functional ladder, whereas in smaller systems he or she might reach the rank of supervisor, director of a facility, or some other designation signifying the complexity of duties and the increase in responsibility. This position is considered professional, as distinct from merely being skilled or technical. The position is concerned with directing a multitude of recreational experiences at a large playground, center, within a treatment center, or assisting in the direction of a regional recreational center. The recreationist is responsible for initiating ideas, planning, coordinating, and providing some supervision to subordinate employees as well as to recreational activities. Work is performed with all age groups. Particularly, there must be brought to these experiences a professional attitude toward participants, along with specialized skills and preparation for meeting the needs of many people and conducting activities designed to satisfy such needs. Some latitude is given the recreationist in this position for exploration of new programming experiences. Much of the work will be performed upon the recreationist's own initiative, and he or she is obliged to widen the scope of activities to meet the particular needs of potential and actual participants.

Examples of services to be performed by the recreationist on this level may be seen from the following list: initiates, plans, organizes, and coordinates a great variety of recreational activities in a center or other recreational facility and analyzes the recreational needs of people living in the neighborhood or residing in the institution who utilize the facility and its program. Such analysis is used for immediate and future recreational plans. The recreationist performs services of a civic and recreational nature for the local neighborhood as well as other community organizations; provides, upon request, individual and group guidance on civic, social, or recreational matters within the area served by the facility; supervises the issuance and collection of recreational supplies, materials, and equipment; sees to the maintenance and proper utilization of such items as are issued; is authorized to give general supervision to subordinate personnel and volunteers for the proper performance of assigned tasks; may hold in-service educational activities or assist in developmental studies of the facility and the area which it serves; attends such staff conferences, clinics, workshops, professional meetings, and other educational programs as may be required for professional growth and development.

Specialists

Specialists are those personnel who have excellent technical proficiency in some recreational category, e.g., art, crafts, dance, drama, music, nature study, etc., beyond that usually found in the personnel employed by recreational agencies. Such workers may be recreationists or they may be part-time employees whose talents and skills allow them to be utilized by the recreational agency. Specialists are responsible for developing a comprehensive activity according to their specialization and also offering instructional classes to employees of the agency in their particular skill so that a wider participating group can be reached.

Specialists in outdoor education or nature study would ordinarily have skill and knowledge concerning nature lore, Indian lore, astronomy, botany, geology, camping, survival, conservation, woodcraft, campcraft, entomology, and other applicable knowledge relating to this broad area. Specialists in arts and crafts might be well versed in drawing, painting, sketching, sculpturing, clay modeling, ceramics, wood, metal, or leather crafts, weaving, sewing, crocheting, knitting, and other art or crafts skills necessary for the provision of recreational experiences. They must have a high personal proficiency and be able to instruct others as well.

Specialists in drama would ordinarily be required to have knowledge and skill in the design, production, and direction or presentation of various kinds of drama including puppetry, marionettes, shadow plays, and live stage productions, as well as some experience in set and stage design, lighting, make-up, skits, stunts, radio scripts, pageants, parades, and other activities analogous to this special area.

Specialists in dance would normally be expected to have skills in folk, square, country, social, tap, ballet, modern, clog, or other types of dance. Such personnel might also be called upon for choreography, rhythmics, or leadership in certain musical activities.

Specialists in music should have skill and talent in the playing of one or more instruments, have a working knowledge of a large variety of instruments, and be able to organize, instruct, and conduct classes in rhythm-band, group and choral singing, band concert, or other instrumental or vocal group presentation. They should have knowledge and skill in directing musical games and be able to work with and coordinate musical activities with dance and drama experiences.

Other specialists may also be employed within the recreational agency to provide part-time instruction in various athletic areas, such as archery, aquatics, boating, basketball, tennis, riflery, and other activities that require special knowledge or skill. While it is true that few recreational agencies employ all of these specialists, there appears to be a growing need for them as agencies go wider afield to offer experiences that will enable participants to achieve satisfaction in meeting their unique needs.

The above descriptions, then, are those of the day-to-day line workers on the functional level within recreational agencies of all kinds. Terminology differs from agency to agency; but in the main the functions, duties, and responsibilities in the examples provided are those which typically and normally are the concern of the personnel operating on this level. Essentially, they are all recreationists, professionally educated and prepared to assume the positions and prerogatives carried by their assignment in departments of recreational service. They are differentiated only in terms of the applied experiences and talent which causes them to be retained and promoted within the agency.

The classifying of program positions has usually been oriented toward community or public departments of recreational service. However, with the growth of a new specialization to meet the needs of those citizens who are confined to medical institutions for emergency, chronic, long-term, or custodial care and treatment, and/or adapted recreational service positions are also included. Additionally, recreational services for armed forces personnel, industrial workers, resort operations, and similar agencies also contain similar positions and function.

The Supervisory Level

In the field of recreational service, the position classification between program or functional worker and administration has been termed supervisory. Within the hierarchy of a department, the supervisor stands as the mediating member of the agency. The supervisor functions (a) to execute decisions made by administrative personnel; (b) to interpret agency philosophy, policy, practices, and scope to subordinate workers in the functional positions; and (c) to act as spokesperson and buffer between the program worker and the administration, and thereby bring to the program personnel a better understanding of administrative practice. The supervisor allies with neither the administrator nor with the functional workers, but serves as the counselor to both, interpreting decisions downward through the chain of command and explaining the needs and objectives of workers upwards. It is the function of the supervisor to offer such expert and technical assistance both to the administrator and the functional workers that success in various spheres of work assigned to them is more likely to be attained. The typical duties of the supervisor are outlined in Table 2.

Table 2. *Supervisory Level Duties*

1. Has general supervision of all personnel operating in the program in an assigned area.
2. Plans, organizes, promotes, and supervises particular recreational activities within a given area.
3. Supervises, educates, and evaluates all subordinates.
4. Conducts in-service educational programs for all assigned personnel.
5. Oversees maintenance of the physical plant in the area of jurisdiction.
6. Prepares appropriate publicity for assigned aspect of the program.
7. Prepares whatever reports or records are required by superiors concerning area of assignment.
8. May represent the department at conferences, community meetings, or other speaking engagements dealing with the concerns of the area of assignment.

The process of obtaining cooperation from groups or individuals and coordinating such activity toward established desirable objectives is supervisory. This aspect of leadership arises in the formulation of recreational policies, in the planning and evaluation of the program, in the selection and education of workers, and in the community organization and operation. It has generally been considered that the focus of supervision is on the improvement of instructional and educative processes for the production of more effective, efficient, and competent recreational personnel through the development of their capacities and abilities. However, supervision as a leadership process in recreational service is neither the exclusive property of supervisory personnel nor of any level within the recreational service system. As a process whereby expert technique is used to provide the best possible arrangement of facilities and experiences for public and patron benefit, supervision may be performed on every level where valid leadership is to be found. The functional worker supervises the recreational activities of participants and on occasion co-workers. The executive or administrator may also exercise supervision in the performance of his or her responsibilities. No one person has sole claim on the ability to supervise or in the use of supervision for the daily fulfillment of on-the-job living. It may be that each worker is his own best supervisor, because only when the individual is able to self-supervise, will he develop optimum maturity as a professional person.

Supervision is characterized by the following functions in the field of recreational service:

1. The exercise of leadership and the awareness of leadership ability in others with attendant stimulation of that capacity whenever it is discovered.

2. The study and improvement of the activities presented in the recreational program, the materials, supplies, equipment utilized in the program, leadership methods, and group processes developed as a result of agency initiation.

3. The interpretation of recreational and agency objectives within the system as well as to the community at large. Internally this may be considered as the guidance and instruction of recreational personnel and volunteers. Externally, it is part of the public relations function utilized to explain the purpose and operation of the agency.

4. The determination of the individual worker's ability and inclination for learning new methods of activity presentation and for accepting work suggestions or advice.

5. The assistance of workers in their professional development, the instilling of objective reactions toward the work situation and the problems which may confront the worker; and the analysis and instruction of professional objectives and the stimulation of dedication toward this field of service.

6. The in-service education of recreational personnel and improvement of their personal work habits. This may take the form of individual or staff conferences, observation of better-prepared workers, utilization of a professional library, prescribed attendance at clinics, workshops, conferences, or other learning situations, or any additional techniques which may be imparted to the worker.

7. The field observation and personal interview of staff personnel and program operation for the purpose of aiding in the improvement of worker technique and for recommending desirable changes in the program related to the findings. This function is carried on through the analysis of records and reports as well as inspection and examination of the methods used by workers.

8. The education and improvement of supervisory personnel and the evaluation of the technical efficiency of supervision accompanied by recommended needed modifications. This latter aspect of supervision is urgently required if the supervisor is to be current in his knowledge and techniques. Thus, there is an implication of self-supervision as well as the need for consistent objective appraisal of supervisory tasks and expertness.

The Administrative Level

Positions on the administrative level may carry either line or staff connotations, but usually refer to the management of some specific function and the personnel assigned to that activity throughout the agency. Administrative level personnel have normally been associated with the execution of policy and the methods utilized for the swift and effective operation of the day-to-day assignments for which their phase of the agency is responsible. To this end administrative personnel are concerned with all items of a material nature which interact with personal capacities for maintenance of a high and beneficial output of energy in the provision of a worthwhile program of recreational activities or in the functions which assist in the production of recreational services. Table 3 sums up the typical duties of administrative personnel.

Administrative agents may be called by many titles, among which are director, manager, general or area supervisor, and assistant. However they are called, they perform the same functions at the same level within the system. Some may be charged with staff responsibility—personnel or office manager; others may be responsible for the provision of technical assistance to line personnel so that the latter can perform more effectively. Still others who facilitate the making of decisions by shouldering some of the more routine and time-consuming duties are charged with the handling of the daily operations of the agency. This means the execution of policy statements into actions and subsequently recreational service. In some instances they may be called upon to act in the absence of the executive, but in the main they assist the executive with technical and special aid.

The administrative level personnel function under the direction of the agency executive, as full assistants to the executive or in charge of one complete phase of the agency's operations. Such a person will serve as director in the daily operations of an entire department, or some

Table 3. Administrative Level Duties

1. Assists in the administration of the department as assigned by the executive.

2. May be deputized for the executive in his or her absence.

3. Assists in the development of maximum efficiency of the department.

4. Assists in the management of personnel who are assigned to the jurisdiction.

5. Develops budgetary materials and accounts for any financial allocations or revenues which accrue to the jurisdiction.

6. Gives appropriate direction to subordinate staff.

7. Evaluates subordinates in order to achieve whatever improvement in the work is necessary.

8. Has responsibility for the condition of the physical plant under jurisdiction.

9. Appraises the recreational program for effectiveness and improvement.

10. Assists in the development of a public relations program.

segment of it, with broad latitude to make decisions and recommendations, subject to review and acceptance of the executive and with authority for the implementation of policy, development of the section for which responsibility is granted, and management. Administrative personnel participate in the formulation of policies, i.e., make recommendations and suggested improvements, which govern the administration and operation of the department, thereby releasing the executive for more important considerations of the top policies to be examined and adopted. The administrator then frees the executive for the essential function of coordinating and conducting the relationships of the department with the numerous other departments, governmental bodies, private agencies, citizens, parent-teacher, social, labor, professional, and other organizations and groups. Certain administrators may also participate in some duties peculiar to the executive and act in his or her stead during any absence.

Administrators engage in such functions as: (1) establishing methods to govern the control, collection, and distribution of donations, gifts, bequests, grants, endowments, and awards for recreational purposes; (2) assembling data, statistics, and other information, making studies and analyses, and preparing comprehensive reports and recommendations; (3) assisting in the preparation of the annual report; (4) helping in the negotiation, preparation, and administration of regular, periodic, and special forms or agreements for the department with other agencies; (5) assisting in the management of complex and delicate public relations situations; (6) after collection and examination of technical and advisory narrative data, preparing numerous federal, state, local, or regional requests for information or assistance; (7) assisting the executive in such ways as are necessary and directed; (8) assuming such of the executive commitments as the executive may not be available to keep; (9) consulting with the executive on most matters in preparing the preliminary and full agenda of the department; (10) assisting in the formulation and preparation of the annual departmental budget; (11) being on call to assume the duties and responsibilities of the executive in the event of sickness or absence.

The administrator has general supervision over the recreational personnel connected with his or her phase of agency operation and through these workers over the functioning of the recreational service program. The administrator assists with the operation of the department's central office, may prepare correspondence for the signature of the executive, and reviews all correspondence originating with the office or going to the executive for action. The administrator performs all of those activities which are necessary for the maintenance of a high degree of efficiency in providing the service for which the department was created and has the responsibility for executing such procedures which insure the continued operation and competent functioning of the central office.

The preceding paragraphs indicate a conglomeration of activities which are performed by administrative personnel. However, it should be understood that one individual would not be expected to have all the knowledge or technical skills to be able to function in every category listed. Instead, it must be realized that several persons are employed in various capacities, depending upon their abilities, prior experiences, technical proficiency, and the size of the agency. Thus, personnel on the administrative level might be employed in positions requiring responsibility for office management, personnel management, fiscal (budgetary) management, maintenance, planning administration, or program administration.

As a specialist in some aspect of recreational service, the administrative worker has a professional obligation and a positional responsibility to assist in keeping the executive informed not only of the problems and need of his own division, but also of developments and achievements in the entire field which have a bearing on the area of his technical expertise. If the administrative worker has performed all those tasks which are required to make the agency more effective and still finds that his efforts are being frustrated due to deficiencies or incompetencies in equipment, facilities, or personnel beyond his control, it is his duty to bring these matters to the attention of the executive and to make definite recommendations for their improvement.

The Executive Level

When mention is made of the executive level, it is well to keep in mind that the word *executive* implies more than manager, director, supervisor, or coordinator. The executive is the individual solely responsible for the operational effectiveness and efficiency of others. This individual assigns tasks and directs and controls all aspects of the project, program, or agency operation. He or she has the final responsibility for the execution of work performed by all personnel within the organization. The roster of executive level duties appears in Table 4.

In the choice of executive, care must be taken not to select only on the basis of technical proficiency, prior experience, and knowledge. While these criteria are important to the executive position, administrative skill and a capacity for work are also significant and necessary attributes. The executive level demands (a) a high degree of administrative ability. The executive must be able to sustain all operations smoothly, actively, and effectively; (b) to comprehend and utilize the applicable principles of organization and direction; (c) to appreciate the requirement for equitable personnel practices and recognize the need for sound personnel and human relations; and (d) to follow concepts of leadership i.e., clearly see objectives, plan with subordinates the procedure to follow for the execution of these aims, delegate the requisite authority to those who are assigned the responsibility for performing various aspects of the program, and set limits to insure that his ideas are being followed.

In selecting an executive, it is important to choose someone with the ability to identify and focus on significant problems rather than someone who would dissipate his efforts on minor problems that could be better handled at lower levels. The executive, then, has the skill to view conditions from long range and plan accordingly.

The following compilation of facts relates to the executive's office in connection with the various types of organizational structures to which the executive may be attached. Regardless of whether there is a board, council, or commission with ultimate responsibility for the provision of

Table 4. Executive Level Duties

1. Directs the operation of the department in accordance with established policies.
2. Promotes maximum efficiency of departmental operations.
3. Develops and promotes personnel policy.
4. Plans for the physical enhancement of department property and such additions as are found necessary to carry out the goals of the department.
5. Controls and is accountable for all fiscal operations of the department.
6. Continuously evaluates all personnel of the department.
7. Continuously appraises the departmental program of recreational services.
8. Continuously monitors the physical plant of the department.
9. Speaks for the department in any sensitive situation or where representation is necessary before higher authority.
10. Implements and directs an effective public relations program.

recreational service to the institution or community, or if the executive simply reports to a managing authority (mayor, city manager, hospital administrator, warden, or other official), the duties, responsibilities, and powers, as defined below are typical of the work which is performed.

Subject to legal review by a higher authority, if there is one, the chief executive of the recreational department, agency, or system, has direct and unshared responsibility for the effective and efficient functioning and operation of the system. He or she is responsible for the general organization, administration, management, and supervision of the department as a whole and its employees, and exercises all necessary powers incident thereto. The executive is always associated with the management and control of personnel practices, fiscal administration, methodology, and the plans and operations of the overall recreational program.

When there is a board, the executive occupies a seat on the board, attends all meetings of the board and its committees, and has full privilege to speak and express opinions and suggestions on all matters before that board. The executive compiles, collates, and prepares for board examination the minutes of all meetings, the annual report of the system, the annual budget message and statements, and all estimates for appropriations; prepares annual, periodic, and special reports of recreational services provided throughout the community, agency, or institution;

analyzes, collects, and assembles such information as may be useful by the board; recommends to the board such actions as will promote recreational services to the potential clientele of the agency.

The executive is responsible for the progressive development of recreational service throughout the institution or community, in accordance with most approved principles, methods, and practices in the field of recreational service. He or she keeps abreast of new developments and improvements by a complete study of available factual material, and applies that which is advantageous. The executive's functions may be divided into eight spheres: personnel management; program management; maintenance management; financial management; records management; educational administration; planning, research, and development; and negotiation. While most of these functions are specifically delegated to subordinates and specialists for execution, the final responsibility for them resides with the executive. Outlined below are specific activities normally associated with each of the executive functions.

1. **Personnel Management.** The executive has the responsibility for recruitment, in-service education, and supervision of all personnel; development of equitable personnel practices; the periodic appraisal and evaluation of workers; and the maintenance of proper working conditions for personnel of the agency.

   a. Authorized to employ such part-time and special employees that may be necessary to carry out the recreational service functions for the fulfillment of the provisions of this responsibility.

   b. Authorized to suspend for cause, pending investigation of the merits of the case, any employee for a period of not more than 30 days.

   c. Authorized to accept the resignation of any employees, to grant leaves of absence, to make all assignments, to sign or countersign payrolls and to perform such other managerial duties which may be required.

   d. Has administrative and technical supervision over all other employees of the agency.

The executive will also be concerned with the promotion of morale and group spirit of lay and professional groups of the community or institution working on recreational problems which have interest for them. He or she will have knowledge of group dynamics and attempt to promote the desire to work cooperatively in the solution of common problems among the individual concerned. He or she will further assist in the development of the individual abilities to contribute to group effort.

2. **Program Management.** The executive's objective is to facilitate effective recreational services through a program of activities which will actually satisfy the recreational needs of people.
   a. **Program planning** is the interpretation of philosophy and policy into concrete experiences of a recreational nature. Such practices will be initiated from the interests and demands of clientele as well as selective criteria necessary for the provision of the program.
   b. **Program direction** is concerned with the management of personnel and materials in a coordinated manner so that specific duties will be carried out with a minimum of friction and optimum service. This phase of the work is executed through a system-wide utilization of records, periodic inspection and observation, reports of supervisors, staff conferences, and the analyses of studies related to the departmental program.
   c. **Program balance** is concerned with the maintenance of a well-rounded, full range, yearly program offering a variety of activities in which nearly all may participate. Thus, each age, sex, racial, ethnic, social, economic, or other identifiable group is served without discrimination as to types or variety of experiences.
3. **Maintenance Management.** The executive is responsible for the planning, design, construction, and maintenance of all recreational areas and structures which constitute the physical property of the system; must be aware of and utilize the latest materials and design ideas for the instruction and proper placement of new facilities; must choose designs for structures and spaces which will offer maximum opportunity for use by clients.
4. **Financial Management.** The executive is responsible for all budgeting and spending. It is upon his or her extimates of services to be provided, programs needed, and personnel to operate the system that appropriations will be based.
5. **Records Management.** The records and reports submitted by program personnel are utilized for making periodic studies and surveys for the continuous improvement and guidance of personnel.

    a. The executive is obliged to develop or design and approve forms for records and reports in relation to the handling of departmental business to ensure continuity by personnel and to facilitate the process whereby information may be readily obtained.

    b. The executive sets up inventory procedures for the control of office, program, maintenance, and administrative supplies, materials, and equipment.

    c. The maintenance of records, central files, and field files, as well as adequate filing systems for the preservation of correspondence, studies, and legal papers of all kinds is also part of the executive's function.

6. **Educational Administration.** Public education and interpretation deals with the dissemination of information to potential clients on matters of interest to them. Where there is some question as to policy statements, various activity offerings, and justifications for agency priority schedules, these must be clarified. Public relations, as an outgrowth of education, is concerned with the reduction of conflict situations between the agency and its constituents. Since the executive is the chief public relations officer of the department, it is up to him to establish a procedure by which the agency is interpreted to potential clients.

7. **Planning, Research, and Development.** As chief officer for the recreational service agency, the executive must necessarily be involved in the study, survey, and analysis of the condition of recreational needs, both personal and physical, of the community or institution, and must compile and otherwise assemble and report on such information pertaining to recreational service. Thus, he or she will do whatever is appropriate to generate the required information so that this function is successful.

8. **Negotiation.** The chief executive may be required to negotiate, prepare, and administer regular and periodic agreements for the agency, public, quasi-public, and private agencies or individuals for the purposes of enhancing the recreational services within the institution or community through the development of recreational programs for all. This will probably involve the coordination and utilization of such physical property or personnel as these contacts indicate.

As we have seen in this chapter, in the field of recreational service the levels of leadership are divided among functional workers, supervisors, administrators, and executives, all of whom are recreationists in the professional sense. The basic function of the recreationist within any recreational service agency is in working and communicating with and understanding human beings and their individual behavior patterns—to the extent that such patterns are understandable. Recreationists must determine the interests and needs of those whom they will serve and then perform those specific duties and responsibilities which will enable people to satisfy their recreational needs. While it is true that no one recreationist is highly skilled in all phases of recreational activity, he should know where to turn for the needed skills and for available resource materials.

Although the range of leadership is great—from complete direction to passive appreciation—the ability of the participants will dictate the recreational role within any given set of experiences. The highly successful recreationist is one whose followers are not aware of being led. In many instances success within a given group may be attained only by working through others. All levels of leadership deal with other individuals, so that different personalities are brought into close contact, either to clash or to harmonize. The recreationist will attempt to promote relationships which build morale and group spirit to achieve goals.

Chapter 25

CAREER OPPORTUNITIES
AND PROFESSIONAL ORGANIZATIONS

J ob opportunities in the field of recreational service are many and
varied. According to a recent estimate there are now about 6,000
annual vacancies. Positions are available at all governmental levels and
with a variety of agencies in the public and private sectors. The recreationist can choose from a broad spectrum of settings according to: age
group to be served, skills to be taught, type of clientele (hospital, penal,
industrial, school, armed forces, tourist, etc.), and geographic preference.
Employment opportunities are increasing both at home and abroad.
Salaries in the growing field of recreational service depend upon the
degree of experience and the professional preparation the individual
has had. In general, salaries also reflect the economic ability of a given
state, city, or region to pay for these services. Salaries of between $20,000
per year for a beginning worker without experience to $80,000 per year,
and sometimes higher, for the highly experienced executive are illustrative of the range. In this chapter we survey the types of recreational
positions in detail, and conclude with a look at some of the long-
established professional organizations in the field.

Employment in Recreational Service

The personnel employed in recreational service agencies of all types
is determined by the nature and amount of work to be performed.
Generally, there are three more or less distinct operating functions:
(1) organizing, operating, and conducting recreational programs; (2) planning, maintenance, and construction of recreational facilities; and (3) those
duties related to the business and clerical work of administration. These
positions and terms of employment of the recreationists are the proper
object of this section.

Employees hired to perform duties directly related to the provision of recreational services in terms of a complete program of recreational activities are specialists who may be presumed to have had pre-entry preparation of the type required by their specialities. Although the uniqueness of the recreationist lies with his or her orientation to the field of recreational service as a generalist, additionally, the several abilities which are involved in the organizational aspects of recreational experiences for agency clientele also indicate that he or she is a specialist.

Positions in the field of recreational service are not as standardized as some of the more established professions. Yet, there is a tendency toward the standardization of duties and functions, if not titles, in the public field and to a lesser extent in the private sector. An examination of the titles used by many cities and other jurisdictions which are carrying on this work shows a high degree of unanimity concerning titles of employment as well as duties and responsibilities.

The duties of persons employed by recreational agencies vary because of the differences in size of operations, funds available for programming, the number, size, and type of facilities operated, and the conduct of the program. In many instances the job tends to conform to the recreationist within the position rather than like so many standardized positions in commerce or industry where the employee conforms to the job.

Jobs in Public Agencies

The public services of a recreational nature are rendered through such facilities as libraries, playgrounds, national, state, county, and local parks, and other recreational plants, centers, and facilities. These services, however, tend to go far beyond the mere provision of physical facilities. They include the organization and promotion of public recreational activities and the supervision of these varied experiences.

The following is a description of the titles generally used and the responsibilities usually assigned to each type of position within the public agency:

1. **Superintendent.** The chief executive officer of a department, division, or bureau, having unshared responsibility for the organization, direction, administration, planning, and conduct of the entire system; usually responsible to a municipal governing authority which may be a city manager, mayor, council, or legally constituted board.

2. **General Supervisor.** Administrative officer responsible to the superintendent and/or assistant superintendent for a geographic portion of the municipality of a group of facilities of similar type, their personnel

and the general program of activities carried on therein; or of some specific function generally applicable to all centers, e.g., Supervisor of Playgrounds, Centers, etc.

3. Supervisor of Special Activity. Staff officers responsible for special phases of any given program. Responsibilities of these employees vary greatly and depend upon the scope of the entire program, the size of the agency, and the number of specialists who are available. Examples of such personnel responsibilities might be Supervisor of Dramatics, Nature Study, Arts and Crafts, Music, or other activities as required.

4. Director of Facilities. Line officers in charge of directing a center or other large facility and the employed personnel and program administered therein. Usually these personnel are responsible to a general supervisor, if there are a number of similar facilities to warrant the employment of one.

5. Leaders. Line personnel functioning on a face-to-face basis who, under the close direction of facility directors or assistant directors, exercise general oversight of program activities of children and adults who participate at a center, playground, or other recreational facility. Such employees may conduct, instruct, or provide resource information in any given activity of the facility program.

6. Specialists. Personnel who instruct in specific activities, usually at more than one facility or center, whose responsibility is limited to the instruction or organization of a particular activity, e.g., tennis, dance, or archery.

Jobs in Quasi-Public Agencies

Various types of community organizations are prominent in the promotion of community recreational services. While such agencies are organized for community betterment, they are not supported by tax funds. Indeed, much, if not all, of their operating expenses is made up of small private donations as well as from the United Way, United Givers Fund, and other donative type sources. Such agencies may be proclaimed a public service, as the National American Red Cross, or be created by a public agency, as are police and fire department athletic leagues. They may provide services only to a specific group, as do college or university student unions (usually as a campus recreational center), or they may serve the immediate needs of a small portion of a municipality's population, depending upon their location, as do neighborhood houses. However they are constituted, they serve in an important capacity for bringing recreational service to some segment of the population in the community. Agencies such as the police athletic leagues are organized primarily for recreational purposes. In the social settlements type the primary purpose may be the elevation of home life or neighborhood living. These are usually denoted as "character building agencies" or, more recently, as "group work agencies," the latter term signifying that they employ informal educational and recreational techniques in group activity.

The quasi-public agencies make an important contribution to American leisure in several ways. Their programs are definitely for the improvement of standards of recreational living. They pioneer in new fields of social work which sometime are later accepted as public functions. (The first playgrounds, for example, were conducted by private social work agencies.) Their ability to go far beyond what the public agency can do (regulated as it is by public control) may provide for more rapid advances in the enhancement of human leisure programs. They relate to the work of recreational leadership thousands of adults who assume responsibilities as lay volunteer workers. This constitutes an education process in itself which serves as a support to all programs for better recreational service.

The American National Red Cross is an outstanding example of an agency which offers career opportunities to recreationists. Among the recreational positions found in this quasi-public agency are the following:

1. **Club Director.** Organizes, administers, and conducts clubs.

2. **Assistant Club Director.** Assists the Director and substitutes in the director's absence.

3. **Club Program Director.** Operates the recreational program within the club.

4. **Assistant Program Director.** Assists the Director and substitutes in the Director's absence.

5. **Recreational Staff Assistant.** Performs face-to-face recreational leadership in various activities within the club program.

6. **Clubmobile Staff Assistant.** Performs face-to-face leadership in various recreational activities in an outdoor environment.

7. **Hospital Recreational Worker.** Plans, organizes, and conducts a varied program of recreational activities for patients in military hospitals.

8. **Hospital Staff Aide.** Performs face-to-face recreational leadership functions in military hospitals.

Jobs in Private Recreational Agencies

Churches. The church has always exercised an important influence upon leisure activities. Historically, it has sanctioned certain forms of leisure activities and has censored and supressed others. Since, generally speaking, the attitude of the church has been liberalized, the church provides through its many activities opportunities for recreational expression. To some extent the church services themselves may be regarded as recreational, inasmuch as they provide emotional outlet and occasion to give expression to cultural impulses. Recreation may be a part of worship. The church offers the setting and stimulus for social participation in a wide variety of group activities—choral and congregational singing, Christmas and Easter pageants, forums, group discussions, entertainments, suppers, and Sunday school picnics. Not a few churches have provided gymnasiums, social halls, and playgrounds, and have made their plants the centers of recreational activities for their congregations, especially the children and youth. The church must, therefore, be recognized as being among the most important agencies serving recreational needs. Churches employ recreationists to organize programs.

Unions, Fraternal, Civic, Professional Clubs. Fraternal orders, labor unions, civic clubs, professional and business societies, country clubs, the Young Men's and Women's Christian Associations, The Hebrew Associations, the Catholic Youth Organization, and women's clubs must also be recognized as playing important parts in filling the need for recreational pursuit. While they are organized primarily for benevolent and civic service purposes, it may be noted that such activity constitutes a part of recreational experience. Associated with such primary activities within these organizations, however, are may secondary social activities which embody much of their programs and which add interest and zest to membership.

The influence of these organizations may be inferred from their size.[1] It is estimated that fraternal societies in America have a total membership of about 19,000,000. The total membership of civic service and women's clubs is over 60,000,000, of all denominations of churches, 120,250,000, and of labor unions, 21,987,108. The total membership of the various Y organizations and youth-serving agencies of this type is said to

---

[1]Deborah M. Burek, ed., *Encyclopedia of Associations,* Vol. I, 26th ed. (Michigan: Gale Research Company 1992), pp. 1149–1344, 1843–2302, 2321–2344, also U.S. Bureau of the Census, *Statistical Abstracts of the United States* 1991 (U.S.G. P.O.: Washington, D.C.), 1991.

exceed 35,800,000 persons.[2] In addition to the recreational outlets which these agencies afford their own members, who are predominantly adults, they frequently sponsor and provide some funds for programs of a recreational character for children.

Besides the organizations whose interest in recreational activity is incidental to their main purpose, there are several types of private organizations in the community whose main purpose is the promotion of recreational experience. These differ from voluntary agencies in the fact that they require payment of dues, fees, tithes, or other charges for their support. In some cases, a few of the private organizations, because they are clearly seen to be organized for community betterment, draw a small amount of support from voluntary contributions and other philanthropic sources. Even where the most prominent portion of their program may be said to be recreational in nature, they are not, strictly speaking, recreational agencies, but utilize recreational activity as a means of enticement and as a program through which their primary aims are accomplished.

These agencies are primarily interested in children and youth, but in recent years have widened their service to include individuals of all ages. Some provide buildings, grounds, and equipment for varied recreational activities, but all have well-formulated programs designed to contribute to the improvement of behavior. In the past, and to some extent now, these organizations have been spoken of as "character building agencies," but more recently as private recreational agencies, as in the case of the Y's.

Industrial. Industrial recreational opportunities are growing. Recreationists in industry are primarily concerned with recreational guidance, planning and conducting comprehensive programs for workers and their families. In general the job titles of industrial recreational workers generally follow those of other private agencies, i.e., director, program worker, staff assistant. Positions within this field may be secured through several sources. Some workers utilize the resources of the National Industrial Recreational Association; others may apply directly to the corporation, company, plant, or union in which they may wish to work. Many recreational workers are selected from within industrial plants so another method for gaining entrance may be through the personnel department

---

[2]Mark S. Hoffman, ed., *The World Almanac and Book of Facts* 1992 (New York: Scripps Howard), pp. 549–562.

of the company. With experience, recreationists rise through several positional levels, including assistant director, specialist, recreational director, and occasionally to Director of Personnel if their experience has included personnel work along with their recreational functions.

Institutional. In institutional settings of all kinds, e.g., penal, hospital, or church, whether they are of the public, quasi-public, or private type, there exists the need for professional personnel working in recreational service. The position levels correspond to those of other public or community titles, and the duties and responsibilities for planning, conducting, or leading recreational activities are the same. The difference between the institutionalized setting and the community setting is the goal toward which the program is oriented. Thus, the recreationist in the penal institution gears the program to help in social rehabilitation, while the therapeutic recreationist is concerned with assisting patients in terms of physical or mental rehabilitation. In instances where the individual has been disabled since birth, the recreationist provides activities which may enrich the daily living of that person. Such assistance is habilitation rather than rehabilitation. The church recreationist orients his/her program toward the teachings and character development inherent in the philosophy of his/her denomination.

Youth Services. Recreationists have a wide range of choices if they desire employment in youth organization work. Of the many national organizations performing youth services of a recreational nature, some of the best known are the YMCA, YWCA, Boy and Girl Scouts of America, Camp Fire Girls, Boys Clubs of America, YMHA, YWHA, CYO, Jewish Community Centers of the Jewish Welfare Board, 4-H Clubs, Future Farmers of America, Future Home Makers of America, sponsored by the United States Department of Agriculture, and the United Christian Youth Movement. On the local governmental or community level are countless police and fire department athletic leagues, and many civic service clubs employing professionals to guide youth service activities.

Youth-serving agencies usually function as private or quasi-public organizations, assisted by philanthropic funds or by membership dues. There are, however, governmentally organized youth-serving agencies as well. The rapid growth of membership in such agencies surely indicates their importance. Almost four million boys and men are enrolled in some phase of Scouting, while membership in the Girl Scouts numbers over 2,000,000 girls and 600,000 adults. More than 2,000 professional workers are employed to guide the activities performed by these individuals. Four hundred thousand members participate in Boys' Club activities, which employ a professional staff of nearly 5,000 full-time and part-time workers. More than 3,000 professional workers serve over 3,000,000 YMCA members, two-thirds of whom are under twenty-five years of age, while the YWCA employs nearly 3,000 professionals.

Additionally, some general agencies have youth divisions or include youth services as part of their program. The American National Red Cross and the Jewish Neighborhood Houses fit in these categories, employing about 2,000 professional personnel.

Organizations such as those indicated above vary in their position classification and titles, but they correspond in terms of structure. Typical positions in the youth-serving agencies are as follows:

1. **Executive Director** (also called General or Executive Secretary). The chief professional worker of the agency, responsible directly to the agency board. In very small agencies, is usually the only professional employed; but in most places professional assistants are employed, the number depending upon the clientele served. The executive director serves as advisor to the board, is the chief financial officer of the agency, and is responsible for the physical plant and its maintenance. Also supervises and provides in-service education to all employees and volunteers.

2. **Program Director.** (Activities Director, Boy's or Girl's Work Secretary, and other titles). Chiefly responsible for scheduling and planning all of the activities initiated by the Director and the Board. Responsible for recruiting and preparing volunteers to assist in carrying out the various activities of the overall program. Sometimes there is an assistant program director who may work closely with either boys' or girls' activities. The largest agencies may have directors for adults as well as youth.

3. **Physical Activity Director or Secretary.** Responsible for all of the physical activities conducted by the agency. May instruct in water safety classes and physical fitness classes and organize teams and leagues for various athletic activities. Usually coordinates work with community recreational services.

4. **Camp Director.** Responsible to the executive director. In charge of carrying out the camping program. Responsible for all phases of the camp activity, including maintenance of the physical property, and the health, welfare, and safety of all campers. May also direct the activities program.

5. Specialists. Where there is a need for further diversification of responsibility, personnel who are specialists in specific activities or phases of program may be employed, e.g., group director for clubs, social director, etc.

REGIONAL. Agencies that work within geographical areas or regions rather than in centers may have positions corresponding to the following:

1. Field or District Executive. Under the direction of the executive director or secretary, the field executive is responsible for conducting all operations in his area. Duties include organizing new units, coordinating the program through local leaders, supervising existing programs, and assisting with in-service programs, camping activities, and similar matters. Generally, this position is a traveling assignment with the executive shuttling between several communities of the jurisdiction.

2. Field Worker. Work is similar to that of the executive and more intensive, but area is smaller with fewer units.

PRIVATE CLUBS. Other types of employment, e.g., in private agencies, may be seen from the following list of titles used in private recreational clubs.

1. Club Manager. Serves as the general manager in charge of the complete facility and its personnel. Is responsible for obtaining new members for the club, conducting sales promotion, recruiting, and public relations as directed by the board of directors. Responsible for planning, promoting, and organizing a comprehensive recreational program for the membership of the club. Carries out the policies of the club as established by the board of directors and serves as technical advisor to the board.

2. Recreational Leader. Responsible for the organization, development, and personal leadership of a variety of activities as assigned by the club manager. Organizes, promotes, leads, and teaches a variety of recreational activities, including crafts, low-organizational games, sports, dancing, story-telling, nature study, and informal group singing. Consults with individuals and groups to determine interests and needs. Organizes and acts as advisor to clubs and groups. Assists in recruiting, preparing, and supervising seasonal, part-time, or volunteer personnel.

3. Activity Specialist. Responsible for one special activity, e.g., arts and crafts, dramatics, etc. Organizes, teaches, and conducts an activity requiring technical knowledge. Serves as staff person to the Recreational Leader and supplements knowledge on specific occasions such as play productions or the staging of a pageant.

EMPLOYMENT TITLES

The following position titles are utilized for all agencies providing recreational programs on an organized basis for public, quasi-public, or private groups. These agencies require:

Administrative

    Superintendent of Park and Recreational Services
    Superintendent of Recreational Services
    Assistant Superintendent
    Commissioner and Assistant Commissioner
    Director, Assistant Director, or Chief Deputy Director

Supervisory

    General Supervisor of Recreational Services
    Area Supervisor of Recreational Activities
    Supervisor of Sports or Athletics for Men or Women

Program Specialist

a. Arts and Crafts
b. Sports and Games
c. Aquatics
d. Dance
e. Dramatics
f. Outdoor Education and Camping (nature Oriented)
g. Music
h. Public Relations
i. Special Projects/Events
j. Volunteers and Services

Program Director

    Director of Recreational Center
    Director of Playground
    Director of Recreational Services for a school system
    Service Club Director
    Camp Director
    Therapeutic Recreational Service Director (Activities Director)
    Minister of Education (church recreational service)
    Director of Activity Therapy
    Program Director of a college Student Union
    Industrial Recreational Services Director
    Playstreet Director (police athletic league)
    YMCA, YWCA Program Director

Leader/Instructor

Playground Leader
Youth Services Supervisor
Pool Supervisor/Manager
Beach Supervisor/Manager
Golf Links (course) Manager
Camp Counselor, Camping Specialist
Boy Scout Leader
Consultant
Coordinator of Recreational Service
Educator

The status and prestige of recreationists is being enhanced and upgraded as more people realize the need for such professional persons. Without good leadership, well-educated and professionally qualified, there can never be worthwhile recreational programs. The field needs the dedication of competent and intelligent people to service the growing demand for organized recreational experiences. This is the unlimited potential for future recreationists.

Professional Organizations

Every field of human service which aspires toward professional status inevitably forms some kind of association. By organizing, the field brings together disparate elements, provides some measure of standardized practice, develops a code of ethics, initiates conferences wherein the practitioners can transmit the techniques common to the field, and offers a united front so that the message of the field's intent and value to society becomes well known. Each ascendant professional field must take its cue from the practitioners of law and medicine. It must create a highly organized body which speaks authoritatively for all practitioners within the field on matters of public interest and concern. The organization may then be able to command considerable influence in the several state legislatures, as well as in the Congress, where the full majesty and power of the law can be brought to bear for the benefit of those who practice. The presumption of such activity is that what benefits the practitioners will also redound to the benefit of those whom they serve.

When the field achieves an eminent status, the professional association often attempts to seek state sanction through certification or licensing procedures designed to assure competency among the field's workers. Through its various interest groups the association develops basic educational standards. These are translated into formalized curricular offerings in institutions of higher education, which may then seek accreditation from whatever authority generally deals with that specialization.

Professional associations police their own members. Not only is there an attempt to transmit the best practices possible, but there is usually considerable pressure on the part of peers to uphold ethical standards of conduct. Professional organizations, whether international, national, regional, or state, all have the same intent: to foster the acceptance of the field as a socially significant and valuable contributor to the welfare of all people who are served, and the maintenance of educational and experiential levels which are expected to provide guidance for superior performance by practitioners.

The field of recreational service continues to strive for excellence and to aspire toward professional status. In this regard, there are many organizations representing or serving the field in some way. Many of these groups are highly specialized and may serve only a limited membership. However, other organizations have large memberships and many affiliated groups representing specialized areas. A sampling of these organizations is discussed in this section.

Recreational Service Organizations

National Recreation and Park Association. The NRPA is perhaps the best known recreational service organization. It was formed in 1966 by the merger of the following organizations: the *American Institute of Park Executives,* the *American Association of Zoological Parks and Aquariums,* the *American Recreation Society,* the *National Conference on State Parks,* and the *National Recreation Association.*

The National Recreation and Park Association (1601 North Kent Street, Arlington, Virginia 22202) is an independent, nonprofit service organization dedicated to the advancement and enhancement of the recreational service movement and to the conservation of natural and human resources. The Association is directed by a 63 member board of trustees that meets several times a year. It has a professional staff of specialists in parks, recreational activities, conservation, and associated fields. Additional professional representatives divided into district offices across the United States provide personal consultant services to park and recreational service agencies at the municipal, county, state, and regional levels.

The NRPA has an active membership of almost 17,000 including: citizens interested in recreational activities, parks, zoos, and conservation of natural resources and wildlife; parks and recreational service commissioners and board members; professional park and recreational leaders; government and private recreational and park agencies. Data on its membership makeup is shown in Table 1.

According to their specific interests, most NRPA members are also affiliated with one of six professional and volunteer branches: the American Park and Recreation Society; the National Conference on State Parks; the National Therapeutic Recreation Society; the Society of Park and Recreation Educators; the commissioners and board members of park and recreational agencies, and the National Student Branch.

As a service organization, NRPA works closely with public and private park and recreational agencies at the national, state, and local levels to foster the progressive development and wise administration of resources, facilities, programs, and personnel. Because of this close liaison, the Association serves as a repository for a vast amount of factual information on a wide variety of recreational and park topics.

Financial support comes entirely through public contributions, endowments, grants, and membership fees. Much of its income is raised annually through United Fund campaigns.

In addition to special publications, the NRPA issues the following publications at regular intervals:

Parks and Recreation Magazine
Recreation and Park Yearbook
A Guide to Books on Recreation
Playground Summer Notebook
Journal of Leisure Research
Therapeutic Recreation Journal
NRPA Membership Directory
Management aids
Newsletters
Park Practice Program Series

NRPA serves the general public through cooperation with public and private park and recreational agencies. Services to these agencies include the following:

Table 1. NRPA Membership Statistics, March 6, 1992

				Branches							
AFRB	APRS	C-BM	CRTS	NSPR	NAS	NRSB	NTRS	SPRE	LAS	OTHER	TOTAL
715	6703	6468		1117	750	1655	2619	723	1	10	20761
10	71			8			15	14		1	119
79	1053			168			406	91		2	1799
	5			1			6			4	16
	2									1	3
	1									120	121
6	47	1		9			2	1			66
	57										57
	5						5	127			137
		1					10				11
1	20	1		2							24
36	61			306			14	2		1	420
	39			5							44
4	20	3		6		6	4	4		382	429
851	8084	6474		1622	750	1661	3081	962	1	521	24007

AFRB: Armed Forces Recreational Branch
APRS: American Park & Recreation Society
C–BM: Commission and Board Members
NSPR: National Society for Park Resources
NRSB: National Recreation Student Branch
NTRS: National Therapeutic Recreation Society
SPRE: Society of Park and Recreation Educators
LAS: Leisure and Aging Section
CRTS: Commercial Recreation and Tourism Society
NAS: National Aquatic Society

1. Conducts nationwide efforts to acquaint all Americans with the benefits of physical fitness, conservation, beautification, and open spaces for recreational purposes.
2. Acts as a clearinghouse for information among national, state, district, and local public and private agencies.
3. Conducts studies of specific agency problems and recommends solutions.
4. Serves as a consultant on state legislation and policies.

5. Devises and suggests standards for facilities, programs, administration, and budget.
6. Gathers factual information on the present status of parks and recreational services, and forecasts future trends.
7. Works with educational institutions to improve curricula.
8. Sponsors an annual fair of equipment and products.
9. Sponsors national promotional campaigns on behalf of recreational service and parks.
10. Encourages public support for agency policies.

NRPA also offers the following individual services to professionals and non-professionals interested in the park and recreational service movement:

1. Helps professionals keep abreast of new ideas and techniques.
2. Conducts schools, conferences, and seminars for professionals.
3. Sponsors national and regional congresses to provide forums for renowned experts.
4. Maintains a job placement service for professionals.
5. Sponsors an internship program for recent park and recreational service education graduates.
6. Conducts experiments with equipment and programs to evaluate effectiveness and ensure safety.
7. Encourages improvement of recreational opportunities for special groups such as the disabled, infirm aged, and mentally retarded.
8. Provides information to all persons on specific park and recreational activities.
9. Promotes community recognition of outstanding volunteer efforts through an awards program.
10. Encourages individual participation in agency programs.

American Alliance for Health, Physical Education, Recreation and Dance (AAHPERD, 1900 Association Drive, Reston, Virginia 22091). Founded in 1885.

Membership: students in preparation for employment and practitioners in the fields of physical education, dance, health, athletics, safety education, recreational service, and outdoor recreational activities; 45,000 members.

Objectives: To improve recreational participation in the United States. It sponsors district conferences and a national convention every other year. It establishes and promotes personnel and program standards and supports legislation of interest to the profession. It helps recruit and place professional personnel and provides technical and consultative exchange of information services.

AAHPERD Publications:

The Journal of Physical Education, Recreation, and Dance

Research Quarterly

Leisure Today

Bibliographies, conference reports, bulletins, rosters, surveys, and other material

American Camping Association (ACA, Bradford Woods, Martinsville, Indiana 46151). Founded in 1910.

Membership: Camp directors, camp staff, educators, people concerned with the operation of camps and the camping movement; 7,800 members.

Objectives: To further the interests and welfare of children and adults through camping as a recreational and educational experience. The Association expresses the views of camping people at both the national and local levels, in addition to providing leadership in the development of new camping areas. Also, disseminates information on new camping trends, as well as developing standards and operating codes for the improvement of camping practices. It maintains a library and conducts a Campcraft Certification Program.

ACA Publications:

Camping Magazine (published eight times per year)

National Directory of Accredited Camps

Pamphlets, studies, reports, and other publications at various times during the year.

World Leisure and Recreation Association (WLRA). Founded in 1956 as the International Recreation Association; changed to WLRA in 1975.

Membership: Citizens, professionals, and statesmen involved in the world recreational service movement.

The primary objectives of the WLRA are as follows:

1. Serve as a central clearinghouse for the exchange of information and experiences among recreational service agencies of the world.
2. Aid countries to establish central recreational service agencies upon request.
3. Forward the development of a world recreational service movement designed to enrich the human spirit through wholesome use of leisure.

4. Encourage the provision of land and facilities, training of leaders, developing of varied programs, and public interpretation of values of recreational experiences for all age groups everywhere.
5. Provide a medium through which the recreational service authorities of the world may work in unity on common problems.

Services of the WLRA include:

1. Maintains a central office to service the international recreational service organizations of the world.
2. Provides correspondence and consultation services on specific problems.
3. Provides a field service to countries desiring help with central recreational agencies.
4. Provides a field service on specific aspects of program.
5. Encourages the exchange of recreational service leaders among nations.
6. Cooperates with the United Nations and its affiliated agencies.
7. Publishes a bulletin for recreational agencies to exchange information.
8. Aids and encourages programs for leadership training in recreational service.
9. Arranges for international and regional conferences.
10. Encourages the contribution of funds—public and private—to the development of recreational services for all.

Publications: WLRA *Bulletin* and other related materials.

National Employee Services Recreation Association (NESRA, 20 North Wacker Drive, Chicago, Illinois 60606). Founded in 1941 as the National Industrial Recreation Association; changed to NESRA in 1982.

Membership: Athletic and recreational service directors for commercial and industrial firms; 800 members.

Objectives: Advancement of profession and research in areas relating to industrial recreational service.

Services: Maintains library and placement service; operates regional workshops, gives annual awards for best industrial recreational programs.

NESRA Publications:

Recreation Management
President's Bulletin
Manuals and research reports

American Therapeutic Recreation Association (ATRA, 1021 L. Street

NW Washington, D.C. 20036), was established during 1984 as a practitioners guild. This society's membership basically came from the National Therapeutic Recreation Society of NRPA who dissented from the latter group. The association sees itself as the major proponent of practitioner concerns in therapeutic recreational service. Its agenda devolves upon a single minded purpose without the constraints imposed by an overhead organization whose primary objective is park and community based recreational programming.

Whether the ATRA will survive as an independent professional organization depends upon a number of variables; time and money limitations being prominent among others.

Other Organizations: International Federation of Park and Recreation Administration; International Playground Association; Canadian Recreation and Park Association; European Leisure and Recreation Association (ELRA); Israel Leisure and Recreation Association (ILRA); National Community Education Association; National Recreation Sport Association; and various state associations.

A joining together of professionals in a single enterprise serves to unify efforts and offers a method for the forceful presentation of positive information concerning the field. Although there is still some scattering of energy and a number of groups to which professionals give time and financial support, there is rapidly being accepted a single master organization at the national level which can do much to promote the entire recreational service movement.

SELECTED REFERENCES

Chapter 1

1. Butler, G.D., *Pioneers in Public Recreation* (Minneapolis: Burgess, 1965).
2. Chubb, M. and H.R. Chubb, *One third of Our Time? an Introduction to Recreation Behavior and Resources* (N.Y.: John Wiley, 1981).
3. Danford, H.G. *Recreation in the American Community* (N.Y.: Harper, 1953).
4. Doell, C.E. and G.B. Fitzgerald *A Brief History of Parks and Recreation in the United States* (Chicago: The Athletic Institute, 1954).
5. Dulles, F.R. *A History of Recreation: America Learns to Play* (N.Y.: Appleton-Century-Crofts, 1965).
6. Gray, D.E. and D.A. Pelegrin *Reflections on the Recreation and Park Movement* (Dubuque, Iowa: Wm. C. Brown, 1973).
7. Knopp, R.F. and C.E. Hartso, *Play for America: The History of the National Recreation and Park Association,* 1906–1965, (Arlington, VA: NRPA 1980).
8. LaGasse, A.B. and W.L. Cook, *History of Parks and Recreation* (Wheeling, W.Va.: American Institute of Park Executives, 1965).
9. MacLean, J.R., J.A. Peterson, and W.D. Martin, *Recreation and Leisure: The Changing Scene,* (Somerset, N.J.: John Wiley, 1985).
10. Kraus, R.G. *Recreation and Leisure in Modern Society* 4th ed., (Glenview, Ill.: Scott, Foresman/Little, Brown, 1990).

Chapter 2

1. Brightbill, C.K. *The Challenge of Leisure,* (Englewood Cliffs, N.J.: Prentice Hall, Inc., 1960).
2. Cohan, H.D. and W.J. Tait, *Education for Leisure,* (Englewood Cliffs, N.J.: Prentice-Hall, Inc., 1973).
3. Godbey, G. *Leisure in Your Life* (Philadelphia: W.B. Saunders and Co., 1980).
4. Nash, J.B. *The Philosophy of Recreation and Leisure* (Dubuque, Iowa: Wm. C. Brown, 1953).
5. Neumeyer, M. and E. Neumeyer, *Leisure and Recreation* (N.Y.: The Ronald Press, 1949).
6. Robeuch, M. *The Nature of Human Values,* (N.Y.: The Free Press, 1973).
7. Smith, D.H. and N. Theberge, *Why People Recreate,* (Champaign, Ill.: Life Enhancement Publications, 1987).
8. Wesland, C. and J. Knight, *Playing Living Learning,* (State College, Pa: Venture Publishing, 1982).

Chapter 3

1. Busby, R.J. *Recreation and Leisure in New Communities,* 3rd. ed., (Phila., PA: Ballinger Publishing Co., 1976).
2. Gulick, L.H., *A Philosophy of Play,* (N.Y.: Charles Scribner, 1920).
3. Lindeman, E.C., *Leisure: A National Issue,* (N.Y.: American Association for the Study of Group Work, 1939).
4. Kraus, R.G. *Recreation and Leisure in Modern Society,* 4th ed., (Glenview, Il.: Scott, Foresman/Little, Brown, 1990).

Chapter 4

1. Butler, G.D. *Introduction to Community Recreation,* 5th ed. (N.Y.: McGraw Hill Book Co., 1976).
2. Godbey, G. *Recreation, Park and Leisure Services: Foundations, Organization, Administration,* (N.Y.: Holt, Rineholt and Winston, Inc., 1978).
3. Hjelte, G., *The Administration of Public Recreation,* (N.Y.: The MacMillan Company, 1940).
4. Hutchison, J.L. *Principles of Recreation,* (N.Y.: The Ronald Press, 1951).
5. Marlow, P. Ed., *Recreation in America,* (N.Y.: H.W. Wilson, 1965).
6. Rainwater, C.E., *The Play Movement in the United States,* (Chicago: The University of Chicago Press, 1922).
7. Steiner, J.F. *Americans at Play,* (N.Y.: McGraw-Hill Book Co., 1933).

Chapter 5

1. Baum, R.A. *Public Interest Law: Where Law Meets Social Action,* (Dobbs Ferry, N.Y.: Oceana Publications, Inc., 1987).
2. Carlson, K.S. *Law and Structure of Social Action,* (Westport, CT: Greenwood Publishing Group, 1980).
3. Carney, T. *Law at the Margins: Toward Social Participation,* (Westport, CT: Oxford University Press, 1991).
4. Freund, E. and R.H. Heinholz, Jr., eds. *The Police Power: Public Policy and Constitutional Rights* (N.Y.: William S. Hein and Co., Inc., 1981).
5. Gifford, D.J. and K.H. Gifford, *Our Legal System,* 2nd ed. (Holmes Beach, Fla.: William W. Gaunt and Sons, Inc., 1983).
6. Robiliard, St. John and J. McEwan, *Police Powers and the Individual* (Cambridge, Mass.: Blackwell Pubs., 1986).
7. Teaford, J.C. *The Municipal Revolution in America: Origins of Modern Urban Government,* (Chicago: University of Chicago Press, 1975).

Chapter 6

1. Benest, F. *Organizing Leisure and Human Services,* (Dubuque, IA: Kendall/Hunt Publishing Co., 1984).
2. Crimando, W. and T.F. Riggar, *Utilizing Community Resources: An Overview of Human Services,* (Orlando, Fla.: P.M. Deutsch Press, 1992).
3. Broger, G.A. *et al, Community Organizing* 2nd ed., (N.Y.: Columbia University Press, 1987).

Chapter 7

1. Edginton, C.R. and J.G. Williams, *Productive Management of Leisure Service Organizations: A Behavioral Approach,* (N.Y.: John Wily and Sons, Inc., 1978).
2. Gibson, J.L. *Organization: Behavior, Structure, Process,* 3rd ed., (Homewood, Ill.: Business Publications, Inc., 1979).
3. Hjelte, G. and J.S. Shivers, *Public Administration of Recreational Services,* 2nd. ed., (Philadelphia: Lea and Febiger, 1978).
4. Kraus, R.G. and J.E. Curtis, *Creative Management in Recreation, Parks, and Leisure Services,* 5th ed., (St. Louis, MO: Time Mirror/Mosby College Publishing, 1990).
5. Litterer, J. *Organizations: Structure and Behavior,* 3rd ed., (N.Y.: John Wiley and Sons, Inc., 1980).
6. Sessoms, H.P. *Leisure Services,* 6th ed. (Englewood Cliffs, N.J.: Prentice-Hall, Inc., 1984).

Chapter 8

1. Bedeian, A.G. *Management* (Dryden Press, 1986).
2. Walton, M. *Management and Managing* (Harp C, 1984).
3. Adair, J. *Management Decision Making* (Ashgate Publishing Co., 1985).
4. Miringhoff, M.L. *Management in Human Service Organization* (MacMillan, 1980).
5. Gannon, M.J. *Management: Managing for Results* (Wm. C. Brown, 1988).
6. Johnston, R. (Ed.) *Management of Service Operations* (Spris-Verlag, 1988).
7. Anderson, C.R. *Management: Skills, Functions and Organization Performance* 2nd ed., (Wm. C. Brown, 1988).
8. Palumbo, D.J. and S. Maynard-Moorly, *Public Administration,* 2nd ed. (Logman, 1990).
9. Barton, C.R. and W.L. Chappell, *Public Administration: The Work of Government* (Scott Foresman, 1985).
10. Lyne, D.J. *Public Employee Benefit Plans,* 1989 (International Foundation for Employment, 1990).
11. Shivers, Jay S., *Introduction to Recreational Service Administration* (Phila, Pa: Lea and Febiger, 1987).

Chapter 9

1. Mayo, H.B., *Finance,* 2nd ed., (Niles, IL: Dryden Press, 1986).
2. Benjamin, J.L. *Financial Accounting,* 9th ed., (Houston, TX: Dame Publications, 1990).
3. Clark, T.M., *et al,* 2nd ed., *Financial Handbook for Mayors and City Managers* (New York, NY: Van Nostrand Reinhold, 1985).
4. Braswell, R., *et al, Financial Management for Not For Profit Organizations,* (New York, NY: Wiley, 1984).
5. Wacht, R.F., *Financial Management in Nonprofit Organizations,* (Atlanta, GA: Georgia State University Business Press, 1984).

Chapter 10

1. Flynn, R.B. (ed.) *Planning Facilities for Athletics, Physical Education and Recreation,* (Reston, VA: The American Alliance for Health, Physical Education, Recreation, and Dance, 1985).
2. Gold, S.M. *Recreational Planning and Design,* (N.Y.: McGraw-Hill, 1980).
3. Groefe, A., F. Kuss, and J. Vaske, *Recreational Impacts and Carrying Capacity,* (Washington, D.C.: National Parks and Conservation Association, 1987).
4. Hultsman, J., R.L. Cottrell, W. Zaks-Hultsman, *Planning Parks for People,* State College, PA: Venture Publishing, Inc., 1987).
5. Kelsey, C. and H. Gray, *The Feasibility Study Process for Parks and Recreation,* (Reston, VA: The American Alliance for Health, Physical Education, Recreation, and Dance, 1986).
6. Marshall, L., *Action by Design,* (Washington, D.C.: American Society of Landscape Architects, 1983).
7. Molnar, D.J. and A.J. Rutledge, *Anatomy of A Park,* 2nd. ed. (Prospect Heights, Ill.: Waveland Press, Inc., 1992).
8. Petersen, D.C. *Convention Centers, Stadiums, and Arenas,* (Washington, D.C.: The Urban Land Institute, 1989).
9. Rutledge, A.J. *A Visual Approach to Park Design,* (N.Y.: John Wiley and Sons, 1985).

Chapter 11

1. Carpenter, G.M. and Howe, C.Z. *Programming Leisure Experience,* (Englewood-Cliffs, N.J.: Prentice-Hall, 1985).
2. Corbin, H.D. and William E. *Recreation Programming and Leadership,* 4th ed. (Englewood-Cliffs, NJ: Prentice-Hall, 1987).
3. Edginton, C.R., Hanson, C.J. and Edginton, S.R., *Leisure Programming,* 2nd ed., (Dubuque, Iowa: Brown and Benchmark Publishers, 1992).
4. Farrell, P. and Lundegren, H.N. *The Process of Recreation Programming,* 2nd. ed., (N.Y.: John Wiley and Sons, 1983).

5. Kraus, R.A. *Recreation: Program Planning-Today,* (Glenview, Ill.: Scott, Foresman and Company, 1985).
6. Meier, J. and Mitchell, A.V., *Camp Counseling,* (Madison, Wis.: Brown and Benchmark Publishers, 1993).
7. Patterson, F.C. *A Systems Approach to Recreation Programming,* (Columbus, Ohio: Publishing Horizons, Inc.), 1987.
8. Rossman, J.R. *Recreation Programming,* (Champaign, Ill.: Sagamore Publishing, 1989).

Chapter 12

1. Bittel, L.R. and J.W. Newstrom, *What Every Supervisor Should Know,* (N.Y.: McGraw Hill Book Co., 1990).
2. Broadwell, M. and R.S. House, *Supervising Technical and Professional People,* (N.Y.: John Wiley and Sons, Inc., 1986).
3. Catt, S.E. and D.S. Miller, *Supervision: Working With People,* 2nd ed., (Homewood, Ill.: Richard D. Irwin, Inc., 1990).
4. Emanuel, H.M. *et al, Supervisory Skills* 2nd. ed., (Malvern, Pa.: Insurance Institute of America, 1990).
5. Gillespie, K.R. *Creative Supervision,* 2nd ed., (Fort Worth, Tx.: Dryden Press, 1989).
6. Imundo, L. *The Effective Supervisor's Handbook,* (Watertown, Mass.: AMACOM, 1991).
7. Kadushin, A. *Supervision in Social Work,* (N.Y.: Columbia University Press, 1992).
8. Levesque, J.D., *The Human Resource Problem-Solver's Handbook,* (N.Y.: McGraw-Hill Book Co., 1991).
9. Plunkett, W.R., *Supervision: The Direction of People at Work,* (Needham Heights, Mass.: Allyn and Bacon, Inc., 1992).
10. Simpson, W.F. *et al, Essentials of Supervision,* (Malvern, Pa.: Insurance Institute of America, 1991).

Chapter 13

1. Baskin, O.W. and C. Arnoff, *Public Relations: The Profession and the Practice,* 3rd ed., (Dubuque, IA: Wm. Brown, and Benchmark, 1992).
2. Dilenschneider, R.L. *Power and Influence: Mastering the Art of Persuasion,* (Englewood Cliffs, NJ: Prentice-Hall, Inc., 1990).
3. Dotz, D.J., *Publicity and Public Relations,* (Haupauge, N.Y.: Barron's Educational Series, 1990).
4. Dwyer, T.W., *Simply Public Relations: Public Relations Made Challenging, Complete and Concise!* (Stillwater, OK: New Forums Press, Inc., 1992).
5. Ramacitti, P.F., *Do-It-Yourself Publicity,* (Watertown, Mass.: AMACOM, 1990).

6. White, J. *How to Understand and Manage Public Relations: A Jargon-free Guide to Public Relations Management,* (North Pomfret, VT: Trafalgar, 1992).

Chapter 14

1. Bingham, R.D. and C.L. Felbinger, *Evaluation in Practice,* (White Plains, N.Y.: Longman Publishing Group, 1989).
2. Chambers, D.E. *et al, Evaluating Social Programs* (Needham Heights, MA: Allyn and Bacon, 1991).
3. Fitz-Gibbon, C.T. and L.L. Morris, *How to Design a Program Evaluation* 2nd ed., (Newbury Park, Cal.: Sage Publications, Inc., 1987).
4. King, J.A. *et al, How to Assess Program Implementation* 2nd ed. (Newbury Park, Cal.: Sage Publications, Inc., 1987).
5. Kraus, R. and L. Allen, *Research and Evaluation in Recreation, Parks, and Leisure Studies* (Columbus, Ohio: Publishing Horizons, Inc., 1987).
6. Love, A.J. *Internal Evaluation: Building Organizations from Within* (Newbury Park, Cal.: Sage Publications, Inc., 1991).
7. Lundegren, H.M. and P. Farrell, *Education for Leisure Service Managers,* Philadelphia, PA: Saunders College Publishing, 1985).
8. Nagel, S.S. and W. Dunn, eds. *Policy Theory and Evaluation Concepts, Knowledge, Causes and Norms,* (Westport, CT: Greenwood Publishing Group, Inc., 1990).
9. Patton, M.Q., *Qualitative Evaluation and Research Methods,* 2nd ed. (Newbury Park, Cal.: Sage Publishing Inc., 1990).

Chapter 15

1. Blam, G. and D. Simpson, *Political Action: The Key to Understanding Politics* (Athens, Ohio: Ohio University Press, 1984).
2. Flanagan, W.H. and N.H. Lingale, *Political Behavior of the American Electorate,* 6th ed., (Dubuque, IA: Wm. C. Brown, 1987).
3. Allen, C. *Political Campaigning: A New Decade,* (Phila, PA: Packard Press Financial Pub., 1990).
4. Harrigan, J.J. *Political Change in the Metropolis,* 3rd. ed., (Glenview, IL: Scott/Foresman, 1985).
5. Little, G., *Political Ensembles: A Psychosocial Approach to Politics and Leadership,* (Athens, Ohio: Ohio University Press, 1985).
6. Thompson, D.F., *Political Ethics and Public Office,* (Cambridge, MA: Harvard University Press, 1987).
7. Adler, R. *Politics and Media* (New York, NY: St. Martin Press, 1988).
8. Harrigan, J.J. *Politics and Policy in States and Communities,* 3rd ed., (Glenview, IL: Scott/Foresman, 1988).

Chapter 16

1. Bonevac, D. *Today's Moral Issues: Classic and Contemporary Perspectives* (Mountain View, Cal.: Mayfield Publishing Co., 1992).
2. Brandt, R.B. *Morality, Utilitarianism, and Rights,* (N.Y.: Cambridge University Press, 1992).
3. Dawley, A. *Struggles for Justice: Social Responsibility and the Liberal State,* (Cambridge, Mass.: Harvard University Press, 1991).
4. Eldridge, W.D. *Some Thoughts on Social Responsibility,* (Lonhorn, MD: University Press of America, 1991).
5. Elster, J. and J.E. Roemer, eds. *Interpersonal Comparison of Well-Being* (N.Y.: Cambridge University Press, 1991).
6. Paul, E.F. *et al* eds., *The Good Life and the Human Good* (N.Y.: Cambridge, University Press, 1992).
7. Rakowski, E. *Equal Justice,* (N.Y.: Oxford University Press, 1991).
8. Rauch, J. *Kindly Inquisitors: The New Attacks on Free Thought.* (Chicago: University of Chicago Press, 1993).

Chapter 17

1. Arena, J.M. and M.B. Settle, *Child Safety is no Accident* (N.Y.: Berkeley Publishing Group, 1991).
2. Charette, R., *Risk Management,* (N.Y.: McGraw Hill Book Co., 1989).
3. Cox, J. and N. Tait *Reliability, Safety and Risk Management* (Stoneham, MA: Butterworth-Heinemann, 1991).
4. Handmer, J. and E. Penning-Rawsell, *Hazards and the Communication of Risk* (Brookfield, VT: Ashgate Publishing Co., 1990).
5. Morrison, D.A. *Risk Management and Loss Control Manual for Local Government* (Seattle, Wash.: Sound Resource Management, 1989).
6. Seuling, B. *Stay Safe, Play Safe,* (Lake Worth, Fla.: Western Publishing Co., Inc., 1991).
7. Shivers, J.S., *Recreational Safety: The Standard of Care* (Cranbury, NJ: Fairleigh Dicksenson University Press, 1986).
8. Thomen, J.R. *Leadership in Safety Management* (N.Y.: John Wiley and Sons, Inc., 1991).

Chapter 18

1. Bartlett, R.V. ed., *Policy Through Impact Assessment: Institutionalized Analysis As a Policy Strategy* (Westport, CT: Greenwood Publishing Groups, Inc., 1989).
2. Gaines, S., *et al, Taxation for Environmental Protection: A Multinational Study,* (Westport, CT: Quorum Books, 1991).
3. Harrison, H.S. *National Association of Environmental Risks Auditors Environmental Manual,* (New Haven, CT: H. Squared Co., 1990).

4. Orloff, N. *The Environmental Impact Statement Process: A Guide to Citizen Action* (Arlington, VA: Information Resources Press, 1978).
5. Rona, D.C., *Environmental Permits: A Time Saving Guide* (New York: Van Nostrand Reinhold, 1988).

Chapter 19

1. Carter, M.J. *et al,* *Therapeutic Recreation,* (Prospect Heights, Ill.: Waveland Press, Inc., 1990).
2. Case, M. *Recreation for Blind Adults,* (Springfield, Ill.: Charles C Thomas Publisher, 1966).
3. Crawford, M.E. and R. Mendell, *Therapeutic Recreation and Adapted Physical Activities for Mentally Retarded Individuals,* (Englewood Cliffs, NJ: Prentice-Hall, Inc., 1987).
4. Eddy, J. *The Music Came from Deep Inside,* (Cambridge, Mass: Brookline Books, 1989).
5. Gould, E. and L. Gould, *Arts and Crafts for Physically and Mentally Disabled,* (Springfield, Ill.: Charles C Thomas, Publisher, 1978).
6. Katz, F.L. and E. Katz, *Art and Disabilities,* (Cambridge, Mass.: Brookline Books, 1990).
7. Kennedy, D.W. *et al,* *Special Recreation: Opportunities for Persons with Disabilities,* (Dubuque, IA: Wm. C. Brown, Publishers, 1991).
8. Lepore, M., *Teaching Aquatic Activities to People with Traumatic Brain Injury,* (Lepore, 1991).
9. Schleien, S. and M.T. Ray, *Community Recreation and Persons with Disabilities: Strategies for Integration,* (Baltimore, Md.: Paul H. Brooks, 1988).
10. Warren, B. *Disability and Social Performance,* (Cambridge, MA: Brookline Books, 1988).
11. Wehman, P., ed., *Recreation Programming for Developmentally Disabled Persons,* (Austin, Tx.: Pro-Ed, 1979).
12. Wuerch, B.B., and L.M. Voeltz, *Longitudinal Leisure Skills for Severely Handicapped Learners,* (Baltimore, Md.: Paul H. Brookes Publishing Co., 1982).

Chapter 20

1. American Society of Landscape Architects Foundation and U.S. Department of Housing and Urban Development: *Barrier Free Site Design,* (Washington, D.C.: U.S. Government Printing Office, 1976).
2. Cotter, S.R. and A.H. DeGraff, *Architectural Accessibility for the Disabled of College Campuses,* (Albany, N.Y.: State University Construction Fund 1976).
3. Kopf, P.S., *Access for the Handicapped: The Barrier Free Regulation for Design and Construction in All 50 States,* (N.Y.: Van Nostrand Reinhold, 1984).
4. Jorgensen, J., *Modification of Park and Recreational Facilities for Handicapped Individuals,* (Washington, D.C.: Hawkins and Associates, Inc., 1980).

5. Steinfeld, E. *et al, Barrier-Free Design for the Elderly and the Disabled* (Syracuse, N.Y.: Syracuse University, 1975).

Chapter 21

1. Nusberg, C., *Voluntary Agency As An Instrument of Social Change: Effective Advocacy on Behalf of the Aging* (International Federation on Aging).
2. Prochacka, F. *Voluntary Impulse,* (Winchester, MA: Faber and Faber, 1989).
3. Reeman, D., *Volunteers,* (New York, NY: Berkley Publishing, 1987).
4. Pugliese, D.J., *Voluntary Associations,* (New York, NY: Garland, 1986).
5. Peterson, J.C. *et al, Voluntary Associations: Structure and Process,* (Westport, CT: Greenwood Pub. Group, 1986).
6. Ricard, V.B. *Volunteer,* (New York, NY: Gordon Press, 1985).
7. McCurley, S. *Volunteer Management Policies,* (Downers Grove, IL: Heritage Arts, 1990).
8. Saccomandi, P. and B.R. Hart *Volunteer Skillsbank: An Innovative Way to Connect Individual Talents to Community Needs,* (Arlington: VTNC, 1981).
9. Caroll, A. Volunteer U.S.A., (Long Island City, NY: Fawcett, 1991).
10. Sewell, H. Volunteer Work: *A Comprehensive Guide to Medium and Long Term Voluntary Service,* (Cincinnati, Ohio: Seven Hills Book Dist., 1991).

Chapter 22

1. Blankenship, R.L., *ed. Colleagues in Organization: The Social Construction of Professional Work* (NY: John Wiley, 1977).
2. Bledstein, B., *The Culture of Professionalism* (NY: W. W. Norton, 1976).
3. Etzioni, A., *Semi-Professions and Their Organization,* (Riverside, NJ: The Free Press, 1969).
4. Freidson, E., *Professions and Their Prospects,* (Beverly-Hills, Calif: Sage, 1973).
5. Hayware, F.H., *Professionalism and Originality* (NY: Arno, 1974).
6. Honig, D., *Professional* (NY: Watts, Franklin, 1974).
7. Jackson, J.A., ed., *Professions and Professionalization* (New Rochelle, NY: Cambridge University Press, 1970).
8. Moore, W.E., *Professions: Roles and Rules* (Scranton: Sage, 1970).
9. Redlich, N., *Professional Responsibility: A Problem Approach,* (Waltham, MA: Little, Brown, 1976).

Chapter 24

1. Adair, J., *Effective Leadership: A Self-Development Manual,* (Brookfield, VT: Gower Pub. Co., 1983).
2. Bower, J.L. *The Two Faces of Management: An American Approach to Leadership,* (Boston, Mass.: Houghton Mifflin Co., 1983).

3. Clarke, J.I., *Who, Me Lead a Group?*, (Minneapolis, Minn.: Winston Press, 1983).
4. Culligan, M.J. and S. Derkins, *Back to Basics Management: The Lost Craft of Leadership,* (N.Y.: Facts on File, Inc., 1983).
5. Doll, R.C., *Supervision by Staff Development Ideas and Application,* (Boston: Allyn and Bacon, 1983).
6. Fallon, W.K., ed. *Leadership on the Job: Guide to Good Supervision* (N.Y.: American Management Association, 1982).
7. Hunt, J.G., *et al, Leaders and Managers: International Perspectives on Managerial Behavior and Leadership Research,* (Elmsford, N.Y.: Pergamon Press, Inc., 1980).
8. Lawson, L.G., *et al, Lead On! The Complete Handbook for Group Leaders* (San Luis Obispo, Cal.: Impact Publishers, Inc., 1982).
9. Sergiovanni, T.J., and R.J. Stavist, *Supervision: Human Perspectives* (N.Y.: McGraw-Hill, 1983).

Chapter 25

1. American Alliance for Health, Physical Education, Recreation and Dance, *Opportunities in Recreation and Leisure,* (Washington, D.C.: AAAPERP, 1978).
2. Dorfrin, A., *Jobs in Recreation,* (N.Y.: Lothrop, Lee and Shepard Books, 1974).
3. Evert, J. *Introduction to Hospitality—Recreation Careers,* (Bloomington, Ind.: McKnight Publishing Co., 1975).
4. Henkel, D.D. and G.C. Godbey, *Parks, Recreation, and Leisure Services—Employment in the Public Sector: Status and Trends,* (Arlington, Va.: National Recreation and Park Assoc., 1977).
5. Jensen, C.R., *Recreation and Leisure Careers,* (Louisville, KY: Vocational Guidance Manuals, 1976).

INDEX

609